RED STATE RELIGION

RED STATE RELIGION

Faith and Politics in America's Heartland

Robert Wuthnow

Princeton University Press

Princeton & Oxford

Published by Princeton University Press, 41 William Street, Princeton,
New Jersey 08540
In the United Kingdom: Princeton University Press, 6 Oxford Street, Woodstock,
Oxfordshire OX20 1TW
press.princeton.edu

ISBN 978-0-691-15055-0

Library of Congress Cataloging-in-Publication Data

Wuthnow, Robert.
Red state religion : faith and politics in America's heartland / Robert Wuthnow.
p. cm.
Includes bibliographical references and index.
ISBN 978-0-691-15055-0 (hardcover : acid-free paper) 1. Religion and
politics—Kansas—History. 2. Kansas—Politics and government—History.
3. Political culture—Kansas—History. I. Title.
BL65.P7W88 2011
306.6'61709781–dc22   2011011998

British Library Cataloging-in-Publication Data is available

This book has been composed in Sabon and Century Expanded
Printed on acid-free paper. ∞
Printed in the United States of America

1 3 5 7 9 10 8 6 4 2

CONTENTS

ILLUSTRATIONS

PREFACE

SEVERAL YEARS AGO, I pulled my faded pink and brown *Story of Kansas* from the shelf and read it with considerably more interest than I had in seventh grade. The state's history is replete with tales of bloodshed and sacrifice. John Brown takes his place alongside General Jim Lane and John J. Ingalls. Sockless Jerry Simpson joins Carry Nation and William Allen White. The hall of fame includes Amelia Earhart and Dwight David Eisenhower. Pioneers, farmers, country lawyers, teachers, and merchants settled the heartland. But there were also itinerant preachers, traveling evangelists, priests, nuns, and freethinkers. Mennonites, Quakers, Dunkards, Swedish Lutherans, German Baptists, and vegetarians established colonies. Townspeople built churches by the thousands. People of faith struggled to make their state what they thought it should be. There was no mention of them in the *Story of Kansas*.

Who, then, would have guessed that Kansas would become a leading player in national controversies about religion and politics? Who would have thought that its churches would encourage thousands of protesters to blockade abortion clinics? That its clergy would work for a stiff constitutional ban on same-sex marriage? That its board of education would be embroiled in controversies about evolution and intelligent design? Or who would have guessed that churches played a different role in the famous *Brown v. Board of Education* case? In staging civil rights demonstrations? In advocating populism and opposing war? The fact that textbooks said little about religion made it hard to understand these developments.

The thought that someone must have dealt with these topics led me to some interesting discoveries. One of the state's most distinguished historians, Kenneth S. Davis, wrote a wonderful novel, *The Years of the Pilgrimage*, dealing extensively with religion. But the subject barely comes up in his beautifully written *Kansas: A*

Bicentennial History. Craig Miner's masterful *Kansas: The History of the Sunflower State, 1854–2000* is remarkably comprehensive, but not the place to find much about religion. Robert Smith Bader's plan to follow his authoritative *Prohibition in Kansas* and tantalizing *Hayseeds, Moralizers, and Methodists* with a more complete study of Kansas religion was not realized. There have been important essays on specific topics, from Catholic education to Mennonite farming, yet nothing bringing the larger story together.

That larger story remains to be written. What I have attempted here is more modest. This is a book about the changing connections between religion and politics in Kansas from the Civil War through the early twenty-first century. One would be hard-pressed to find any other place that has voted Republican so consistently over a longer period, or has in recent years been as fraught with controversies about faith's relationship with social and moral issues. Kansas is red state America par excellence. But my aim is not to describe Kansas simply as a breeding ground for religious and political conservatism.

Religion and politics in Kansas have had a complicated history. The two came together on numerous occasions to shape policies and public perceptions. But they often remained separate. There were bigots who aroused the ire of eastern intellectuals, but there were fair-minded leaders in Kansas who did everything they could to inhibit bigotry. For every freak who made headlines there were hundreds of ordinary citizens who quietly practiced their faith. Religion and politics did not occur in a vacuum. People struggled on the open prairie to build churches that would be ornaments to their communities. Then as now, politicians saw advantages in favoring one religious perspective or another. Clergy variously condemned and cooperated with one another. Kansans were sometimes at the center of national politics and at other moments far removed. They felt at times as if the entire nation cared what happened in Kansas. At other times, they figured that Washington might as well be on another planet. All that had gone on before them affected the abortion wars at the end of the twentieth century.

Why should anyone not from Kansas be interested? For more than a century and a half, writers have filed reports informing the rest of the country about what was happening in Kansas. At first the stories were about abolitionists and border ruffians. Then the news was of saloon smashers and Populists. Later it was about creationists and abortion protesters. Thomas Frank's evocative *What's the Matter with Kansas?* captured the attention of a nation wondering if "values voters" were filled with heavenly delusions. It was one of a long line of works that saw Kansas as an exemplary place in which to probe some important aspect of the American soul. That is one reason to be interested in the history of Kansas religion and politics. Kansans were not so different from many other Americans who lived on farms and in small towns far from either coast. If one wanted to understand small-town America, Kansas was the place. Its citizens were mostly white Protestants and Catholics, traditional families proud of their achievements, concerned about their futures, committed to fiscal conservatism, skeptical of big government, and dedicated to preserving what they regarded as simple moral virtue. These were the grassroots sentiments on which red state America was based.

A broader issue is at stake as well. We are a people constantly on the lookout for what is new. We seize on trends, imagining ourselves to be experiencing something that our ancestors would never have understood, and yet wonder if anything has really changed that much. The question of what is new lies at the core of recent debates about religion and politics. Are we in a new era of moral activists shaping politics? Have religion and politics become more contentious than in the past? Or is the present a continuation of the past? One can find arguments on both sides.

Kansas is an interesting location from which to examine the connections between recent religious activism and the past. The state was dominated by moral politics all along. Prohibition was proposed in 1859, became state law well before it passed nationally, and lasted long after it was repealed. Besides Brown and Nation, archconservative Reverend Gerald K. Winrod made his home in Kansas, as did leaders of the John Birch Society. With these precedents, it was hardly surprising that Kansas became famous at the end of the twentieth century for its schoolbook controversies and antiabortion rallies. Indeed, the state provides rich material for understanding how one kind of activism sets precedents for another. But if there were differences—if recent activism is in fact more pervasive—then Kansas is the place to understand these differences.

My argument is that the Republican Party and the centrist conservatism of the state's two dominant religions—Methodism and Catholicism—actually deterred radical religious and political movements from gaining much ground during most of the state's history. They had a stake in doing so, and did it well. The exceptions—most notably the third-party Populist movement of the 1890s and occasional Democratic victories—usually resulted in a broadening of the Republican base. Methodists' competition with Catholics, stemming from theological and liturgical differences, spurred each to found churches as the population grew. They took different sides on Prohibition, which became the principal activity through which Methodists engaged in politics. Prohibition illustrated the tenacity of an issue once it became part of a denomination's identity. It was nevertheless a progressive issue that had little to do with the state's later conservatism. That turn to the Right was bred of Republicans' long isolation from Washington during the Roosevelt and Truman eras. The immediate post–World War II years witnessed an attempted return to normalcy that focused mainly on local communities, churches, and families. The unrest of the 1960s brought churches more directly into the political sphere than had been the case for some time. Campus protests, the Vietnam War, and the civil rights movement added to controversies already taking place within and between denominations. Much of that was new and was exacerbated by the growth of new denominations—at least ones that were new to the state, especially Southern Baptists. All of that set the stage for Religious Right activism to play the important role that it did in subsequent years.

I have traced these developments by drawing from a wide range of sources. I made extensive use of censuses of religious bodies that provided information about churches and church membership—all available as electronic data files. Election results and, in more recent decades, public opinion surveys were indispensable. The Kansas State Historical Society and several denominational archives have accumulated impressive collections of valuable information. Through personal networks I was able to track down letters, diaries, and church histories. Searchable databases of journal articles, magazines, and newspapers as well as electronic collections of oral histories made it possible to identify connections that would have otherwise remained obscure. For the recent period, I drew on more than a hundred new qualitative interviews.

Special thanks to the Woodrow Wilson School of Public and International Affairs, the University Center for Human Values, and the Center for the Study of Religion at Princeton University for generous financial and administrative support; the staff of Firestone Library for assistance with archival materials; the Lilly Endowment over the years for grants and intellectual sustenance; Karen Myers, her staff, Justin Farrell, and Emily Dumler for research assistance; Donna Defrancisco and Jay Barnes for administrative and computing assistance; and my family, for always being there when I needed them.

RED STATE RELIGION

PROLOGUE

ON MAY 10, 1867, suffragist Lucy Stone telegraphed Susan B. Anthony from Atchison in eastern Kansas. "Impartial suffrage, without regard to color or sex, will succeed by overwhelming majorities," she predicted. "Kansas leads the world!" Stone had reason to be optimistic. For the past month, she had been lecturing to enthusiastic crowds at churches and town halls, and enlisting support from community leaders. Leading Congregational and Presbyterian ministers along with editors of newspapers were declaring their allegiance. Two weeks later, the *New York Tribune* echoed her positive assessment: "The young state of Kansas is fitly the vanguard of this cause." From across the Atlantic, John Stuart Mill added his endorsement. "Kansas was the herald and protagonist of the memorable contest, which at the cost of so many heroic lives, has admitted the African race to the blessings of freedom," he wrote, and is now "taking the same advanced position" in the struggle for "social and moral progress."[1]

But other correspondence from Stone was less confident. Many of the state's politicians were on the fence. Republicans, it was feared, seemed to be turning their backs on the movement. By summer's end, when Anthony arrived, the campaign was suffering setbacks. Anthony wrote from Salina on September 12, 1867, that she was "getting along splendidly," having lectured at a new Methodist church, and was heading west the next day to Ellsworth, where soldiers and Indians had just been fighting. She was facing opposition, though, and had run out of tracts.[2] Anthony's concerns were justified. The hope for women's suffrage died later that fall. "Kansas being Republican by a large majority," a leader explained, "there was no chance of victory."[3] Efforts to revive the cause two years later, and again in 1894, failed. Women's suffrage was not achieved until 1912.

Over the years, Kansas became known as one of the most conservative states in the nation. It was one of the first to pass mandatory Prohibition and one of the last to overturn it. Kansas schools regularly included Bible reading and prayer, and by the end of the twentieth century were a battleground for proponents of creationism and intelligent design. In 1954, the U.S. Supreme Court decision in *Brown v. Board of Education*, a case brought to the court on behalf of African American children in Topeka and elsewhere, forcibly ended a long history of segregation. The state made headlines for its assertive opposition to the Supreme Court's decision to uphold abortion rights in *Roe v. Wade* and for subsequent agitation on behalf of the pro-life movement. After two decades of increasingly aggressive mobilization by antiabortion groups, abortion provider Dr. George Tiller was murdered at a church in Wichita in 2009.

What was the matter? Even Kansans were puzzled. In 1896 William Allen White, the *Emporia Gazette* editor who would win a Pulitzer Prize for his essays, observed, "Go east and you hear them laugh at Kansas; go west and they sneer at her; go south and they 'cuss' her; go north and they have forgotten her." More than a century later, native Kansan Thomas Frank picked up Allen's refrain. In *What's the Matter with Kansas?* Frank argued that conservative moral issues, promulgated by preachers and their followers, had become so seductive that citizens were compromising their own economic well-being and intellectual integrity.[4]

The Republican Party was a strong contender among the possible explanations for Kansas conservatism. Kansas and the Republican Party owed their mutual existence to the passage of the Kansas-Nebraska bill in 1854. Over the next century and a half, only two states voted Republican in at least thirty of the nation's thirty-eight presidential elections. One of those two voted Republican in every presidential election from 1968 through 2008. That state was Kansas. On average, Kansas opted for Republican candidates from the state's inception in 1861 by 57 percent—eight points above the national average. In 2008, when Barack Obama beat John McCain by seven points in the popular vote nationally, McCain won Kansas by 15 percent.

Religion was a second plausible explanation for Kansas conservatism. If southern conservatism could be placed at the feet of Baptists, Kansas was from the start dominated by denominations that engaged in revival meetings, promoted enthusiastic experiences of the Holy Spirit, and encouraged believers to abstain from alcohol, live modestly, pray, and look to God for their daily bread. The Middle West Bible Belt was known for Methodist camp meetings, Holiness and Pentecostal revivals, and occasional outbursts of religious fanaticism. For a time the Ku Klux Klan sought to enlist clergy in its bigoted campaigns, and at other times the nativist American Protective Association succeeded. By the end of the twentieth century, Kansas preachers and priests gained notoriety for militant crusades against abortion providers and campaigns against homosexuals.

By many indications, an inquiry into the connections between faith and politics in Kansas would begin and end with arguments about the self-perpetuating power of conservative ideas and leaders in the nation's heartland. In that telling, Kansas would be a case study in the peculiar strength of red state religion. What's the matter with Kansas would be a question capable of shedding light on the persistence of traditionalists everywhere who dig in their heels against enlightened, progressive, egalitarian ideals. But that story is too simple and is not the one I tell in this book.

Consider the following. When Stone and Anthony visited in 1867, "bleeding Kansas" was widely regarded as a state founded by abolitionists who suffered hardship and risked their lives in the antislavery cause. Its citizens included a higher percentage of men of eligible age who had fought in the Union army than any other state. Women's suffrage lost in 1867 because supporters of African American suffrage, including leading African Americans, feared it would weaken the popularity of that campaign. In 1861, the first state legislature granted women the right to vote in school elections, and in 1887, Kansas became the first state in which women voted and held offices in municipal elections. When Kansas adopted universal suffrage in 1912, it was one of the first to do so. Meanwhile, Prohibition had been advanced for the protection of women and children. It was notable, too, that White's jeremiad was not against conservatism but rather directed toward Kansas Populists who achieved impressive victories in the 1890s on behalf of working families and farmers.

None of this is evidence that Kansas was actually a progressive state all along, nor one that somehow lost its way in the twentieth century and became conservative. The truth is more complex. Kansas has been about as Republican as any state could be. Not only did it routinely vote for Republican presidential candidates, but most of its gubernatorial and congressional elections also went Republican, and among all the representatives serving over the decades in its state legislature, more than three-quarters were Republicans. The question was not why Republicans won year after year but instead why they ever lost, why anyone ever ran against them, and indeed why they managed to reform themselves, how they developed and overcame party factionalism, and how they achieved as much for the state as they did. The related question is what role religion played in all this. The casual observer gets it wrong in supposing that Methodists were simply the moral cheerleaders of the Republican Party or imagining that religious fanatics were lurking in every corner. Red state religion was as complicated as red state politics. Piety influenced elections in unexpected ways, promoted moral conservatism decade after decade, and yet kept a sufficient distance from politics that its role could never be easily predicted.

From 1861 through the century's end, Kansas Republicans benefited from the fact of having championed the free state cause and being on the winning side in the Civil War. As settlers poured into Kansas and spread west across the state, Republicans opened law offices, founded newspapers, and ran successfully for local, state, and national offices. Churches were established in nearly every community almost as quickly as towns were plotted and incorporated. Methodists were by far the most successful in starting churches. Their success was emulated by other Protestant denominations that differed in theology, liturgical style, or ethnic background. Presbyterians, Baptists, and Disciples of Christ founded hundreds of churches. Mennonites, Quakers, African Methodists, Unitarians, and Jews started congregations as well. Catholics were Methodists' most serious competitor in terms of numbers of members and potential influence in state politics. Temperance was the most common, but by no means the only issue that brought religious leaders into the political sphere. Laws were passed that protected and encouraged public expressions of faith. But piety was as much a matter of the heart as of politics, and it was broadly understood that religion was to mingle in politics with caution.

The pattern in religion and politics that developed during the nineteenth century was aptly characterized as a moderately conservative Protestant Republican establishment. As the largest denomination, Methodism played an important role in both establishing churches of its own as well as discouraging the smaller independent groups that sometimes appeared as a result of revival preaching and followers seeking personal holiness. Methodists' competition with Catholics to enlist and influence members, perhaps ironically, facilitated these endeavors, and Catholics developed their own institutions and practices that strengthened religious devotion in Catholic communities. Republicans were closely aligned with Methodists and other mainstream Protestants. Candidates frequently gave speeches in churches, and publicly declared their support of temperance and other issues of interest to religious constituents. Republicans' influence was sufficient to win in most elections, yet was never dominant enough to discourage Democrats from running or prevent factions from developing within their own party. Populism gained strong support in the 1890s. Its brief rise to power forced Republicans, with help from church leaders, to adopt reforms that served the party well during the first decades of the twentieth century.

Between 1900 and 1929, Kansas experienced a number of good years in agricultural productivity and undertook an impressive program of modernization. Towns acquired electricity and telephone service, roads and rural mail delivery improved, stores stocked an abundant supply of consumer goods, and farming benefited from mechanization. Republicans led the way in encouraging progress while maintaining their commitment to efficiency in government. Churches constructed larger and more substantial buildings, and prospered from increasing participation as more of the population lived in towns. These were good years to be Republicans, and a time of rising influence for Methodists. Prohibition was understood to be a progressive issue that contributed positively to the state's prosperity. Ratification of the Eighteenth Amendment in 1919 reinforced the view that Kansas was in the vanguard of moral reform.

It is against this backdrop of moral and economic progress in the 1920s that the subsequent redefinition of Kansans' self-image must be understood. The 1930s brought not only the dust bowl and the Depression but also Franklin Delano Roosevelt and the New Deal. At first Kansans supported the New Deal, but after 1936 they became increasingly disillusioned with it. Kansas Republicans, with Alfred M. Landon as their most visible national leader, became a weak opposition party with none of the influence in Washington that they had been used to in the 1920s and before. The churches were suffering setbacks as well. Fundamentalism made inroads. Prohibition was repealed in 1933. Congregations struggled to support their preachers. Extremists used radio broadcasts to attract audiences, and did so among people who disliked Roosevelt and feared the one-party rule they saw in Washington.

Republicans' return to power in the 1950s under Dwight David Eisenhower would seem to have removed Kansans' sense of being in the political wilderness. They had fought wholeheartedly during World War II and taken pride in the fact that Eisenhower was from Kansas. They liked him as president, far better than they did Harry S. Truman or Roosevelt, but more because of who he was than because of his administration's policies. Churches and community leaders shifted their attention increasingly toward local issues. Towns were able to turn again to the modernizing efforts begun in the 1920s. Roads, soil conservation, and especially school construction and consolidation became leaders' preoccupation. Republicans were good at getting these projects started and finding ways to pay for them. They were also adept at providing patronage. Churches focused increasingly on family activities and programs capable of attracting children. It was a time of quiet conservatism.

The 1960s disrupted the calm that communities hoped they had achieved by the end of the 1950s. The demographic center of gravity was no longer on farms and in small rural communities. It was in Wichita, Topeka, and Kansas City. African American and a few white churches in those cities were active in the civil rights movement, playing a role in the events in Topeka that led to *Brown v. Board of Education*, and desegregation efforts in Wichita. The Vietnam War sparked both opposition and support. Barry Goldwater's unsuccessful bid for the presidency in 1964 mobilized leaders on the far Right who would continue to be important in Kansas and national politics through the 1970s. Campuses became sites of antiwar activism in Kansas, as they did elsewhere. Between 1968 and 1970, unrest over the war as well as about racial and gender equality generated increasing activism on campuses along with sharper disapproval in many of the state's towns and suburbs. The churches were drawn into these debates in ways unseen since the Civil War. The mainstream denominations became divided; fundamentalist and evangelical groups with conservative views on social issues grew.

The late 1970s through the early years of the twenty-first century saw a continuation and deepening of the religious and political unrest that began in the 1960s. Conservative Republicans brought questions about teaching evolution to national attention in ways unseen since the Scopes trial in 1925. Abortion became the most hotly contested issue in state politics. Fundamentalist churches now commanded a larger share of the population than ever before. The role that Methodism and other mainstream denominations had played in providing a large centrist tent for many of the state's communities had weakened. Catholics were more numerous and increasingly concentrated in the largest urban areas, and yet sensed that parochial schools were not as influential as they once had been, Mass attendance and adherence to church teachings about birth control was diminishing, and priests and nuns were in short supply.

With outside groups of activists increasingly involved in the state, contentious rallies, demonstrations, legal battles, and political campaigns became the order of the day.

What the headlines missed, though, was the fact that red state religion and politics in Kansas had less to do with contentious moral activism than it did with local communities and relationships among neighbors, friends, and fellow churchgoers. At the grassroots level, conservatism was pragmatic. It did not prevent fiscal conservatives from accepting government funding for roads, schools, nursing homes, and hospitals. It did include a healthy skepticism toward Washington and Wall Street. Kansans had been ridiculed by the eastern press for so long, and had heard stories of Roosevelt's arrogance and New Deal wastefulness so frequently, that it was hard to believe big government was on their side. To be in favor of abortion was to be irresponsible and disrespectful of life. Being against abortion was a reason to vote Republican, and yet year after year, Kansans put Democrats in the governor's office and voted for moderates over conservatives in Republican primaries. They said religion and politics were topics that one did not talk about much, but when pressed to state their opinions, they revealed nuanced views. Abortion might be reprehensible, but Kansans knew there were circumstances when it might be the only reasonable option. A responsible person tried to live right, aimed to teach one's children to do the same, and mostly hoped to get along with friends and neighbors. There was nothing wrong with getting ahead as long as a person also treated others fairly.

If she were alive today, Stone would no longer assert that Kansas leads the way, except perhaps in consistently voting Republican. Yet one can imagine that she would not be surprised with the way the state has turned out. Suffrage took longer to achieve than anyone expected. So did civil rights and desegregation. Suffragists worked for temperance because it was good for women and children as well as good for communities. It took a long time for Kansas to experiment with Prohibition and then find other ways to curb intoxication. In the twenty-first century, meth labs and binge drinking were still of concern in many Kansas communities. Churches still provided venues for public meetings about social issues, just as they did for Stone and Anthony. They were venues in which sit-ins could be practiced and rallies organized. Occasionally they filled people with such passion that violence resulted. Most of the time they were not about politics at all but instead focused on the ups and downs of daily life, helping people mourn and celebrate, and forging social ties that reminded them to be decent citizens.

MURDER AT THE GLENWOOD

ON THE NIGHT OF NOVEMBER 12, 1912, police in Topeka were summoned to the third floor of the Hotel Glenwood, where they found Laura Beers dead in a pool of blood. Witnesses claimed to have heard a quarrel between Mrs. Beers and her husband, to which he freely admitted while maintaining that her death had occurred accidentally. Suspecting worse, police took Mr. Beers into custody, charging him with his wife's murder.[1]

The incident led to one of the most controversial trials in Kansas history, and attracted attention from journalists and readers across the country. The most bizarre aspect of the case was the manner of death. At the coroner's inquest it was determined that Mrs. Beers's lower false teeth had been forced down her throat, causing her to die from suffocation. The other feature that drew attention to the case was that Mrs. Beers's husband was an upstanding Methodist preacher. He had served congregations in Nebraska and Ohio, and currently held a pastorate in Wakarusa and two other hamlets a few miles south of Topeka. News accounts routinely mentioned both the deceased's teeth and her husband's occupation.[2]

Churches in Kansas were well established in 1912. Nearly every community had at least one, and most had several. The Topeka area was no exception. Almost nine thousand people belonged to Protestant churches, and more than a thousand were Catholics. Several of the churches dated to the territorial days. The First Methodist in Topeka, founded in 1855, had more than twelve hundred members. Smaller churches with several dozen members, like the ones that Reverend W. L. Beers pastored, were more typical. The larger churches included members of the state legislature and often hosted lectures by public officials. People from the surrounding communities came by horse and wagon to camp meetings and revivals.

The Beers case was a crime of passion arising from a domestic quarrel. But it also illustrated something important about Kansas politics. Religion was generally more significant in private life than it ever was in the political sphere. People cared about it because they believed their salvation was at stake. It mattered how their children were raised, which church they belonged to, and who they married. They were willing to accept some religious differences, but not others. Those differences influenced who they saw as their friends or foes, what they felt about social issues, and how they voted.

At the trial, which opened five months after the murder and played to a packed courtroom for more than a week, the prosecution argued that Reverend Beers had traveled from Wakarusa to Topeka, where his wife had taken refuge from repeated beatings and verbal abuse, and after quarreling, grabbed her by the left shoulder and pushed her false teeth down her throat until she died. The coroner testified that the dentures had been forced through the muscles of the neck to the outer skin, where they formed a lump as big as a robin's egg. The prosecution further suggested that Mr. Beers was upset by his wife's plans to seek a divorce, had begun planning to kill her several years earlier while living in Ohio, had come up with the idea of false teeth as such an unlikely means of committing homicide that a jury would consider it an accident, and had moved to Kansas knowing that if he were found guilty, he would not hang because the state lacked capital punishment.

The defense contended that Mrs. Beers had become hysterical and begun hitting her husband and screaming, to which he responded by placing his hand over her mouth to quiet her, accidentally causing her teeth to dislodge. "She sprang on me," Beers testified. "She struck and scratched me. The thought came to me that she was getting the best of me." As character witnesses, the defense called members of Beers's church in Kansas and three of his brothers from Ohio—one a banker, one a lawyer, and one a wealthy rancher—and recounted the sad tale of Beers and his first wife living in Nebraska with their eight children, she dying of measles, the nurse becoming his second wife, and he pleading with her to stay with him for the sake of love and their children.[3]

The trial was a riveting spectacle. Prosecution and defense lawyers argued back and forth in the presence of Beers and several of his children, all sobbing audibly from time to time. The deceased's dentures were prominently displayed on a table near the stenographer. But it was not that unusual for Kansans to revel in high-profile criminal proceedings. Still fresh in their minds was the trial of Maggie Davis, who pleaded innocent on the grounds of insanity in the brutal slaying of her boyfriend, and the case of celebrated pickpocket John C. Martin, who allegedly used fall money or bribes to avoid prosecution in several cities. Nor were citizens unused to hearing about sensational activities on the part of clergy. In nearby Lansing, prayer meetings and a revival were spreading through the state penitentiary as the Beers trial unfolded. Topeka itself was home to Charles Parham's Beth-El Bible School, where believers began experiencing the Holy Ghost at the turn of the century and started the movement that led to the famous Azusa Street Revival in California a few years later. The city was also where Congregationalist minister Charles M. Sheldon wrote articles under the heading "What Would Jesus Do?" for the *Topeka Daily Capital*, causing its circulation to jump from twelve thousand to nearly four hundred thousand, including thousands of copies in Chicago and New York City. Shocking as it may have been to see a pastor accused of murder, readers received a steady diet of news about sermons, camp meetings, clergy conferences, and revivals.[4]

Yet there was one aspect of the Beers case—hardly mentioned in news accounts outside the region—that figured importantly in the trial and the local coverage: the accusation that Laura Beers had been killed because of her religion. The story came out that she had been raised Catholic and did not see eye to eye on matters of faith with her Methodist husband, who reportedly hated the Catholic Church with intense bitterness. While living in Nebraska, Mrs. Beers had joined the Methodist Church and been baptized during a revival meeting. She later regretted the decision and wished to return to the Catholic Church, but learned that she could do so only by promising to rear her children in the church. In Ohio she frequently attended the Catholic Church, which embarrassed her preacher husband and intensified their disputes.

The quarrel on the day of her death was over the education of their children, especially their daughter Alice, whom Mrs. Beers wished to send to live with an uncle in Nebraska to attend parochial school. Reverend Beers was adamantly opposed to this idea. It did not sit well with him either that his wife had taken refuge with the Catholic sisters at St. Francis Hospital in Topeka. The prosecution further revealed that while the couple was living in Ohio, Reverend Beers had forcibly retrieved a letter hidden in his wife's bosom in which she mentioned receiving advice from a local priest about her plans to seek a divorce. At the trial, the priest in question related that Mrs. Beers had come to him after her husband knocked her down, dragged her across the room by her hair, and thrust his fingers down her throat.[5]

It was never determined how much the jury may have been swayed by religious sentiments, but there were ample reasons to believe that the story of religious conflict resonated with citizens in the region. A Methodist preacher in Axtell, ninety miles northwest of Topeka, lectured in 1889 in such inflammatory language about the evils of Rome that violence broke out between church members and local Catholics, requiring the mayor to seek a military regiment's intervention to end the bloodshed. In the 1890s, Kansas Protestants were drawn to the American Protective Association, which sloganeered in favor of the little red schoolhouse and home rule against interference from the Vatican. At the Methodists' national conference in 1892 in Kansas City, Methodist leaders heard vehement denunciations of the Catholic religion. "The most wily and dangerous enemy of America and American liberty today is Romanism," a Topeka resident observed a few months later. "Of all the religions in the United States the Roman Catholic stands alone in its determined foreignism." At a subsequent gathering, Methodists passed a resolution to remove the word "catholic" from the creed. In 1899, Kansas Methodists attending their annual convention in Lawrence listened as speakers warned of Romanist evils. "A clamor at this moment rises from Rome for the establishment of an overwhelming system of parochial schools," one announced. "We must cast anchor against this tide driving us before it to destruction on the rocks of the papacy, and the anchor must [include] the Bible in the public schools for one, not one copper of the public money for ecclesiasticism the other."[6]

Two years prior to Laura Beers's death, tensions between Methodists and Catholics reopened on a wider scale. Controversy erupted in February 1910 when former U.S. vice president Charles W. Fairbanks was denied a meeting with the Pope because of allegations that American Methodists in Italy were spreading anti-Catholic propaganda. Soon after, the tension over a planned visit with the Pope by former President Theodore Roosevelt was escalated by what became known as the Merry del Val incident. The incident, in which Cardinal Merry del Val played a prominent role, involved the Vatican setting as a condition for the visit that Roosevelt was not to meet with Methodists in Rome, Roosevelt refusing, the Vatican rescinding its invitation, Methodist leaders attacking the Vatican, and Roosevelt opting not to meet with the Methodists either. After the incident seemed to be over, with a quiet meeting between Roosevelt and a papal nuncio, the fury continued as Methodists in Washington and Italy strongly criticized the Vatican, and an archbishop in the Midwest defended the reprimand.[7]

Reverend Beers's trial ended inconclusively when the jury deadlocked after forty-four hours of deliberation with eight of its members arguing for acquittal and four for a conviction. The disagreement, they explained, had to do with whether the teeth had in fact been forcibly pushed into Mrs. Beers's throat or whether there had not been enough force to indicate an intention to kill. At a second trial six months later, when the key witness who had overheard the Beers quarreling at the hotel could not be located and after several prosecution witnesses could not recall their earlier testimony, Reverend Beers was acquitted. Six months after that, he married the postmistress in Wakarusa and moved to a farm fourteen miles east of Cheyenne, Wyoming, where he held pastorates in several rural Methodist churches. He died in 1921.[8]

Tension between Catholics and Methodists, and with other Protestants, continued long after the Beers trial. Significant as the conflict itself was, the more important aspect was the larger pattern of Great Plains piety that it revealed. Catholic and Methodist churches were by far the dominant religious institutions in the region. They not only competed with each other for local influence, criticized each other, and sometimes engaged in violent attacks, but also encouraged the kind of institution building that shaped the region's politics and inspired its civic sensibilities. Across much of the Middle West, Methodists were sufficiently strong that other Protestant denominations imitated them, or remained truly on the periphery in enclaves defined by nationality, ethnicity, race, and social class. The exceptions were in the northern Plains, where Lutherans played a role comparable to Methodists, and in much of Oklahoma and Arkansas, where Baptists were strong. Church leaders faithfully served their parishes and congregations by preaching, building churches, baptizing children, and burying the dead. They also struggled to create a civic and moral system that conformed to their ideal of U.S. democracy.

The establishment of Middle West religious patterns by Catholics, Methodists, and a few other denominations from the mid-1800s through World War I holds the key to understanding how the region became so thoroughly identified with red state politics in the closing decades of the twentieth century. Catholics, Methodists, and several smaller Protestant denominations resembled one another in having the motivation and capacity to establish churches throughout the Great Plains. They were well organized with clear administrative structures that facilitated church expansion. They also had incentives to promote middle-of-the-road democratic social policies, even though they often differed about the specifics of these policies, and argue against fringe groups and radical factions. The Protestant denominations became identified with the Republican Party, and these loyalties remained strong through the presidential election of 1960, which stirred long-held divisions with Catholics, but by the 1980s were challenged by demographic, economic, and cultural shifts. Only then was it possible for a new brand of religious-political conservatism to emerge, sink roots in well-prepared soil, and eventually even outgrow itself.

CHAPTER 1

PIETY ON THE PLAINS

THE STORY of how Kansas came to be known as a bastion of Protestant Republican conservatism begins in the 1850s when statehood was at issue, and when that issue was central in national politics. This period just prior to the Civil War saw the first alliances between Republicans and Methodists in Kansas. The relationship of religion to politics that emerged in those years continued through the end of the nineteenth century—and shaped much of what happened in the twentieth century. Many parts of eastern Kansas were settled immediately after the Civil War, and counties farther west were inhabited by the mid-1870s. How churches were established in those communities, why town leaders were so eager to have churches, and which religious groups were most successful are important questions for understanding that period of settlement. These were the years in which Methodism and Catholicism became the dominant religious institutions, and in which smaller denominations found ways to have a continuing presence. Towns competed to attract churches. Buildings went up with support from denominations and local donors. At times, it appeared that politicians and church leaders were working hand in hand to pass laws, promote temperance, and start schools. And yet the relationships between churches and public affairs were complicated.

The complications arose from the fact that Kansans were divided about the state being free or having slavery. Republicans' views won out, although not without conflict. Democrats emerged as the weaker party, but with strength in Catholic communities. There were tensions between different Republican factions. Residents naturally brought ideas from their home communities in other states. From the start, there were strong sentiments about how much or how little political discussions should be included in places of worship. Nearly all these complications were evident as Kansas moved toward statehood.

ABRAHAM LINCOLN IN KANSAS

The first presidential candidate to campaign in Kansas was Lincoln, who visited in 1859, fourteen months before the territory became a state. Having spoken so often about Kansas and having heard so much about its struggle for free state sovereignty, Lincoln was eager to see it firsthand. Taking the train across Missouri from Hannibal to Saint Joseph, where he arrived on Wednesday, November 30, he crossed the river to Elwood, Kansas, and gave a brief speech in the Great Western Hotel dining room that evening. The next day, which turned bitterly cold, Lincoln traveled fifteen miles by horse and buggy to Troy, where he gave a speech to a small crowd at the courthouse, and then eleven miles to Doniphan, where the turnout was again sparse and the speech short. On December 2, the reception in Atchison was more enthusiastic. At the Methodist Church that evening, Lincoln lectured to a packed house for two hours and twenty minutes after being escorted there by a brass band. The next day he journeyed on to Leavenworth, where he gave three more lectures, departing for home on December 7.[1]

On the surface, Lincoln's December 2 address at the Atchison Methodist Church merged faith and politics in ways that would be repeated time and again in Kansas history. Methodists had been active in Kansas since 1830, when Reverend Thomas Johnson and his wife, Sarah, established the Shawnee Methodist Mission on the Kansas River approximately fifty miles south of the eventual location of Atchison. In 1839, Johnson opened a school on two thousand acres of prime land. He constructed three large buildings over the next six years that housed as many as two hundred Indian boys and girls, who learned farming, milling, sewing, boot making, and

1.1 Kansas Avenue Methodist Episcopal Church in Atchison, where Abraham Lincoln spoke on December 2, 1859. Courtesy of KansasMemory.org, Kansas State Historical Society, Copy and Reuse Restrictions Apply.

other manual skills. James Wheeler from Ohio founded a Methodist mission in 1843 near present-day Kansas City among the Wyandot Indians. In 1846, when the Methodist Episcopal Church split into northern and southern branches over slavery, the southern wing took control of the Indian missions, including the one run by Johnson, who favored slavery. The Methodist Episcopal Church South secured government funding to establish a Kaw mission at Council Grove in 1849, but the school did not succeed and closed in 1854. Four years later, the northern Methodists successfully established Baker University in Baldwin City, twenty miles south of Lawrence.[2]

Meanwhile, the Shawnee Mission school served as the Kansas Territorial Legislature's headquarters from mid-1855 through the following spring. When the Kansas constitutional convention met at Wyandotte on July 5, 1859, the one clergyman present was a Methodist.[3] The federal census conducted a few months after Lincoln's Atchison visit identified thirty-six Methodist churches in Kansas with property valued at more than forty-five thousand dollars. That was more than the number and total property value of Baptist, Presbyterian, and Roman Catholic churches combined. There were five Methodist churches in Doniphan County, where Lincoln's journey began, and seven in Leavenworth County. Reports from the Kansas Conference of the Methodist Episcopal Church showed even more activity. All told, Methodist services were being held in fifty-one locations throughout eastern Kansas.[4]

The Methodists in Atchison had a fine new building, dedicated on March 8, 1859, at a cost of $3,075. The structure, conveniently located across the street from the courthouse, measured fifty-eight feet long and thirty-two feet wide, and could seat 350 people.[5] Its presiding elder, Reverend James Shaw, had been a prominent Methodist leader in Detroit before coming to Kansas in 1856. Shaw strongly supported the free state cause, and another free state supporter, Reverend Hugh D. Fisher, from Leavenworth, assisted him at the dedication service. The current pastor, Isaac F. Collins, would undoubtedly have been honored to introduce Lincoln and may have expected the oration to reference the divine.

Atchison itself was a "fine growing place," Lincoln wrote to a friend a few months after his visit.[6] With a population of more than twenty-five hundred, Atchison was the second-largest city in Kansas, exceeded only by Leavenworth, twenty-four miles to the south.[7] Atchison served as an outfitting point for ox trains to Salt Lake City and California, taking advantage of its location on a western bend of the Missouri River that reduced overland freight costs.[8] It received freight and passengers from steamboats traveling between Saint Louis and Saint Joseph, had telegraph service, was making plans to be the terminus of the Atchison and Saint Joe Railroad, was well represented in territorial politics, and would soon send one of its citizens to the U.S. Senate.

Interest in politics had been growing since Atchison's incorporation in 1855. The Kansas-Nebraska Act of 1854 repealed the Missouri Compromise of 1820 and allowed people in those territories to decide for themselves about slavery. Atchison was founded by proslavery settlers and took its name from David R. Atchison, the Democratic U.S. senator from Missouri who was a champion of popular sovereignty and the slavery cause. Proslavery forces controlled the town, which became the location of frequent border skirmishes until 1857 when free state leaders who opposed slavery gained the upper hand. When the Kansas Republican Party was organized in May 1859, John A. Martin, the twenty-year-old editor of Atchison's free state newspaper, *Freedom's Champion*, was present, and in July of that year Martin served as secretary of the Wyandotte convention, which produced the free state constitution that was ratified in October.

On the day Lincoln spoke in Atchison, John Brown was hanged at Charlestown, Virginia, for murder and insurrection. During the trial *Freedom's Champion* and its rival, *Atchison Union*, carried story after story recounting the slaughter of Brown's men in southern Kansas and his attack on the federal arsenal at Harper's Ferry. Brown was a person of faith who believed that he was engaged in a holy war. A proslavery preacher killed Brown's son. "The shot that struck the child's heart," abolitionist Reverend Henry Ward Beecher wrote two weeks before Lincoln's speech, "crazed the father's brain." The following May, Lincoln was nominated at the Republican convention in Chicago to run for president. John J. Ingalls, an Atchison lawyer who was a delegate to the Wyandotte convention, served as secretary of the Kansas Senate in 1861 and was later elected to the U.S. Senate on the Republican ticket, succeeding Samuel C. Pomeroy, also of Atchison. Martin went on to become a Republican governor of Kansas. "We have formed a Republican

Constitution," Martin noted a few weeks after Lincoln's visit in 1859, "adopted it by Republican votes, sent a Republican delegate to bear it to the National Capitol, [and] elected Republican State Officers and a Republican State Legislature." No place in the country, he added, was "as thoroughly Republican" as Kansas.[9]

Lincoln's visit to Kansas became standard fare in the state's legends of its origin and political culture. Newspapers periodically commemorated the Wyandotte convention with accounts of what Lincoln said on his visit in 1859 and explanations of why he had not attended the convention itself. Historians recalled the visit as evidence that Kansas had been the recipient, as one wrote, "of much flattering attention from the great men of the country."[10] In 1902, the Kansas State Historical Society collected and reprinted all the accounts it could find of Lincoln's visit from national newspapers, letters, and diaries. Historian Fred W. Brinkerhoff delivered a presidential address in 1945 to the Kansas State Historical Society on the topic of Lincoln's Kansas tour. In the 1950s, textbooks about the state's history included accounts of the visit, and the tour was revisited and extensively reexamined on the occasion of its centennial in 1959. In subsequent decades, standard histories of Kansas continued to describe the famous tour. On the sesquicentennial of the visit in 2009, the state's historical museum in Topeka mounted a special exhibit in its honor.[11] Many of the accounts mentioned the speech at the Methodist Church and some included an image of the church. Kansans' loyalty to the Republican Party had become legendary over the years, and Methodism had become its most popular religion. By all appearances, Lincoln's lecture, which historians agreed was a warm-up for his influential address two months later at Cooper Institute in New York City, symbolized the emerging ties between Kansas religion and partisan politics.

But appearances in this instance are deceiving. A closer look at Lincoln's Atchison visit reveals a more tenuous mingling of faith and politics, and foreshadows the ongoing complexities in this relationship. Although nearly every aspect of Lincoln's tour has been scrutinized, even a stop at the barbershop before leaving Saint Joseph as well as how long each leg of his journey may have taken over muddy or icy roads, the question of what his visit may have said about religion and politics in territorial Kansas has not been sufficiently considered. On the surface, there was little significance to the fact that the lecture occurred at the Methodist Church. It was the only suitable location. The other church that could have accommodated the crowd, a spacious Baptist church of Gothic brick construction, was not quite finished, and there was no public building large enough. Had there been, Lincoln probably would have spoken there, as he did the following evening in Leavenworth. It is important, though, to ask whether Lincoln's visit struck an enthusiastic chord with Atchison's churchgoers or whether it evoked ambivalence.[12]

Had the Baptist Church been ready in time, there is a good chance that its leaders would have in any case been reluctant to host Lincoln. They were as much on the free state side as anyone else, but had reasons to be cautious about Lincoln. Unlike the Methodist denomination, which had a separate congregation in Atchison to which southern Methodists could go, the Baptist Church drew members from both the South and North, and may well have discouraged discussions of politics for this reason. The pastor, Reverend L. A. Alderson from Virginia, had tried unsuccessfully to start a church in Kansas a few years earlier, and had preached again in Virginia for four years before coming to Atchison. Three of the prominent members were sons of the distinguished New Jersey Baptist preacher James M. Challiss, and a fourth son lived in Atchison for several years before returning to the East. William L. Challiss was a doctor and one of the church's most generous donors. George T. Challiss operated Atchison's first dry goods and grocery store, and Luther C. Challiss was in business with George. Luther was a member of Atchison's free state town council at the time of Lincoln's visit and had donated the land on which the Baptist Church stood.[13] Their father encouraged his sons to organize the church in Atchison, and he and his congregation in New Jersey provided funds for the building. Reverend Challis did not favor slavery, but according to his biographer, was "cautious and reserved in his opposition" to it, "greatly deprecated the agitation of this question in religious bodies," and "was disposed to lose his personal responsibility in this matter by regarding the whole question as purely political; with which ministers, as such, had nothing to do."[14] His sons and others in the congregation may have shared his views.

The other influential member of the Baptist Church was Benjamin F. Stringfellow. The Stringfellows were longtime Baptists from Culpeper County, Virginia.[15] Benjamin grew up on his father's plantation, attended the University of Virginia, earned a reputation in Missouri as a fiery proslavery lawyer, served in the Missouri state legislature, and became the state's attorney general. In 1852 he and his younger brother, Dr. John Stringfellow, moved to Weston, Missouri, eighteen miles from Atchison, where they purchased land and encouraged proslavery settlers to move to Kansas. John relocated to Atchison in 1854, and a few months later cofounded the proslavery *Squatter Sovereign* newspaper.[16] On several occasions, the brothers were accused of encouraging violent confrontations with abolitionists.[17] In 1858, John returned to Virginia to settle his father's estate and when war broke out joined the Confederate Army. Benjamin moved to Atchison in 1859 and became a promoter of the new railroad to Topeka. With real estate valued at fifty thousand dollars, he was the richest person in the county and one of the most generous donors to the Baptist Church. He attended Lincoln's speech and after the war became a Republican himself, but at the time was known in the community as a proslavery advocate.[18]

If Baptists may have had mixed sentiments about hosting Lincoln, Methodists did too. Franklin G. Adams, one of the lawyers in charge of arranging the visit, recalled having "considerable difficulty in gaining consent to have a political meeting in a church." He reported that he and his colleague, Judge P. P. Wilcox, "met with such a rebuff and refusal" from the trustees at the Methodist Church that they nearly "lost patience" and used every means of persuasion to gain the trustees' cooperation.[19] One person who may have helped was Colonel Peter T. Abell, on whose donated land the church was constructed. Abell had grown up in Kentucky, converted to the Methodist Church as a young man, and was one of Atchison's founders and leading citizens. In 1855 Abell opposed free staters, but by 1859 his views appear to have moderated.[20] According to Adams, Abell and Lincoln struck up a lively conversation at the hotel the afternoon of Lincoln's arrival, and shared pleasant memories of Kentucky. A second source of support may have been O. F. Short, a free state advocate who was a member of the school board and one of the church's founders. The other person who may have assisted in securing the venue was Pomeroy, Atchison's mayor, a collaborator with Short and Martin in founding Atchison's antislavery newspaper, and a leader of the New England Emigrant Aid Company, which supported free state settlers in Kansas. Pomeroy had been a founding trustee of the Plymouth Church in Lawrence in 1854. He introduced Lincoln that evening.[21]

Although the Methodists may have been more favorable toward Lincoln than the Baptists, it would have been mistaken to regard the two churches simply as rivals. Churches in frontier Kansas were civic organizations that town boosters promoted because they were deemed to be good for the community's economic and social well-being. That necessitated cooperation more than it led to competition. The Baptist Church, for example, received small donations from contributors who were not Baptists.[22] Four of the eight founding members of the Methodist Church were not Methodists and participated with the understanding that they would join their own churches when the opportunity arose.[23] Cooperation was necessary when buildings and pastors were in short supply. It also caused free state sentiments to cross-denominational lines. Before Reverend L. A. Alderson arrived to conduct the inaugural meeting at the Baptist Church, the Methodists' Reverend Shaw had been invited to preach the service. At the Methodist Church, Reverend J. H. Byrd of the Congregationalists, whose church remained unfinished until 1865, preached on alternate Sundays. Pomeroy and his wife, Lucy Gaylord Pomeroy, were Congregationalists, as was Ingalls.[24] Congregationalists were the strongest supporters of the New England Emigrant Aid Company. Another Atchison pastor with Congregationalist roots was Pardee Butler, who affiliated loosely with the Disciples of Christ and failed to launch a church of his own, but became a local hero after a confrontation with proslavery leaders.[25]

Although the different denominations would compete in coming years for members and on theological grounds, it was often the interpersonal bonds and sharing of scarce resources in small towns that brought them together in common cause.

A second complication illustrated by Lincoln's visit was that religious and political loyalties were always conditioned by economic circumstances as well as aspirations. Slavery and states' rights were divisive enough to lead a nation to war, and yet men like Abell and Benjamin Stringfellow—who happened to be law partners— not only shared in schemes to get rich but also changed ideological positions and political affiliations. Whatever their views may have been on slavery and religion, Abell and Luther Challiss invited proslavery advocate John Stringfellow to join as a director of the Atchison and Topeka Railroad Company.[26] Economic incentives were at work with Pomeroy as well. Pomeroy the idealist supported free staters emigrating from the East to Kansas. Pomeroy the realist was in business with investor Theodore Hyatt of New York to develop property on both sides of the Missouri River, gained wealth from land speculation and investing in railroads, and in 1873 was found guilty of bribery and corruption. Pomeroy's funder in the 1850s, Theodore Hyatt, was the brother of Thaddeus Hyatt, who was jailed for refusing to testify against Brown. Theodore was critical of his brother's idealism. Thaddeus the realist, after his release, worked with Pomeroy to solicit food and clothing from churches in the East, and send them to starving pioneers during the harsh winter of 1860 and 1861.[27]

The third point that Lincoln's visit illustrated was that Kansans might become overwhelmingly Republican, but that did not preclude disagreements within the party. In December 1859, it was not that Kansas Republicans opposed Lincoln but rather that they favored William Henry Seward more. Seward had championed the free state cause in Kansas as a leader in the U.S. Senate and was favored to win the Republican Party's nomination for president in 1860. The Kansas territorial delegation pledged its courtesy votes to Seward before the convention, and even when Lincoln triumphed on the third ballot, loyalties to Seward remained strong.

The welcome that Seward received in Atchison when he visited that fall could not have contrasted more with Lincoln's. Martin made no mention of Lincoln's visit in *Freedom's Champion*, yet introduced Seward as the "foremost Statesman of the Age." While Lincoln's audience at the Methodist Church was cordial enough, Seward was escorted not only by the town's brass band but also by a reception committee on horseback, ladies in carriages, three free state committees, and visiting delegations from neighboring towns. Seward's lecture could not have been held in any church. He addressed an audience of four thousand from the balcony of his hotel.[28] He and Lincoln did not differ substantially on the issues. Seward was simply more popular. Leaders like Martin, Pomeroy, and Ingalls came around, serving Lincoln and the Union. But there would always be differences among Kansas Republicans, even though Kansas would long be almost a single-party state.

Never far in the background was a remaining aspect of faith and politics: the tension that would surface again and again between Protestants and Catholics, and that often took on political overtones. After Leavenworth, Atchison was the second-largest Catholic community in Kansas at the time of Lincoln's visit. Overlooking the Missouri River on a ridge just north of town was St. Benedict's Abbey, Church, and school. The land had been donated by Benjamin Stringfellow, presumably not because of any particular religious affinities but instead because he saw the project as a way to enhance the town.[29] Catholics settled in Atchison from Ireland and Germany as well as the eastern states, usually coming to Saint Louis by way of the Mississippi River and then to Saint Joseph by steamboat. In 1860, Atchison's residents included 309 born in Ireland and 184 born in Germany. Most of the residents were in their twenties or thirties. William Shannon, the territorial governor of Kansas in 1855 and 1856, was a Catholic Democrat from Ohio. Republicans were often skeptical of Catholics, figuring them to be in the pocket of Democratic candidates, and in 1854 and 1856 the Know-Nothing movement exploited these fears.[30] But the picture in Atchison was different from partisan politics elsewhere, just as it was among Protestants. St. Benedict's founders were German monks from Pennsylvania. They had little sympathy for the pro-slavery cause.[31]

What did separate many of Atchison's Catholics from Protestants was social class. The Germans were carpenters, stonemasons, butchers, saddlers, blacksmiths, and farmers, putting them on a par with Protestant shopkeepers and farmers, but German Catholics were largely absent from the community's elite. With only a few exceptions, the Irish men worked as unskilled laborers. Many of the wealthier Protestants employed Irish girls as domestics. When class was not an issue, there was evidence of social interaction across religious and ethnic lines, at least if business dealings and employment counted. One of the community's first and most successful residents was Michael C. Finney, who arrived in 1856 from Saint Louis, having immigrated as a young man to New York City from Ireland. Finney was the wharfmaster, owned a general merchandise store, supplied grain and produce to pioneers passing through Atchison, and served on the city council.[32] He and his wife, Katherine Kathrens Finney, raised three children, one of whom, Charles C. Finney, became a doctor and was elected mayor. Her brother, R. D. Kathrens, was a wholesale merchant in Atchison. Her best friend was the wife of Baptist businessperson George Challiss.[33] Another member of the Catholic community was Tom Murphy, known as the "genial Irishman," who ran the Massasoit House, the town's leading hotel, where Lincoln stayed the night of his visit.

But there were also instances of tension and misunderstanding. Several of Atchison's saloons were run by Germans and Irish, and undoubtedly did their share of business with the town's unmarried male population. The temperance movement came later, but churchwomen were already beginning to complain that something needed to be done.[34] *Freedom's Champion* periodically carried stories about Irishmen who were notoriously stupid, poor, or laughable. On one occasion the newspaper reprinted a long story about a girl in another state who disappeared, only to be tracked down by her father, who located her at a convent. The story implied that Catholics and kidnapping went hand in hand.[35]

At the same time, the reality of living and working together in a small town moderated the tensions between Catholics and

Protestants. One episode suggested the potential for getting along. About a year after Lincoln's visit a column appeared in the Atchison *Union*, the town's proslavery paper, praising Benjamin Stringfellow (though not by name) for donating land to St. Benedict's, and thus assisting the "humble order" of Germans and Irish. In reply, an anonymous reader sent a letter to *Freedom's Champion* arguing that the Germans and Irish were in fact "foremost in improving and advancing our city." They were, the letter continued, responsible for "miracles of improvement, of invention, and of boundless development," as opposed to the "bloated aristocracy" who held them in low esteem. Martin published the lengthy letter in full.[36]

Characteristically, Lincoln's visit to Atchison fulfilled only a few of his hosts' expectations. He failed to convert any of Seward's supporters. Ungainly rustic that he was, he nevertheless got along well with the town's gentry and even drew favorable comments from proslavery advocates. If any of the Methodists hoped that he would talk about God, he did not.[37] Tension may have been present between Atchison's Protestants and Catholics, but if any of Lincoln's hosts voiced anti-Catholic sentiments, Lincoln would have disapproved. He strongly disliked the anti-Catholicism of the Know-Nothing Party, expressing this sentiment in an 1855 letter that registered his view of Benjamin Stringfellow as a representative of an "odious and detested class" of slave traders, and then turned to the broader topic of bigotry: "When the Know-Nothings get control, [the national creed] will read 'all men are created equal, except negroes, and foreigners, and catholics.'" Lincoln added, "When it comes to this I should prefer emigrating to some country where they make no pretence of loving liberty."[38]

ESTABLISHING A CIVIC ORDER

The context in which Lincoln's Kansas visit occurred was one of enormous opportunity for settlers, speculators, and entrepreneurs—-opportunity to acquire land and make homes, start towns and businesses, launch churches, and for some, bend the law and exploit their neighbors. The fifty million acres that made up Kansas in 1861 constituted approximately a tenth of the territory that Thomas Jefferson acquired from the French in 1803. Missouri was the first of that territory to be settled, gaining statehood in 1821, growing to a population of 140,000 by 1830, and becoming the most populous state in the region by 1860 with nearly 1.2 million residents. Missouri's population in 1860 included 115,000 slaves, more than the entire population of Kansas. Arkansas became a state in 1836, and by 1860 had a population of 435,000, including 111,000 slaves. The other Middle West states that preceded Kansas were Iowa in 1846 and Minnesota in 1858. Iowa was the second most populous state in the region in 1860 with 675,000 residents, while Minnesota remained much smaller with a population of only 172,000. Nebraska entered the union in 1867, North and South Dakota followed in 1889, and Oklahoma in 1907. Although much of Kansas territory was set aside for Indians from eastern states, white settlers began staking claims in 1854 and 1855, and by 1860 the white population increased to more than 107,000.

The challenges facing ordinary settlers, officials, and church leaders were immense. Laws were difficult to enforce, and elections were uncertain. Popular sovereignty as the basis on which Kansas was to become a free state or embrace slavery resulted in fraudulent elections along with border violence. The decision's significance for the country's future drew Kansas into the national political debate, and made it a topic of profound interest in places as remote as Springfield, Charleston, New York, Boston, and the nation's capital. Horace Greeley, who stopped in Atchison on May 15, 1859 (declaring, "I have long been looking for the West, and here it is at last"), published hundreds of articles in the New York Daily Tribune about the struggles in Kansas and the Republicans' efforts to make it a free state.[39] Three days after visiting Atchison, Greeley addressed the Kansas Republican convention in Osawatomie. The Democratic Party, he said, was a "whited sepulchre," a "grinning death's head," the "den of all abominations."[40]

That Kansas should be a free state was both a plank of the Republican Party and a constant refrain from abolitionist pulpits.

Beecher, the Connecticut preacher who sent Bibles and rifles to Kansas plus helped organize the New Haven colony that settled in Wabaunsee near Topeka, declared on the colony's departure, "You are the seed of Christianity" and civilization. "To go there determined to transplant to its soil that tree of liberty which under God has in older states borne and shook down from its boughs all the fruits of an unparalleled prosperity requires heroic courage." To defend themselves and their liberties, Beecher counseled, "is a duty from which you cannot shrink without leaving your honor, your manhood, your Christian fidelity behind you."[41] On behalf of the colony, C. B. Lines expressed his conviction that "from this settlement there will go out an influence for good over the state that shall be to some extent felt in promoting civil order, just and equal laws, a correct idea of the rights of man, and the value of free institutions."[42]

In towns like Atchison, Lawrence, and Leavenworth, it was not at all certain that the free state cause would prevail. Martin's exuberance at Republicans' triumph in December 1859 was conditioned by the fact that Atchison had participated in three ballots that fall, all of them close, and with Democrats winning in November.[43] In Lawrence a few months earlier, a free state resident wrote to a friend, "The democratic party is a power in this territory, [and] the indications are that it will receive a victory next fall in the elections. The Republicans will be defeated and a democrat to Congress."[44] His prediction was wrong, and Lawrence itself remained a free state stronghold, but it had been plundered by proslavery forces in 1856 and would be again in a few years. On August 20, 1863, Lawrence was sacked and burned by William Quantrill's raiders, who also killed 150 residents. Arriving from Atchison four days later, General Ingalls wrote, "Absolutely nothing remained. Not a yard of calico, a pound of flour or sugar, a nail or a pan or pair of shoes could be purchased in a town where stocks of not less value than a million and a half of dollars were exposed two days before."[45] Leavenworth, in contrast, was known as a proslavery town from its inception in 1855, and in 1857 was the location of some of the most violent attacks against free state residents in the territory. By the time of Lincoln's visit in 1859 Republicans held six of the town's twelve council seats, but Democrats hung on to the office of mayor, and rancor between the two parties resulted in at least one melee with paving stones thrown and shots fired. All of Leavenworth's delegates to the Wyandotte convention were Democrats.[46]

Smaller towns were drawn into the partisan conflicts as well. Residents near Doniphan, where Lincoln spoke in 1859, remembered Benjamin Stringfellow arriving during an election in 1855 with a band of proslavery Missourians and threatening anyone who voted for a free state candidate.[47] Although Doniphan was a free state town in 1859, its delegate to the Wyandotte convention was a Democrat. One of Troy's delegates was a Democrat, and the other an independent. Near Shawnee Mission, Greeley's stagecoach took him through Olathe—a "smart village," he wrote, "destined to become a place of considerable size and importance."[48] Olathe sent a Republican to the Wyandotte convention and a Democrat, who left soon after and served in the Confederate Army. Fifteen miles from Lawrence, Lecompton flourished from 1855 to 1859 as the territorial capital, but quickly declined when Republicans rose to power and relocated the legislature to Topeka.[49]

When Kansas adopted a free state constitution and soon after entered the union on the side of the North, the Republican Party became almost synonymous with righteous virtue, while anyone who opposed it was considered a lawless ruffian most likely from Missouri. Such "ruffians" were responsible for Kansans' travail and would be forever held in disrepute. Thoroughly armed Missourians, Greeley declared, "swarmed across the unmarked border whenever an election was impending, camping in the vicinity of most of the polls, whereof they took unceremonious possession, and voting till they were sure that no more votes were needed, when they decamped, and returned to their Missouri homes."[50] Democrats, others complained, were a sham party, engaged in pettifoggery, and repugnant, conniving, and fraudulent.[51] The first meeting of the Kansas state legislature, a delegate recalled, "killed everything that had a pro-slavery, Democratic, tinge to it." The free state

Republicans, he observed, "came to Kansas for a holy purpose and were not to be balked in their intentions."[52] Kansas Republicans won every race for the U.S. Senate and every gubernatorial election except one for the next thirty years.

But the task of creating towns as well as establishing farms and homes was a matter of creating a civic order that went well beyond the immediate conflicts separating free state and slavery proponents. As government agents negotiated treaties with Indians, surveyors mapped counties, townships, and sections. Town companies formulated charters, sold shares, elected officers, and purchased property. Lots were platted and advertised to attract settlers. Land offices opened to record claims. Courthouses, stores, and churches had to be built, town councils elected, school boards established, and schools constructed. Within a year of its founding, a promising town usually had a law officer, revenue for developing and maintaining streets, a jail, a post office, a hotel, a school, and several stores. One of Atchison's first tasks was to construct a "lockup" of sturdy cottonwood logs. Another was to decree that tippling shops would remain closed on Sundays.

The resources that settlers brought with them included not only the rugged entrepreneurial spirit about which so much would be written but also their knowledge of social institutions. Like the rest of the Louisiana Purchase, Kansas benefited from being settled well after the nation's basic laws and patterns of government were established. The Land Ordinance of 1785 created the system of counties and townships that the Middle West territories and states later adopted. Iowa modeled its effective system of public schools on Ohio's, and Kansas and Minnesota modeled theirs on Iowa's. Schooling and literacy rates were high in the northern states from which a large number of Kansans came, especially Illinois, Indiana, New York, Ohio, and Pennsylvania. Literacy was also high among the English, Canadian, and German immigrants who made up a majority of Kansas' foreign-born population.[53]

Notorious as it was for border violence, Kansas was led by citizens with experience in passing laws and creating civic organizations. Men like Pomeroy and Father Henry Lemke in Atchison were examples. Pomeroy was a schoolteacher, merchant, and antislavery lecturer, and served a term in the Massachusetts legislature prior to becoming an agent for the New England Emigrant Aid Company. Lemke arrived in Kansas at the age of sixty, almost destitute and ready to sink into semiretirement, but having bought and sold land in significant quantities as well as founded the town of Carrolltown, Pennsylvania. Lemke knew surveyors and merchants, and secured the initial funding for St. Benedict's Abbey.[54] Other examples included the Stringfellows and Challis brothers, who brought experience in law, medicine, and business.

A year before it became a state, Kansas included more than eight hundred residents working as lawyers, public officials, and teachers. Another thousand were merchants or doctors. These occupations represented a small fraction of the total labor force composed mostly of farmers, farm laborers, craftspeople, and artisans. Yet compared with other parts of the Middle West, the rate of involvement in these professions was high. The rate of lawyers in the labor force, for example, was more than twice as high in Kansas as in Missouri or Arkansas, both of which had been states for several decades. It was also higher than in Minnesota and Iowa. The rate of merchants and public officials was higher in Kansas than in any of these states. Kansas ranked second among the five states in having the highest rate of physicians and second in the rate employed as printers. Overall, Kansas was significantly above the five-state average for six of the seven professions.[55]

The churches contributed to establishing civic order in the region's towns and farming communities. As in Atchison, churches provided a public space in which lectures could be given and visiting dignitaries hosted. Church functions included sermons, classes, social gatherings, and business meetings. The one that clergy and lay members themselves would have placed first was serving as a public expression of their faith. Clergy embodied the faith as its most visible specialists. Church leaders in eastern states sent clergy to the Middle West to preach, perform the sacraments, preside at weddings and funerals, organize congregations, solicit funds, and erect buildings. Nationwide there was 1 pastor for every 838 people in 1860. In Kansas the ratio was considerably better: a pastor for every 518 people, or almost 40 percent better than the national average. Iowa was the only other Middle West state that came close.

Clergy gravitated to Iowa and Kansas for the same reasons that lawyers and doctors did, although with far less hope of earning a decent living. Newly available land meant a growing population, which in turn created opportunities to preach, start churches, and minister to the needy. These opportunities were also present in Missouri, where the population increased by four hundred thousand in the 1850s. And yet it was interesting that the ratio of clergy to population in Kansas (and Iowa) was significantly better than in Missouri. The difference was partly that Missouri was already more settled. In smaller measure, Kansas and Iowa also benefited from the impending struggle over slavery. Congregationalists, for example, established eight churches in Kansas and seventy-one in Iowa by 1860, but none in Missouri. Northern Methodists in Missouri lost property and pulpits to southern Methodists when the denomination split in 1846, forcing some deposed clergy to relocate to Kansas and Iowa, and later to Nebraska. In 1860, approximately 40 percent of the clergy in Kansas were Methodists.[56]

PUBLIC RELIGION

Church buildings provided the other public expression of piety in plains communities. Small or large, churches served as sanctified space, set apart for worship and governed by concerns that sometimes restricted their use—as the Atchison Methodist trustees' reluctance to host Lincoln illustrated. Tall steeples were far less common in the Middle West than in New England, not only because they were expensive, but also because fire and cyclones destroyed them. Churches nevertheless were architecturally distinct, often resembling one another from town to town and across denominations. An edifice demonstrated both a financial commitment and the congregation's expectation that its presence would continue.

Buildings went up quickly when donors could be found, but in many instances were delayed by high costs, scarce materials, poor crops, and uncertain population flows. The comparison of Kansas with Missouri and Iowa in this regard is instructive. By 1850 Missouri had a church building on average for every 750 people, and that rate held steady in 1860. Iowa had one church building for every 996 people in 1850, and the ratio improved to one building for every 711 people in 1860. In contrast, Kansas had only one building for every 1,105 people in 1860.

Even in prosperous towns like Atchison, Leavenworth, and Topeka the difficulties were evident. Nine churches were constructed in Atchison between 1858 and 1868, with five years elapsing on average after a congregation organized until its building was finished and in use. Among the eleven churches constructed in Leavenworth between 1857 and 1873, the average was 4.7 years, and in Topeka where the population rose rapidly as a result of the state capital locating there, the average was 3.3 years among the eleven churches built by congregations organized between 1855 and 1870. Of the thirty churches in the three towns, only eight were completed within a year of the congregation being organized. Eleven took at least five years.

In no instance was a building completed without one or more pastors being intimately involved. Delays occurred when congregations failed to grow, when finances fell short, and from adverse weather. The First Congregational Church in Topeka highlighted the difficulties. Organized with a membership of sixteen in 1856, the congregation raised seven hundred dollars and laid a foundation nine months later. A year after that, the walls were up yet funds were lacking to add a roof. In June 1859, a storm demolished the rear and side walls. The American Congregational Union provided three hundred dollars that fall and rebuilding began the following spring, only to be halted by another violent storm that caused the south wall to collapse. The building was finally dedicated on January 1, 1861. Three months later it hosted the first meeting of the Kansas state legislature.[57]

Although drought, the harsh winter of 1860–61, and the Civil War slowed population growth, the Homestead Act in 1862 and a series of treaties with Indian leaders facilitated new immigration at the close of the war. The population of Kansas tripled from 107,000 in 1860 to 364,000 in 1870.[58] As new land attracted streams of migrant settlers, the rise in the number of clergy could not keep pace. Nationally, the balance of population to clergy edged up from 838 persons per pastor in 1860 to 858 in 1870, but in the Middle West the shift was more dramatic. The number of people to pastors rose in Kansas from 518 to 676, in Iowa from 532 to 746, and in Missouri from 926 to 990. But if the ratio of clergy to population mattered, it was not yet the case, at least not in Kansas and Nebraska, that there was an actual shortage of clergy relative to the number of congregations. In 1870 there were 578 clergy in Kansas, 530 organized congregations, and 301 church buildings. In Nebraska there were 183 clergy, 181 organized congregations, and 108 buildings. That did not mean that every congregation had its own pastor. Many did not. It did, however, set Kansas and Nebraska apart from Missouri, where churches outnumbered clergy by a ratio of 5 to 4; Minnesota, with a ratio of 4 to 3; and Iowa, where the ratio was almost 2 to 1.[59]

With immigrants arriving from nearly every state as well as many ethnic and national backgrounds, Kansas was denominationally diverse from the start. The ninety-seven established churches in 1860 included thirty-six Methodist, thirteen Baptist, eleven Episcopal, eight Congregational, seven Presbyterian, seven Union (interdenominational), six Christian (Disciples of Christ), and six Roman Catholic congregations. In addition there was one Lutheran church, one Cumberland Presbyterian church, and one Friends meeting house. By the time the next official tally was taken in 1870, census officials decided that the previous count may have been misleading because some churches were included only if they had buildings, while others were counted simply because they claimed to be organized. Thus, the new census takers were instructed that a church "to deserve notice in the census must have something of the character of an institution," adding that it "must be known in the community in which it is located," and should have "something permanent and tangible to substantiate its title to recognition."[60]

Acknowledging that churches having these qualifications might or might not have buildings, the 1870 census counted church organizations and edifices separately, included the seating capacity and value of the latter, and hedged its numbers by stating that the results would differ from those reported by denominations—which frequently was the case. The 1870 figures suggested that churches in Kansas were three to five times more numerous than in 1860, and had become more diverse. Besides the denominations represented in 1860 there were two synagogues, a Unitarian church, a Universalist church, and a Mormon congregation. Not fully captured in the census were further distinctions such as those between German and Swedish Lutherans, German and Irish Catholics, and African American and white Baptists.

Besides the fact that denominational diversity was a reality, the freedom to practice a religion of one's choosing was officially recognized. The state's constitution adopted at Wyandotte in 1859 specified that "the right to worship God according to the dictates of conscience shall never be infringed; nor shall any person be compelled to attend or support any form of worship; nor shall any control of or interference with the rights of conscience be permitted, nor any preference be given by law to any religious establishment or mode of worship." The constitution further declared that "no religious test or property qualification shall be required for any office of public trust, nor for any vote at any election, nor shall any person be incompetent to testify on account of religious belief."[61] These clauses followed the section of the constitution that decreed Kansas free of slavery, and were preceded by the statement that the people of Kansas were "grateful to Almighty God for our civil and religious privileges." The wording was similar to that of Ohio's constitution of 1850, which the delegates adopted as their model, and closely resembled phrases in the Minnesota and Iowa constitutions of 1857.[62]

In practice, religious freedom was the minimal condition for multiple denominations to establish churches in Kansas, but it is important to understand that much more was involved than a so-called free market of religious competitors. Where competition could plausibly be said to have mattered was in church construction: in town after town, church leaders broke ground for church buildings within a few months of one another. But there was no indication that each successive structure was an attempt to outlavish local rivals. Faced with rapid population growth or the hope thereof, church leaders had little reason to imagine themselves competing for scarce resources. The challenge was rather to make enough congregations available to attract settlers and provide them with worship facilities when they came. The competition was with rival towns more so than among denominations. This was the reason that church leaders so often cooperated in launching new congregations, and why land speculators like Luther Challiss and Benjamin Stringfellow could be persuaded to donate property.

With 166 organized congregations and 74 buildings valued at $316,000, Methodists were the largest denomination in 1870, just as they had been in 1860. When the Kansas Conference of the Methodist Episcopal Church met at Paola in 1871, its leaders reported having 243 preachers among their number and Sunday school classes involving 10,683 children.[63] Baptists were second in size, with ninety-two congregations and fifty-six buildings valued at $247,000, and Presbyterians third with eighty-four congregations and fifty-five buildings valued at $277,000. There were forty-three Congregationalist churches with twenty-six buildings and thirty-five Christian churches with sixteen buildings. Episcopalians had only fourteen parishes and nine buildings, but on average had structures valued at more than $6,300 each, compared to edifices averaging between $4,000 and $4,500 among the other denominations.

Roman Catholics were listed as having thirty-seven parishes and thirty-four buildings valued at $513,000. That included the Cathedral of the Immaculate Conception in Leavenworth completed in 1868 at a cost of $200,000 under the direction of Bishop John B.

Miege and assisted by Santa Fe bishop John B. Lamy, who in 1927 was to become the inspiration for Willa Cather's acclaimed novel *Death Comes for the Archbishop*. The cathedral's location was an instance of church leaders understanding the value of competition among rival towns. Bishop Miege initially approached the Wyandotte Town Company for a donation of land near the future site of Kansas City, Kansas, and when offered a small unattractive lot went on to Leavenworth, where he was given five acres in a desirable part of town. Father Anton Kuhls of Kansas City later lamented, "All the grand ecclesiastical buildings of Leavenworth would be [here], and the fate of our town would have been different today, if our land company had taken another view of this matter."[64]

Methodists' success in launching new congregations during the 1860s in greater number than any other denomination owed much to the famed circuit-rider system, in which itinerant clergy traveled from village to village holding meetings in homes, stores, and when weather permitted outdoors. Even with clergy as abundant as they were in Kansas, the circuit system facilitated planting churches in new locations. Especially as the population spread to central and western Kansas, clergy traveled long distances by horse or on foot, and organized congregations by conducting services wherever they could find interested settlers. But it is crucial not to associate itinerancy only with Methodism. Itinerant clergy from western Missouri performed Episcopal services in eastern Kansas. Baptists used itinerancy too, and although quite different in many other respects, so did Catholics. By 1860, the monks at Atchison Priory had developed three circuits involving twenty-three mission stations, which they visited at least once a month. Like their Protestant counterparts, the monks rode forty or fifty miles a day, and relied on networks among the faithful to provide lodgings and host meetings.

An 1862 letter to a Catholic circuit rider between Atchison and Omaha illustrated the details and character of the networks involved. "Go from here to Rockbluff about eighteen miles from Nebraska City and ask after Mr. Haskins the owner of the flouring mill," it instructed. "If you find him he will invite you to say Mass on Saturday. From Rockbluff go to Plattsmouth and ask after

1.2 Cathedral of the Immaculate Conception at Leavenworth during construction
in 1867. Courtesy of KansasMemory.org, Kansas State Historical Society, Copy
and Reuse Restrictions Apply

Mr. Gottfried Fickler, a German butcher. He will tell you what you
have to do. You can say Mass and preach there on Sunday." The
itinerant was to visit the bishop in Omaha the next day to inquire
about a German settlement at Helfna, then travel to West Point and
Fontanelle, where a Mr. Hancock would be able to give directions
to another settlement across a river near a sawmill, and so on.[65]
The circuit riders were known for weathering hardship and holding
meetings in drafty barns, but as this letter reveals, their work also
depended on careful planning and strategic contacts.

Unlike colonial churches that benefited from government
funding, congregations in the Middle West were voluntary organizations supported by tithes, pledges, and subscriptions. As civic

organizations, churches nevertheless engaged in activities that had
political implications, and church leaders looked to government to
implement and enforce laws deemed favorable to church teachings
and ideals. In 1868, under the governorship of Methodist reverend Nehemiah Green, the Kansas legislature passed a series of laws
defining "crimes against public morals and decency," including
bigamy, incest, adultery, removing or receiving a dead body from
its place of interment, and gambling. The laws further stipulated
that performing any work other than acts of necessity or charity
on the first day of the week was a misdemeanor carrying a fine of
up to twenty-five dollars, and that selling merchandise or operating
a tippling shop on Sunday was punishable by up to fifty dollars.
Highlighting an issue posed by religious meetings, the statute most
directly concerned with religion specified that selling or disposing
of "any spirituous or other liquors," or "any article of traffic whatever," within one mile of "the place where any religious society or
assembly of people are collected or collecting together for religious
worship in any camp or field meeting" was a misdemeanor carrying
a fine of up to one hundred dollars. Finding the wording overly restrictive, the legislature amended the law in 1876 to exempt tavern
keepers operating at their regular places of business and anyone
having a written permit from the managers of the religious assembly to sell provisions to the persons attending.[66]

SERVING THE COMMUNITY

The issues that brought church leaders and politics together most
often were abolition and temperance. Abolition was pressed by
Congregationalist leaders such as Pomeroy of Atchison and John
Ritchie, the colorful Topekan who assisted John Brown on at least
one occasion and was active in the Underground Railroad. It was a
principal reason for the New England Emigrant Aid Association's
efforts to assist settlers, many of whom were Congregationalists. It
was also the official position of the Kansas Methodist Conference.

Consistent with the stance of the northern branch of the denomination, Kansas Methodists deemed slavery a great evil, and declared in a resolution drafted by Atchison's Isaac F. Collins and adopted by the conference in 1858 that no slaveholder was to be admitted to the church's membership.

Intemperance, the same conference decreed, was "one of the most formidable and widely extended evils with which the Church and society have to contend." Ministers and members were encouraged to work toward passing and sustaining "a prohibitory liquor law in our Territories."[67] At the Wyandotte convention, Congregationalist Ritchie proposed unsuccessfully to include a Prohibition clause in the constitution.[68] Prohibition was also attempted with varying success through local legislation. In Lawrence, for example, the town's constitution included a provision against the sale of intoxicating drinks, and the statute was stiffened by popular referendum in 1855. Two years of failed enforcement, however, during which seven saloons were established, persuaded the churchwomen who felt most deeply about the issue to take matters into their own hands. In 1857 they formed the Temperance Vigilance Committee, a citizens' organization seeking to influence local elections and law enforcement.[69]

Besides abolition and temperance, churches' efforts in the areas of education and social welfare brought them into the political sphere. At the primary level, public school curricula typically included Bible reading and prayer. The churches were also active in initiating institutions of higher education, such as Baker University in Baldwin and Bluemont Central College, the predecessor of Kansas State University in Manhattan. Relief assistance from public funds was supplemented through the efforts of Pomeroy, Thaddeus Hyatt, and others to solicit support from eastern churches. Joint religious and governmental efforts were also made to assist the needs of the blind and deaf. For instance, in 1871 the state of Kansas contributed five thousand dollars to "Protestant and Catholic asylums" in Leavenworth. That was small compared with the state's nearly fifty-four thousand dollar budget for insane asylums, but not insignificant relative to the six thousand dollars that the state spent establishing a normal school in Leavenworth or the twenty-seven hundred dollars it provided for the new agricultural college in Manhattan.[70]

With faith and politics so intertwined, it was thus crucial that the two domains remained as separate as they did. Delegates to the Wyandotte constitutional convention decided to include the clauses guaranteeing the separation of church and state with no dissent, and apparently little discussion. Clergy could scarcely refrain from preaching about slavery, but it was preaching that the Methodists' conference called for, not clergy involvement in legislation. Despite an appeal from Lyman Beecher in 1855 for clergy to participate more actively in the New England Emigrant Aid Society, only four embarked on the journey to Kansas, and one returned immediately, leaving the work of settlement and antislavery agitation almost entirely in the hands of lay leaders. The reluctance in Atchison to host a political speaker in the Lord's house probably was not atypical. Church members were certainly among those who voted for the free state constitution, but churches themselves were segregated, and proposals were made to prevent African Americans from settling at all in Kansas.

If race complicated the connection of faith and politics, schooling and relief attempts followed simpler lines of delineation. Unlike Missouri and Arkansas where private schools organized by churches and funded through subscriptions became popular in the 1850s, schooling in Kansas and Nebraska followed the pattern in Ohio, Iowa, and Minnesota of public support through revenue from land and taxes, and supervision by elected county and township officials. Protestant churches focused their educational efforts on Sunday school programs, and were content that Bible reading and prayer were a regular part of public school activities. The Catholic schools in Atchison and Leavenworth offered training for a small number of younger scholars, but were oriented chiefly toward higher learning in preparation for the priesthood and careers in business. Higher learning was the aim of institutions like Baker University and Bluemont Central College as well. Relief efforts looked to churches for support in times of emergency, but poor farms, insane asylums, and institutions for the blind and deaf were established and operated by the state and county governments.

Notwithstanding the fact that Kansas was overwhelmingly Republican and Protestant, and that Methodists were the largest group of Protestants, there were demarcations then that separated faith from politics, and caused the two to mingle through shared convictions more than from organized electoral or legislative efforts. The issue that deviated from this pattern was temperance. Although it would be two decades before the state adopted Prohibition, settlers struggled to restrict saloons and intoxicating liquor from the start. If the intent was to limit Catholic influences and foreign immigration, as historians would argue, those were not yet the issue. It was rather that Kansas was truly the frontier where lawlessness often prevailed and was deemed by citizens to be aggravated by drunkenness. Settlers associated drunkenness with danger from Indians and border ruffians, and saw it as a threat to their families and towns.

Frank A. Root was a boarder at the rooming house in Atchison run by John Martin's parents. He worked among the drivers who ran ox teams to California and wrote later of life in frontier Kansas. "Frequently I saw drivers while sitting on the box and riding with them," he remarked, "when they were so drunk that the wonder to me was how they ever kept from tumbling off the seat." Root especially remembered a dinner at which Paul Coburn, the stage company's agent, became "gloriously drunk," proceeding to paint the place red with his six-shooters, destroy the chandelier, and leave the room in shambles. Not much later Coburn killed a man in a Denver saloon.[71] On her journey to Atchison in 1857, Lucy Gaylord Pomeroy spent the Sabbath in Quindaro, a free state town on the Missouri River, where she observed the ladies circulating a petition to stop the sale of intoxicating drinks and rejoiced that a public meeting was initiated on the subject.[72] It was not surprising that towns like Quindaro, Lawrence, and Topeka looked favorably at temperance efforts.

But it would be misleading to conclude that piety in those early years of Kansas settlement was primarily about temperance, abolition, or even church building. Faith was fundamentally a part of settlers' struggle to survive, face illness and bereavement, and make sense of why they had come to a land of unrelenting hardship. Scarlet fever and typhoid wiped out entire families. Women routinely died giving birth. Men who got lost in blinding snowstorms froze on the open prairie. With death so near, faith offered assurance of eternal life. It was the same piety that soldiers wrote of from their encampments during the Civil War, and that pioneer women in Nebraska and Minnesota described as they wrote of loneliness and illness on the treeless plains. They prayed, questioned God, and hoped to meet their departed loved ones in heaven. A church meeting at a settler's cabin was an opportunity to socialize and exchange news. The traveling pastor or priest brought people together, performed weddings, visited the sick and dying, and buried the dead. Church connections facilitated courtships and helped when the unexpected happened.

An episode that illustrated the value of church connections occurred in Leavenworth in 1859. Maria Maher, a young unmarried Catholic woman working as a domestic servant, became pregnant. The father was a young man in the community whose identity and intentions were apparently unknown to her employer, Thomas Ewing Jr., a lawyer and landowner who served in the territorial legislature and was destined to become a general in the Union army. In keeping with customs of the day, the bishop arranged for Maher to go to Saint Louis, where she would be able to live in confinement and receive help from one of the Catholic charitable institutions. Ewing offered his assistance as well, inviting her to write if she needed financial aid and giving her the name of an attorney who would work with her in negotiating with the young man in question. Further, Ewing suggested that if the young man was Catholic, it would be advisable to consult with the sisters or a priest before involving an attorney. Ewing himself was not Catholic, but his mother and three of his siblings were, which probably explained his knowledge of how best to handle the situation.[73]

The role of faith in sustaining early settlers was particularly evident in women's diaries and letters. Julia Hardy Lovejoy kept a diary from 1854 to 1856, chronicling her departure from New

Hampshire at the age of forty-two with her husband and daughter as well as her life as a pioneer in Kansas. Like many women, she found it difficult to leave home and family. Her loneliness was compounded by the fact that her husband was a Methodist preacher who spent months at a time traveling and serving in other stations. On the journey the Lovejoys' five-year-old daughter, Edith, contracted measles and died. Julia was pregnant and nearly died giving birth to a son. She confided often to her diary that she was heartbroken, alone, ill, weeping, and praying. Her prayers were for strength and understanding, the health of her son, and her own desire to be with God in heaven.

In 1859, after three years of writing nothing, Lovejoy resumed her diary. Her husband was still away, her house half finished, and she was sometimes too sick to stand up, but her son was alive and healthy. She was thankful. God was with her and indeed, she felt, had been revealed to her in a special way. "I shouted from a full soul," she wrote, "and even at a late hour in the night, with none but my little boy with me, I feared the neighbors might hear my shouts of praise—God has saved me from sin—the witness is clear with not one doubt—glory to His blessed Name!" She felt confident about her ability to face the trials before her. "His grace will help me to overcome, and vanquish all thro' Jesus' Name." Lovejoy was filled with praise. "To Him, I commit my interests, for time and for eternity," she stated, "and subscribe with my own hand, to His faithfulness. Amen, and Amen."[74]

CHURCH EXPANSION

A century and a half after Lovejoy wrote those words, scholars and church planners were fervently engaged in debating the sources of church expansion. One interpretation held that churches grew best when sparked by denominational competition. Another argued that strictness in doctrine and morality encouraged growth. Yet another emphasized the importance of sheer demographic expansion through frequent childbearing. Some earlier contentions were still in play, such as churches growing because of revival meetings, or from people moving to towns where transportation was easier and chores were lighter. All of these interpretations held some merit. The fact was that church expansion occurred for differing reasons under differing circumstances, though. Between 1870 and 1890, the rapid population growth that took place in Kansas provided opportunities for churches to expand, but it was also challenging to start congregations on treeless prairies where cyclones and blizzards prevailed. Competition may have encouraged growth, yet some rivalries ran deep in the bones while others hardly mattered at all. Certainly it was critical for church leaders to invest scarce resources wisely.[75]

By the end of the Civil War, church construction in Kansas had ground almost to a halt. Quantrill's raiders destroyed churches in Lawrence and Wakarusa. Young men who might otherwise have gone to the seminary became army volunteers. The Kansas Methodist Conference reported only sixty-eight clergy in 1863, down from seventy-four in 1861, after having increased from forty-seven in 1858 to eighty-five in 1860. Having doubled its membership between 1858 and 1860, the church grew only from 3,932 members in 1861 to 4,184 in 1863. For all denominations, the war delayed church building. Fort Scott near the Missouri border was typical. Presbyterian, Episcopal, and Catholic congregations organized there in 1859 and 1860, but they did not complete buildings until after the war, and Methodist, Baptist, and Congregational churches failed to be constructed until 1870. As the war ended, denominational leaders in the East were conflicted about sending additional funds to Kansas versus putting them to use in rebuilding war-damaged churches in other parts of the country. In 1865 Pomeroy, now a U.S. senator, told a national meeting of the Congregational Union that churches in Kansas would likely succeed on their own and that sending ministers to the South should be a higher priority.[76] Methodists, Baptists, and Presbyterians were already sending northern pastors to fill southern pulpits.[77] Under these circumstances, it was impressive that the religious census of 1870 counted as many churches in Kansas as it did.

The 530 congregations and 301 church buildings recorded in the 1870 census were scattered among the forty-five counties that made up the eastern half of the state and accounted for 97 percent of its population. County for county, the number of congregations, edifices, sittings, and value of church property reflected population size more than anything else.[78] Leavenworth County, with more than thirty-two thousand residents, was the most populous, and had sixty congregations and forty church buildings. Douglas County, where Lawrence was located, was second with more than twenty thousand residents, forty-two congregations, and twenty-one church buildings. Atchison County's growth had slowed as trade crossed increasingly into Kansas from Kansas City, Missouri, but the county still ranked third with more than fifteen thousand residents, eleven congregations, and ten church buildings.

The three counties that had significantly more congregations than would have been expected on the basis of population alone were Linn, Coffey, and Anderson, all in eastern Kansas about fifty miles south of Lawrence. There were twenty-nine congregations in Linn County, nineteen in Coffey County, and fifteen in Anderson County. These three counties were denominationally diverse, suggesting that competition may have driven church growth. There was a simpler explanation, however. These were counties lacking a central town of any notable size, such as Atchison or Lawrence, but with populations scattered among smaller towns, such as Mound City, La Cygne, Pleasanton, Burlington, Le Roy, Colony, Greeley, and Garnett. As a consequence, each of the major denominations launched several congregations in the same county.

Over the next two decades, the most important factors accounting for new congregations continued to be population growth and the number of towns founded in each county. There were 4,920 organized congregations and 2,854 church edifices in Kansas in 1890, nearly ten times as many as in 1870. Unlike the earlier census, the one taken in 1890 also attempted to tally church members, which were reported as 335,575 or an average of 68 per congregation.[79] Between 1870 and 1890, the total population of Kansas increased from 364,390 to 1,427,095. Counties with larger populations had the highest number of organized congregations, and when population was taken into account, counties with more towns had a larger number of congregations than counties with fewer towns.[80]

Keeping up with a population that was growing at the rate of more than 50,000 new residents a year was no small task. Settlements remained small and scattered. Farm families lived miles from town. It helped that settlers were eager to have churches, and that town companies and railroad officials were often willing to donate land. It was also important that denominational bodies headquartered in eastern states were able to train and send pastors as well as provide loans for buildings. But church leaders had to be careful about investing scarce resources wisely. Many more towns were started than survived. By 1890 more than 1,800 towns were in existence, but as many as 6,000 had been attempted, and fewer than 400 had the required number of 250 residents to legally incorporate.[81] It was risky to build a church in a town that might die a few years later and expect a pastor to exist on the donations of a handful of members. It was equally difficult to know how large a church to build, and it was sometimes necessary to discipline pastors whose work was ineffective.

Churches affiliated with small denominations frequently began within ethnically distinct settlements. Abundant land made Kansas an attractive location for these settlements. Purchasing or homesteading farms on adjacent tracts enabled settlers to assist one another, gave them a common identity, ensured that they would speak the same language, and greatly increased the chances of being able to initiate their own church and support its pastor. In 1868, the Chicago Swedish Company purchased land in McPherson County in central Kansas and established the town of Lindsborg. The population grew to six hundred by 1880, and the town was home to a Swedish Lutheran church, three other Lutheran churches, a Swedish Methodist church, and a Swedish mission church. McPherson along with neighboring Marion and Harvey counties became the location of Russian immigrants, who arrived in 1874 and formed Mennonite churches. Other settlements that established distinct ethnic churches included Bohemian colonies in Marion and Ellsworth counties, Dunkard colonies in Norton and Gove counties, and Quaker settlements in Lawrence, Haviland, and Wichita. One of the more unusual religious settlements was a colony founded in 1877 in Delphos, Ottawa County, by spiritualists from Wisconsin. Another was a settlement in western Kansas along the recently completed Kansas Pacific Railroad that named itself Collyer in honor of Chicago Unitarian reverend Robert Collyer. Not all the colonies formed churches or survived. One that did not was a vegetarian settlement that arrived in Allen County in 1855 and lasted for only a year.

Jewish settlements in Kansas included some of the characteristics that distinguished other ethnic enclaves, including distinctive customs and origins. The 1890 census identified approximately 300 Jews living in Leavenworth, 100 in Wichita, and 50 in Topeka. Another 150 lived in Kansas City, Missouri, and approximately 500 in Omaha. Newspapers of the day carried routine stories about Hebrew Harvest Fairs, plays featuring Jewish themes, and Jewish weddings and charitable activities. An informed non-Jewish reader would have gained the impression that U.S. Jews mostly lived in New York City, Jews in other countries were frequent victims of persecution, and local Jews were hardworking and generous. There were suggestions, too, that Jews were rich, greedy, bigoted, or superstitious. Kansans expressed their sense of being exploited by eastern banks in anti-Semitic references to Shylocks, bloodsuckers, Judases, and hawk-billed Jews. At the same time, religious misgivings of the kind separating Protestants and Catholics were remarkably infrequent, at least in published accounts. The rabbi in Leavenworth was described as a liberal-minded person who got along well with non-Jewish leaders. Congregations were less often referred to as synagogues than as Hebrew churches.[82]

Racial barriers created enclaves of a different sort. Segregated congregations that were known at the time as "colored" churches were organized in Leavenworth in 1861, Lawrence and Wyandotte in 1862, Atchison in 1867, and Topeka in 1868. During the 1870s, the state's African American population increased from seventeen thousand to forty-three thousand. Growth was especially rapid between 1877 and 1879 as "Exodusters" fled Reconstruction in the South on steamboats bound for Missouri and Kansas. African Methodist Episcopal churches in the East held services at which donations for the cause were solicited while audiences sang "John Brown's body lies a-mouldering in the grave." Churches and freedmen's associations in Kansas also provided assistance, but white residents were at best ambivalent about the new arrivals. In 1879, the governor organized an effort to raise voluntary relief funds and relocate African Americans from Wyandotte, where many were arriving, to Lawrence and Topeka. By 1882 there were colored Baptist, Congregational, Methodist, and Catholic congregations in Lawrence, and colored Baptist, Methodist, Presbyterian, and independent churches in Topeka. Exodusters settled in western Kansas as well, organizing communities in Morris and Graham counties, including Nicodemus, where an African Methodist Episcopal congregation began in 1885 and continued until the 1950s.[83] In 1890, approximately 2.5 percent of the state's church members belonged to African American churches.

Among white settlers, Methodists continued to outnumber all other adherents. In 1890, 37 percent of white Protestants statewide were Methodists, and 92 percent of them were affiliated with the northern branch of the Methodist Episcopal Church. Baptists were a distant second with 14 percent of the white Protestant membership. Presbyterians and Disciples of Christ each made up 10 percent of white Protestants. Six percent of white Protestants were Lutherans, divided among eight different conferences. Another 6 percent were United Brethren, and 5 percent were Congregationalists. The remaining 12 percent of white Protestants were scattered among more than a dozen smaller denominations, including the Episcopal, Seventh-Day Adventist, Mennonite, and Moravian churches along with the Church of God and the Reformed Church of America.[84]

The sizable number of Methodists reflected the religious composition of the states from which the majority of Kansans came. In

1880, three-fourths of non-foreign-born Kansans from other parts of the country had been born in just seven states: Illinois, Indiana, Iowa, Missouri, New York, Ohio, and Pennsylvania. Methodists were by far the largest denomination in each of these states, accounting for 32 percent of their churches.[85] That elevated the likelihood that in any Kansas community, a sufficient number of people willing to start a church would already be Methodists. It also increased the chances that new congregations could secure funding from eastern Methodist conferences. In 1879, for example, the secretary of the church extension board of the New York Methodist Conference wrote with satisfaction that more than a million people had crossed the Missouri River in the past eighteen months, churches seating three to four hundred people could be built there for a thousand dollars, loans were being repaid on schedule, and the board had enough cash on hand "to secure the erection of a hundred houses of worship every year for all time."[86]

Seemingly inexhaustible resources did not deter Methodist leaders from employing strategies aimed at maximizing success in establishing churches. Churches built with borrowed money gave borrowers and lenders an incentive to plan well. Applicants were required to file information about current and expected membership, the size of their town and its anticipated population increase, and their plans for repaying the loan. Starting as so many did with fewer than a dozen members, fledgling congregations were able to construct buildings sooner and less expensively by borrowing and securing funds from church conferences than from eastern banks. In 1890, four-fifths of congregations in eastern Kansas where towns were better settled had buildings, while in the remainder of the state the proportion was fewer than half.[87] The interval between organizing a congregation and putting up a building was protection against investing assets in the wrong place when towns flourished and died as often as they did. Despite the fact that organized congregations typically had fewer than seventy members when buildings were dedicated, the buildings were usually constructed to hold two or three times that many, which added to the cost, but anticipated and encouraged growth.

Most buildings were constructed of wood, and many used a standard floor plan and architectural design. The signature of Methodism became its square churches with a bell tower and entry in one corner, a pulpit in the opposite corner, and convertible space at the rear of the sanctuary for a single classroom. In later years, more substantial brick buildings would replace many of these churches, but for now John Wesley's admonition a century earlier that churches "be built plain and decent" was the order of the day. Like so many of Wesley's practices, plain churches helped ensure that Methodism would be the faith of common people. If churches were too expensive, "the necessity of raising money will make rich men necessary to us," Wesley wrote. "And then farewell to Methodist discipline, if not doctrine too."[88]

It was not true in Kansas, as was sometimes claimed elsewhere, that there were more Methodist churches than post offices. But Methodists came closer than any other denomination to having a church in every town. Each district had at least one pastor assigned to hold meetings at gatherings too small to support their own pastor, and it was not uncommon for the pastor of an established congregation to be responsible for a second one. Towns that became county seats had the best chances of surviving. Nearly every county seat had a Methodist church by 1890—and the five that did not were in western counties with sparse populations. Inevitably, churches failed when rail lines went in unexpected locations, when grasshoppers and cyclones wreaked havoc, and when towns lost population. But the result of this winnowing process was to locate surviving churches where they were most likely to succeed. In 1890, incorporated Kansas towns that had a Methodist church averaged 1,172 residents, or almost three times as many as towns without a Methodist church. Larger towns were in a better position than smaller towns to not only grow but also serve as regional markets for area farmers and maintain a population sufficient to keep a church in business. By 1940, the towns where Methodist churches were located in 1890 had become four times the size of towns where Methodist churches were absent in 1890. It

1.3 Bucklin Methodist Church, an example of the church buildings that were constructed in small Kansas towns between 1870 and 1910. From the author's collection.

was not that growth was caused by the presence of a church; rather, churches were well located to benefit from this growth.[89]

Although population had an impact on them, churches' survival and success depended especially on the presence as well as work of qualified clergy. The ratio of clergy (across all denominations) to the population improved in Kansas from one for every 675 people in 1870 to one for every 535 people in 1890, and that ratio was better than in any of Kansas's neighboring states or the nation as a whole.[90] The 2,665 clergy in Kansas nearly equaled the number of churches with buildings, but fell far short of the number of organized congregations, accentuating the need to utilize scarce personnel wisely. Methodists enlisted volunteer exhorters and untrained local preachers when necessary, and deployed licensed pastors as widely as possible. A listing of 125 Methodist posts spanning a large portion of northern Kansas in 1893 showed that 80 percent were filled with licensed pastors and the remainder were to be supplied by the presiding elder. Seven pastors were serving in circuit posts, and four others held appointments in more than one congregation. In keeping with the itinerancy system, two out of three pastors were serving a different congregation a year later. The conference was also adapting to wider change. Twenty-one of the pastors in 1893 were no longer in the conference in 1894, and forty-three pastors were new. By 1897, forty-two of the pastors serving in 1894 were gone, and forty newcomers were present.[91]

Itinerancy was based on the principle that pastors relinquished the right to decide on the location of their labor and a congregation surrendered its claim to that decision as well. It granted the bishop or presiding elder the authority to place pastors in positions that best served the conference or district. Pulpits were filled that would otherwise have remained vacant, and a pastor's performance in one position could become the basis for a better or worse assignment in the next. The hierarchy of rewards was suggested by the pattern of assignments. Congregations in small, unincorporated towns were likely to be filled with pastors serving in a provisional or temporary capacity. Pastors with regular appointments in small towns hoped eventually to receive appointments in larger towns. Having attained a congregation in a larger town, pastors anticipated being able to move to a town of similar size. There were, however, limits to how well a presiding elder could satisfy these expectations. Small towns greatly outnumbered larger ones. Some pastors were more deserving than others. Effective pastors were also needed to start new ministries.

It was not surprising that pastors awaited the announcement of appointments at annual meetings with more than casual interest. Pastors routinely faced hardship caused by the large circuits that they were expected to cover and the meager support their charges were able to contribute. Many were determined to make converts and establish churches if they were permitted to stay another year, while others desperately wished to relocate.[92] "The room became very quiet," an observer at an annual meeting in 1891 wrote. "The brethren were interested, very; some tried to look unconcerned; some smiled in a gruesome way; some looked very anxious, for preachers are but human, anyway." They would soon know if they "would remain where they were already pleasantly situated or go again among strangers and perhaps to a hard and tollful circuit." As the bishop read the list of appointments, the observer noted that "a good many faces changed their expressions."[93]

The Southwest Kansas Methodist Episcopal Conference illustrated how itinerancy worked in practice. The conference covered approximately 36,000 square miles, and extended from east of Wichita west to the Colorado line and from north of McPherson south to the Oklahoma Territory line. A total of 249 pastors served in the conference at one time or another between 1883 and 1903. Although the maximum time that a pastor was permitted to serve at a particular church was three years, the average time served was only two years. Of the 897 moves these pastors made, 48 percent involved going to a town in which the population was larger than that of the town in which the pastor presently served, 42 percent involved relocating to a smaller town, and 10 percent involved no change in the town size. Fortunately for pastors serving in the smallest towns there was a good chance of moving to a slightly larger one. For example, among pastors in towns with only 100 people, the next church these pastors served was in a town averaging 562 people, and among pastors in towns averaging about 300 people, their next church was in a town averaging almost 700 people. There were fewer chances of moving up among pastors in larger towns because most towns were small. The chances of at least staying in a town of a similar size were improved by the fact that for every pastor, three others retired, died, or left the conference after five years.[94]

COOPERATION AND COMPETITION

While differences of doctrine and styles of worship separated Protestant denominations from one another, there were numerous instances of imitation, sharing, and mutual endeavor. A popular way of promoting church involvement was through revival services held on successive weekday evenings and featuring a guest preacher. Methodists used them to good effect throughout Kansas, drawing on the initiative of circuit preachers and presiding elders, and sometimes working with larger organizations. One such organization was the National Camp Meeting Association for the Promotion of Christian Holiness, which began in 1867 in Philadelphia, met in Vineland, New Jersey, a year later, and in 1870, produced a spin-off that established permanent facilities in Ocean Grove, New Jersey. Preachers from Ocean Grove traveled to Kansas that summer, and held meetings in Kansas City, Leavenworth, Lawrence, and Oswego. The ten-day meeting in Oswego was so successful that the Methodist Church there followed it with a series of revivals, at which it was reported that "hundreds were brought to Jesus and the work of holiness."[95]

But other denominations also held revival meetings of their own, and local churches often joined forces in sponsoring them. Baptists, Disciples of Christ, Mennonites, Quakers, and Presbyterians all held revivals. The years following the grasshopper invasion of 1874, as large-scale immigration to Kansas resumed, seem to have been especially favorable for revivals. Evangelical revivals swept through Friends meetings in eastern Kansas in 1876, causing dissent between those who favored them and those who were opposed.[96] In Republic County, revivals that same year led to new churches being formed among Swedish immigrants, while in McPherson County revivals were being conducted among Russian Mennonite immigrants.[97] Similar meetings were spreading through Cowley County among Methodists, Baptists, and Congregationalists.[98]

Revivals continued in the 1880s, bringing to the Midwest itinerant preachers with success in organizing large-scale crusades in eastern cities. One of the largest revivals occurred in Kansas City in 1888 under the leadership of evangelist Samuel Porter Jones, a Methodist preacher from Georgia who was later said to have been the inspiration for much of the wit of Will Rogers. The two-week crusade drew nightly audiences of five thousand from eastern Kansas and western Missouri as well as from Kansas City itself, and was widely supported by churches of several denominations. Taking Jesus's invitation to "Come unto me" as his text, Jones pointedly argued that the call transcended doctrines and creeds. "I'm glad it does not say 'Whosoever believeth in the Methodist creed . . . the Presbyterian creed [or] the Baptist creed.' It is faith which saves souls." At the conclusion of each lengthy service, Jones appealed to the masses to join their respective churches. "I want every man or woman who'll say, 'I'll join the Christian church, or the Baptist church, or the Methodist church, to come forward and give me their hands.' We'll have the Presbyterians first. Now, all who agree to join [come forward]."[99]

In quieter ways, Protestants worked across denominational lines to provide space for new congregations, hold community meetings, and organize special programs. These activities were well illustrated in southeastern Kansas among the Methodists, Baptists, Congregationalists, and Presbyterians of Winfield, a town of 472 residents in 1870 that grew to more than 5,000 by 1890. Church buildings were used for public meetings about schools and railroads as well as for Masonic suppers and installation ceremonies. The Presbyterian minister occasionally preached at the Baptist Church, and the Baptist minister returned the favor. Dedication services of new buildings typically included brief addresses by all the community's clergy. Each year the churches cooperated in holding a union service on Thanksgiving. During the Christmas holidays, Presbyterians and Methodists each held festivals to which the entire community was invited. The Presbyterian festival, at least one time, was held at the Methodist Church. That was the year an intoxicated man disrupted the event, causing the women of both churches to increase their participation in the temperance movement.[100] By 1886, the Methodist and Presbyterian women were hosting capacity crowds at lectures of the Women's Christian Temperance Union (WCTU). The Winfield churches had also formed a YMCA, were hosting literary lectures and concerts at the Opera Hall, and were holding joint meetings among Sunday school children.[101]

In other locations, cooperative Sunday school efforts ranged from small congregations holding joint classes or hosting programs at schools when church buildings were lacking, to enlisting children for larger purposes. The former was evident in Rosedale, a small town in Wyandotte County where nearly three hundred youngsters were involved in the Union Sunday School in 1882, and Lincoln Center, where seventy-five children met every Sunday at the Presbyterian Church for a Union Sabbath School sponsored by the town's Presbyterian, Lutheran, and Methodist churches. Cooperation was often evident in newly settled communities in western Kansas. In Garden City, for example, Congregationalists, Methodists, Presbyterians, and United Brethren initiated a Union Sabbath School that drew children from the entire community, and resulted in the formation of a union church. Larger cooperative programs were illustrated in 1872 when churches in Lawrence, Leavenworth, and Topeka held mass meetings in each town to which Sunday school children were invited, and then deployed to scour the streets for vagrants, gamblers, and hardened individuals who they could invite to church. In Lawrence, nearly two thousand children and adults attended the meetings, and in Topeka, the afternoon sessions at public schools were canceled for four days to allow children to participate.[102]

The formal cooperation and interchange that was so frequently evident among Protestant denominations seldom extended to Catholics. The Kansas State Census of 1875 estimated membership in the Roman Catholic Church at approximately thirty-seven thousand, making it the largest religious body in the state. Catholics outnumbered Methodists by almost fifteen thousand. The difference was partly because Catholic membership included children while Methodist membership did not. That was considerable at a time when approximately 28 percent of the state's population were children age thirteen or younger. And yet, if children were subtracted, Catholics still outnumbered Methodists by more than four thousand members. Insofar as numbers mattered, Catholics were in the best position to counter Methodists' influence and pursue an alternative pattern of church growth.[103]

In several respects Catholics and Methodists were quite similar. Both were organized under the authority of a bishop, who was responsible for assigning pastors and approving plans for church expansion. Both were engaged in mission work among Indians well before Kansas became a state, and both had been among the first to found colleges in territorial Kansas. Both sought to be the faith of the common people and provide for the spiritual needs of a rapidly expanding settler population. And both employed circuit pastors to start and minister to new congregations as well as carefully plan where to construct buildings. By 1875, there was at least one organized Catholic congregation in 88 percent of the state's counties, and at least one organized Methodist congregation in 83 percent of the counties. The most expensive structures of both denominations were in Leavenworth. For the state as a whole, there also was a significant positive correlation between the value of Catholic and Methodist churches in each county, the number of Catholic and Methodist congregations, and the number of Catholic and Methodist members.[104]

By 1890, Catholics were still the Methodists' closest competitors in terms of size and influence, counting 67,000 members and making up 21 percent of the state's total church membership. Both were highly successful in organizing new congregations and constructing new buildings. But Methodists were more successful. In fifteen years, Catholics founded 165 new congregations, built more than 200 churches, and added 30,000 members. In the same period, Methodists started more than 600 congregations, constructed 638 buildings, and increased their total membership by more than 60,000. Methodists averaged twelve congregations per county, while Catholics averaged only three congregations per county.[105]

The growth patterns of the two denominations reflected different strategies that in turn could be traced to differences in location, resources, and ethnic origin. Methodist clergy were appointed to stations where they served alone or in the company of a spouse; Catholic clergy, in contrast, were more often assigned to locations served by fellow priests or monks. Atchison, where three monks were in residence by 1859, and where the number grew to four priests, a deacon, four clerics, and five monks by 1864, was an early example.[106] Clustering was advantageous not only for the company it provided celibate clergy but also for dividing labor, maintaining discipline, founding schools, and attracting Catholic settlers. It worked especially well in eastern Kansas, where settlements were closer, counties more populous, and schools and missions better established.

In 1875, the ratio of Catholics to Methodists was highest in Leavenworth, the seat of the bishop and the location of an estimated four thousand Catholic residents, the majority of whom were Irish and German.[107] Catholics were also well represented in Wyandotte, Neosho, and Pottawatomie counties, where missions among Indians had been present since the 1840s. St. Mary's in Pottawatomie County developed a cluster of Catholic organizations that included its Indian mission, the Sacred Heart Convent, and a large church capable of seating a thousand people. Between 1875 and 1890, the Catholic population of Pottawatomie County doubled to more than four thousand and was served by seven parishes. A further advantage of clustering was enabling funds to be raised from donors interested in establishing prominent Catholic institutions, such as in Atchison, where the priory was funded largely by King Ludwig I of Bavaria. For a well-educated priest or monk interested in teaching, or a prior aiming to become an abbot, serving in a well-funded institution was clearly a desirable choice.

Clustering took on added importance as settlements spread west. Besides continuing to create locations in which schools could be established, it became a way to attract and minister to ethnically distinct immigrant populations. Early westward migration followed the Kansas Pacific and Santa Fe rail lines, and resulted in settlements in railroad towns and at forts. In 1890, the ratio of Catholics to Methodists was still highest in Leavenworth County (better than ten to one), but the second-highest ratio (almost ten to one) was in Ellis County in western Kansas, where almost two thousand Catholics lived. Forty-two percent of Ellis County's population in 1870 was foreign born, one of the highest percentages in the state, and it remained one of the highest two decades later with 26 percent foreign born. Nearly all the foreign-born residents were from Russia. The Russian immigration began in 1875, following the drought of 1874 that reduced Ellis County's population to less than a thousand, and over the next two years brought more than twelve hundred settlers who established five separate farming communities. Nearly all were Volga Germans fleeing the conscription of their sons into the Russian army. By 1890, five Catholic churches and a monastery had been built. St. Fidelis Church in Victoria, begun in 1881, became the location of a later structure, which at the time of its dedication in 1911 was the largest church west of the Mississippi River.[108]

Two other counties with high ratios of Catholics to Methodists were Cloud in north-central Kansas and Barton in west-central Kansas. Cloud's population included more than 1,000 residents born in Canada, the largest of any county in the state. Barton's population was largely native born, but included nearly 2,000 residents of German and Austrian origin. By 1875, the Catholic population of Cloud County was estimated at about 1,000, and that number increased to more than 2,400 by 1890. Barton County's Catholic population grew from 250 in 1875 to more than 1,500 in 1890. Cloud County was the location of the Sisters of St. Joseph motherhouse founded in 1884 in Concordia by four sisters of the French order that made its way to the United States in the 1830s. Within a few years the motherhouse was staffing schools, hospitals, and orphanages in Kansas. In 1887, Concordia became the administrative center of the northwestern Kansas diocese. Barton County's Catholic population was served in Ellinwood by a small network of itinerant priests, who founded churches in Ellinwood, Great Bend, Odin, Claflin, Dubuque, and Olmitz between 1877 and 1882.[109]

The clustering pattern in which the Catholic population developed had two potential implications for the relationships between Catholics and Methodists, or with other Protestants. On the one hand, clustering amounted to geographic segregation, which reduced the likelihood of tensions arising in local communities. The extent of this segregation was evident in the fact that in 1890, 26 of the state's 105 counties did not include a single Catholic church building, and in ten others with a single building the number of Catholics was fewer than one hundred, lowering the chances that a priest was in residence. Although there were Catholic families in many of these locations, these were counties in which there was little visible presence of the Catholic community, either in the form of a building or in the person of a resident priest. Moreover, nearly all these counties were in the western half of the state. On the other hand, clustering reduced opportunities for positive face-to-face interreligious contact, and raised the likelihood of Protestants and Catholics viewing one another, as it were, from a distance. This was perhaps especially true in western Kansas, where travelers could view Catholic churches from miles away while identifying communities such as Ellis and Ellinwood as Catholic enclaves.[110]

Tensions between Methodists or other Protestants and Catholics seldom flared into the kind of violence that erupted in Axtell in 1889. The traveling Methodist minister in Axtell who preached on "Romanism is not of God" probably would not have been heckled had he not lectured again the next evening on the evils of Catholicism, and the melee may not have led to the militia setting up artillery around the church had the Catholic hecklers not been arrested.[111] But state law since 1876 mandated that anyone who "shall disquiet or disturb any congregation or assembly of people met for religious worship" was guilty of a misdemeanor, and subject to a hundred dollar fine or three months in jail.[112] It was also the case that every Methodist preacher would have been familiar with their denomination's stance toward basic Catholic teachings and practices. "The Romish doctrine concerning purgatory, pardon, worshipping, and adoration, as well of images as of reliques, and also invocation of saints," the *Doctrines and Discipline of the Methodist Episcopal Church in America* explained, "is a fond thing vainly invented, and grounded upon no warrant of scripture, but repugnant to the word of God." *Doctrines and Discipline* further taught that preaching in a "tongue not understood" by the people was "plainly repugnant to the word of God," and that five of the seven Roman Catholic sacraments were merely the work of a "most corrupt priesthood, whose only aim was to enrich and aggrandize themselves."[113]

Misgivings between Protestants and Catholics usually surfaced in quieter ways than they did in Axtell. In 1872, Methodist pastor D. P. Mitchell—an organizer of the mass Sunday school rally in Topeka—became concerned that a Catholic legislator was petitioning to give Catholic prisoners at the state penitentiary the right to attend Catholic religious services. The idea, Mitchell wrote to the editor of the *Topeka Commonwealth*, smacked of Brigham Young's religious right to have fifty wives and would surely divide the prison into twenty factions. Catholics "first attacked the common schools in this country," he added, and then "abandoned the schools on the ground they were Godless." In his view, this was simply another instance of "Romanism" pitting itself against an "open Bible and a free education."[114] Whether that was true or not, the issue of schools was indeed a bone of contention among Catholics as well. Writing from Leavenworth in 1871, Father Thomas Butler praised nearly everything about Kansas, but noted an "ignorance of religion" and "carelessness in the great affair of the salvation of the soul," which he attributed to the public schools. "From one end of the year to the other the name of Almighty God is never uttered by the teachers," he wrote. And yet Catholics were required to support "the schools to which they are opposed." He considered this to be a great injustice.[115]

In the years since Lincoln's visit to Atchison, Kansas had entered the union as a free state and a bloody war had cost the lives of thousands of young people. After the war, settlers flocked to Kansas, populating its fledgling towns and creating opportunities for hundreds of new churches to form. Denominational diversity and freedom of religion prevailed. Church leaders and public officials worked to establish a system of government that encouraged public morality as well as upheld law and order. Methodists were clearly in the majority in religion, and Republicans dominated state politics. But if the die that would shape later relations between religion and politics was being cast, it was not by any means fixed. What was to follow would be the work of a generation of institution builders who had strong opinions about what their churches and government should and should not do. Among the clearest fault lines were the divisions between Methodists and Catholics. Each had leaders who questioned the theology of the other, and who sometimes used their influence in local politics to get their way.

It was not that Catholics and Protestants were unable to get along. Just as they did in Atchison, they mingled at public meetings and did business together. Sometimes they married across religious lines, as Thomas Ewing's parents did. But it did not help that Catholics and Protestants so often hailed from different national backgrounds, spoke different languages, lived in different communities, sent their children to different schools, and buried their dead in different cemeteries. Nor was it the case that misgivings occurred only when such differences were present. In the small German community of Alma, thirty miles west of Topeka, Catholics completed a fine church of native limestone in 1877. A year later the German Lutherans constructed theirs a half block away, facing the structure north despite the fact that south would have been the more logical direction. A legend that persisted more than a century later was that north was selected so the Lutherans could exit the church on Sundays without having to "see the damned Catholics."[116] In other instances, religious differences mapped onto painful memories of troubles in the past. William James Milliken staked a claim in southeastern Kansas near Edna in 1871, and served as a teacher and superintendent at several Methodist schools. Years later he wrote in his autobiography that his grandfather, an Orangeman, had been beaten by a Catholic mob and was unable to do much work afterward. The bitterness in his family remained strong.[117]

CHAPTER 2

AN EVOLVING POLITICAL STYLE

COMPETITION BETWEEN METHODISTS AND CATHOLICS would periodically become an influence in Kansas politics, but its immediate
effect in the 1880s and 1890s was to reinforce a moderately conservative civic ethos across the state. Whatever their disagreements
might be, Methodists and Catholics alike had a stake in promoting what they regarded as good citizenship. Congregations brought
people together, creating what later scholars would call social capital, helping them to make friends, conduct business, and care for
the needy. Church buildings were widely regarded as adornments to
thriving towns and were routinely mentioned in newspaper stories
as laudable achievements. Public lectures and even revival meetings
focused on issues of the day, and sought to uplift the moral tenor of
the community. Temperance meetings may have been Protestants'
way of keeping Catholics at bay, but Catholic leaders also sought to
curb the evils of intoxication. "The one great fault here, as at home,
is love of intoxicating drinks," Father Butler wrote from Leavenworth. "No doubt, want and misery engendered that vice amongst
our people in 'the old country'; but unfortunately, it follows many
over here, and some men who possess qualities that might have
raised them to a high position in the great country have fallen in
the dust through their inordinate love for liquor." If drinking could
be curbed, he argued, the natural intelligence of Irish immigrants
would ensure their rise to the ranks of "leading men of America."[1]

The most important way in which Methodists and Catholics
exerted a conservative influence in their communities was by restraining the excesses of fringe religious groups. As the two major
religious institutions, both were capable of exercising a stabilizing

role in this regard and both had an interest in doing so. Indeed, their interest was probably heightened by the competition between them. It did Methodists no good if Catholics could point to excesses on the Protestant side, and the same was true among Catholics when Methodists were disposed to be as critical as they were. On the Catholic side, policing largely took the form of caring for residents among the Catholic population who might otherwise become burdens to the wider community. It involved priestly visits to saloon owners, quiet relocation programs for unwed mothers, orphanages, hospitals, food, and clothing for indigent immigrants, and church services for immigrants who did not speak English. It also consisted of efforts to maintain the boundaries separating Catholics and Protestants, especially cross-denominational marriages that posed conflicts about child rearing and led to incidents like the famous false-teeth murder in 1912. Separate schools and firm rules about confession, weddings, and funerals helped to affirm these demarcations.

Among Protestants, the necessity to rein in fringe religious practices was even more demanding. Revival meetings that sometimes whipped crowds into an emotional frenzy were especially in need of strict control. In her account of life in territorial Kansas, Sara Robinson described a Methodist camp meeting that she attended in the countryside near Lawrence. "There was a large gathering of people," she wrote, "and the services would be impressive were it not for the continued 'Amens,' in shrill as well as deep guttural tones, which the zealous worshippers are sounding in one's ears from all quarters."[2] In his reminiscences of the overland stage business, Atchison's Frank Root described a parody of an old-fashioned revival that reflected some of the misapprehension in which the meetings were held. The parody suggested that preachers were not above bamboozling their audiences and that drinking was sometimes occasioned by the events.[3] It was perhaps with good reason that Kansas law prohibited the selling of spiritous liquor near religious gatherings.

Although Methodists were particularly active in sponsoring revivals, they also shouldered the responsibility for keeping them within bounds. Announcements of upcoming revivals often vouched for the credentials of the guest speaker, noting their education and previous engagements. After the fact reports typically stressed that the speaker was not a sensationalist, the arguments had been profoundly logical, the crowd had been orderly, and some of the town's prominent citizens had been present. By implication, these stories communicated to those who had not attended the revivals that nothing untoward had happened and indicated to future participants what the expected behavior should be. Proper behavior was also expressed through stories of outrageous episodes that served as cautionary tales. Tales of drunken and glutenous evangelists, participants going insane, and good citizens being harangued served well for this purpose. One such incident took place in 1886 following a revival at Havensville, a small town north of Topeka. Four men reportedly went insane from the excitement of the meetings. On the way home one of the men attacked his companion, Sam Gordon, age sixty, tore out Gordon's heart, and ate it.[4]

Besides policing revivals, the leaders of Methodism and the other established churches guarded against fringe sects emerging and heretical teachings appearing, especially from their own clergy. It was an understatement to say that Methodism was orderly. *Doctrines and Discipline* specified rules of proper conduct for clergy and members down to the finest detail, including how singing should be done at meetings. The aim was perfection in holiness. A person might join at a revival service to escape the eternal hellfire that the preacher depicted, but members expected that faith would assist them in leading better lives in this world as well. Holiness was achieved through clean living along with a dedication to one's faith and family. Yet the quest for holiness led not only to sobriety and hard work but also the kind of emotional closeness to God that Lovejoy portrayed in her diary. Seeking and hearing the voice of the Lord presented believers with opportunities to deviate from the strict authority of the church.

In the 1880s, quasi-independent holiness movements were becoming a matter of growing concern to Methodist officials. The National Camp Meeting Association that spurred a revival in

Oswego in 1870 grew into a truly national enterprise. Local camp meetings led to the formation of the Southern Kansas Holiness Association in 1880, the Kansas Western Holiness Association in 1883, statewide rallies in 1888 and 1889, and the formal organization of the Kansas State Holiness Association in 1891. Editors of Methodist periodicals and bishops in Kansas, Missouri, and as far away as New England issued repeated warnings against the darkness as well as fanaticism of holiness associations. At a meeting in Salina, the Kansas bishop described a pastor who had gone crazy with zealotry. The bishop in Missouri warned that the advocates of "come-outism" were a menace to the church. The warnings only succeeded in attracting believers to the holiness meetings.[5]

It was in this context that Methodist, Baptist, and Presbyterian ministers began dealing with other disruptions in their congregations and communities. The Church Triumphant was a small sect in Illinois founded by George Jacob Schweinfurth, a Methodist preacher who broke with the denomination, and claimed himself to be sinless, capable of performing miracles, filled with the Holy Spirit, an equal of Jesus, and the voice of a new dispensation for the church. In 1889, elders in a Kansas City Presbyterian church excommunicated one of Schweinfurth's followers, Mrs. L. A. Ward. The incident spurred Ward and fellow members of the Church Triumphant to attend meetings at other churches in Kansas, posing as interested newcomers and then testifying on behalf of Schweinfurth's teachings. At one Methodist church, the disturbers were reportedly promptly furnished with a "free escort away from the place."[6]

The Church Triumphant—or Beekmanites as they were called—was not the only source of new ideas in matters of faith. In 1869, a young lawyer who had fought in the Confederate army moved to Atchison with his wife, a French Catholic from Saint Louis, was admitted to the bar, served in the Kansas legislature in 1871 and 1872, and became the U.S. district attorney of Kansas in 1873. Following a divorce and several years of heavy drinking, the attorney experienced a religious conversion, was ordained as a Congregationalist minister, and in 1882 moved to Dallas, where he became one of the most widely known proponents of dispensationalist theology. His name was Cyrus Ingerson Scofield. His annotated Scofield Bible became one of the most widely used texts in fundamentalist churches.[7] Another innovator was Charles Parham, a young Methodist preacher in Iowa who was affiliated with the holiness movement. In 1895 Parham would break with the Methodists, and in 1898 he moved to Topeka, where his ministry initiated the modern Pentecostal movement.

A third innovator was less successful. Her name was Anna Spafford. In 1881 Spafford and her husband, a prominent lawyer in Chicago, sold their possessions and with a dozen fellow believers departed for Jerusalem to await the Lord's second coming. A decade later, her husband having died and Jesus not having returned, Spafford sent an agent back to the United States to recruit new disciples with sufficient means to keep the colony in business. In Lebanon, Kansas, near the exact geographic center of the United States, the agent persuaded a well-to-do farmer, Joseph Meyers, and his extended family to join the colony. It was never clear why they went and how they fared at the colony. But in Smith County, their departure provided grist for serious concern. Reports circulated that the Meyers's family had surely been duped by the "greatest slicker and talker" ever seen, a cunning person who exercised "hypnotic control" over people. The trouble, reports said, was people acting on impulse, noting that one of Meyers' neighbors, John Dixon, ran to join the departing group wearing only one of his shoes. Word spread that the Meyers were barely surviving on boiled rice and wanted to return but could not. An appeal was made via Governor John W. Leedy to President William McKinley for help, but the colony was said to have hurled epithets at the U.S. emissary. The hair of a Meyers's relative who stayed behind was rumored to have turned white almost instantly from worry. Another relative, folks said, wisely chose to join the Methodist Church. Mr. E. D. Hyde issued the strongest warnings against the group. He was a devout Methodist who advertised his faith by painting Bible verses in large letters on the Lebanon grain elevator. There was no escaping the lesson of the Jerusalem colony. Fringe groups were dangerous.[8]

PRAIRIE POLITICS

For the generation that populated Kansas after the Civil War, local and state politics were so thoroughly dominated by the Republican Party that there was little need in most instances to reinforce it through the support of religious appeals. Certainly the strength of the party did not lie in its ability to hold meetings at Methodist churches or secure pastors' endorsements. Farmers on land acquired under the Homestead Act knew they had the party of Lincoln to thank. The agent who arranged preemption and the lawyer who wrote up the title were in most counties Republicans. A merchant doing well in a railroad town had the Republican administration to appreciate for bringing railroads through Kansas. The newspaper in that town was probably a Republican one. A Union army veteran was likely to vote for a fellow Republican veteran. Veterans' pensions came from the Republican administration, and pension appeals went to Republican officials. The party controlled judgeships and school boards, elected most of the state's legislators, and sent these leaders on to become governors and congresspeople. The question was not why Republicans stayed in power but rather how Democrats or third-party candidates could ever mount an effective opposition.

Democrats were down but not completely out. Republican candidates seldom ran unopposed even in the most heavily Republican districts. There were Democratic leaders who had been on the proslavery side before the war and who quietly retained their party affiliation when the cause was lost. Others held office in eastern states as Democrats before migrating to Kansas and perhaps thought it better to let the South secede than to follow the radical Republicans into war. There were also loyalties driven by local politics and business interests. In towns like Atchison and Leavenworth, an aspiring official might run on the Democratic ticket because of a falling out with Republican leaders, or in hopes of capturing the Irish or German vote. Others ran when an incumbent died or was caught in a legal scandal.

The Democrat who achieved the greatest success, eventually becoming governor, was George Washington Glick, an Atchison attorney. His brief rise to power was the exception that demonstrated Republicans' strength. Glick was from a prominent family in Fairfield County, Ohio, where his father was a prosperous landowner and three-term county treasurer. Glick himself was nominated to run for Congress on the Democratic ticket in Ohio in 1858, but campaigned for a state senate seat instead. Defeated in that election, he moved to Atchison, bought land, and established a successful law practice. By 1870 he was the fourth-richest person in Atchison County, exceeded only by his partner, Alfred G. Otis, and William Challiss and Benjamin Stringfellow. Promising to promote railroad development, he was elected as a Democratic representative to the state legislature from 1863 to 1868, and ran for governor in 1868. The Republicans' strength was clearly evident in the results. Glick earned only 34 percent of the vote, winning in only three counties, and losing his home county by more than two hundred votes.[9]

The Glicks were longtime German Lutherans, settling in Ohio before the Revolutionary War and through their patronage establishing what became known as the Glick Church west of Greencastle. Being Lutheran was hardly a factor in George Glick's politics in Kansas, although it did locate him outside of Methodism, distanced him from Methodists' temperance inclinations, and put him in the more liturgical wing of Kansas churches. Glick grew up speaking German as well as English, which gave him an advantage in dealing with Atchison's German Catholic community. Through his brother Charles, who was a friend of Father Kuhls in Wyandotte, he had connections there too. Glick's largest margins of victory in 1868 were in Wyandotte County, where he won 52 percent of the vote, and newly settled Ellis County in western Kansas, where he won 73 percent of the vote. Although he lost Leavenworth County by three hundred votes, he captured 66 percent of the vote in Leavenworth's heavily Irish third ward.[10]

Glick was an unlikely figure to gain further prominence in Kansas politics. After his defeat in 1868, he continued in public service as county commissioner and state legislator, but concentrated on his expanding business interests, becoming a director of the Union Pacific Railroad, developing his six-hundred-acre Shannon Hill farm near Atchison, and building the Glick mansion, which was considered one of the finest houses in eastern Kansas for the next half century. His victory in the gubernatorial election of 1882 proved that a Democrat could win in Kansas if circumstances were sufficiently unusual. What made these circumstances unusual was an alliance between faith and politics that gave some Republicans pause even as it mobilized others. Like much of what influenced elections in these years, this alliance reflected the complicated politics of railroads, settlement, and liquor.

The principal wedge issue in the late 1870s—and the one that would bring electoral success for Glick—was Prohibition. The idea of imposing a constitutional ban on the sale of intoxicating liquor had continued since the proposal's initial failure at the Wyandotte convention in 1859. Methodist and Presbyterian clergy discussed temperance at annual conferences, and from time to time supported third-party Prohibition candidates. Churchwomen periodically held temperance rallies and campaigned against local saloons. By the late 1870s, these rallies and campaigns were connecting women with temperance advocates in other states. A temperance rally at the Bismarck Grove picnic grounds two miles northeast of Lawrence in September 1878 drew an estimated fifty thousand participants during eight days of meetings. Speakers included Methodist pastor Mitchell (the organizer of children's rallies in Topeka) and Republican leader John P. St. John of Olathe. The event was partly a holiday for residents from Lawrence, Topeka, and neighboring towns who idled among concessionaires selling jewelry, candy, lemonade, tobacco, and even liquor. It was mostly politics mixed with heavy doses of religion, including a prayer meeting on the first day and revival hymns sung throughout the week. The event was only outdone by another gathering one year later, when upward of seventy-five thousand people attended a twelve-day rally at the same location.[11]

St. John had gained a reputation in the state legislature starting in 1873 as a strong proponent of Prohibition. In 1878, he captured the governorship by a 54 percent margin, winning a majority or plurality of the vote in every county except Leavenworth and Wyandotte. His win gave Kansas Republicans their tenth-consecutive gubernatorial victory. In 1880, St. John was reelected with a 58 percent margin, winning all counties except Ford, where it was assumed that Dodge City's cowboys and saloon keepers were responsible for a narrow twenty-three-vote loss. Two other counties—Atchison and Leavenworth—were closely contested, but St. John prevailed in the former by fifty votes and in the latter by thirty-five. In both 1878 and 1880, counties in which a larger percentage of the population was Catholic were significantly more likely to vote for St. John's Democratic opponent, while counties with larger proportions of Methodists were more favorably inclined toward St. John.[12]

In 1880, temperance advocates succeeded in placing a Prohibition amendment to the state constitution on the ballot. With Governor St. John's support and vigorous campaigning by temperance groups, the measure passed by 7,837 votes, or a 52 to 48 percent margin, securing at least 57 percent of the vote in twenty-eight counties, but sustaining fewer than 50 percent in twenty-seven others. The ablest proponents of the amendment were members of the Kansas chapter of the WCTU, which formed at the Bismarck Grove meeting in 1878. The WCTU included "Christian" in its title, drew on social networks in congregations, denounced liquor as sin, and yet derided it chiefly as a threat to women's safety, children's livelihood, family security, and community standards. The state's Methodist, Baptist, Congregational, and Presbyterian clergy along with the Kansas State Teachers' Association also endorsed the amendment.[13]

Historians would later argue that the appeal of Prohibition in 1880 was as much about nativism and ill feelings in rural areas against cities as it was about alcohol. Whether that was true or not remains in doubt, but one thing was clear: the vote on Prohibition divided strongly along religious lines. Taking account of differences in population and nativity, counties with larger percentages of Methodists were more likely to vote in favor of the amendment, and counties with larger percentages of Catholics were more likely to vote against it. In Pawnee County, which at the time had the highest proportion of Methodists, 70 percent voted for it, while in Leavenworth, Atchison, Barton, and Wyandotte fewer than a third did.[14]

Passing Prohibition was one thing; implementing it was another. Despite the support it received from Republicans and Methodists, the effort to put Prohibition into practice exposed underlying misgivings. Manufacturers and distributors along the state's eastern border complained that liquor would now be imported from Missouri. Others contended that voluntary compliance and local enforcement had been more effective, and should be continued. Methodist teachings emphasized temperance as a matter of personal discipline more than as an item of law enforcement. The church's tradition encouraged voluntary moral and social support among its members, and respect for boundaries separating church and state. The temperance movement posed questions of gender equality and suffrage that were new to many husbands and fathers. Methodist shopkeepers and railroad bondholders could imagine that strict enforcement of Prohibition would dampen business and deter settlers from coming to Kansas. There were concerns simply about St. John himself, whether he was devoting too much of his administration's attention to the liquor issue, and whether it was good for any governor to have a third term.[15]

Glick was the Democrats' best hope to displace St. John. He was known as a party loyalist and opponent of Prohibition—at least its rigid enforcement, if not the principle as well. Glick believed that Prohibition discouraged German immigration to Kansas, was the work of busybodies, and should not be enforced even it were the law. "No man with a spark of manhood or honor in him," Glick once said, "would inform on another who had sold him intoxicating liquor."[16] He stood a good chance of capturing the Catholic vote in Atchison and Leavenworth, appealing to German voters, and garnering support in communities that were calling for a system of state railroad regulation. Republican newspapers sought to diminish him through unfavorable comparisons of his service record in the Kansas militia, which included being wounded at the Battle of the Blue, with St. John's record as a lieutenant colonel in the Illinois Volunteer Infantry. Glick won, but with only 46 percent of the vote. His largest margins were in Atchison, Leavenworth, and Ellis counties. He also won significant margins in Pottawatomie and Barton. Ford County cast fewer than a thousand votes, but more than 70 percent were for Glick.[17] "Illustrious Kansas," mourned the Republican-oriented *Topeka Weekly Capital*, had "gone into the dark backward abysm of time."[18]

Glick's tenure as governor lasted only two years. During that period, temperance advocates argued more strongly than ever that Prohibition was not a moral or spiritual issue but instead a matter of practicality. Against criticism from eastern newspapers, they published statistics demonstrating the beneficial effects of Prohibition. The state's population and value of its property were up. Arrests were down. The death rate was down. Sidewalks were clean. In two years alone, commitments to the state penitentiary fell 90 percent.[19] In 1884, fellow Atchison resident John A. Martin, the longtime editor of *Freedom's Champion* and a member of the national Republican committee since 1868, ran against Governor Glick and won 55 percent of the vote. The two candidates split the vote in Atchison County, but Glick outdistanced Martin by large margins in Leavenworth, Barton, and Ford counties, where Catholic voters were numerous. Glick's largest margin was in Ellis County, winning 68 percent of the vote. His win in those counties was credited to his opposition to Prohibition and support of German immigration. Ellis County residents had special reason to favor him. In January 1884, one of the county's Volga German residents, a man named Goubleman, was charged with sixteen counts of selling liquor and convicted on one count. Within a week he was charged again on ten counts, fined fourteen hundred dollars, and sentenced to six months in jail. Maintaining that the trial and sentence were unfair, Goubleman's fellow residents petitioned the governor, who in response granted Goubleman a pardon. Republican critics charged that Glick had done the same in Pottawatomie and Barton counties.[20]

County-to-county comparisons of gubernatorial election results showed that several factors protected Republican candidates in the 1880s against Democratic opponents like Glick. One factor was the Republicans' strength in less populated rural counties. Another was the party's appeal to native-born residents in contrast to the Democrats' strength among German immigrants. But controlling for these factors, the effects of religion remained. The percentage of residents who were Catholic versus Methodist had significant and opposing effects on gubernatorial outcomes from the late 1870s through the 1880s.[21] Glick's short stint as governor showed that Republican dominance was not inevitable, but it also revealed the religious fault lines running through Kansas politics. Methodists and Protestants from smaller denominations who shared their views on temperance, especially Baptists and Presbyterians, could be counted on to support Republican candidates, while Catholics and a few others, such as German Lutherans, were more likely to favor Republicans' opponents.

The debate over Prohibition sharpened these differences between religious groups. Explicit accusations and counteraccusations between Protestants and Catholics nevertheless remained relatively infrequent.[22] The reason was that Catholics were not a sufficient political threat to Prohibition to make much of a difference, and both they and the Protestants advocating Prohibition knew it. Catholic numbers were sufficient to swing a few counties in the Democrats' direction, but not enough to matter much in the long run. Except when other factors surfaced, as they did in 1882, Republicans could count on winning a majority in almost every county. To the extent that reform and enforcement needed to be mobilized, the proponents of Prohibition knew their real work was to persuade Republicans. There was nothing to be gained by either

Catholic leaders speaking against Prohibition or Protestants making religion any more of an issue than it was.[23]

In 1884, St. John became the first Kansan to run for U.S. president, entering on the Prohibition ticket against Republican James G. Blaine and Democrat Grover Cleveland. The Republican Party was not ready to endorse Prohibition despite a petition with two hundred thousand names on it submitted by WCTU leader and suffragist Frances E. Willard.[24] The nation was not ready either. St. John received only 1.5 percent of the vote. Meanwhile, Governor Martin became Prohibition's strongest supporter in Kansas, extolling its benefits for families, schools, churches, and communities. He was reelected in 1886, winning nearly every county, and losing by more than 10 percent only in Atchison, Ellis, Leavenworth, and Wyandotte. "The public sentiment in Kansas is overwhelmingly against the liquor traffic," Martin reported in 1887. "Thousands of men who a few years ago opposed prohibition, or doubted whether it was the best method of dealing with the traffic, have seen and frankly acknowledged its beneficent results and practical success."[25]

POPULISM AND RELIGIOUS POLITICS

With Prohibition settled for the time being, a different dynamic entered Kansas politics in the 1890s and challenged Republican dominance, principally through the Populist appeals of third parties. These appeals weakened the support that Republican candidates enjoyed among Methodists and other conservative Protestants by emphasizing the differences between faith and politics, and indeed by exercising the voice of piety in criticizing government. This was a critical stance grounded not only in prophetic religion but also in the state's understanding of its origin and history. The dominant motif of that history was of course "bleeding Kansas." People had died, towns had been sacked, and militias had been raised in the cause of freedom. Kansas, John Brown, Abraham Lincoln, abolition, the Union army, and the Republican Party were all woven together in this telling of the state's history. Kansas had achieved statehood though the bloodshed of its martyred heroes. *Ad astra per aspera*—to the stars through difficulty—was the state's motto. A secondary motif, though, was implicit in the primary account. All the struggle and sacrifice would have been unnecessary if the government in Washington had behaved properly in the first place.

Government's main offense in this telling was overturning the Missouri Compromise of 1820 through the passage of the Kansas-Nebraska Act of 1854. The Missouri Compromise admitted Missouri as a slave state, Maine as a free state, and excluded slavery from the former Louisiana territory north of the 36'30" parallel. Under that arrangement, slavery would never have been at issue in Kansas. The act of 1854 assumed that Nebraska would likely be admitted as a free state and Kansas as a slave state, but because the matter was to be decided through popular sovereignty, it resulted in the bloody struggles that ensued. The federal government's further offense was in providing no assistance to restrain the violence. Kansans were left at the mercy of marauders from Missouri. Whatever defenses they could mount had to be of their own making.

Brown, as Kansas' most famous martyr, fit neatly into this story. He was not only a figure in the struggle against slavery; Brown was also a hero for taking action into his own hands. The day after Brown was hung, *Freedom's Champion* in Atchison declared that the "chief moral responsibility" for Harper's Ferry was not Brown's but rather President James Buchanan's, whose "high-handed attempts to force slavery upon a free people, by violence and bloodshed," had led to the attack. Brown was remembered in Kansas as having been convicted and hanged by the federal government. He became a larger-than-life ordinary citizen who had seen his friends in Kansas killed and had risen to the occasion. The famous John Steuart Curry mural, commissioned in 1937 for the state capitol in Topeka, depicted Brown towering in the foreground, exercising his First Amendment right to carry the Bible in one hand, his Second Amendment right by holding a rifle in the other hand, and rising in anger above conflicted symbols of a divided government—the stars and stripes along with the Confederate flag, both of which appear small and ineffective in the background.[26]

As settlers populated Kansas, they were confronted at every turn with government seeming to be on their side yet in reality proving less than fully effective. Settlers on the Osage reserve in southeastern Kansas were removed from land they thought was theirs because of uncertainties in government treaties. In northeastern Kansas, settlers looked without success to the federal government for assistance against drought and starvation. Regulation proved ineffective against exploitative interest rates charged by eastern banks and did nothing to curb periodic financial panics. Railroad companies were given huge tracts of land on which they did not have to pay taxes. Railroad magnates got rich, pulling strings in New York and Washington or so it seemed, while towns invested in risky bond schemes and farmers paid exorbitant freight rates.[27]

It was hardly surprising that populism spread across the state in the late 1880s. During the previous decade crops had been good, homesteading had risen steadily, railroads made it easier to ship grain to markets, and land could be purchased in many parts of the state from speculators, railroad companies, and school boards for less than four dollars an acre. But in the 1880s shifts in weather, crop yields, and prices resulted in dramatic reductions in farm earnings. Following increases for nearly a decade, the gross value of Kansas wheat declined steadily from almost thirty million dollars in 1882 to less than five million dollars in 1887.[28] Meanwhile, wheat farmers became more dependent on export markets, which fell by two-thirds, and rail shipments, which remained costly.[29]

A study conducted in relatively prosperous Harvey County near Newton showed that the gross farm income in 1890 averaged $600 for the year, hired labor and machinery repairs averaged $150, taxes averaged $70, and interest averaged $90, leaving only $290 for an average family of seven, or a mere 11¢ a day per person. That was about the same as an unskilled pieceworker could earn in Leavenworth or Topeka. It was better because farm families could raise their own food, but less dependable because of weather and crop failures.[30]

Rainfall fluctuated as much as 50 percent from year to year, and was at near-drought conditions across the state in 1882, 1886, and 1890.[31] Hiram H. Young was trying to eke out a living raising corn in Cloud County about eight miles south of Concordia in 1890. In early July he wrote of hot dry wind making the corn look discouraging. By the end of the month, more wind and high temperatures convinced him the corn was lost. "Good bye corn," he wrote. "We did our best to get you. But failed. A great amount of hard work lost without any return. 7 in our family. 95 acres of corn gone. Hard winter in store for us. It will take grit and economy to winter here."[32]

Grit and economy frequently necessitated borrowing. By 1890, 46 percent of the farms in Cloud County were mortgaged. That many or more farms were mortgaged in thirteen other counties. Statewide, 34 percent were mortgaged. To entice buyers, the railroad companies offered land in the early 1880s with deferred payments for two or three years on the interest and principle. Those payments were now coming due. A temporary boom in land prices encouraged other buyers to take out mortgages. Much of the investment reflected the transition from open prairie to working farms. In the 1880s, improved farmland in Kansas increased from eleven million to more than twenty-two million acres.

Mortgages were as much a curse as a blessing. The interest rate on mortgages statewide in 1890 was slightly above 8 percent. In western Kansas, where the risks of failure from drought and wind were higher, the rate was 10 percent. That was the going rate, but it seemed high to farmers whose net earnings were only 6 percent of their land's value. The larger problem was the regularity with which payments had to be made. Sharecroppers, who comprised a quarter of the state's farmers, had it better in bad years because the landlord shared their misfortune. Mortgage holders did not. In 1890, it is estimated that more than fifty-three hundred farms were sold through sheriff's auctions in foreclosure proceedings.[33]

The Populist movement emerged as an effort to ameliorate the harsh economic conditions that farmers were experiencing. Calling itself the Farmers' Alliance, it began in homes and country schoolhouses, gaining momentum as it identified reforms that could be made through the political process. By 1890 it was functioning as the People's Party, having determined that the established party machinery was in the hands, as a leader stated in 1891, "of men living in the towns, and connected in one way or another, to a greater or less degree, with railroads and with corporations engaged in the business of lending money for people in the East [and] powerfully in opposition to the interests of the farmers."[34]

The People's Party took as its primary objective the reform of banking and monetary practices that it deemed were responsible for the high mortgage rates. These reforms included abolishing national banks, expanding the supply of money through printing paper currency and coining silver, and reducing or eliminating brokerage charges on mortgages through a direct government lending program. In addition, the party called for a more equitable taxation of railroad assets and the closer regulation of shipping rates.[35]

Populists did not preach lawlessness, as their opponents frequently charged, but they did argue that government was unresponsive to common demands for justice, or was downright against seeing it come about. There was a familiar thread connecting populism to the rhetoric of abolition and the legacy of John Brown. Sockless Jerry Simpson—who claimed that the rich wore silk stockings and he wore none—was one of Kansas' strongest voices for Populist reform. Simpson maintained that loan agents and bankers were exploiting farmers by charging exorbitant rates, selling the mortgages to their friends in the East, and swaggering about town as great financiers. It was a case, he said, of the oppressors wielding power "through military force, the Church, by controlling money, trade, commerce, transportation, through cunningly devised schemes of legislation, [and] chattel slavery." The struggle in Kansas was a rebellion against this selfish brutality. "Is it any wonder," Simpson asked, that the men who followed 'old John Brown' into Kansas, on the principle that it was wrong to rob the black man of the fruits of his toil, should rebel when their own welfare is at stake?"[36]

Near Concordia, Hiram Young joined the alliance in June 1890, paying a quarter for his dues and taking his neighbor the next time

2.1 An 1891 magazine depiction, criticizing Populism as a "Party of Patches," shows William Peffer and Sockless Jerry Simpson among its leaders. Courtesy of KansasMemory.org, Kansas State Historical Society, Copy and Reuse Restrictions Apply

it met. Soon he was attending once or twice a week, and reporting large and enthusiastic crowds. Most of the meetings lasted past ten o'clock and some until midnight. Cigars were a nickel. Camaraderie was free. His wife's principal outings were to the Christian Church where Reverend Peter Bushong preached on Sunday mornings and Mrs. Bushong lectured on Sunday evenings. Hiram's outings were on Thursday and Saturday evenings to the Farmers'

Alliance. In October he attended a statewide meeting in Topeka, and a few weeks later was serving as a county official in the new party. That fall, almost two thousand of his neighbors in Cloud County voted for the Populist candidate for governor, beating the Republican candidate by more than five hundred votes.[37]

The official policy of the Farmers' Alliance and People's Party toward religion was to be nonsectarian, encourage people of every denomination to participate, and disallow discussions of religion at meetings on the grounds that these would lead to dissension. That did not deter the movement from meeting at church buildings when no other space could be found. It did reduce the chances of members making religious appeals or enlisting clergy on their behalf. Yet there were exceptions. One was Reverend Isom P. Langley, an Arkansas Baptist who was ordained in 1869, preached in Little Rock and several other locations in the 1870s while earning a law degree, and in the 1880s served as editor of several leading labor newspapers. In 1886 he ran unsuccessfully for Congress, and thereafter lectured throughout the Midwest and South on behalf of the Farmers' Alliance. Langley spoke freely about the relationship of faith to the Populist movement. True faith, he argued, was to be found in the example of Jesus feeding the hungry. It was expressed in the call to follow the Golden Rule and treat one another as equals. But pastors and priests were more concerned about theological distinctions than about caring for the poor. The result was injustice in politics as well as religion. "If the Christian ministers of the United States had the moral courage to preach the religion of Jesus Christ instead of yielding to the influence of Mammon-worshipers," he charged, "our political organizations would not dare to neglect the demands of the people."[38]

Langley's outspokenness was facilitated by the fact that he did not occupy a regular pulpit, and thus was free of denominational strictures against mingling faith and politics. The same was true of Reverend Alden C. Hillman, a Methodist pastor in Salina who served as state chaplain of the Kansas Farmers' Alliance. Hillman was ordained in Illinois in 1860, but never held a position as a regular pastor. He taught at Southern Illinois University in Carbondale and joined the faculty of Kansas Wesleyan University in 1883.[39] Other clergy held opinions about populism, and sometimes voiced them at official gatherings. A few months after the People's Party held its first national meeting in Cincinnati in May 1891, the Methodist Episcopal Church sponsored an ecumenical meeting in the nation's capital at which "social problems" were discussed. Speakers debated the merits of eight- and ten-hour days, and whether conglomerates were good or bad for society. There was general agreement that the laboring classes prospered best when Prohibition was enforced.[40]

In May 1892, Kansas delegates journeyed to Omaha to attend the Methodist Episcopal General Conference. The Farmers' Alliance was stronger in Nebraska than in Kansas, and so it may have been expected that the gathering would include a discussion of farmers' concerns in its program. Reverend Thomas Hanlon of Pennington Seminary in New Jersey introduced a resolution calling on the church to show greater sympathy for the laboring millions. "The laboring classes are drifting away from the church," he said. "Our church is made up of women to a large extent. The men are drifting away from it. We must take a stand on this great question affecting capital and labor." An observer reported that he was vigorously applauded from the gallery. The resolution, however, was simply referred to a committee, and the conference turned to questions about the seating of delegates and districting of bishops. Six weeks later, the Populist Party held a national convention in Omaha at which it invoked the blessing of Almighty God in its struggle to represent the interests of working people.[41]

Clergy who may have considered supporting the Populist movement found themselves in ambiguous circumstances at best. In February 1890, Catholic clergy received a Lenten pastoral letter from Bishop Louis Fink in Leavenworth with instructions that the letter was to be read to their congregations. The bishop expressed concern over the farm population's distress, and its fears of losing house and home. "It seems that almost every industry in our country is protected in order to amass riches in the hands of the few by which the many will have to suffer," he wrote, adding, "The only classes not protected are those that would seem to need it most, the laboring men and the farming population." Yet he declared that no Catholic could become a member of the Farmers' Alliance. The alliance was in his view anti-Catholic, a secret society dabbling in religion, "setting up men in place of God," and opposing Jesus Christ and the church.[42]

In a striking reversal four weeks later, Bishop Fink circulated a letter to the diocesan clergy withdrawing his objection to the Farmers' Alliance. Realizing the danger of having the bishop against it, the Kansas alliance had sent a delegation to assure the bishop that any rules contrary to the Holy Church would be done away with at the party's next convention. Most important was revoking the rule that local meetings be conducted as secret societies. With that understanding in place, Catholics were now free to join the Farmers' Alliance. "I wish it God Speed in its honest aims," the bishop wrote. But it was the initial message that carried the day. In the 1890 elections for governor and senator, counties with higher percentages of Catholics were significantly less likely to vote Populist than counties with lower percentages of Catholics.[43]

If Catholic signals were mixed, the message from Protestant leaders was that politics and pulpits should be separate, at least when it came to populism. At their state conference at Emporia in September 1891, Kansas Methodists adopted a resolution declaring the People's Party unchristian, and its organization a menace to the church and nation. Two weeks earlier, seven members of the Bethany Lutheran Church in Lindsborg were excommunicated for holding Farmers' Alliance membership. Although the church had been hosting Republican rallies on Sunday evenings for several years, the pastor explained that the members were expelled solely because the alliance was a secret society, and as such was unchristian and unrepublican. The church, he said, "has not taken any part in politics, nor does it intend to."[44]

The Methodist pastor who most clearly demonstrated the church's stance against populism by violating it was Reverend Jeremiah D. Botkin, one of the denomination's most accomplished temperance campaigners and camp meeting speakers. Botkin was the presiding elder of the Southwest Kansas Methodist Conference headquartered in Wichita, a frequent speaker at Bismarck Grove revival meetings, and in 1888 was nominated to run for governor on the Prohibition ticket. Prohibition was a worthy cause that any Methodist should have been able to support. But Botkin's candidacy threatened to divide the Republican vote and increase the chances of a Democratic victory. Botkin received a visit from Reverend Bernard Kelly, the presiding elder of the Southeast Kansas Conference in Emporia, who met with him for three hours in an effort to dissuade him from running. Kelly argued that it was inappropriate for a pastor to seek public office and asserted that Botkin's plans were the source of growing concern among their fellow Methodist ministers. Not persuaded, Botkin described Kelly's visit as having more to do with politics than with the church. "I propose to make my canvas thoroughly and show up Republican hypocrisy," Botkin explained. "I would not think I was doing my duty unless I did." Opting for Prohibition over Republicanism, some of his fellow clergy campaigned for him. But Botkin secured only 2 percent of the vote while his Republican opponent won handily with 55 percent.[45]

Had that been his only foray into politics, Reverend Botkin would likely have remained in the church's favor. Whatever reservations that Reverend Kelly may have had about mixing religion and politics seem to have faded too, for a year later Kelly accepted an appointment from the new Republican administration as a district pension agent. Botkin continued as the presiding elder and a Prohibition speaker, gaining notoriety on one occasion for calling the Wichita police commissioner—who happened to be a prominent Methodist elder—a perjurer and scoundrel. But in 1894, now as pastor of the Wellington Methodist Church, Botkin made the politically, if not professionally, risky move of abandoning the Prohibitionist party and joining the Populists. No sooner was the switch made than several members of his congregation accused him of "preaching politics." As the dispute escalated and clergy called for his resignation, Botkin left the congregation, declaring himself against those unwilling to "think politically outside of a certain old musty mold."[46]

A week later, the *Topeka Daily Capital* published a letter from Reverend Botkin's younger brother, Tom, a Republican living in Galena near the southeast corner of the state. "I have always admired his manly stand against the evils of intemperance and the encroachments of the rum power," Tom wrote. "Imagine my surprise [at] his entry into the populist camp." Now, Tom said, his brother was friends with a "rotten outfit [of] gamblers and whisky sellers." How any "honest Christian man" could support such an "immoral and indecent" party was simply a mystery, he added. Another story appeared in the *Topeka Daily Capital* two weeks later under the headline "Botkin Is Radical." The reporter asked Botkin how he could possibly reconcile his Methodism with anarchistic views. "I am a Christian socialist," Botkin replied. "I believe that the title to all land lies in God Almighty and that no man has a right to land in fee simple."[47]

Jerry Botkin, as he now called himself, moved to Neodosha, ran unsuccessfully for congress on the Populist ticket in 1894 and ran again in 1896. With other Populist candidates he stumped the state by rail as well as horse and wagon, stopping in farming communities to speak at Fourth of July celebrations and county fairs. At the Leonardville Korn Karnival, Botkin spoke for two hours to an enthusiastic crowd of more than a thousand. Leonardville was a farming community. Many of its residents were from Germany or Switzerland. Nearly half of their farms were mortgaged. It had taken them a decade to secure the money to build a small Methodist church and the Zion Evangelical church that later united with it. People were out of work, and businesses were going under. They knew what Jerry Botkin was talking about.[48]

In William Allen White's famous 1896 essay "What's the Matter with Kansas?" the Emporia editor wrote that the Populists "raked the old ash heap of failure in the state and found an old human hoop skirt who has failed as a businessman, who has failed as an editor, who has failed as a preacher, and we are going to run him for Congressman-at-Large." That was White's view of Botkin.[49] But Botkin was elected along with five other Populists to the U.S. House of Representatives, where he served ably from 1897 to 1899 as one of the few Methodist clergy ever to hold national office from Kansas. As the Populists' strength diminished, Botkin ran unsuccessfully for congress in 1902 as a Democrat and then governor on that ticket in 1908. In later life, he served for two years as warden of the state penitentiary and returned to the pulpit ministry, preaching at the Methodist Church in Winfield. His years in politics demonstrated that it was possible for a Methodist pastor to support the Populist cause, but illustrated equally the difficulties involved. There were pressures against taking stands that generated discord among fellow clergy and upsetting the dominance that Republicans so often enjoyed.

PROTESTING AGAINST INEQUALITY

The inequality that Populists identified between people of means and ordinary farmers and laborers was a reality for church members along with the pastors who served them. Vast differences in resources were evident among Methodists themselves, whose unrivaled success in establishing churches drew members spanning the social spectrum. The First Methodist Church in Topeka, a reporter wrote in November 1889, included "a dozen or twenty men who are worth from a quarter of a million to a million dollars, and a grist of smaller fellows who modestly boast of fifty or a hundred thousand." The church building was worth thirty thousand dollars, and the pastor was earning a handsome salary of thirty-five hundred dollars. At the opposite extreme, Reverend J. D. Baker was a pastor in north-central Kansas, serving United Brethren congregations in four counties from 1880 until 1885, and after that working under Methodist auspices. These communities were fully settled by the late 1870s. Rail service had been established, land improved, and homes built. More than fifty modest church buildings had been constructed. In 1890, Baker wrote to his presiding elder that it had been a hard time. Drought had ravaged the area for three consecutive years. Few crops had been raised, and there was no seed for the coming season. His pay for the year totaled eighty-seven dollars. Another pastor said there had been much sickness in the area. A Woman's Home Missionary Society officer visited the region, and confirmed that people were living in such poverty that donations of food and clothing were desperately needed.[50]

Farmers drawn to populism were keenly aware of the differences between their own communities and churches serving more affluent congregations in larger towns. "While poverty, ignorance, and starvation walk around under the shadow of these temples of worship," a writer near Winfield observed, "a minister at $10,000 a year talks to a crowd of bankers and stock gamblers, who go out during the week and lay all kinds of schemes and devices to defraud and impoverish the people." There were humble people who attended church when they could and if one was available, and then there were aristocratic churches attended by people wearing fine clothes.[51]

Differences in the value of church buildings reflected differences in members' ability to pay. The Methodist Church in Leonardville cost $2,000. The Methodist Church in Atchison, built in 1873 to replace the one that Lincoln spoke at in 1859, cost $25,000. Statewide, the average value of more than sixteen hundred churches among the five leading Protestant denominations in 1890 was $2,872. But county averages varied from less than $1,500 to more than $7,500, and the variation was only partly a function of population or location. Churches in Rice County, for example, averaged $3,400, but in neighboring Stafford County less than $2,000. Pawnee in western Kansas averaged more than $3,600, while neighboring Rush County averaged about $1,400.

The vote for Populist candidates also varied from county to county. In 1890 the Populist candidate for governor, J. F. Willits, captured 36 percent of the vote statewide, up from only 11 percent in 1888. But the 1890 vote ranged from 10 percent or less in nine counties to more than 50 percent in sixteen counties. In that election as well as the elections from 1888 to 1894 for governor, senator, and president, economic factors clearly affected county-to-county variations in voting for Populist candidates. Indeed, the one factor that consistently affected voting patterns was the percentage of farmers in the county whose land was encumbered with mortgages. But the other factor that impacted voting patterns was the average value of church buildings: the higher the value, the less likely the county was to vote Populist. That was true in all the elections from 1890 to 1896, and was especially so in 1890, when Populists were most clearly distinguished from both Democratic and Republican candidates. It was true taking account of differences in mortgage holding and the value of farms. The church effect did not mean that pastors in more expensive churches were preaching against populism. It did reflect the fact that influential members of these churches were more likely to be among the community leaders who resisted populism.[52]

It fell to Populist leaders themselves to draw connections between the central issues with which they were concerned and any arguments that might be grounded in religious faith. The central issues were economic, having to do with the money supply, freight rates, mortgages, and tariffs. Unlike Prohibition, which had always been framed as a moral issue and thus of relevance to the churches, populism was harder to define in moral terms, easier to be excluded from pulpits on the grounds that it was political, and indeed advanced by its own leaders as a scientific approach to farming, government, and trade. And yet populism's appeal was grounded in moral claims about fellowship, harmony, unity, working together, and pursuing common aims because they were good, virtuous, and right. It was these claims that sometimes gained expression in biblical themes, in references to abolition and slavery, and hence in the language that led Bishop Fink to worry that populism itself was a kind of religion.

On the national stage, William Jennings Bryan connected faith and moral politics as much in what was said about him as through his own words. Bryan's mother was a devout Methodist, his father was a Baptist, and Bryan himself attended services regularly at both churches before joining the Cumberland Presbyterian Church at age fourteen following a revival meeting. Placing Bryan's name in nomination for president in 1896, Diplomatic Consul Edward C.

Little of Kansas asserted that the "ark of the covenant of human freedom which John Brown of Osawatomie" established in Kansas was now being transferred to Bryan of Nebraska. The nation would have to choose between being ruled by the almighty dollar or almighty God, Little said, and Bryan would be like the young Joshua bidding the sun and moon to stand still while he "fights the battle of human freedom." At campaign appearances, other speakers introduced him as a fearless champion of the people endowed with God's blessing and guided by God's omnipotent hand. Bryan himself alluded often in his talks to biblical imagery, most notably in his speech against the gold standard, in which he declared, "You shall not press down upon the brow of labor this crown of thorns, you shall not crucify mankind upon a cross of gold."[53]

The Kansas leader who most clearly expressed populism's moral and religious themes was William Alfred Peffer. Peffer was a modest man who advertised the fact that he owned a mortgaged farm in southeastern Kansas, but who also edited the widely circulated *Kansas Farmer*, and was a lawyer and an effective public speaker. He was an Episcopalian, a Bible scholar, and a teetotaler. His chest-length beard resembled Brown's and gave him the look of an Old Testament prophet, though he was milder than Brown in tone and style, and was a keen student of farm economics and trade policy. In 1890 he ran as the People's Party candidate for U.S. Senate, winning with nearly 141,000 votes or approximately 18,000 more than his Republican opponent. He was widely described as the first senator from Kansas to be elected with no indebtedness to the Republican Party, although Republican newspapers quickly argued that he was really a Republican on most issues and Prohibitionist leaders hailed him as one of theirs. In an address to the Kansas state legislature when his victory was announced, Peffer reiterated the Populists' call for government that was responsive to the people, equal and just taxation, and free trade, noting (to cries of "amen") that "a just God in heaven would not permit" the middle classes to disappear. Near the speech's end, he expressed "supreme gratitude to the Father of all mercy, from whom all blessings flow, for this dispensation of his blessing." And on a lighter note, asking for pardon "inasmuch as I am not a minister," he observed that when he reached the senate, he would do just what someone said they would do when they got to heaven: "I will go right in and just sit down wherever God tells me." The speech received thunderous applause from the legislature's Populists.[54]

Peffer was not resorting to religious language casually. After a year at Dickinson College in Pennsylvania he farmed in Indiana, moved to Missouri and then Illinois, served as a second lieutenant in the Illinois eighty-third regiment, and practiced law in Clarksville, Tennessee, until 1870, when he moved to Kansas.[55] In 1869, he published a 226-page epic poem in the style of Walt Whitman titled *Myriorama: A View of Our People and Their History, Together with the Principles Underlying, and the Circumstances Attending, the Rise and Progress of the American Union.*[56] Like Whitman, Peffer was profoundly influenced by the Civil War and interested in what it meant for the future progress of the nation. But unlike Whitman's "Passage to India," *Myriorama* emphasized progress far less, and dwelled considerably more on the devastation wrought by the war and the continuing problems the nation faced. Of women in Tennessee he wrote how they had "prayed o'er mangled bodies of their murdered dead," and of gray-haired men how they had been "pulled and dragged about from tree to tree behind a crazy mob," and then hanged or shot. The poem graphically described the martyred dead, ruthless hate, burning houses, and starving refugees. The language pulsed with blood-soaked battlefields, the chains of slavery, fire and swords, smoke, tears, and grief.[57]

Through it all Peffer saw the hand of God, guiding, calling people to obey, demanding courage and sacrifice, offering comfort and eternal life, and requiring that justice and mercy be done. The tone was not of blind belief but rather Joblike questioning. Virtue, justice, reason, and wisdom adjudicate the delicate debate that transpires over slavery, and determines that it should end, despite uncertain knowledge of the complexity of human life, because all are God's offspring. Humanity is vain, easily deluded, beaten down, and yet capable of hanging on and even expressing gratitude in humble ways. "That arm?" the wife asks her returning husband.

"At Chicamauga left," he answers. "But you are left, thank God," she says. The leg is wood, but he is alive. There is more of struggle and humility than of heroism. People can only do so much. They must uphold the law and seek liberty, leaving the rest to God. The final verdict is that "God rules over all" and "directs the whole for purpose of His own." Progress comes only as people conform to God's law and will.[58]

Near the poem's end, Peffer celebrates Ulysses S. Grant becoming president in the 1868 election, and momentarily allows himself Whitmanlike reveling over the transcontinental railroad and the trans-Atlantic telegraph cable. But those thoughts turn his attention to the continuing dangers of avarice and pride. "Have war and victory had their full fruition yet?" he asks. Or will national decay prevail? "What now remains to do?" Anticipating his later work on behalf of the Populist movement, he answers:

The moral world is full of work. Across
The growing nation cast your eye and see
The wretchedness and want, privation and
Distress in countless phases shown. The poor
On every hand need help; reach out your hand
To struggling poverty. The fallen, and the low,
Go down to them; go, help them all to rise;
Go, ease the aching world of pain, and on
The ruins of a wicked past raise up,
By good you do to humble, needy man,
A monument for Virtue's eye to scan.[59]

A DIVIDED PARTY

The Republican Party rebounded from the defeats it suffered at the hands of Populist organizers in the 1890s. In 1898, Republicans regained the governorship and all but one of the state's eight seats in the U.S. House of Representatives, and two years later won back both seats in the U.S. Senate. But populism was the most effective challenge Kansas Republicans had faced since coming into power in 1861, and its success was not to be diminished or easily forgotten. In the presidential race of 1896, running on the fusion People's and Democratic ticket, Bryan bested Republican McKinley by more than twelve thousand votes in Kansas, or a margin of almost 4 percent. Republicans lost gubernatorial races in 1892 and 1896, and over the decade edged out Democrats and Populists by a margin averaging only 3 percent. That compared with an average margin of 31 percent from 1862 to 1872, and 16 percent from 1874 to 1888. Even when Republicans won, the reality was increasingly evident that they could be beaten. They held the governorship only 56 percent of the time in the 1890s, compared with 93 percent of the time before that. From 1861 to 1889, Republicans represented Kansas in the U.S. House of Representatives 98 percent of the time, but during the 1890s that proportion fell to 47 percent. For three decades every seat from Kansas in the U.S. Senate had been held by Republicans, but in the 1890s that representation declined to 39 percent. Peffer's win was the biggest shock of all. His victory occurred at the expense of John J. Ingalls, the revered Republican statesperson who had played a prominent role in the Wyandotte constitutional convention of 1859, designed the state seal, been elected and reelected to the U.S. Senate for eighteen years, and served as its presiding officer.[60]

Faced with the need to either retrench or reform, Republicans opted to do both. Retrenchment involved discrediting the Populists in every way possible, and demonstrating that Republicans after all were the party of peace, order, and prosperity in Kansas. The Republican-led Board of Regents dismissed the president and four faculty of the Kansas Agricultural College in Manhattan for advocating populism. Republican newspapers argued that Populists were radicals, anarchists, and floppers who had deserted their party, and thus could not be trusted. Newspapers in New York, Chicago, and Los Angeles previously known for favorable reports about Kansas investment opportunities—newspapers that later ridiculed Kansans for their conservatism—asserted that Kansas was filled with wild-eyed socialists. Populism brought to mind Emile Zola, Karl Marx, and the revolutions of 1848. Kansas Republicans warned that eastern sources of finance would dry up. Farmers in western Kansas, leaders contended, would find their mortgages called and lose their land overnight. Other leaders took a different view that also disparaged populism. The foreclosures that Populists worried about, they maintained, were rare, and mostly the result of mismanagement, bad weather, and even drunkenness. A couple of good crops and the mortgages would all be paid off. Meanwhile, Republicans would do what they could to keep banks from going under and encourage railroad officials to take their public responsibilities more seriously.[61]

The Republicans' ability to fight back was greatly facilitated by having been in power for so long. Candidates ran on their credentials, which meant having served in the Union army and having been appointed to a judgeship or local office, such as postmaster or pension agent. Those credentials were powerful enough that Populists and Democrats relied on them as well, but usually with fewer offices or appointments to show. It was notable that Populists were able to organize local Farmers' Alliance meetings, especially among farmers who lived apart and had to travel on muddy roads to attend. But Republicans regularly got together at meetings of the Masonic lodges that were present in nearly every town, Grand Army of the Republic reunions, and church. To counter the alliance meetings, there were also Commercial Clubs and newly formed Republican Clubs. Law and Order Leagues emerged in smaller towns, and though never as active as in other parts of the country, the American Protective Association stoked anti-Catholic and nativist sentiments.[62]

The Republican Party that regained power in 1900 was nevertheless quite different than the one that had held nearly unrivaled influence during the 1870s and 1880s. In reality, the conditions to which Republicans had to respond in the new century to claim power posed new challenges. Most evident was the fact that earlier Republicans had not experienced the threat of populism, or the possibility that a third party could emerge and win on its own steam or fuse with Democrats. The earlier threat had come solely from Democrats, and was more easily countered by reminding Kansas voters that Democrats were for slavery, fought on the wrong side, and countenanced border ruffians from Missouri, and if that were not enough, were soft on temperance and loyal to Rome. The new reality was that few Kansans in 1900 had actually experienced the Civil War. The earlier Republicans could run as war heroes, but at the turn of the century any Republican candidate under the age of fifty could not.

Social conditions were changing as well. Suffrage for women in state and national elections was not achieved in Kansas until 1912, but the state constitution of 1861 guaranteed women the right to vote in school board elections, and that right was extended to all municipal elections in 1887. By the early 1890s, agitation for complete suffrage was in full swing. The only towns of any size in 1880 were Topeka, Leavenworth, and Atchison, all within sixty miles of one another, and thus giving Republican officeholders in Topeka easy access to their constituents. By 1900 Kansas City, Kansas, was the largest city in the state, and Wichita was larger than Leavenworth and Atchison. Topeka's population was still growing, but Leavenworth's and Atchison's were almost stagnant. Kansas City had become the center of rail service and shipping, and it was booming in conjunction with the rise of meatpacking and the emergence of Kansas City, Missouri, as a manufacturing and distribution hub. The state's population was also continuing to grow. The population in 1900 totaled almost 1.5 million, an increase of 50 percent since 1880. Twenty-six new counties had been organized. Thirty-two of the state's 105 counties included urban residents, up from only 16 in 1880. There were only 51 towns in 1880 with populations of at least 1,000; in 1900, there were 107. Besides the urban concentrations around Topeka and Kansas City, there were regional centers, such as Hutchinson, Salina, Newton, Fort Scott, and Emporia—all capable of expressing new political interests. With only twenty-three hundred miles of track serving the state in 1879, towns everywhere were lobbying for more. With nearly nine thousand miles of mainline track in 1900 and two thousand miles of auxiliary track, the question had become one of regulation instead of additional mileage. There was also growing inequality, not only between farms and towns, but also in agriculture itself. In 1900, 14 percent of the state's farms had five hundred acres or more, up from only 1 percent in 1880. Twenty-nine percent of farms were rented, up from 14 percent in 1880.[63]

While many of these changes reinforced the official doctrine that Kansas was prospering, they also created new constituencies and opportunities for Republican leaders to tailor their appeals to these constituencies. Between 1900 and 1914, at least three distinct factions vied for party control. The one that most clearly represented the old guard became known among its rivals as the Republican machine. Its leaders were older, held office longer, were mostly Civil War veterans, represented the party at national meetings as well as in the state, and vehemently opposed nearly everything the Populists' stood for. They were closely aligned with two of the state's wealthiest leaders, Cyrus Leland Jr. and Morton Albaugh.

Leland was a Civil War veteran who served under General Ewing, chased and killed some of Quantrill's border ruffians following the raid on Lawrence in 1863, and after the war served as a delegate to the state legislature from Doniphan County and worked for Ewing's election to the U.S. Senate. Albaugh came to Kansas in the early 1880s, served as a school principal and newspaper editor in Kingman, organized the county's local Republican efforts in the late 1880s, and was elected chair of the party's state committee. In 1895, Albaugh and his wife built an expensive home near the capitol in Topeka, and joined the town's elite of railroad owners, doctors, and politicians. In 1898, he was credited with organizing the campaign that overthrew the Populists and returned the Republicans to the governor's office and legislature. When asked if there were any personal friends he would take care of, Governor-elect William Eugene Stanley replied, "Yes one. Mort Albaugh, chairman of the state committee, may have anything he asks for." Albaugh also organized the successful campaigns for governor of W. J. Bailey in 1902 and 1904. Under the leadership of Leland and Albaugh, the Republican machine secured funds from the state's wealthiest residents, selected delegates and candidates for office in closed-door meetings, and rewarded the faithful with judgeships and appointments to commissions in charge of railroads, charities, and public lands. There were numerous instances, Leland later recalled, of money changing hands in return for political favors.[64]

The faction that arose in opposition to the Republican machine became known as antiboss Republicans or simply as insurgents. They were younger, and less likely to have fought in the Civil War or come to Kansas as pioneers, and yet were able to match or exceed the establishment in education, wealth, and accomplishments. Behind the scenes, the most powerful insurgent was David W. Mulvane, an honors graduate from Yale University who in 1900 at the age of thirty-five owned a ranch near Troy in Doniphan County, practiced law in Topeka, and had worked up the party's ranks to become commissioner of pensions and a delegate to the national Republican convention. Mulvane was the son of Joab Mulvane, a wealthy Kansas banker, landowner, railroad magnate, and outspoken Republican. The younger Mulvane achieved the further good fortune in 1906 of marrying wealthy New York widow Helen M. Drexel, and by the time he died was said to have amassed an estate of more than a million dollars. In 1900 he wrested control of the Kansas party from Leland, installed friends from Wichita and Chanute among the delegation to the national convention, and backed former Salina editor and Abilene attorney J. R. Burton to represent Kansas in the U.S. Senate. Burton was elected and served until 1906, when he returned to Kansas and took up farming.

In 1904, Mulvane supported Edward Wallis Hoch as a reform candidate for governor on the Republican ticket. Hoch was elected and won again in 1906 despite a minor scandal involving the governor allegedly kissing a former governor's wife. Hoch had been too young to fight in the Civil War, but came to Kansas with his older brother in 1872, settling first in Barton and then in Marion County, and working as a printer. Being seen as an outsider of humble background served Hoch as a candidate to challenge the Republican machine. Hoch gained attention in 1900 when the machine rigged a vote to deprive him of becoming state printer and again in 1902 over a controversy with the machine involving state delegates. As governor, Hoch spoke frankly of the "multiplicity of useless offices and extravagant waste of the people's money" under the previous Republican administration, and called for a thorough examination of public records. He also worked for congressional reapportionment and replacement of the spoils system by a professional system of civil service.[65]

LAW AND ORDER

The third faction in Republican politics was a grassroots movement for law and order, focusing especially on the need for stricter enforcement of Prohibition. The law and order movement was not directly involved in the selection of candidates, but through local activities influenced the party's role in state and national politics. Law and order meetings grew in popularity in the late 1880s as citizens responded to what they perceived as lax implementation of the state's prohibition against package houses, dram shops, and liquor joints. At a meeting in June 1890, a large crowd met at the First Methodist Church in Salina to demand the jailing of local jointists and argue against resubmission of the Prohibition amendment for possible revision. In Leavenworth, a local branch of the International Law and Order League met for a similar purpose. Angry citizens in Leonardville organized a Law and Order League in 1897 following the killing of the town's sheriff by a gunman assumed to be in violation of the liquor law.

Advocates of law and order became increasingly concerned in 1898 when Governor Stanley declared himself in favor of a local option law rather than mandatory Prohibition. Neither the machine Republicans nor the insurgents in subsequent administrations seemed intent on strict enforcement. It was in this context that violent saloon-smashing episodes led by WCTU activist Carry Nation erupted in 1901 and 1902. Senator Burton said that Nation was a mere molehill and Kansans would eventually abandon saloons when they grew tired of them. But Nation brought national attention to the issue and Kansas. Soon Republican leaders were again voicing their approval of Prohibition. "The growth of temperance sentiment has been marvelous," Governor Hoch told the legislature in January 1905. "The business world is now practically a great temperance society."[66]

The churches' relationship to politics in the decade and a half before World War I was evident in all three factions of the Republican Party. Special censuses of religious bodies conducted in 1906 and 1916 confirmed that churches were doing well. By the latter date there were 610,000 church members in Kansas, representing an increase of more than 260,000 in twenty-six years. Methodists still outnumbered all other Protestant denominations by margins of two or three to one, and remained well ahead of Roman Catholics. The biggest change since 1890 was that nearly all congregations had their own buildings, and instead of small frame structures of the kind that John Wesley and Francis Asbury had imagined, the average building was valued at between $5,000 and $6,000, and a growing number were of brick construction.[67] Among the machine Republicans, Governor Stanley, who served as a Methodist Sunday school superintendant and Bible teacher in Wichita, was the most visible Methodist representative. "Many children of Wichita, now grown into manhood and womanhood," a reporter wrote in 1898, "received their first Scriptural instruction from him."[68] The anti-boss Republicans were connected with Methodism as well. Joab Mulvane was a board member of the First Methodist Church of Topeka, which later named its educational building in his honor, served as a trustee of Baker University, and reared his children in the church. Grassroots law and order Republicans were also aligned with the churches.

Churches were the preferred venues for law and order meetings. A meeting in January 1898 at the First Presbyterian Church of Emporia was typical. The town's Methodist, Congregational, and Presbyterian churches jointly sponsored the meeting, which was presided over by the Law and Order League's president. Each of the pastors gave a vigorous talk on behalf of temperance. The featured speaker was Lieutenant Governor James A. Troutman. Three years later, following a joint smashing episode led by ministers in several of the surrounding towns, the Emporia clergy held a mass meeting demanding the legal closure of local joints. The same day, a meeting of the McPherson district Methodists in Lyons resolved to deplore lawlessness, and yet "approve the methods of Mrs. Carry Nation and all bodies of saloon smashers." Law and order Republicans in Hutchison succeeded in nominating their own slate of candidates for city offices against "regular ticket" nominees. That spring, the statewide Kansas Methodist Conference adopted a resolution against "the law-defying, vice-breeding saloon," and expressed hope that the recent revival of interest in law and order would continue. That expectation increased with Governor Hoch in 1905—a better Methodist, they hoped, than Governor Stanley had been—and rose further in 1908 when Governor Hoch addressed the Methodists' general conference in Baltimore on the merits of Prohibition.[69]

Under other circumstances the factional differences among Republicans might have weakened the party, but in Kansas events proved to be in its favor. From 1900 through 1912, Republicans held the governorship continuously, elected all the state's U.S. senators, and elected all but one of the state's members of the U.S. House of Representatives. The machine faction retained some of its power, selecting insider Alfred W. Benson to fill Senator Burton's position in 1906 after Burton was convicted of corruption. The reformers succeeded in instituting a primary election law that opened the selection of candidates to a popular vote. The law and order faction witnessed a rebirth of its appeals for strict enforcement of Prohibition. In 1914, well-known Republican Arthur Capper became governor, winning by a nine-point margin, and two years later was reelected by a twenty-three-point margin.[70]

As Republicans flourished, there were fewer instances in which the churches became directly involved in political controversies. Methodist clergy raised eyebrows even among their own members by banning football at Baker University in Baldwin, but rescinded the ban a few years later, and were pleased to see the town described in the *Washington Post* as a place where "crime is a thing almost unknown" and a "good lecturer or preacher can draw a big audience any time." At a gathering in Chicago in 1910, former governor Hoch described himself as a temperance man and a teetotaler. "It is as much a Christian's duty to vote as it is to go to prayer meeting," he said. Back in Kansas few would have disagreed about it being their duty to vote. They would merely have asserted the importance of attending prayer meeting as well. Lee Bloomenshine grew up near Wichita in the town that named itself Mulvane in gratitude for the Mulvane family's help in securing a railroad. He remembered the town being a "church community" with Methodists occupying the largest brick building on Church Street and traveling evangelists setting up tents for revival meetings in the town park. Mary Potter Boyd was a member of the Methodist Church in Corbin, not far from Winfield. It was not the political meetings or temperance rallies that stayed in her memory years later but rather the Sunday school classes, worship services, Christmas Eve programs, and Ladies' Aid gatherings to make quilts for the needy and take food to the sick. The point of it all, she said, was trying to live "right with our Lord and with our fellow men."[71]

FOR THE CHILDREN

The one issue that sparked continuing controversy was education. By the end of the nineteenth century more than 380,000 pupils were enrolled in Kansas public schools, representing 83 percent of the state's children age five through eighteen. More than 10,000 teachers were employed, and the total expenditures on primary and secondary education exceeded $4 million. The kindergarten movement was just beginning, but in Topeka the T. E. Bowman Memorial Kindergarten Training School for teachers and mothers had been established to promote a "better understanding of the practical teachings of Jesus Christ." In addition, there were more than twenty-four public and private normal schools, preparatory institutes, and colleges. Baker University in Baldwin with 500 students was the largest of the denominational institutions. Others included Ottawa University, founded by Baptists in 1865; St. Mary's Academy in Leavenworth, founded by the Sisters of Charity in 1870; Highland University in Doniphan County, founded by Presbyterians in 1878; the College of Emporia, founded by Presbyterians in 1882; Bethany College in Lindsborg, founded by Lutherans in 1882; Kansas Wesleyan University in Salina, founded by Methodists in 1886; Cooper Memorial College in Sterling, founded by United Presbyterians in 1887; and Friends University in Wichita, founded by Quakers in 1898.[72]

Darwinism was an emerging issue that surfaced occasionally in educational debates, and was dealt with summarily when it did. In 1901, at Kansas Wesleyan University, the institution's Methodist trustees removed natural sciences professor Frank D. Tubbs on charges of espousing evolution. "I am a consistent believer in evolution as the method which God has employed to bring things about in this world," Tubbs explained, adding, "I don't believe God has gone about His work in a haphazard manner."[73] His appeal was unsuccessful. A year later, the Kansas Methodist Conference charged Reverend Granville Louther of McPherson with heresy for disseminating subversive doctrines alleged to be atheistic and evolutionist. Louther's views rested less in natural science than in holiness teachings that God was in the process of evolving higher life-forms from lower ones.[74] For the greater part, worries about evolution lay well in the future.

Of larger concern was the proper place of biblical instruction in the public schools. Ostensibly religion was to be separate from public education, just as it was from government, but how that was accomplished was a matter of interpretation. The Kansas Constitution affirmed that "no religious sect or sects shall ever control any part of the common school or university funds of the state."[75] The Kansas wording anticipated an amendment to the U.S. Constitution proposed in 1875 by Maine Republican James G. Blaine, which asserted that "no money raised by taxation in any State for the support of public schools, or derived from any public fund therefor, nor any public lands devoted thereto, shall ever be under the control of any religious sect; nor shall any money so raised or lands so devoted be divided between religious sects or denominations." The amendment passed in the House of Representatives by a margin of 180 to 7, but failed to achieve the necessary two-thirds majority in the U.S. Senate. Eleven states subsequently passed laws similar to the Blaine amendment. Kansans had no need for one. They did, however, favor Blaine in his unsuccessful bid for the presidency against Cleveland in 1884. Observers attributed Blaine's defeat to the phrase "Rum, Romanism, and Rebellion," which his proponents used to characterize Cleveland, with the inadvertent result of Catholics in New York and New Jersey giving Cleveland the winning margin. There was no backlash in Kansas. Blaine secured 58 percent of the popular vote statewide, winning a majority in all but four counties, two of which were Ellis and Barton.[76]

The question of religious instruction emerged anew in the 1890s over concerns that public monies were being used to promulgate Catholic doctrine in Indian schools. In 1896, both houses of the U.S. Congress debated proposals to halt or phase out government funding of these sectarian institutions. "The Catholic church has some rights," Representative James S. Sherman of New York argued. "Any sect" should receive funding, he said, that would "reach down and attempt to shed light into the minds of the dusty little wards of the nation." The House of Representatives nevertheless voted to end funding, and the measure was put into effect several years later.[77]

In Kansas, concern focused less on government funding than on provisions governing religious instruction. An 1876 statute referring to first- and second-class cities declared that "no sectarian or religious doctrine shall be taught or inculcated in any of the public schools of the city," but clarified the restriction by stating that "nothing in this section shall be construed to prohibit the reading of the Holy Scriptures." For second-class towns, the wording further stipulated that the Holy Scriptures should be read "without note or comment." An 1897 statute about the purchase and use of textbooks provided that "no text-book shall be adopted that contains anything of a partisan or sectarian character." But if it seemed clear enough that religion was not to be taught, the difficulty was that "sectarian" did not exclude those elements of religion about which every reasonable citizen was assumed to agree, and the Holy Scriptures in practice meant the King James Bible used in Protestant churches.[78] Romish teachings were sectarian; Methodism was not. The school day routinely began with the Lord's Prayer and passages from the Bible, and the occasional student who refused to participate risked suspension.[79]

These tacit understandings were not shared in all communities. In 1885 the school board in Concordia, where a significant minority of the population was Catholic, resolved that Bible reading, prayer, and religious exercises of any kind should be prohibited in the public schools. That clarification extended the statutory provisions to exclude prayer and reading from either the Protestant or Catholic Bible. But the state attorney general overturned the board's action on the grounds that it had no power to make such rulings, and even if it did, the ruling was contrary to public policy. Citing a Cincinnati case argued before the U.S. Supreme Court, the attorney general observed that "sectarian instruction" was not permitted, but that "moral and religious instruction as well as intellectual and scientific" was appropriate.[80]

A decade later, questions of sectarian influence were still at issue in many parts of the nation and increasingly were directed against Catholics. The American Protective Association revived efforts to pass the Blaine amendment and ran advertisements in hundreds of newspapers, asking, "Do you believe in maintaining and perpetuating our public school system and public institutions? Are you opposed to all attempts to use our public funds for any sectarian purpose?" In Pennsylvania, the Pittsburgh Board of Education adopted a resolution banning any public school teacher from appearing in the garb of any religious order. In Topeka, a secret society calling itself the Junior Order of United American Mechanics organized in order to shield Americans from foreign influences, "uphold the public school system of the United States," and "prevent sectarian inference." It was joined by the Patriotic Sons of America, another nativist organization in Topeka devoted to keeping the public schools free of sectarian influences. In Kansas City, the American Protective Association circulated a petition demanding that only Protestant teachers be employed.[81]

The underlying concern among both Protestants and Catholics was that children needed to be exposed to sound moral and religious values, and be protected from heresy. "The Catholic church today forbids its members to hear heretical teachers or to read heretical books, and even the 'Holy Bible' is not allowed to be freely read," a Topeka resident complained in 1889. "Protestants," the same writer observed, "are really but little less tolerant than Catholics in regard to extending the domain of knowledge into the realm of heresy." The writer argued that this lack of tolerance was ultimately rooted in the terrible consequences "for time and eternity" that would flow from exposure to incorrect teachings.[82] As the new century began, educators met in Topeka to consider what the schools' role should be. There was general agreement that the struggle between good and evil was increasing, but disagreement about addressing it through greater attention to the Bible, or better instruction in literature and science.[83] That debate would continue for many decades.

Nearly a half century had passed since Lincoln spoke at Atchison, since Catholics and Protestants there constructed their respective churches and got along with one another better at certain times than at others. Both traditions flourished over the years, adding members in the tens of thousands and building churches in every county. Methodists had clearly enjoyed the stronger hand in politics, although they had never entirely gotten their way or for that matter embraced the Republican Party quite as warmly as later observers would sometimes imagine. In the meantime, Catholics and Protestants alike deplored drunkenness, and sometimes accused the other of voting for public officials incapable of upholding law and order. Both were at times critical of secret societies and on other occasions willing to encourage them. Each was wary of gains that the other might be making. In 1900, Kansas Methodists read that their church's leaders applauded enthusiastically when a speaker in

New York City said the Pope presided over a "land of superstition and priestcraft," and turned any educated person into "a cringing beggar with a monkey and a grind organ." That indictment was mild compared to one passed later by a Presbyterian assembly in Kansas City. The Church of Rome, it declared, "is, and always has been, a menace or a blight to civil and religious liberty of every kind wherever it has obtained a foothold."[84]

What mattered more to ordinary Kansans, if public officials had it right, were schools and taxes. The evolving political style was profoundly pragmatic and centrist, drawing on clergy and community leaders to restrain radicalism, and giving citizens ample opportunities to disagree about how best to govern themselves. On the one hand, the state proudly advanced its system of common schools, constructed buildings by the thousands, and required children to attend. This was the path to progress and prosperity. On the other hand, better schools meant higher taxes. Governor after governor encouraged lawmakers to find ways to keep government expenditures low. That was a key doctrine of Republican policy. It rankled Catholics that they were being asked to support the public schools with no remuneration for their own. It bothered Protestants that Catholics were intent on developing a separate system of education. Were that not enough, children's souls were at stake. In which religion would they be trained? In which would they find salvation? That was the issue that Laura Beers and her Methodist husband argued about that fateful evening in 1912. In rare circumstances it could lead to murder.

CHAPTER 3

REDEFINING THE HEARTLAND

NEVER ONE TO SHY FROM HYPERBOLE, ex-senator John J. Ingalls declared in 1896 that Kansas was the "nucleus of our political system," the "core and kernel of the country," "indispensable" to the nation's inspiration and improvement, unmatched in the ample rewards of its industry and the conditions of its prosperity. "Its arithmetic is more dazzling than poetry," he opined. Historians would have difficulty describing it in ways that did not strain the "capacity of human credulity."[1] The speech occurred as Populists advanced a far different picture of Kansas prosperity. But if Ingalls's rhetoric was less than compelling as an assessment of the current conditions, it presaged the optimism that was to prevail in coming decades. Progressivism was rooted in the realization that the material aspects of life were indeed improving. The new century offered Americans hope that science, industry, better roads, schools, and even new methods of farming would advance civilization. No one then could foresee how armed aggression in Europe and an economic catastrophe at home would derail the train of progress.

Republicans, Democrats, Methodists, Catholics, and members of small denominations all held strong opinions of what had made Kansas great, and what would keep its beacon shining bright. Kansans seldom thought of themselves as part of an identifiable progressive movement, at least not one with a capital P. Theirs was rather a conviction of being important participants in the noble experiment of U.S. democracy. They took pride in being among the first to grant universal suffrage to women. There was satisfaction in being at the crossroads of the nation, neatly located along the major rail arteries connecting East Coast cities with the growing populations of

110

California and Oregon. It was inspiring to see highways following the rail lines and be hailed as the nation's breadbasket. Prohibition was touted as a positive factor in the state's advancing economic climate and low prison population. Towns were rapidly acquiring electricity, mechanization was changing agriculture, crop yields were improving, and better churches were being built. It was possible for Kansans to argue that thrift, self-sufficiency, and wholesome living all were the keys to their continuing success. It was just as sensible to imagine that these virtues would sustain the heartland in hard times—better perhaps than intervention from easterners who knew little of the Middle West.

But Kansas was to experience a long slide from being the "kernel of the country," to becoming a mere outpost far from the centers of national economic and political influence. The shift was rooted in economic and demographic changes, but was primarily a matter of cultural redefinition. Kansas was attacked so often and so pejoratively by leaders in other parts of the country—and by some within Kansas itself—that it came to be viewed as a cultural wasteland, a place where only freaks and fanatics could survive. By the time this redefinition was finished, it would be hard for anyone in the nation's burgeoning coastal cities to imagine that Kansas had ever been anything but marginal. It would be difficult to retrieve the state of mind that existed in the 1920s when economic conditions and educational aspirations were rising, and when being a progressive Republican state created opportunities to be heard in Washington. But to understand Kansas politics and religion during the latter decades of the twentieth century, it is essential to retrieve that sense of pride and indeed the perception of centrality that existed among Kansans in the 1920s, and then to observe how those faded in the 1930s.

On those rare occasions in the nineteenth century when the Kansas Republican Party lost power, it regrouped and made a comeback in the next electoral cycle. Voters were independent enough that they periodically abandoned the dominant party, but smart enough to return when they saw that it was in their interest to do so. Temporary defection from the Republican Party happened again in 1932 and 1936 as Kansas voters opted for the agricultural policies of the New Deal. They soon were disappointed, however, and became increasingly worried about the distant arrogation of power in Washington. By the time a member of the Grand Old Party returned to the White House in the 1950s, Kansas Republicans had been out of step with national politics for more than two decades. Their sense of being marginal and somehow needing to be an oppositional voice was a function of having been out of power during that time. That sense of separation from Washington would continue for a long time.

For the churches, being the faith of political outsiders was not as consequential as it was for Republican leaders. Although it was initially a difficult pill to swallow when the nation abandoned the Prohibition stance that many churchpeople avidly believed in, the separation of church and state was strong enough to inhibit radical efforts that otherwise may have arisen from frustration. Religious leaders turned with some relief to the spiritual and congregational activities that were always more central to their calling. Churches struggled through the Depression, and some closed their doors forever, but the majority survived. Cooperation and tolerance increased, yet so did theological and denominational diversity. It was nevertheless a time of uncertainty for religious leaders. The question was whether to engage with the political turmoil of the period, or hunker down and ignore it.

HARVEST OF PROGRESS

If a single year could be identified when Republicans' and Methodists' influence peaked, it would be 1924. Former two-term Republican governor Arthur Capper was serving in the U.S. Senate, having won 64 percent of the vote in 1918 and achieving a 70 percent victory in the 1924 election. Senator Charles Curtis, who had won in 1914 with only 35 percent of the popular vote, was reelected on the Republican ticket for a six-year term in 1920 with 64 percent of the vote. In the 1924 gubernatorial election, Republican Benjamin Sanford Paulen ran against incumbent Democrat Jonathan McMillan Davis. Paulen received 49 percent of the vote, Davis got 28 percent, and William Allen White, who ran as a third-party candidate, received 23 percent. Seventy-five percent of the state legislators were Republicans, and Republicans held seven of the state's eight seats in the U.S. House of Representatives. In the 1924 presidential race, Calvin Coolidge and Charles Dawes swept into office over John Davis and Charles Bryan, winning in all but twelve southern states and carrying Kansas by a 62 to 24 percent victory over the Democrats. Four years later, as he campaigned to succeed Coolidge, Herbert Hoover looked back on the Republicans' accomplishments with pride. Republican policies had encouraged efficiency, promoted better schools, increased home ownership, and strengthened the "spiritual energy of our people." Republicanism, he said, had improved the life of the farmer and the farmer's wife, defended equal opportunity, and stood for religious tolerance. The sum, he concluded, was a "gigantic harvest of national progress."[2]

Methodists could view the landscape with a special sense of accomplishment as well. In 1920, the Eighteenth Amendment to the U.S. Constitution went into effect, implementing the national prohibition of liquor sales that Methodists and other religious groups had worked so long to achieve. Between 1920 and 1924, Kansas Methodists expanded their hospitals in Wichita, Hutchinson, Salina, and Kansas City, and approved plans for a large hospital and home for the aged in Topeka. Church statistics showed that the Wichita area experienced the largest growth in Methodist membership of any district in the country. Near Kansas City, the Quindaro Methodist Church drew up plans for a new building that would include a radio receiving station, motion picture apparatus, dining hall, kitchen, and basketball gymnasium complete with showers and spectators' gallery. In the nation's capital the Methodists constructed a building in 1923, the only nongovernmental structure on Capitol Hill, at a cost of $650,000 to house the denomination's national headquarters along with its Board of Temperance, Prohibition, and Public Morals. Remarkably, the Russian Soviet government under Vladimir Ilyich Lenin that same spring lauded the U.S. Methodists for their interests in worker protection and invited three of the bishops to Moscow to help reorganize Russian churches. The visit did not materialize, although one bishop traveled by himself to Russia and was subsequently defrocked. Meanwhile, Methodist officials announced major gains in China including reports of conversion among four thousand members of the Chinese army.[3]

It was a banner year for the Kansas economy in 1924. The state's farmers produced nearly 153 million bushels of wheat, a record crop double the 1923 season, and achieved an average yield per acre that would be exceeded only twice in the next two decades. Farm income overall topped the previous year by 30 percent. Seventeen percent of Kansas farms had tractors in 1924, up from fewer than 10 percent five years earlier. Automobile registrations grew to 412,000, an increase of approximately 40 percent in four years. Although most of the state's roads were still poorly maintained, paved highways grew from 1,100 miles in 1921 to more than 1,400 in 1924. More than 100 new petroleum companies were founded, 18,000 wells were in operation, and more than 28 million barrels of crude oil were produced. As towns put up streetlights and residents wired their homes, electricity generation grew from 270 million kilowatt hours in 1917 to 557 million kilowatt hours in 1924, and served more than one-third of the state's population. Nearly 80 percent of farm dwellings had telephone service, the highest proportion in the nation. Statewide, 88 percent of Kansas children were enrolled in school, for a higher proportion than in New York, Massachusetts, or any Eastern Seaboard state.[4]

Republicans deftly situated themselves as the party of Kansas' proud past, and the architects of its current and anticipated future progress. Senator Curtis personified the continuity. Born of mixed Indian and European American parentage, and raised on the Kaw reservation, he became the state's first Native American to win national office. He attended high school in Topeka, became the Shawnee County prosecuting attorney in 1885, and was elected as a Republican to the U.S. House of Representatives in 1893. He served in the U.S. Senate from 1907 to 1913, returned to the senate in 1915, became its majority leader in 1925, and was vice president under Hoover from 1929 to 1933. Continuity and progress were equally evident in the state's other long-serving Republican senator. Capper was the son of devout antislavery Quaker teetotalers who settled in Kansas before the Civil War as well as the son-in-law of Kansas pioneer, Civil War general, and former governor Samuel J. Crawford. Capper gained statewide prominence as publisher of *Capper's Farmer*, a five-cents weekly newsmagazine that eventually reached a readership of three million across the Middle West, and earned him enough money to purchase the *Topeka Daily Capital*, launch several radio stations, and establish a foundation for crippled children. He served as governor from 1915 to 1919, and as senator from 1919 to 1949.[5]

After regaining power at the end of the nineteenth century, Kansas Republicans had the good fortune of holding office when the state's economy was expanding, but they also implemented programs that facilitated nearly unbroken electoral victories for three decades. The primary election law of 1908 made it easier for new candidates to run for office, and civil service reform further curbed the worst excesses of the patronage system. Uniform accounting practices were instituted, banking laws were developed, and laws regulating public utilities were established. "Kansas has made more progress in constructive, beneficial legislation during the past four years than any state in the Union," Governor Walter Roscoe Stubbs proclaimed in 1909. Four years later, Democratic Governor George Hartshorn Hodges was less complimentary toward the Republicans' accomplishments. Calling for additional improvements, he noted that "remarkable changes in sociological and economic conditions" had taken place that required "new and progressive methods." Capper's administration from 1915 to 1919 was marked by efforts to improve government efficiency at the county and township levels, by combining or abolishing boards, and strengthening the merit system in civil service. As women's suffrage and labor unrest drew attention to human welfare issues, Capper proposed measures to assist mothers and children, regulate working hours, strengthen workers' compensation, establish rural savings and loan institutions, and improve schools. The State Board of Administration was reorganized to coordinate management of the state's educational, benevolent, and penal institutions, a state mining commission was established, and a state highway commission was created.[6]

From 1919 to 1923, Capper's emphasis on efficiency and human welfare continued under the administration of Governor Henry J. Allen. Allen had run on the Progressive ticket against Capper in 1914, winning in the Wichita area, but losing statewide by a four-to-one margin. As governor, Allen reflected the growing sentiment in rural America that efforts to staunch the unrest evident in Bolshevism and the Industrial Workers of the World movement should include expanded home and farm ownership, a just system of taxation, an industrial court, and an improved system of workers' compensation. Allen favored a progressive state income tax, exemptions from attorney's fees for injured workers, closer inspection of mines, and a constitutional amendment for women's suffrage. His administration initiated a commission to revise the general statutes of the state, reorganized and expanded the public utilities commission, and created a bureau for child research at the University of Kansas (KU).[7]

It was significant for Kansas Republicans that their party held power in Washington during much of the first third of the twentieth century as well as in Topeka. The succession of McKinley, Theodore Roosevelt, and William Taft, interrupted by Wilson, and followed by Warren Harding, Coolidge, and Hoover gave Republicans the White House in three-quarters of those years. In the legislative branch Republicans held a majority in both houses from 1895 to 1911, in one house from 1911 to 1913 as well as from 1917 to 1919, and in both houses again from 1919 to 1933. Republican majorities facilitated the rise of Curtis and Capper to prominent committees, and elevated Kansans' sense that their views were shared outside the state. In 1926, Capper was featured on the cover of *Time* magazine. Capper had successfully cosponsored the Capper-Volstead Act of 1922, which gave farmers the right to form voluntary cooperative associations and exempted them from antitrust laws. He was said to receive more mail than any other member of Congress. In 1927, both he and Curtis were considered as possible candidates for president.

CONSOLIDATION AND EXPANSION

For Kansas churches, these were years of quiet consolidation and further expansion. The Methodist Church continued to lead all other denominations with 177,000 members in 1926, an increase of 69,000 since 1906. Roman Catholics remained their closest competitor with 171,000 in 1926, an increase of 78,000 in 20 years. Disciples of Christ were a distant third with 77,000 members in 1926; Northern Baptists were next with almost 55,000 members, followed by Presbyterians with 50,000. Smaller denominations included Missouri Synod Lutherans with 25,000 members, United Brethren with 18,000, Congregationalists with 15,000, various African American Baptist churches with a total membership of 15,000, Mennonites with 11,000 members, and Episcopalians with almost 10,000.[8]

Shifts in the location of church members largely followed changes in population from rural areas and small towns to larger towns and cities. In 1900, only 22 percent of the state's population lived in towns of 2,500 or more, and fewer than 6 percent lived in cities of 25,000 or more. By 1920, those proportions grew to 35 and 13 percent, respectively, and over the next decade to 39 and 17 percent, respectively. The counties in which Methodist membership grew faster than would have been predicted based only on membership in 1906 and total population growth were generally ones with larger towns, such as the counties in which Wichita, Topeka, and Salina were located. Catholic membership also shifted. Whereas Methodist growth was largest in Wichita, Catholic increases were greatest in Kansas City, Kansas, reflecting an influx from Kansas City, Missouri, and other cities. Growth also remained strong in Marysville and Ellis, but declined in other traditional centers of

Catholic strength, such as Leavenworth, Atchison, and St. Mary's. On the whole, changes in Methodist membership mirrored county-to-county shifts in population, whereas Catholic membership became increasingly concentrated in the state's larger urban centers. Catholic increases also reflected a disproportionate representation of Catholics among recent immigrants.[9]

The growth among Methodists and Catholics confirmed some contemporary interpretations of what was happening, and belied others. It fit impressions drawn in Chicago, Saint Louis, and other large cities that urban centers were gaining new churches as well as increasing church membership. Wichita alone had twenty Methodist churches by 1926, nearly half founded in the past decade. But rural churches were faring better than observers sometimes imagined. The reason in Kansas was that relatively few churches in the 1920s were actually located in open country. They were in small towns where the original nonnative settlers had been able to secure lots and build parsonages, and the churches that survived were in towns that had successfully weathered the uncertainties of rail lines and crop failures. Approximately 50 percent more of the state's towns were large enough to be incorporated in 1920 than they were in 1900, and of the towns that were incorporated in 1900, approximately three-quarters were larger by 1920. Among incorporated towns with a Methodist church in 1900, population on average increased by nearly 50 percent between then and 1920. That growth, even in the smallest towns, helped churches survive and add members. It also helped that townspeople could more easily walk to church, and less often had morning and evening chores than farmers did, that wealthier farmers could drive, that roads were better, and that pastors could travel more frequently to make home visits.[10]

Sermons of the day focused on familiar biblical themes, and although pastors undoubtedly made reference to current events, explicit political topics were rare. The exceptions occurred during the war years when pastors spoke more often than at other times about patriotism, and on Sunday evenings when pulpits occasionally became lecture halls for discussions of moral issues that bordered on the political, such as the church's relationship to Masonic lodges, the influence of science, the scourge of drunkenness, the need to understand tuberculosis, the evils of smoking and playing poker, the rising threat of the Ku Klux Klan, and the role of Christianity in commerce. Far more common were sermons on such topics as the birth of the savior, the twenty-third psalm, treasures in Christ, Christian service, the good Samaritan, Jesus's love of children, the Crucifixion, the resurrection, and the Second Coming of Jesus. Connections with daily life were evident in the themes of other sermons, such as finding peace, practical Christianity, what God means to me, doubt, godly parents, growing old, dealing with danger and death, and our eternal home. By the mid-1920s some of the larger churches in Kansas City, Wichita, and Topeka were offering motion pictures for young people, receiving or transmitting radio broadcasts, and staging dramatic performances. In small-town churches, Sunday services included congregational singing and prayer, and educational classes for children were increasingly popular.

There was little indication of what people believed or how they approached God in their private moments, but studies in other settings suggested that faith in the existence of God was pervasive. Anthropologists Robert and Helen Lynd conducted one of the most telling studies from 1923 to 1925 in Muncie, Indiana. Like towns in Kansas, Muncie was an overwhelmingly Republican community in a predominantly Republican state. It was smaller than Topeka, larger than Hutchinson, and mostly Protestant. People varied in how often they attended church, but believed in God as the creator and sustainer of life, and looked to Jesus for salvation. The value of being a Christian and trying to do God's will were taken for granted. When asked, "What does one believe in if one is a Christian?" the Lynds wrote, residents were inclined "to think the questioner was joking, a condition reflecting the general tendency to accept 'being a Christian' as synonymous with being 'civilized' or 'an honest man' or 'a reputable citizen.'" That would likely have been the response in Kansas as well.[11]

The occasional unbeliever was likely to be treated as the proverbial village atheist—an outcast to be prayed for and invited to revival meetings. But in small communities, where neighbors valued getting along almost as much as getting to heaven, a different norm sometimes prevailed. A telling incident occurred in 1927 in southwestern Kansas, where Caroline Henderson, a freethinker who joined the United Brethren Church to find community, suddenly became the focus of attention at a revival meeting. When the traveling evangelist asked if anyone did not believe in hell, Henderson raised her hand. Infuriated, the evangelist placed a match under her hand and announced that she now knew what it would feel like to burn in hell. But that was not what surprised her. In the days and weeks that followed, the congregation accepted her as cordially as she had been received before the incident.[12]

Faith and politics intersected most frequently, just as they had in the nineteenth century, in speeches given at churches by public officials. Methodist governor Hoch, who spoke often at church meetings, was succeeded in 1909 by Methodist Stubbs, who did the same thing. "There was a time when I considered it a disgrace and was ashamed to speak the name of God in the presence of other men," Governor Stubbs confessed to an audience at the First Christian Church in Topeka, "but I have long since learned that it is an honor to recognize the Creator of the Universe." Converted at the age of seventeen, Stubbs claimed to know from personal experience that "Christ can save a man and keep him from sin." Stubbs was followed by Hodges, a Democrat from Olathe who claimed membership in the Disciples of Christ Church. Like Stubbs, Hodges was an ardent defender of Prohibition and was credited with turning his party toward a strict enforcement of the state's prohibitory laws.[13]

After Hodges came Capper, whose Quaker background disposed him to be less outspoken about his faith than several of his predecessors, but who traveled with a Methodist gospel team and lectured at churches on behalf of Prohibition. "I am not afraid of the church in politics," Capper told an audience at the Methodist Church in Atchison in 1915. "The church perhaps has no place in what we ordinarily call 'partisan politics,' but more and more are political issues becoming moral issues and we must look to the church and its leaders if they are in truth 'leaders of men' not only to fire men's souls with zeal for righteousness in the abstract, but stand adamant for specific, definite measures that tend to righteousness and faithful, earnest, patriotic service in public affairs." Two years later in New York City, Capper singled out the Methodist Church for particular praise, calling it "the American church militant." Methodists were "ever engaged," he said, "in raising the American standards of law and order and citizenship." In quieter ways Capper encouraged the kind of citizenship he associated with faith. His farm journals carried "What Would Jesus Do?" essays by his friend Charles M. Sheldon as well as syndicated Sunday school lessons and sermons by other pastors. Contemporaries said Capper's faith was evident in his fair-mindedness, charitable activities, and Quaker-bred opposition to war. *New York Times* correspondent W. G. Clugston called him "America's greatest Christian statesman."[14] Capper's successor as governor, Allen, was another gospel team participant, belonged to the Methodist Church, and served for several months as a YMCA volunteer in France at the end of World War I. During his tenure in Topeka, Allen lectured at churches and assisted in John D. Rockefeller's campaign to organize and raise money for the Interchurch World Movement. In a 1922 essay published in the *Kansas City Star* titled "Why I Go to Church," Allen asserted that "no sensible man" would want to live in a community that did not enjoy the "constructive safeguards which civilization receives from the church."[15]

Prohibition remained an issue that brought governors and church leaders together in a common cause, and yet it was less often the moral aspects of intoxication that were the point of intersection than Prohibition's practical benefits. "Prohibition has demonstrated that the most expensive revenue any state can collect is the saloon license tax," Governor Hodges said at the annual convention of the American Anti-Saloon League in 1913. Money that used to be spent on liquor, he explained, "now goes into happy homes, public schools and civic improvements." In a special bulletin issued by the national Temperance Society of the Methodist Church in 1915, Governor Capper defended Kansas Prohibition on the grounds that it "added real value to every acre of Kansas land"

and was endorsed by the state banking association. Capper further argued that Prohibition "promotes social welfare and reduces to a minimum economic waste." The state legislature, he wrote, confirmed his views by resolving "that the state of Kansas is cleaner, better, more advanced in mental culture and stronger in moral fiber and conviction; that her homes are happier and more comfortable, her children better educated than ever before in her history; that crime is less prevalent and poverty less general; and that all this is due largely to the fact that the saloon is an outlaw." Three months later, the *Kansas City Star* remarked in an editorial that competitive companies could achieve the "highest efficiency" by refusing to "bother with the man who drinks." Capper signed the "Bone Dry Law" in February 1917, prohibiting the possession of liquor within the state and restricting shipments of liquor into Kansas by out-of-state vendors.[16]

Although later critics of Prohibition would tag it regressive, its defenders in the 1920s viewed it as a forward-looking effort in which Kansas proudly led the way. This perspective united political and religious leaders even when working in their separate domains. In the political sphere, the Democrats' brief rise to power in 1913 led Republicans to institute reforms just as they had to regain ascendancy in 1899. Capper had lost to Hodges in 1912 by only thirty-five votes—a loss some blamed on Reverend Botkin spreading innuendos about advertisements in Capper's publications. In the 1914 race, Republicans felt confident of winning on the grounds that Hodges had failed to reduce taxes. Republicans also expected women, voting for the first time in a statewide election, to favor the Grand Old Party. Impressionistic exit polling, however, suggested that women in fact favored the Democratic slate, and Allen's entry on the Progressive ticket resulted in Capper winning with only a plurality of 40 percent. In the previous campaign Capper had styled himself a progressive Republican, but now the press associated him with the party's old guard. "Mr. Capper is supporting a ticket of standpatters," White wrote. "Mr. Capper is quietly tangoing up and down the keys of the party organ, making no more noise than a cat in a cream pitcher."[17]

3.1 Kansas Governor Arthur Capper signs the "Bone Dry Law" that prohibits possession of liquor within the state, February 23, 1917. Courtesy of KansasMemory .org, Kansas State Historical Society, Copy and Reuse Restrictions Apply.

It was against those criticisms, and needing to win over Progressives and Democrats as well as divided Republicans in the state legislature, that Capper set a program of reform in motion. Emphasizing his credentials as a successful businessperson, he contended that politics should be removed from the hands of professional politicians and become more businesslike. Economy and efficiency were the watchwords, and were to be advanced by a new commission under that heading. There should be fewer laws, useless boards should be eliminated, and taxes reduced. The time had come to move forward. "Our present system of public service was born in the days of the stage coach and the blunderbuss. It is utterly incapable of keeping step with the quick march of modern progress," Capper said in a major speech to the Commercial Club of Leavenworth three months into his first term. Many changes would be needed to make government "cleaner, better, more adequate" and lower the tax burden. "It is not the work of a day or even of one administration. It requires study of the most scientific nature, and statesmanship of the highest order."[18]

FORWARD-LOOKING INITIATIVES

During his two terms in office Capper's calls for efficient, business-like government and lower taxes played against the backdrop of rising prices fueled by wartime expenditures. The cost of living for food, clothing, and basic household necessities rose 96 percent nationwide between 1914 and 1919. Fortunately for Kansas farmers, wheat rose from 95¢ to $2.41 a bushel over the same period. But the cost of land and machinery increased at the same rate, state and local taxes doubled, and the national debt climbed from slightly over $1 billion to more than $25 billion. Efficiency, though, was necessitated as much by wartime scarcity as by rising prices. "We must prevent waste of every kind," Capper told a Baptist audience in 1917. In maxims reminiscent of Benjamin Franklin, he called on his listeners to "do our daily tasks a little more diligently, a little more efficiently." It was important, he said, to economize on time, labor, material, and even food, keep physically fit, be always careful, and live simply. There was no room for slackers. Meanwhile, the state's legislative agenda began focusing on human welfare items, including more generous appropriations for normal institutes and universities, improved primary and secondary schools, public hygiene, and child labor protection. While adding to the state's budget, these were measures necessary to increase Kansas citizens' individual contributions. New laws stiffened penalties for the possession of intoxicating liquor, banned the sale of cigarettes, limited work in mines to an eight-hour day, reformed the state's prisons, and provided for the creation of an office of state fire marshal.[19]

The 1918 election that brought Allen the governorship instituted further innovations. Allen secured the support of the Republican machine during the primary, including that of longtime party boss Albaugh, who agreed to head the campaign. But Albaugh's death left the campaign in the hands of Harvey Motter, a traveling salesperson from McPherson who had worked for Allen in the 1914 election. As editor and publisher of the *Wichita Beacon*, Allen supplied the same business credentials and visibility that Capper had as publisher of *Capper's Farmer*. Allen was in France with the YMCA, however, which meant that the campaign could not rely on the usual round of stump speeches at picnic grounds and county fairs. The party's success over the previous four years at instituting civil service reform also reduced its chances of winning with old-fashioned promises of patronage. Motter enlisted the help of fellow traveling salespeople, and organized the state's first campaign truly in the hands of local volunteers and paid for with local donations. It became the model that both parties employed in future elections.[20]

Church leaders implemented similarly forward-looking initiatives. In 1915, the Federal Council of Churches of Christ in America launched a movement called the National Abstainers' Union to rid the nation of liquor through the use of new "economic, scientific, and educational" means. Among its leaders were Governor Capper and Kansas senator Joseph L. Bristow. The federal council, new in 1908, was itself an initiative to promote cooperation among the major Protestant denominations. Its founding delegates included Kansas governor Hoch. In 1916, four years after universal suffrage was achieved in Kansas and three years before the Nineteenth Amendment was approved nationally, the Methodist Church adopted a resolution submitted by Kansas Supreme Court justice John Marshall and eight other signatories declaring itself in favor of granting the political franchise to women. Six months later, Topeka Methodist reverend Dr. Clarence True Wilson took up residence in the nation's capital as general secretary of the Methodist

Board of Temperance, Prohibition, and Public Morals and initiated litigation against liquor advertising. Near the end of Capper's term as governor, the WCTU added its voice to the national campaign for children's welfare and health by initiating an educational campaign about the ill effects of nicotine.[21]

New efforts in church circles were by no means limited to crusades for social and moral reform. As in government, practical initiatives occurred as well. Northern and southern branches of the Methodist Episcopal Church formed committees in 1924 to take steps toward eventual reunification. Two years later, northern Presbyterians undertook a sweeping reorganization of the denomination's national boards. The increasing availability of automobiles and better roads facilitated travel to regional as well as national conferences, which in turn forged a stronger national identity among denominations. Gospel teams toured more easily, and young people's rallies broadened their appeal. Dealers advertised better church attendance as an important benefit of automobile ownership. Church buildings added electric chandeliers and hosted touring musical groups. Larger congregations in Kansas City and Wichita began staffing offices with full-time secretaries. Long favorable toward efficiency, church leaders now advocated it more in organizing missionary endeavors, hospitals, and colleges. Clergy and lay leaders received instruction in how to canvas neighborhoods for new members with greatest efficiency. At a gathering of church workers in Kansas City, participants learned how to apply standards of efficiency to children's Sunday school programs.[22]

Efficient, well-organized Sunday schools were part of churches' larger efforts to meet the challenges of changing social conditions. These changes were most evident in Kansas City and Wichita, where an industrial labor force was emerging, and the mining communities of southeast Kansas. Although Prohibition was widely favored as an effective weapon in the arsenal against poverty and labor unrest, other measures also were seen as necessary. Churches supplemented legislative programs through voluntary charitable activities. These activities included organizations for youth, such as the Boys Welfare League, and initiatives to encourage improved public health practices. In 1921 churches in Kansas City, for example, sponsored educational programs during the city's health week, and in 1922, joined Jewish women's groups and life insurance companies in raising money to assist the Visiting Nurses Association.

Labor issues surfaced in 1919 when ten thousand miners in southeast Kansas struck for higher wages and shorter hours. With only a two-week fuel supply in much of the state, Governor Allen closed schools, took over the mines, called out the National Guard, enlisted volunteers, and set up an industrial court to enforce compulsory arbitration. Three years later when six hundred railroad workers struck at Horton, the question of strikes and arbitration was reopened. The industrial court was controversial from the start, evoking opposition in 1920 from local and national labor unions, resulting in a highly publicized debate in New York City between Governor Allen and labor leader Samuel Gompers, and playing a role in Democrat Davis's gubernatorial win in 1922. Church leaders were divided. In 1920, Pittsburg Methodist pastor George E. Satterlee stumped on behalf of Governor Allen's reelection and in favor of the industrial court, while clergy in Wichita sided with the opposition. African American leader W.E.B. DuBois counseled black clergy to press harder in both parties for antidiscrimination measures in labor proposals. In 1921, the Presbyterian general assembly heard U.S. secretary of labor James J. Davis call for greater church involvement in bridging conflicts between employers and employees. A year later the National Catholic Welfare Council was formed to study the issues, and in Kansas City Bishop Thomas F. Lillis spoke in favor of the industrial court. Closest to the conflicts in Pittsburg and Horton, congregations debated the issues, and in several instances split or reprimanded pastors for taking stands on one side or the other.[23]

The greatest embarrassment to the state's drive for efficiency and progress was the resurgence of the Ku Klux Klan. The Klan's hooded members and blatant nativism reminded Kansans of an era many hoped was gone. Yet its appeal was related to the

hyperpatriotism that emerged during the Great War. Seven pacifists, including one who would gain later notoriety, were arrested
after a meeting at the Topeka Unitarian Church, convicted, and
imprisoned. Kansas Mennonites were intimidated into purchasing
war bonds in violation of pacifist convictions. Stung by accusations
of being unpatriotic, German Lutherans, Baptists, and Methodists
shifted to English-language services. Governor Capper kept a file
on so-called slackers who were suspected of being disloyal to the
war effort. Prohibition advocates whispered that brewers were se-
cretly sending money to the kaiser. At the end of the war, nativism
continued in the form of red-baiting labor organizers and accusing Russian Kansans of being Bolshevik sympathizers. It was in
this context that the Klan began staging mass rallies, some with as
many as five thousand participants. The Ku Klux Klan also visited
churches, typically interrupting Sunday services with handfuls of
white-robed intruders who offered a brief statement on behalf of
Americanism or silently placed an envelope of cash in the preacher's hand.[24]

Analysts in later years would argue that the Klan's activities
bolstered Protestantism in its long struggle against the Catholic
Church, especially as immigration brought more Catholics to U.S.
shores, and that it contributed to Paulen's 1924 gubernatorial victory in Kansas. But the truth was more complex. Although it was
true that the Klan flourished in communities where anti-Catholic
and nativist feeling ran strong, it was also the case that church leaders and public officials denounced the organization plus sought to
limit its influence. In July 1922, amid labor unrest at railroad shops
and conflicts among merchants over Sunday closing laws, Governor Allen threatened to call out troops if a Klan rally in Arkansas
City took place as announced. "We'll have no such foolishness in
Kansas," he declared. Two days later, Allen issued a proclamation
banning gatherings and parades by anyone in masks, and set in
motion a successful effort to outlaw the Klan. The Federal Council
of Churches castigated the Klan in 1923 as an organization em-
bodying "many of the evils which the church has been decrying
for years." In 1924, William Allen White, a recent recipient of the

3.2 *Emporia Gazette* editor William Allen White runs for governor in 1924 to arouse opposition to the Ku Klux Klan. Courtesy of KansasMemory.org, Kansas State Historical Society, Copy and Reuse Restrictions Apply.

Pulitzer Prize for an essay defending freedom of speech in labor issues, turned his editorial wrath toward the Klan, calling it a menagerie of "Grand Goblins," "Titans," and "whang-doodles." White ran as an independent in the gubernatorial race to draw attention to the Klan's indignities. "The thought that Kansas should have a government beholden to this hooded gang of masked fanatics, ignorant and tyrannical in their ruthless oppression," he said, "is what calls me out of the pleasant ways of my life, into this distasteful, but necessary, task."[25]

CHURCH AND STATE

In retrospect, the first quarter of the twentieth century was the period that writers would contend had facilitated a dramatic secularization of U.S. society. It was a time, these writers would suggest, when institutions became more clearly differentiated from one another and more highly specialized, when the authority of religion weakened and participation in churches declined. It was a new era in which the public role of religion became more private. But if that was happening elsewhere, there was little evidence that it was occurring in Kansas. The separation of church and state was well in place when the state came into existence in 1861, and little about this distinction changed. Preachers seldom ran for political office, but did so occasionally, and officeholders or seekers of office spoke and held meetings at churches. Other than the few Catholic parochial schools, education was under the state's auspices, yet included Bible reading and prayer. Some writers would later remember that Buddhists and Muslims had been present at the World's Columbian Exhibition in Chicago in 1893, and argue that this was the dawn of a new post-Christian epoch. Still, when Buddhists sought to erect a shrine in a public park in 1925, church leaders and government officials uniformly declared themselves opposed. "This is a Christian land," one Methodist proclaimed. That was in New York City. Back in Kansas drought-stricken farmers sometimes prayed for rain, earning ridicule from critics who thought they were hopelessly superstitious, but these farmers also invested in shelterbelts and terraces, constructed irrigation canals, and supported scientific agricultural-experiment stations.[26]

If church and state ran in separate yet occasionally converging channels, the period nevertheless witnessed an enlargement of civil society that had important ramifications for the role of religion. Kansas had always been a state rich in civic organizations. Masonic lodges and other fraternal organizations emerged as quickly as churches did, and were supplemented with veterans' associations, book clubs, and temperance leagues. A person aspiring to public office was wise to join as many of these organizations as possible and use the networks involved to attract votes. The number and variety of these voluntary associations proliferated, though, offering citizens wider venues for networking. Between 1886 and 1925, state charters were granted to a total of 3,361 civic and agricultural associations, fairs, lodges, clubs, guilds, and benevolent organizations. During the same period, 3,550 charters were granted to churches. But only 34 percent of all religious and civic charters granted from 1920 through 1925 went to churches, whereas 54 percent did prior to 1900. Automobiles and better roads made it easier for members of these other associations to hold regional and statewide meetings at which social and political issues were discussed. By 1925, these associations included everything from butchers' and pharmaceutical associations, to societies for crippled children and disabled veterans, to organizations of women lawyers, swine breeders, artists, bottlers, book dealers, children's welfare advocates, taxpayers, sports and automobile enthusiasts, social workers, pacifists, and marching bands.[27]

The claim that religion retreated from public prominence into the private realm during this period was especially interesting. On the surface it was hard to assert that religion had become any less public, at least not at the very time when religious leaders were advocating successfully for national Prohibition. It nonetheless was the case that religion had long been most important in helping ordinary people make sense of their lives, give thanks for their blessings, meet with like-minded believers, christen their children, face illness, and mourn their dead. Women were most at risk of dying in childbirth, most involved in caring for the sick, and most exposed to financial hardship when a husband died or lost a limb. It surprised no one in 1916 when statistics showed that women were far more likely to be church members than were men. And yet the public and private realms were always connected. Women talked with other women, read newspapers, and participated in campaigns for temperance and suffrage.

The early decades of the twentieth century brought public and private interests together in new ways, especially for women. Secondary education was becoming increasingly available, and in farm communities girls typically attended high school in larger numbers than did boys. Suffrage meant not only that women voted but also that officeholders paid more attention to child labor protection, support for widows, and public hygiene. Improvements in medical practices reduced infant mortality, but these changes were new enough that the chances of having had a stillborn baby, a sibling or cousin who died from a childhood disease, or a mother or aunt who died giving birth were still high. Public health reports, such as a study in western Kansas showing that few expectant mothers received proper medical care, further sensitized women to the continuing dangers. In the 1920s, Kansans were keenly aware of the influenza epidemic that had erupted in 1918 in Fort Riley, possibly spreading there—later writers would suggest—from a farm in Haskell County, and claiming an estimated fifty million lives worldwide. Five years later, Kansans whose own families may not have been affected read that Governor Davis was gravely ill with influenza, heard varying reports that germs did or did not spread the disease, and wondered when the next outbreak would occur.[28]

Besides influenza, the risks that prompted ordinary people to mindfulness of life's brevity included tuberculosis, which still claimed more lives than influenza; paralysis, which Senator Capper's efforts on behalf of crippled children kept in the public eye; and of course accidents. In rural communities, accidents were caused by everything from threshing machines, tractors, and mechanical hay balers, to automobiles, cyclones, blizzards, and fires. After the devastating Chicago fire of 1871, residents of large and small towns alike paid greater attention to the risks of fire. Traveling salespeople added lightning rods and fire insurance to their portfolios, and actuarial services calculated the risks involved. In Kansas, fire losses covered by insurance reached nearly eight million dollars in 1924, seven times the amount in 1900. As losses mounted, the insurance companies enlisted churches, schools, and public officials to promote fire prevention techniques. Starting with war preparedness drills between 1914 and 1917, these efforts expanded from municipal and state campaigns to federal programs. In 1924, President Coolidge declared October 5 to 11 national fire prevention week. Citizens acquired safety tips to help them extinguish or avoid fires, and learned that carelessness was the greatest single cause of fire. A good wife, husband, or parent was obligated to prevent fires, and was more likely than ever to feel at fault if an accident occurred.[29]

In 1924 Elmer E. Monroe was living with his wife, Susie, and their children on a farm in Rice County, north of Lyons. Elmer had come to Kansas from Illinois with his parents in 1882 when he was six years old. His uncle, Simon Monroe, was one of the county's first settlers, arriving in 1873 as an ordained local elder and licensed Methodist preacher. It was said of Reverend Monroe that "his life was a rebuke to sin and an example of what God can do for a man." By his death in 1913, he had performed more weddings and preached more funerals than any other person in the county. It was not surprising that the rest of the Monroes were Methodists. Despite bad crops in the 1890s that sparked interest among their neighbors in the Populist Alliance, the Monroes saved enough money to send their children to college. In 1893, Elmer's older sister, Nellie Monroe, graduated from Southwestern College, a Methodist institution in Winfield. His brother, Olney, attended there in 1894, and the following fall Elmer went to Kansas Wesleyan in Salina. Nellie wrote to him in late September that year. "How do you like Salina? Do you have any Y.M.C.A. at the college? Or do you go downtown to church services? I hope you have a nice place to room under good Christian influence." She concluded the letter with some sisterly advice: "I am quite confident you will be faithful to your school work, but don't slight your Christian work or duties. Your Christian work is all that will count in the next world." Pregnant at the time and knowing the risks that women faced bearing children, Nellie may especially have had the next world on her mind. The next spring Nellie died giving birth.

Elmer came back to Lyons and became a partner in the town's furniture store. Times were good. From 1900 to 1910, the town's population grew from seventeen hundred to nearly twenty-one hundred and the county's farmland tripled in value. Streetlights were installed around the town square, and a country club and nine-hole golf course were being planned for south of town. On Christmas Day 1910 Elmer married Susie Crawford, the daughter of his business partner, and in 1915 they moved to the farm north of Lyons where Elmer had grown up. Susie was known in the community as a woman who lived a consistent Christian life. She and Elmer belonged to the Ebenezer Methodist Episcopal Church, a country congregation four miles northwest of Lyons. Susie was one of the congregation's most faithful and loyal workers, serving as a teacher and primary superintendant in the Sunday school. In 1924 she and Elmer had a son, age eleven, and two daughters, ages nine and five. On the morning of October 30, Susie was attempting to light the kitchen stove to fix breakfast when the stove exploded. While trying to put out the fire, she succumbed and died that evening at the Lyons hospital. She was thirty-nine. The capacity-crowd funeral was held at the large Christian Church in Lyons around the corner from her father's furniture store. Elmer continued farming and eventually remarried. Ironically, tragedy also claimed his life. In 1955 a field caught fire near his home, and Elmer, now retired, drove out to see if he could be of help. Smoke made it impossible to see that the fire had destroyed a wooden bridge. Elmer's pickup truck crashed into the dry creek bed. He crawled out, suffering from internal injuries, and died a few minutes later. Like the rest of his family he was a lifelong Methodist.[30]

HUNKERING DOWN

A provisional consensus about the meaning and value of being modern was clearly in place by 1928. In government, the harvest of progress that Hoover described meant the kind of programs that

Capper and Allen had instituted in Kansas. It involved the promotion of good roads, child welfare, and public safety. It necessitated periodic reforms to keep taxes low and ensure that programs were efficient. In religion, it meant informed clergy who spoke to the changing needs and interests of their congregations, and leaders who updated their churches and worked with other denominations to expand ministries among children and young people as well as start churches in suburbs and cities. In personal life, it was an expectation that material progress could be achieved through hard work and good planning. A responsible person could anticipate setbacks and yet reasonably expect that the improvements of the past would continue.

As if to signal their understanding of this consensus, the Republicans selected Kansas City as the site for their 1928 national convention. Delegates came by train to hobnob with Reed Smoot of Utah and Charles Eastman of Rochester, admire the beautiful Marion Marjorie Scranton of Pennsylvania, and respond to the call, Who but Hoover? The meetings took place in Convention Hall on the Missouri side, but Kansans basked in the nearby glory. A reporter covering the assembly figured out that 40 percent of the nation's oil along with much of its beef, corn, and wheat were being produced within a day's journey of the place. This was the nation's agricultural center, the source of its fuel and food. The region was equally noted for its manufacturing, fledgling aircraft industry, ample golf courses, and commodious public parks. The people were what Republicans aspired to be, idealistic and industrious, practical-minded good-spirited go-getters.[31]

The point was not that everyone in Kansas agreed about politics and religion, or shared equally in the state's progress, but instead that there was an underlying sentiment about what it meant to be doing well. That sentiment was especially evident in citizens' commitment to education. Communities shut down one-room country schools, embarked on consolidation programs, and paid higher taxes to support new high schools. Families like the Monroes considered it worthwhile to send their children to college. Public officials worried about the rising costs of higher education, but overcame their concerns with expectations that the state would benefit from investments in engineering, business, and agricultural science. Religious leaders approved larger budgets for church colleges, and invented new arrangements for upholding students' moral and spiritual values within public institutions. At KU in Lawrence, a student religious center, later dubbed Purity Palace, was established early in the century by a local Presbyterian pastor with the help of several faculty and Dr. James Naismith, the famed basketball coach. In 1916, when Billy Sunday visited the campus, the evangelist declared his love for Kansas and pledged to preach its glory to millions of people. Chancellor Frank Strong reciprocated. "I believe in revivals," he said, "and in Billy Sunday because he believes in the One who speaks with authority, and in this time of world crisis it is well to remember that there is only One who speaks with authority."[32]

In the decades following Sunday's visit, clergy and educators would become divided over fundamentalist claims, but at the time criticisms focused on what several of the KU faculty described only as Sunday's vulgarity and sensationalism. It was plausible to believe, as Chancellor Strong did, that faith and reason were compatible. That view was widely shared among church leaders as well, perhaps especially among Methodists, who argued that their tradition's emphasis on the centrality of an experiential relationship with God circumvented creedal disputes. At its 1928 general convention in Kansas City, the denomination's board of bishops said as much, asserting that advances in scientific knowledge were to the glory of God and should not be criticized by preachers. "If the preacher assumes to answer every adversary of Christianity, he will make the place a battlefield instead of a sheepfold," the bishops observed. Preachers were advised to avoid an "arrogant mechanistic philosophy" or a "despotic traditionalism."[33] Symptomatic of an accommodating spirit, Methodist leaders at the same Kansas City meeting proposed to move "without reservation or condition" toward an organic union with the Presbyterian Church.[34]

Acceptance of Roman Catholics was a different matter, causing some observers to imagine that Protestants' lingering misgivings were fueling their interest in interdenominational cooperation. But discussions of religious tolerance as a positive value became more explicit. Ironically, it was Alfred E. Smith's unsuccessful bid in 1928 for the presidency—the first Roman Catholic to run for the nation's highest office—that prompted these discussions. Smith's candidacy provoked anti-Catholic sentiment in many parts of the nation, expressed in pamphlets, flyers, political cartoons, newspaper columns, and speeches at Ku Klux Klan rallies. Accusations ranged from claims that Smith would destroy the public schools, to allegations that his religion was autocratic and subservient to Rome. Smith carried only eight states, losing to Hoover, who received 58 percent of the popular vote nationwide and 72 percent in Kansas, the highest proportion of any state. In Kansas there was evidence that religion mattered. The only county that Smith won was Ellis, and the only other county where he received at least 40 percent of the vote was Leavenworth—both traditional Catholic and Democratic strongholds.

Hoover's showing in Kansas was enhanced by having Senator Curtis as a running mate, but was impressive nonetheless because Hoover's agricultural proposals were unpopular with many of the state's farmers. Yet it was unclear if voters' rejection of Smith was particularly driven by anti-Catholicism, rooted simply in the state's long tradition of voting Republican, or a renunciation of Smith's opposition to Prohibition. County variations in Kansas revealed a statistically significant relationship between the percentage of voters who opted for Hoover and the percentage against repealing Prohibition. Counties with higher percentages of Catholics voting for Smith pointed to religion's role, but it was not the case that ones with larger proportions of Methodists opted for Hoover. An analysis of election results in several other states by sociologist William F. Ogburn suggested that Prohibition was probably the decisive factor. Some religious leaders shared that view, maintaining that Prohibition was a legitimate political issue, but a candidate's personal faith was not. Patrick H. Callahan, secretary of the Association of Catholics Favoring Prohibition, described the campaign as a "distinct gain in the direction of tolerance" and "an improvement in our social relations." Methodist bishop and Federal Council of Churches president Francis J. McConnell echoed Callahan, arguing that tolerance was a mark of Christian advancement and that "salvation depends on a personal devotion to an inner spiritual ideal." In Chicago, clergy associated with the city's church federation agreed that right-minded citizens should "not carry doctrinal matters into their exercise of suffrage."[35]

Hoover himself took the high road, perhaps figuring that anti-Catholicism would be present anyway, but knowing that tolerance was the more appropriate stance for the official campaign. Of Quaker stock, Hoover claimed that he knew about religious persecution from the troubles his tradition had experienced. "I stand for religious tolerance both in act and in spirit," he said in his acceptance speech on August 11, 1928. "The glory of our American ideals is the right of every man to worship God according to the dictates of his own conscience." Six weeks into the campaign, Hoover repeated his plea for religious tolerance as anti-Catholic statements surfaced among his grassroots supporters. "Religious questions have no part in this campaign," he said. Ex-governor Allen, who directed publicity for the campaign, took the same position, asserting that the Republican National Committee did not endorse any criticisms of Smith's faith. Running mate Senator Curtis also argued for religious tolerance when it was discovered that despite his lifelong affiliation with the Methodist Church, he had been baptized Catholic on the Kaw reservation. In his inaugural address on March 4, 1929, Hoover again called for "tolerance of all faiths" as a mark of good citizenship and strong government.[36]

The Wall Street crash in October 1929 was the clearest sign that all would not be well for Hoover's administration. In Kansas, economic conditions generally remained favorable through the end of the year. Wholesale and retail prices for food and household commodities stabilized after 1924. Hard winter wheat in the Kansas City market averaged $1.03 a bushel, down from $1.43 in 1925, but farmers planted more acres, harvested a record crop of nearly 178 million bushels in 1928, and produced a decent crop of 138 million bushels in 1929. In the manufacturing and commercial sectors only 198 businesses failed in 1929 out of nearly 37,000, which was one of the lowest rates in the nation. There was a continuing sense of confidence as well. With Hoover in the White House, Curtis occupying the vice presidency, and Senator Capper now accompanied in the U.S. Senate by former governor Allen as Curtis's replacement, Kansans enjoyed enough power in Washington to forestall any fears they may have had that progress was passing them by. "The Kansas farmer is no hillbilly," a reporter for the *New York Times* observed in August 1929. "He has a radio, motorcars and hired help. He farms with power machinery, has his books audited, makes a confidant of his banker and thinks about his own affairs."[37]

The economic decline that was to become the Great Depression took hold between 1930 and 1932. With 61 percent of the state's population living in rural areas, and farmers accounting for more of the labor force than manufacturing, wholesale firms, and retail employment combined, changes in agriculture were particularly important. Having planted more wheat and harvested less in 1929 than in 1928, farmers sowed almost 1 million more acres the following year. In 1931 a record yield of 19 bushels an acre, up from 13 the year before, resulted in a bumper crop of nearly 240 million bushels. With supply far exceeding demand, the price of wheat plunged from $1.08 a bushel in January 1930 to 33¢ a bushel in January 1933. That year fewer acres and poor yields resulted in a crop almost three-quarters smaller than in 1931. A wheat farmer with gross income of $1,000 in 1928 would have received $522 in 1931 and only $280 in 1933. Other aspects of the state's economy did not suffer as badly but reflected the decline. Electricity consumption fell by 12 percent between 1930 and 1933. Hourly wages decreased by 19 percent. The number of manufacturing and commercial establishments diminished by 10 percent. Automobile registrations declined by 13 percent. Disbursements for rural highway construction and maintenance dropped by 25 percent. A kind of uncertainty set in among Kansans as a result. As one observer wrote, there was "a haze of economic, political and sociological" confusion. "No one in any walk of life is quite smug about anything."[38]

In the 1932 presidential election FDR ran against Hoover and won by a landslide. Hoover secured only 40 percent of the popular vote and won only six states, all in the Northeast. Kansas turned in the lowest margin for Roosevelt of any Middle West state, and yet gave him a 54 to 44 percent victory. Ninety-one of the state's counties went for Roosevelt while only fourteen favored Hoover. Roosevelt's strongest showing was in Ellis County, winning 75 percent of the vote. Farmers were disappointed with Hoover's efforts to stabilize wheat prices, and oil company executives were angry that stronger tariff policies were not in place to protect the state's independent producers. Hoover's emphasis on voluntary assistance offered little comfort to drought victims. Even Capper and Curtis seemed unable to sway the president's mind on policies important to the state. Roosevelt was an eastern city person who Republicans argued had no understanding of rural life in the Middle West. But he was better to have on the Democratic ticket, Kansans figured, than Smith, and he at least offered hope of change. Fears that Roosevelt would end Prohibition remained, but the campaign worked to keep repeal from becoming a central issue, and the state Democratic Party vowed to oppose attempts to weaken Prohibition.

Roosevelt's victory was accompanied by that of Wichita attorney George S. McGill, who won a U.S. Senate seat for the Democrats, and Democratic success for three of the state's seven representatives in the House, including University of Chicago–trained lawyer and insurance executive Kathryn O'Loughlin of Hays, the state's first congresswoman. As if to punctuate his party's defeat, longtime Republican leader David Mulvane suffered a cerebral hemorrhage and died the day after the election. One bright spot for the Republicans was that Capper had been reelected to the senate in 1930, although with a smaller margin than in 1924. The other cause for celebration was that oil executive Landon beat incumbent Democrat Harry H. Woodring in a tight three-way race for governor.

Religion's public role in the state's 1932 campaigns was notable by its near absence. On the eve of the election, the Lawrence WCTU chapter sponsored a lecture on behalf of Hoover and Landon at which prominent Topeka pastor and author Charles Sheldon warned that Democratic victories would hasten Prohibition's repeal. But the state WCTU refrained from endorsing either of the major parties' candidates, instead opting to encourage voters to send postcards to the winning candidates expressing continuing support of the Eighteenth Amendment. Republicans and Democrats alike organized local campaign offices, enlisted support from women's groups, sponsored programs with musical entertainment, and hosted speakers who talked of farm prices and relief efforts. If churches were an important factor anywhere, it would have been in Winfield, a center of Methodist activity for more than half a century and home to Southwestern College, where a cousin of Landon was president. Landon and Woodring campaigned there repeatedly, socialist Norman Thomas lectured at the campus, and Vice President Curtis visited only days before the election. But the only campaign-related event as the election drew near was a Sunday evening discussion of the candidates sponsored by the young people of the Free Methodist Church. Sermon topics and meeting announcements at the town's other churches gave no indication that the election was to be discussed. A local Democrat saw humor in the silence. Observing that a reelect Hoover rally in another state opened with prayer, she quipped that with millions out of work, the Republicans should "know it's a time for prayer."[39]

The Republicans' setbacks may have been disappointing to Protestants, who were used to being on the winning side, but religious leaders had troubles of their own. One that directly affected Kansas arose from scandals within the Anti-Saloon League, a national organization founded in 1893 by Chicago Congregationalist pastor Howard H. Russell. Though less widely known than the WCTU, the Anti-Saloon League worked closely with local churches, supplying them with speakers to address Prohibition issues and soliciting funds from church members. Its leadership was composed of leading Methodist, Presbyterian, and Catholic clergy, business-people, and public officials, including Senator Capper. With passage of the Eighteenth Amendment in 1920, the league continued its efforts to ensure that Prohibition was enforced. In 1925, however, the league's state superintendent, Methodist pastor John G. Schaibly, accused Kansas state supreme court justice Richard J. Hopkins and two other officials, including a fellow Methodist minister, of misusing league funds to pay for campaign expenses. Controversy continued into the following spring with Schaibly's resignation and innuendos flying on all sides. Pastors whose churches had supported the league were embarrassed, but also hoped publicity about the incident would not provide ammunition for anti-Prohibition forces. Sheldon suggested that all churches in the state withhold contributions until the issue was fully investigated. Reverend Charles R. Weede, a pastor in Rice County, went further, declaring that the damage was "irreparable" and calling for the league to "quit business."[40]

FUNDAMENTALISM AND THE GREAT DEPRESSION

If the league scandal evoked restiveness, fundamentalism did so even more. The movement developed far from the Middle West, most visibly through *The Fundamentals*, a series of booklets published in California from 1910 through 1915, with funding from oil millionaire Lyman Stewart and through the leadership of theologian J. Gresham Machen from Princeton Theological Seminary in New Jersey. By 1924, when Methodist bishops agreed that controversy should have no place in their denomination, fundamentalism had spread widely among Northern Baptists and was being advanced among Presbyterians under the able leadership of Pittsburgh pastor Clarence McCartney, elected that year as moderator of the General Assembly. Free Methodists and Southern Baptists had gone on record as supporters of biblical fundamentals, and at least one faculty member at William Jewell College in Missouri near Kansas City had been fired. Fundamentalists affirmed that the Bible was literally true and that Jesus was the divine Son of God. They were especially troubled by what they regarded as radical modernist preaching in influential urban pulpits. One of the first organized efforts in Kansas to combat these modernist influences was an overture passed by the Larned Presbytery requesting that the General Assembly remove the denomination's business offices from New York City in order to curb the strength of the city's modernists.[41]

Fundamentalism gained additional visibility in 1925 as a result of the trial of high school teacher John T. Scopes in Dayton, Tennessee, which pitted Bryan for the prosecution against Clarence Darrow for the defense. For several years Bryan had been stumping the country on behalf of God and against apeism, as he put it, arguing that the Bible should be believed cover to cover, Jonah really spent three days in a whale's belly, and biologists' claims about evolution were pure fiction. In Bryan's view, a person either believed in the Bible or sided with radicals in the cities and universities who did not. In the Middle West, the trial and the controversy surrounding it elicited varied responses. Some maintained that it was possible to be a conservative Christian without opting for fundamentalism and church teachings should be hospitable to scientific investigation. Yet for many who saw Bryan as an advocate for the common person, the choice was clear. "From evolution we gain darkness," a Methodist pastor in Kansas City explained. "From the Bible we gain light."[42]

Bryan's death five days after the trial cost fundamentalism one of its most effective advocates, but did not derail its popularity. Over the next few years laws were passed in several states against teaching evolution, including one in neighboring Oklahoma; clergy and college professors, including several in Kansas, were dismissed on charges of heresy; and organizations such as the Defenders of the Faith and the World League of Christian Faith, both founded in Kansas, attracted growing numbers of adherents. One of the more ambitious of these organizations was the Flying Fundamentalists, founded by Reverend Gerald B. Winrod of Wichita to educate voters in the United States, France, England, South America, and

Australia. Likening his campaign to the struggle for Prohibition, Winrod became known for his anti-Semitism and ran unsuccessfully for the U.S. Senate in 1938.[43]

In a state where religion had been so well supported for so long, it was nearly unimaginable that anyone would rise in opposition to fundamentalism—and yet some did. One who emerged with such extreme passion that he became an easy target for fundamentalists like Bryan and Winrod was Reverend Leon Milton Birkhead. Trained at Drew Theological Seminary and Columbia University, Birkhead was a Methodist pastor in the Saint Louis area from 1912 to 1915 before accepting the pulpit of the First Unitarian Church in Wichita. Soon Birkhead became known as a gifted speaker willing to take on controversial topics ranging from the divinity of Jesus to the need to move past outmoded creeds. He championed John Dewey's views of secular education, and conducted Unitarian revival meetings in Kansas City, Denver, and Oklahoma City. In 1917 Birkhead moved to the All Souls Unitarian Church in Kansas City, and in 1925 traveled to Dayton, Tennessee, in hopes of assisting Darrow. When Winrod ran for the senate, Birkhead led the campaign against him.[44]

The most significant difficulty that church leaders faced in the 1930s was the Great Depression itself. Financial support for Methodist pastors in Kansas was 40 percent lower in 1934 than in 1930, and the total giving was down by 58 percent. The worst decline occurred in northwest Kansas, where giving dropped by 73 percent. Support and giving rose slightly with improved agricultural conditions in 1935, but fell again and remained low through 1939. Reductions of this magnitude made it impossible for the denomination to appoint new pastors. At a meeting in 1932 nine pastors hoped to be appointed, and none were. Sparse finances reduced attendance at clergy conferences, made it harder to host visiting evangelists, and curbed enrollments at denominational colleges. At Baker University, salaries were cut 25 percent in 1934 and cut again in 1935. Kansas Wesleyan in Salina filed for bankruptcy and took years to recover. St. Mary's College closed its doors and became a Jesuit seminary. Congregations reverted to earlier patterns of holding services without a regular pastor. Other congregations provided milk and eggs in lieu of cash, and offered vegetables from members' gardens, if anything grew. In the 1920s, churches had modernized by constructing new buildings or adding new class-room wings, but in the 1930s such plans were put on hold. Nation-wide, churches spent $153 million on new construction in 1925, but less than $18 million in 1933.[45]

Churches in western Kansas suffered the most. In Coldwa-ter, where some of the worst dust storms occurred, the Christian Church supplemented meager offerings with pound parties at which canned goods and farm products were given for the preacher. "One year green beans had been plentiful," a member recalled, "so the minister and his wife cheerfully ate green beans all winter even though neither one liked them." The daughter of a Holiness pastor in Logan County remembered that the little stone church where thirty people worshipped was heated by burning cow chips. Too poor to buy antifreeze, members kept radiator fluid warm on the church stove during services. In Liberal, a Methodist pastor re-ported that dust storms lasted for fifty-four days in 1934 with little interruption, emergency hospitals were established at churches, and people died of measles and dust pneumonia. The roof of one church caved in during the Sunday morning service from three tons of dust. "For weeks," he wrote, "our churches barely existed."[46]

The 1936 Census of Religious Bodies reported that the to-tal church membership in Kansas was 691,438, a drop of 7 per-cent from the number recorded in 1926, and the total number of churches had declined from 4,530 to 3,686, a decrease of 19 per-cent. These were startling results in view of the fact that censuses from 1870 through 1926 had registered steady increases in abso-lute numbers and membership as a percentage of the population. But the truth was that nobody knew for sure how much church membership was down or how many churches may have closed because of the Depression. The 1936 census was widely criticized at the time as well as by later scholars for being poorly financed and administered, and for failing to secure adequate cooperation from church officials. In Kansas, the results suggested that Baptist and

Presbyterian memberships were stable from 1926 to 1936, but that Methodists suffered a loss of more than 35,000 members and shut down 40 percent of their churches. Yet a closer inspection of the results showed that three counties did not include Methodist data at all, and eighteen others, mostly in one district, were suspiciously low given stable populations and later membership figures. If these counties were excluded, Methodist memberships in the remaining counties were down modestly compared with 1926.[47]

Other factors compounded the difficulty of assessing church statistics. Methodists kept records as well as any denomination, but congregations sometimes met without clergy and did not report members to conference officials. That was more likely in the 1930s, when finances made it impossible for some congregations to support pastors. Baptist memberships may have stabilized partly because Northern Baptists were absorbing members from German and independent Baptist congregations. Catholic memberships continued to be estimates based on baptisms and population rather than actual participation. Smaller denominations sometimes did not keep records at all. The one thing that seemed clear was that church membership was not growing.

The lack of growth was not surprising. In previous decades, increases in church membership had been the result of population gains, better roads, improved transportation, and migration from farms to towns and cities. Even in farming communities, residents moved often enough that revival meetings were necessary to attract newcomers. In the 1930s these dynamics changed. Having grown by nearly 112,000 people in the 1920s, the Kansas population declined by nearly 80,000 in the 1930s—a decrease of approximately 4 percent. Twenty-five counties declined by at least 15 percent, while several counties in which cities were located continued to grow. In addition, the oil industry resulted in population increases in Barton, Rice, Russell, and Ellis counties. Churches and church membership adapted to these changes, but the overall effect was an absence of growth.

By 1936, Republicans' dominance of Kansas politics was at the lowest ebb it had been since the state came into existence. The state's representation in Congress was almost evenly divided between the two parties. In Topeka, Republicans retained a majority in both houses of the state legislature but Democrats had a 40 percent minority. It became increasingly evident to voters as the Depression continued that Republicans' arguments for rigorous economic policies, such as cutting government bureaus and reducing taxes, needed to be supplemented with other programs. After several false starts, Roosevelt's New Deal farm policies were gaining popularity, and relief was being distributed to the jobless and needy. In October 1936, as Roosevelt crossed Kansas on a whistle-stop tour making eight speeches in two days, large numbers turned out to hear him speak. A gathering in Olathe was estimated at ten thousand, or more than twice the town's population. People came, bringing their children, just to say they had seen the famous man, but many appreciated what he was doing for them as well. Roosevelt acknowledged that his farm policies were a bit like those of automobile makers who brought out a new model each year, yet insisted that change was necessary and each model was better than the last. "He started putting his loving arms around the farm people," a farmer in central Kansas said fondly of Roosevelt years later. "He knew they were important."[48]

Roosevelt was careful about what he said in Kansas, where so many voters were Republicans. To an audience of seventeen thousand in Wichita, he praised Kansas as a "great farming state" and quipped that he had recently "dared to talk farming" to a New York City crowd. "I told them that one of the best things that had come out of these three years was the realization by city dwellers that they could not be prosperous until the farmer was also prosperous." He avoided mentioning any Republicans by name, but argued that speculators and "individualism run amuck" were the root of the nation's problems, then asserted that his policies were saving drought-stricken cattle, reducing bank robberies, eliminating unsafe banking practices, assisting rural schools, and improving farm-to-market roads. His only reference to religion was a pledge of support for Americans' "freedom to worship God in their own way."[49]

3.3 Kansas Republicans celebrated in Topeka on July 23, 1936, as Governor Alfred M. Landon was selected to be the party's candidate in the presidential election against incumbent Franklin Delano Roosevelt. Courtesy of KansasMemory.org, Kansas State Historical Society, Copy and Reuse Restrictions Apply.

Republican hopes for a better tomorrow lay principally with Alfred Landon, who despite Roosevelt's rising popularity, won the 1934 gubernatorial race in Kansas by a 52 to 47 percent margin, and was the only Republican governor in the country to achieve reelection. Landon's victory brought him national attention and secured him the Republican presidential nomination in 1936. His nomination was a proud day for Kansas Republicans, reminding them of better times and filling them with hope for renewed influence in national politics. But Landon campaigned ineffectively, carried only two states, failed even to win his home state, and later made fun of his historic loss by observing, "As Maine goes, so goes Vermont." His race nevertheless illustrated Kansas Republicans' capacity to adapt yet again, not with electoral victory as the result, but to the realities of the Depression and so as to effect the party's longer-term recovery. Landon was a sagacious, energetic liberal

Republican who had opted for Theodore Roosevelt as a progressive in 1912 and had favored William Allen White for governor in 1924. He was known as an astute businessperson, balanced the state budget, and had the added benefit of being a Methodist. As governor, he worked with Senator Capper and the state legislature to implement New Deal policies, and as a presidential candidate failed to attract more votes partly because his views did not differ substantially from FDR's on social programs.[50]

White captured the spirit of Kansas politics in 1936 when he observed that "party lines are loosely drawn," while "factional lines are tighter." That made it possible for Democrats to win from time to time, and gave Republicans the ability to bob and weave as factional interests changed. Disputes among public utility companies, over farm policies, and about government expenditures could all be accommodated. Moderately liberal Republicans like Landon and Capper could make the best of it by mediating among the contending interests. "Kansas political leaders ride in good cars," White observed, "live in decent houses with wide, bluegrass lawns under elm trees, with flower-bordered gardens; belong to the country club, play a fair hand of bridge, a little poker, take a little drink at odd times and vote for prohibition."[51]

There was little in Landon's failed campaign, Roosevelt's administration, or the tenure of Democrat Walter August Huxman, who succeeded Landon as governor, to bring religion as directly into Kansas politics as it often had been in the past. That was in itself notable. The one aspect of religion that continued to be of some importance was the gap separating Catholics and Protestants. Nationally, an estimated 78 percent of Catholics were for Roosevelt compared with 46 percent of Baptists, 43 percent of Methodists, and only 37 percent of Presbyterians and Episcopalians.[52] An early Gallup poll showed that respondents who said they would not vote for a qualified Catholic were less likely to have voted for Roosevelt than respondents whose views were more favorable toward Catholics, taking account of other differences such as age, gender, and occupation. But Kansans mostly voted their pocketbooks, empty as they were, in hopes that Roosevelt's policies would bring relief. The ones who voted for Republicans in the state legislature figured that the majority party was in a better position to get the job done. Toward the end of his life, Landon was asked how he would describe himself politically. "Practical progressive," he said. That was an apt description of Kansas politics in the 1930s as well. Voters were perplexed but hopeful, a reporter observed, and willing to try anything at least once. They cautiously followed Roosevelt's lead because there was no other, and yet they figured relief would come as much from rain as from Washington, and in the meantime, the only way to survive was to work hard and spend as little as possible.[53]

In their own ways, the Landon and Huxman administrations demonstrated that politics and faith were separate, and could remain that way even in the most challenging times. Although he was a Methodist and the grandson of a preacher, Landon attended worship services irregularly, and did not talk about his faith as openly or speak at churches the way that Capper and Allen did. Huxman was the son of a lay Swedenborgian preacher-farmer and a member of the Disciples of Christ Church, but his campaign benefited less from church connections than from his leadership as a tax attorney in Hutchinson and a member of the Kansas State Tax Commission. Both governors emphasized efficiency and accountability in state administration. A legislative council was established in 1933 to investigate problems of general welfare, and a research unit of the council was added a year later. Other initiatives included a soil conservation commission, a social welfare board, and the Homestead Rehabilitation Corporation. New Deal programs instituted in Kansas included emergency relief efforts that were administered through hospitals, schools, and separate boards, but seldom through churches. The Works Progress Administration supplied jobs and built infrastructure. Strapped as they were financially, churches provided some voluntary assistance to their members, but had few resources to expend on moral and political issues. To be sure, there were occasional contretemps about dancing and decency in motion pictures, yet those largely failed to gain traction.[54]

Journalists would speculate later that people surely had turned to God during the Depression and hard times led to surging interest in the churches. But the Lynds, returning to Muncie, Indiana, in the 1930s, found no evidence that the Depression was bringing people closer to God or sparking an increase in church participation. There was no proof of that happening in Kansas, either. Asked if religious interest in their communities had increased or decreased during the 1930s, 32 percent of Kansans polled in 1941 said it had decreased, while only 13 percent said it had increased. Families dealt with the gnawing misery of dust storms and meager incomes as they did other challenges, facing them with gritty determination. The responses were as varied as the people themselves. John Steinbeck captured some of the variation in *The Grapes of Wrath* as he described the Joad family's inherited affinity with the Holiness tradition, the simple kindness of unholy people, and the Christlike figure of Jim Casey. Sinclair Lewis's *Elmer Gantry*, based on observations of preachers in Kansas City in the 1920s, expressed aspects of fraud and ambition that remained in the 1930s. Decades later, writer Timothy Egan toured western Kansas, eastern Colorado, and the Oklahoma panhandle, trying to reconstruct how people may have responded to the dust storms of the 1930s. From scattered conversations he imagined some of the people believing God was punishing them for killing rabbits on Sunday, others thinking Armageddon had come for sure, and still others praying desperately for God's mercy knee-deep in dust. It made for interesting reading but was mostly conjecture.[55]

Better evidence came from oral histories, like the ones that historian Pamela Riney-Kehrberg collected in southwest Kansas, and from residents' memoirs and pastors' reports. Riney-Kehrberg found that church attendance declined during the Depression as people struggled to pay for gasoline and were embarrassed to appear in worn-out clothes. Contributions faltered to the point that several churches fell into bankruptcy. Nevertheless, churchgoing provided hope and comfort, as did family ties, motion pictures, and gatherings with neighbors. People had faith that rain would come again, not because they expected God to respond on cue, but because it had always rained in the past.[56]

Other accounts exhibited the range of beliefs and practices. A Baptist in Rice County recalled the security of daily prayers along with her father reading "a portion of God's Word as we all sat quietly and reverently." A Presbyterian in Hutchinson said he thought a lot about whether there really was a God, and concluded that there had to have been a creator, the best explanation of people's relation to the creator was the Bible, and faith had to take over from there. In contrast, a man who grew up near Mankato remembered his father reading *Capper's Farmer* in the evenings and the family going to church occasionally on Sundays, but school and lodge activities were more important than religion. A western Kansas farmer said people "lived very much as they had before the Dust Bowl," but with schools and churches sometimes closed, and neighbors pulling together to help one another a bit more than usual. A farmer in Meade County whose crops failed repeatedly worked himself to exhaustion trying to stall the raging erosion. "I have never made it a practice to labor on the Sabbath," he wrote, "but I was now in no position to choose my working days. I kept going all day Sunday." "God only knows" what the average family "has faced in these terrible days and long nights," a Methodist pastor in western Kansas mused. People attended his church when they could, but that was not always possible. "No one attempted to travel any distance except in case of necessity," he recalled. "When they could go it was as between two very close mountains only one could not see the top." Weather was not the only obstacle. There was also the desire to hunker down in the face of gnawing insecurity. "The surface of the earth seemed down hill all the time," he said. A person felt like "he was just about to slip off of something head first."[57]

SIMIAN PEASANTS

Apart from the Depression and the Republicans' weakening influence, a further dynamic took root during the 1930s. At the time it was hardly important, and yet it became part of the context in which the state's conservative religious and political movements were to be understood a half century later. This was the view that

Kansas abandoned its forward-looking vision sometime during the dust bowl, and turned to an old-fashioned traditionalism that included the narrow-minded religious bigotry of Winrod and the Flying Fundamentalists. How that could have happened was hard to understand when events of the 1930s were considered carefully. It was difficult to reconcile with the fact that Methodism was the dominant religious influence in the state, and Methodism generally avoided or restrained radical fringe ideas. It ran counter to the evidence that church participation did not increase during the Depression, and political and economic interests were less influenced by religion than they had been in the past. It was contradicted by the fact that a majority of Kansans voted for Roosevelt in 1932 and again in 1936, rejecting their own native son in doing so, and that Landon and Capper were among the New Deal's liberal Republican allies. Yet it was a view promulgated enough by critics at the time that it became part of the state's subsequent image as a bastion of radical conservatism.[58]

There had always been critics of Kansas who viewed it in one way or another as a backward, undesirable, pitiable place. Their criticisms could be used whenever the occasion arose to make the point that Kansas was anything but modern or progressive. Early writers placed Kansas smack in the middle of the Great American Desert. Later ones wrote that it was overrun with jackrabbits and tumbleweeds. Some of the negative imagery was self-inflicted. In the 1890s Kansas secretary of agriculture F. D. Coburn kept a file of apocryphal stories about winds strong enough to blow whiskers off a man's face, crops so heavy that fields caved in, and tornadoes powerful enough to skin a goat. In the Populist era, Kansas came in for criticism not only for bad weather but also for breeding malcontents like Peffer and Simpson. "Kansas with her universal and never-cured bellyache," the *Los Angeles Times* editorialized, "where is there anything else like her on the face of this green earth?" White's 1896 "What's the Matter with Kansas?" essay, written in a fit of pique against populism, was brought out again and again as evidence that the state's own citizens despised it. Even at the apex of Republican influence and economic improvement,

Kansans occasionally found themselves on the defensive. At a hotel in Southern California in 1923, the editor of a small-town Kansas newspaper was forced to respond yet again to White's famous question. "Nothing," he bellowed. "Kansas is the political experiment station of America. Try it on in Kansas and if it doesn't work there it won't work anywhere."[59]

The political experiment most at issue in the 1920s was of course Prohibition. As long as Prohibition was defined as a moral issue, its ultimate justification lay in commonsense biblical interpretations of temperate living. But it had always been defended on utilitarian grounds as well. The Eighteenth Amendment put Kansas in the national spotlight as the place where Prohibition had been tried and tested. If banning liquor was of practical social benefit, Kansas had decades of experience to prove it, and if there were flaws, they should be abundantly evident.

In 1925, correspondent Elmer T. Peterson conducted an extensive investigation of how Prohibition was faring in Kansas and reported his observations in *McClure's Magazine*. Peterson avoided easily refuted claims that Prohibition was responsible for population growth and economic prosperity. His report acknowledged that the Eighteenth Amendment was not popular with everyone, and liquor could be smuggled into the state or manufactured in homemade stills. It was important, Peterson argued, to understand that the state was handling Prohibition in a practical, fair-minded way, contrary to misinformation being circulated in eastern cities. "Newspapers, motion pictures, vaudeville sketches and other means of propaganda carried a furious wave of prohibition jokes," Peterson wrote. "A flashy wave in the 'smart Aleck' sets has deceived some observers and leads them into the curious and obvious error of supposing that the total consumption of liquor is greater than ever before." That claim was untrue in Kansas, Peterson concluded. It was also wrong, he contended, to regard Kansas proponents of Prohibition as throwbacks. Of Allen, he said, "Nobody who knows this fighting ex-governor who blazed a new trail by his establishment of a state industrial court can believe that he is bound down by outgrown tradition."[60]

But other writers were less charitable in interpreting what was happening in Kansas. Pundit H. L. Mencken became one of the state's harshest critics. In a 1927 essay Mencken argued that Prohibition was failing miserably, not merely from lax supervision, but also from corruption and overzealous enforcement. This was a view shared by many in Kansas on both sides of the liquor issue. Mencken pressed the point, though, by imagining Kansas and Mississippi as the places where the worst problems were occurring. It was "by the votes of the simian peasants of such backwaters," he argued, "that the rest of us are afflicted with the farce of law enforcement." It would properly serve the farmers and "half-witted Negroes" who lived in these places, Mencken averred, to send thousands of evangelical clergy and people in holy orders to shut down their illicit stills.[61] Others castigated Kansas in less acerbic tones. Countering earlier claims that Prohibition promoted progress, the argument was now advanced that Prohibition inhibited it. That was all the more plausible as the Depression set in. "The facts show that the state has failed to progress," a critic of Prohibition asserted in 1931, "crime has become more prevalent," "penal institutions have been filled to capacity," population and incomes were sagging, and there was a shocking increase in insanity.[62]

Roosevelt's election in 1932 greatly increased the chances that Prohibition would be repealed, and public sentiment seemed to be moving rapidly in that direction. Kansas was now an interesting case to illustrate what had gone wrong. Even there, critics charged, it had been impossible to stop people from drinking. Kansans were not only wetter than they claimed to be but there was also something unmistakably distasteful in their holier-than-thou attitude. Perhaps something deeper was at stake in Kansas moralism than just hypocrisy about liquor. Another of White's essays provided a starting point. White had argued that Kansas, settled as it was by ardent Congregationalists from New England, was the last bastion of American Puritanism. Through its struggles to become a free state it had taken a strong either-or orientation toward human existence, White maintained, and had mapped that perspective onto the good-or-evil battle for Prohibition.

If that view was correct, critics suggested, Kansas was now desperately clinging to an old-fashioned Puritanism, even as the rest of the nation became more sophisticated and enlightened. Mildred Adams, who visited Kansas shortly after Roosevelt's victory in 1932 and concluded that Kansans were fighting a rearguard cultural battle that included strong nativist orientations, ably advanced this contention. For several decades, she wrote, the Methodists and Presbyterians of Kansas had gradually been displaced by new settlers from Europe who did not agree with them, and who menaced their comfortable theory that Kansas was homogeneous. The issue was larger than Prohibition. Kansans' way of life was unraveling, and that was making the state's inhabitants confused and resistant to the inevitable march of history. Modernity was happening mostly in bustling urban centers, leaving a befuddled rural population behind.[63]

Evenhanded descriptions of Prohibition described the competing sides as dry and wet, and typically observed that there were thoughtful citizens in all parts of the country who favored one view or the other. As polling began, evidence to that effect showed that even in Kansas, views were divided. A Literary Digest poll in 1930 revealed that 58 percent of Kansans favored the enforcement of Prohibition, 23 percent wanted modification, and 19 percent preferred repeal. In 1932, the poll asked only about continuance or repeal, and found that Kansas was almost evenly split with continuance favored over repeal by less than .5 percent. Nevertheless, Kansas was one of only two states (the other being North Carolina) in which continuation was favored even by a slight majority and thus was labeled in the press as Prohibition's last defender.[64] Kansas was not only dry but also symbolized a wider struggle between the rural and urban United States. Adams suggested that the new European settlers were as threatening to native Kansans as "the cosmopolitan populations of our great cities." Mencken wrote that it was the "civilized city man" who suffered because of "yokels" and "peasants" in Kansas and Mississippi. Kansas was no longer the national nucleus that John J. Ingalls imagined it to be; it was instead part of the reactionary countryside fearful of the truly civilized Americans who lived in cities.

The worst public relations setback that Kansas experienced during the initial years of the Great Depression was the repeal of Prohibition in 1933. It was unclear if Kansans believed that what had worked in their state was necessarily good for the entire country. But the state had been identified for so long as Prohibition's leading proponent that any other position would have seemed contradictory. "We are in the midst of a confusing reaction," Allen confessed. Nobody knew quite what to think. An older generation that had fought for Prohibition felt betrayed, and a younger generation felt that not enough was being done to move forward. What perhaps saved the churches some embarrassment was that the national discussion since 1920 had turned increasingly toward the practical costs and benefits of Prohibition, and away from claims about its morality. Prohibition proponents argued that it was good for business, while detractors said it generated crime and lost the government potential tax revenue. When Prohibition was repealed, church leaders could take some solace in the view that morality had not been repudiated but rather that economic considerations had finally prevailed. There was further comfort among those church leaders who favored it in the fact that Kansas itself voted in 1934 to keep Prohibition in force. That vote nonetheless reinforced the sense that Kansas was out of step with the rest of the nation. "When Kansas voters reaffirmed their state's fifty-four-year-old prohibition policy," observed historian Robert Smith Bader, "they became even more vulnerable to national charges of being 'backward,' 'unprogressive,' 'unsophisticated,' even 'antediluvian.'"[65]

As if it weren't enough to be on the wrong side of Prohibition, Kansas was an easy target for critics who regarded it as a cultural wasteland because of its economic troubles. Social scientists contended that Kansas farmers lacked ambition and had no understanding of modern bookkeeping. *The Plow That Broke the Plains*, a documentary film depicting barren fields against a sound track of popular religious music, proclaimed that farmers themselves were to blame for their problems. Journalists speculated that Kansas farmers were becoming restless fanatics who would resort to Wild West antics like they had in the 1890s. Motion pictures such as *The Worst Woman in Paris?* and *The Washington Masquerade* portrayed Kansas as a rustic place of naive simplicity against the glamour and excitement of urban life. Writers described Kansas as a faraway place of dirt and misery, where people rolled up the sidewalks at night and spent their weekends in church. "Kansas," essayist Meridel LeSueur observed in *Scribner's Magazine*, "I have seen your beauty and your terror and your evil." The state was filled, she wrote, with revivalists, dreary villages, shambling houses, and ravished prairies.[66]

In 1936, Kansas again found itself in the national spotlight as a result of Landon's bid for the presidency. Landon and Roosevelt refrained from caustic personal attacks, but the two men conveyed vastly different public personas, which were reinforced by their campaigns and the press. Roosevelt was the epitome of cosmopolitan sophistication: born and bred among wealthy old New York families with ties to former presidents and business leaders, educated at Groton and Harvard, connected to Wall Street, a frequent visitor to Europe, and conversant in French and German. He was a gifted public speaker who carefully tailored his messages to the interests of each audience, spoke with an authoritative cadence, and exuded an air of confidence. Landon was a plain man who prided himself on that fact. He was the son of a family with no political connections, a KU graduate, a person from a rural state who worked in the oil industry, and was known mostly for having balanced the state's budget. Landon's potential as the Republican standard-bearer was his ability to show the common people that he was one of them. But he was no match to Roosevelt for anyone preferring vibrant leadership and sophistication.

Landon's candidacy reinforced the notion that Kansas was a cultural hinterland. At the Michigan Democratic state convention in May 1936, Postmaster General James Aloysius Farley, the national chair of the Roosevelt campaign, belittled Landon as a political nonentity from a "typical prairie state." Republicans responded angrily, calling the statement a slur, and arguing that it illustrated the view of people with "Little Lord Fauntleroy training" who never attended public schools and regarded everyone west of the Hudson as "rubes." Farley denied having meant any disrespect to the prairie state, but others intensified the onslaught against Landon. In radio addresses, labor leader John L. Lewis described Landon as a "quavering, quaggy dummy." Landon was a person of small accomplishments, Lewis chided, who "halts and stumbles over the most simple phrases of our common tongue" in uttering his bewildering "nocturnal babblements."[67]

In Washington a whispering campaign attacked Landon's record as a liberal Republican, alleging that he was in the pocket of the state's old guard. Whether Landon was liberal or not, the picture that emerged was not in contrast with other Republicans but rather with Roosevelt, and in that comparison even fair-minded observers pegged Landon as the more conservative of the two. Landon embraced an "old-fashioned political philosophy" of economy, thrift, honest dealings, and work, wrote correspondent Franklyn Waltman of the *Washington Post* after visiting the Republican candidate in Topeka and claiming to have developed a sympathetic bond with him. It made sense to Waltman that a person from the Sunflower State would see the world this way. These were simply "the rugged virtues of the pioneer and the covered wagon days."[68]

Despite Landon's and Roosevelt's reluctance to talk about it, religion became part of the attacks fielded on both sides in the 1936 contest. A whispering campaign also emerged in New York City, accusing Landon of being anti-Semitic and suggesting that he would not appoint Jews to his administration if elected. The Landon camp responded quickly by pointing out that a year earlier, Landon had been one of five governors to express concern about the plight of Jews in Germany and had long been an ardent foe of the Ku Klux Klan. As the innuendos continued to fly, prominent Jewish leaders and rabbis in New York, Boston, Pittsburgh, and Kansas City endorsed Landon, and asserted that there was no evidence to indicate that he was anti-Semitic. In a Labor Day speech in Wichita Landon denounced religious intolerance, and a few weeks later issued a public statement in Topeka in which he declared, "I have no use for any elements who are endeavoring to bring racial prejudices and religious bigotries into American life, and state frankly that I disclaim the support of any such organizations or groups."[69]

Religious leaders nevertheless expressed their views freely and openly. In Wichita, Winrod's preaching seemed increasingly similar to Nazi propaganda. In Michigan, Father Charles E. Coughlin gained national attention by calling for third-party opposition to Landon and Roosevelt alike. In Kansas City, Reverend C. E. Chapman, presiding elder of the Kansas district African Methodist Episcopal Church, dubbed the New Deal a failure, and called for a return to "ordinary horse and buggy common sense." Landon, he said, would be like Moses leading the nation out of its wilderness of economic and political chaos. A statement by Yale Divinity School dean emeritus Charles R. Brown to the Connecticut Conference of Congregational and Christian Churches played especially well in Kansas newspapers. "With a playboy in the White House, a mere opportunist who caters to popular feeling and whose chief desire is to make himself agreeable, who openly disregards his promises, who acts as the wind blows and who does not know what to do," Brown said, "thoughtful people of the North, South, East and West are considering the importance of having a more desirable type to control the economic order."[70]

The question was whether Kansans in 1936 were swayed enough by campaign rhetoric to behave as cultural reactionaries or whether they were guided by other considerations. Operatives in both parties figured economic considerations would prevail. As one quipped, farmers would find two letters in their mailbox: one from Republicans about an obscure constitutional issue, and the other from the Democratic administration with a check enclosed. Which would be more persuasive?[71] But it was not so much government checks as it was improved farm prices that mattered in Kansas. Taking account of voting patterns in 1932, the best predictor of county variations in 1936 voting was wheat. Indeed, wheat was a better predictor than even how counties had voted in 1932. Counties in which a higher percentage of farmland was in wheat were the most likely to vote for Roosevelt, and counties with the lowest percentages were the least likely. The reason was not hard to find. When Kansas farmers went to the polls in November 1932, wheat was at a record low of 32¢ a bushel. In November 1936, when they returned to the polls, wheat was selling for $1.14 a bushel. The region that benefited most extended across the southern half of the state from around Wichita on the east to Garden City on the west. In seventeen of these counties, where at least 30 percent of farm-land was in wheat, the vote for FDR increased from 55 percent in 1932 to 60 percent in 1936. That was a higher proportion than in Roosevelt's home state of New York, or New Jersey, Pennsylvania, or any state in New England.

Other than wheat and how they had voted in 1932, the only factor that mattered much in the 1936 election was having a native son on the ticket, not religion and not Prohibition. At a meeting in Topeka in October 1935 prior to Landon receiving the nomination, the Kansas Republican leadership discussed a strategy that would hopefully appeal to wheat growers but win additional support by including a strong statement about Prohibition. It was unclear what that statement could be because repeal had changed the debate con-siderably and eastern Republicans were opposed to any position that sounded too dry. The hope was that the Kansas delegation might be asked to draft the statement, as it had in 1932, and could write something sufficiently ambiguous to appeal to both sides. "While they realize that no plank can be expected which will advo-cate the restoration of the Eighteenth amendment," an observer at the meeting wrote, "they feel that there is a way to the hearts of the Kansas Prohibitionists. This way is by making the Republican de-nunciation of the Democratic administration of the present liquor laws just as hot as possible."[72]

But when Landon became the nominee, the need to win votes on the basis of Prohibition all but disappeared. Democrats who favored Prohibition, such as *Lyons Daily News* editor Paul Jones, shifted their allegiance to Landon anyway, and the state's Method-ists refocused their efforts toward opposing a measure in the Kan-sas legislature legalizing the sale of beer with 3.2 percent alcohol content rather than one limited to .5 percent. County variations in 1936 voting showed a small statistical relationship between voting to retain Prohibition in 1934 and voting against Roosevelt in 1936, but this relationship disappeared when voting patterns in the 1934 gubernatorial race were taken into account. County variations also evidenced no effect in 1936 voting attributable to the proportion of counties' population that was Catholic.[73]

NOVEL MOVEMENTS

If it was untrue that Kansas was quite as reactionary as some of the debate about Prohibition and Landon made it out to be, the Depression nevertheless opened the door for smaller political and religious movements to emerge, just as had been the case in the 1890s. None of these movements gained sizable followings, and only a few easily fit preconceived notions of what Kansas reactionaries might be like. Their existence demonstrated merely that the established parties did not speak for everyone. It was little known even at the time, but Landon was not the only Kansan in the 1936 presidential race. The other native son was Earl W. Browder.

Browder was a native of Wichita and was one of the seven pacifists arrested in Topeka after a meeting there at the Unitarian Church during World War I. A month later, he was arrested again for refusing to register for the draft and served a year in jail. On his release he moved to Independence, Missouri, where he formed a socialist community, and then to Kansas City, where he edited a labor newspaper. In 1922, Browder was arrested by federal agents during a raid on the convention of the Trades Union Educational League in Chicago and charged with having escaped from Michigan during a raid on a Communist Party meeting. Browder became the Communist Party's presidential nominee in 1936 and selected James W. Ford of Harlem as his running mate. At the nominating convention attended by a crowd of twenty-five thousand in New York City, Browder assailed both major parties as part of the "growing forces of fascism and reaction." He was hailed as the new John Brown of Osawatomie.[74]

President Roosevelt freed Browder from jail in 1942, after he had served fourteen months of a four-year term for passport fraud, and in 1952 *Time* described him as the number one Communist in the United States. In 1936, Browder received a mere .5 percent of the vote only in New York and California, and .25 percent only in Washington and Vermont. He was not on the ballot in Kansas. The results were only slightly better for Norman Thomas, who received 2,770 votes as the Socialist Party candidate, and William Lemke, who earned 497 votes as a write-in candidate for the Union Party.[75] The poor showing of minority parties in Kansas contrasted sharply with results in other states, including Minnesota, Massachusetts, and Rhode Island, where in each case Lemke received 6 percent of the vote, and North Dakota, where he garnered 13 percent. It differed from earlier contests in Kansas, when Populists, Prohibitionists, and progressives all ran successful campaigns. Landon's place on the ticket undoubtedly kept restive Republicans in the fold, but it also helped that party lines were as loosely drawn as White said they were and yet exercised enough discipline to deter renegades.

The possibility for novel movements to circumvent party discipline was most evident in the use of new communication technology. Ever since territorial days, newspapers had been the best way of publicizing ideas and earning candidates visibility. From John A. Martin in Atchison to William Allen White in Emporia, and from Peffer's *Kansas Farmer* to Capper's role in the *Topeka Daily Capital* and *Capper's Farmer*, and Allen's *Wichita Beacon*, newspaper publishing had been an effective means of gaining political stature. Radio was the new mechanism for acquiring influence. It was not entirely independent, as Capper's involvement in radio illustrated, but it increasingly provided an additional outlet for unconventional as well as conventional ideas.

The first radio station in Kansas was KFH, licensed in Wichita in 1922, the same year that the station WDAF was launched in Kansas City by the *Kansas City Star*, and two years after the nation's first broadcast station commenced operation in Pittsburgh. Radio's capacity to reach large audiences was evident in 1924, when the first broadcast from a station at KU was heard in twenty-two states. By the 1930s, Kansans were listening to music from Carnegie Hall and lectures by Senator Capper from the nation's capital on the Columbia Broadcasting System. In 1932, the state's first third-party candidate to run largely on the basis of popularity gained through radio was Dr. John R. Brinkley, who received almost 245,000 of the 800,000 votes cast that year in the governor's race. Brinkley established a questionable medical practice in Milford, Kansas, in 1918 that involved implanting testicular goat glands in male patients to restore sexual virility. He set up a radio station in 1923 that broadcast live musical performances, and featured himself as a medical lecturer and adviser. After losing his license in 1930, Brinkley carried on his broadcasting and advertised himself for governor by establishing a radio station in Mexico across the border from Del Rio, Texas. He was said to have earned $12 million by 1938.[76]

Brinkley's location outside the United States was effective until 1939, when the Mexican government took control of the station, in giving leaders espousing unorthodox ideas a platform. The Kansan who used the facility regularly was Gerald Winrod in his unsuccessful bid for a senate nomination in the 1938 primary and as a promoter of pro-Nazi propaganda about Jewish Communist conspiracies. Winrod's views represented the extreme anti-Semitic reactionary stance that writers feared was bound to flourish in the nation's hinterland. Elsewhere, radio was the springboard for other leaders to advocate views critical of the major parties' positions. Father Coughlin, broadcasting from Royal Oak, Michigan, was said to have reached a weekly national audience of forty million in 1936 as he opposed Roosevelt and Landon, supported Lemke's third party, espoused nativism, and railed against Jews and Communists. "May he take his radio cohorts with him," an editorial in *Barron's* declared, "for they are out of place when they try to interfere with the affairs of the older parties."[77]

Defection from the established religious denominations was relatively uncommon, just as it was in politics from the major parties. Yet there was enough movement of this kind that it could be looked on as a harbinger of things to come. While membership among Methodists, Catholics, Baptists, Presbyterians, and Lutherans was at best static between 1926 and 1936, the numbers affiliated with several smaller denominations shot up dramatically. There were thirty Assemblies of God churches in 1926 with approximately seventeen hundred members, and by 1936 the number of churches had risen to seventy-six and the membership exceeded four thousand. The Nazarene Church increased its congregations from sixty-two to eighty-six over the same period, and its membership rose from fewer than twenty-five hundred to more than fifty-four hundred. In the Church of God Andersonville branch the number of congregations was constant, but the membership climbed from fewer than fourteen hundred to almost twenty-one hundred. None of these denominations was large, yet their growth was significant. While several denominations were even smaller, they also registered notable increases in membership. The Churches of God and Saints of Christ claimed nearly five hundred members. Membership in the largely African American Churches of God in Christ grew to more than twelve hundred. Pentecostal Assemblies, Pentecostal Holiness, and Pilgrim Holiness numbers also increased.[78]

None of these denominations was particularly active in politics. They differed from one another and mainstream denominations in specific theological interpretations, prophetic views about past and future events, and styles of worship. They would have fit neatly into the category that theologian H. Richard Niebuhr termed "churches of the disinherited" in his 1929 treatise, the *Social Sources of Denominationalism*, although Niebuhr did not mention any of them by name. They grew during the Depression in Wichita and Kansas City as well as in out-of-the-way railroad and farming towns as laborers were displaced by the hard times that swept over the nation. In coming years writers would argue about whether these groups were reactionaries driven by a fear of modern ways or whether they were merely finding an alternative path to the divine.[79]

It would be the 1950s before seeds sown during the Depression sprouted into movements against liberalizing trends in religion and politics. Even then, the state's centrist conservatism would be strong enough to rein in most of the potential followers of these movements. In the meantime, daily life inched forward against the ever-looming prospect of war. Methodists met in Kansas City in 1939 and effected the north-south merger they had worked toward for more than a decade. While continuing his Unitarian pastorate, Reverend Birkhead served as the national director of the Friends of Democracy, an antipropaganda organization, and became one of the strongest opponents of Coughlin. Winrod's political aspirations were thwarted again, this time by Kansas Republican leader John Hamilton, serving as chair of the Republican National Committee.

The 1940 primaries fielded a large number of Republican and Democratic hopefuls for local office, and although the turnout was light, Kansans showed up in record numbers in the general election to give Wendell Willkie a decisive victory. They regarded Willkie as an adopted native son for having taught school briefly in Coffeyville and voted for him to prevent Roosevelt from having a third term. There was fear that Roosevelt was leading the nation toward war, and Kansas Republicans as well as Methodists at their general conference in 1940 went on record in favor of peace. When war came at the end of 1941, isolationist sentiments all but disappeared. Methodists joined Catholics, Jews, and other Protestants in vigorously supporting the war effort. Mennonites who conscientiously objected were sent to a camp near Colorado Springs to serve as noncombatants. Kansas consistently turned in high rates of contributions to the Red Cross.[80]

Near Hutchinson, a young woman set out to join her husband in Florida, where he was stationed with the U.S. Navy. Her brother was somewhere in Europe with the U.S. Army. She received censored V mail from him now and then. She would learn eventually that he was in battles in North Africa and Sicily, and was among the first to land on Omaha Beach during the Normandy invasion.

Her brother would be severely wounded during the Battle of the Bulge and spend more than a year in military hospitals after the war. But that was all in the future. As she headed through Wichita and across southwestern Missouri into Arkansas, she worried about the old car she was driving, and the recapped tires that had not been replaced during the Depression and could not be replaced now because of the war. She used the spare tire somewhere in Tennessee. She noted the segregated restaurants, the Negroes toiling in cotton fields, the unemployed, the hoboes, and the hitchhikers. Her diary at the start reflected the continuing realities of the Depression. In the coming months it captured the changes wrought by the war.

Away from home she recorded news from her sister, sisters-in-law, and women friends back in Kansas. They all had brothers, husbands, and friends in the service. She referred to them by their initials. V is in Texas. He has to take a physical. If he passes, he will be shipped overseas. L is being sent out soon to fly a light plane. N writes that E was home after being in the hospital and her spirits are better. Later, N writes that E is somewhere in the Pacific. Tojo threw everything he had at us, E reported. I got my leg hurt, had an operation on my arm, he said. A few months later her diary recorded E's death. She wrote: E had elephantitis caused by an insect, his limbs swelled two or three times their natural size, and then he died. He was on Guadalcanal, a ranger.

She was a woman of faith who went to church and prayed that her husband would not be sent overseas. Her prayers were answered. She and her husband were able to stay together for the war's duration. As they settled and resettled, they found churches that reminded them of home. She was used to reading the Bible and taking notes on the sermons she heard. In her diary, however, she replaced biblical notes with quotes from the letters she received from her brother. She preserved the quotes, wondering if each might be the last. He wrote of possibly having to make the supreme sacrifice: "I hope we are not called upon to make such a sacrifice, but if we are, I only hope and pray that we are given strength to meet it." In another letter, he said that his sergeant told them only a handful would return from a mission. She recorded the lines that her brother quoted next from Alfred Lord Tennyson:

> If e'er when faith had fall'n asleep,
> I heard a voice, "Believe no more,"
> And heard an ever-breaking shore,
> That tumbled in the Godless deep;
> A warmth within the breast would melt
> The freezing reason's colder part,
> And like a man in wrath the heart
> Stood up and answer'd, "I have felt."

It was a time of trial, so different from what she had known in Kansas, a time for courage. She was pregnant. It would be a challenge to raise a family, maintain the faith she held so dear, find her way in whatever the world was to be when the war was finally over.[81]

CHAPTER 4

QUIET CONSERVATISM

In 1952, Dwight David Eisenhower was elected on the Republican ticket to be the thirty-fourth U.S. president. Kansans voted for their native son over challenger Adlai E. Stevenson by a 69 to 30 percent margin, the largest spread of any state except North Dakota and Vermont. After years of being in the political wilderness, the state had finally come again into its own. Eisenhower represented the best that Kansas had to offer. He was an accomplished war hero and yet a plain spoken man of the people. His family was made up of ordinary folks from Abilene. He was a fiscally conservative Republican who believed that government should be efficient and concerned mainly with the country's military protection. Even though Eisenhower was not a Methodist, he was a Protestant from churchgoing stock. It was a proud moment to be from Kansas.[1]

Yet two decades of being a predominantly Republican state with a Democratic administration in Washington had taken its toll on the Kansas psyche. The state's love affair with Roosevelt's policies was brief. If people elsewhere viewed the New Deal as a great bless-ing, Kansans were more likely to regard it as a wasteful intrusion of government bureaucracy. Roosevelt was an arrogant easterner whom Kansans feared would become a dictator. They followed him reluctantly on the path of war. When war came, they poured themselves into it, commiting themselves wholeheartedly to the war effort. They became part of the great generation that later writers would extol as heroes as well as self-sacrificing community build-ers, parents, and citizens. They were all of that. And still, they were never convinced that Roosevelt had their best interests at heart or that Truman's administration would be much better.

The earlier sense that Kansas was out of step with the nation was defined increasingly as a gap between local communities and Washington. The nation's capital seemed more removed at the very time when communication technology, better transportation, and pressing international issues should have made it seem closer. Eisenhower could have provided the connective tissue, and he did to some extent, but only because Kansans liked him as a person, and separated those feelings from their views of his administration's policies. The state's continuing role as the nation's breadbasket along with its increasing importance in defense and manufacturing was another potential link that nevertheless served to alienate the local public from Washington rather than strengthen a bond. Kansas Republicans had been the opposition party for so long that it was hard to take a different stance even when Washington became Republican again.

This distance from Washington was accompanied by a stronger commitment to local communities. Towns became more precious as centers of daily interest and focal points of nostalgic longings for a simpler time. Residents increasingly regarded their communities as hometowns, the site of ancestors' graves, and places where real or imagined pioneers had struggled to carve civilization from the raw unforgiving prairie. Towns were the headquarters of an increasingly busy round of school activities for families with children. The school mascot and weekly, if not daily, sports activities stamped each town with a tangible identity. Townspeople flocked enthusiastically to football and basketball games, hailed victorious athletes as local heroes, and mourned defeats as if some deep tragedy had befallen the entire community. It was important too for adults to be involved in the town's civic activities, which included everything from booster clubs and service organizations to park improvement committees and churches.

For the middle-class people who worked in town or farmed nearby, church participation was a signature of respectability. The brick churches near the center of town sponsored civic events, and provided occasions for women to work together during the week on service projects and families to give their children proper moral as well as spiritual instruction. For residents who fell below the respectable middle class, there was ample room to find alternative places of worship. The down-and-out knew there was little hope of being heard in Washington. They could retreat from politics except to vote now and then without much sense of feeling that things should be otherwise. The tension was more acute for the middle-class residents. They were better educated and informed, able to anticipate sending their children to college, and yet were uncertain if they were anything but bystanders in national affairs. They could choose to be Democrats, and some did, or they could remain loyal Republicans, with concerns that even their party was not quite as responsive or effective as it should be.

In the background, threats of Communist infiltrators and Russian missiles added uncertainties that prompted a few to join ultraconservative patriotic organizations. There was probably some truth in the observation that cold war insecurities encouraged heartlanders to pray more often and attend church more faithfully. The more interesting fact was that people retreated into a quiet centrist conservatism that was relatively more bipartisan and apolitical than would have been expected, especially in a state with such a long Republican history. The conservatism of the period included rare hints of the more aggressive political and religious movements that were to brand the region as part of the red state Middle West in later decades. The mood was distinctly different than during the dust bowl and World War II, and yet it deeply reflected the growing sense in those earlier years that the nation was moving in a new direction and leaving the heartland behind.

GRASSROOTS RESENTMENTS

The increasing feeling of political isolation in Kansas was evident by the end of Roosevelt's second term. Although the New Deal kept banks from failing and assisted the jobless, its agricultural policies generated as much discontent as cooperation. Wheat that had been above a dollar a bushel when Kansans voted to reelect Roosevelt in 1936 was selling for fifty cents a bushel by late summer in 1938. Farmers interviewed at the state fair in Hutchinson that September expressed deep misgivings about the Agricultural Adjustment Act. Its rules capped the amount of wheat that could be planted and was doing nothing to raise prices. A newly organized Farmers Liberty League, capturing resentment reminiscent of Populist appeals in the 1890s, gained adherents in the wheat-growing counties. A letter writer to Senator Capper observed, "The farmer should be allowed to run his own business which he can do better than any brain-truster in Washington. The man who has a farm is getting tired of being dictated to." Red tape was hurting townspeople who depended on farmers' income as much as farmers themselves. Others were unhappy with the state's new sales tax, which had been approved reluctantly as a condition for receiving federal welfare funds and increased state spending for social welfare twelvefold. Still others were dissatisfied that more aggressive steps were not being taken to develop the state's oil industry.[2]

In a survey conducted in November 1938, Roosevelt received disapproval from 40 percent of the respondents in the Middle West, the same proportion as in the nation at large, but in Kansas 59 percent disapproved, and among those who had been for Landon in 1936 the proportion rose to 83 percent. Another survey showed that 50 percent of Kansans thought Roosevelt's mistakes were so great that his usefulness was over or that two more years of him in office would be a calamity for the country. A farmer in Mitchell County expressed the prevailing sentiment about Roosevelt: "When we needed government help, he was fine. But when we didn't we were left with all that government red tape and regulations, telling you what you could and couldn't do. That was no good. Farmers hate to be told what to do." At the polls that fall, Kansas voters punished the Democrats by reducing their representation in the state legislature from 40 to 20 percent, electing Republican Payne Ratner for governor over incumbent Democrat Huxman, sending Republicans to six of the state's seven seats in the U.S. House of

Representatives, and replacing Democrat McGill in the U.S. Senate with Republican Clyde M. Reed.[3]

The dissatisfaction with Roosevelt's programs stemmed from more than just the desire to be free of government constraints. Kansans recognized as clearly as anyone else that needy families were being helped. But federal programs were less effective in stabilizing farm incomes that were so heavily dependent on weather and international markets than they were at providing employment for workers in cities, and initiating the huge mining projects and reservoirs that played such a key role in western states. What Kansans in small towns and on farms observed were government programs that either did not work or backfired. Tenants were pushed off farms by the bankers who owned the farms, so that the bankers could receive government payments. Day laborers who worked for twenty-five cents an hour saw Works Progress Administration workers leaning on their shovels for forty cents an hour. "The New Deal programs cost lots of tax dollars, and many of them accomplished little," a farmer near Pratt observed, "or even worse, they failed by increasing the problems they were created to solve."[4]

It was evident that Kansas Republicans were opposed to the Roosevelt administration's policies, but unclear what shape that opposition would take. Reverend Winrod, whose poor third-place showing in the 1938 Republican primary nevertheless earned him fifty-three thousand votes, represented one extreme. Winrod was a complicated figure, as much an opportunist as a bigoted ideologue. Besides his radio program and print publications, he pastored an independent fundamentalist congregation in Wichita and cultivated connections with California fundamentalist Reverend William Matthews, who awarded Winrod an honorary doctorate from a fledgling seminary operating through the Calvary Baptist Church in Los Angeles. Winrod visited Germany, where he became enamored with Nazi propaganda, and because of his antiwar stance persuaded the Mennonite press in Kansas to publish his work. He accepted the anti-Semitic policies of the National Socialists as justified efforts to save Germany from Jewish bankers, radicals, and Communists.

4.1 Reverend Dr. Gerald B. Winrod's Defenders of the Christian Faith congregation in Wichita in 1953. Courtesy of the Howard Eastwood Collection, Wichita
State University Libraries' Department of Special Collections.

Winrod's Sunday evening radio broadcasts repeated slurs voiced by
anti-Semites in New York and Chicago about Jew-o-Crats and the
Jew Deal.[5]

Winrod's arguments resonated among Kansans who disliked
Roosevelt and were themselves of German descent. Two factors
distinguished the counties in which Winrod received the highest
proportion of Republican primary votes in 1938: counties with the
highest percentages voting against Roosevelt in 1936, and those
with the highest percentages of German-born residents. These were
also counties in which farms were small and a higher than average
percentage were mortgaged.[6] It was not that these Kansans wanted
Germany to win. A poll conducted in November 1938 showed that
only 12 percent nationally favored Germany in a war with Russia,
while 57 percent opted for Russia, and 28 percent were undecided.
In Kansas the percentage favoring Germany was even lower.[7] It was
rather that Winrod attracted supporters who opposed Roosevelt,

hoped that war could be avoided, and were drawn by his apocalyptic religious appeals that included forecasts of massive bloodshed in Europe. Winrod's extremism, though, was roundly criticized and contested by other Kansans. A committee of prominent Protestant pastors from Wichita, Topeka, Kansas City, Ottawa, Atchison, and Garden City denounced him as a fascist, and asked that an inquiry be made into the sources of his campaign funds. Methodist pastor Reverend Jesse C. Fisher, who was widely known in western Kansas, ran against him, and White paid for newspaper advertisements castigating Winrod's religious intolerance. The Republican Party leadership, fearing that a Winrod victory would turn voters into Democrats, backed his opponent, Reed.[8]

The challenge that moderate Kansas Republicans faced was sorting out the various strands of administration policies with which they disagreed. Besides farm policies and lingering concerns in some quarters about the liquor trade, there were serious misgivings about Roosevelt seeking to pack the Supreme Court, expanding the federal bureaucracy, and positioning himself for a third term. The war in Europe and looming prospect of U.S. involvement compounded these questions. Fears of Communism posed worries about supporting Joseph Stalin. Anti-Semitism was enough a part of local folk culture that efforts had to be made to combat it. Amid discussions of totalitarianism in Europe, it was not uncommon for concerns about authoritarianism in Washington to be raised. Above all, citizens wondered if there were ways to support the European allies of the United States without becoming directly engaged in the war itself. "Why try so hard to teach our children to be peaceful, and true, honest, useful citizens, only to have them sent overseas later to shoot down their fellowmen just to help some quarrelsome fools' fight?" a mother asked. "I think all of them should refuse to go, and all mothers should refuse to bear any more children only to be butchered like cattle every twenty years or so." Reverend Sheldon, now in his eighties, held a similar view. "War is the most wicked, wasteful, stupid, cowardly and unchristian activity of the human race," he told church audiences. Outside the Topeka post office, Sheldon and a group of churchpeople erected an eight-foot sign, against objections from the U.S. Department of the Treasury, condemning war and calling for it to be abolished.[9]

Senator Capper expressed the views held by many Republicans in the Middle West toward the Roosevelt administration. In 1932, Capper had argued that Hoover embodied the kind of leadership the nation needed to stabilize the dollar, reform the financial system, and bring about a dramatic reconstruction of agricultural and welfare policies. When Roosevelt won, Capper declared it time for "all of us to support the government and cooperate with the administration in leading the country into better times." He hoped that farm prices could be raised and employment could be increased at the same time that governmental expenditures were reduced. Capper supported the Agricultural Adjustment Act as a temporary measure, favored the regulation of securities transactions and utilities, and called for governmental programs to support the elderly. His greatest concern and strongest reason for supporting Landon in 1936 was that Roosevelt seemed intent on centralizing legislative and judicial power under the executive branch, and creating a dangerous and wasteful governmental monopoly over business and society.[10]

Capper conceded that war in Europe was inevitable, and by 1938 was firmly convinced that the nation needed to strengthen its defenses while avoiding becoming directly involved. He favored strict neutrality and a constitutional amendment empowering the public to decide by popular referendum when to go to war. He had long believed that greed among the rich and powerful was the source of economic woes in the United States, and would lead to war if left unchecked. Capper favored a steep progressive income tax to curb war profiteering, opposed expanding the navy, and argued repeatedly that war would turn Roosevelt's administration into a dictatorship. Over the next two years, as Roosevelt prepared the nation for war and public opinion shifted in that direction, Capper became known as one of the country's leading isolationists. He belonged to or regularly corresponded with such groups as the Keep America out of War Congress, World Peaceways, the National Council for the Prevention of War, the Women's International League for Peace and Freedom, and the America First Committee.[11]

Capper's long years in the U.S. Senate may have given Kansans a sense of being well represented in the nation's capital. It was said that voting for him became as habitual in farming communities as chewing tobacco, and that he routinely received endorsements from labor leaders, business owners, Protestant pastors, and Catholic priests alike. Certainly his views on farm policies were widely known, and even children were drawn to the cartoons, columns, and serialized romance stories in his publications. He was nevertheless best understood as an expression of Kansans' political and cultural distance from Washington. He was the mild-mannered, soft-spoken fiscal conservative who promised to be a "free man" and "not be a rubber stamp" for any group or party. He represented the outsider in Washington who stood for simple moral principles and the common person against the ambitions of big-city people on the East Coast and complicated warmongering dictators in Europe. Capper came only reluctantly to support Roosevelt's preparations for war in the months before Pearl Harbor, and during the war continued to voice concerns about the administration's arrogation of power even as he supported the nation's military efforts. He retired from the Senate in 1949 and died in 1951. Eulogies and editorials described him as something less than a great statesman who overstayed his time in Washington, yet fully embodied the state he represented: kindly, unassuming, a bit bashful, old-fashioned, and rural, a man from a place and time that seemed oddly remote.[12]

Landon's failed bid for the presidency in 1936 left him in the unenviable position of being the state's leading Republican and the party's most outspoken opponent of Roosevelt's policies. Landon was a generation younger than Capper, had a higher national profile by virtue of having been the party's standard-bearer, and took the occasion repeatedly to criticize the Democratic administration. In May 1940 Roosevelt selected Frank Knox, Landon's running mate in 1936, to become U.S. Navy secretary in an effort to build bipartisan support for war preparations. Roosevelt invited Landon to a meeting at the White House with the intent, it was rumored, of asking him to serve as war secretary. Landon departed for Washington by train from Topeka, but in Chicago received a message that Roosevelt had canceled the meeting. Landon's subsequent attacks on administration policies were sometimes attributed to the disappointment arising from this event.

Landon was already a fierce critic, however. While campaigning on behalf of Kansas Republicans in 1938, he warned that candidates should not be "yes-men" who played into "the Washington tendencies toward running everything." In 1939, he criticized Washington's farm policies, and challenged the administration to acknowledge more openly the "mass brutality" taking place in Europe along with the "horrors being lived by the Jews of Austria and Germany." As the 1940 election cycle began, Landon accused Roosevelt's followers of attempting to "deify" the president and predicted that an effort to nominate him for a third term would produce "howls all over the place." When he learned that Roosevelt was nominating Knox as navy secretary, his response was to call on fellow Republicans to maintain themselves as a strong opposition party. It may have been this call that prompted Roosevelt to rescind Landon's invitation to the White House.[13]

There was a decent chance in 1940 that Roosevelt might not win a third term. An insightful essay written by Dr. Stanley High and published in the *Saturday Evening Post* in 1937 revealed the potential weaknesses that the Democratic Party faced in 1940. High was a Methodist from Nebraska who served as a flier in World War I, worked for the Methodist Board of Foreign Missions after the war, edited the nondenominational *Christian Herald*, lectured on behalf of Prohibition, and supported Hoover in 1932 before joining Roosevelt's team and becoming one of the president's inner circle. In 1937 he occupied a desk at the White House, and was charged with winning support for the administration's policies among Republicans and dissident Democrats. In High's estimation, Democratic strength resided in a coalition that squared uneasily with his own Middle West Methodist inclinations. There was the solid South, which High described as "unashamedly reactionary," and the northeastern city machines run by people in politics "not because of the issues but because of the spoils." Roosevelt's victory and reelection, High believed, was attributable in large measure to the nation's economic crisis, and the president's policies had proven to be more liberal than the party's conservative leaders had expected. High predicted that the result would be a continuation of Roosevelt's policies through a realignment of the political system. Increasingly, Democrats would be the party of economic and political liberalism, while Republicans would represent conservatism. Liberalism would be a new coalition favorable toward centrally administered government programs, big business, big labor, and social welfare, while conservatism would be the position of farmers, small business owners, and opponents of government spending. History seemed to be on Roosevelt's side, High thought, but conservatism might carry the day.[14]

As Republicans gathered in Topeka for Kansas Day celebrations in January 1940, there was optimism that power in Washington could be regained. The party was well represented in the state legislature and Congress, and was effectively organized at the grass roots through Republican women's clubs, youth clubs, Negro assemblies, and veterans' organizations. House minority leader Joseph W. Martin Jr. came out from Massachusetts, and Colonel Theodore Roosevelt spoke on behalf of presidential aspirant Thomas E. Dewey of New York. Kansans were solidly against peacetime military conscription and in favor of curbing discretionary presidential power. Landon argued that Roosevelt's administration was the most "butter fingered" in U.S. history and predicted that voters would no longer be "mesmerized by the golden voice from the White House." A statewide survey three months later showed a solid 56 to 44 percent majority for the Republicans, and local interviews indicated that sentiment against Roosevelt was driven by rising fears of his administration involving the nation in Europe's war, continuing dissatisfaction with government farm policies, and growing resistance to the idea of Roosevelt serving a third term. A week before the election, Republican newspapers in Kansas carried a political cartoon labeled "Which?" On the left side was an image of Willkie dressed in a modest business suit, one hand on the Bible, raising his other hand to be inaugurated. On the right side was a depiction of a fat-jowled Roosevelt in kingly robes being coronated with a crown topped by a "3." Roosevelt received nearly a hundred thousand fewer votes in Kansas that fall than in 1936, resulting in a 57 percent win for Willkie. But Kansas was one of only ten states that went for Willkie. It would be a Republican state in a predominantly Democratic country for at least another four years.[15]

A minor incident in 1940 illustrated Kansans' conflicted sentiments about their state. John Steuart Curry's newly completed mural of John Brown, commissioned three years earlier, produced an outcry from the Kansas Council of Women, which passed a resolution objecting to its depiction of tornadoes, lawlessness, and "freaks," and its failure to showcase Kansas as a "law-abiding, progressive state." The following year, the Kansas legislature passed a resolution that prevented Curry from finishing the trilogy of his murals. The view that Kansas was law abiding and progressive was one side of the story. The other side was expressed in the larger-than-life image of Brown that Curry captured so effectively. A Kansan viewing it in 1940 could imagine Brown as an angry citizen of the prairie rising to be heard against the backdrop of an unresponsive government. Brown was lawless because he had to be. Neither party understood his passion. He was truly in the wilderness where steely self-determination had to stand tall against an alien world.[16]

But the person who most nearly reflected how Kansans felt about Washington—or who symbolized what the outside world imagined Kansans felt—was William Allen White. Known nationally as the Sage of Emporia, White lectured at Harvard and in New York City, toured the capital in Washington, wrote books, and captured journalists' attention through his pithy remarks at tony dinner parties and his editorials in the *Emporia Gazette*. White was an attractive representative of the rustic Middle West because of his native drawl, deadpan humor, and above all, willingness to hold Washington and both political parties in contempt. During the 1938 election, he chastised Republicans for their inability to operate an effective opposition party. "We are forever running to the fire when the siren sounds," he declared, "forgetting that we're not the brave fire laddies!" Amid heated debates in 1939 about neutrality legislation and an embargo act, White illustrated his disdain of government by asserting, "We need a three-inch rain in Kansas more than we need any piece of legislation." His view, which he carried through by lending his efforts to voluntary organizations, was that government's efforts were at best limited.[17]

In 1938, White served as cochair of the Provisional Council against Anti-Semitism, an interfaith organization responding to the persecution of Jews in Germany, and promoting racial and religious tolerance in the United States. A year later he headed the National Nonpartisan Committee for Peace through Revision of the Neutrality Law, with members including leading churchpeople, college presidents, and newspaper editors. In 1940 he chaired the Committee to Defend America by Aiding the Allies, an organization aimed at deflecting the United States from entering the war directly. He lectured against religious prejudice for the National Conference of Christians and Jews, and served with Willkie and editor Henry R. Luce on the board of the United Church Appeal. When he retired from public service a few years later, writers took the occasion to cast him as a symbol of the state in which he lived. It was not so much his recent involvement in voluntary organizations that drew their attention as his capacity to represent a bygone era unfamiliar in New York or Washington, and yet presumed to exist in distant Kansas. He exemplified what it meant to be a small-town conservative Republican, a symbol of the neighborly Middle West, a Christian Protestant Kansan, a person of common sense, an isolationist, a quiet, courageous, God-fearing man from an unusual place, and a true provincial inlander.[18]

Roosevelt's victory in 1940 and Pearl Harbor a year later placed Kansas Republicans and the citizens who supported them in the ambiguous situation of needing to rally under the banner of national unity and at the same time feeling they had no say in national politics. The result was an array of mixed responses through formal and informal channels organized by communities, churches, and civic organizations. Isolationism all but disappeared. By November 1941, a national survey showed that 70 percent of the public nationwide favored doing "everything we can to defeat Germany, even if this means getting into the war ourselves." Opinion in the Middle West and Kansas was nearly the same.[19] Between 1940 and 1945, more than 225,000 men and women from Kansas served in the armed forces, and more than 5,400 made the supreme sacrifice. Major air bases were established in Salina, Hutchinson, and Wichita; ammunition was produced near Olathe; Kansas City and Wichita became major producers of aircraft; Fort Riley became an important training center; and Fort Leavenworth earned the distinction of being the location where seven German prisoners of war were hanged.[20]

Voluntary organizations launched before the war continued and adapted to the changing national climate. An isolationist speech given in Des Moines by Charles Lindbergh in which the famous aviator made anti-Semitic references led to an interfaith movement, including clergy members in Kansas, organized to speak against religious intolerance. Reverend Birkhead's Friends of Democracy organization intensified its publicity against Winrod, Father Coughlin, and others suspected of being soft on fascism. Colored Methodist Episcopal clergyman Bishop Arthur Hamlett of Kansas City, Kansas, led an effort in his denomination to organize postwar peace proposals. Catholic Charities volunteers met to plan programs to curb juvenile delinquency in homes upset by military service. For pastors in rural communities, it was a time for older people and women to gather for worship as well as remember their loved ones. In locations near rapidly expanding military production facilities the challenges were different. "People flocked to church in great numbers," the pastor of a new Baptist Tabernacle in Wichita recalled. "Hearts were heavy and sad as nearly everyone had a loved one on the battlefield and they were seeking help and comfort. At almost every service the Tabernacle was packed and it was not unusual to see anywhere from six to fifteen or even twenty people accept Christ at each service."[21]

In 1944, Kansans again found themselves on the losing side in national politics. Kansas was one of only twelve states in which Republican challenger Dewey prevailed against Roosevelt's run for a fourth term. Sixty percent of Kansans voted for Dewey, giving him the largest margin of any state. Anti–New Deal sentiments were so strong that even former Democratic governor Woodring formed a committee opposing Roosevelt and his "Palace Guard." Capper and Reed continued in the U.S. Senate, and Republicans won all six of the state's seats in the U.S. House of Representatives. Kansans further expressed their displeasure with the administration in Washington by punishing Democratic candidates for state offices. Ninety-six percent of the state legislators were Republican.[22]

That fall a new play, *Bright Star*, opened at the Call Board Theater in Los Angeles. The play was about a typical farm family in Kansas, the Jesmers, whose son escapes the dull prairie farm life to travel in Europe and brings home a sophisticated bride, who then languishes under the harsh insensitivity of his mother. It was a saga, reviewers observed, about the humdrum existence of a plain people who suffered from a lack of imagination. Many in Kansas would not have shared that view, but an astute observer of local politics offered a similar reflection on the fall election results. Happy that Kansas was solidly Republican, the writer nevertheless conceded that "Kansas is out of step with the nation and has gone to the dogs politically." The state had "turned thumbs down on everything that carried a Washington odor." If Republicans were ever again to win a national election," he predicted, "it will be necessary to use Kansas as the guinea pig to demonstrate and promote grassroots resentments."[23]

THE SENATOR FROM PENDERGAST

Roosevelt's death on April 12, 1945, left the White House to Vice President Truman, a middle westerner from Missouri whose home-spun small-town style should have made Kansans feel more at ease in national politics than they had for more than a decade. The difficulty was that Truman was a Democrat who promised to carry on Roosevelt's policies. The added worry for middle westerners was that Truman was widely regarded as a product of Kansas City's corrupt political machine run by boss Thomas J. Pendergast. The popular version of the story of how Truman became known as the senator from Pendergast was that Pendergast helped Truman win his first bid for public office as the eastern district judge of Jackson County in 1922, and that in 1934 Pendergast bragged that he helped Truman, who was still relatively unknown, win a seat in the U.S. Senate just to "demonstrate that a well oiled machine could send an office boy to the senate." Pendergast was said to be so influential in Kansas City that his people were able to assist any newcomer find housing, get a job or start a business, and decide how to vote. That ability to help with jobs and business was especially valuable during the Depression. Pendergast benefited directly from the New Deal, which he said netted him about a billion dollars, because most of the Works Progress Administration contracts for municipal buildings and roads in Kansas City went to his companies without competitive bids. In 1939, the corruption behind Pendergast's machine was exposed during a highly publicized trial that resulted in Pendergast being sent to prison for income tax evasion.

By all accounts, Pendergast played no role in Truman becoming the vice presidential candidate in 1944, but the Pendergast machine continued to operate in Kansas City, and the political bosses of other cities, including Saint Louis, New York, and Chicago, threw their support to Truman. How much the Pendergast connection may have influenced Kansans' views of Truman was impossible to gauge, but the *Kansas City Star*, which was widely read in eastern Kansas, had a crucial role in publicizing the Pendergast affair. The story of big-city corruption played especially well in small towns and rural areas. In 1937, President Roosevelt received a telling letter from a farmer near Ransom in western Kansas. The farmer felt that the current soil conservation program was working better than the original Agricultural Adjustment Act that had been struck down by the Supreme Court. But he thought that Roosevelt's attempt to change the Supreme Court would set a dangerous precedent. He explained, "We shudder to think what fun some of your election supporters, Pendergast of Kansas City for instance, could have following such a precedent." A woman from Cawker City in north-central Kansas recalled, "We knew all about Kansas City and Pendergast. We didn't want to be identified with *that*."[24]

Early in his tenure as president, Truman reached out to Landon as well as Hoover and Dewey, and Landon reported favorably after the meeting that Truman hoped to develop a foreign policy that would unite both parties. Truman's approval rating nationally in Gallup polls stood at 88 percent when his presidency began. A year later, however, only 32 percent of the public approved of his performance as president. His popularity sank so rapidly and so low that some within his own party suggested that he should resign. It did not help that Truman had attended Pendergast's funeral a few days after being sworn in as vice president, the only elected official to do so, and his reputation was damaged further in July 1946 when he pardoned former Pendergast allies convicted of voter fraud. "The political morals of the Pendergast gang still dominate the White House," a Kansas City attorney charged.[25]

Undoubtedly the response to Truman in Kansas reflected some of the state's long-standing grievances toward Missouri, and to an even greater extent, the widening gap between small towns and cities. A 1944 poll showed that Roosevelt and Truman held a solid 58 percent majority among voters in Middle West cities of fifty thousand or more, but were favored by only 41 percent of farmers and small-town residents. Among Kansas counties, the Democratic vote was positively correlated with population size in 1940 and 1944—something that had not been true in 1936. Population in the greater Kansas City area swelled to more than half a million during World War II. The Pratt and Whitney plant alone employed more than twenty-four thousand workers making warplane engines. More than forty thousand were employed in other defense industries. Ford and General Motors assembly plants became major suppliers of military vehicles. In addition, the huge Kansas City stockyards and packing plants were processing as many as fifty thouasnd cattle a day. Many of the city's workers were African Americans, included a small but growing number of Hispanics, or were women from small towns and farming communities.

In 1943, under pressure to ease the hiring of nonunion workers at war production plants, the Kansas legislature passed a law requiring unions to list personnel and finances, strike only on approval of a majority of their members, avoid boycotts, and conduct picketing peacefully. The law was substantially similar to ones passed or discussed in eight other states, and was opposed by Landon and former governor Ratner. Labor leaders regarded it as strongly antagonistic to unions. The *Manchester Guardian*, describing it as a severe antiunion measure, called it an example of the ultraconservatism that existed in Kansas. Besides labor unrest, Kansas City was known in the region for its extremes of wealth and poverty, its racial tensions, a spate of highly publicized abductions and murders, and its history of speakeasies and saloons. When the musical *Oklahoma!* opened in 1943, audiences in New York were amused by the thought of everything being "up to date in Kansas City," with a seven-story skyscraper being "about as high as a buildin' orta grow," but rural Kansans would have noted the line about "a big theater they call the Burley-Que," the region's notorious strip joint. These were among the negative connotations with which a president from Kansas City had to contend.[26]

But Truman weathered the storm of his first year in office, gained popularity by presenting a strong front against the spread of Communism in Eastern Europe, conducted a successful whistle-stop campaign in 1948, and was elected over Dewey by more than two million votes. He was less than persuasive in Kansas. On a tour in June he stopped in Dodge City, Hutchinson, and Newton, and then in Emporia, where he paid brief homage to White and pledged to authorize a commemorative stamp honoring the late editor. Truman encouraged farmers to remember that things were better than they had been in 1932, but at each stop he argued that there should be more liberals in Congress—a plea that surely fell on deaf ears. A Gallup survey on the eve of the election, which wrongly predicted a Dewey victory and became one of the most embarrassing moments in polling history, correctly indicated that sentiment in Kansas, Nebraska, and Vermont was running strongly against Truman. Kansas voted 54 percent for Dewey and 45 percent for Truman. The margin was smaller than in either of the two previous presidential elections, but Kansas was still out of step with Washington. The disappointment was compounded by the fact that a strong grassroots movement for Eisenhower, whom Senator Capper had tried to persuade to run in 1944, had emerged among Kansas Republicans. Eisenhower, though, was not yet ready.[27]

HOMETOWN RELIGION

The sense of political distance from Washington that prevailed in the late 1940s was compatible with a renewed emphasis on homes, hometowns, and hometown churches as the essential ingredients of Middle West life. Kansans could sympathize with the Joad family's search for a new home in the 1940 film rendition of *The Grapes of Wrath* and were able to resonate with Dorothy as they watched *The Wizard of Oz* in 1939, declaring to Toto, "There's no place like home." If homes were a refuge to be protected during the Depression and longed for from distant places in World War II, they were finally a dream to be realized after the war. The rising number of children drove, in large measure, the centrality of home, community, and church. During the 1940s, the total population of Kansas rose less than 5 percent, but the number of children age fourteen and younger shot up 77 percent. By 1950, more than a quarter of the state's population was under fifteen years of age. That meant a heavy emphasis on family and school activities. To meet the demand for better education, Kansas instituted a statewide program of school consolidation. In 1942 there were 7,782 schools, and by 1950 that number had shrunk to 4,267. One- and two-room country schools were phased out, and replaced by town schools with graded classrooms from kindergarten through eighth grade and secondary schools with programs organized by subject matter. These larger, centralized schools made it possible to better accommodate children's and parents' interests in music and sports. Schools that had once served as meeting places for occasional gatherings of farmers increasingly became the focal point of regular after-school and weekend activities for towns and neighborhoods.[28]

Most Kansas communities in 1950 were small. Among the nearly six hundred incorporated towns, 80 percent had fewer than fifteen hundred residents, and only seven had more than twenty thousand. Small towns were becoming smaller, while medium and larger towns were growing. Nearly half the towns with fewer than fifteen hundred residents were smaller in 1950 than they had been in 1940. Two-thirds of towns with five to twenty thousand residents were growing, as were all the larger towns. Nevertheless, 75 percent of the state's population still lived in towns of fewer than twenty thousand or on farms. In small communities of that kind schools served as common points of reference. Children attended the same high school and perhaps even the same elementary school. Teachers were well known in the community, and parents saw one another at school events. The typical small-town newspaper devoted far more front-page coverage to school news and athletic scores than to national news or politics.[29]

School consolidation had significant implications for community relations. The school administration in Kansas was from the start under the jurisdiction of elected county superintendants and local boards, which in turn were required to conform to state laws specifying standards for teacher certification, instruction, and building maintenance. But school elections became increasingly important in the 1940s and 1950s. Consolidation generated resistance in some communities, and forced others to raise taxes to build new schools. Issues that could previously be fought out at the township level now required discussions involving larger and more diverse populations. Racial segregation was officially permitted only in the state's largest cities, but was practiced de facto in many smaller communities through patterns of residential segregation, if racial diversity was present at all. The landmark *Brown v. Board of Education* Supreme Court decision of 1954 included plaintiffs in Topeka.[30]

Larger school districts also reopened long-standing questions about religious practices. Bible reading and prayers that may have been favored in smaller local communities were more likely to be challenged in larger and more diverse districts. Questions of funding for busing and textbooks became more important for the 9 percent of the state's schoolchildren in 1950 who were enrolled in private schools, including at Lutheran, Mennonite, Quaker, and Catholic schools. Although much had been said in public forums about the need for religious tolerance, misgivings between Protestants and Catholics remained. The memoir of a woman who moved from the largely Protestant town of Council Grove to work at a military aircraft plant in Kansas City during the war was revealing in this regard. City life was in many ways an uncomfortable and eye-opening experience for her. She became acquainted with "women who drank, dated, and slept around," including one who became pregnant and had an abortion. Happily, she met a fine young man from Topeka, and in 1944 they decided to marry. "John had three strikes against him in my parents' eyes," she recalled. "He was Catholic and they thought all Catholics worshipped the Virgin Mary. There were no Catholics in our neighborhood. I do not remember seeing a Catholic Church in Council Grove, though I am sure there must have been one." She could smile about it later. "John and I confronted my parents. John confessed he had a drink occasionally and liked to dance. Dad was ill and incapable of using a shotgun."[31]

For churches, the emphasis on children and schools reinforced the emergence of what most aptly may have been termed the activity church. Although churches had served as gathering places for public events since territorial days, the usual round of activities during most of the state's history was limited to Sunday morning and evening worship services, Sunday school classes on Sunday morning, and the occasional prayer meeting or revival service. Better buildings located in towns, electricity, and automobiles made it easier for churches to host additional meetings, such as ladies' auxiliary gatherings and service clubs. After World War II, better cars, fewer people doing farm chores, an improved economy, and children in the home encouraged churches to sponsor a wider round of regular activities. Insofar as clergy competed with one another for members, these activities were prompted by intercongregational rivalries. Yet it was just as apparent that the true competitor was the school. Churches organized youth groups and sports teams the way that schools did, hosted guest lecturers, and sponsored community-wide meetings at the school gymnasium or auditorium. Not to be outdone by schools' homecoming festivities during the fall football season, churches also began sponsoring homecoming weekends, during which former pastors and longtime members were honored, and extended families, visitors, and townspeople were invited to attend.

Courtland, Kansas, was a town of about 370 residents in 1947. Like many towns of its size, Courtland was smaller than it had been before the Depression, but now that the war was over it was growing slightly. There were young families with children, and more of the area's farmers were living in town. Nearly everyone belonged to one of Courtland's four churches. The Methodist Church on Main Street, completed in 1893 at a cost of $2,200, was the largest. The Church of Christ and the Covenant Church were a few blocks away. The Church of Christ had been built in 1893 following a series of revival meetings. Swedish immigrants founded the Covenant Church in 1890, after settling in Republic County in the 1870s and 1880s. They met in schoolhouses and homes for nearly a decade before erecting a building in the country, and later moving it into the town. They held services in Swedish until 1922. The Lutheran Church outside of town also had roots in the Swedish immigration. The Courtland schools supplied children with a rich offering of extracurricular activities, including basketball tournaments, track meets, plays, concerts, and district musical competitions. To keep up, the churches expanded their programs as well. Each of the churches had a youth organization that met on Sunday evenings. The Methodist Church held periodic full-day youth rallies that brought in teenagers from neighboring high schools. All the churches sponsored films, radio broadcasts, gospel teams, concerts, visiting speakers, panel discussions, and cleanup days.[32]

Courtland's churches were as pivotal to the community's local identity as its ethnic heritage was. The *Courtland Journal* carried

church announcements on its front page as well as listings of sermon topics and paragraphs by each of the town's ministers giving a
précis of the sermon's content or a short meditation. It was not uncommon for readers of these paragraphs to find admonitions about
the importance of seeking God, honoring God, attending church,
and giving thanks for God's blessings. Community news items included notices of who had visited whom on Sunday after church,
who had chaired a church committee, and who had helped shingle
a church roof. Each week the full text of the syndicated International Sunday School Lesson appeared. On the Thursday before
Easter, the front page was filled with a giant cross, inscribed with a
drawing of people flocking to a church along with listings of each
congregation's special Easter services, sermon titles, and hymns.
The week was to include a comedy put on by one of the youth
groups, a missionary drama, several special children's services, a
breakfast, classes for all ages, and a training class for children's
Sunday school teachers. "He is risen," the newspaper announced in
large block letters.[33]

Politics played a key role in Courtland, too. Residents followed
war news on the radio, learned of casualties, read Drew Pearson's
"Washington Merry-Go-Round" column in the newspaper, and
kept up on legislation affecting farms, roads, and schools. When
Japan surrendered in 1945, the Courtland community met for
Thanksgiving and prayer at the Methodist Church. In state and national elections, the citizens mostly voted for Republicans because
they favored the GOP's views on farm issues. But there was a gap
even between those Republican proclivities and local interests. Republic County had been a center of Populist activity in the 1890s.
In the 1940s local elections still tilted toward People's Party candidates. These candidates won because they were known as trusted
leaders who put the community first. Sometimes they were elected
as write-in candidates. Churches were what connected residents
to the world outside Courtland, perhaps to a greater extent than
did politics. As long as anyone could remember, Courtland's pastors had gone to district clergy meetings, and it was common for
churches to host visiting speakers.

To those continuing connections were now added activities that would prove increasingly important in small towns in the coming years. The guest speakers included college professors who told local youths about the significance of attending college and what it was like being a student. Concerts featured choirs from these institutions. Some of the speakers brought firsthand news of church activities in other countries. A missionary from Venezuela described her work. A speaker told how churches in Europe damaged during the war were rebuilding. Other events featured topics that would eventually play a role in reshaping the contours of local religion and politics. The special speaker at the Covenant Church in February 1947 was Dr. Paul W. Rood, president of the World Christian Fundamentalist Association, a nondenominational organization that advocated biblical literalism and opposed teaching evolution. At the Methodist Church that month, the adult Sunday school class studied a lesson about race relations provided by the denomination and took up an offering for Negro students in Little Rock, Arkansas.[34]

Comity existed among most of the Protestant denominations across the state, such that it was common for each to sponsor its own youth group and guest speakers, and yet cooperate in organizing Reformation Day, Thanksgiving, and other special worship services. Ministerial alliances became popular, working together to address community problems and often to place holiday greetings in community newspapers. The four-member ministerial alliance in Courtland, for example, secured the school auditorium in March 1947 for a community-wide screening of *The God of Creation*, a film produced by the Moody Bible Institute in Chicago about the creation of the world. In other towns, clergy participated in organizing countywide church associations with the assistance of the Kansas Council of Churches. In Barber County, for instance, the first such meeting was held in 1948 at the Kiowa Methodist Church, and featured workshops on children's and youth ministries with guest speakers from Topeka and Oklahoma. That year, the Kansas Council of Churches also sponsored a meeting in Lawrence that launched the State Council of Civil Rights to combat racial discrimination by coordinating the efforts of local ministerial councils, veterans groups, and civic organizations. Church teachings prohibited Catholic churches from participating formally in Protestant ministerial alliances and councils, but neighborly relations bridged the gap in some communities. One of Courtland's pastors spoke fondly of a Catholic chaplain with whom he had served during the war. In other towns, Catholic masses were advertised alongside Protestant worship services, and priests in some communities made efforts to explain Catholic distinctives, such as teachings about the Virgin Mary and saints, to the wider Protestant public. It was also common for communities to sponsor Christian holiday events, newspapers to emphasize them, and businesses to participate.[35]

The activity church drew people in and made them feel good about participating in a way that politics seldom did. Public officials in Washington were remote, bureaucratic, more often than not from an alien party, and seemingly more interested in big cities and international affairs than in the struggles and aspirations of small-town inhabitants in the Middle West. Even in Topeka, the elected Republicans who ran the state were usually better educated and richer than the common person. The churches, in contrast, held regular meetings at which ordinary people sang and prayed together with their neighbors. A neighbor with musical talent was likely to sing in the church choir or play the piano. Covered-dish dinners and church picnics punctuated the annual calendar. Church basements provided the venue for Home Demonstration Unit meetings and Post-War Emergency Program instruction. For those who still cared about liquor problems, churches not only sponsored small WCTU meetings but also hosted rallies with featured celebrities, such as track star Glenn Cunningham, the "temperance tornado" from Emporia who set the world mile record in the 1930s. Having a person like that come to town affirmed the community. "We're just good solid citizens," a rally participant in Elkhart explained.[36]

In 1948, agricultural economist F. D. Farrell undertook an investigation of churches in small Kansas communities. He selected three churches in communities not unlike Courtland: one in northeast

Kansas, one in southeast Kansas, and one near Hutchinson in central Kansas. Each of the churches held regular Sunday school classes and worship services attended by anywhere from 100 to 250 people, and each of the pastors conducted more than a dozen weddings and funerals a year, plus made upward of 100 home visits. In addition, the congregations sponsored women's service organizations, men's clubs, and youth fellowship groups; hosted 4-H Club and YWCA meetings; organized special programs at the community high school; and held meetings about homemaking, soil conservation, agriculture, roads, and school improvement. When Farrell interviewed members about why they participated, the top reasons were that it was good for the children, provided opportunities for worship and fellowship, and served the community.[37]

The extent to which church life was part and parcel of Kansas towns was seldom more evident than at holidays. Kiowa southwest of Wichita near the Oklahoma border, with a population of about fifteen hundred in the late 1940s, and WaKeeney in western Kansas, with a population of approximately two thousand, were typical county seats. Both suffered during the dust storms of the Depression, but benefited from rising wheat prices during the war and were experiencing some population growth as a result of the postwar baby boom. Kiowa's well-established congregations included Methodist, Catholic, Christian, and Congregational churches, the Church of Christ, and the more recent Assembly of God Church. WaKeeney had Methodist, Baptist, and Presbyterian churches, three Lutheran churches, the Seventh-Day Adventist Church, the Church of God, and the Assembly of God Church. The congregations in both towns sponsored a busy round of weekly activities, including adult and junior choirs, youth groups, girls' groups, men's groups, women's aid societies, and supper clubs.

It was not that residents spent all their waking hours at church, though. Farmers gathered on rainy mornings at the coffee shop and gossiped with their neighbors at farm auctions. Men and women belonged to their respective lodges. Parents attended school programs and cheered the home team on Friday evenings. It was rather that church activities related seamlessly with the rest of community life. The Community Choral Society was an avocational musical association that included singers from Kiowa and five neighboring towns. Its Palm Sunday performance of *The Crucifixion* at the grade school auditorium under the direction of the high school vocal music teacher drew a large audience from the towns represented. Holy Week services were held each noon that week at the Lawrence Motor Company. WaKeeney celebrated Advent with such spirit that it became known as "the Christmas city of Kansas." Each December the ministerial alliance erected a massive Christmas tree, supplemented by lights and garlands extending in all directions, at the intersection of Main Street and Russell Avenue. The annual Christmas Festival of carols and hymns played to an overflow audience at the high school auditorium. There was no question that Christmas was a religious holiday as opposed to merely a seasonal event. It was the "nativity of the Christ Child" that worked "an awesome magic on men's souls" and produced a "new stirring of faith," the local newspaper declared in a front-page message. Businesses added greetings of their own, wishing the community not only happiness and prosperity but also encouraging readers to attend church on Christmas Day. Nearly all the town's businesses cooperated in sponsoring the ministerial alliance's weekly page of announcements and spiritual advice. "The church can make a better you and a better me," the page advised. "The church is the salvation of mankind."[38]

It was one thing to argue that churches could shape lives; it was quite another to understand exactly how this happened. Presumably parishioners flocked to churches hoping for salvation and then lived better as a result. A "better you and a better me" resonated with Methodist perfectionism and wider emphases on self-improvement. Were it possible to know what people actually believed, it would have been reasonable to imagine that faith affected their values in these ways. That was what Harvard psychologist Gordon Allport contended, asserting that the truly devout developed an "intrinsic religiosity" that sustained them in good times and bad.[39]

But that view missed the social role of churches. It overemphasized individuals' private beliefs and underemphasized their communities. Rare insight into the social dimension of religion came from another Kansas town. In 1948, a team of researchers led by a couple, psychologist Roger G. Barker and Louise Barker, established a field station in Oskaloosa, Kansas. Forty-five miles northeast of Topeka, Oskaloosa was a community of about seven hundred when the Barkers arrived. Other than the fact that it was a county seat, it was in no way special. Small by most standards, it was actually somewhat larger than the median Kansas town. The community and surrounding farms were catered to by eighty-five businesses. Seventy percent of its residents had been born and reared in Jefferson County, and nearly all the remainder were native to the Middle West. Ninety-nine percent owned a radio, and nearly every family subscribed to a daily newspaper. They loved hamburgers, potatoes, white bread, and apple pie. The field station's purpose was to study child development among the town's hundred or so schoolchildren. But as the Barkers observed community life from their second-story window near the center of town, they became interested in how and where people congregated. That interest led them to initiate the most extensive investigation of public social interaction ever to be conducted in any community.[40]

The study began in July 1951 and continued for a year. The researchers recorded every setting and public activity in which every resident of Oskaloosa participated. If there was a meeting at the school, they wrote down how many people attended and how long the meeting lasted. If there was a choir rehearsal, they did the same. They surveyed the stores to see how much time people spent shopping. They recorded gatherings in the park, visits to the dentist, auctions, elections, and funerals. In all, they registered more than 5,000 different activities in 538 different settings totaling approximately 1 million person-hours.[41]

One of the principal conclusions was that the residents of Oskaloosa spent an enormous amount of time performing the basic activities necessary to keep their community functioning. It was not that they were especially engaged in activities outside their homes. If they spent a million hours collectively in community settings that year, they spent five million in family settings. Nor was it the case that they were particularly involved in voluntary community service, such as helping at the fire station or library. The most common activities took place in business settings, and consisted of working and shopping. Still, the researchers were impressed that in a small town, it took the involvement of nearly everyone to get things done. That included maintaining the streets, keeping the lights and phones working, stocking the grocery shelves, selling shoes, and organizing holiday parades—all of which might have been done more efficiently, the researchers speculated, in a larger town. And what needed to be done seemed to have increased. Compared to an earlier generation, there were more classes at the school, more after-school activities, and more athletic events. Residents were holding meetings to discuss such topics as water fluoridation and soil conservation. They were going more often to the dentist. There was a cancer control committee and a polio support group. There were bowling leagues and people were eating out more than their parents would have dreamed of doing.

It all took time, but it also generated community spirit. In interviews, the researchers found residents filled with quiet pride about their homes, lawns, and town. They knew its history, rooted for its teams, and championed its amenities. "Our people are housed, not in crowded apartments, but largely in comfortable homes of their own," one of the residents boasted. Oskaloosa, he said, "offers unexcelled opportunities for quietude of mind and growth of soul."[42]

The study especially illuminated the role of government. As was true in other towns, ordinary Oskaloosans spent only a few minutes each year at the polls. Republicans usually won, and it was easy to think that politics had little to do with daily life. But if politics seemed remote, there were constant reminders of its importance. Seventy of the town's four hundred employed adults worked for the state, federal, county, or city government. There were twenty-six different government offices in Oskaloosa. These offices dealt with everything from law enforcement to taxes to vehicle maintenance to agricultural subsidies. Sixty percent of all the activities in Oskaloosa, the study concluded, in some way involved government.

Compared with what else they did, Oskaloosans spent relatively little time at church. Of the million person-hours recorded, about 4 percent were in church settings, while 51 percent were in business settings, 24 percent were in school settings, and 9 percent were in government settings. That was hardly surprising. Services were held Sunday mornings and evenings, but during much of the week the churches stood empty. And yet by other indications, the churches were important. Seventy-five percent of the residents were members of one of the town's three churches: 34 percent were Methodists, 37 percent were Presbyterians, and 4 percent were African Methodists. In addition, 7 percent belonged to churches out of town. Only 15 percent were unchurched. Twenty-five percent of Oskaloosa women regularly attended missionary society meetings. There were numerous father-son and mother-daughter banquets, Sunday school programs, and choir rehearsals. The researchers found that 750 copies of church publications circulated each month, more than two per family.[43]

The more important conclusion about religion, however, was implicit in the study's findings. In towns the size of Oskaloosa, churches were integrated into the community not only by the amount of time that residents spent at church, or even by the impact of church on their private beliefs, but through overlapping social networks. Worshippers saw and greeted one another during the week as well as on Sundays and at church meetings. It would not have been uncommon for the church choir director to teach music at the high school. The church organist may have given piano lessons after school. The minister would have belonged to the Rotary Club and was a volunteer firefighter. A church usher ran the drugstore. A deacon was the mayor. A Sunday school teacher lived next door.

Students of social networks argue that norms are enforced most effectively when a person's associates not only know that person but also know each other. You are then subject to what your Sunday school teacher neighbor says to the deacon behind your back. Or what the organist knows about your children and can tell the minister. A study just east of Kansas in a small Missouri town in 1945 noted the power of such networks. "The religious control of morals operates mainly through gossip and the fear of gossip," the author wrote. "People report, suspect, laugh at, and condemn the peccadilloes of others, and walk and behave carefully to avoid being caught in any trifling missteps of their own."[44] That was probably true in Oskaloosa and most small towns.

Oskaloosa was atypical of Kansas towns in that it had no Catholics. It was typical, though, in being populated almost entirely by white Americans and being dominated by churches affiliated with well-established mainline denominations. Its Methodists and Presbyterians spanned the range of occupations and income levels represented in the community, and left little room for upstart congregations to emerge. Methodists knew Presbyterians, and Presbyterians knew Methodists. The African Methodists were separated by race. But all three of the churches offered venues of respectability for the town's residents.

Statewide, the distribution of membership among Kansas denominations remained similar to the figures obtained in 1936. Having decided that it was no longer appropriate to ask questions about religion, the U.S. Bureau of the Census turned the task over to the National Council of Churches, the ecumenical organization that replaced the Federal Council of Churches in 1950. Information collected by the National Council of Churches in 1952 showed Methodists still well in front of all other Protestant denominations with nearly 227,000 members, followed by Roman Catholics with almost 209,000. The Christian Church (Disciples of Christ) came in third with almost 99,000 members, American Baptists claimed 67,000, the Presbyterian Church (U.S.A.) almost 60,000, and Lutheran churches 59,000. With the added participation of such well-established denominations as Congregationalists, Evangelical United Brethren, and Episcopalians—each with more than 20,000 members—the typical ministerial council could claim to represent a large share of the inhabitants of most communities. This was the religious situation in Kansas as Eisenhower's presidency began.[45]

I LIKE IKE

Eisenhower grew up in Kansas, went off to West Point after high school, and was away from Kansas for most of his adult life. When he returned for a visit to his boyhood home in Abilene in 1945, he was the victorious Allied Expeditionary Force commander who had crushed the enemy, and was being feted in London, Paris, and New York City. Eisenhower arrived at Abilene's Union Pacific train station on the evening of June 21 to an exuberant crowd of ten thousand, twice the town's usual population. As the band played "Hail, Hail, the Gang's All Here," the mayor handed Ike a key to the city and the general pressed through the crowd toward his hotel. "He was like a pied piper," an observer noted. "I'm coming home and I'm glad to be here," Eisenhower said. "When I get out of this uniform this is the country I'm coming back to," he promised. The next day, a crowd of twenty thousand assembled for a parade in his honor. After the floats, marching bands, veterans, and farm implements all passed the reviewing stand, Eisenhower addressed the gathering. "The proudest thing I can claim," he declared, "is that I am from Abilene."[46]

It was not surprising that Kansans were ecstatic to see Eisenhower. He was their own, the boy who made good. As reports of his military successes in Europe grew, his stature as the state's most famous citizen had increased. Legends circulated that Ike had whipped the toughest boy in town while growing up in Abilene and that he hoped to become a Kansas farmer when the war was over. The Kansas committee of the Golden Rule Foundation named his eighty-three-year-old mom as the state mother of the year. Abilene hired a professional decorator to doll up the town in preparation for Eisenhower's homecoming. Townspeople planted flowers and made sure their lawns were freshly mowed. There were rumors that a museum would be built in his honor and that he might run for president. Whether he would or not, his presence told the world that the Middle West was important after all. In a speech in Kansas City, he disputed the criticism that the region was isolationist. Eisenhower was living proof that it was not. With proper attention to its civic duties and training its youth, he predicted, the Middle West would continue to be a source of moral leadership for the nation.[47]

Having been in the political wilderness for so long, Kansans were desperate to hear this. They would have been happy enough for affirmation from a traveling temperance leader or an itinerant evangelist, but this was so much better. The old sense of being out of step with the nation, and with being the object of ridicule, continued with sufficient force that affirmation was sorely needed. "Air just full o' slander darts from the busy Eastern marts," complained a Kansas poet. Karl Menninger, the renowned psychiatrist in Topeka, wrote that the state suffered from an inferiority complex. Social scientists administered IQ tests to see if farm children in the region might indeed be inferior. The writer Kenneth S. Davis, who would gain acclaim for his biographies of Eisenhower and Roosevelt, observed of his native state that it seemed to have bought into the most unflattering depictions of itself. Kansans viewed themselves as the inhabitants of a dreary landscape, a place of unremitting monotony, he argued. It was probably from sheer boredom that the state periodically erupted in political and religious fanaticism. Davis believed that Eisenhower might spark an awakening in the Kansas temperament. With better schools, bigger towns, and stronger connections to the outside world, the state could move beyond the "phony" appeals of its Prohibitionist past. Davis was less confident, though, that Kansas could ever escape its ingrained backwardness. Its best hope was probably to stand as a beacon of individual self-reliance, even as the rest of the nation moved toward a greater understanding of interdependence and collective responsibility.[48]

Eisenhower was difficult to understand as a symbol of self-reliance, at least if his accomplishments were viewed as part of the most massive military undertaking in history. It served better to put him back in his boyhood home, and in that setting, emphasize his family's simple religious faith. Many of the biographies written during and after his presidency mentioned the family's religious affiliation barely in passing. Davis's biography, published in 1945, reflected Davis's intimate knowledge of Kansas and dwelled at length on Eisenhower's religious roots. Those roots were in the Anabaptist tradition that brought groups often persecuted in Germany, the Swiss cantons, and elsewhere in Europe to the United States, where they formed various Mennonite, Amish, Dunkard, and Brethren faith communities. The Eisenhowers were affiliated with the River Brethren, whose name originated from the group's proximity to the Susquehanna River in Pennsylvania. In 1879, approximately three hundred River Brethren relocated to Kansas, settling near Hope and Abilene in Dickinson County. They located near other German-speaking settlers, bought farms, and started businesses. There was a strong ethic of individual moral and spiritual responsibility, according to Davis, as well as strong loyalty to fellow brethren. Eisenhower and his brothers were raised on daily prayer and Bible reading along with weekly attendance at worship services. Both parents were said to be quite dedicated in their study of the Bible, and several members of the Eisenhower clan were preachers.[49]

Kansas churchgoers who read of Eisenhower's boyhood faith may have overlooked Davis's observation that Dwight seemed to have rebelled against his strict upbringing and taken a more rationalistic approach to religion as he matured. Eisenhower's father was said to have developed a kind of mystical orientation toward biblical prophecy, and other accounts suggested that his parents became interested in the teachings of Jehovah's Witnesses. Eisenhower himself did not become a church member until 1953, when he joined the National Presbyterian Church in Washington. His most famous statement about religion, amplified in writer Will Herberg's widely read reuse of it in *Protestant-Catholic-Jew*, was that "our government has no sense unless it is founded in a deeply felt religious faith and I don't care what it is." That view undoubtedly reflected something of Eisenhower's own exposure to different faith

4.2 Dwight D. Eisenhower speaking to a crowd in Abilene, Kansas, June 6, 1952.
Courtesy of KansasMemory.org, Kansas State Historical Society, Copy and Reuse
Restrictions Apply.

traditions, but it was also a prevailing sentiment, Herberg believed,
in the heartland and throughout the nation. This was especially
evident from the wider context in which the statement occurred.
Eisenhower's remark, with the clarification that Americans believed
in the "Judo-Christian concept," was made in an address criticizing
the Soviet leadership for its disavowal of religion.[50]

The 1952 presidential campaign, in which Eisenhower ran
against Adlai E. Stevenson, put religion and religious tolerance

squarely in the public eye. On repeated occasions, Eisenhower insisted that religious faith was a necessary underpinning of democracy. He criticized the French for emphasizing reason at the expense of faith. Eisenhower insisted that the United States had to be strong in its spiritual convictions to prevail in the struggle against the Soviets. He argued that it was difficult to deal with the Soviets because they had no understanding of religion. It was important, he believed, for the United States to experience a spiritual revival. At the same time, Eisenhower acknowledged that people held different views toward religious creeds and needed to unite in what they could perceive as underlying principles. "Even those among us who are, in my opinion, so silly as to doubt the existence of an Almighty, are still members of a religious civilization," he told an audience in New York City. "I didn't mean to come before you and be evangelical," explained Eisenhower. But it was critical, in his view, for people to live up to their duty as citizens according to the basic teachings of religion. If we can do that, he said, "we will have self-reliant citizens."[51]

Religious leaders were pleased not only that Eisenhower spoke favorably of religion but also that both candidates stressed religious tolerance. Protestant, Catholic, and Jewish leaders praised Eisenhower and Stevenson for avoiding bigotry, highlighting the "brotherhood of man and the Fatherhood of God," and serving as role models of acceptable civic and religious decorum. At a dinner in 1953, the Anti-Defamation League of B'nai B'rith honored Eisenhower with its Democratic Legacy Award. "The deep things that are American are the soul and the spirit," Eisenhower told the group. "The individual is dignified because he is created in the image of his God. Let us not forget it." As his presidency unfolded, the spirit of tolerant religious promotion remained evident. Without much dissent, "under God" was added to the Pledge of Allegiance and "In God We Trust" was inscribed on the nation's currency. Eisenhower's secretary of agriculture, Ezra Taft Benson, held a high position in the Church of Jesus Christ of Latter-day Saints, but his prominence in the church seldom resulted in anti-Mormon sentiments being voiced. Benson reportedly opened Eisenhower's

regular cabinet meetings with prayer. More visibly, a group calling itself the International Council for Christian Leadership initiated the annual National Prayer Breakfast in which the president,
congressional leaders, and other public officials participated. The
council's president was Kansas senator Frank Carlson.[52]

How Kansas participated in the national mood of religion in
the service of U.S. democracy was more ambiguous than may have
seemed evident on the surface. Citizens in places like Kiowa and
WaKeeney, where religion was integral to community life, were certainly at home with having God recognized on the currency and
in the nation's capital. It was easy enough in communities with
prevailing Christian majorities to imagine that everyone believed
in the same God. Yet that presumption was rooted in a tacit agreement not to say too precisely what exactly one believed about God.
Eisenhower was the perfect role model. He did not disclose much
of what he personally believed, other than to say he was convinced
of the Almighty's existence. That was the spirit in which the prayer
breakfasts were held in Washington and acknowledgments of God
were added to the currency. It fit well with holiday greetings in
Kansas newspapers encouraging people to count their blessings and
attend church. The prayers that Benson used to open Eisenhower's
cabinet meetings were silent ones. The tacit agreement was that
nobody needed to talk loudly about what they believed specifically,
as long as nearly everyone believed. It did not satisfy everyone, of
course. There were believers with stronger views about the differences separating Protestants from Catholics, Christians from Jews,
believers from atheists, and one denomination from another. For
all his professed faith in the importance of religion, Eisenhower's
brand of faith was too general for many.

But it was not so much his attitude toward religion as his personal style that made Eisenhower attractive to the Kansans who
embraced him as one of their own. He was an uncomplicated
person, journalist John Gunther wrote, a man with simple spiritual values who believed in personal dignity and moral integrity.
Simplicity was the best part. After years of struggle in a complicated war and faced with an increasingly complex world, there was

nothing more desirable than being able to live an uncomplicated
life in a small town in the middle of the United States. That was
the true meaning of liberty, a Kansas high school student wrote, "a
thing of the spirit," being free to worship, think, hold one's opinions, and have a family. Kansans liked Eisenhower's boyish smile,
and the slow, deliberate manner in which he addressed them on
their new black-and-white television sets. They liked the fact that
he spoke of self-reliance, and voiced concerns about government
red tape and large bureaucracies. His gift—the same gift that Ronald Reagan would manifest to a far greater extent—was his ability
to be a president and commander in chief who people nevertheless
regarded as a Washington outsider. For the truth was that Kansans
who liked him as a person did not care much for many of his policies. They fretted that Washington was still dictating what farmers
could and could not do without maintaining an adequate program
of price supports for wheat, or helping enough to insure against
losses from the periodic droughts and dust storms that continued
in the 1950s. It was troublesome that men were being drafted again
so recently after the last war and that the specter of Communism
was spreading.[53]

The state's Republican leaders naturally assumed that their own
voice would be much stronger in Washington than it had been for
two decades. But these expectations went largely unrealized. On
January 16, 1953, Eisenhower gave a controversial farewell address at Columbia University, assailing campuses for harboring red
subversives, and the same day nominated Kansas newspaper man,
C. Wesley Roberts, to chair the Republican National Committee.
Roberts was known in Kansas as an old-fashioned party loyalist
who knew how to manipulate patronage to the party's advantage.
There will be "one direct lane to a place on the federal payroll,"
an observer in Topeka explained. "It will lead from the county
committee to the court house, state house and the White House."
Three weeks later Alvin McCoy, a correspondent for the *Kansas
City Star*, learned that Roberts had received an eleven thousand
dollar fee from an insurance company for helping the company sell

a tuberculosis sanitarium near Norton to the state. A subsequent inquiry by a state legislature committee determined that the sanitarium's title already belonged to the state, and in any case, Roberts was not appropriately designated as a public relations counsel or consultant to the company, and thus should not have been entitled to a fee. Both the governor and the White House initially rose to Roberts's defense, but as the allegations became stronger and the event gained attention in national newspapers, Roberts's tenure as Republican National Committee chair was terminated. McCoy received a Pulitzer Prize for exposing the scandal. In Topeka, the Republican leadership fell into factions over the issue.[54]

Meanwhile, Eisenhower appointed lame-duck Kansas congressman Albert M. Cole to head the Federal Housing Administration, an appointment that was instantly criticized in Kansas, where Cole's farm policies had proven too unpopular for him to be reelected. Better views were held of Congressman Clifford Hope, who had served since 1943 and had risen to chair the House Agriculture Committee, except that Hope defended Secretary of Agriculture Benson's policies, which were also unpopular. These concerns contributed to Democrat Floyd Breeding's narrow victory over Hutchinson Republican John Crutcher as Hope's replacement in 1957.[55]

The one bright spot for Kansas Republicans was that Representative Carlson won a seat in the U.S. Senate in the 1952 election. Carlson was a devout Baptist from Concordia who had served first in the state legislature, then the House of Representatives from 1935 to 1947, as governor from 1947 to 1950, and then again in the House of Representatives from 1950 to 1952. He supported Eisenhower and was considered a progressive Republican. He was also known as a churchgoer, but relatively few would have been aware of his role in the International Council for Christian Leadership. The council was founded in 1944 by Abraham Verheide, a Methodist evangelist from Seattle who conceived of it as an informal organization working behind the scenes to build personal relationships among Christians in government, business, and labor. It did, however, issue statements condemning materialism, encouraged Christians to put their faith into practice, and sponsored prayer groups attended by Republicans and Democrats.[56]

A WELL-QUALIFIED CATHOLIC

By the end of the twentieth century, writers would look back at the 1950s and imagine that ultraconservatism in Kansas had originated during the cold war. There was little evidence of that. The legacy that influenced later conservatism was rather the sense of disenfranchisement that grew during the long years of Roosevelt's and Truman's administrations. It was partly the distance that ordinary people felt when faced with government regulations and taxes they did not understand, or for which they did not see a need. It was compounded for citizens who instinctively voted Republican and knew that their party was incapable of effecting policies in Washington. Whether Roosevelt could have lessened the estrangement by leaving office sooner or working harder to build bipartisan support was uncertain. The fact that it continued under Eisenhower suggested that it was rooted in grassroots resentments deeper than partisanship alone could explain.

The irony is that grassroots resentments were almost overcome in 1960, not only because Richard Nixon came so close to winning against John F. Kennedy, but also because Kansas politics had become increasingly bipartisan by the end of the 1950s. The shift was insufficient to eradicate the divisions that had separated Catholics and Protestants for so long. Unsurprisingly, three Kansans voted for Nixon for every two who voted for Kennedy. And yet that was a smaller Republican margin than in either of the two previous presidential elections, and four years later Kansas joined the rest of the nation in voting for Democrat Lyndon Johnson. These developments were destined to have a profound influence on the unsettled politics of the remainder of the century. They were in turn the result of two underlying changes: greater cooperation among the state's major religious bodies, and greater division within the state's dominant political party.

The changes in religion were easiest to describe because they were already evident in the activity churches of the late 1940s as well as the interdenominational efforts of the 1920s and 1930s. The view that Kansas was the home of religious freaks along with such abominations as the Ku Klux Klan and the bigotry of Winrod would lead writers to emphasize these features of Kansas religion. The dominant reality was quite different. The established churches were such centrist organizations that radical movements on the far Right or far Left emerged rarely, and only to the extent that they could form independent organizations. Methodists, Disciples of Christ, Presbyterians, Lutherans, and other major denominations generally worked to restrain these upstarts, either by opposing them frontally, or arguing that they were mingling religion and politics. From the Kansas Council of Churches, organized in 1921, to church leaders' denunciations of the Ku Klux Klan and Winrod's anti-Semitism, to calls for religious tolerance in political campaigns, the message was to support a civic-minded faith that did not stray far from organized worship and prayer. It was usually in the Republican Party's interest to support the churches in these efforts, thereby reinforcing the status quo while promoting community improvement. The activity church fit the prevailing pattern by encouraging participation in congregations as well as directing attention toward local communities, families, and children.[57]

The one aspect of community religious life that was difficult to reconcile with this congenial centrist orientation was the gap between Catholics and Protestants. The two had been taught to be suspicious of each other for so long that it was sometimes hard to find common ground. Catholics were still regarded by some Protestants as worshippers of the pope, and some Catholics feared Protestants were trying to convert them, or shut down their churches and schools. In 1956, misgivings were reinforced when Bishop Mark K. Carroll prohibited students from the southeastern Kansas diocese from enrolling in undergraduate psychology and philosophy courses offered at colleges and universities not under church control, for fear that students would be brainwashed and lose their faith. But there were also mitigating factors. Catholics had come to Kansas about the same time as Protestants, and the two were seldom distinguishable in terms of social class. By the 1950s, ethnic differences were less important, and the majority of Catholic youths attended public high schools. In small towns Protestants might still dictate the content of community-wide Christmas and Easter events, but in larger towns like Hutchinson, Salina, and Wichita, it was harder for any religious group to carry this much influence.

In the 1950s the largest concentrations of Catholics were in Kansas City and Wichita, but the majority of Catholics were dispersed throughout the state. Counties with a higher-than-expected growth in the numbers of Catholics ranged from Brown, Johnson, and Nemaha in the northeast, to Butler, Cherokee, and Crawford in the southeast, to Finney and Ford in western Kansas. That dispersion meant Catholics and Protestants were living as neighbors in most communities. If church rules and local customs deterred Protestant ecumenical organizations from including Catholics, the different traditions could at least demonstrate basic agreement by sponsoring similar activities. The fact that Catholics and Protestants held worship services at the same hour on the same day of the week, placed similar announcements in local newspapers, and sponsored youth fellowships with similar names implicitly communicated that the two traditions were not so fundamentally different after all. There were also instances in which Protestants and Catholics cooperated in common humanitarian efforts. The most notable of these was the Christian Rural Overseas Program. This program was organized in 1947 to supply food and other farm products to needy people in foreign countries. In 1948, during Carlson's tenure as governor, Kansas Protestants and Catholics worked together in soliciting enough wheat, flour, and dried milk to fill a sixty-car train.[58]

Whatever mutual understanding existed between Protestants and Catholics, it was not enough to preclude religious differences from becoming an important factor in the 1960 presidential election. Members of the Church of Christ, such as the ones in

Courtland and Kiowa, heard sermons about the dangers of Catholicism and were invited to consider arguments against having a Catholic president printed in the denomination's *Gospel Advocate*. Members of Southern Baptist churches received similar advice from the Baptist press. The American Council of Christian Churches, an organization of fundamentalist denominations, met in Kansas City that spring and unanimously passed a resolution disapproving of a Roman Catholic for president. At a meeting in Hutchinson in March 1960, Kennedy received a standing ovation, but afterward, when asked if religion would be a source of opposition, a member of the crowd confided, "It's hidden, it's ugly, but it's there."[59]

The sentiment against Kennedy's Catholicism was by no means limited to conservative denominations in the nation's heartland. In New York City Norman Vincent Peale, the well-known author and pastor of Marble Collegiate Church, led an organization called the National Conference of Citizens for Religious Freedom to oppose Kennedy's election. News reports nevertheless suggested that anti-Catholicism was especially rife in the Middle West—more so, some claimed, than in the South—and embedded so firmly in Middle West culture that if it appeared on the West Coast, it was probably because of the dust bowl émigrés who lived there.[60] A Gallup poll in May 1960, though, showed that the speculation was only partly correct. Asked "If your party nominated a generally well-qualified man for president, and he happened to be a Catholic, would you vote for him?" 77 percent of the respondents nationwide said yes, 22 percent of the respondents said no, and 1 percent of the respondents were unsure. In the Middle West, the percentages were exactly the same as for the nation at large. It was the South where a substantially larger minority of people (38 percent) said they would not vote for a well-qualified Catholic. Among Kansans, 85 percent said they would vote for a well-qualified Catholic—the same proportion as in the Northeast and on the West Coast.[61]

The fact that one in every five or six voters would oppose a well-qualified person from their own party simply on religious grounds testified to the legacy of misgiving between Protestants and Catholics. Yet there were signs that these doubts were diminishing. One was that the same Gallup question asked in 1940 had shown a significantly higher level of opposition than in 1960. A second was that the tacit agreement forged during the Hoover and Smith campaign in 1928 against open expressions of religious bigotry had remained. A third was the work of Protestant, Catholic, and Jewish leaders to promote greater understanding and cooperation. The fourth was Kennedy's own declaration that a president's personal faith convictions could be distinguished from the more formal public duties of office governed by the constitutional separation of church and state. The cultural groundwork for that distinction was clearly in place. It was evident in Eisenhower's orientation toward religion as a private belief expressed in generic recognition of the Almighty, and was the implicit understanding that encouraged mainstream churches in Kansas communities to act as if their similarities were more important than their differences.[62]

Because Kennedy was the Democratic candidate, there was little reason for Kansans to think through the deeper conundrum of voting for a Catholic if that person was a Republican. They were inclined toward Nixon because they nearly always voted Republican and because he was Eisenhower's vice president. Still, the presidential election could not obscure the fact that Republican dominance was weakening in Kansas. The shift was especially evident in the state legislature, where Republican seats declined from 85 percent in 1952 to 61 percent in 1958, and in gubernatorial elections in which the popular vote for Republican candidates declined from 58 to 46 percent over the same period. The 1956 victory of George Docking, a Baptist from Clay Center who had been a Republican until 1932, and his reelection in 1958 made him the first two-term Democratic governor in the state's history.

The Republicans' decline was surprising in view of the fact that it occurred during the cold war and Eisenhower's tenure as president. The factors that contributed to this decline included voters' dissatisfaction with Eisenhower administration policies, and the factionalism among Kansas Republicans that became evident during the Roberts scandal and by 1956 had become an all-out war. But there were crucial economic and demographic factors as well.

The late 1940s and 1950s witnessed more departures from farming than in the 1930s. Older farmers retired, marginal farmers with small acreage quit, and even the more prosperous farmers experienced wide fluctuations in annual yields and earnings. The result was fewer farmers overall and dissatisfaction with farm policies among those who remained. The state's economy shifted increasingly toward nonagricultural trade and manufacturing, towns and cities became more significant, and parents looked increasingly toward sending their children to college. The impact on politics was to both reinforce Democratic segments of the electorate, especially in the increasingly populous and influential urban areas of Wichita and Kansas City, and evoke calls for legislative reforms to more fairly represent the changing interests of the population.[63]

Docking's reelection in 1958 demonstrated that economic issues were uppermost in voters' minds. He outmaneuvered Republican challenger Reed by pledging to repeal the .5 percent increase in the state sales tax enacted by the Republican-controlled state legislature, thus presenting himself as the fiscal conservative in the race. That fall's ballot included a controversial amendment to the state constitution that guaranteed nonunion employees the right to work. The amendment was favored by owners of small businesses and farmers seeking off-farm employment, but was opposed by union leaders, union workers in Kansas City and Wichita, and Governor Docking. Proponents mounted an advertising campaign showing that the amendment would benefit a wide spectrum of the population. Appeals emphasized individual freedom and self-determination against the threat of urban labor bosses telling people what to do. In an unusual move, a group of clergy members and educators rose in opposition to the amendment. The educators were nearly all from KU and the University of Wichita. The clergy were a coalition of Catholic priests and Protestant ministers from Wichita, Topeka, and the Kansas City area. Similar right-to-work measures failed in other states, but Kansans approved it by a large margin.[64]

Kansas celebrated its centennial on January 29, 1961, nine days into Kennedy's presidency. It was a conservative state devoted to individual freedom and fiscal restraint, far from the centers of national power, with little influence in Washington, and yet happily committed to the affairs of local communities, schools, and churches. By some appearances this was the same orientation toward politics that had been present for a century, but in major respects it was quite different. The prevailing sentiment was decidedly more bipartisan than it had been from the 1860s through the 1920s, and significantly less oppositional than it was during most of the 1930s and 1940s. The quiet conservatism of the 1950s was neither complacent nor marked by overwhelming cold war insecurities. There was the lingering sense of displacement from having been politically distant from Washington and out of sync with national trends. But the Eisenhower years evoked a centrist bipartisan style that most Kansans could embrace. It worked well for members of the established churches, and did reasonably well at including Democratic representation while retaining Republican dominance. It may have seemed almost perfect, but Kansans knew better. Nothing that good could last.

CHAPTER 5

AN ERA OF RESTRUCTURING

ON THE AFTERNOON OF MARCH 18, 1968, forty-two-year-old Senator Robert F. Kennedy journeyed by motorcade to Lawrence. Two
days earlier, following a surprisingly strong second-place finish by
challenger Eugene McCarthy against President Johnson in the New
Hampshire primary, Kennedy had announced his candidacy for the
Democratic presidential nomination. Speculation about the effects
of Kennedy's entry was feverish. Would he be able to win in the
primaries against McCarthy and Johnson? Was it a gamble worth
taking? Would his involvement weaken the Democrats and make
it easier for a Republican to win? Inside KU's massive Allen Fieldhouse, where Kennedy was to speak, students anxiously awaited
his arrival. The crowd of sixteen thousand that usually filled the
arena swelled to twenty thousand as chairs were set up on the pol-
ished basketball court and every aisle was taken up. Neatly dressed
students from the nearby business school sat next to self-described
hippies from humanities departments farther up the hill. While
some of the students wore Reserve Officers' Training Corps uni-
forms, others carried antiwar signs. Homemade banners for Mc-
Carthy and Nelson Rockefeller mingled with ones for Bobby.[1]

Eventually Kennedy arrived, late from having addressed a crowd
at Kansas State, and was introduced by Governor Robert Docking.
After teasing the crowd that he had come only to bring love from
Kansas State, Kennedy spoke of the growing restlessness in the nation about the war in Vietnam. He criticized the administration and
called for a new direction in bringing the war to a conclusion. On
the flight back to Washington he mused to correspondent Jimmy
Breslin, "Did you ever see anything like it? You can hear the fabric

ripping. If we don't get out of this war, I don't know what these young people are going to do." A KU student wrote the next day, "For a Republican state, Kansas sure gave him a hearty welcome. He's being practical about the war and negotiating, unlike Johnson and Nixon. I'm convinced to vote for him."[2]

Kennedy's visit punctuated a restructuring of Kansas religion and politics that was already in evidence by the late 1960s, and would continue for at least two more decades. The quiet conservatism of the 1950s gave way to activism borne of concerns about the escalating war in Vietnam and the struggle for racial equality. To these concerns were added questions about government's changing role in the provision of social welfare, controversies about the constitutionality of school prayer, and shifting standards of sexual morality and gender relations. Across the heartland, residents increasingly found themselves on one side or the other of these issues.

The fact that Kennedy spoke at campuses was indicative of changes in the composition and orientation of the electorate. The post–World War II baby boomers were coming of age and were attending college in rising proportions. Students had mobilized in large numbers during the 1964 election, and with the subsequent enfranchisement of eighteen to twenty year olds were poised to be even more important in 1968. Concerns that had once seemed distant, such as "Vietnam, race riots, selective service, psychedelic drugs, [and] parental, social and economic pressure for a good degree," a KU student wrote, now seemed much closer to everyday life.[3] Off campus, significant changes were also occurring. Growth in Wichita and around Kansas City, coupled with a decline in small towns and farms, pushed the center of gravity in state politics further in the direction of urban interests. Neither political party could be assured of continuing victories. The place of Catholics, Methodists, and other established denominations shifted as well. Confronting difficult social issues exacerbated intradenominational divisions and contributed to the growth of smaller independent churches.

By the 1980s, Kansas may have appeared to the casual observer as the same bastion of white Protestant Republicanism it had always been. But a closer inspection would show that politics had become more contentious and religion more divided. Congregations that had been satisfied in the 1950s to focus on activities within local communities were more often engaged in national politics and confronted with controversies within their denominations. The earlier sense of being out of step with the dominant national culture was reanimated for some, while others found it harder to imagine that Kansas was different from anywhere else. Both the religious and political climate became more conducive to activist social movements, and these movements in turn shaped both religion and politics. The turmoil of the 1960s and early 1970s became a prelude for a new alignment of conservative religious and political interests, and that alignment produced what would become known as the Religious Right. It was not that Kansans had lost their senses, as some charged, or that they had found their souls, as others hoped. To a remarkable degree, what Kansans thought of themselves and how they regarded their state were less important than during most of the state's history. Kansas nevertheless posed interesting questions for political analysts, just as it frequently had in the past. Was it a place where someone like Bobby Kennedy could win? Or was it better understood as a state in which only conservative Republicans were taken seriously?

STIRRINGS ON THE RIGHT

The first signs of a new conservatism in Kansas politics had few connections with religion and differed so little from the prevailing grassroots orientation toward politics that it largely went unnoticed. When President Kennedy was assassinated on November 22, 1963, Kansans responded in shocked horror with the rest of the nation and in the ensuing months turned to support Lyndon Johnson in carrying out the slain leader's unfinished legislative agenda. In the 1964 presidential election, Kansans gave Johnson a 54 to 45 percent victory over Arizona Republican Barry Goldwater, who carried only his home state and five other states in the deep South.

It was the first time that Kansas had gone to the Democratic column since voting for Roosevelt in 1936. Goldwater scared enough of the moderate Eisenhower Republicans that they voted for Johnson or refrained from voting at all. But Goldwater did appeal to a substantial number of voters, and his loss spurred them to action aimed at perpetuating a distinctly conservative voice in state and national politics.

The southern states that voted for Goldwater in 1964—Louisiana, Mississippi, Alabama, Georgia, and South Carolina—had all voted for Kennedy in 1960 and were won over to Goldwater by white voters unhappy with the civil rights movement. Racial politics would play a role in Kansas as well, but Goldwater's strength in the Middle West lay chiefly in concerns about Communism and support for fiscal conservatism. Kansans had voted for Nixon in 1960, not only because he was Eisenhower's vice president, but also because he promised to be tough on Soviet and Chinese aggression. On Kennedy's watch, the nation experienced the Cuban missile crisis, the humiliating Bay of Pigs disaster, a buildup of the Soviet nuclear arsenal, and the spread of Communism in Indochina. If residents of small Kansas towns had been able to imagine themselves far from the front when World War II began, that was no longer the case.

In 1954, McConnell Air Force Base in Wichita became the location of a $22 million construction project that turned it into a Strategic Air Command (SAC) facility serving as the coordinating point for a ring of eighteen nuclear-armed Titan II missile silos constructed at a cost of $80 million within a fifty-mile radius of Wichita. Meanwhile, in 1948 Forbes Air Force Base near Topeka had become a SAC base, trained bomber crews during the Korean War, and in 1961 became the center of operations for nine Atlas missile silos. Schilling Air Force Base in Salina underwent a similar transformation, providing bomber and gunnery training during World War II, becoming a SAC base in 1951, receiving upgrades of more than $250 million in the late 1950s, and during the Cuban missile crisis in 1962 maintaining twelve Atlas F intercontinental missiles on high alert. Elsewhere in the Middle West, SAC bases with ballistic missile support and long-range bomber capabilities included facilities in Knob Noster, Missouri; Grand Island, Kearney, Lincoln, and Omaha, Nebraska; Altus and Clinton, Oklahoma; Blytheville, Arkansas; Rapid City, South Dakota; and Minot and Grand Forks, North Dakota.[4] With so much military activity, it was hard for anyone in the Middle West to avoid imagining the worst. Farmers knew about land taken by the government for intercontinental nuclear missile silos, townspeople could see and hear the large bombers overhead, and schoolchildren learned to duck and cover as part of civil defense drills.[5]

During the 1964 presidential campaign few Americans denied that Communist aggression was a serious issue, but the public was divided about what should be done about it. A national study conducted during the two months prior to the election showed that 38 percent of the public favored doing something to rid Cuba of its Communist government, while 50 percent thought that the Cuban people should handle their own affairs, and 12 percent held some other view. Opinion was divided among both Republicans and Democrats, although those who had voted for Nixon in 1960 leaned more toward intervention in Cuba than those who had voted for Kennedy. The study also asked if farmers and business owners should be allowed to trade with Communist countries or not. This was a controversial topic, especially in the Middle West, because of grain exports to Russia and China. The survey found that 38 percent of Americans favored doing business with Communist countries, 56 were opposed, and 6 percent were undecided.[6]

Goldwater was more outspoken about Communism than his moderate Republican primary opponents, who included New York governor Rockefeller, Henry Cabot Lodge Jr. of Massachusetts, and Pennsylvania governor William Scranton. "Extremism in the defense of liberty is no vice" became the most memorable line of his acceptance speech at the 1964 Republican convention. That statement provided grist for President Johnson to assert that Goldwater's militancy could lead to nuclear war—a theme emphasized in the famous Daisy advertisement showing a young girl counting daisy petals and ending with a mushroom cloud in the background. By November hardly anyone expected Goldwater to win, but he continued to attract a sizable minority among voters who felt that Communism should be strongly resisted. In the study just mentioned, 39 percent of Middle Western respondents who opposed doing business with Communist countries said they planned to vote for Goldwater, while only 12 percent of those who favored trading with Communist countries did.[7] These responses were consistent with Goldwater's campaign advertisements in the region, which stated clearly that "trade with Communist countries is not in the interest of the United States," and were confirmed by interviews with farmers at the Kansas state fair in Hutchinson. Although he lost in Kansas, Goldwater received a warm welcome during a campaign stop in Wichita and won at least 50 percent of the vote in 40 of the state's 105 counties. His showing was especially strong in counties that had voted for Winrod in the 1938 Republican primary.[8]

Goldwater's candidacy was widely regarded as a contributor to the conservative movement that was to gain power in the coming years. Reagan's nationally televised speech in support of Goldwater late in the 1964 campaign helped him win the California governorship in 1966. Other Goldwater supporters included George H. W. Bush and conservative activist Phyllis Schlafly. The Kansas Republican leadership was divided. Former governor Fred Hall worked against Goldwater in the California primary, Governor John Anderson Jr. favored Rockefeller, and Congressman Hope worked on behalf of Lodge. But Goldwater supporters including Congressman Bob Dole and prominent Johnson County business leader Gordon Greb were amply represented among the eleven hundred leaders who gathered in Topeka in April 1964 for the Kansas Republican Convention. During the campaign, one of Goldwater's most active supporters was KU law student and former KU student body president Jerry Dickson, who headed the College Service Committee of the Young Republican National Federation. Dickson was succeeded by two other Kansans, Reuben McCornack, also a KU student body president, and Tom Van Sickle, a state senator. Van Sickle led what was known as the conservative syndicate faction of the Young Republicans, became the national head of the American Council of Young Political Leaders, was prominent in the movement to draft

Reagan for president in 1968, and served on the board of the American Conservative Union.[9]

Other conservatives worked outside the Republican Party. Separatist Conservative Party organizations emerged in Kansas, New York, and California during the 1962 gubernatorial elections. In 1964, the Kansas Conservative Party ran an independent candidate for governor (who received fewer than 2 percent of the vote) and eventually backed Goldwater for president when the National Conservative Council endorsed the Republican ticket. In 1966, Kansas Conservative Party delegates listened as national chair Kent Courtney urged followers to take a stronger stand against missiles that he said still existed in Cuba, termed Democrats Communists, and called President Johnson a National Socialist dictator. The Kansas Conservative Party supported controversial Alabama governor George C. Wallace for president in 1972. Leaders of both the Kansas Conservative Party and the conservative movement among Young Republicans had forged stronger ties with conservatives in the South during the previous decade.[10]

With several notable exceptions, religious leaders played few roles in organizing these conservative efforts, contrary to what critics at the time believed. The main exception was Billy James Hargis, a conservative Protestant pastor who preferred "Mr." to "Reverend," and led a ministry headquartered in Tulsa, Oklahoma, that included a regular radio broadcast on over four hundred stations and a magazine, *Christian Crusade*, with a circulation of a hundred thousand. Hargis had no direct connection with Kansas, other than his geographic proximity, but had received assistance in starting his radio ministry from Reverend Winrod and had received an honorary doctor of divinity degree from a Puerto Rican seminary founded by Winrod. Hargis began his radio work in 1950, and in 1953 was enlisted by Reverend Carl McIntire, who headed the fundamentalist International Council of Christian Churches, to supervise a project using balloons to drop Bibles behind the iron curtain. A year later Hargis began publishing essays for Winrod, and by the decade's end was gaining attention in the Middle West and beyond through his magazine articles, broadcasts, books, and conferences. Hargis warned of the dangers of Communism and liberalism, which he regarded as equivalent, if not related, threats to the nation, and called for personal repentance and salvation. Observers who scanned his literature expecting it to be the same as Winrod's, found it remarkably free of racism, anti-Catholicism, and anti-Semitism. Hargis's relevance to the restructuring of religion in Kansas would become evident later as a contributor to the division between conservative and liberal Protestants as well as new connections between the Middle West and South.[11]

Hargis was intimately involved with several conservative groups that included religious elements but were less overtly faith based than his own. In 1959 he was elected president of We the People, a national bipartisan coalition of anti-Communist, antilabor, and anti–New Deal conservatives that met annually in Chicago starting in 1955. We the People withheld support from Eisenhower in 1955 and 1956, honored Goldwater in 1958, and hosted Goldwater as its keynote speaker in 1959. Hargis gained notoriety in 1960 as the source of a controversial anti-Communist publication used by the U.S. Air Force, and in 1961 enlisted John Birch Society founder Robert Welch and four congresspeople associated with the National Conservative Coalition as We the People speakers. That year Hargis toured the country by bus to give speeches at municipal auditoriums about Communist infiltration, grew his staff in Tulsa to fifty, and commenced construction of a new headquarters on the city's outskirts.[12]

His widening circle of activities in 1961 included organizing a secret fraternity among conservative congresspeople, serving on the John Birch Society advisory board, working with Democratic senator Strom Thurmond of South Carolina to combat Communists in the military, and supporting Goldwater allies in the Phoenix city council election. The following year, Hargis sponsored conferences and institutes in Oklahoma and Colorado that included lectures by fundamentalist Baptist Bob Jones Sr. and a film narrated by Reagan about U.S. prisoners during the Korean War. He shared the We the People platform in 1963 with former Agriculture Secretary Benson and National Committee for Economic Freedom chair Willis E.

Stone, and in 1964 threw the weight of his *Christian Crusade* behind Goldwater's candidacy. It was widely believed that some of Goldwater's strength in the Middle West was from voters who followed Hargis's radio broadcasts and read his magazine.[13]

Groups with objectives similar to Hargis's included McIntire's International Council of Christian Churches, which claimed to represent the three hundred thousand members affiliated with fourteen fundamentalist denominations, and a fledgling independent movement organized by Denver Southern Baptist real estate developer Gerri von Frellick to encourage political participation by fundamentalist Protestant laypeople. McIntire's work included a weekly paper, the *Christian Beacon*, and five-day-a-week broadcasts on more than five hundred radio stations, while von Frellick's functioned on a smaller scale but claimed to include leaders in seventeen states. Another movement that gained widespread attention was the Christian Anti-Communism Crusade, which originated in 1953 in Waterloo, Iowa, under the leadership of local radio evangelist W. E. Pietsch and former McIntire associate Fred C. Schwarz, moving to southern California a few years later and continuing through the 1970s.[14]

How appealing these and other conservative movements may have been to the general public was difficult to ascertain. One indication was a study of Lawrence, conducted by historian Rusty L. Monhollon, who concluded that "through an intricate web of fraternal and civic organizations, church and work associations, and personal relationships, a grassroots anticommunist movement flourished in Lawrence through the 1960s and 1970s." Monhollon found groups such as the Lawrence Committee for a Free America and the Save America from Communism Council working with churches, the American Legion, and the Veterans of Foreign Wars to host public lectures and films as well as organize anti-Communist political meetings. Other indications came from surveys. A poll in 1964 showed that approximately a quarter of adults in the Middle West had heard of Schwarz's Christian Anti-Communism Crusade, the same proportion as in the nation at large. Among those who had heard of it, about a third regarded it favorably and a tenth were highly favorable. That meant perhaps 2 to 3 percent of Middle West residents who were strongly supportive of the group.[15]

More important than grassroots interest, though, were the networks that developed among influential business and political leaders who favored Goldwater in 1964, and continued to support conservative causes in the coming decades. Among these leaders was Texas oil executive H. L. Hunt, who attended Christian Anti-Communism Crusade meetings in Dallas, founded the International Committee for the Defense of Christian Culture, and provided major funding for Hargis's *Christian Crusade*. Others included former Major General Edwin Walker, who ran unsuccessfully with Goldwater's support for governor of Texas in 1962; Governor Wallace, who organized conservatives in Alabama on behalf of Goldwater; and investor and former GOP representative Howard Buffett, who sponsored Schwarz's Christian Anti-Communism Crusade rallies in Omaha.[16]

Besides taking a strong stand against Communism, Goldwater conservatives were adamant opponents of what they saw as wasteful big government programs and government interference in the marketplace. These were familiar themes in Kansas, fundamental to the criticisms that Capper and Landon had voiced so often toward Roosevelt, and consistent with the state's ideological distance from Washington bureaucrats. But they were arguments that returned stronger than ever in the 1960s because of rising taxes, and amid expanding expenditures for social welfare under the Kennedy and Johnson administrations. Nowhere were contentions against big government more clearly articulated than in the October 27, 1964, speech that catapulted Reagan to prominence as a potential Republican Party leader.

The speech was given to an audience in Los Angeles assembled for the purpose of showing that an audience was in fact present and was broadcast on national television through funding from corporate backers. Reagan had been giving three or four speeches a day, six or seven days a week, on behalf of Goldwater. He had much of the half-hour lecture memorized, and delivered it well. The speech peppered the audience with statistics and anecdotes demonstrating the government's ineptitude in one area after another. Eight minutes into the speech Reagan blasted the administration's farm policies, undoubtedly to amens from sympathetic viewers in Kansas. "The wheat farmers voted against a wheat program. The government passed it anyway," he chided. Turning to government's assault on freedom in cities and towns, he discussed the Area Redevelopment Agency initiated in 1961 to address poverty in distressed areas. Then he mentioned Kansas specifically. "They've just declared Rice County, Kansas, a depressed area. Rice County, Kansas, has two hundred oil wells, and the 14,000 people there have over 30 million dollars on deposit in personal savings in their banks." An authority on presidential rhetoric wrote that "The Speech," as it became known, threw facts and anecdotes at the audience so fast that they had no time to consider the substance, and could only respond by following the speaker's tone of outrage and incredulousness. Reagan's Kansas anecdote elicited loud groans and laughter from the audience followed by a long round of applause. Only after that interruption was he able to deliver the punch line: "When the government tells you you're depressed, lie down and be depressed."[17]

If viewers in Rice County were watching closely enough to have caught what Reagan said, they must have been stunned. Rice County had voted Republican for as long as anyone could remember, opting for GOP candidates by 70 percent in the past three presidential elections. So Reagan's anecdote could not be interpreted as a jibe at Rice County residents but rather at the phony bureaucrats in Washington who had no knowledge of Kansas. And yet it was an odd remark because it implied that Rice County residents were freeloaders. It also may have revealed that Reagan himself had little understanding of rural Kansas. If it were true that two hundred oil wells existed, nearly all the revenue would have gone to corporate owners and speculators in Wichita and Tulsa. The average family was living on less than five thousand dollars a year, and 20 percent had annual incomes of less than three thousand dollars. Unemployment was up because one of the county's two salt mines had just closed. And if anybody checked Reagan's statistics on bank holdings, they would have found him in error by a factor of three.

Whatever they may have thought of the speech, Rice County's voters defected in droves from Goldwater when they went to the polls the following week. In votes for Goldwater compared with votes for Nixon in 1960, only one other county registered as great a decline. Even Congressman Dole, who won reelection, lost by a sizable margin in Rice County to challenger Bill Bork.[18]

The truth was that ordinary Kansans had mixed feelings about government programs. It was good to be self-sufficient, and it was easy to imagine that bureaucrats in Washington were wasting taxpayers' hard-earned dollars. But it was reassuring to know that government funding was available for farm subsidies, soil conservation programs, Social Security, roads, schools, job training, housing for the elderly, and community development. A woman who grew up in north-central Kansas, not far from Rice County, recalled how relieved her parents were in the 1960s to have Social Security available. They were farmers, she said, with sinking crop prices and expensive machinery. "It wasn't until they started getting Social Security that they had any regular income at all." In her community, people were glad when a representative from the Social Security Administration hosted meetings at the courthouse to explain the procedures. In Mankato, where oil wells were nonexistent and average incomes were significantly lower than in Rice County, a group of farmers and merchants worked for several years to open a $1.2 million meatpacking plant, and succeeded only because of a loan from the Small Business Administration. In Rice County, 97 percent of farmers had been won over to government wheat allotment programs by 1964. They worried that Goldwater would end the programs and criticized Dole for failing to understand farmers' interests. In other communities, nursing homes and housing for senior citizens were being built with the help of government grants. Through state and federal partnerships, other programs were also expanding. Under Republican governor Anderson, for example, medical assistance for the elderly more than doubled between 1963 and 1964, and expansion occurred in mental health assistance, higher education, highways, and economic development as well.[19]

Still, there were opinion leaders whose interests were served by arguing that government was inherently incompetent, if not downright wasteful. This claim was especially appealing to members of the John Birch Society, which emerged in 1958 and had as many as a hundred thousand members nationwide by 1964. The John Birch Society gained a reputation for being staunchly anti-Communist, which indeed it was, but the organization's antipathy toward government was equally important. Robert Welch, the society's founder, grew up in North Carolina, attended the U.S. Naval Academy and Harvard Law School, and earned a fortune as the manufacturer of such well-known confections as Sugar Daddies, Junior Mints, and Pom Poms. A convert to Unitarianism, he retained enough of an affinity with his fundamentalist Baptist upbringing to select World War II Baptist missionary John Birch, killed in 1945 by Chinese Communists, as the namesake for his conservative organization. Welch believed firmly that government control was bad for the economy. He was close to being a libertarian in his economic views, and saw similarities between Communism in the Soviet Union and government bureaucracy in the United States. He opposed participating in the United Nations, fearing that organization was a step toward one-world totalitarianism.[20]

His cofounders were self-made businesspeople like himself, such as William Grede of Grede Foundries in Milwaukee, A. G. Heinshohn of Cherokee Mills in Tennessee, J. Howard Pew of Sun Oil in Philadelphia, and Fred C. Koch of Koch Industries in Wichita. Reared in Texas, Koch was a wealthy oil executive who made a fortune developing Russia's oil industry after failing to receive a potentially lucrative patent from the U.S. government. By the early 1960s, Koch Industries was the largest company in Kansas and would soon become the second-largest privately owned firm (after Cargill Industries) in the nation. Koch's association with the John Birch Society was relatively minor, but his influence in conservative politics was to grow, and be carried on nationally through the foundations he established and the work of his sons, Charles and David, both of whom would emerge as prominent civic leaders and philanthropists in their own right.[21]

Following so closely on concerns evoked by Senator Joseph McCarthy's investigations and the House Un-American Activities Committee, the John Birch Society came under scrutiny almost immediately by writers on the Left who feared it would exacerbate right-wing bigotry. Watchdog organizations collected pamphlets, monitored radio and television broadcasts, and sponsored polls to determine how much of an impact it was having. Prominent intellectuals, including historian Richard Hofstadter, political scientists Seymour Martin Lipset and Alan F. Westin, and sociologists Daniel Bell and Nathan Glazer wrote exposés of the extremism that was increasingly termed the radical Right. Catholic and Jewish leaders wrote essays denying Welch's claims that his organization included Catholics and Jews. In much of the commentary, writers identified the movement with religious fundamentalism, noting the involvement of Hargis and its similarities to Schwarz's Christian Anti-Communism Crusade. They also associated it with the Middle West, where pent-up feelings of being left out and left behind were presumed to be at work yet again. "The Birch Society has developed a thoroughly satisfying way for the thin-lipped little lady from Wichita," Westin wrote, "to work in manageable little daily doses against 'the Communists.'" Subsequent investigations demonstrated that neither of these impressions was valid. Unlike Schwarz's organization, which disproportionately attracted fundamentalist Protestants, John Birch Society supporters were no more likely to be fundamentalist Protestants than were other Americans, and they were more likely to be from the West Coast and South than from the Middle West. There was nevertheless one characteristic of Birch supporters with which conservative Kansans probably agreed: they were negatively disposed toward the "eastern establishment."[22]

In the aftermath of Goldwater's defeat, conservatives who supported him lost ground among Kansas Republicans but continued to have an active voice in the state. That voice was evident in two key elections. In 1966 Dole was reelected to the House of Representatives, and in the primary conservative incumbent Senator James B. Pearson defeated a liberal Republican challenger. The uncertainties that Kansas Republicans faced, however, were evident in a different way in another important race. Governor William H. Avery, a Republican farmer from Clay County who had been elected governor in 1964 after serving for a decade in the U.S. Congress and opposing construction of the Tuttle Creek Dam, was defeated by Democrat Robert Docking, the son of former governor George Docking. Avery attributed his defeat to having sponsored an unpopular state withholding tax, but observers said other issues were troubling voters as well, including the Vietnam War, campus unrest, and race relations.[23]

FROM DESEGREGATION TO BLACK POWER

Seventeen days after Bobby Kennedy's visit in March 1968, comedian Bill Cosby was performing at Hoch Auditorium on the KU campus when word came that Dr. Martin Luther King Jr. had been assassinated in Memphis. Cosby exited the stage for ten minutes, phoned his condolences to the King family, and then continued with a subdued performance to the stunned audience. In the days and weeks that followed, Kansas was not spared the unrest that erupted in cities and on campuses across the nation. Confrontations occurred at KU, in Lawrence, Wichita, and Kansas City. King's assassination was "the ultimate slap in the face of blacks in America," a man who was a student at East High School in Wichita at the time recalled. "Several hundred black students went across Douglas to a drive-in restaurant frequented by whites," he remembered. "A few minutes later several hundred whites showed up and fistfights began." Citizens in the state's small towns and all-white suburbs who had thought of the civil rights movement as a phenomenon of the South were surprised to discover that it was not. Whatever they may have thought about *Brown v. Board of Education*, it was easier to imagine that racial issues in the state had been settled in 1954, if not decades earlier, than to grasp their continuing significance.

Yet in reality, race was becoming increasingly important in Kansas politics, and was gaining more attention in some of the state's churches than at any time in the recent past.[24]

When the U.S. Supreme Court ruled in 1954 that segregated schools were unconstitutional, only fifteen schools in Kansas were segregated, representing approximately 2 percent of the state's 362,000 students. Although the case had been pending since 1951 when the U.S. District Court of Kansas ruled that the inferiority of segregated schools had not been demonstrated, the Topeka School Board ended segregation in September 1953, eight months prior to the Supreme Court's decision. The court's ruling did not put an immediate stop to segregation or ensure that African Americans received equal education in Kansas. Schools in Wichita, Kansas City, Topeka, Olathe, and smaller towns remained unequal in many instances because of districting and segregated housing. That was true in neighboring states as well, especially Missouri and Oklahoma. In 1956, when a national poll asked how the "government in Washington" was doing in terms of "being concerned about white and colored children going to the same schools," only 24 percent of middle westerners said it was "going too far." That was lower than the 35 percent nationally and well below the 51 percent of rural dwellers in other parts of the country who felt the government was going too far. Nearly half of middle westerners (47 percent) thought that the government was doing about the right amount, and 29 percent thought it was doing too little. In short, there was little evidence that middle westerners were disturbed that *Brown v. Board* was changing things in a way that would prove disruptive.[25]

A year later the controversy over school desegregation in Little Rock, Arkansas, when Governor Orval Faubus employed National Guard troops to impede integration of Central High School and President Eisenhower brought in soldiers from the U.S. Army to escort students, resulted in public opinion becoming more divided. A national poll conducted in late September 1957, found 42 percent of the public in support of Faubus's action and 47 percent opposed. A second poll two weeks later showed that 58 percent of the public supported Eisenhower's handling of the situation, while 31 percent disapproved. In a third survey half of the public agreed that the "government in Washington should stay out of the question of whether white and colored children go to the same school" and nearly half disagreed. In the Middle West 39 percent agreed, while 53 percent disagreed.[26]

For most Kansans, racial issues were more relevant to how they thought about national politics than to policies affecting their own communities. Twenty-three of the state's counties included no African Americans at all, and another forty-five included fewer than a hundred. Two-thirds of the state's ninety-one thousand African Americans lived in just three counties—Sedgwick, Shawnee, and Wyandotte—the locations of Wichita, Topeka, and Kansas City. It was in these communities that race relations became contested aspects of local and state politics. Wichita became the site of a successful desegregation effort in July 1958, when student members of the National Association for the Advancement of Colored People (NAACP) Youth Council organized a series of sit-ins at the Dockum Drug Store, which was part of the large Rexall chain. The Kansas legislature passed a civil rights law in 1959 banning racial discrimination in the state's hotels, motels, restaurants, and other places of public accommodation, but failed to pass legislation about fair employment practices and public housing. In 1960, the NAACP Youth Council used tactics similar to the ones in Wichita against segregated restaurants in Kansas City, Missouri—with mixed success.[27]

Churches and church leaders played a role in Kansas civil rights efforts, just as they did in the South. In 1956, the Kansas-Missouri Conference of the Colored Methodist Episcopal Church adopted a strong civil rights resolution condemning discrimination, and encouraging members to join the NAACP and become more active in pressing for voter registration. Later that year, two hundred white and African American clergy from Kansas, Missouri, and Nebraska met in Kansas City to consider practical steps toward improving race relations. One of the most active leaders was Mrs. O. M. Blount, the wife of state legislator William H. Blount and a lay member of the African Methodist Episcopal Church in Kansas City. Mrs. Blount served as vice president of Kansas United

Church Women and worked on behalf of civil rights organizations until her death in 1959. In Wichita, several churches contributed directly to the antisegregation activity in that city. The racially mixed First Unitarian Universalist Church included founding members of Wichita's Urban League, sponsored an experimental community theater group that performed about racial topics, and sent delegates to address the state legislature about fair employment practices. Several of its members staged sit-ins at Dockum's as early as 1952.[28] The Fairmount Congregational United Church of Christ, located near the Unitarian Church, was active in organizing the Kansas Anti-Discrimination Committee and the Urban League. Several of its members participated in the 1958 sit-ins at Dockum's. Organizations that participated in other civil rights activities during the 1950s included the Wichita Council of Churches, United Church Women, the YWCA, a spin-off organization of the YWCA called the Community Committee on Social Action, the Wichita Ministerial League, Congregation Emanu-El, St. Mary's Baptist Church, Brotherhood Presbyterian Church, and St. Peter Claver Roman Catholic Church.[29]

Studies of civil rights activism in other parts of the country have shown that churches contributed in several specific ways. They provided lay and clergy leaders who were trained and supported in congregations, and who acquired a vocabulary that inspired them to take action. The church buildings were set apart as sanctified spaces in which people could nurture one another, share their grievances, and learn civic skills such as speaking in public, leading meetings, and organizing programs. In these spaces, young people who may have had few opportunities to develop leadership skills elsewhere could practice, find role models, and gain self-confidence. Youth programs, church schools, Bible study groups, and opportunities to participate in choirs served in these ways. Black churches often served especially well as spaces of empowerment, giving members a chance to acquire skills denied them in other contexts. Sometimes the churches set themselves apart from their neighborhoods so completely that they became a refuge rather than a resource for community action, but in other instances they encouraged leaders to

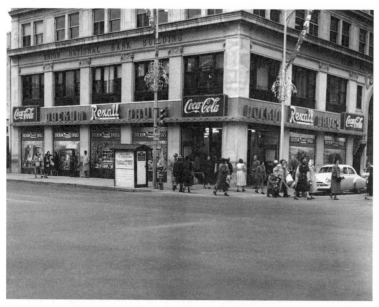

5.1 The Dockum Drug Company in Wichita, circa 1955, where the NAACP Youth Council sit-ins resulted in desegregation in 1958. Courtesy of the Tihen Collection, Wichita State University Libraries' Department of Special Collections.

develop networks with other organizations in and beyond the community. Members of congregations sometimes developed a sense of obligation to help others and work for social justice because of the assistance they received from their churches. They learned about opportunities to engage in social action and picked up ideas from successful efforts in other churches.[30]

Churches played all these roles in Kansas. A principal reason for the success of the sit-ins at Dockum Drug Store in 1958 after failed attempts in previous years was that the NAACP Youth Council leaders used the basement of St. Peter Claver Roman Catholic Church for several weeks prior to the sit-ins to practice. They role-played how to respond to threats, intimidation, waitresses' requests, the store's management, and the police—memorizing instructions such as "do not strike back" and "turn the other cheek." An important factor in motivating the sit-ins was the mother of Emmitt Till, the black teenager from Chicago who was beaten to death in Mississippi in 1955, visiting Wichita and speaking at the New Hope Missionary Baptist Church. The success of the Wichita sit-in led to ones in Oklahoma City in 1958 and again in 1959, the Kansas City sit-in, and events in Arkansas and Saint Louis, which preceded the much-publicized 1960 sit-in in Greensboro, North Carolina. Ron Walters who headed the Dockum's sit-in credited his interest in community activism to his mother, Maxine Walters, who became active in St. John Episcopal Church's outreach program to the homeless and served as a civil rights investigator on the Kansas Commission of Civil Rights.

Like Mrs. Walters, other Kansas civil rights activists gained support from their churches. In Arkansas City, a butcher named Virgil E. Watson who worked at the local packing plant became an ordained minister in the Church of God in Christ in 1954 after serving five years as a lay pastor. Feeling a calling to work for social justice, he became a member of the Kansas Civil Rights Commission and eventually was elected as the first African American mayor of Arkansas City. In Chanute, Roberta Thuston was a leader in the Church of God in Christ, having grown up singing in church choirs and leading prayer groups. She became active in civil rights work in 1952 and served as president of the local NAACP chapter. "I was a Christian and I thought I should do all the good I knew how to do," she said. A cross was burned on her lawn, and her church was set on fire, but she persisted as a community leader, and was instrumental in desegregating public accommodations and securing low-income community housing. Others included Manhattan's Rosa Hickman, who did not engage in community activism but served as official mother of the Baptist Church that provided a haven for African American members during segregation, and Reverend Stacy Hopkins, who played a critical part in desegregating Ottawa as pastor of Bethany Chapel Baptist Church.[31]

A rather different relationship with civil rights activism was evident in Lawrence at St. Luke African Methodist Episcopal Church. The congregation began during the Civil War though the efforts of African Americans and white abolitionists. A half century later Langston Hughes, who would become the famous Harlem writer, attended the church while living in Lawrence and wrote about it later in *The Big Sea*. In keeping with its heritage, St. Luke became one of the community's leading supporters of desegregation, freedom marches, and the work of King's Southern Christian Leadership Council. Another connection with civil rights activity outside Kansas emerged through the work of attorney Donald Hollowell. Born and raised in Wichita, Hollowell experienced repeated discrimination growing up in the 1920s and 1930s, and was disillusioned by the constant humiliation. He later described himself as a tough guy who as a child went reluctantly to church but was drawn by its message. "Finding Christ," he said, "removed the bitterness," and the Kansas toughness became a "resolve guided by love." He joined the military at Fort Leavenworth, attended Lane College in Tennessee on a scholarship, and was inspired by Paul Robeson to pursue a "sacred call" as a civil rights lawyer. After earning his law degree from Loyola University in Chicago, he returned to the South and became one of the region's best-known civil rights attorneys.[32]

There were two important church connections in the famous *Brown v. Board of Education* case. One was with St. John African Methodist Episcopal Church in Topeka, the historic congregation founded by ex-slaves in 1868. Oliver L. Brown, the father of third-grader Linda Brown, became the lead plaintiff in the case. At the time, many believed Brown appeared first among the thirteen plaintiffs because his name began with B. But another plaintiff, Darlene Brown, would have preceded him. The reason Oliver was chosen was that he was a male head of an intact family, held a steady union job as a welder for the Santa Fe Railroad, and was respected in his community. That respect derived especially from the fact that he was Reverend Brown, the assistant pastor at St. John African Methodist Episcopal Church.[33]

The connection went deeper, though. The case began four years before it reached the Supreme Court when Lucinda Todd contacted the NAACP because her daughter Nancy was excluded from a white school near their home. Todd was an active member at St. John's. That was how she knew Oliver. It was also how they knew Zelma Henderson, another plaintiff in the case. And it was where

Sharon Woodson, two years younger than Linda Brown, remembered receiving strength as she dealt with the challenges of being the only African American in her newly integrated classroom.[34]

The other church connection involved Charles Scott, a childhood friend of Oliver as well as the attorney who selected and represented him. His father, Elisha Scott, a nationally known civil rights attorney who served with Charles on the Brown case, was the son of black Exodusters who settled in Tennessee Town in Topeka. In 1896, Elisha attended a kindergarten, the first founded west of the Mississippi, established by Central Congregational Church pastor Charles Monroe Sheldon, who was working with low-income families in Tennessee Town and a year later would publish the bestseller *In His Steps*. The talented six year old captured the preacher's attention, and Sheldon became his mentor through graduation from Washburn Law School in 1916. In honor of Sheldon's assistance and friendship, Scott named his son Charles Monroe Sheldon Scott.[35]

Broader though still tentative steps toward supporting racial equality took place in the 1960s. Kansas Methodist Episcopal leaders voted in 1963 to end a quarter century of separate annual conferences for white and black congregations. Kansas Disciples of Christ churches moved to end racially separate conventions at about the same time. In Lawrence, members of the Ninth Street Baptist Church and the Plymouth Congregational Church were instrumental in organizing a fair housing committee, and initiating interracial neighborhood fellowship groups. In 1964, United Church Women circulated petitions in congregations in Lawrence, Topeka, and Wichita in support of nondiscrimination in housing, and at the organization's national meeting in Kansas City, Missouri, declared themselves opposed to the John Birch Society, the Ku Klux Klan, White Citizens Councils, and other extremist organizations that "breed suspicion, division, and hatred." The General Assembly of the United Presbyterian Church approved a resolution in 1965 opposing state laws banning interracial marriages, which proponents hoped could serve as a statement against racism without seeming to encourage interracial marriage. A similar effort to

5.2 Tennessee Town Kindergarten in Topeka, organized by Dr. Charles M. Sheldon (right), attended in 1896 by Elisha Scott who, with his son Charles Monroe Sheldon Scott, served as attorneys in the 1954 *Brown v. Board of Education* lawsuit. Courtesy of KansasMemory.org, Kansas State Historical Society, Copy and Reuse Restrictions Apply.

find a middle ground occurred in 1966, when the Kansas Council of Churches attempted unsuccessfully to mediate a rift between the Kansas NAACP chapter and Governor Avery's Commission on Civil Rights over allegations of cronyism.[36]

Colleges and universities became another focal point of civil rights organizing. Although Kansas colleges and universities admitted black students from 1870 onward, segregation and exclusion from many campus activities continued through World War II. Occasionally these practices were contested, such as at KU in 1927 over discrimination against black athletes, and in 1939 when black students were denied admission to a Count Basie concert. But activism increased during the early 1960s and especially in 1965 as violence against marchers in the South intensified. On March 9, 1965, white segregationists in Selma, Alabama, attacked Reverend James Reeb, a thirty-eight-year-old Unitarian pastor who had grown up in Russell, Kansas. Reeb died two days later. King eulogized him as a person who "dared to live his faith." Students in Wichita held a mass memorial service for Reeb. Methodist, Catholic, and interdenominational campus ministries at KU and Kansas State organized carloads of students to spend spring break and the summer participating in southern civil rights activities along with rebuilding firebombed churches. Mennonites at Bethel College in Newton did the same. Southwestern College students in Winfield initiated an effort to desegregate the town's barbershops. At KU, more than a hundred students were arrested after occupying the chancellor's office in protest of racial discrimination in the school's sororities and fraternities. The pastor of St. Luke African Methodist Episcopal Church assisted those who could not raise the twenty-five dollars to post bond. Following their release, the students regrouped at the Wesley Methodist Student Center and eventually won most of their demands. The lawyer who represented the students, Chester I. Lewis Jr., was a graduate of KU Law School and had been a Dockum Drug Store sit-in organizer in 1958. By 1965, Lewis was president of the NAACP in Wichita, and was successfully pressing for complete desegregation of the city's all-black schools and bringing civil rights lawsuits against some of the city's leading corporations. Lewis resigned from the NAACP three years later and endorsed the black power movement.[37]

Black power was the political slogan of a younger cohort of civil rights activists, including Stokley Carmichael of the Student Nonviolent Coordinating Committee and Bobby Seale of the Black Panther Party for Self-defense. Its adherents were critical of the NAACP and the Southern Christian Leadership Council, more favorably disposed toward the use of violence in some instances, and in other cases, more interested in black nationalism and separatism. Public opinion was polarized beyond the divisions already present concerning desegregation and nonviolent civil rights activism by the rise of black power, the assassination of King, and the violence that occurred in cities and on campuses.

Other than in Wichita, Kansas City, and a few other communities, most Kansans experienced these activities through television and newspapers, rather than in their congregations or schools. Church members knew that King had enlisted the support of church leaders and evoked resistance from others. Congregations heard clergy condemning riots or speaking against the conditions causing them. Readers of church periodicals would have learned of contentious gatherings of Episcopalians, Catholics, Baptists, or Presbyterians at which different views of the civil rights movement were debated. Parishioners may have been asked to contribute money to emergency civil rights funds or learned that their denomination's participation in the National Council of Churches was helping to finance civil rights demonstrations. They would likely have read that helmeted police used tear gas in Kansas City's Swope Park to quell rioters in 1967, and that three days of violence in 1968 left six of the city's residents dead and more than five hundred in jail. They may have noticed clergy in clerical collars marching in Kansas City and being confronted by police. Many may have favored the Disciples of Christ's pledge to help the poor, but been shocked to learn that the denomination applauded the black power movement and endorsed revolutionary civil disobedience. They may have felt sympathy with Roman Catholics in Cincinnati who walked out of a sermon on racial justice or a Lutheran businessperson in Kansas City who said it was not Jesus's way to get involved in social issues.[38]

Seventy-five miles southwest of Kansas City, Garnett was a town of three thousand surrounded by wheat fields and grassland, and populated by Methodists and Catholics, Presbyterians and Baptists. Its claim to fame was that it was the home of the oldest church pew manufacturing company in North America. Otherwise, it was an ordinary Middle West town. George Gallup called it a barometer community. So in October 1968, the *New York Times* sent its Washington correspondent Nan Robertson out for a visit. Robertson discovered a peaceable kingdom, like something from a Victorian novel, where crime was nonexistent and African Americans almost were too. The residents nevertheless were concerned about crime and moral decay, government spending and inflation, rebellious youth and racial tensions. They were especially troubled by the racial unrest they saw daily on the television news. "I can see how the Negroes want their rights," a twenty-six-year-old

Methodist woman said, "but after they get them, why won't they work to keep their jobs like white people do?" A liberal Democrat at the Presbyterian Church said there was talk at her church that "those colored folks aren't going to get it—whatever 'it' might be—until they prove themselves."[39]

At the polls two weeks later, Garnett cast 57 percent of its ballots for Nixon, 33 percent for Hubert Humphrey, and 10 percent for Wallace. Whatever they may have felt about African Americans and the push for civil rights, they were not ready to endorse Wallace. He was a "hothead," a Garnett resident said, who would "throw us into a greater civil war than we have." They were afraid of him, another resident explained, because "he'd stir up the colored people if he were elected." Statewide, Garnett proved to be a good barometer. The Kansas tally was 55 percent for Nixon, 35 percent for Humphrey, and 10 percent for Wallace. Garnett's views of African Americans also reflected wider sentiments. In a national poll, 63 percent of white Americans thought Negroes had "less ambition than whites," and 67 percent felt that Negroes were "asking for more than they were ready for." A large minority of whites also believed that African Americans "wanted to live off handouts," "had less native intelligence than whites," and "kept untidy homes." At least 40 percent of whites held these views.[40]

In the Middle West the prevailing mood was deeply ambivalent. On the one hand, there was widespread awareness among white voters that times were changing, and that they also needed to change. White voters said they supported African Americans' right to live wherever they wanted and understood that most African Americans wanted desegregation. On the other hand, white voters overwhelmingly thought the civil rights movement was pushing ahead too quickly, regarded it as mostly violent, and believed it was hurting African Americans more than it was helping them. The least charitable interpretation was that white voters wished the civil rights movement would simply go away. A more nuanced interpretation was that public opinion, like the civil rights movement itself, was complex. People could be swayed by what they saw on television or heard at church. Or their views could be driven by underlying fears, personal anxieties, and values that had little to do with the issues at hand. They might vote Republican, as they had always done, and worship at the Methodist or Catholic Church. But they could easily find themselves disagreeing with a political candidate or a person of the cloth. In the meantime, civil rights was not the only unsettling issue.[41]

NIXON AT KANSAS STATE

If the civil rights movement affected Kansans mostly from a distance, the Vietnam War brought national politics painfully closer to home. In 1963, fewer than 16,000 U.S. troops were stationed in Vietnam. That number climbed to almost 130,000 by early 1965, and peaked at 543,000 in April 1969. Another 50,000 were stationed in Thailand. Fort Riley, where the First Infantry trained for jungle patrol in summer heat and helicopters practiced sorties over the Kansas hills, became one of the major centers of deployment. In total, 3.4 million U.S. soldiers served in Southeast Asia during the war, nearly 2.6 million within the borders of South Vietnam itself. More than 300,000 were wounded, and 58,156 died. By the end of 1965, 32 soldiers from Kansas were dead. Over the next three years the number of deaths rose from 57 in 1966 to 102 in 1967, and to 183 in 1968 before declining to 137 in 1969. By the time it was over, 627 soldiers from Kansas were dead, mostly in their early twenties. Nearly every community—from small towns like Hope, Anthony, Lindsborg, and Larned, to metropolitan Wichita, Lawrence, Topeka, and Kansas City—suffered losses. They were men like twenty-four-year-old Steve Train from Lindsborg, whose plane was shot down in 1970; twenty-three-year-old machine gunner Patrick O'Brien from Liberal, who died from small-arms fire in 1967; and twenty-two-year-old Lance Corporal David Helson from Hutchinson, who died in a mortar attack in 1968.[42]

As casualties mounted, the war became increasingly unpopular. Disapproval of President Johnson's handling of the war rose in national polls from 22 percent in September 1965 to 57 percent in February 1968. Initially the Middle West appeared to be solidly in favor of halting the Communists' aggression. But by early 1966 when President Johnson resumed the bombing of North Vietnam, the situation was coming to be viewed as a quagmire. Force was needed, people said, mainly to prevent U.S. casualties from becoming even worse. "We are asking our boys to fight with one hand tied behind their backs if we don't bomb the enemy's sources of supply," one Kansan explained. Interviews in Dodge City showed that opinion was divided. Sergeant Frank Sanchez Jr.'s death when Vietcong fire downed his helicopter brought the war home. The community filled Our Lady of Guadalupe Church for the funeral Mass.[43]

The war was on everyone's minds. Young men were enlisting to avoid worse assignments as draftees. Enrollment at the junior college was up as students sought deferments. Merchants and farmers were being affected by late deliveries and personnel shortages. A young wife whose husband was in boot camp had no income. A mother said she was "scared green" they were going to draft her son. "I can't even watch pictures of fighting and wounded soldiers on television," she said. Seventy percent of the letters from Dodge City to Congressman Dole's office were about the war. People "want to know what's going on" and "when it's going to end," Dole reported. "They're about evenly divided between escalation and negotiation." Amid the concerns there were nevertheless strong indications of patriotism. "We just can't do enough for those soldiers," a Presbyterian woman observed. "The attention those draft card burners have gotten makes me so mad I could spit fire."[44]

By July 1967 the mood in Dodge City, like the sentiment nationally, was decidedly more negative. Two more young men from the community—twenty-two-year-old Phillip Hines and twenty-six-year-old Charles Hemmingway—had become casualties of the war, and more than five hundred from the area were serving in Vietnam. "You can't plan anything for the future with something like this hanging over you," a young man said. A woman whose husband was in Vietnam said, "It seems silly to be fighting when there's so much to be done here at home." A poll at the high school, where people had been satisfied with the war a year before, showed serious doubts about it now. "There's a strong undercurrent of change here," the mayor said. "People are beginning to question everything—especially what our leaders tell us and the wisdom of going ahead in Vietnam." An antiwar group calling itself Western Kansans Concerned about Vietnam published a full-page ad encouraging readers to express their dissent to neighbors, clergy, and elected officials. The Presbyterian woman who had been hawkish was more conflicted. She opposed an antiwar resolution passed by her denomination, but admitted she was weary of the war. "I'm awfully tired of not getting anywhere." Her pastor was uncertain what to do. "Privately I think this war is a sin," he said, "but I can't stand up in front of my congregation and say this." Congressman Dole, who supported the war, was worried too. "This unrest is going to be felt by somebody," he mused, thinking about the next election. "I just hope it isn't me."[45]

But if the public was becoming restive about the war, there were misgivings about efforts to oppose it. A national poll in April 1968 showed that only 37 percent of the public approved of churches becoming involved in social and political issues, such as the urban crisis, Vietnam, and civil rights, while 59 percent disapproved. The reaction to public demonstrations was even less positive. A poll in November 1969 found that only 19 percent of the public approved of groups that had been "holding public protests against the United States' involvement in Vietnam," while 77 percent disapproved. In Kansas, liberal Republican representative Robert Ellsworth challenged incumbent conservative Republican Pearson in the 1966 Kansas primary for a seat in the U.S. Senate. Ellsworth criticized President Johnson's handling of the war in a highly publicized speech in Great Bend. But Pearson, who supported the war, fended off Ellsworth's challenge and retained his seat in the general election. Dole's bid for the state's other senate seat in 1968 was successful by a 60 to 39 percent margin. He won handily even in Dodge City, where he received 57 percent of the vote. Democratic governor Docking won reelection, but only by 52 percent, having been put in the spotlight in 1967 by a visit to Vietnam at the request of President Johnson.[46]

Johnson's decision not to seek reelection, which he announced near the end of a nationally televised speech on March 31, 1968, set the stage for the Democratic contest among Kennedy, McCarthy, and Humphrey. The day before Johnson's announcement, Kennedy had won a minor victory at the Democratic state convention in Topeka when Governor Docking persuaded the delegates to remain uncommitted until the national convention in Chicago in August. The *Kansas City Star* had been increasingly critical of Johnson and taken a more dovish position toward the war all spring. Kennedy's speeches at KU and Kansas State had gained favorable publicity, and there was optimism that he could beat Johnson and go on to win the general election even in the staunchly Republican farm belt states. His assassination in Los Angeles on June 6 left the race principally between Humphrey and Nixon, with Wallace as the strongest third-party contender. Nixon's victory in November temporarily tilted public opinion more favorably toward how the war was being handled. Polls conducted in spring 1969 found about half the public approving of the president's handling of the situation in Vietnam, about a quarter disapproving, and the remainder with no opinion. A year later almost half still approved, but because enough of those who previously had no opinion became negative, disapproval was almost as common in several polls as was approval.[47]

The increasing polarization could be traced to policies toward the war itself and wider events. A sizable majority of the public wanted the war to end, but opinion was divided about how to achieve an honorable settlement. People wondered whether a settlement could in fact be achieved, how much the South Vietnamese government could be trusted, and who should participate in peace talks. The wider events included civil rights demonstrations, race riots, and campus unrest. Major protests took place during spring 1968 at Columbia University, Howard University, the University of Wisconsin at Madison, and the University of North Carolina at Chapel Hill. On August 24, leaders of the National Student Association representing 1.7 million students on 366 campuses met at

Weber Hall on the Kansas State campus in Manhattan. Association president Edward Schwartz said there was a "very deep-seated revolutionary feeling" among the students and predicted that "there will be protests all over the place." In Chicago at the Democratic National Convention demonstrations were already under way. The next evening an estimated 10,000 protesters clashed with 1,000 police. More than 500 protesters and police were injured in the ensuing melee. When asked what they thought of the event, 56 percent in a Gallup poll the following week said they approved of the way that the Chicago police dealt with the young people, 31 percent disapproved, and 13 percent had no opinion.[48]

Differences of opinion among young people themselves were in quieter ways increasingly evident in clothing, grooming, lifestyles, and sexual behavior. A few miles from Lawrence, a group calling themselves the Kaw Valley Hemp Pickers lived communally in a rented farmhouse, wrote poetry, dropped acid, and relished in free love. On the KU campus, students and administrators were embroiled in controversy about birth control. State law had been amended in 1963 to give married women access to the pill, and public funding for family planning services became available in 1965. By 1968, the question was how much access unmarried women should have and what role the university health service should play in providing birth control. Religious groups joined with administrators and health officials in weighing the issue. Most of the campus ministries sided with Planned Parenthood and the Women's Liberation Front in arguing for wider access to birth control, while several of the organizations, including the Catholic chaplaincy and Campus Crusade for Christ, took the opposing view. The debate continued for several years, during which time the campus roiled with debates about gender equality, gay and lesbian activities, sexual freedom, and marijuana.[49]

How alien these discussions were to Kansans in small towns and even to college freshman from these towns was suggested in conversations conducted by journalist Douglas E. Kneeland during summer 1968 in Smith Center, a town of twenty-seven hundred near the historic geographic center of the United States in Smith

County. Smith Center had been a hotbed of populism in the 1890s, but like the rest of the state had voted Republican in nearly every election since then. Kneeland was surprised to see no yard signs or bumper stickers for Nixon. But residents were intensely interested in what was happening in the wider world. They were disturbed by the changes they saw, and doubtful that they could do anything about them. "This is real conservative country out here," the local newspaper editor told him. "Folks are really concerned about these riots in the cities and lawlessness. They want to restore law and order somehow." They were troubled by the war, yet unsure which of the presidential candidates, if any, could be trusted to move the situation in a better direction. At a Lions Club dinner, men joked that "fellows on Wall Street" had probably already decided the fall election. There was just a "feeling of helplessness," one of the men said afterward. "We have so little to say about the way things are going." That seemed true even in their families. Most of the young people, they explained, were "pretty good kids," and the community took pride in its consolidated high school. It had a winning football team, and most of the young people were going on to college after high school. Yet they were facing challenges and temptations that their parents had never experienced. College was an alien world. Careers were uncertain. The young people knew they would encounter protesters and people from different racial and ethnic backgrounds. They imagined being free to make new choices. "You could wear a miniskirt," a seventeen year old told Kneeland, "but we don't. If a girl was real nice and went to church all the time and she wore a miniskirt once, that would be the end of her reputation."[50]

Earl Jackson was teaching high school near Smith Center in 1968. The changes taking place among his students worried him. He was a child of the Great Depression. As a teenager, he worked on farms herding cattle and lifting hay bales. His dream was to own a farm, but after serving in Korea and coming home with shrapnel in his leg, he worked his way through college and went into teaching. He expected a lot from his students. The tests in his history and French classes were among the toughest in the school. He was just as tough after school as a coach. Jackson gave the boot to any player caught drinking or smoking. The war bothered him. He knew what war was like. Years later the disrespect that the soldiers received still made him angry. "These boys came home and they were called names," he said. It was the "hippie group generation. They hated the soldiers." That was not all that upset him. Everything was changing so fast. Youngsters, he feared, were growing up on television, not learning to work hard enough, and unsure of their moral grounding. Jackson wondered where it was all headed.[51]

The question uppermost on young people's minds was how best to pursue their dreams. Miniskirts and birth control were relevant to the extent that they affected a girl's reputation. The war was relevant because it posed both risks and opportunities. Farmers' sons had diminishing expectations of being able to farm. College students who sold pots and pans to cover tuition and worked as oil field roustabouts in the summers wondered if there would be jobs in Wichita or Kansas City when they graduated. However abhorrent the war may have been, the military offered a chance to gain skills and earn respect. Joining the army was more honorable in small towns than becoming a dissident. A woman who grew up on a dairy farm in eastern Kansas said her main dream in high school was to get married. She wanted a man who was a conservative Baptist like herself. She hoped he would not be a farmer. A woman from western Kansas recalled wanting to be a beautician and raise good children like her mother had. She was overjoyed when her boyfriend at Fort Hays State College asked her to marry him. A man from Fredonia said he "didn't progress very well" in high school, but loved 4-H club and started raising hogs in ninth grade. He just "wanted to get started and get to work." A woman in Hoxie whose husband spent a year in Vietnam said their dream was to return to their hometown and do whatever they could. They ran a motel. A man who wound up in Pratt thought about being a theology student, but decided they "were all draft dodgers" and he "didn't want to be associated with that." He majored in business, served in Vietnam, and got a job in a chain store when he returned.[52]

The hope that normalcy would soon return with Nixon's victory was not fulfilled. The war continued. Inflation soared, and jobs diminished. On October 15, 1969, opponents of the war organized protests and teach-ins in cities and on campuses across the nation. In Lawrence, meetings to plan the day's events were held at the First United Methodist Church, the day itself began with a breakfast at the First Christian Church, workshops were held at the high school and on the KU campus, and the day concluded with a town meeting at which withdrawal and the moral impact of the war were discussed. More than 100 people attended the town meeting, and an estimated 5,000 students participated in a rally earlier in the day. The events elicited criticism as well as support. Residents declared themselves part of the silent majority whose lives were focused on children and jobs. They supported the president, and were fed up with protests and demonstrations. A month later an antiwar demonstration in Washington, DC, on November 15 drew an estimated 500,000 participants, and a West Coast demonstration in San Francisco attracted 250,000 protesters. About 300 Kansans took part in the Washington demonstration. In Lawrence, 150 people held a small demonstration and 300 participated in a teach-in on campus. Criticism was again evident as residents flew flags to show their patriotism, and the newspaper editorialized that demonstrations gave "aid and comfort to the enemy" and did "harm to the national climate."[53]

Unrest continued the following spring. On May 4, 1970, members of the Ohio National Guard opened fire on unarmed protesters at Kent State University, killing four students and wounding nine others. Two students were killed in a similar incident at Jackson State College in Mississippi. Meanwhile, bombing in Vietnam increased and fighting spread as U.S. forces invaded Cambodia. In response to the escalation, more than four million students on more than 450 campuses went on strike. KU's "Days of Rage" began several weeks earlier when a homemade bomb exploded at Anchor Savings near the campus. A few days later the Kappa Sigma fraternity house was set on fire, and the Gambles store in downtown Lawrence was firebombed and destroyed. A firebomb ignited a major blaze at the student union on April 20 that burned out of control for several hours and caused nearly a million dollars in damage. The Kent State killings in May resulted in a large demonstration on campus and a smaller one at which police used tear gas against students blocking a highway near campus. By the end of June, some fifty firebombings and acts of arson had taken place in Lawrence.[54]

Against this backdrop, President Nixon traveled to Kansas in September 1970 to give a major address at Kansas State in Manhattan. A few days before the Kent State killings Nixon had derided campus protesters as "bums." Everyone expected the protests to continue in the fall. It was uncertain whether Nixon would accept Kansas State's invitation. But the event was part of the university's distinguished Alfred Landon lecture series. Previous speakers included Reagan, George Romney, Nelson Rockefeller, and General W. C. Westmoreland. Aides decided that Kansas State was a safe bet for the president—maybe the only campus in the country that was.[55]

The speech took place on September 16, 1970, at Kansas State's Ahearn Fieldhouse, to a capacity crowd of 15,500 students, faculty, and invited guests, while hundreds more listened outside on loudspeakers. Landon came out of retirement to introduce the president, and Nixon praised him as one of the great elder statesmen in the United States. Nixon then spoke at length about the bombings and burnings on the nation's campuses, likening them to Palestinian guerrilla terrorism. He described the current situation as a great "moral and spiritual crisis." Destructive activists selfishly seeking their own way, he said, were a cancerous disease spreading against the responsible majority, and threatening the fabric of U.S. higher education and society. "What corrodes a society even more deeply than violence itself is the acceptance of violence," he remarked. "When this happens, the community sacrifices more than its calm, and more even than its safety. It loses its integrity and corrupts its soul."[56]

The audience responded enthusiastically to the lecture, interrupting it repeatedly with extended applause. But several hecklers tried to disrupt the speech with taunts about the war. Initial reports said there were forty hecklers, and that as soon as they had been identified, they would be suspended. Then it was determined that the number was twenty or perhaps fifteen, and that the students would not be suspended, either to avoid turning them into martyrs or because there was insufficient evidence. Word soon spread that heckling had also occurred among the faculty. One of the hecklers was the distinguished historian and Eisenhower biographer Stephen E. Ambrose, who had joined the faculty that fall. Ambrose was distraught that Nixon's focus was on campus violence when headlines that morning described record bombings in Southeast Asia. He and his wife, he wrote later, became social outcasts in Manhattan following the incident. He took a position at Louisiana State University in New Orleans the following year. More than three decades later, an investigation of FBI files discovered that the supposed student hecklers were not from Kansas State at all but instead were members of an out-of-town antiwar organization that the FBI had been monitoring and knew were planning to attend Nixon's lecture. None of that, though, was known at the time. Commentators everywhere focused on the event itself. Was the heckling justified? Or did it underscore Nixon's concerns?[57]

Reactions showed how easy it was for an out-of-the-way campus where nobody expected anything controversial to happen to be drawn into the national debate. Nixon's supporters were delighted with the speech. Wealthy Chicago insurance executive W. Clement Stone teamed up with *Reader's Digest*, Pepsico, and Warner-Lambert Pharmaceuticals to have the speech rebroadcast on national television. A national poll showed that 90 percent of the public thought campus protests were completely or mostly unjustified, while only 3 percent thought they were completely justified. In a Harris survey, 64 percent of the public blamed campus unrest on "irresponsible students who just want to cause trouble." In yet another poll, 24 percent of the public said campus protesters were the main reason that the war itself was going badly.[58]

Realizing the issue's public relations potential, President Nixon emphasized law and order in speeches throughout the fall, and Vice

President Spiro Agnew stepped up the barrage against campus dissidents. Not to be outdone, more than a hundred Democrats in the U.S. House of Representatives condemned the hecklers, calling their actions "abhorrent to anyone who believes in free speech." Critics of the administration naturally saw the incident differently. In the *New York Times* Tom Wicker, acknowledging the hecklers' rudeness, stressed that dissent is "all too often strong-armed into silence these days." Nixon should have condemned police riots and violence against protesters, Wicker observed. And if anything was corroding the soul, it was the administration's continuing violence in Vietnam. That was similar to Ambrose's criticism. Another Kansas State faculty member, associate professor of history Bruce S. Eastwood, said that Nixon's speech had been singularly unhelpful: "Speak with the air of a moralizing preacher in fundamentalist country and ovations follow."[59]

It was not that Nixon spoke literally as a preacher but rather that the president described the mood in the United States as a spiritual and moral crisis—a theme to which he returned again and again in coming years. The audience in Ahearn Fieldhouse would have understood, or at least assumed that they did. How a person felt about the United States ran deeper than whether the war in Vietnam was going well or badly. A good American was a person who played by the rules and knew right from wrong. To be spiritual was to believe in something, to rise above petty self-interest and cynicism. Win or lose, Nixon said, there had to be a dogged spirit of determination. Kansans could imagine that was part of their character, the pioneer spirit that ran in their blood.

Perhaps it was the same message that they heard in their houses of worship. Words like "spiritual" and "moral" were sufficiently ambiguous to apply equally to Methodists and Catholics, Baptists or Quakers, and could suggest a relationship with God or simply an aspect of a person's character. They were the same words that evangelist Billy Graham used when giving his own Landon lecture a few years later. The spiritual crisis had become so pervasive, Graham said, that people were filled with despair. "It's time to believe

again, time to hope again, time to stand up and be counted again,"
he declared. "You can only do it if you have peace with God."[60]

DIVISION IN THE CHURCHES

Parishioners may have been searching for peace with God, but
it was not a propitious moment to be finding it in the pews. The
1960s divided religion in ways unseen since the Civil War. The divisions cut through denominations and congregations, separating
churchgoers into ideological camps that mapped less neatly onto
geographic regions, as had been the case a century earlier, than
along demographic and partisan lines. Clergy and lay members
who leaned in one direction on Goldwater conservatism typically
leaned in the same direction on racial issues and the Vietnam war,
while those with opposing views on one topic frequently held opposing views on other topics as well. In Kansas, it was not so much
that large numbers became vocal proponents of either side. It was
rather that people who hewed to the middle found kindred spirits
more on one side or the other. The fault lines were not entirely
new. And yet they increasingly offered a new vocabulary of religious self-designation. A person who previously claimed only to
be a Methodist or Catholic was now more likely to identify as a
conservative or liberal Methodist or Catholic.

Scholars would later debate whether the restructuring that
took place during these years cut mostly between denominations
or through the middle of them, and whether the tensions became
worse, affected a lot of people, or were limited to a few. In reality,
the dynamics were complex enough that it was helpful to see how
they played out in specific locations. Kansas was particularly interesting because it became identified with the Religious Right, but the
path it took was by no means straightforward.

The remarkable staying power of Methodism during most
of the state's history was an important consideration. In 1980,
when the next tally of religious bodies was conducted, the United

Methodist Church was still the largest Protestant denomination in Kansas with 262,000 adherents. Presbyterians ranked a distant second with 78,000 adherents. Of the other established denominations, American Baptists were next with 73,000 adherents, and the Christian Church (Disciples of Christ) followed with 69,000. The Lutheran Church Missouri Synod had 58,000 adherents. And the Evangelical Lutheran Church in America included 46,000 adherents. Methodists, in short, were far more numerous than any other Protestant denomination. Indeed, there were as many Methodists as Presbyterians, Baptists, and Lutherans combined.[61]

Methodism's numerical strength continued to reside in the state's less populated areas. By 1980, half of the state's overall population was concentrated in just seven counties, but only a third of the state's Methodists were in those counties. Two-thirds were living in smaller areas. It was no accident that this was the case. Over the past century, Methodists had worked hard to establish churches in smaller towns. Theirs were often the first and largest churches in these communities. During the Depression and World War II, when many of the smaller towns declined, Methodist churches remained active. Having been the largest congregation in town gave them an advantage in retaining members and staffing programs as populations diminished. After World War II, when many of the state's rural areas declined further, that pattern continued. Among the fifty counties that declined the most, Methodists fared better in forty-six than would have been expected from population trends alone. Membership either grew or declined less than the overall population. The population of Jewell County, for example, declined by nearly half between 1950 and 1980, but the number of Methodists increased by almost a quarter. In contrast, Methodism did less well in areas that were growing. Membership increased, but not as much as the population growth would have suggested. For example, the population of Johnson County multiplied more than fourfold, but Methodist membership increased less than threefold.[62]

As rural areas declined, Methodist churches sometimes closed their doors forever. Yet that did not occur as often as might have been expected. In the fifty counties that experienced the greatest decline, the population dropped by 26 percent between 1950 and 1980, but the number of Methodist churches decreased by only 10 percent. Keeping churches open wherever possible had two effects. It diminished the likelihood of members drifting away to other churches or becoming unaffiliated. And it meant that congregations typically remained small. The average size in these declining counties in 1980 was 263. In contrast, relatively few additional congregations were initiated in the fastest-growing areas. Johnson County had only three more Methodist churches in 1980 than it did in 1950, the number in Sedgwick County increased by nine, and the number in Shawnee was unchanged.[63]

Methodists' commitment to small towns was well illustrated by a Methodist pastor who entered the ministry in 1980 after having taught school for several years. He served successively in towns with populations of 150, 350, 700, 250, 1,800, and 2,800, never staying more than four years before the bishop moved him to another charge. After more than two decades, he received an appointment at a church of 450 members with an average attendance of 185 in a town of 3,600. Asked what he would have to do to further improve his situation, he said he would have to leave the ministry. This was as high as he could expect to advance. He was happy to have made it to the top. Of course there were a few large Methodist churches in the cities, but those were out of reach for all but the most fortunate clergy. The rotational system served well as long as the population of small towns held steady or grew. But it would become a deficit when the population began shifting to urban areas. When that happened, Methodists were at a disadvantage compared with newer independent churches or ones with greater congregational autonomy. Pastors of those churches could be entrepreneurs, and if they were successful, stay in one place for as long as they wanted, and see their congregation grow larger and larger.[64]

Methodists were distinctive but not unique. Several of the other established denominations followed similar patterns. American Baptists, the Christian Church, the Lutheran Church Missouri Synod, and the Evangelical Lutheran Church in America all remained disproportionately concentrated in the state's less populated counties.

In smaller communities, the tacit cooperation evident in towns like Courtland and WaKeeney in the early 1950s continued. Members of churches that closed were forced to join other congregations, but there was little evidence of aggressive efforts on the part of one denomination to grow at the expense of another.[65]

With their numerical center of gravity in the state's rural areas, the established denominations were positioned to reflect the social and political values of these communities. These were mostly Republican strongholds dependent on agriculture, concerned in many instances about declining population and uncertain farm prices. They were shielded from the racial issues in cities and insulated from campus disturbances. Churches in small communities relied extensively on lay involvement, and emphasized hometown networks and loyalties. In relating to their denominational conferences and presbyteries, churches in rural areas held numerical superiority, but were at a disadvantage in shaping church policies compared with leaders from large urban congregations.

In 1969, a young sociologist reared in Pratt published what became an influential book about the growing tensions in Protestant churches. In *The Gathering Storm in the Churches*, Jeffrey K. Hadden examined national survey data showing differences in attitudes toward social issues among clergy and laity. On theological issues, such as the divinity of Jesus and understandings of the Bible, clergy and laity held similar views. But on social issues the two diverged. Clergy were generally more liberal on civil rights questions, more favorable toward government-sponsored social welfare programs, and more inclined to vote Democratic than Republican. Hadden's data did not enable state-by-state comparisons, but several of his findings were suggestive of what was probably happening in Kansas. One was that the differences between clergy and laity on social issues were more pronounced among the large middle-of-the-road denominations, such as Methodists, American Baptists, and Lutherans, than among smaller conservative denominations. Another was that clergy in wealthier, better-educated congregations tended to be more liberal than those in poorer, less well-educated congregations. It would not have been surprising to find that clergy in large congregations in Wichita or Topeka held different views from those in small towns like WaKeeney, Pratt, or Oskaloosa.[66]

Other writers were finding patterns similar to Hadden's. A study of campus clergy found them to be dramatically more engaged in civil rights and antiwar activism than congregation-based clergy within the same denominations. The campus clergy were younger, and their views were shaped by the turmoil among students. They were also safely insulated from the social and financial pressures that clergy faced in other settings from laity who may have been disturbed by what they saw on campuses. Another study showed that church members with strong local orientations differed from members with cosmopolitan outlooks. The ones who focused mostly on their hometowns, followed local news with interest, and limited themselves to local friendships were less tolerant as well as more likely to harbor racial and ethnic prejudice than their counterparts with broader outlooks. In other studies, differences in education levels played a similar role.[67]

None of these studies suggested that a straightforward division would have existed in Kansas simply between churchgoers in smaller rural communities and those in larger urban areas. The tendency was there, though. It was reinforced by another aspect of where the established denominations' strength lay. There were relatively few opportunities or incentives for entrepreneurial fundamentalist preachers to start new churches in small communities. There may have been an Assembly of God congregation or a Holiness church that had emerged during the Depression. But with a declining population as well as established Methodist and Baptist congregations spanning much of the theological and social spectrum, an enterprising preacher would have been better advised to work elsewhere. The opportunities were much greater in larger, rapidly growing urban areas. Especially in communities where Methodists were failing to start new churches fast enough, or where migration and social class were producing sharper distinctions among the inhabitants, the likelihood of being able to launch a new kind of church was much greater.[68]

In 1946, a small group of Southern Baptists saw Kansas as a promising mission field in which to start new churches. Unlike Methodists, who merged their northern and southern branches in 1939, the division between northern American Baptists and Southern Baptists continued. Southern Baptists were the more conservative of the two. They held more often to a literal interpretation of the Bible. They preached that Jesus was coming soon to reward his own followers and punish evildoers. With strength among white southerners, they were frequently resistant to desegregation and critical of the civil rights movement. The group that formed the Kansas Convention of Southern Baptist Churches in 1946 had been part of a Southern Baptist association in Oklahoma. It met at a small church in Burden—a town of about 500 located 60 miles southeast of Wichita—that had been affiliated with the Oklahoma association since 1919 when the congregation broke ties with Northern Baptists over the denomination's participation in the ecumenical Interchurch World Movement.[69]

The 1952 census of religious bodies reported more than 8 million Southern Baptists nationwide, making it second in size only to Methodists. Large numbers of Southern Baptists were located to the south and east of Kansas. There were more than 1,200 Southern Baptist churches in Oklahoma with nearly 400,000 members; 1,700 churches in Missouri with 390,000 members; 1,100 churches in Arkansas with 270,000 members; and 3,500 churches in Texas with 1.4 million members. Kansas had only 39 Southern Baptist churches with 15,000 members. The impact of geography was evident in the location of these churches. Most were situated on the southern and eastern borders near Oklahoma and Missouri. Eleven were in Cherokee County, 5 in Crawford, 5 in Cowley, 4 in Montgomery, 4 in Sumner, and 3 in Labette. It was also apparent that Southern Baptists were targeting urban areas where the population was growing. Wichita was the largest urban area near the Oklahoma border and had long ties with Oklahoma, first as a cattle town, then as a staging ground for settlers moving to Oklahoma, and more recently through the oil industry. There were 18 Southern Baptist churches with more than 5,000 members in Sedgwick County alone. Southern Baptists were also experiencing success starting churches in Kansas City, Topeka, Hutchinson, and Salina.[70]

By 1980, Southern Baptists had become a major factor in Kansas religion. Seventy-nine new churches were organized during the 1950s, fifty-four more were added in the 1960s, and forty-one more in the 1970s. There were 73,000 members in 1980—equal to the number of American Baptists, and more than the Christian Church, Lutheran Church Missouri Synod, or Evangelical Lutheran Church of America. The effect of geography was still evident. In nearly half the state there were no Southern Baptist churches at all, while memberships in counties along the Oklahoma border had grown significantly. Most of the growth, though, was concentrated in the state's largest urban areas. Indeed, two-thirds of Kansas Southern Baptists lived in the state's most populous counties. A third lived in the Wichita area. The second-largest concentration was in Johnson County, where commuters to Kansas City were swelling the populations of Olathe, Overland Park, Shawnee, Leawood, and Lenexa.[71]

Southern Baptists were not the only theologically conservative churches that were growing. Many were independent congregations founded earlier in the century by pastors inspired by the work of Dwight L. Moody, Ira Sankey, and other revivalists. Like Parham's group in Topeka at the start of the century, a few were Pentecostalists seeking gifts of the Holy Spirit. More described themselves simply as Bible-loving Christians. In Salina a group calling itself the City Bible Hall began meeting in 1929, grew rapidly in the 1930s, became the Salina Bible Church in 1944, and grew significantly again in the 1950s and 1960s. Other churches begun in the late 1920s and 1930s included the Wichita Bible Church and the Topeka Bible Church. Pastors and members of independent churches networked with one another through the American Conference of Undenominational Churches, a confederation of fundamentalists founded in 1923, and through fellowships of independent Baptists, regional conferences, and programs sponsored by the Moody Bible Institute in Chicago. Colleges and institutes in which aspiring pastors, Sunday school teachers, and missionaries could receive training in a few months at relatively little cost played an important role in the growth of independent churches. These included the Wichita Bible Seminary, founded in 1926; the Kansas City Bible Institute, founded in 1932; the Topeka Bible Institute, founded in 1937; and the Midwest Bible and Missionary Institute in Salina, founded in 1938. By 1980, the Topeka Bible Church had an annual budget of a hundred thousand dollars and was staged to become one of the city's largest congregations. The Wichita Bible Church had grown to more than a thousand members by the early 1960s.[72]

Like Southern Baptists, Bible churches advertised themselves as truer to fundamental Christian doctrines than the larger established denominations, and emphasized their independence from organizations such as the Interchurch World Movement and the National Council of Churches. With little outside support, pastors had a strong incentive to locate in communities where growth could be expected and then work hard at recruiting members. That pattern was evident among Assemblies of God churches as well. From fewer than nine thousand members statewide in 1952, the denomination grew to almost twenty-five thousand by 1980. Like Southern Baptists, Assemblies of God leaders targeted urban areas. Membership in Wichita and Kansas City increased fourfold, and in Johnson County it multiplied tenfold.

The other dynamic in these years affecting church affiliations was a response to denominational mergers. These included the 1957 union of Congregational Christian churches with Evangelical and Reformed ones, the 1958 union of United Presbyterians with the Presbyterian Church (U.S.A.), the 1960 merger of three Lutheran denominations to form the American Lutheran Church, and the 1971 merger of Evangelical United Brethren and Methodist churches. In each instance members unhappy with the proposed mergers held out, formed new denominations, became independent, or joined other churches. The restructuring of the Christian Church, finalized in 1968, had similar consequences. By 1980, approximately forty-five thousand members were affiliated with the new conservative Christian Churches and Churches of Christ denomination, while sixty-nine thousand remained affiliated with the Christian Church. The shift was especially pronounced in several western Kansas counties, where all the Christian Churches went with the more conservative branch.[73]

In most of the less populated counties, the older established denominations were still in the majority in 1980. About two-thirds of all Protestants in these communities belonged to Methodist, Presbyterian, American Baptist, Evangelical Lutheran, Christian, Episcopal, Mennonite, Friends, or United Church of Christ congregations. The other third were Southern Baptists, Christian Churches and Churches of Christ, Churches of Christ, Assemblies of God, Church of God, Nazarene, Free Methodist, Foursquare Gospel, Brethren, or members of several smaller denominations. The exceptions in which conservative groups were a larger proportion were generally in the southeast, where Southern Baptists were more numerous, or in western Kansas, where Christian Churches and Churches of Christ were strong. The established churches enjoyed two advantages in smaller communities in addition to the fact that they had usually been there longer. On average, each congregation was about twice as large as was true for the conservative congregations. And they were used to sharing pulpits, participating in ministerial councils, and cooperating in community-wide events. The newer conservative churches' advantage was that they often secured greater commitment from their members in terms of participation and giving.

In absolute numbers, the conservative denominations' strength was in larger urban communities. The Topeka area included more than 12,000 members in 40 congregations affiliated with conservative denominations in 1980. Kansas City, Kansas, along with the surrounding suburbs in Wyandotte and Johnson counties included approximately 100 such churches with more than 35,000 members. In both Topeka and Kansas City, membership in the older established denominations still outnumbered membership in these conservative churches by more than double. The situation in Wichita was different. Wichita had more than 130 conservative congregations, as many as the old-line denominations did, and each of the two categories included approximately 60,000 members.[74]

A study of Wichita in 1958 identified religious patterns that probably continued in the 1960s and 1970s. Only 4 percent of the city's families did not have a religious affiliation. Methodists and Baptists were the largest denominations with 21 and 19 percent of the population, respectively. Twelve percent were Catholics. Most of the remaining families were in smaller Protestant denominations. The sharpest differences that the study documented were that Methodists, Presbyterians, Episcopalians, Lutherans, Disciples of Christ, and Congregationalists tended to live in census tracts with above-average incomes. In contrast, Baptists, Assemblies of God, Church of God, Church of Christ, Brethren, Salvation Army, and Pentecostal members were disproportionately concentrated in lower-income census tracts.[75]

Wichita had grown during the 1950s by more than eighty thousand people, with many of its newest residents taking blue-collar jobs in the city's burgeoning aircraft industry, and during the 1960s and 1970s would grow by another thirty-five thousand. In 1980, a third of its labor force was employed in manufacturing, 10 percent of its families were below the poverty line, and 43 percent of the city's adults had not graduated from high school. One-fifth of the residents were newcomers in the past five years. That gave churches with aggressive outreach programs ample opportunities to grow. Wichita included not only small neighborhood churches in rented storefronts and basements but also large, potentially powerful congregations like Tabernacle Baptist, with a thousand members in 1960, and Metropolitan Baptist, organized in 1962 with more than eighteen hundred charter members.[76]

Theological differences among the various denominations were evident from national studies. A 1964 study, for example, found that 85 percent of Southern Baptists and 87 percent of members in smaller sectarian churches believed that faith in Jesus was necessary for salvation, compared with 56 percent of Methodists and 53 percent of Presbyterians. These differences set the stage for tensions between conservative and moderate denominations, and showed that moderate denominations were potentially divided among members whose views on basic theological teachings differed.[77]

Theological differences emerged as overt tensions in 1960 when Billy James Hargis declared that "communists and communist fellow-travelers have successfully infiltrated our churches." The National Council of Churches was implicated in Communism, Hargis charged, and was using its influence to weaken the Christian faith. Thirty of the ninety-five scholars involved in the council's Revised Standard Version of the Bible, Hargis said, were affiliated with Communist fronts and Communist projects. The accusation resulted in an angry retort from the National Council of Churches. But in Wichita, the board of deacons of the largest American Baptist congregation in the country voted to withhold its thirty-three thousand dollar contribution to the denomination as a protest against its council membership. Two years later, fifteen hundred people upset with their denominations met at Southeast High School in Wichita to plan the new Metropolitan Baptist Church.[78]

In 1962, another potentially divisive issue emerged when the U.S. Supreme Court ruled by a six-to-one majority in *Engel v. Vitale* against the inclusion of prayers in public schools, and strengthened its interpretation a year later in *Murray v. Curlett*. Kansas was one of eighteen states with laws specifically authorizing Bible reading and prayer in public schools. Constitutional lawyers differed as to whether the ruling prohibited the mention of God in the morning recitations of the Pledge of Allegiance or formulaic prayers in patriotic ceremonies. Devout Kansans were reassured that the government had not turned completely against them as they watched Senator Carlson joined by evangelist Billy Graham and President Kennedy at the National Prayer Breakfast. But they were scandalized when Madalyn J. Murray, the woman who brought the suit that resulted in the Supreme Court's 1963 decision, announced plans to establish a radio station, printing press, and colony for atheists on a farm in Kansas near Stockton. By 1964, efforts were under way to pass a constitutional amendment reinstating prayer and Bible reading in the public schools. The amendment was opposed by the National Council of Churches, but favored by Hargis, McIntire, and many other conservative leaders. In 1972, the amendment was still an issue in Kansas electoral campaigns.[79]

While Protestants were debating school prayer and versions of the Bible, Catholics were experiencing changes of their own. The 1950s had been a decade of incomparable growth in Kansas dioceses. Membership in the Salina diocese rose from 40,848 to 53,410, an increase of 31 percent, and the Kansas City diocese grew from 80,000 to 120,500, an increase of 51 percent. The Wichita diocese numbered 68,849 in 1950, and was divided in 1951, leaving 78,477 members in the eastern part that continued to be known as the Wichita diocese, and 25,850 in the new Dodge City diocese, or an overall increase of 52 percent. Much of the growth was from the post–World War II baby boom, which continued to produce high birthrates into the mid-1960s. That increase, however, affected the several Kansas dioceses differently. In the largely rural Salina diocese, the number of children enrolled in Catholic elementary schools declined by about 10 percent, whereas enrollment in the combined Wichita–Dodge City diocese increased by 68 percent, and in the Kansas City diocese it rose by 91 percent.[80]

The 1960s were dominated by the sweeping reforms instituted by the Second Vatican Council between October 1962 and December 1968. These included a revision of the liturgy to include greater lay participation and incorporate the use of vernacular languages. Other statements repudiated anti-Semitism, and opened the opportunities for greater interfaith cooperation with Protestants and Jews. The council, though, did not condone the use of birth control other than through natural means or alter clerical celibacy policies. National studies found Catholics deeply divided on these issues. A study in 1963, for example, revealed that 42 percent of Catholics accepted the church's position on birth control and divorce, while the remainder disagreed. A follow-up study in 1974 found that only 18 percent agreed. In the former study, 71 percent said that they attended Mass weekly, while in the latter study only 50 percent did.[81]

If there was diminishing participation and eroding support for church teachings, as these studies suggested, the sense of decline was compounded in Kansas by demographics. Although the total number of Kansas Catholics increased by 22 percent between 1960 and 1980, that was significantly smaller than the 47 percent growth experienced from 1950 to 1960. And by nearly every other measure the church was not as strong as it had been. The number of priests dropped 25 percent between 1960 and 1980. There was a decline of two-thirds in the number of sisters teaching in Catholic elementary schools. The number of children in Catholic elementary schools fell by 50 percent, and 73 of the state's 163 schools were closed.

These were changes driven by larger dynamics in the state and nation. The farm population was declining. Small towns were losing population. Fewer young people were becoming clergy or joining religious orders. The baby boom was diminishing. And Catholic fertility rates that had been higher than among Protestants in the past were converging as younger Catholics were defying church teachings about birth control. But having invested so much in Catholic schools, and having focused so much attention on family life and children, the sense of decline was acute for many Catholic leaders. By 1980, more than half of Catholic marriages performed in Kansas were defined as interfaith—and that did not include marriages performed outside the church. The Catholic schools that remained were larger and better, but it worried some that only a third of the teachers in these schools were sisters.[82]

The one bright spot was that Kansas Catholics were increasingly concentrated in the largest urban areas, and thus poised to be a continuing influence as these communities grew. Not only were the Wichita and Kansas City dioceses considerably more populous than the Salina and Dodge City ones, but Wichita and the environs of Kansas City were increasingly the dominant centers of their dioceses. In 1980, 52 percent of Catholics in the Wichita diocese lived in Sedgwick County, up from only 35 percent in 1950. Half the Kansas City diocese was concentrated in Wyandotte and Johnson counties.

In the coming decades, the Kansas bishops would have to make difficult decisions about closing parochial schools in rural areas and finding ways to staff parishes in small towns with fewer priests. They would also have to address the needs of increasingly diverse communities like Dodge City, Garden City, and Liberal, where the meatpacking industry was attracting large numbers of immigrants, and compete in places like Wichita, Olathe, and Overland Park with large conservative Protestant churches. Meanwhile, Catholics and Protestants alike were faced with such divisive issues as civil rights activism, campus unrest, changing attitudes toward sexuality and gender, and continuing debates about the Vietnam War.

The 1970s put some of these issues to rest and raised others. The 1973 Supreme Court decision in *Roe v. Wade* would be the issue with the longest consequences for religion and politics in Kansas as in much of the nation. Watergate was a blow for Kansans who had voted to reelect Nixon in 1972 by a large—68 to 29 percent—margin over George McGovern. Gerald Ford's 1974 pardon of Nixon and Jimmy Carter's Southern Baptist credentials, though, were not enough to undermine the state's Republican base. Kansans voted for Ford over Carter in 1976 by 52 to 45 percent. It helped that Ford's running mate was Bob Dole. In Congress, Republicans held both of the state's senate seats and four of its five seats in the House. These Republicans consistently received heavily favorable ratings by conservative political action groups and largely unfavorable ratings by liberal groups. The Democrats' strength resided in Wichita and Kansas City, and was sufficient to secure a narrow gubernatorial victory in 1974 for Democrat Robert F. Bennett.[83]

Bennett reflected both the ambitions and frustrations associated with the restructuring taking place in Kansas during the 1960s and 1970s. A Presbyterian who grew up near Kansas City and served as mayor of suburban Prairie Village, he was considered a bit too intellectual to relate well to ordinary folks—a flaw that lost him a second term in 1978. He tried to balance the state's tradition of rugged individualism with enough government intervention to promote the common good, and like his Republican and Democratic predecessors, sought to govern on an "efficient and economical basis." He found himself at odds with a growing number of ideological and political interest groups on both the Right and Left. Changing the way that "the cow gets from the field to the barn," he said, gets them all stirred up.[84]

CHAPTER 6

THE RELIGIOUS RIGHT

THE PARISHIONERS were sitting quietly that Sunday morning waiting for the worship service to begin. It was Pentecost Sunday, not one of the more important days of the liturgical calendar, but a time for the church to be reminded of God's indwelling spirit of love. The padded pews, the hushed reverence as people took their seats, the sunlight filtering in through stained glass, and even the subdued serenity of the wood-and-brick sanctuary were conducive to silent reflection. There was a brief commotion somewhere outside near the front of the church. An usher came forward, asked the worshippers to remain seated, and whispered to one of the women. It was Jeanne, a longtime member of the congregation who sometimes sang in the choir and often served on committees. She followed the usher to the rear of the auditorium. Under the portico by the front door her husband lay dead. He was serving as a greeter that morning, handing out bulletins, and was supposed to have come sit with her like they had been doing nearly every Sunday for thirty years. He was not only her husband but also her best friend. She called him Buddy. But that morning a lone gunman came to the church and killed her husband with a single bullet to the head.

The murder of Dr. George Tiller took place on May 31, 2009, at the Reformation Lutheran Church in suburban Wichita. As one of the region's few providers of legal late-term abortions, Tiller had been the focus of frequent attacks by antiabortion activists. They had bombed his clinic, blockaded it, glued its doors shut, tried to murder him, threatened his staff, harassed his patients, picketed his home, and invaded his church. It was a holy war, they said. They brandished Bibles and sang hymns as they peopled the blockades.

They held prayer vigils and organized meetings at churches. Clergy helped mobilize the crusade. They were saving innocent babies from being slaughtered.

Pro-life groups in Kansas and around the country issued statements deploring Tiller's murder. They denied having in any way been involved in motivating his death. They also gave thanks that his practice was no longer in business. Operation Rescue held a prayer service. It was a bittersweet moment, participants said. Their work in Wichita was over. It had not ended as they imagined it would. But they could go home now and think about other things. It was time, their leaders said, to move on to Nebraska and focus their attention on a clinic there.[1]

No issue brought churches as directly into the political sphere during the late 1980s and 1990s as abortion. Clergy and parishioners organized pro-life groups, hired lobbyists, participated in demonstrations, and were arrested. They set up watchdog committees, published newsletters, and launched Web sites. Leaders hosted public officials whose views they endorsed and banned others from appearing in their churches. A few religious leaders took the other side, participating in pro-choice events and working to provide family assistance.

The struggle lasted for years. It was furthered not only by deep religious convictions but also by each side experiencing small gains that raised hopes and kept activists motivated. Unlike anything since the temperance movement a century earlier, abortion was fought at all levels of local, state, and national government. Few Kansans had abortions or knew anyone who did, but the issue seemed to come up everywhere—from sex education classes in middle schools to municipal hospital boards to bills before the state legislature to presidential elections. It dominated, but did not crowd out, issues that also drew wide interest in the religious community, including prayer and Bible reading in schools, and especially how evolution should be taught.

Had it not been for the struggle over abortion, the Religious Right in Kansas would have still gained national attention because of its role in encouraging the Kansas State Board of Education to approve science standards that downplayed the teaching of evolution. The decision made Kansas a laughingstock among scientists, educators, and journalists across the nation. It also posed questions requiring more serious scrutiny than they usually received. Why was Kansas such a hotbed of religious conservatism? What role did long-standing antipathy toward the federal government play? In what ways did it matter that independent evangelical Protestant churches were now on the same side of many issues as conservative Roman Catholics?

MOBILIZATION ON THE RIGHT

The Tiller clinic in Wichita opened in 1975, bringing the total number of abortion providers in Kansas to twenty-three, up from nine two years earlier. More than fourteen hundred abortions were performed in the state that year, about half with Kansas residents. Although the Supreme Court's 1973 *Roe v. Wade* decision protecting a woman's right to choose an abortion would be debated with increasing intensity, abortion was far from being a front-burner issue in the mid-1970s. The top concerns in national polls were inflation, crime, and corruption in government. Carter's victory over Ford the following fall was widely attributed to the public's desire for national healing in the wake of the Watergate scandal.[2]

In Kansas the issues of greatest concern were spiraling prices, high interest rates, rising taxes, and uncertainties about the fate of federal revenue-sharing programs. Agriculture was particularly worrisome, as output fell 27 percent in value from 1973 to 1976. Legislators debated measures to improve schools, fund higher education, reduce tax burdens on the elderly, provide welfare services for the poor, and adjust tax inequities between rural areas and cities. Penal reform, civil rights, and the death penalty were among the issues discussed. Republicans controlled the state legislature, but Democrats held the executive branch. In national politics Dole had been damaged by Watergate, having served as Republican National

Committee chair from 1971 to 1973, and was reelected to the senate in 1974 by only a few thousand votes.[3]

Church leaders in the mid-1970s had plenty on their minds besides abortion. Questions about the relative growth or decline of their denominations were of particular concern. In a widely circulated *National Catholic Reporter* article, sociologists Andrew M. Greeley and William C. McCready described a drastic decline in Mass attendance among Catholics. In a single year, the proportion attending weekly fell from 61 to 48 percent. The sharpest declines were among parishioners in their thirties and forties—those most likely to be rearing children. Among Protestants the alarm was sounded by United Methodist minister and National Council of Churches official Dean M. Kelley, who observed that nearly every old-line Protestant denomination was losing membership, after having gained members during the 1950s and usually for much longer. Methodist membership, for example, peaked at approximately eleven million in 1965 and declined by more than a million over the next decade. Presbyterian membership fell by about 10 percent over the same period. Episcopalians and memberships in the United Church of Christ declined by more than 20 percent. In contrast, Southern Baptists, Assemblies of God, Jehovah's Witnesses, and Mormons had grown.[4]

Kelley argued that denominations' growth or decline could be explained by theology. Liberal churches were declining, he said, because they demanded too little of their members, and thus gave them no reason to belong, while conservative churches asked for more and got more in return. That argument resonated with concerns about the growth of new religious movements. These included groups with roots in ancient Eastern religions, such as Transcendental Meditation and Zen Buddhism, which flourished on campuses during the unrest of the Vietnam War. There were also authoritarian cults that seemed to be faring particularly well. Among these were Scientology, which was flourishing in California under the leadership of L. Ron Hubbard, who perhaps ironically, was said to have conceived the group while living in Wichita in the early 1950s, and the Unification Church or Moonies, which also had an ironic connection with Kansas through a campaign donation that Dole unknowingly accepted from a leader of the group in 1970. Both movements worried church leaders not only because they attracted youths but also because they seemed to validate Kelley's thesis that rigid authoritarianism caused religious organizations to grow.

The more important concern with which Kelley's contention resonated was whether churches themselves were suffering because of having become too liberal. The declining denominations were all associated with the theologically liberal National Council of Churches. Moreover, Kelley's data showed that the more liberal of these denominations declined most. The United Methodist Church, for example, was losing members while the Wesleyan Methodists were gaining; similarly, the more liberal Reformed Church in America was losing people while its conservative counterpart, the Christian Reformed Church, was growing. That was the situation in 1975 when William Phelps Thompson of Wichita was elected National Council of Churches president. A Beloit native who had graduated from McPherson College and the University of Chicago Law School, Thompson was an elder in the First Presbyterian Church of Wichita and had served since 1966 as the chief administrative officer of the United Presbyterian Church. He was known as an astute parliamentarian capable of adjudicating the tensions between theologically conservative and theologically moderate or liberal Presbyterians. The National Council, he said, was facing a "tough climate." Declining numbers in its member denominations were causing financial difficulties, and these were exacerbated by controversial stands on divisive social issues. But Thompson's stand on these issues was clear. A moderate Democrat, he had fought right-wing McCarthyism in the 1950s, supported the civil rights movement in the 1960s, was an outspoken opponent of the Vietnam War, believed in full equality for women, and favored stronger ecumenical ties among Protestant denominations and with Catholics.[5]

Liberals like Thompson faced growing opposition from conservatives upset by what they saw as misguided theological and social initiatives. For example, the Presbyterian Lay Committee formed in 1965 in opposition to the denomination's proposed revision of its core statement of confessional beliefs, which was adopted in 1967, and in coming years served as a conservative voice against clergy involvement in civil rights and antiwar activism, women's ordination, and gay rights. Other conservative groups included the Lutheran Laymen's League, Concerned Presbyterians, Methodist organizations such as Circuit Riders and the Good News Movement, and Episcopal groups such as the American Church Union and the Foundation for Christian Theology. Methodists, Presbyterians, Lutherans, and Disciples of Christ all experienced losses of individual members and whole congregations to conservative denominations. Among Southern Baptists, fundamentalists advocating biblical literalism and opposed to women's ordination were mobilizing against moderates. Catholics saw the formation of conservative groups such as Concerned Catholic Parishioners, a Chicago organization opposed to new catechisms in Catholic grade schools, and Una Voce, an organization to promote the continued use of the Latin Mass. Church leaders were also troubled by the rise of religious television, which they feared would weaken congregational participation as well as strengthen the influence of popular televangelists such as Oral Roberts, Jim Bakker, Jerry Falwell, and Pat Robertson.[6]

Until the mid-1970s, most of the tension among Protestants and Catholics focused on issues that grew from and directly affected church programs. The creeds and confessional statements to which members were asked to subscribe when they joined churches, whether women were allowed to preach, the language in which Mass was said, who would be elected to denominational offices, and how a church's finances would be used were all issues that mattered to the collective lives of congregations. But having mobilized groups within the churches to argue on one side or the other of these concerns, denominations had the mechanisms available to engage in broader issues. Clergy and lay leaders learned the importance of building networks, securing funding, forming caucuses, establishing special interest organizations, registering these organizations as legal tax-exempt nonprofit entities, putting out newsletters,

sending direct mail, lobbying at denominational meetings, and securing publicity. It was less a matter of inventing new strategies
than of updating familiar methods, and adapting them to a more
contentious and activist political climate. These were the strategies
used to organize civil rights sit-ins and campus demonstrations
against the Vietnam War. They were readily adapted by religious
groups fearing that the Internal Revenue Service was going to tax
churches, the Federal Communications Commission was imposing
restrictions on religious broadcasting, or the Supreme Court was
eliminating prayer and Bible reading from schools.

Abortion emerged as a topic of concern to religious organizations in the context of these wider disagreements about theology,
church governance, and clergy involvement in social issues. As one
of many issues it was seldom the most important, but after *Roe v.
Wade* it gained prominence both in church teachings and political
campaigns. The Catholic Church, affirming a position stated in the
Pastoral Constitution on the Church in the Modern World at the
Second Vatican Council that human life begins at conception, along
with Greek Orthodox churches, was firmly opposed to abortion,
equating it with infanticide and calling it an unspeakable crime.
Fundamentalist McIntire of the International Council of Christian
Churches took the same position, as did the Church of the Brethren
and many of the smaller groups represented by the National Association of Evangelicals. In 1971, Southern Baptists favored legislation allowing abortion under such conditions as rape, incest,
and danger to the mother's health, but over the next several years
shifted toward a stronger policy of opposing abortion.

Between 1966 and 1972, most of the denominations affiliated with the National Council of Churches adopted statements
favoring a woman's right to choose, although there was enough
disagreement that the council itself did not formalize a position.
Methodists, Presbyterians, American Baptists, the United Church of
Christ, and the Lutheran Church in America argued that the matter
should be decided between a woman and her doctor. They encouraged the establishment of responsible counseling services, while
acknowledging that pastors and members in their denominations

held varying views, and should be guided by prayerful reflection and discussion. Reform and Conservative Jewish leaders adopted similar views. While *Roe v. Wade* affirmed the position of groups favoring choice, opponents initiated efforts to resist, including boycotting and picketing clinics and hospitals at which abortions were performed, denying communion to proabortion church members, writing to public officials, and testifying at congressional hearings. By 1974, right-to-life groups were organized across the country, and were countered by coalitions of Christians and Jews under the umbrella of such organizations as the Religious Coalition for Abortion Rights, Catholics for a Free Choice, and the National Abortion Rights Action League.[7]

Until 1971, Kansas law stipulated that abortions could be performed only in hospitals accredited by the Joint Commission on Accreditation of Hospitals and only on approval by three physicians. The federal court in Kansas City ruled in 1972 that both statutes were unconstitutional. The action eased the availability of abortions and at the same time alerted opponents of abortion that stronger efforts might be needed to prevent the further liberalization of access. With no required waiting period for nonresidents, Kansas became one of the region's major abortion providers. More abortions were performed in Kansas in 1973 than in Missouri, Iowa, Nebraska, Arkansas, and Oklahoma combined. Adjusted for the total population, the rate in Kansas was three times the rate in Nebraska, seven times the rate in Missouri, and twenty-five times the rate in Oklahoma. *Roe v. Wade* eased neighboring states' restrictions, but in 1974 the rate in Kansas was still triple the rate in Nebraska, Missouri, and Oklahoma.[8]

In 1974, abortion surfaced as an issue in the hotly contested senate race between Dole and Congressman Bill Roy. With the taint of Nixon and Watergate working against him, Dole tagged Roy as a proponent of abortion. It was an easy assertion because Roy was a doctor who had actually performed abortions and had spoken in Congress against restricting federal funds to abortion providers. It also made sense as a strategy for saving Wichita, which otherwise would likely have voted Democratic. Wichita was the home of the

Kansas Birthright Center, a right-to-life crisis pregnancy and advocacy group founded in 1971, and there were more than forty thousand Catholics and almost twenty-five thousand Southern Baptists who could be courted by a pro-life appeal. Roy struck back by campaigning hard in the Kansas City area, speaking at churches, and emphasizing President Ford's pardon of Nixon. A statewide poll suggested that abortion could be the decisive issue for one voter in six. Soon campaign ads were appearing in newspapers bearing the title "Vote for Life!" and depicting a skull along with "abortion" and "euthanasia" on the two crossbones. By the weekend before the election, windshield pamphlets were showing bloody fetuses in garbage pails.

Dole scored a 70 percent victory in his home county and won thirty-three other small counties by at least 60 percent, but was beaten badly in Topeka and Lawrence, where Roy was well known and negative reaction to Watergate was acute. Had it not been for Wichita, Dole likely would have lost the election. That was evident in comparisons with the gubernatorial race. While Democrat Robert Bennett achieved a margin of seventeen thousand votes in Sedgwick County in the contest for governor, Dole held Roy's edge to fewer than twenty-three hundred votes. On the national scene, where a majority of pro-life candidates lost, Dole's victory not only stood out but also helped position him to become Ford's running mate in 1976. "I did not know how to handle the abortion issue," Roy said later, "how to say to a Roman Catholic, 'Yes, I have done some legal abortions.'"[9]

When the Republican National Convention met in Kemper Arena in Kansas City, Missouri, in August 1976, abortion emerged as a front-burner issue. Reagan, President Ford's strongest competitor for the nomination, endorsed the idea of a constitutional amendment to ban abortion. The human rights subcommittee of which Dole was a member added a plank to the party's platform promising to protect the right to life of unborn children. The platform condemned the idea of teens being able to have abortions without parental consent and endorsed voluntary prayer in schools. Meanwhile, the Democrats nominated Carter, a self-described born-again Southern Baptist who was personally opposed to abortion, but the party did not include an endorsement of a right-to-life amendment in its platform. Its failure to do so evoked an immediate protest. Scheduled to give the benediction at the Democratic National Convention, Reverend Robert N. Deming of the Cathedral of the Immaculate Conception in Kansas City, Missouri, sent a letter saying that he would be unable to do so as a matter of conscience. As the campaign developed, Dole hammered Carter not only on abortion but also by arguing that the Democrat wanted to impose taxes on church-owned hospitals, schools, senior citizen homes, and orphanages.[10]

Carter's victory in November nevertheless reflected favorable margins among Catholics and Southern Baptists as well as union and blue-collar workers and in the South. He scored wins in twenty-six counties in Kansas—the strongest in Wyandotte County among Kansas City residents, and nearly all the rest in western counties. The Ford-Dole ticket triumphed in the Wichita area by nearly six thousand votes. Analysts saw Carter's win as a repudiation of the view that sentiments about abortion could sway elections. But that did not dissuade activists from trying. In 1977, Southern Baptists circulated antiabortion materials in thousands of congregations and pledged to work more closely with Catholic leaders, who redoubled their efforts to achieve passage of a right-to-life amendment. The 1978 midterm election served as a test case for targeted pro-life activism. In Iowa, the Prolife Action Council succeeded in defeating Democratic senator Dick Clark, who refused to support a right-to-life amendment, by distributing three hundred thouand brochures in churches across the state. Similar efforts occurred in Minnesota. Besides engaging in electoral politics, activists took to the streets. In 1979, sixty thousand demonstrators marked the sixth anniversary of *Roe v. Wade* in the nation's capital. Many of the marchers were from Catholic churches, schools, and Knights of Columbus organizations. But churchgoers remained divided on the issue. A study of Catholics found 47 percent supportive of the church's stance against abortion, while 44 percent thought the church should "relax its standards forbidding all abortions under any circumstances."[11]

The abortion debates of the late 1970s were accompanied by conflicts over homosexuality and the Equal Rights Amendment (ERA). In 1977, Wichita passed a civil rights ordinance that included a provision that would prevent discrimination in housing, employment, and public accommodations on the basis of sexual orientation. The ordinance was similar to one in Dade County, Florida, that an organization called Save Our Children, with support from televangelist Falwell and North Carolina senator Jesse Helms, and led by Southern Baptist Anita Bryant, a former Miss Oklahoma and popular recording artist, publicized and succeeded in overturning. Bryant turned her attention to Wichita, asserting that "if homosexuals were allowed their civil rights, then so would prostitutes, thieves, or anyone else." Reverend Ron Adrian and members of the Glenville Baptist Church organized Concerned Citizens for Community Standards of Wichita, which distributed pamphlets stating that "our community could become a haven for practicing homosexuals, lesbians, prostitutes and pimps," and warning that "homosexual teachers, social workers or counselors [can] encourage sexual deviation in children." The issue quickly became one of "church against church and neighbor against neighbor," a resident recalled. Catholic and mainline Protestant leaders favored retaining the ordinance, while Baptists and other conservative clergy from Wichita and neighboring towns supported Adrian. At the polls citizens voted five to one to overturn the ordinance. News of the result evoked a large protest demonstration in San Francisco and discouraged an attempt to pass a similar ordinance in Chicago.[12]

The ERA barring discrimination on the basis of gender was first proposed by suffragist leaders in 1923, and put forward as a U.S. Senate Joint Resolution the same year by Kansas Senator Curtis and Kansas representative Daniel R. Anthony Jr. After years of tepid support by Republicans and resistance from Democrats, the ERA was approved by both houses of Congress in 1972 and endorsed by President Nixon. Both parties supported efforts to achieve ratification by three-quarters of the state legislatures in their 1972 platforms. Kansas was the seventh of twenty-two states to ratify the amendment during the first year. Of its neighboring states, Missouri, Oklahoma, and Arkansas did not ratify it, and Nebraska and South Dakota rescinded their ratifications.

In 1972 Phyllis Schlafly, who had supported Goldwater and run unsuccessfully for president of the National Federation of Republican Women in 1967, founded the Eagle Forum in Saint Louis and launched a national movement to derail the ERA's ratification. In 1976, the Republican national platform committee found its members deeply divided over the issue. Anti-ERA activists proclaimed that it was a satanic measure that should be aborted. Delegates to a conference in Topeka from July 15 to 17, 1977, narrowly turned back a movement for rescission in Kansas. Across the state, conservative women had become mobilized by a desire to protect the family against what they perceived as radical feminism. Twelve miles east of Lawrence in the small town of Eudora evangelical Church of Christ member Barbara Hanna, inspired by the work of Texas evangelical Lottie Beth Hobbs, founded Kansas Citizens against the ERA. There were "strong religious reasons" to oppose the ERA, she said, but it was important not to be viewed narrowly as a religious organization because women of "many denominations" were involved.[13]

Hundreds of women, influenced by Schlafly, Hobbs, and Hanna, and more often simply on their own, wrote to their elected officials in opposition to the ERA. An analysis of the letters by historian Kristi Lowenthal revealed the range and depth of their concerns. They were worried that women would be drafted for military service, motherhood was no longer respected, and men would become less responsible in their families than they already were. They disliked the National Organization of Women, which they variously associated with promiscuity, lesbianism, and abortion. Many expressed their concerns with references to biblical teachings. A woman's place, they said, was in the home and her God-given role was to be a helper for her husband. The concerns were reasonably formulated, Lowenthal concluded, not the views of a lunatic fringe. They also resonated with a long-standing theme in Kansas history. Like the Roosevelt administration that so many farmers despised in the 1930s, the ERA smacked of intervention by arrogant outsiders who did not understand or appreciate local culture. It "stirred up fears of the federal government interfering in family relationships," Lowenthal wrote.[14]

GOVERNMENT IS THE PROBLEM

Important as it was, abortion was not the reigning issue at the end of the 1970s. Neither was the debate about gay rights, feminism, or family values. Kansas Republican Keith Sebelius, campaigning for reelection from the "Big First" congressional district in 1978, captured the prevailing mood. "With inflation, big government, and problems in farm country," he declared, "it is easy to become discouraged and to lose faith." It was time, Sebelius argued, for a new direction. "We cannot afford apathy and cynicism. We have no alternative but to renew the fight for common sense and a fair shake in Washington." The nation was on a spending treadmill, leading to a "social welfare state." That was the same problem that women concerned about the ERA feared. It was the threat from federal government. Reagan had been talking about it since his speech for Goldwater in 1964. "Government is not the solution to our problem," Reagan said in his inaugural address in 1981. "Government is the problem."[15]

How people with that view could have decided that government should police abortions was a question scholars would ponder in later years. But the point was not that government should disappear. "It is not my intention to do away with government," Reagan said in the same speech. The point was that government had somehow escaped serving the common people. "We have been tempted to believe that society has become too complex to be managed by self-rule, that government by an elite group is superior to government for, by, and of the people," he explained. It was the sentiment that Kansans had expressed in the late 1930s toward the New Deal and resembled the populism of the 1890s. People once again were called on to respond in small ways by organizing locally, by coming together not to replace government but rather to retrieve control of it. That was an attractive message at a time when inflation was running in double digits and the federal deficit was skyrocketing. Abortion was enough of a concern in its own right. It was more of a worry because ordinary citizens felt a renewed need to take charge of what was happening in their communities.[16]

There was little doubt in 1980 that Reagan would carry Kansas. He received 58 percent of the vote statewide, compared to 33 percent for Carter, and was victorious by a two-to-one margin in forty-four of the counties. His only loss was in Wyandotte County, where African American voters were largely unpersuaded by Reagan's arguments, if not overtly offended by his strategy of courting white voters in the South. But in western Kansas more than 70 percent of the voters went for Reagan. He won even in traditionally Democratic Ellis County. The only question early in the campaign was whether the state's senior senator could launch a credible challenge in the primary, but Dole withdrew from the race and endorsed his rival. With two brief appearances in the state, Reagan received 63 percent of the primary vote, Anderson 18 percent, and Bush Sr. 13 percent. In announcing his candidacy, Reagan emphasized the nation's hunger for spiritual renewal, and pledged a return to principles of self-reliance and morality. Government, he said, should uphold and not undermine institutions that are "custodians of the very values upon which civilization is founded—religion, education, and above all, family." These were themes he returned to again and again. The government was living too well, he said. It was fat and extravagant, had usurped powers, and imposed itself on people. Most problems "could be solved by the people themselves, if they were given a chance."[17]

Local candidates in Kansas elections took up similar themes in 1980. They advertised themselves as "someone you can talk to," a person who would "make your voice heard and respected," "a real dirt farmer," a father of a "month-old daughter," and a candidate "familiar with you and your concerns." Photographs showed them playing softball or riding a tractor, and might include a child wearing a T-shirt that said, "Vote for my dad." They asked for votes not so much because of their experience in public office but instead as someone who "has raised his family here," a person "wary of giant companies," against "needless government interference," who believes "the federal government is taking over" as well as an opponent of "government regulation" and an advocate for families, capable of giving ordinary people a voice. They were willing to represent the "average working man," apply "common sense," "limit state spending," and "control high taxes." Some noted that they were "right on family issues," and had been endorsed by the Pro Family Forum or a right-to-life group.[18]

Elsewhere abortion continued to draw attention, more often in minor skirmishes than through mass mobilization. Hopeful that Reagan's victory signaled a more conservative perspective, activists worked quietly in more than a dozen states on parental consent or notification bills affecting minors, and on legislation to cut off the public financing of abortions or restrict the reasons for which procedures could be performed. In Missouri, Kansas City attorney Judith Whittaker's chances of becoming a federal judge were scuttled after conservative groups accused her of being too liberal on the ERA and abortion. Yet despite efforts in Missouri to discourage abortions, the number performed annually doubled between 1974 and 1981. That was also true in Nebraska, Oklahoma, and Arkansas. In Kansas the rate was constant. Right-to-life groups formed in Topeka and Emporia, but one of the few instances in which the topic gained wider publicity was when a coach at Wichita State University allegedly financed an abortion for a player's girlfriend. The 1982 gubernatorial race between Republican incumbent John Carlin and Wichita businessperson Sam Hardage was fought entirely on other grounds. "Abortion was never an issue," Carlin said later. "It was my tax increase recommendation versus his."[19]

But broader developments were occurring that would bring religion and politics together in new ways. Anticipating Democratic victories in the 1982 midterm elections, and dissatisfied with Reagan's failure to take a more active role in balancing the federal budget and supporting a constitutional ban on abortions, conservative leaders persuaded Reagan to address the issues. One of the leaders was North Carolina senator Helms, who had not only been active in opposing gay rights but also worked against the ERA and had been considered as a running mate for Reagan in the 1980 election. In 1982, Helms was spearheading proposals in Congress to institute a federal flat tax, balance the budget, and return voluntary prayer to public schools. He was also attempting to circumvent the need for a constitutional ban on abortions through the Helms Human Life Statute, which would define embryos from the moment of conception as persons and thus afford them rights. Utah senator Orrin Hatch, who worked for Reagan's election in 1980 and sponsored the Hatch Human Life Federalism Amendment, joined Helms in this effort. The Hatch and Helms proposals were popular among pro-life members of Congress, but were not supported by economic conservatives, including Goldwater and Kansas Republican Nancy Kassebaum. Ironically, it was the Kansas State University lecture series named in honor of Kassebaum's father, Alfred Landon, at which Reagan chose to speak about abortion.[20]

Accompanied by Senators Kassebaum, Hatch, and Dole, and with ninety-five-year-old Landon in the audience, Reagan addressed the capacity crowd in Manhattan on September 9, 1982. Unlike Nixon in 1970, Reagan was interrupted only by applause as protesters carrying placards attacking his nuclear arms policies were cordoned outside the auditorium. After leading the crowd in singing "Happy Birthday" to Landon, Reagan spoke of the need for faith and courage for people to believe in themselves. He enumerated recent economic accomplishments and made fun of "so-called experts" who predicted that oil prices would rise to a hundred dollars a barrel. He then turned to abortion, acknowledging that it was controversial, and couched it in the context of both religion and his arguments against big government.

The United States, he said, was one nation under God, and he prayed it would be the protector of freedom as God's will on earth. He called for a crusade of national renewal, a return to bedrock values, to the faith of early settlers who asked that God would work his will in their daily lives, to standards of right and wrong, the Ten Commandments, and the Golden Rule. It was impossible, he contended, to have morality without religion. But the "runaway growth of government" was undercutting religion, and destroying people's ability to meet their own needs through their churches, schools, and communities. He criticized the Supreme Court's expulsion of God from the classroom and said he favored voluntary prayer in schools. The nation had a sacred duty, declared Reagan, to protect the innocent human life of an unborn child. It should be protected as every other person by the right to liberty and the pursuit of happiness. God wants us to wake up, he warned, and maybe is running out of patience. The time had come for spiritual revival, for a strengthening of spiritual ties in families and communities. Federal spending needed to be reduced, and programs pruned. People had something that was often in short supply in government: common sense. It was time, he said, to put the "American people back in charge of your country again."[21]

On the surface, the speech included everything that conservatives in Kansas wanted to hear. In a cadence noticeably slower than the one he used in criticizing Rice County to a Los Angeles audience in 1964, Reagan calmly reassured the audience at Kansas State that he was sincerely opposed to abortion. Churchgoers could deduce that he was a person of faith who viewed abortion as a matter of importance to God-fearing people. But the speech was more of an endorsement than a plan of action. The president had chosen not to make abortion the central theme of his lecture but rather to include it among a list of topics that ranged from balancing the federal budget to engaging in a reasonable series of arms reduction talks. A listener disposed to see big government as the problem could understand that it was to blame for abortion, but could be left wondering whether to do anything about it or focus on other matters entirely. It would have been tempting to conclude that energies should be devoted to families, churches, neighborhoods, and schools, as they had been in the 1950s.

Thus it was not surprising that little was done in Kansas to mobilize large-scale activism against abortion until later in the decade. What did occur was the formation of two lobbying organizations, Right to Life of Kansas, founded in Topeka in 1981, and Kansans for Life, organized in Wichita in 1984. In addition, pregnancy counseling centers encouraging alternatives to abortion were established between 1973 and 1987 under the names of Birthright, Birthline, and Pregnancy Crisis in Wichita, Topeka, and nine other locations throughout the state. These organizations served as the basis of an effort that would eventually become well institutionalized. They concentrated specifically on abortion prevention, were not churches or multipurpose religious organizations, and had separate legal status as nonprofit associations. They operated on small budgets sustainable through donations and volunteer time. Their activities were framed by the reality of *Roe v. Wade* along with statutes governing when and under what circumstances abortions and pregnancy counseling could be provided. Legislative efforts proceeded with the hope of clarifying uncertainties or reducing gaps in existing statutes. In 1985, the Kansas Senate considered a proposal to require all babies born during attempted abortions to have medical treatment and be placed in the custody of the state's welfare agency, and the following year debated the measure again while passing a bill requiring girls sixteen or younger seeking an abortion to have a parent's consent. In the 1986 race for governor between Republican Mike Hayden and Democrat Tom Docking, Kansans for Life endorsed Hayden and Right to Life of Kansas endorsed neither. Hayden won, but neither candidate said much about abortion, and observers believed the election to have been decided largely by economic issues and party loyalties.[22]

By 1988, abortion was gaining wider attention than it had during most of the preceding decade. Pope John Paul II had toured the United States for ten days the previous September, and ended his visit with a sharply worded speech in Detroit about the necessity of respecting and protecting "every human being from conception until natural death." The National Association of Evangelicals applauded the pope's statement. The Southern Baptist Christian Life Commission called for stronger preaching against abortion, and renewed its efforts to shape legislation and open crisis pregnancy centers. Fundamentalist Reverend Falwell was staging rallies at state capitals, during which pro-life and abortion rights activists sometimes clashed. In the Kansas legislature, proposals to stiffen parental consent laws were still discussed, but abortion was proving to be sufficiently thorny that lawmakers and activists alike were frustrated. An estimated 150,000 people gathered in Washington in November 1989 to hear speeches for and against abortion rights. Smaller events were held in 150 cities, including one in Topeka that drew 1,000 participants. A representative survey of Kansans that fall gave ammunition to both sides. Abortion rights leaders were reassured by a majority of those surveyed expressing approval of the state's current policies and saying they would not want *Roe v. Wade* overturned. Opponents of abortion noted that a majority favored parental consent for teenagers seeking abortions, wanted doctors to perform tests to determine whether fetuses could survive outside the womb, and approved of abortions only in cases of rape or incest, or if the mother's life was in danger.[23]

The renewed activity that fall was driven primarily by the Supreme Court's decision in *Webster v. Reproductive Health Services* on July 3, 1989, that a Missouri law regulating the conditions under which abortions could be performed was not unconstitutional. The Missouri law restricted the use of public funds for abortions, and set limits on where abortions could be performed and by whom. The law also included a preamble stating that "the life of each human being begins at conception," and "unborn children have protectable interests in life, health, and well-being." Much of the testimony before the Supreme Court focused on medical evidence about fetal development and indications by which physicians could determine the viability of fetuses beyond twenty weeks of pregnancy. Opponents of abortion considered it a victory that the testimony educated the public about the personhood of fetuses and that the court did not challenge the definition of human life included in the law's preamble. The most important result of the decision, however, was opening the way for states to pass laws about abortion, and indeed necessitating that they do so.[24]

The *Webster* decision was not only an opportunity for abortion opponents to mobilize to affect state legislation. It was also a crucial step toward bringing about the new relationship between individual citizens and government that President Reagan described in his speech at Kansas State and on many other occasions. Reagan's emphasis on churches, schools, neighborhoods, and families was more than rhetorical. It was an associationalist vision of democracy akin to the one that Alexis de Tocqueville articulated following his visit to the United States in the 1830s. Voluntary associations, Tocqueville argued, prevented centralized government from becoming totalitarian by enabling citizens to perform many of the tasks needing to be done in their communities, such as caring for the sick and organizing schools, by themselves. In Reagan's view, the antidote to big government was not individualism. Although he spoke of freedom and self-reliance, his stress was on what conservative social theorists at the time were calling mediating structures. Churches, schools, neighborhoods, and families were the local organizations through which citizens empowered themselves. *Webster* gave people on both sides of the abortion issue a reason to mobilize through these mediating structures. Organizing meant protecting families and local customs. It also meant enlisting clergy and other community leaders to shape policy.[25]

With Missouri's restrictions upheld, Kansas groups on both sides of the issue felt the need to become more active. Two hospitals in Kansas City, Missouri, quit performing abortions except when mothers' lives were at risk, leading officials to believe that more abortions for Missourians were likely to be performed in Kansas. In Wichita, abortion rights activists formed the Pro-Choice Action League, which included Catholic members who disagreed with the church's strong antiabortion stance. "The church's basic position on abortion is crystal clear," Reverend Ronald Gilmore, vicar general of the Wichita diocese, said. The state's bishops called on Catholic legislators to oppose abortion, but stopped short of threatening excommunication if they did not. For its part, the legislature considered, but did not approve, a measure prohibiting abortions at the KU Medical Center in Kansas City, Kansas, and tabled a bill that would have extended the parental consent requirement to seventeen year olds. Heated discussion of the proposal focused on whether the measure would result in more legal abortions or create a back-alley abortion industry. The Kansas Supreme Court fueled

the controversy by determining that a fetus was not a human being under the state's homicide laws. A lobbyist for Right to Life of
Kansas saw the decision as an opportunity for a law to the contrary
that might have far-reaching implications. Democratic representative Kathleen Sebelius presaged controversies that would return
during her term as governor by registering opposition to the idea.[26]

While bills and court rulings were being discussed in Topeka,
the most significant aspect of the growing controversies over abortion was little recognized: its ability to necessitate responses from a
wide range of local institutions. Despite the fact that relatively few
women were seeking abortions, the issue was sufficiently complex
that it had to be considered by almost everyone in a leadership
position. In this respect, it was quite different from an issue like
women's ordination that mainly affected churches, or a controversy
about zoning that might involve a single neighborhood. Abortion
was discussed in churches because clergy and parishioners associated it with questions about the sanctity of life. It arose in the
courts because the slaying of a pregnant woman posed the question of whether one murder or two had been committed. It affected
discussions of appropriations for the state's universities because of
the medical center question. In Wichita, the county Board of Health
was drawn into the controversy by questions about its approval of
Planned Parenthood as a provider of family planning counseling.
Catholic staff at St. Francis Hospital in Wichita had to decide if they
could exempt themselves from performing abortions. The Wichita
School Board was drawn into the debate by questions about a new
sex education curriculum. All of these issues were being debated in
fall 1989. Meanwhile, protesters were starting to make their voices
heard by taking to the streets.[27]

THE WAR IN WICHITA

On Saturday morning, July 15, 1989, seventy-nine protesters were
arrested for blocking an east Wichita abortion clinic's entrance.
The clinic was the Women's Health Care Services, operated by

Dr. George Tiller. It was not the first time that trouble had occurred at the clinic. Protesters had distributed antiabortion literature and conducted sidewalk prayer vigils there for years. The clinic was bombed in 1986. The arrests in 1989 were the third such incident in recent months. The organizer, Michael Dodds, headed a coalition called the Wichita Rescue Movement. Besides enlisting local activists, the coalition brought in protesters from Oklahoma, Nebraska, and West Virginia. They were coordinating with Operation Rescue, Dodds said, to organize a national event in Wichita in the next few months.[28]

That event did not materialize until 1991. The intervening months were marked by a continuation of local controversy. On January 8, 1990, Governor Hayden offered proposals about abortion for legislative consideration that included restrictions after twenty-two weeks of pregnancy, parental consent for teens under the age of sixteen, permitting abortions at KU Medical Center, and an increase in funding for sex education in public schools. The governor's affirmation of abortion on demand during the first twenty-two weeks of pregnancy and failure to recommend tougher restrictions on other points was roundly condemned by antiabortion spokespersons. Two weeks later, protesters led by Baptist pastor Fred Phelps prayed outside the statehouse to mark the *Roe v. Wade* anniversary, while 150 abortion rights advocates attended a meeting sponsored by the Religious Coalition for Abortion Rights and the Kansas Choice Alliance at the First Presbyterian Church. On February 10, 1990, more than 200 abortion opponents protested at Tiller's clinic in Wichita, and 68 were arrested. The event coincided with a Planned Parenthood lecture by *Roe v. Wade* attorney Sarah Weddington. That fall, in a reversal of usual party orientations, Democratic state treasurer Joan Finney ran on an antiabortion platform and defeated Republican governor Hayden. "I'm a Catholic," she told supporters, and "sick of abortion." In Wichita, evangelical clergy under the leadership of Assembly of God pastor Cecil Adams formed a political action committee called Evangelicals for Good Government in hopes of filling Republican Party posts with antiabortion leaders.[29]

The Summer of Mercy, as abortion opponents called it, began on July 15, 1991, following a week of field training in late June sponsored by the Pro-Life Action Network under Dodds's direction and with Operation Rescue's assistance. Over the next three months more than twenty-five hundred arrests for trespassing, loitering, and disorderly conduct would be made in conjunction with the civil disobedience that occurred—by far the largest number in the state's history. Dodds, a thirty-six-year-old Wichita resident who was intent on putting his Christian faith into practice, had been arrested twenty-five times over the past four years for participating in antiabortion protests in various cities. His arrests, he said, were among the "most enriching experiences as a Christian" he'd ever had.

Operation Rescue was a national organization, founded in 1987 under the leadership of Randall Terry, who also considered himself a devout Christian and often used biblical language in describing his efforts. The organization blockaded a New Jersey clinic in 1987 and gained national attention a year later by blockading clinics in Atlanta during the Democratic National Convention. By 1991 it was troubled with lawsuits, fines, injunctions, and jail sentences, and uncertain of how to proceed. Its newly appointed field director, Reverend Keith Tucci, decided that responding to Dodds's appeal for help in Wichita would be a wise move. Wichita was smaller than most of the cities in which blockades had been attempted thus far, and was farther from major media markets that could provide the publicity that fed volunteers and money to the organization, but it was large enough, was easily reached by air and bus, already had active local antiabortion groups, and was in the heartland, where conservative churches were plentiful and strong. Most important, it had at least one clinic that performed late-term abortions. That was good, because public sentiment against so-called baby killing was easier to arouse when late-term abortions were involved.

Between a thousand and fifteen hundred abortion opponents arrived that week from all over the country. Throughout the week, protesters gathered outside Tiller's and two other clinics to pray, march, and confront patients as they entered or left. Several dozen of the protesters picketed Tiller's home outside Wichita. During a Wednesday evening service at the Lutheran Church that Tiller attended, a group of protesters led by a Baptist minister from Louisiana stormed into the church and disrupted the meeting. On Sunday, July 21, more than three thousand people gathered for competing rallies, one sponsored by Operation Rescue, the other by abortion rights groups under the leadership of the Pro-Choice Action League. The next day, rows of protesters six deep blockaded Tiller's clinic carrying signs and waving plastic fetuses. An African American woman emerging from the clinic, where she was being treated for a minor illness, was confronted by a white woman, who shouted, "Even back on the plantation, the masters let you people live. Even massa let you live." Police arrested some of the protesters the next day. Rain thinned the crowd, but the demonstrators were not discouraged. Having succeeded temporarily in forcing the clinics to stay closed, the organizers declared their intention to continue. "Hey, why stay a week?" Terry asked. "Let's stay a month. Let's stay the summer. Let's see how long we can stay."[30]

During the second week, Tiller obtained a preliminary injunction from federal district judge Patrick F. Kelly, a Catholic Democrat and law school friend of Dole, to prohibit protesters from blocking access to his clinic. The judge ordered U.S. marshals to assist in carrying out the order. Mayor Bob Knight and Chief of Police Rick Stone, both of whom were personally opposed to abortion, cooperated by directing police to arrest protesters using the minimum force necessary. More than a thousand arrests were made that week. After a one-day lull the protests continued for a third week, during which a quarter of the entire Wichita police force were enlisted and another nine hundred arrests were made. Protesters sang, prayed, read passages from the Bible, and shouted epithets about slaughtering babies. Abortion rights spokespersons accused them of bleary-eyed zealotry. Operation Rescue spokesperson Patrick Mahoney, a Presbyterian pastor from Florida who had flown in to assist in leading the effort, saw it differently. "The abortion battle is not going to be decided in the trendy urban centers," the reverend said. "Wichita is the heartland of America. Wichita embodies what we will see in the next three to four years." Terry responded from his jail cell, where he was spending a week for violating the judge's restraining order, "The challenge before us is to use this street-level momentum and take back the state legislatures all over the country. The sky is the limit of the potential here."

The trajectory of any social movement is precarious. People have to be motivated to take part in the first place and then given enough hope to stay with it. Operation Rescue's initial success in Wichita was the result of a strategic decision to focus its attention on Tiller's and the two other clinics. The goal was not simply to protest abortion in general or overturn *Roe v. Wade* but rather to stop abortions from happening at three specific locations. With more than a thousand people from across the country, it was a matter of overwhelming force coming to bear against a few doctors and their staffs. The point, moreover, was not to protest but to instead rescue. It would count as a major success if a clinic could be shut down for good. But even if one baby's life could be spared, that was a major achievement. A rescuer could go home or stay another day feeling that something important had been accomplished. The question was whether the momentum could be sustained.

At the end of the third week, the unrest showed no signs of dissipating. Friday of that week Governor Finney arrived from Topeka and gave an antiabortion speech at an Operation Rescue rally. On Saturday, Bishop Eugene Gerber of the Wichita Roman Catholic diocese attended the clinic blockade and declared his support for the protesters. Eighty of the persons arrested that day were clergy. The following Monday Judge Kelly responded by raising the stakes. He would arrest the governor and the bishop if he had to, and fill jails across the state, he said. He released Terry and Mahoney from jail, but required Operation Rescue to post a hundred thousand dollar bond to cover damages that might eventually be awarded to the clinics. Any local clergy who urged supporters to block entrances to clinics were also required to post a hundred thousand dollar bond.

The threat backfired. The following day Reverend Joe Wright of the Central Christian Church, one of the largest evangelical churches in the city and a headquarters of antiabortion organizing, declared that Judge Kelly was mocking the church and trying to intimidate it from preaching against "blatant sin." He and fifty clergy, mostly Catholics, evangelicals, and fundamentalists, who claimed to have the support of at least fifty more, joined the blockade at Tiller's clinic the next day. "We cannot be silent," said Reverend Tom Macy of the First Evangelical Free Church, "as long as the abortion industry continues the premeditated killing of children." "Now the church is rising up," said Reverend Thomas F. Scaletty of St. Jude's Catholic Church. Christians who knew "abortion is murder," he declared, were now beginning to act like Christians. "I felt the Lord was speaking to me," a lay member reported. "Why am I just standing here" when some guy is killing babies. In a further response, Operation Rescue lawyer Jay Sekulow enlisted the U.S. Department of Justice in an effort to request the U.S. Circuit Court of Appeals in Denver to overturn Judge Kelly's restraining order. The arrests stopped. Judge Kelly persuaded abortion rights activists from other locations not to enter the fray. Operation Rescue's top leaders left town, and the mayor asked local clergy members to spend a day or two planning their next steps rather than taking immediate action. Three days later the battle resumed.

This time the churches were more active than ever. Journalists estimated that there were probably at least 500 religious organizations in the region that were capable of getting involved on one side or the other. The Catholic Diocese of Wichita included more than 100 churches, 30 schools, over 150 priests, and 100,000 parishioners, more than half of whom lived in Sedgwick County. Every parish included an annual "Respect Life Sunday," and several sponsored monthly rosary vigils at Tiller's clinic. Although Bishop Gerber did not condone civil disobedience, he attended rallies and encouraged members to confront their conscience about the right to life of unborn children. Sedgwick County included more than 300 Protestant churches totaling approximately 150,000 members. More than 30,000 were Southern Baptists. Another 20,000 belonged to Assembly of God, Evangelical Free, Nazarene, or conservative churches like Central Christian. Of the conservative pastors, 150 were affiliated with the Wichita Alliance of Evangelical Churches, an organization founded in 1988 by clergy members unhappy with the city's Interfaith Alliance. Led by Reverend Dick Kelsey, a former Bible salesperson, Christian school administrator, and political activist from Indiana and Alabama who ran a Christian retreat center near Wichita, the alliance encouraged its pastors to be active in the antiabortion effort. "If preachers don't take a stand," Kelsey said, "then we don't have a right to be called preachers."[31]

Many clergy refrained from becoming involved. Pastors of Methodist, Presbyterian, and Lutheran churches sometimes hosted abortion rights meetings, but more often found their congregations divided on basic views toward abortion and conflicted about the continuing unrest. That was true in some of the evangelical churches as well. At the large Immanuel Baptist Church, Reverend John Click was opposed to abortion, yet thought efforts should be directed toward the courts and through legislative action rather than in the streets. Reverend Titus James of the North Heights Christian Church, an African American congregation, believed a more effective approach was to teach people about the proper role of sexual behavior. Reverend Jack Middleton, pastor at Wichita Bible Church, was pro-life, but knew Tiller and sought to maintain cordial relations with him.[32]

On August 14, seventy-five clergy opposed to abortion met to discuss plans for further action following the departure of Operation Rescue, which was expected before the month's end. While praising Operation Rescue for igniting their consciences, the pastors decided to discontinue blockading clinics. Two days later, representatives of twenty-five local and state antiabortion groups met in Wichita and formed a coalition, named Hope for the Heartland, to carry on the work. Among the groups represented were Right to Life of Kansas, Life Inc., Kansans for Life, Physicians for Life, and the Wichita Alliance of Evangelical Churches. The coalition pledged to use educational and legislative means rather than clinic protests to achieve its aims, and planned a large stadium rally on August 25 to mark the departure of Operation Rescue and the beginning of a new phase. The next day, however, other leaders continued the blockades. More than three hundred protesters took part, and nearly half were arrested. Another hundred were arrested two days later, including Operation Rescue's Reverend Mahoney, who was returning from a trip to the East Coast. Meanwhile, a coalition of twenty abortion rights groups formed as Wichita Voices for Choice and promised to counter any continuing protests by Operation Rescue. Hope for the Heartland's stadium rally took place as planned, except that it had to be moved to a larger venue. The crowd was estimated at twenty-five thousand. The keynote speaker was television preacher Pat Robertson, who had run for president in 1988 and was closely associated with the antiabortion movement. "We will not rest until every baby in the United States is safe in his mother's womb," Robertson declared.[33]

Had it been up to the leaders of Hope for the Heartland, the war in Wichita would have ended in August and the campaign against abortion would have entered a new phase. Instead, the conflict continued for another month and a half. In early September, Judge Kelly sought to end the blockades through a compromise that involved lifting the injunction as long as protesters limited the number present at any given time, and promised not to deter patients and employees from entering for more than a stipulated period. Tiller refused, and the injunction stayed in effect. Dodds, whose Wichita Rescue Movement had taken over from Operation Rescue, threatened that the blockades would resume. More than fifty protesters were arrested blockading the Wichita Women's Center the next day. A week later protesters invaded one of the clinics. In October, protesters who wished to keep the blockades going invited an Operation Rescue leader to return. The leader was arrested at the airport, but the protesters held prayer vigils and blockades in Wichita and Overland Park. That Sunday, more than thirteen thousand abortion opponents formed a nine-mile "life chain" through Wichita in protest of "an industry that kills more than a million babies every year."[34]

SHIFTING THE FOCUS

The struggle to shut down Wichita's abortion clinics was far from over, but the tactics among conservative religious and political leaders shifted in 1992. Whereas the Summer of Mercy blockades had been the dominant focus in 1991, attention broadened in 1992 to a wider range of issues. Hope for the Heartland fulfilled its promise of seeking reform of abortion policies through legislation. That left the blockade effort in the hands of smaller groups of activists in Wichita. Terry's attention turned toward planning mass events in other cities the following summer and raising support through his radio program. The Wichita Alliance of Evangelical Churches included concerns about schools and family values among its top issues. With the fall elections looming, the question increasingly became one of mobilizing influence within the Republican Party and promoting conservative Christians for public office. As these wider efforts continued over the next several years, it was easy to believe that the Religious Right was gaining enormous power in Kansas politics. But in reality, a movement that takes on too many diverse issues finds it harder to accomplish its goals and sustain its momentum.

Concerns centering on public schools had been simmering since the late 1970s, when the antigay rights movement warned of homosexual teachers perverting children. ERA opponents worried that schools were debasing traditional family values, and there were periodic controversies over sex education curricula, books in school libraries, and advertisements by abortion clinics in high school newspapers. Interest in private schools was growing as a result. Central Christian Church founded its Central Christian Academy in 1982 and gained full accreditation in 1986. Calvary Christian School began holding classes in 1984 under the leadership of a former Baptist from Oklahoma and in cooperation with Calvary Chapel, a nondenominational evangelical church. After declining enrollments and school closings during the 1960s and 1970s, the Catholic Diocese of Wichita added three new schools during the 1980s and witnessed a 14 percent increase in enrollments. In 1988, conservative Wichitans were disturbed by the public schools' new sex education program, which included discussions of masturbation, homosexuality, and birth control in the middle school curriculum.[35]

When he organized the Wichita Alliance of Evangelical Churches in 1989, Kelsey was trying without much success to sell motivational skills videotapes to the public schools. Having no African Americans in the tapes, he felt later, may have been one of the problems. With fifteen years of administration at Christian schools in Indiana and Alabama under his belt, though, he was concerned about broader issues in the public schools. Wichita was not as conservative an environment as he had been led to believe. The schools, he said, were teaching humanistic values rooted in what he described as a new age philosophy, and there appeared to be a general decline in traditional values. Kelsey hoped that the alliance would change things. Besides opposing abortion, its agenda included reforming the schools, challenging a proposed liberalization of gambling laws, and discouraging a local cable company from showing Martin Scorcese's controversial film, *The Last Temptation of Christ*.[36]

The occasion for the alliance to become more directly involved in school matters arose during the heat of the antiabortion blockades, and probably would not have aroused interest from religious groups had it not been for their involvement in the blockades. In August 1991, a group of Wichita parents organized a petition drive to force a recall election of two school board members, charging that they were engaged in a personal vendetta against the school superintendant that was costing the district and occurring in violation of open-hearing laws. By November, the group had secured more than twenty-four thousand signatures and the recall election was scheduled for April. One of the two board members facing recall, Darrel Thorp, was known to have an evangelical Christian background and was opposed to abortions. Thorp was reluctant to make either an issue, but conservative supporters decided to emphasize them. Kelsey argued that the superintendant was promoting a humanistic philosophy in the schools and that Thorp was resisting it. The alliance went to bat for Thorp, using its network to launch Pastors for Quality Education, and enlisted the support of several antiabortion groups, including Life Inc. and its political action committee, Lifepax. Thorp, they maintained, was a fine Christian, a "strong spokesman for traditional Christian values" against the rising tide of godless humanistic philosophies. Their efforts did not prevail. Thorp became the first Wichita School Board member in history to be recalled. But his supporters, citing high turnout and the fact that 45 percent of the voters wanted him to stay, vowed to continue the struggle for Christians in public office.[37]

While the recall campaign was occupying some of the clergy leaders' attention, others sought to capitalize on the lessons of the previous summer, but in ways that might bridge the divide between pro-choice and pro-life constituents, or at least demonstrate that other issues were important. The major event of the winter was a citywide crusade held at the Kansas Coliseum in Wichita on February 22. Project Freedom, a coalition of government and private sector groups concerned with teen violence, gang membership, and drug abuse, organized the event. The coalition included Big Brothers and Big Sisters, Kids across America, the Catholic Diocese of Wichita, and more than a dozen clergy spanning the denominational spectrum from Nazarene and Baptist to Methodist and Presbyterian. More than nine thousand teens attended the event, which included a prayer meeting, evangelistic lectures, and a contemporary Christian rock concert.[38]

The main result of the antiabortion activism of the previous summer was the passage of a new state law stiffening abortion restrictions. The law raised the previously proposed age at which parental consent was required for an abortion to include any unmarried woman under the age of eighteen. It stipulated that a woman would not be allowed to have an abortion if the fetus was capable of living outside the womb unless the woman's life was in danger or the fetus was severely deformed. Those determinations were left to the attending physician, but were understood to apply to third-trimester pregnancies. A woman seeking an abortion was also required to receive counseling about the procedure's risks, alternatives to having an abortion, how well developed the fetus was, and available community resources for carrying the baby to term, and she was then required to wait at least eight hours after counseling before having the abortion. The law further responded to the unrest in Wichita by preventing cities or counties from passing their own laws regulating abortion, and increased the penalties for blockading clinics.[39]

The new law was more restrictive than abortion rights groups wanted, but did not satisfy the strongest abortion opponents either. The Wichita Rescue Movement continued its vigils and demonstrations at Tiller's clinic and the Wichita Women's Center, contending that it was fulfilling a biblical mandate to combat evil, escalated the confrontations by picketing pro-choice offices, demonstrating in front of the private residences of abortion rights spokespersons, and threatening a boycott of one of the community's largest hospitals. With fewer round-the-clock demonstrations and less police surveillance, incidents perpetrated by antiabortionists, presumably acting on their own, began to include gluing doors and door locks, spray-painting clinics, attempted arsons, and other acts of vandalism. As the warm weather returned, a group calling itself Lambs of Christ planned to resume the protest activities of the previous summer at Tiller's clinic. The Pro-Choice Action League rented a house two doors from the clinic to monitor the activities. On June 5, 1992, city workers erected snow fences as a barricade around the clinic. The next morning, twenty police and several dozen abortion rights activists faced off against two hundred antiabortion demonstrators. A man from Oklahoma calling himself Jonah said God told him to come to Wichita. A woman drove by and sprinkled holy water on the grass. A man nailed a huge wooden cross to the bed of his truck. Another man came from Oregon, having just spent five years in prison for bombing a clinic there. One of the clinic's volunteers opened a bag on the grass and found a hand grenade. Protesters said she had probably put it there herself.[40]

Protests continued throughout the summer under the leadership of the Wichita Rescue Movement and Lambs for Christ, but on a far smaller scale than in 1991. Under the new Kansas law, demonstrators faced arrest for interfering with a lawful business or criminal trespass, tougher sentences, and requirements to post higher bonds. Activity shifted increasingly toward efforts to elect antiabortion candidates to local positions in the Republican Party and the primaries as well as secure victories in the general election in the fall. Candidates sometimes fretted that other issues were being ignored, but more often advertised their credentials as supporters of choice or opponents of abortion. A reporter covering the campaign observed that the candidates were "constantly on edge as they try to dodge the pitfalls of being labeled, denounced or misunderstood."[41]

The churches played a more active role in the 1992 election than at any time in Wichita's history. The associate pastor at the Tabernacle Baptist Church, Eric Snell, ran for a seat in the state legislature as an outspoken opponent of abortion and foe of big government. The Republican candidate for Congress, Eric Yost, spoke frequently at churches and to pastors' groups about his opposition to abortion, support for tax breaks to help parents send children to church-operated schools, and desire to return prayer to the public schools. Countering Yost's emphasis on traditional Christian values, Democrat Dan Glickman also spoke at churches, denied that he was pro-choice yet argued that big government should stay out of his relationship with God and moral decisions, and asserted that the nation needed spiritual renewal. Kansans for Life placed political pamphlets on churchgoers' windshields in Catholic, Baptist, and Evangelical Free parking lots. Hope for the Heartland distributed brochures in churches, urging members to take action on behalf of the "right" candidates. Wichita Rescue Movement leader Bryan Brown formed a group called Godarchy, meaning "God rules," to encourage conservative antiabortion Christians to "wake up" and run for office. Clergy were generally cautious about endorsing candidates from the pulpit, but saw no reason to keep silent in other contexts. As a Southern Baptist preacher, Tim Boyd of Mulvane, observed, "Endorsing candidates when you are not in the pulpit is another thing." Bringing national publicity to the campaign, Reverend Falwell, preaching at the Immanuel Baptist Church, denounced the National Organization for Women as the "National Organization of Witches," and described Planned Parenthood and the National Education Association as "anti-family bigots."[42]

The conservatives' efforts were not a complete success. Snell was not elected. Glickman won, although by a smaller margin than in previous elections. Of the twenty-two Sedgwick County candidates endorsed by Kansans for Life, twelve were victorious and ten lost. But the Kansas Republican Coalition for Life, a group inspired by

Schlafly and Robertson, estimated that abortion foes and members of the Religious Right succeeded in winning 255 of the 308 precinct committee positions in Sedgwick County, which gave them hope for the future. The key, a spokesperson for the coalition said, was "getting sympathetic churchgoers registered to vote and involved." Statewide, Republicans solidified their control of the legislature, ousting twelve incumbents to establish a sixty-six-seat majority in the House, and gaining five seats for a total of twenty-seven in the Senate. In the presidential race, Bush beat Clinton by 39 to 34 percent, with Ross Perot taking 27 percent of the vote. Only ten counties opted for Clinton.[43]

With a majority in both houses of the state legislature, Republicans sought to strengthen regulations on abortion through measures extending the waiting period from eight to twenty-four hours, changing the definition of fetal viability, and banning the French RU-486 abortion pill. In Wichita, the rescue movement brought Operation Rescue leader Mahoney to speak at a church conference and help mobilize summer plans. Hopes were elevated by rumors that two of the three clinics might be closing and a U.S. Supreme Court ruling that the Reconstruction-era civil rights law used to ban Ku Klux Klan activities could not be applied by federal judges to antiabortion blockades. Yet Operation Rescue's major campaign that summer was to be held in Minnesota and six other states.[44]

Wichita's antiabortion leaders quietly rejoiced that the news of Dr. David Gunn's killing by an abortion protester in Florida was causing Kansas abortion providers to be more cautious. Rather than focusing its efforts solely on blockades, for which arrests could still be made under Kansas law, Operation Rescue encouraged a range of tactics. Homes were picketed, billboards and posters were used, letters were sent to doctors' and nurses' relatives and neighbors in their hometowns, and disruptions were staged at their churches. As the movement splintered into smaller, less easily coordinated groups, and protesters considered more inventive ways of stopping abortions, the risks of the Florida incident being repeated increased. That risk was heightened when Wichita leader Dodds, along with more than a dozen activists in other cities, declared that the killing in Florida should be treated as a justifiable homicide. On August 19, 1993, Rachelle Renae Shannon of Grants Pass, Oregon, fired two shots from her .32 caliber pistol at Dr. Tiller as he drove away from his clinic, wounding him in both arms. "It was the most holy, the most righteous thing I've ever done," Shannon said. As Tiller recuperated, Catholics in Wichita commemorated their annual "Respect Life Sunday," evangelical Protestants formed a human chain in the shape of a cross to protest abortion, and activists picketed Tiller's home.[45]

But if all attention seemed to focus on abortion, that clearly was not the case. The Religious Right was increasingly expanding its reach to a wider portfolio of conservative causes. Groups such as the Kansas Education Watch Network, Kansas Family Values Coalition, School PAC, and Concerned Parents were running conservative Christians in school board elections, lobbying against measures that might discourage homeschooling, and stirring enough opposition to new curricula and educational testing reforms that superintendants and school board members held a meeting in Topeka to discuss "dealing with pressure groups." At the Central Christian Church in Wichita, Concerned Women of America hosted public officials speaking about conservative family, educational, and electoral issues. In the state legislature, conservatives prepared measures they hoped to introduce in 1994, opposing what they viewed as preferential treatment for gays, favoring abstinence-based sex education, allowing teachers to talk about God, and establishing a voucher program permitting parents to use state funds to send children to private schools. Falwell's visit, which focused on moral decay, homosexuality, and family values more than abortion, was indicative of the Religious Right's wider concerns.[46]

Robertson, giving the Landon Lecture at Kansas State, emphasized similar themes. Calling the feminist movement a "socialist, anti-family political movement that encourages women to leave their husbands, kill their children, practice witchcraft, and destroy capitalism," Robertson declared that true Christians everywhere were under assault. Like Reagan four years earlier, Robertson saw big government as the underlying problem. Ignoring the federal

government's considerable role in acquiring, organizing, and defending the land that became Kansas, Robertson lauded the pioneers who settled the state. "And you know something?" he said.
"They did so without the Department of Covered Wagons in Washington, D.C."[47]

Efforts to broaden the scope of Religious Right activism continued through the 1990s, inspired by general opposition to the
Clinton administration, and through national organizations such
as Operation Rescue, Falwell's Moral Majority, Schlafly's Eagle
Forum, and Robertson's Christian Coalition. Having eased federal
restrictions on abortion clinic blockades, the Supreme Court ruled
in 1994 that racketeering laws could be used to prosecute protesters for damage at clinics as well as inhibit intimidation, bombings,
and other violent acts. A statewide poll in 1995 showed that rank-
and-file Kansans were conflicted about abortion. Thirty-eight percent thought it was always wrong, 19 percent said it was usually
wrong, and 40 percent said it was right or neither right nor wrong.
Seventy percent favored keeping the state's current practice of allowing a woman to make her own decision about whether to have
an abortion. But a majority revealed that the debate was polarizing
public opinion. A third said their support for abortion rights had
increased, while an equal number said their opposition to abortion
had strengthened.[48]

In 1997, the state legislature passed a compromise bill aimed at
increasing a "woman's right to know" by requiring written material along with a face-to-face consultation between patients and
their doctors, but that left unresolved important questions about
late-term abortions and did not prohibit abortions performed to
prevent mental as well as physical endangerment. Neither side was
entirely satisfied, but the measure offered a respite to citizens weary
of the controversy, and eager to concentrate on such perennial issues as crime and taxes.[49]

In the 1998 gubernatorial race, the Religious Right's imprint was
strong. Seventy-nine percent of Kansans polled said moral decay in
their communities was a major concern, more than said the same
about crime or taxes, and 72 percent were interested in candidates'

positions on moral values. When asked about broadening the rights of gays and lesbians, 64 percent said they were opposed. Incumbent Republican Bill Graves emphasized his role in passing tougher restrictions on abortion, declared he was against same-sex marriage, and promised to combat obscenity and strengthen families. Not to be outdone challenger David Miller, campaigning under the slogan "Restoring Kansas Values," said his core beliefs were based on his faith in God, proclaimed that all abortions were wrong except when the mother's life is at risk, promised to take away the mental health exception in the abortion law, called sodomy a sin, and pledged himself in favor of returning traditional values to the schools.[50]

QUESTIONING EVOLUTION

As Republicans celebrated Governor Graves's reelection in 1998, the central issue bringing religion and politics together was shifting increasingly from abortion toward the schools and specifically to evolution. In 1999, the Kansas State Board of Education voted six to four to revise standards for teaching science to make room for criticisms and possible alternative explanations for human origins in lessons about evolution. The decision put Kansas in the national spotlight as an object for derision unlike anything it had experienced since the 1920s. Critics recalled White's question, "What's the matter with Kansas?" The state that had nurtured John Brown and Carry Nation, the state that had retained Prohibition long after its repeal and had recently witnessed one of the most sustained battles against abortion clinics, was now apparently revisiting Bryan's crusade against Darwin.

The Religious Right's relationship to the board of education controversy resembled its role in the antiabortion movement. Conservative churches served as venues in which concerns about the public schools were raised. Pastors encouraged members to vote, run for office, and attend meetings at which political issues were discussed. Large congregations hosted community-wide meetings and served as magnets for conservative activists from smaller churches. Special interest groups sent speakers to talk at church meetings and placed campaign literature on windshields in church parking lots. Many of the leaders who pressed for a revision of the science curriculum were connected with the antiabortion groups and churches in which these groups were active.

In other ways, the role of religion in the evolution controversy was quite different from the antiabortion movement. Giving high school students a chance to criticize evolution was very different, even to those who cared most, than preventing unborn children from being murdered. The case was simply harder to make that the belief in evolution contradicted religious faith in the same way that abortion violated the sanctity of life. In practical terms, critics of school policies had found it difficult to mobilize because concerned parents opted out by homeschooling their children or sending them to private schools. Nobody cared enough to blockade school entrances, get themselves arrested, or shoot teachers.

The possibility of affecting school policies lay in the fact that mass mobilization was not needed. Robertson's Christian Coalition had been arguing since his unsuccessful bid as a presidential candidate in 1988 that stealth tactics could be used effectively in local elections. Stealth tactics involved elections in precincts or districts small enough, and with sufficiently low voter turnout, that Christians could win with the help of fellow Christians from a few churches, or even from one large congregation. School boards were prime locations for stealth tactics. Church members frequently had credentials as teachers, many had children, and districts generally found themselves short on qualified candidates willing to serve. Conservative Christians had been successful in other states and some Kansas communities at getting themselves elected to local boards.

The Kansas State Board of Education presented a rare opportunity for conservative Christians to gain influence in the 1990s. Its ten members had been split five to five for several years between conservatives and moderates who opposed each other on a wide range of issues. A single new member could shift the balance. The board was in this respect like the U.S. Supreme Court, where major decisions were often decided by one vote, except that board members were elected for four-year terms. Usually at least two or three of the members from rural districts were reliably on the conservative side. That meant the decisive contests happened in populous urban districts. One was Wichita, where the antiabortion campaign had mobilized conservative Christians to take over a large element of the Republican Party. The other was Johnson County, with its own history of antiabortion activism on a smaller scale against clinics in Overland Park and Kansas City, and dozens of large conservative congregations.

For conservative churchgoers in predominately white middle-class suburbs of Wichita and rapidly growing upscale communities such as Overland Park, Olathe, Leawood, Lenexa, and Shawnee, school reform was a more comfortable issue than abortion. A well-educated, thoughtful person who opposed abortion could agree that Operation Rescue was too radical and that shooting abortion doctors was deplorable. It was better to vote periodically for conservative candidates and leave it to the legislature to do the rest. School reform was something in which a reasonable, law-abiding citizen could become involved, believing it actually mattered to the education one's children or grandchildren were receiving. There was no risk of mingling with people carrying hand grenades and posters of bloody fetuses. And yet it was a way to put one's faith into practice, especially if one believed, as Robertson argued, that Christianity was under assault.

In 1987, the Supreme Court ruled in a seven-to-two decision that a 1981 law in Louisiana requiring schools that taught evolution to teach creationism as well was unconstitutional. Requiring the teaching of creationism, the justices argued, served a religious purpose, and thus violated the constitutional principle of separation of church and state. Although many Religious Right leaders disagreed with the court's ruling, the Kansas controversy developed with an understanding that any similar attempt to introduce creationism explicitly into school curricula would be struck down. In fact, concerns about curricula emerged largely around other issues.

During the Reagan and Bush administrations, national discussions of education focused on reducing federal involvement and curtailing the power of teachers' unions. Districts in Kansas confronted questions about values and diversity, sex education, and whether new emphases on personal expression and self-esteem were undermining a traditional focus on basic skills.

In the early 1990s, these issues became the impetus for a number of special interest groups, including the Family Action Network, Kansas Coalition for Academic Excellence, Kansas Family Research Institute, Citizens for Excellence in Education, and the Kansas chapters of Concerned Women of America. As a follow-up to Wichita's 1991 Summer of Mercy, Life Inc. and Kansans for Life encouraged conservative Christians to take over local school boards. An anti-abortion activist from Wichita, Ruth Heitsman, ran unsuccessfully that year for a seat on the Kansas State Board of Education. The Central Christian Church in Wichita hosted guest speakers advising parents how to influence school officials. Concerned Women directed its lobbyist in Topeka to oppose a new Quality Performance Accreditation plan that the organization said was harmful to traditional values. Robertson gave the effort national publicity by featuring it on a broadcast of his *700 Club*. A frustrated state legislator complained that the "religious right wants to create their own new world order [and] wants to take young minds and limit their development, knowledge and understanding."[51]

In 1996, Linda Holloway of Shawnee ran for a seat on the Kansas State Board of Education, having tried unsuccessfully in 1994 for a position in the state legislature against incumbent Republican Phill Kline, an attorney who was to play a leading role in subsequent efforts to shut down the Tiller clinic in Wichita. Holloway was a soft-spoken forty-six-year-old grandmother with a master's degree and more than twenty years as a teacher. She was a former Southern Baptist who enjoyed listening to Christian radio and was a member of Grace Christian Fellowship Church, a nondenominational evangelical congregation founded in the early 1980s by a pastor trained in business administration with a graduate degree from Falwell's Liberty University. The church stressed a contemporary style of worship, featuring inspirational praise music and uplifted hands, and was committed to "raising up Christians who are life-giving instruments of change for God." Reluctant to reenter the political fray, Holloway decided to do so with the encouragement of her pastor. She hoped to use her position on the board to promote academic accountability and revise the Quality Performance Accreditation program, which she described as "fuzzy wuzzy." She won the primary by ten thousand votes and the general election by more than twenty thousand, giving her a 59 to 41 percent victory over independent challenger Richard G. Spears.[52]

It was not a time for immediate change. Worried by conservatives' gains, moderate Republicans discussed a constitutional amendment eliminating the board of education, or giving the legislature greater control over it—similar to proposals that had failed in 1974, 1986, and 1990. As a newcomer, Holloway spoke rarely and worked to secure a reputation for careful research. Although she favored voluntary school prayer and had reservations about sex education curricula, she raised neither issue. After attending a meeting sponsored by Concerned Women of America in 1998 at which sex education was discussed, Holloway and fellow conservatives introduced a new sex education program that focused on abstinence and required parents to give written consent for students to participate in the course. The board deadlocked five to five on the proposal.[53]

The prospect for conservative change improved dramatically in 1999. Holloway became the board's president, and conservatives achieved a six-to-four majority. After months of hearings, during which a committee of scientists and educators prepared a lengthy statement of recommendations, the board approved a different set of science standards that did not include evolution and left it to local school boards whether to include evolution in science curricula at all. The campaign against the scientists' committee began in earnest in January 1999, when Celtie Johnson, a Prairie Village homemaker and outspoken critic of sex education in the schools, learned that new science standards were being studied. Johnson asked fellow church members to get involved by speaking at public hearings.

A group formed that included several adherents of creation science. The group enlisted the help of Mary Kay Culp, associate director of Education for the Kansas Catholic Conference. Culp had been the president of Missouri Right to Life, was experienced in bringing pro-life issues to the attention of parishioners and legislators, and had been tracking what she regarded as worrisome trends in national educational policies about teaching evolution for several years. She was especially troubled that the new policies seemed destined to undermine religion by equating it with myth and superstition. The group met at the home of Tom Willis, president of the Creation Science Association for Mid-America, near Kansas City and began drafting an alternative proposal. Willis, who regarded the "scientific fraternity in America" as "little more than a religious cult," held deep misgivings about the evidence for evolution, but also understood the importance of keeping whatever the group proposed free of explicit references to creationism and religion.[54]

The board members who voted for approval of the revised standards viewed the decision as a reasonable compromise that would encourage teachers and students to engage in frank discussion of evolution's scientific strengths as well as weaknesses. Scott Hill, a rancher from Abilene, figured it would give districts latitude about what to teach. He assumed they would still use textbooks that included evolution. Baptist Steve Abrams, a veterinarian from Arkansas City who served on the board of a center providing alternatives to abortion, cited the possibility of teaching innovative cosmological theories that challenged conventional understandings of time. Harold Voth, a Mennonite from Haven, explained that he was influenced by the number of people urging him to delete standards about evolution. Holloway said a close reading of the scientific evidence suggested that the case for evolution across species was not as compelling as the case for evolution within species. The board's decision, in her view, "broadened academic freedom and free inquiry." Presbyterian Mary Douglass Brown, a retired teacher from Wichita, thought the entire debate was a tempest in a teapot. She said the whole matter could have been avoided if the board had stated emphatically that evolution is a theory. Not surprisingly, none of the measure's supporters saw themselves as dogmatic or narrow-minded. They wanted students from conservative religious backgrounds to feel welcome in classroom discussions and at the same time wanted the schools to offer excellent education for everyone. They denied criticisms that their aim was to promote creationism, but conceded that the long deliberations posed thorny questions they would just as soon have avoided. "I've been ridiculed ever since I've been on this board for my faith," Holloway said at one of the hearings, almost in tears. "It's not about faith," a scientist replied. "It's about science."[55]

Reaction to the board's decision came from all sides. A few conservative clergy and proponents of creation science spoke in favor. Phillip E. Johnson, a critic of Darwin from the University of California at Berkeley, showed up at the Overland Park Church of Christ to applaud the decision. A Baptist preacher in Topeka said, "Evolution is just bad science." A Hare Krishna leader from Kansas City praised the board for its "bold and brilliant step in rejecting Darwin's evolutionary theory." Dr. John D. Morris, president of the Institute for Creation Research in California, declared that the board's decision was a heroic stand against promoting "naturalism in the name of science, to the detriment of good education as well as student well being." The new standards, he said, would encourage students to "think critically" and "keep their minds open."[56]

But the overwhelming response was negative. Governor Graves called the decision a "terrible, tragic, embarrassing solution to a problem that did not exist." The chair of the committee of scientists that advised the board said the decision was a "travesty to science education." A moderate member of the state legislature termed it a "strong breach of good sense." A Lutheran pastor from Osborne wrote to the *Salina Journal* that "a Judeo-Christian moral obligation exists to vigorously study how Creation works," which he took as a mandate to study science and take its conclusions seriously, however uncomfortable they might prove to preconceived notions. A parent pleaded that the Religious Right not try to teach creationism to her children. A group of KU students, picketing the board's offices, asked if it might also want to declare the earth flat.

A statewide poll found that only 21 percent agreed with the board's decision. Most of those polled believed in evolution. Eighty-one percent said that dinosaurs lived millions of years ago, and 65 percent said fossil evidence demonstrates that sea creatures evolved into land creatures.[57]

Fears that Kansas would be a national laughingstock proved accurate. "What does a single cell organism and the Kansas Board of Education have in common?" a comedian asked. "The same number of brain cells." Kansas was a state where cousins could marry, said another. It was not the Land of Oz but rather the Land of Odds, quipped yet another. Rumor circulated that a high-tech company from another state canceled plans to relocate to Kansas and that graduate programs were advising new PhDs not to take jobs in the state. Scientists across the country sent letters to the board and wrote editorials defending evolution. CNN's *Crossfire* hosted a face-off on the topic between Falwell and paleontologist Stephen Jay Gould. The *Baltimore Sun* dusted off Mencken's most derisive observations from the 1920s to describe the Kansas decision: "It serves notice on the country that Neanderthal man is organizing in these forlorn backwaters of the land."[58]

The ridicule propelled a strong reaction against the decision. Guided not only by outside criticism but also by the centrist pragmatism that had been so much a part of the state's culture from the beginning, Kansans distanced themselves religiously and politically from what they viewed as an extremist element in their midst. Voters ousted two of the board's conservative members in 2000, and the newly constituted board approved new science standards that reinstated evolution the following February by a seven-to-three vote. Holloway received a warm endorsement from Senator Sam Brownback and raised nearly ninety thousand dollars in campaign funds, including small donations from Kansans for Life, Phillip Johnson of Berkeley, and the creationist Discovery Institute in Florida. Her moderate Republican challenger, Sue Gamble, was nevertheless victorious in the primary by a three-to-two ratio. Holloway turned to work in her church, broadcast a daily education feature on Christian radio, and with the assistance of her pastor, founded a private Christian academy.[59]

The Religious Right was down but not out. In 2004, conservative members once again gained a majority on the Kansas State Board of Education, and in 2005 the board rewrote the science standards using language similar to 1999. Just as had happened before, voters reacted by reducing the number of conservatives on the board in 2006, resulting in criticisms of evolution being eliminated from the science standards in 2007. In the interim, churches went about their business of hosting worship and nurturing faith, but a few conservative congregations continued to host creation science meetings and put forward biblical literalists for public office. In 2008, Holloway's pastor at Grace Christian Fellowship Church joined a network of more than two-dozen conservative pastors to challenge Internal Revenue Service rules forbidding churches from endorsing political candidates.[60]

CHAPTER 7

CONTINUING THE STRUGGLE

WHILE the Kansas State Board of Education debated evolution to the point that many of the state's citizens grew weary of hearing about it, conservative church leaders in Kansas continued the struggle against abortion and expanded their activities to include opposition to same-sex marriage. Unlike the early 1990s, when the Religious Right threw everything it had into making the right to life an issue that would arouse thousands of activists, the ensuing years required action that could be sustained by fewer numbers and with less support from the general public. By the decade's end, it was clear that the Religious Right was moving into a new phase. It could win small victories by keeping up the pressure on local clinics and in the state legislature. It could make a difference by deploying its resources carefully in local and state elections. Political action could command the attention of clergy some of the time, but had to be in the hands of lawmakers, lobbyists, and special interest groups most of the time. The board of education's temporary success in bringing creationist criticisms to bear on the state's science standards was symptomatic of the changes taking place. Success could be achieved in small increments at strategic moments. Setbacks were as likely as gains.

The word most descriptive of these changes was institutionalization. A social movement becomes institutionalized when it acquires the ability to secure resources capable of sustaining itself indefinitely, and when it is able to set its own goals, then define its own criteria of success toward meeting those goals. Institutionalization usually includes quieter tactics and a lowering of expectations, and thus is often mistaken as a decline of movement strength when in fact it is just the opposite. An institutionalized movement's strength lies in the fact that experienced professionals do more of the work, and the work they do focuses increasingly on the day-to-day business of administering formal organizations. Inevitably these organizations are shaped not only by their leaders but also by the contexts in which they occur.

By the late 1990s, the Religious Right's activist phase of the 1980s was largely replaced on the national stage by a more enduring emphasis on institution building. Falwell's Moral Majority disbanded in the late 1980s, and was replaced by the larger and more effective Christian Coalition under the direction of political organizer Ralph Reed. Falwell himself turned more of his attention to presiding over Liberty University, which was training the next generation of conservative religious and political leaders. Robertson's Christian Broadcasting Network evolved into an empire that included the Family Channel, which Robertson sold in 1997 for $1.9 billion; Regent University, with graduate programs in broadcasting and law; and Operation Blessing, an international humanitarian relief agency. The Southern Baptist Convention successfully elected fundamentalists to its top posts for more than a decade, rid its seminaries of moderate faculty, and supported aggressive church expansion domestically and abroad. Conservative evangelical megachurches, such as Willow Creek in suburban Chicago and Calvary Chapel in Southern California, grew from single congregations into large networks of affiliated independent congregations. In Colorado Springs, James Dobson's Focus on the Family was reaching thousands of households through radio broadcasts and newsletters featuring conservative religious and social issues. The Family Research Council under the leadership of Tony Perkins was a $10 million organization engaged in fighting abortion, homosexuality, and pornography, and promoting traditional Judeo-Christian values. In Washington, the National Prayer Breakfasts, congressional prayer meetings, and the smaller behind-the-scenes group known as the Fellowship that Senator Carlson had helped establish were more active than ever before.

But institutionalization is never accomplished without costs. Activist leaders who launch movements and build successful organizations eventually burn out, retire, and die. Their successors are more likely to emphasize efficient management than activist mobilization. New issues emerge; the political climate changes. Well institutionalized as it was in the late 1990s, the Religious Right experienced these changes during the following decade. Its strength was by no means spent, but its activities in the early twenty-first century were marked as much by this transition as by its previous gains. Unable to enlist the active support of most Kansans, it nevertheless captured enough of the energy of conservative clergy and lawmakers that it was a phenomenon to be reckoned with, by friends and foes alike.

THE CHURCHES AND ACTIVIST NETWORKS

As the twenty-first century began, conservative church leaders in Kansas commanded enormous resources. Statewide approximately 1,800 conservative Protestant congregations included nearly 420,000 adherents. That number accounted for nearly a third of all churchgoers in the state. Southern Baptists added approximately 5,000 members during the 1990s, bringing the total to more than 100,000. The independent Christian churches that had separated from the Disciples of Christ grew to nearly 57,000, for an increase of almost 10,000 in the same decade. Catholics with more than 400,000 members, up from fewer than 370,000 members in 1990, made up a second third of the church going public. With conservative Protestants, that meant nearly two-thirds of Kansas churchgoers belonged to denominations in which opposition to abortion was part of church teachings. The remaining third belonged to old-line Protestant denominations, totaling approximately 458,000 adherents. Most of these denominations were smaller than they had been a decade earlier. Methodists, who outnumbered Catholics during much of the state's history, were now half as numerous and had declined by more than 30,000 during the 1990s. American Baptists were now only two-thirds as numerous as Southern Baptists. Adherents of Christian churches affiliated with the Disciples of Christ were slightly less numerous than adherents of independent Christian churches. Presbyterians, who numbered approximately 50,000, had declined by 20 percent in ten years.[1]

Besides the shifting balance of denominations, the state was affected by a continuing redistribution of its population. Sixty-five percent of Kansas towns lost population during the 1980s and 1990s. Small towns in rural areas were most likely to lose population. Even among towns with 5,000 to 20,000 residents in 1980, 45 percent declined. In contrast, 85 percent of towns with populations of at least 20,000 in 1980 grew. Wichita, which annexed thousands of acres of surrounding land as the population expanded, grew from 279,000 in 1980 to 351,000 in 2000. In Johnson County, Lenexa increased from 18,000 to 40,000, Leawood grew from 13,000 to nearly 28,000, Overland Park climbed from 82,000 to 149,000, and Olathe mushroomed from 37,000 to 93,000. As a result, the center of gravity of a state that had long thought of itself as predominantly rural, was increasingly urban. Sedgwick and Johnson counties alone made up a third of the state's population, and together included more residents than ninety-one of the state's smaller counties combined.[2]

The growth of Sedgwick and Johnson counties relative to the rest of the state affected the churches in three ways. First, it was an important factor in the decline of Methodism and the other old-line denominations that had planted and retained churches in small towns, but now found the populations of those towns dwindling. Of the 567 Methodist churches in Kansas, for example, 55 percent were in towns of fewer than fifteen hundred residents—a majority of which were declining in population—while only 17 percent were in towns of twenty thousand or more. Second, the redistribution of population contributed to the growth of Southern Baptists, independent Christian churches, Assemblies of God, and other conservative denominations that targeted urban areas as their primary locations during the 1950s and 1960s. This growth was facilitated by the fact that the new residents were especially likely to have come from Oklahoma, Texas, and Missouri, where conservative churches were numerous. For instance, the location of Southern Baptist churches in Kansas was almost a mirror opposite of Methodist locations. Only 19 percent of the three hundred Southern Baptist congregations were in towns of fifteen hundred residents or less, while 42 percent were in towns of twenty thousand or more. And third, many of the residents in Sedgwick and Johnson counties were newcomers who could most easily be attracted by large seeker-oriented, family-friendly congregations with special programs for all ages. In a state used to having congregations with fewer than three hundred members, it was now possible for entrepreneurial pastors to build institutions ten times that size. Doing so could give a church of that size considerable influence in shaping the spiritual climate of not only its members but also the wider community.[3]

The largest Protestant congregation in Kansas was the Church of the Resurrection, a congregation of ten thousand members with an eight million dollar annual budget on ninety acres in suburban Leawood. Founded in 1990 by a handful of families that met at a funeral home, the church benefited from the dedicated leadership of its pastor, Reverend Adam Hamilton, and the fact that Leawood was one of the most upscale of Kansas City's rapidly growing suburban communities. Large homes and excellent schools attracted well-educated professionals working at high-tech firms, such as Sprint and Garmin, or one of the area's many pharmaceutical companies, hospitals, and research centers. The Church of the Resurrection demonstrated that a congregation could become large and gain considerable influence in its community without aligning itself with the Religious Right. It was a Methodist congregation that attracted newcomers from Missouri, Arkansas, Oklahoma, and Texas, where being Methodist was a way of not being Southern Baptist, and from smaller communities where people had grown up in mainline denominations. Like other Methodist churches, its members included Republicans and Democrats who held varying opinions about abortion and other social issues. Its pastor believed that reasonable people could and should disagree with one another. He preached occasionally on controversial issues being debated in the denomination, such as abortion and homosexuality, and encouraged parishioners to understand the complexity of seemingly black-and-white issues. The congregation took pride in being a mixture of liberals and conservatives. It sponsored small fellowship groups in which people could voice their opinions among trusted others and focused its formal programs on activities around which there was substantial agreement, such as a strong children's education department, high-school-age ministry, short-term overseas mission trips, tutoring, and neighborhood assistance for a low-income community in Kansas City.[4]

The largest Catholic congregation in Kansas was the Church of the Magdalen on the northeast outskirts of Wichita. The parish home of more than sixteen hundred families, Magdalen occupied a thirty-acre site that included a nearly new fifteen million dollar sanctuary, rectory, gymnasium, and school for more than five hundred students. The parish facilities served as a venue for occasional meetings about abortion, school curricula, and other social issues, but like the Church of the Resurrection Magdalen focused largely on family activities about which parishioners could agree rather than on controversial topics. Much of its energy went into its school and related family-oriented programs, such as marriage counseling, classes about natural family planning, Moms' Day Out meetings for mothers with young children, a compassion program for needy families, home fellowship groups, a youth ministry, and children's activities. Like other Catholic parishes, Magdalen's involvement in pro-life issues was largely institutionalized through routine diocesan-wide activities. These included special Sundays during which prayers were said for the unborn, and networks through which members could sign up for trips to Topeka or Washington on the anniversary of *Roe v. Wade*. A survey of members showed that the top reasons for attending were the parish's proximity to their home, its friendliness, the reputation of its clergy, and its school. Eighty percent felt that the parish did a good job of appealing to a diverse range of groups and interests.[5]

7.1 The Church of the Magdalen in suburban Wichita is one of a growing number of megachurches in Kansas. Photo by author.

The Church of the Resurrection and the Church of the Magdalen had avoided the conflicts that shaped older congregations during the 1960s and 1970s. A congregation deeply influenced by these divisions was Wichita's Central Christian Church. The congregation, founded in 1879, was formally organized by the Disciples of Christ in 1880, played an important role in the formation of an institution of higher learning called Garfield University in 1887, and in 1896 tried unsuccessfully to hire Populist leader Mary Lease as its pastor. In 1922 the congregation of 400 members, which included 5 listed in the Social Register, constructed a large new building at its downtown location. In 1943 fire gutted the church, and a new building seating 800 was completed three years later. During the 1950s and 1960s the congregation grew steadily to nearly 2,000 members, but increasingly was at odds with what it perceived as theological liberalism in the Disciples of Christ denomination. In 1980, a majority of the members left and founded the new Central Christian Church as a nondenominational congregation in the northeastern suburbs. The 150 or so who remained with the denomination stayed at the downtown site, and with dwindling numbers disbanded in 2005. The new suburban congregation with approximately 600 charter members called Reverend Joe Wright, a Baptist from Kentucky, as its pastor in 1987. Under Wright's leadership the church grew to 3,000 by the end of the century, when it constructed a massive new 3,250-seat sanctuary and education center marked by a 10,000-pound gilded cross on its 28-acre campus. It was also under Wright's direction that the Central Christian Church became active in the antiabortion movement. During the 1991 Summer of Mercy campaign, it not only sponsored meetings and enlisted participants for the blockade but was also said to have raised $90,000 for Operation Rescue's expenses. In 1996, Wright made headlines and received more than 18,000 letters after offering a prayer at a session of the Kansas House of Representatives confessing on behalf of the state to worshipping multiculturalism, rewarding laziness with welfare, and killing the unborn.[6]

The megachurch most similar to the Central Christian Church on social issues was the Immanuel Baptist Church of Wichita. Affiliated with the Southern Baptist Convention, the congregation was a struggling inner-city church in serious decline when it called Reverend John Click from Houston in 1971. Click was on the fundamentalist side of the conflict between conservatives and moderates that divided the denomination in the 1980s, and as president of the Kansas-Nebraska Convention of Southern Baptists led the effort to secure the conservatives' victory in Kansas. He joined Wichita's anti–gay rights campaign in 1978, launched a television ministry, and helped form the Wichita Alliance of Evangelical Churches with Kelsey in the late 1980s. When Click retired in 1997, his Immanuel Baptist Church included more than three thousand members at its south-central location and at least that many at several satellite congregations. His successor, Reverend Terry Fox, also from Texas, continued the church's expansion, and became an ally of Reverend Wright in opposing abortion and homosexuality.[7]

In Johnson County, the congregation that most nearly resembled the Immanuel Baptist Church was the First Family Church of Overland Park. Located on sixty acres barely three miles from Church of the Resurrection, the First Family Church was founded in 1996 by Reverend Jerry Johnston, a Kansas City native who at nineteen started an evangelistic organization called Jerry Johnston Ministries and dreamed of becoming the next Falwell. With an ample mailing list and an affiliation with the Southern Baptist Convention, the congregation attracted six hundred to its first service at a rented auditorium and doubled within a year. Falwell visited in 1997 to help boost the effort, and by 1999 the church had assets of nearly four million dollars and plans to become much larger. Over the next three years, Johnston constructed a large church valued at more than twelve million dollars and grew the membership to more than three thousand. His success earned him appearances on the *Today Show* and the *O'Reilly Factor*. He increasingly became known not only as the leader of one of the nation's fastest-growing megachurches but also as an outspoken critic of abortion and homosexuality.[8]

Besides the leadership of pastors like Johnston, Wright, and Fox, the Religious Right had at its disposal several well-honed mechanisms for exercising political influence. These included statewide organizations with more than a decade of lobbying experience, such as Kansans for Life and Right to Life of Kansas; parachurch organizations through which activism could be mobilized, such as the Knights of Columbus, parochial schools, and church-related colleges; legal, medical, and health policy professionals associated with the state's large Catholic-owned Via Christi hospital system; and numerous special interest groups such as Avenue for Life, Black Americans for Life, Christians for Life, Feminists for Life, Life Choice Ministries, and Lutherans for Life. An additional resource was the fact that churches served in Kansas as common polling sites during primary and general elections. In Sedgwick County, for example, twenty-seven of the thirty-six polling sites were at churches. Although churches were required to cover religious artifacts, an investigation by a coalition of civic groups showed that violations frequently occurred. It was impossible in any case to disguise the fact that a building with a large cross in front was indeed a church.[9]

Kansas was by no means the most religious place in the nation— church attendance and belief in God were still higher in the South— but there was plenty of potential for conservative religion to mingle with politics. A study in 2000 showed that 54 percent of Kansans wanted religious leaders to become more active in running for public office and 46 percent wanted "Christian fundamentalists" to have more influence in shaping public opinion. While only 25 percent thought clergy should address political issues from the pulpit, 79 percent thought religious organizations should express their views on social issues, and 88 percent thought political candidates should talk publicly about their religious views.[10]

What the Religious Right did not enjoy was uncontested influence within the Republican Party. A poll of registered Kansas Republican voters in 2000 showed that 45 percent identified themselves as moderates or liberals while 55 percent said they were conservatives. Thirty percent of all Kansas Republicans said they identified with the Religious Right, but the proportion was only 16 percent among moderate Republicans compared to 43 percent among conservative Republicans. Conflict between the two Republican factions had been deepening since 1995, when conservatives gained control of the state chairship and a majority of precinct committee representatives. Governor Graves's denunciation of the board of education's 1999 decision to downplay evolution in the state's science standards reflected his broader frustration at conservatives' influence. In the 1998 gubernatorial primary Graves's challenger, conservative David Miller, was the former head of Kansans for Life and the current Republican Party state chair. Graves beat Miller three to one, but Miller ran an aggressive campaign accusing Graves of failing to protect innocent unborn children and drew substantial support from the Religious Right, including an endorsement from Focus on the Family's Dobson. Compounding the tension was the fact that Miller's temporary replacement as party chair was conservative board of education member Abrams, also a strong pro-life advocate.[11]

ELECTING GEORGE W. BUSH

On the national stage, the presidential race in 2000 between Texas Governor George W. Bush and Vice President Al Gore was viewed as a victory for the Religious Right. Bush declared himself to be a born-again evangelical Christian, and received warm endorsements from Falwell, Robertson, Richard Land of the Southern Baptist Convention, and Charles Colson of the Prison Fellowship, while Gore talked little about his faith, despite having gone to a seminary and holding membership in a Southern Baptist congregation. But in Kansas, the Religious Right had little to do with the election—so little that its near absence warrants explanation.[12]

It was a foregone conclusion that Kansas, historically the most Republican of Republican states, would opt for Bush. Since defecting to Johnson in 1964, Kansas had given Nixon a 20 percent margin in 1968 and a 38 percent margin in 1972. It gave Ford a 7 percent victory in 1976, and Reagan a 24 percent win in 1980 and a 33 percent win in 1984. Bush Sr. received a 13 percent margin in 1988 and a 5 percent edge in 1992, and favorite son Dole an 18 percent victory in 1996. It was hardly necessary for the Religious Right or anyone else to work hard at turning out the vote for Bush Jr. in 2000. Bush's campaign staff knew that. They sent him to Missouri eleven times, including several stops in Kansas City, Missouri, but none in Kansas.

But there was more to it than that. In February 1999, more than a year and a half before the 2000 election, Governor Graves threw his weight behind Bush. Graves knew Bush and considered him a fellow moderate Republican as well as a personal friend. There were rumors that Graves might be in line for an appointment as the secretary of agriculture to replace Kansas Democrat Daniel Glickman, who held the position since 1995. With the support of moderate Republicans who were now in the majority, the state legislature took the unusual step of declaring that Kansas would not hold a presidential primary. The reason given was that the state could not afford one. That was a plausible explanation. As a result of lowering taxes and increasing spending, Kansas was running a deficit— the only state that was. Still, that was not the only advantage of not having a primary.

Disgruntled by moderate Republicans' recapture of power in 1998, conservative Republicans hoped to do better in the next election. They formed the Kansas Republican Assembly in January 1999 and helped organize the National Federation of Republican Assemblies. The group tried to persuade the legislature to reconsider a presidential primary, and when that failed suggested Republican caucuses similar to ones in Iowa in which conservative candidates often fared well. That suggestion also failed. At a June rally in Johnson County, the Kansas Republican Assembly featured conservative presidential candidates Pat Buchanan and Alan Keyes along with Eagle Forum leader Schlafly. The assembly held a convention in October in Kansas City attended by conservative delegates from thirty-three states. Family Research Council president Gary Bauer, flat-tax advocate Steve Forbes, Buchanan, and Keyes addressed the convention. Bush campaigned in Missouri but did not attend. Nor did any of the moderate Kansas Republicans.[13]

When Bush secured the nomination, the Kansas Republican Assembly fell in step with its moderate colleagues in supporting his election, but did so with muted enthusiasm. Its one success at the Republican National Convention, prompted in part by the concern that Bush's stance against abortion was wavering, was to ensure that a strong pro-life plank remained in the party platform. Analysts considering the principal issues in the campaign predicted that a Bush administration would have little effect on Kansas agriculture or the aviation industry, but might help oil and gas. In an apparent confirmation of this point, Bush's main donors in Kansas were not social conservatives but rather oil and gas producers. As November approached, there was concern among party leaders nationally that a low turnout might cause Bush to lose the popular vote even if he won the electoral college. In Wichita mainstream churches encouraged citizens to vote, perhaps hoping to assist Gore, but conservative churches were notably silent. Clergy said they were reluctant to get involved for fear of violating the separation of church and state. It was better, they said, to focus on spiritual renewal than on partisanship. Whether the Religious Right or some other factor was responsible, the turnout among registered voters in Kansas was 7.4 percent lower than in 1996, 17.8 percent lower than in 1992, and 4.3 points below the level it would achieve in 2004. Taking account of differences in the total registration, 120,000 fewer Kansans voted in 2000 than should have if the 1996 rate had been attained.[14]

If Kansas conservatives' admiration for Bush was tepid, his victory nevertheless encouraged the Religious Right to believe that more would be done in Washington on their behalf than had been during the Clinton administration. One of the new president's first announcements was that faith-based community initiatives would receive greater support. Another, which coincided with the twenty-eighth anniversary of *Roe v. Wade*, was to reinstate the Reagan-era executive order, termed by critics as the Mexico City gag rule, which banned federal money for organizations that promoted abortions overseas. In the U.S. Senate, Pat Roberts and Brownback were not due for reelection for another two years, and both were clearly on the conservatives' side. Roberts ranked among the ten most conservative members, and Brownback among the fifteen most conservative, according to a study by the *National Journal*. In the U.S. House, former KU miler Jim Ryun of Topeka ranked among the top twenty-five.[15]

The more important consequence of Bush's easy win in Kansas was to give the Religious Right time to regroup. Among the difficulties that conservatives faced in the state legislature was the fact that it met in regular sessions only ninety days a year, and was subject to frequent shifts in the balance of power between conservatives and moderates. In 1999, about fifty of the legislators formed the Kansas Conservative Caucus, modeled after one in Texas that had been in operation for fifteen years, as a kind of think tank to study and bring a conservative perspective to legislative proposals. The caucus included two key aspects of conservatives' effort to better institutionalize themselves. It formalized a coalition that brought together religious conservatives under the rubric of protecting family values with fiscal conservatives interested in limited government, free enterprise, and individual liberties. It also served as a legal entity that could hire a full-time staff person, which members hoped to pay from campaign contributions, to look out for conservative interests. That person was Joan Hawkins, a recent graduate of the

KU Law School and a Catholic, one of twelve children, who was a firm opponent of abortion. The think tank proved difficult to sustain because the state ethics commission ruled that legislators could not use campaign funds to support it, but the effort spawned an ongoing conservative organization called Kansas Legislative Education and Research. Hawkins moved on to become the head of Kansans for Life. Kansas Legislative Education and Research's executive director was attorney and tax expert Bob L. Corkins of the Kansas Public Policy Institute who had also worked as a lobbyist for the Kansas Chamber of Commerce. Corkins went on to become commissioner of the Kansas State Board of Education.[16]

The regrouping that began in 1999 bore dividends in 2002. In the Republican primary, conservative Tim Shallenburger ran for the gubernatorial nomination against Wichita mayor Knight. Still fuming over Knight's role in arresting abortion clinic blockaders in 1991, Operation Rescue West in Wichita denounced Knight as "an enemy of the child and Christians." Shallenburger was a banker from Baxter Springs who had been in the state legislature since 1987 and was currently serving as state treasurer. He was also a Baptist raised in the Nazarene Church who kept a framed copy of the Ten Commandments in his office, opposed abortion, and was critical of efforts to keep religion out of public schools. He captured 41 percent of the primary vote to Knight's 26 percent, and beat Knight even in Wichita. For the state attorney general nomination, conservative Protestant Phill Kline received support from Kansans for Life and strong church backing—including flyers on windshields in church parking lots calling his opponent, State Senator David Adkins, an "abortionist and evolutionist," and challenging readers to think how they would "answer Jesus" for their vote. Kline beat Adkins 50 to 39 percent. In other contests, Kristian Van Meteren of Ozawkie, who served as executive director of the Kansas Republican Assembly, successfully ran his mother, a creationist who publicized her disbelief in evolution, for the board of education, and in western Kansas a conservative from St. Francis whose campaign stoked anti-Hispanic sentiments won another board of education race. In the general election Shallenburger lost to Kathleen Sebelius, but Kline won as attorney general, and the two board of education candidates were successful in returning a conservative majority to the board.[17]

REGULATING ABORTION

In July 2001, abortion opponents marked the tenth anniversary of the Summer of Mercy in Wichita by calling for a summer of protests and blockades of Tiller's Women's Health Care Services clinic and Wichita Family Planning, the one other clinic that remained open. Operation Save America, as the protest planners called the effort, held nightly meetings at Wichita's Word of Life Church, encouraged participants to show up at the clinics, and drew up an "Emancipation Proclamation" they hoped the mayor would sign, stating that all children should be protected from the moment of conception. But the event proved disappointing to its organizers. Attendance at the nightly meetings was smaller than expected. Other than an aging priest who showed up with holy water at Tiller's clinic, few clergy joined the anticipated blockade. Only five arrests were made during the week. The mayor was conveniently out of town when representatives arrived at city hall. The Summer of Mercy had cost the city eight hundred thousand dollars in law enforcement expenses. This one cost only thirty-two thousand dollars.[18]

It was not that activists had grown weary or that the public had become any less opposed to abortion. It was rather that other means were being used. Nobody expected *Roe v. Wade* to be overturned or all abortion clinics to be shut down. There was a sense in Topeka that a basic legal framework had been established governing abortion, and now implementation was the issue. Lawmakers had pressing matters to address other than abortion. The tax structure, budget deficit, and schools were higher priorities. Clergy had different priorities too. Churches in small communities were struggling to maintain programs and keep pastors despite declining memberships. The emerging megachurches had their hands full with zoning board hearings as well as meetings with architects and construction companies. Antiabortion activists shifted increasingly toward regulation and to a lesser extent toward providing alternatives to abortion. After five years of planning, an alternative crisis pregnancy center called Choices Medical Clinic opened in 1999 next door to the Tiller clinic in Wichita. In the legislature Overland Park representative Tim Carmody, who had proposed a covenant marriage bill similar to one passed in Louisiana and favored by the Family Research Council, sponsored an unsuccessful amendment to a medical bill aimed specifically at revoking Tiller's license to practice medicine. The following year Carmody and fellow lawmaker Tony Powell of Wichita introduced bills designed to more closely regulate late-term abortions, and ban intact dilation and extraction abortions.[19]

The clause that abortion opponents were most intent on overturning was the one in Kansas law that permitted late-term abortions to be performed not only if a woman's physical health was endangered but also to prevent mental anguish. Opponents said the clause opened the door for any woman and her doctor to claim an abortion was necessary, while pro-choice leaders alleged that it indeed preserved the right for a woman and her doctor to choose— a right they said should not be exercised lightly yet was important in extreme cases of incest, rape, and abuse. The issue gave clergy members an opportunity to weigh in on both sides of the issue, insofar as examples of mental anguish could be drawn from pastoral counseling, but offered little help in resolving the impasse that had divided religious groups since *Roe v. Wade*. If anything, it shifted more of the debate to health professionals, lawyers, and legislators, whose job it was to write technical language that was both constitutional and satisfactory to constituents.[20]

The election of Kathleen Sebelius, an abortion rights supporter, as governor in 2002 demonstrated the degree to which issues other than abortion were on voters' minds. "From Johnson County to the western border," political analyst Martin Hawver wrote during the campaign, "the abortion issue is either one that candidates believe has been put to rest, or one that pales in significance to the business of balancing a budget, financing schools and making sure that the next session of the Legislature does something that will provide seniors with prescription drug cost assistance." With Sebelius in office, it seemed likely that legislation further restricting abortions would be vetoed. The opportunity to take more aggressive action now lay with Attorney General Kline.[21]

Kline's emphasis on abortion during the campaign, including a promise to seek a court order proclaiming that life starts at conception, worried Dr. Tiller enough that Tiller spent more than a hundred thousand dollars on behalf of Kline's opponent. As attorney general, Kline issued an opinion in June 2003 that any child under the age of sixteen seeking an abortion necessarily had engaged in sexual relations that were illegal under Kansas law. "As a matter of law," Kline wrote, "such child has been the victim of rape or one of the other sexual abuse crimes and such crimes are inherently injurious." It was thus incumbent on any health provider knowing of such circumstances to report them to the proper authorities, Kline argued. The opinion had far-reaching implications. To date, abortion opponents had been stymied in obtaining information about the medical circumstances under which abortions were performed because of privacy laws protecting doctor-patient relationships. Kline's opinion opened the door to soliciting such information. It also placed doctors in legal jeopardy for failing to report the alleged illegal sexual relations of minors. The doctor most at risk was Tiller. His patients' medical records could now be subpoenaed to determine if any of his patients were under sixteen at the time of conception, and if so, Tiller could be prosecuted for failing to report them. Abortion activists hoped the opinion would finally result in Tiller being forced out of business.[22]

In October 2003 Kline's opinion prompted the Center for Reproductive Rights, a national organization headquartered in New York City, to challenge the Kansas law on the grounds that it violated constitutional guarantees of privacy. The challenge was successful, thereby preventing Kline from using the law against Tiller. Other efforts to reduce abortions achieved mixed results. Centers encouraging alternatives to abortion increased. New centers included the Pregnancy Service Center in Salina in 2001, the Heartbeat Pregnancy Center in Beloit and the Open Door Pregnancy Center in Hutchinson in 2002, the Augusta Pregnancy Care Center in 2003, and Your Choice Pregnancy Resource Center in Shawnee Mission in 2004. In 2002, the Vatican stepped up its pro-life efforts under the direction of Philadelphia cardinal Anthony J. Bevilacqua, and expanded its advertising, lobbying, and parish educational programs. Among the church's activities, the Wichita diocese hosted a conference on family values at which Pennsylvania congressman Rick Santorum encouraged the thirty-five hundred participants to "walk the walk" in opposing abortion. In Washington, Kansas senators Brownback and Roberts along with Representatives Ryun, Todd Tiahrt, and Jerry Moran were among those helping to bring about a ban on intact dilation and extraction abortions, and were pressing for stronger parental notification laws. In Topeka, Kline appointed longtime antiabortion activist Bryan Brown to head the state's Consumer Protection Office. But lobbyists failed to persuade the legislature that abortion providers should be required to post warnings about the risks of breast cancer, and a bill to manufacture "Choose Life" license plates failed. Governor Sebelius vetoed a bill that would have established exceptionally tough safety standards for abortion clinics. Statistics on abortions remained subject to competing interpretations. On the one hand, the state's seven clinics (down from fifteen in 1991) performed 10 percent fewer abortions in 2004 than in 1999, and 85 percent were first-trimester procedures. On the other hand, the number in 2004 was higher than in 1995 or 1985, and included nearly five hundred late-term abortions.[23]

As the discussion of abortion focused on specific regulatory measures, the broader frustrations with government and the public's concerns about moral decay that abortion often symbolized remained. Public officials sought small ways to demonstrate their commitment to upholding traditional religious values. A proclamation declared that one week each February would be known as Kansas Christian Heritage Week. Attorney General Kline visited churches on weekends and formulated a ruling that city council representatives could meet for prayer to seek the Lord's guidance without having to abide by open-meeting requirements. Conservative civil liberties attorneys defended the image of Moses on the KU seal, argued for ways to return the Ten Commandments to public buildings and voluntary prayer to the schools, and debated whether police could use biblical language to elicit confessions from suspects. The September 11, 2001, attacks temporarily diverted attention from school prayer, sex education, and abortion, but reinvigorated the conviction that something was wrong with the United States. Clergy contended that moral discipline and military resolve was needed. They debated pacifism and just war principles, and discussed the pros and cons of action in Afghanistan and Iraq. A few ventured the opinion that God's wrath was at hand.[24]

THE CAMPAIGN AGAINST GAY MARRIAGE

From late 2003 through 2006, discussions of same-sex marriage stole most of the attention that religious leaders had previously devoted to abortion. Same-sex marriage moved to the forefront, following years of quieter debates about homosexuality, when questions making their way through the courts converged with debates in the nation's largest religious denominations. In September 2003 as Attorney General Kline was considering his next moves against abortion, the American Civil Liberties Union brought a sodomy case before a Kansas appellate court. The plaintiff was Matthew Limon from Paola, just south of Johnson County. Limon had been convicted of having sex at age eighteen with a fourteen-year-old boy and was serving a seventeen-year sentence. Kansas was one of more than a dozen states with sodomy laws that had just been invalidated by the U.S. Supreme Court in June. Kline's office notified law enforcement officials that sodomy could no longer be prosecuted, but filed a statement in the Limon case affirming the state's law against sex with minors. In January 2004 the Kansas court ruled against Limon, arguing that an eighteen-year-old adult could be punished more severely for engaging in homosexual sodomy with a child than heterosexual sex with a child. While the decision was pending, a Massachusetts court ruled that a ban on same-sex marriage was unconstitutional.[25]

The Supreme Court ruling against sodomy laws and the Massachusetts decision alerted conservative lawmakers to the possibility that legislative action could be needed to head off efforts to legalize same-sex marriage. President Bush asked White House attorneys to look into drafting laws that would define marriage exclusively as a union between a man and woman. Senate majority leader Bill Frist of Tennessee announced that he would support a constitutional amendment banning same-sex marriage. The Vatican called on legislators to oppose same-sex marriages. Protestant denominations were facing the different but related challenge of deciding whether to ban openly gay clergy from holding church positions. In 2002, the Presbyterian Church decided after a bitter struggle between liberals and conservatives that resulted in presbytery-level voting not to overturn a ban on gay clergy. In 2003, the Episcopal Church approved its first openly gay bishop and affirmed acceptance of same-sex blessing ceremonies. The United Church of Christ, Methodists, and Evangelical Lutheran Church of America initiated churchwide discussions at the same time.[26]

The debate over gay ordination and same-sex unions evoked strong responses in Kansas churches. In Wichita, Reverend Fox said the Supreme Court's decision on sodomy was contrary to God's laws. Presbyterians in the area voted two to one against gay ordination, and at the Central Christian Church, Reverend Wright became one of the city's most outspoken opponents of same-sex marriage. In Topeka, the twelve-hundred-member Plymouth Congregational Church voted to embrace same-sex unions. So did the Peace Mennonite Church, but Westboro Baptist preacher Phelps staged noisy antigay demonstrations. "Cry aloud," Phelps said, quoting the prophet Isaiah, "lift up thy voice like a trumpet and show my people their transgression." In Salina the Reverend Steven Baines, a Unitarian pastor, started an organization to oppose a constitutional ban. Two of Hutchinson's leading Methodist pastors spoke in favor of gay rights, while in Garden City several churches displayed signs opposing gay rights. The controversy was not restricted to churches in the larger towns. In the small western Kansas community of Gove, population ninety-nine, the seventy-member Methodist Church split over concerns about the denomination's direction on same-sex marriage, gay ordination, and allegations of paganism. Litigation over the church property ensued. A field researcher who visited the community several years later observed neighbors who had been fellow church members still refusing to speak with one another.[27]

The Gove story was unusual only because the different views split the congregation. Around the state, churchgoers expressed their opinions in newspaper editorials and letters. Opponents of same-sex marriage said it violated God's law: "God created us with a need for the opposite gender." Some said it would be detrimental to children. "I see nothing but confusion and chaos," wrote one. Another predicted it would lead to polygamy. Supporters argued that gay couples were no threat to heterosexuals and should have the same rights as everyone else. A constitutional ban on gay marriage, a writer counseled, would be no more effective than was Prohibition. Some saw a ban as an intrusion of religion on government. It would be like living under a Muslim government, one person said. Someone else asserted that this was the reason the nation's founders had left religion out of the constitution. Others noted similarities to earlier laws against miscegenation.[28]

With sentiment this divided, President Bush's call in late February 2004 for Congress to begin the process of passing a constitutional amendment against same-sex marriage appeared unlikely to gain traction except among conservative Republicans. Senator Brownback immediately cosponsored an antigay marriage bill in the senate, and Congressmen Ryun and Tiahrt sponsored a companion bill in the house. Ryun saw the measure as a necessary curb against an activist court. Tiahrt viewed it as upholding a sacred institution "established by God in the book of Genesis." But critics thought it unlikely that a national amendment would ever be approved and wondered if the idea was merely a ploy to improve conservative turnout for Bush in key battleground states. Democratic congressman Dennis Moore thought the matter should be left to the states. Wichita's Reverend Mike Poage, a United Church of Christ pastor, said the idea was nothing more than a legalization of discrimination. Even Republicans were hesitant. Senator Roberts thought the matter had already been settled in Kansas. Representative Moran said there were many options worth considering. A national poll found that opinion was indeed divided. A slight majority opposed legalizing same-sex marriage, but fewer than half favored a constitutional ban. A poll in Kansas revealed a similar pattern. While 39 percent said they strongly favored a federal constitutional ban on gay marriage, 33 percent said they were strongly opposed.[29]

The well-institutionalized resources of the Religious Right sprang into action. On March 5, the Kansas House of Representatives approved an amendment to the state's constitution defining marriage as "constituted by one man and one woman only," but two weeks later the Kansas Senate failed to endorse the proposal. Reverend Fox vowed that the measure would come before the senate again before it adjourned or the legislators who voted against it would be punished. "We feel the majority of the Senate paid no attention to the religious community," he said. "Our intentions are to intensify our work." Although the state's laws recognizing marriage as existing only between one man and one woman had never been challenged, Fox and other pastors were worried that they might be. The pastors felt it would be harder for gay activists to overturn an amendment to the state constitution.

To prevent Kansas from becoming the Massachusetts of the Midwest, Fox formed a statewide network of about a hundred pastors and planned to apply pressure on legislators to pass a bill placing a constitutional ban on same-sex marriage before the public. Several days later, the pastors met with more than two hundred supporters in Wichita to consider the next steps. They agreed to lobby legislators personally and bombard them with emails from conservative church members. They would avoid separation of church and state entanglements by stopping short of endorsing candidates, but would use every other means at their disposal. The pastors agreed to preach on the topic, make phone calls, and circulate petitions in their churches. They also agreed to push for an amendment that banned not only same-sex marriage but also legal recognition for same-sex civil unions and domestic partnerships. "We will not compromise on anything less," Fox said at a meeting in Topeka.[30]

Reverend Wright of the Central Christian Church, who joined Fox in leading the effort, agreed. Same-sex couples should not be eligible for any of the benefits enjoyed by married couples. "We feel that an amendment to the constitution would provide protection from the recent trend of activist judges imposing their liberal bias on both the state and federal levels," Fox and Wright wrote in a joint op-ed essay in the *Wichita Eagle*. Homosexuals should not receive health or insurance coverage for their partners, they argued. The issue should not be treated as a matter of civil rights, they said, but as a biblical moral issue. "Same sex physical relations are unnatural and contrary to the institution of marriage designed by God." When several pastors in Wichita published a letter disagreeing, Fox declared that they were "out of step with the Bible." Wright said there were now two hundred pastors in Wichita who opposed gay marriage. They represented a huge majority of the public, he claimed. But a poll of Wichita-area residents showed that 43 percent supported a same-sex marriage ban while 45 percent opposed the idea.[31]

On Saturday, May 1, 2004, the Kansas Senate approved a constitutional amendment banning same-sex marriage, but the following Tuesday the Kansas House fell five votes short of achieving the two-thirds majority needed to place the measure on the ballot in the fall. Fox, Wright, and their supporters had spent much of the previous week in the statehouse holding prayer meetings and rallies, speaking to reporters, and monitoring the legislative discussions. They vowed to make good on their threat to punish legislators who voted against the ban. "The body of Christ will hold you accountable," Fox said. Although nothing had changed to make same-sex marriage any more legal in the state than it had been since 1867,

Fox regarded the vote as a blow to the Bible and marriage. Over the summer he and Wright traveled the state, speaking at churches and county fairs, and giving dozens of interviews. They implored fellow pastors to host voter registration drives during Bible study classes. Fox said that he would not endorse candidates but instead would announce which candidates he was voting for. In July, Congressman Tiahrt preached at the Immanuel Baptist Church about the biblical view of marriage and importance of voting for a constitutional ban on alternatives to this view. A few weeks later, Attorney General Kline held a conference at Reverend Johnston's First Family Church in Overland Park to tell pastors how close they could come to the line separating church and state without losing their tax-exempt status.[32]

The August primary resulted in conservative victories in several key races, including three in which moderates who voted against the ban in May were defeated. In September, Falwell appeared with Wright at the Central Christian Church and with Johnston at the First Family Church to bolster their efforts. Abortion and a constitutional amendment to ban same-sex marriage, Falwell said, were the most crucial issues in the fall election. Fox and Wright were elated by the election results. The turnout was 80 percent among registered voters in Sedgwick County and better than expected statewide. Republicans won 72 percent of the state senate seats and 66 percent in the house. In thirteen other states with constitutional bans against same-sex marriage on the ballot, all thirteen were successful. President Bush edged out challenger John Kerry by 3 percentage points nationally and won by 26 percentage points in Kansas. Bush's margin was 58 points among white evangelical voters in Kansas.[33]

To help ensure that Kansas would ban same-sex marriage, reverends Wright and Johnston met with several hundred of the amendment's supporters in Topeka on January 10, 2005, for the opening session of the legislature. "This is the heartland of traditional values," Wright told the crowd. "We are going to wake up our congregations until Kansas has a marriage amendment," Johnston added. Following the rally, groups of four toured the statehouse, pausing to pray at intervals along the way. Two hundred visitors staged a counterrally. Democrats feared that the Republican-led legislature might postpone consideration of the amendment in order to bring it to voters in 2006, when a strong turnout among conservatives could hurt Governor Sebelius's reelection chances. But three days later, the senate approved the proposed amendment by a vote of twenty-eight to eleven. Before the house voted, committee hearings were held in which testimony was given on both sides, including statements favoring the amendment by Attorney General Kline, Concerned Women for America representative Marsha Strahm, and Reverend Bob Hanson, who headed the Kansas-Nebraska Convention of Southern Baptists. The house voted eighty-six to thirty-seven on February 2 to adopt the proposed amendment and place it on the April ballot.[34]

As the April 5 election approached, pastors Fox, Wright, and Hanson, along with Senator Brownback, ran radio and newspaper ads encouraging people to vote for the amendment. Opponents calling themselves Kansans for Fairness countered with ads signed by nearly a hundred clergy. But with the help of a hundred thousand dollar contribution from the Knights of Columbus, amendment supporters were able to outspend opponents by four to one. Voters approved the amendment by a 70 to 30 percent margin. "This is the way God intended things," a Wichita voter explained. "I based my vote on the Bible," said another. "I have to laugh when I hear homosexuals say they were born that way," another remarked. "It is their own decision and the wrong way of life. They should accept that it's not normal and is a sin and change their way of life." It was a singular victory, Fox said, that would take gay marriage "out of the hands of some liberal activist judge." The one thought dampening the celebration was that the margin in Kansas was smaller than in kindred Bible-believing states. Oklahoma's amendment passed by 76 percent, and Mississippi's by 86 percent.[35]

The other concern among conservative pastors was what to do next. Pastor Wright felt the effort had been energizing. Reverend Fox hoped the twelve hundred pastors they had pulled together to advance the amendment could stay connected. Hope of overriding

Governor Sebelius's veto of rigid sanitary standards for abortion clinics flourished briefly, but failed to gain much interest among clergy or sufficient votes in the legislature. There was talk of mounting a campaign against casino gambling and gearing up to defeat Sebelius in 2006, but neither idea sprouted wings. In Washington, the Family Research Council, recognizing similar uncertainty about the future, tried to broaden its appeals to include concerns about generalized threats to freedom of religious expression. But in Wichita, the leadership that had played such an important role in the campaign for a constitutional amendment was facing an even deeper transition.[36]

With a regular weekend attendance of more than three thousand, the Central Christian Church was flourishing, but Wright had been there for twenty years. He was sixty-three, and the hectic schedule over the past two years on behalf of the constitutional amendment had been taxing. He decided it was time to retire. The new pastor, Reverend David Welsh from Lexington, Kentucky, said he would address moral issues from the pulpit, but he did not expect to be an activist like Wright. Welsh's passion was preaching. He was known for his work with children's ministries and efforts to enhance the worship experience. Under his leadership, the Central Christian Church would continue to reach young people through Christian gospel concerts, and minister to low-income families and the homeless, but Wright's retirement left Wichita without one of its most vocal advocates of church involvement in hot-button political issues.[37]

The transition at the Immanuel Baptist Church was more contentious. With little advance notice, Fox resigned in August 2006. Initially tight lipped about the departure, lay leaders revealed unhappiness in the congregation over Fox's frequent absences from the church and what they perceived as increasing arrogance. Activism, some felt, had taken too much of his attention. As one member explained, "You don't need to tell me [about abortion] every Sunday for fifty-two Sundays in a row." Further revelations suggested that Fox may have improperly diverted church funds into his radio ministry, which he conducted with Wright at a cost of ten thousand dollars a month. The trouble did not end there. Having agreed in principle to a kind of noncompetition clause that church leaders said prevented him from pastoring any church within seventy-five miles, Fox instead initiated a new ministry in Wichita with a crowd of about five hundred. The ministry was located at a theme park called Wild West World in which Fox invested personal funds. But within a year the theme park filed for bankruptcy, leaving doubts about its financial consequences and longer-term effects on Fox's ministry.[38]

Reverend Johnston of the First Family Church might have been describing Fox's troubles when he remarked, "Whenever God's work is being built, Satan sends opponents." But Johnston was talking about his own difficulties. By the end of 2006, the First Family Church had grown to more than four thousand members, had a seventeen million dollar annual budget and a global television ministry, and was planning a new sanctuary that would seat seven thousand. Members were leaving, though, and questions were being raised about financial accountability. Contributors who thought they were supporting one program discovered their funds had been used for a different one. Real estate dealings were emerging that Johnston apparently had not wanted disclosed. He had several for-profit businesses. And he was living far more extravagantly than some of his members considered appropriate for a man of God. There was little doubt that the First Family Church would weather the storm, but the questions cast Johnston in a different light than had been true during the constitutional amendment campaign.[39]

EVOLUTION REVISITED

The side issue that took center stage just as Christian conservatives were celebrating the passage of the constitutional amendment against same-sex unions was the ongoing back-and-forth debate about evolution. Despite negative reactions to the board of education's downplaying of evolution in 1999, conservatives regained enough momentum to achieve a five-to-five balance with moderates in 2002. In 2004, conservatives picked up an additional seat to reclaim a six-to-four majority. That opened the door for another round of discussions in which critics of evolution squared off against its defenders. On the surface, the debate was simply a repeat of the one in 1999. Yet both sides had taken lessons from the previous controversy and were influenced by wider developments in the Religious Right.

With the enormous mobilization that occurred in 2004 around the ban on gay marriage, it was surprising that the Religious Right seemed nearly invisible in renewing the criticisms of evolution. The reason, as in 1999, was that different tactics were needed. Passing a constitutional amendment required two-thirds majorities in both chambers of the state legislature and a majority vote among the public. The institutional resources that mattered were large churches like Central Christian, Immanuel Baptist, and First Family. With huge budgets and staffs of dozens, head pastors such as Wright, Fox, and Johnston could travel the state, spend time in Topeka, and host radio programs. They could print flyers, host voter registration drives, bring in Falwell, and publicize their views to thousands of churchgoers. Little of that was needed to influence the board of education. Board members usually won or lost in primaries in their districts in which turnout was low, and often ran unopposed in the general election. Campaign contributions seldom totaled more than ten thousand dollars,and were used mostly for yard signs and ads in local newspapers. The role of explicit appeals to religion was also different. In campaigning against gay marriage, it helped to say that God intended marriage to be heterosexual. In criticizing evolution, it would have helped to argue that God was the creator of everything. That was what a majority of Kansans believed. The issue, however, was not what people believed but rather what could be taught in public schools. It was better to keep religion in the background.

The main difference between 1999 and 2005 was the introduction of language about intelligent design. Textbooks and instructional manuals that previously emphasized creation, creator, and creationists were edited to substitute words about design. Intelligent design networks replaced creationist institutes. Proponents of intelligent design argued that they were not trying to affirm the existence of God. They were merely convinced that life was sufficiently complex that it could not have happened through random mutations and natural selection. The complexity seemed to them better explained as the outcome of a design. The quest was not to demonstrate that a designer existed, only to muster evidence of design. If that could be shown, the existence of a designer could be inferred, and it was then up to religious leaders to say who that designer may have been. As far as intelligent design was concerned, its defenders claimed to be neutral as to the designer's identity. It could have been a space alien, they said, although it seemed more plausible that it was probably the biblical God.

Intelligent design had several advantages as a rhetorical strategy. It gave the appearance of being neutral about religion. It claimed to be in the spirit of scientific investigation. It was also a kind of dual code that could be used in conjunction with theological assertions in church settings, but severed from those connections at school board hearings. But there were two difficulties. One was that proponents had been so used to talking about creation and how intelligent design was consistent with their faith that they had to be careful. If these religious connections slipped in, the courts could rule that they were trying to bring religion into the public schools. The other problem was that hardly any solid evidence in support of intelligent design could be found in reputable science journals. These difficulties went a long way toward explaining how intelligent design as an alternative to evolution was advanced.

The strategy that emerged had three prongs. The first involved contending not that intelligent design should be taught but instead that criticisms of evolution should be. This was the argument for open-mindedness and free inquiry that had been used in 1999. The second was to maintain that the lack of evidence in reputable science journals was the fault of scientists rather than of deficiencies in the evidence itself. Evolution had gained such hegemony among scientists, the reasoning went, that critics could not receive a fair hearing. And that was where the third prong came in. The matter should be decided democratically through public meetings at which people with alternative views were invited to express their opinions.

School board meetings were the perfect venues in which to implement these strategies. Meetings were conducted by democratically elected officials and by law were open to the public. At the end of the day, board members would make the decision about science standards based on positions that had gotten them elected in the first place. As long as the courts could not easily strike down the decisions, it could safely reflect a board member's views. Incumbents were more easily elected than challengers, and in any case a board member had at least four years to serve. A board member did not have to be a scientist or claim to understand all the scientific evidence. It was necessary only to argue that reasonable people should be open-minded. In a state where nearly everyone believed in God and a large majority went to church, it was unnecessary to say anything about God. Faith was part of the woodwork. It was also easy to imagine that the scientific evidence in those elite scientific journals was not quite as solid as the experts said it was. The experts did not understand or appreciate the heartland's values. Experts were like the activist judges who approved of gay marriage in Massachusetts—the Left Coast, as some called it.

The Kansas State Board of Education was prepared to take evolutionists to task when sessions began in January 2005. The conservative majority included Arkansas City veterinarian Abrams, who had played a prominent role in 1999 and now chaired the board, and John Bacon of Olathe, also on the board since 1999. Bacon was a certified public accountant who had beaten his opponent in the 1998 Republican primary by only twenty-four votes, but won handily in the general election and was reelected in an uncontested race in 2002. The 2002 election added conservatives Connie Morris of St. Francis, Iris Van Meter of Thayer, and Kenneth Willard of Hutchinson. The newly elected conservative in 2004 was Kathy Martin of Clay Center.

The six conservatives had solid credentials not only as community leaders but also as Christians and defenders of conservative
positions on key issues. Abrams was known for his opposition to
abortion and vote in 1999 to downplay evolution. Bacon, whose
father had been a leader in the Prohibition Party, was a graduate
of MidAmerica Nazarene University, an active church member, and
had been on the conservative side in 1999. Morris was a born-again
Christian who spoke often about her spiritual awakening at the
Calvary Full Gospel Church and love of Jesus. Van Meter held a
degree in Christian education from the Kentucky Mountain Bible
College, served on church boards, and during the 2002 campaign
stated that she did not believe in evolution. Willard, an insurance
executive from Hutchinson, raised in Oklahoma and Missouri, and
educated at a church-run high school, praised the board for its conservative stance on evolution during his campaign in 2002. Martin
was a conservative Catholic who served as a Eucharistic minister
and parish council chair at Saints Peter and Paul Church in Clay
Center. Backed by the Kansas Republican Assembly, she felt that
creation should be taught alongside evolution.[40]

Arguments about intelligent design were being directed at the
board from retired Johnson County lawyer John Calvert, a born-
again former agnostic who directed the Intelligent Design Network
with cofounder and fellow Christian William Harris. Trained in nu-
trition and biochemistry, Harris had begun to question theories of
human origins while working on his doctorate, but had not thought
much about the topic until the mid-1990s. Both he and Calvert
claimed to have been influenced by the work of Discovery Institute
writer Phillip Johnson. By 2001, the Intelligent Design Network
was attracting attention in national media for its challenges to evolution, and by 2004 could claim to be a broad-based organization
with groups in at least eight states. As an informal adviser to the
board's science standards committee in 2004, Calvert persuaded
eight of the twenty-six committee members that they should take
a more outspoken stance against evolution. In a departure from
the committee's long-standing custom of working until an apparent
consensus was achieved informally, the eight proposed that formal

votes be taken so that dissent could be registered, and when that suggestion was turned down opted to write their own minority report. Neither Calvert nor Harris thought there was sufficient research for intelligent design to be explicitly included in science curricula, but were persuaded that aspects of life, such as the intricacy of cell structure, were too complicated to have occurred naturally. As Harris put it, "[We] believed that the standard naturalistic, materialistic, unguided, undirected, blind interactions of matter and motion that explained how life came to be so diversified were just woefully inadequate and were philosophically driven, not derived from evidence."[41]

At a public meeting in Salina on January 27, 2005, the science standards committee considered more than a dozen proposals to revise the current standards for teaching science. The recommendations were put forward by Harris of the Intelligent Design Network, and ranged from a proposal that members vote by secret ballot to more substantive recommendations focusing on the inclusion of specific words and seemingly minor revisions with potentially large implications. One of the most far-reaching recommendations was a modification of the definition of science from "seeking natural explanations" to "explanations of natural phenomena." Vice president Jack Krebs of Kansas Citizens for Science, an organization of teachers and scientists founded in 1999 to combat conservatives' influence, led the opposition. Science could only produce natural explanations, Krebs asserted, while explanations of natural phenomena could include attributions to supernatural influences and thus should not be part of a science curriculum. The committee sided with Krebs. None of Harris's proposals were approved.[42]

A week later, energized by the legislature's approval of placing an amendment banning gay marriage on the ballot, pastors Fox and Wright announced that they would use their thousand-member conservative clergy alliance to "weigh in on" the debate about evolution. Whether that pledge of support made any difference was unclear, but a few days later conservative board of education members invited Attorney General Kline to a private meeting for advice about what they could legally do to advance their agenda apart from the board's normal procedures. Kline offered to defend the board if it voted to require stickers in all science texts stating that evolution was only a theory—a measure that had recently been struck down in Georgia. By a six-to-four vote, the board also decided to form a special panel composed of three board members to solicit their own testimony from experts critical of evolution and post the alternative report drafted by the minority group of the science standards committee on the board of education Web site for public comments.[43]

Over the next two months, as conservative pastors called on churchgoers to vote on April 5 against gay marriage, the discussion of evolution and intelligent design drew increasing attention. At a public hearing near Wichita, three hundred people showed up to argue the merits and demerits of each side. Passionate editorials and letters to the editor began appearing in Kansas newspapers. Science teachers testified on both sides, giving the impression that the matter was truly up in the air even among experts, but critics of intelligent design presented evidence to the contrary. A survey conducted a few years earlier by educator John Richard Schrock was publicized, showing that only a quarter of Kansas high school biology teachers favored giving equal time to creationism, significantly fewer than in Illinois, Kentucky, and national polls. Meanwhile, the Intelligent Design Network was gaining wider attention because of curriculum revision controversies in Ohio, Georgia, and Pennsylvania. The debate about origins of life, Calvert told the *Washington Post*, was "the most fundamental issue facing the culture." Fox agreed. "Creationism's going to be our big battle," he said. "We're hoping that Kansas will be the model, and we're in it for the long haul."[44]

Hearings and public debates continued for most of the year. At one level, they focused on the technical aspects of evolutionary science itself, and ranged from paleontology to cell biology to genomics. The central question was whether the available evidence pinned down or left open crucial aspects of human origins. The board called for a lengthy series of public meetings at which defenders and critics of evolution would be given an opportunity to testify. At first, the majority members of the science standards committee said they would not appear because they had already had such meetings and the results were in their report. But when it became evident that their failure to appear would put the majority members in a negative light, they relented. At a different level, what was communicated implicitly became as important as what was stated explicitly. Each of the board's meetings was conducted with absolute adherence to proper procedure and in an atmosphere that privileged public decorum. The message was that people who fundamentally doubted that evolution was credible were nevertheless supremely reasonable. Critics saw it differently. They worried as they had in 1999 that Kansas was a national laughingstock and would lose in competition for high-tech industries. It was shameful, critics charged, that Kansas would now turn out students unprepared for college. Religious fanaticism was surely to blame. Yet for the Religious Right the process was clearly a net gain. Without high-profile preachers playing much of a role at all, conservative churchgoers in well-educated communities like Wichita and Overland Park could feel good about themselves. They were folks who favored good logic, critical thinking, and rational debate. They were not the narrow-minded dogmatists. "The zealots of evolution have become the new American Inquisition," the pastor of a conservative nondenominational church in Salina observed. It was "in the courts and in the smoke-filled rooms of higher learning," he said, that a movement "to completely remove God" was taking place.[45]

On November 8, the board of education adopted new science standards by a six-to-four vote. The new standards called on local school boards, school administrators, and classroom teachers to adopt their own curricular revisions, and encouraged students to consider criticisms of evolution that would help them understand the range of scientific views and improve their critical thinking skills. The board's science standards said that the theory of evolution should specifically be criticized for the "lack of empirical evidence for a 'primordial soup,'" the "lack of adequate natural explanations for the genetic code," its failure to account for the sudden emergence of organisms near the time the earth became habitable, and various discrepancies in molecular evidence and the fossil record. The board members who voted for the new standards saw the outcome as a strike against dogma and denied that religion was being promoted. As Willard put it, he was pleased to be "on the front edge of trying to bring some intellectual and academic honesty and integrity" to the standards. "The science standards are not about faith," board chair Abrams asserted. "It's not about what's in Scripture."[46]

The board's decision did not end the controversy. On December 5, 2005, less than a month after the decision, two men in a large pickup truck tailgated KU professor Paul Mirecki on a road south of Lawrence, forced his car to the side of the road, and when he stopped, beat him with their fists and a metal object. Mirecki was chair of the religious studies department. He had angered religious conservatives with an email criticizing "fundies" and offering to teach a course about the deficiencies of intelligent design. Following the beating, Mirecki canceled plans for the course and resigned as the department head. In Wichita, Fox applauded Mirecki's resignation. Two weeks later evolution gained national attention when U.S. District judge John Jones ruled in a closely watched case in Dover, Pennsylvania, that the school board had erred in inserting intelligent design into the curriculum. Critics of the Kansas board's decision hailed the ruling as a defeat for intelligent design. Board members reaffirmed that their decision was different, though. The Kansas science standards did not include intelligent design, they said, and in any case local boards would have to make their own decisions.[47]

In 2006 moderates reclaimed control of the state board, as Van Meter retired and Morris was defeated. How science was to be taught was indeed going to be a wait-and-see matter. Around the state, teachers and school administrators expressed views ranging from adamantly defending the science of evolution, to arguing that it should be taught as a theory, to suggesting that alternative approaches be included. They were less interested in what the state board decided than in giving students the best education possible. "You know," said one superintendant, "the state board fusses and

7.2 Mourners at Wichita's Old Town Plaza following the shooting death earlier that day of Dr. George Tiller, May 31, 2009. Photo by Ann Williamson, courtesy of the Topeka Capital Journal.

they go back and forth about deemphasizing evolution and emphasizing intelligent design. But I bet anywhere in the whole state it hasn't made one iota of difference. It's crazy the way it has all played out."[48]

THE DEATH OF DR. TILLER

By all indications, the gunman who killed Dr. George Tiller in May 2009, Scott Roeder, whose email name was ServantofMessiah, acted alone. Investigators determined that Roeder had visited Tiller's church the week before, when Tiller was scheduled to be ushering, only to discover that Tiller's plans had changed. Roeder was known to have been at the church at least once or twice previously, and could easily identify Tiller from photos on antiabortion Web sites. Roeder was also known to have glued locks shut as well as caused other damage at Tiller's clinic and a clinic near Kansas City. The murder closed a chapter in the struggle against abortion in Kansas. It also revealed how intensely the battle had been waged on both sides.[49]

One of Tiller's classmates, who swam on the swim team with him at East High School in Wichita, remembered his persistence. Tiller had a strong backstroke, was exceptionally dogged in his swimming, and was determined to become a doctor like his father. Others who knew Tiller said the attacks wielded against him and his clinic over the years strengthened his resolve to keep the clinic open. After his death, hundreds of former patients sent tributes about his courage in assisting them through one of the most difficult decisions of their lives. "He was a pro-woman zealot," Congregation Emanu-El's Rabbi Michael Davis, who had known Tiller for years, said. "People were touched by his character and his beliefs and his passion for what he was doing." It was clear that he had been more than a provider of late-term abortions. To friends and foes alike, Tiller had long been the symbolic vortex of a fierce contest between good and evil.[50]

After the Religious Right's gains in 2005 against same-sex marriage and evolution, attention returned to abortion with renewed intensity. Much of the emphasis was driven by Kline's bid for re-election in 2006. Kline's supporters applauded his failed efforts to secure health records from minors seeking abortions, while opponents said his crusade against Tiller had become a misguided vendetta. Kline's staff contacted pastors around the state, asking to speak at churches. A leaked memo said he hoped to find money among churchgoers to help fuel his campaign for attorney general. "Pastor Jerry Johnston's church. Must get on calendar," the memo advised. "Must rework Joe Wright and Terry Fox," the memo continued. "Must get in their pulpit and have them personally host a reception to match Tiller's blood money." But the perception of being too aggressive on abortion, and crossing the line separating church and state, worked against Kline. His opponent, Democrat

Paul Morrison, outspent him by a million dollars and won by 58 to 41 percent. Days before leaving office, Kline filed thirty misdemeanor charges against Tiller, alleging illegal late-term abortions at his clinic, but the Sedgwick County district attorney dismissed the charges. Not content to let matters rest, a coalition of thirty-five Wichita clergy members asked the legislature the following spring to invoke a little-known statute ordering the new attorney general to prosecute Tiller. The call went unheeded.[51]

Abortion figured in Sebelius's campaign for reelection as well. Her opponents attempted to tie her to Tiller by noting that Tiller had attended a dinner hosted by the governor. Kansans for Life Political Action Committee endorsed Republican challenger Jim Barnett and actively reminded voters of his pro-life record throughout the campaign. One of Kansans for Life's largest donors was the Heart Political Action Committee, which in turn received significant contributions from Koch Industries in Wichita. Sebelius nevertheless outspent Barnett four to one, and was reelected by a margin of 58 to 40 percent.[52]

With Kline out and Sebelius reelected, it appeared to some observers that the Religious Right was finished. "Abortion rights, economic justice, stem cell research and a more humane society are winning issues," a former Kansan wrote in *Ms. Magazine*. There were indeed signs that the public was tiring of conservative church involvement in politics or at least was more interested in other topics, such as taxes, schools, jobs, and the Bush administration's unpopular war in Iraq. Old-line Protestant churches under the leadership of Methodist and Lutheran pastors organized Kansans for a Faithful Citizenship to urge voter participation across a wider political spectrum. In Wichita, an interfaith group's monitoring of conservative churches' political activity resulted in the Internal Revenue Service warning the Spirit One Christian Center that it could lose its tax-exempt status. During the election, signs criticizing Governor Sebelius and attorney general candidate Morrison were posted in front of the church. Catholics United for the Common Good, a pro-choice organization, publicized a report suggesting that more could be done to curb abortion by helping mothers and children than by campaigning against clinics. In parishes across the state, attention turned increasingly from abortion toward the rights and needs of new immigrants.[53]

But behind the scenes, quieter efforts were taking place in Wichita that illustrated how firmly antiabortion activities had become institutionalized in some of the area's churches. Once a year on the anniversary of *Roe v. Wade*, ten to twelve buses left Wichita carrying pilgrims to the nation's capital for the annual March for Life and to attend a legislative seminar sponsored by the National Committee for Human Life Amendment. Youths were especially encouraged to participate. On the first Saturday of each month, members of the Wichita diocese were invited by the Respect Life and Social Justice Office to attend a rosary at Tiller's clinic "for the intention of an end to abortion and the establishment of a culture of life in our society." One was scheduled for the Saturday after he was killed. During business hours, activists held a banner that read "Please Do Not Kill Your Baby" above the entrance to Tiller's parking lot, handed out literature, and asked to speak with patients. Churches coordinated sign-up sheets to make sure the coverage was complete. A network of six hundred activists kept a log of each person they contacted. Rejoicing occurred when it appeared that someone had been dissuaded from having an abortion.[54]

It was not surprising that Kansans felt strongly about abortion, even if they were not involved in efforts like those in Wichita. For more than a quarter century, the state's residents had heard that abortion was an unspeakable evil. The Knights of Columbus and Catholic parishes posted signs along country roads reminding the public that "Abortion Stops a Beating Heart" and "No Baby Should Die by Choice." Signs in remote rural communities told the rare teenager there who might be considering an abortion to "Choose Life, Your Mother Did." Passersby were treated to huge photos of babies accompanied by the reminder, "We All Started Small," and appeals for "Adoption Not Abortion" near signs calling the faithful to "Hail Jesus" or announcing "Jesus I Trust in You." Abortion was the antithesis of life. To oppose it was, as sociologist Kristen

Luker discovered in a definitive study of antiabortion sentiments, to be in favor of motherhood, babies, innocence, homemaking, and traditional values.[55]

But that was not all. Abortion symbolized what was wrong with the United States. The problem was not just that babies were being slaughtered, horrendous as that thought was. It was rather that anyone who failed to condemn abortion was contributing to the fundamental downfall of society itself. If baby killing was condoned today, something much worse would happen tomorrow. The threat was real. "We will subvert ourselves to chaotic self-destruction as a nation," a supporter of Attorney General Kline explained. "Woe to the woman who does not repent of this vile abomination!" a Catholic antiabortion Web site proclaimed. "She has walked the road to eternal damnation and hell."[56]

Remarks in candid personal interviews were less strident, and yet drew a seamless line from abortion to larger problems. A priest in western Kansas blamed Anglos having abortions for Hispanics taking over his parish. Another priest described abortion as "an indication of permanent insanity." Yet another, who saw Kansas as the "abortion capital," said abortion was "the scourge of this country," the "ruination of family life," and the source of "low moral standards." Laypeople, Catholic and Protestant alike, connected abortion with permissiveness, self-interest, materialism, and worse.[57]

For those who associated abortion with an all-pervasive moral demise, Tiller's death was a step in the right direction. While they may have found it deplorable, they saw it as a kind of justice. "I thought that [it] was a good thing," a man who saw legalized euthanasia as the next step after abortion said when asked about Tiller's shooting. "He was a goofball," the man explained. "I'm surprised he made it as long as he did." At a church fifty miles from where the shooting took place, shocked members discussed how to think about it. One ventured that this was the reason people should carry guns to church. Another said Tiller had it coming. Yet another wondered if Tiller's church worshipped Satan. More extreme sentiments appeared in anonymous blogs. "One less Nazi as far as I am concerned." "I'm not weeping for the scumbag." "He's rotting in the very special place in hell that he so richly earned."[58]

Although such remarks sounded like knee-jerk hatred, the depth of concern about abortion among staunch pro-life activists was not thoughtless. A priest in Wichita who said abortion was the most serious moral problem in the United States and boasted that Wichita sent one of the largest delegations in the country to the annual March for Life demonstrations in Washington commented that he had become seriously committed to the cause in the seminary. During a retreat about the topic he "cried buckets of tears." He connected his brother, who had been a premature baby, with the thought that his brother might have been aborted. He knew a little girl who doctors said would be "severely deformed," but was now "beautiful, healthy, happy." He loved his little nieces and nephews. It made him happy to hear about young men talking girls into having their babies and giving them up for adoption, instead of undergoing the trauma of an abortion. When he goes to Washington, he visits the Holocaust Museum. It reminds him that Jews were not considered human beings. "It's the same kind of connection with a person who cannot talk, what we call the silent scream. This baby is moving away from the forceps that are going to rip it apart. The baby can't speak for itself, so we do." It did not surprise him that Tiller was killed.[59]

And yet the more common perspective on abortion was not the one expressed by extremists or radical elements of the Religious Right. It was rather a rejection of abortion tempered by a practical attitude toward human reality. "I'm against abortion," a teacher at a Catholic school explained, "but I personally believe there are circumstances where it should be permissible." He favored the church speaking against abortion, but felt the topic should not be a driving force in national or community decisions. A Catholic woman who ran unsuccessfully for the state legislature took a similar position. She said that she absolutely would not have an abortion even if she were carrying a brain-dead or severely damaged baby, but thought women who might feel differently should have the right to make their own decision. The difficulty came when the priest who served her communion every Sunday distorted her position during the legislative campaign. She stopped attending at that point. Another woman who was "definitely opposed to abortion" and was troubled by "young girls getting pregnant," felt that it was the girl's responsibility to have the baby and the community's responsibility to provide support. She thought that antiabortion marches were pointless. Her way of helping was to donate money to a home for pregnant teens.[60]

These views were typical. Nearly everyone thought that abortion was wrong, and yet few regarded it as the sole issue guiding their political decisions or deriving from their religious convictions. They felt strongly enough about it that given the option, they would vote for a pro-life candidate over one who was pro-choice. But it bothered them when antiabortion activists took to the streets. They thought it was uncalled for when a church official suggested that the governor should not be allowed to receive communion because of her views. Underneath it all was the desire to live in a community that upheld both goodness and mutual respect. Goodness was what people strived for in their lives and hoped for in their neighbors. Respect put a human face on goodness. It acknowledged not only differences of opinion but also that people sometimes made bad decisions.

Earl Jackson, the wounded Korean War veteran who detested antiwar protesters in the 1960s, was about the last person anyone would have expected to temper principles with pragmatism. A lifelong churchgoer who worried that the society was becoming "anti-Christian," he demanded toughness of his students, and strictly enforced his no drinking and no smoking policy. "I hate abortion," he stated flatly, "don't get me wrong, it's terrible." But after years of working with young people he had become reflective. "If you've ever seen what some kids have gone through," he said, "you wonder if abortion is the worst thing." He talked about girls at his school who were abused by their stepfathers. He recalled children in Korea starving to death or being killed with bombs. "One thing I always say to my kids in school," he said. "The women are having the babies, not the men. So let the women decide and tell the men to shut up."[61]

In Overland Park, Ellen Bryl, a mother of five who was actively involved in St. Michael the Archangel Church, took a similar view. "Oh, I'm very much against it," she exclaimed when asked about abortion. "As people of God we have a moral obligation to take the gift he gave you." She had gone to fund-raisers for pro-life groups. She also thought there were exceptions to the pro-life stance, however, especially when the mother might die. And she was adamantly opposed to the activities of pro-life extremists who used violence or drove around in trucks displaying gory pictures of fetuses. "I talk about the flip side of it," she said. "I think people need to be able to teach their children their own way."[62]

SWATCHES OF PURPLE

On May 21, 2004, former president Clinton came to Lawrence to deliver the inaugural Dole Lecture for the Robert J. Dole Institute of Politics on the KU campus. It was a moment for humor to transcend the bitter rivalry that had pitted the two representatives of their parties against each other in the 1996 presidential campaign and on many other occasions. Dole joked that the institute might have been a presidential library had it not been for Clinton. Clinton quipped that the audience that afternoon in Allen Fieldhouse probably represented 95 percent of the state's Democrats. It was also a moment for bipartisan goodwill. Clinton praised Dole's service to the nation, and said he agreed with Dole on more issues than the media and Washington partisanship had permitted them to admit publicly. Clinton argued that both parties needed to move beyond the acrimony that had overtaken the country. True conservatism, he said, meant trying to solve problems in the private sector as well as through state and local government before turning to the federal government. Yet "slowly, over the last twenty years, a bitter anti-government, anti-tax feeling, combined with the Religious Right has essentially defined government differently." Extremism had gained too large a role. To move toward a "more perfect union," he contended, Americans needed to focus on "shared benefits, shared responsibilities, and shared values."[63]

The audience warmed to Clinton's humor and appeals for national unity. In the aftermath of 9/11, Kansans were responsive to the call to work against extremism. It was probably true that most of the audience were Democrats. But a Republican at the event found himself agreeing with Clinton as well. "He had us in the palm of his hand," the man remembered. The audience interrupted Clinton repeatedly with applause. If nothing else, the visit was a reminder that not everyone in Kansas was a Republican. In 1996, nearly 390,000 Kansans had voted for Clinton. When Kansans went to the polls in 2004, more than 430,000 voted for Kerry, and one voter in two claimed to be either a Democrat or an independent. Sebelius received nearly 492,000 votes in 2006. And in 2008, Obama received more than 514,000 votes. Kansas would probably never be a blue state, commentators agreed, but there were swatches of purple.[64]

Clinton's criticism of the Religious Right was also a reminder, just as Jackson's remarks about abortion were, that right-wing activists did not exclusively define religion in Kansas. There were houses of worship with quite different orientations, such as the Buddhist temple in a former convenience store in Garden City, where Vietnamese made up an increasing share of the community's packaged-meat-processing employees, and the mosque in a modest frame building in suburban Wichita that painted over its sign after 9/11 for fear of being bombed. The state's congregations included two synagogues in Wichita and seven in the Kansas City area. There was the Metropolitan Community Church of Wichita that welcomed gay and lesbian members, and the Unitarian Universalist Fellowship of Topeka that championed environmental sustainability and stronger action against racially motivated hate crimes. There was the bishop in southwest Kansas who was working for just immigration laws, and the Catholic sisters who were quietly helping undocumented workers.

Few of the activities at these other houses of worship had as much impact on legislation as the Religious Right's efforts against abortion, gay marriage, and teaching evolution. It was nevertheless the case that religious organizations played other roles in their communities, and these activities were influenced by the political climate created by the Religious Right. Even conservative Protestant congregations developed programs that in effect took the Religious Right's agenda for granted, and then worked to differentiate themselves from that agenda and focus members' interests on other activities.

The Church of the Resurrection, the ten-thousand-member Methodist megachurch in Leawood, illustrated the relationship between conservative theology and programs differing from the Religious Right's. The congregation publicly described itself as "evangelical," but as "moderates rather than fundamentalists," and affirmed that it regarded the Bible as "the authoritative guide for faith and practice," while valuing the intellect and modern science. In a community where 68 percent of the residents were college graduates, the Church of the Resurrection appealed to a different kind of evangelical than, say, the Immanuel Baptist or Central Christian churches did in Wichita, where only 25 percent held college degrees. That was an important reason for Reverend Hamilton's emphasis on complexity—the gray areas as opposed to black-and-white ones. But the church also underscored its Methodist identity, viewing itself as being squarely in the best of this tradition. With Wesley, it stressed equipping Christians to live faithfully and aspire toward godly perfection. In contrast to earlier Methodists, there were no revival meetings and no hellfire-and-brimstone sermons, but small Bible study and fellowship groups carried on the tradition of class meetings. Two-thirds of the congregation's members were previously unchurched, attracted by the modern equivalent of revivalism: a focus on programs of relevance to busy, well-educated professionals with families.[65]

The church specifically differentiated itself from the Religious Right in two ways. It addressed a broader range of controversial issues from the pulpit and in home discussion groups. For example, knowing that many newcomers attended its Christmas and Easter services, it advertised forthcoming sermons at these services, such as a series on "the gospel and stories making the news" for which the church's staff members and television newscasters would meet each week to identify the lead story. That strategy provided a rationale for talking about war, the death penalty, traffic congestion, crime, taxes, and other issues besides abortion and gay marriage. The church also differentiated itself from the Religious Right by providing alternative programs through which interested members could be involved. Many of those programs were international, and included sending more than two-dozen teams of short-term mission volunteers to Central America, Africa, or Eastern Europe. Other programs were domestic, ranging from post-Katrina volunteer efforts in New Orleans to low-income economic development in Kansas City.[66]

Pastors at other conservative churches suggested that strategies similar to those at the Church of the Resurrection were being implemented. The Religious Right's issues were so well known that pastors could in effect disagree or argue that other matters needed attention. "We have no interest in fussing and fussing about abortion clinics," the pastor of a rapidly growing evangelical congregation remarked. "We need to help prostitutes get off the street, we need to help single mothers fix their cars, we need to give young women a reason to not abort babies." His church focuses increasingly on helping poor neighborhoods and working in other parts of the world. "Poverty, the environment, and access to the means of life—affordable housing, beneficial food, education—are moral issues," another conservative pastor explained, "that are as important as hot-button issues like homosexuality and abortion." Defining himself as a "pro-life liberal," he said a church like his that is against abortion also has to be involved in supporting adoption services along with working to combat sexual abuse and poverty. "It doesn't make sense to force people to have children they may not be able to support," he said, "without providing some opportunity for those children to experience the life that God intends for us all."[67]

Catholic leaders often expressed similar views. They never said they disagreed with the church's position on abortion, and yet abortion was seldom their parish's top priority. Father Joe Eckberg at the Holy Cross Parish in Hutchinson was typical in this respect. With twelve to fourteen hundred people attending Mass each weekend, and at least that many more registered, he was busy. "It's shocking," he said, that people do not look at abortion "as killing an innocent human being." He voted for McCain instead of Obama for that reason, and was worried that Obama was going to require Catholic hospitals to perform abortions. But Eckberg was more concerned about the larger problems of secularism and materialism. Weaning middle-class people from their dependence on fancy cars and vacation homes was essential, he believed. The parish was working with the St. Vincent DePaul Society to help the poor in Hutchinson. There was a Catholic Credit Union to assist Hispanic immigrants. In cooperation with another parish, young people were going on short-term mission trips to do volunteer work at a low-income community on the Texas-Mexico border. As part of the Wichita diocese, which offered free tuition to parochial schools for all members in good standing, the Holy Cross Parish was heavily invested in supporting its elementary school. As for the Religious Right, Eckberg distanced himself from fundamentalists. They were too narrow in their views of evolution, he thought. Although he considered himself a Republican, he felt that both parties were "messed up." Special interest groups bothered him. An ideal candidate, he said, would be "morally conservative" but concerned about "taking care of the poorest of the poor."[68]

But even when they disagreed with the Religious Right or held different priorities, religious leaders were influenced by it. Most typically they felt that they could not express their views openly or fully to their congregations. "Don't quote me by name," a pastor said. "I'm against the war in Iraq, but I would never say that to my congregation." Another kept it a secret that he considered himself an independent instead of a Republican. "Don't tell anyone I'm a Democrat!" another pleaded. Yet another said privately that she thought gay marriage should be legal, but had never discussed this view with her congregation. Clergy also worried that church programs were overly concerned with personal morality, and not focused enough on larger economic issues such as poverty and the environment that needed to be addressed through the political process. They were finding ways to serve in their communities and were encouraging churchgoers to consider the complexities of social issues. The Religious Right, though, was still the elephant in the room.

EPILOGUE

A CENTURY AND A HALF after Abraham Lincoln lectured at the Methodist Church in Atchison, the principal questions for those of us who ponder the relationship of faith and politics in the twenty-first century are these: What are the decisive turning points that with hindsight can be said to have shaped the region's political climate—to have produced, in this instance, one of the reddest of the nation's red states and led to the Religious Right's lengthy ascendancy? And what broader conclusions can be drawn from this history about the contested place of religion in U.S. politics?

The changes that have taken place in Atchison since Lincoln's visit are so striking that one's attention necessarily focuses on these discontinuities. The Methodist Church moved to a new location in 1870, and has undergone numerous renovations since then. The little abbey that Father Lemke struggled to establish grew into St. Benedict's College, an elementary school, and three parishes. The depot where Lucy Stone telegraphed Susan B. Anthony was rebuilt in 1880, and a century later became a historical museum. The narrow bridge across the Missouri River was recently replaced by an impressive four-lane span, and a new hospital has been constructed. With only twenty-six hundred people in 1859, Atchison has grown to a town of more than ten thousand, but is no longer an important regional hub. Where residents once boasted of having more millionaires per capita than anywhere in the region, layoffs and plant closings have hit hard at the local economy. Roads, houses, jobs, and transportation are all quite different than in earlier years. It is easy to miss what has not changed.

And yet there are important continuities. Lincoln's visit is a reminder that politics comingling with religion is nothing new. Houses of worship in the nation's heartland have always been places to discuss political issues. Church leaders, like the Methodist laypeople who reluctantly agreed to host Lincoln, have long been worried about politics and religion mixing too much. It was significant that Lincoln spent time in Atchison and Leavenworth, and regretted being unable to visit Topeka. Those were the urban centers of the day, and were critical points of influence even in a part of the country that was overwhelmingly rural, just as Wichita and the suburbs of Kansas City would be decades later. In 1859, Kansas was important as a symbol of something larger than itself. Lincoln visited not to secure decisive votes but instead because Kansas was associated with the cause of freedom. That sense of Kansas as somehow representative of the nation's heartland, at times progressive and at other times hopelessly old fashioned, would remain. Nearly everyone in Kansas in 1859 was from somewhere else. In the twenty-first century, that was still the case for four out of every ten of its residents. Whatever Kansas stood for, it was connected with other places. The warm reception that Lincoln received in Atchison underscores the fact that the Republican Party has appealed to Kansas voters for a long time. That Seward was even more popular than Lincoln is but one of many examples over the years of how divided Republicans were. Governor Glick's mansion in Atchison, now an elegant bed and breakfast, is a tangible reminder that Democrats could also be victorious.

These continuities complicate the task of explaining the Religious Right's prominence in Kansas politics at the end of the twentieth century. It could be argued that the die was cast in 1854, when the Missouri Compromise merged the new Republican Party and free state Kansas in a common cause. A precedent for the moral politics of antiabortion activists can be found in 1859, when the Wyandotte convention considered adding a Prohibition clause to the Kansas Constitution. Further precedent could be seen in statutes protecting church services and revival meetings, and in laws about prayer and Bible reading in public schools. It would not be unreasonable to assert that Methodist and Catholic missions shaped the territory before it became a state, and that free state settlers brought a moralistic mind-set that would guide its founding institutions. The fact that Kansas did not fulfill Lucy Stone's prediction of voting for women's suffrage in 1867 could be viewed as a harbinger of what was to come.

All of these precedents played handily into interpretations of later developments. Kansas waging war against Darwin at the start of the twenty-first century was not all that surprising to many observers because Kansas had been the home of Carry Nation. If Kansas voted for McCain and rejected Obama, it was the same state that had pitted Landon against FDR. It had produced Eisenhower and supported Nixon. It was not unthinkable that a state in which Prohibition dominated public discussion for half a century would be a place where antiabortion activism would prevail as well. Roeder taking matters into his own hands, some argued, was no different from John Brown attacking Harper's Ferry.

None of those interpretations is satisfactory, though. Religion and politics in Kansas cannot be understood as conservatism in one era dictating conservatism in the next. Kansas was favorably disposed toward Republican candidates from the start, but all of its territorial governors were Democrats, and many of its settlers were weak on abolition. The Prohibition proposal in 1859 was voted down. The separation of church and state was written into the Kansas Constitution. Only a few of the Methodist and Catholic missions survived. Kansas became one of the first states to vote for women's suffrage. Republicans fought each other as viciously as they did Democrats. Populists took advantage of the conflicts and attracted far greater support than Carry Nation ever did. Kansans voted twice for FDR, once rejecting their native son in doing so. They were at best ambivalent about John Brown.

It was true that religion flourished in Kansas, but not for the reasons that scholars sometimes imagined. Church growth could not be understood as the result of a religious market in which sects and denominations simply worked hard to outdo one another. Competition was important in other ways. Towns competed with one another to attract businesses and residents. Their investors were the ones who stood to gain, and they were the ones who encouraged churches to be built in their communities. The most acute rivalries were often between Methodists and Catholics, as the state's two most influential religious traditions. The leaders of each found ways to cultivate and protect their own constituencies, and thus to reduce outright conflict. The competition that remained had a moderating influence on both, encouraging each to combat sectarian upstarts and support civic engagement.

The motif that most characterized the region was a pervasive skepticism toward big government. "Big" usually referred to the federal government in Washington, but sometimes meant the establishment in Topeka as well, including elite Republicans. Skepticism did not mean that citizens refused to vote, or that they failed to understand the need for laws, military protection, and government services. It was rather the complaint of citizens who knew that government was frequently inept in doing what they thought it should be doing. It was present among the first settlers who believed that Washington was responsible for bleeding Kansas. It was a large part of the Populists' appeal in the 1890s. It deepened considerably during Roosevelt's long tenure in the White House.

If one decision could have prevented the incipient distrust of Washington from thickening, it might have been Roosevelt selecting Landon as war secretary in 1940 instead of canceling Landon's invitation to the White House. That would have silenced Landon's criticisms and demonstrated that the administration was more bipartisan than most Kansans believed. But an even better step would have been Roosevelt foregoing a third term. Kansans had abandoned the GOP to vote for Roosevelt twice, and yet by 1938 frustration with the New Deal was festering to the point that Roosevelt's East Coast arrogance was about all that Kansans could see. The prospect of a third term furthered their distaste for Washington. That sentiment continued for decades.

Antipathy toward Washington would likely have been less acute had Kansans somehow avoided the scorn heaped on them by the eastern press. Having thought of themselves as progressive northerners who favored the Union, it was particularly offensive to be lumped with Mississippians as moralistic hayseeds who disbelieved in evolution and gravitated to fundamentalism. Kansans saw themselves as moderate Methodists and Catholics who favored strong schools and good farms, and who promoted temperance because it was sound economic policy. It was distasteful to find themselves on the wrong side of arguments about Prohibition, government welfare, and the need to become involved in World War II. When Reagan began criticizing big government much later, his attacks struck a resonant chord in Kansas. Those chords were easily amplified when the Religious Right warned of activist judges on the Left Coast seeking to destroy the heartland's basic values.

A second enduring motif was the heartland's faith in associational grassroots democracy. Associational democracy meant that families, churches, schools, and community organizations were the core ingredients of civic life. They tempered the rampant individualism that afflicted the Wild West and moderated the aggressive pursuit of self-interest that midwesterners saw in eastern bankers. Associations were the leavening agent that Tocqueville said prevented the United States from sinking into an unpalatable, undifferentiated mass. It worked well in small towns. New England had its town meetings and the Western Reserve sparkled with frontier villages when Tocqueville visited. Kansas was settled by folks from those other regions. It had the advantage of coming later, when state constitutions along with patterns for town charters and schools had all been worked out. Associations took shape as Masonic lodges, clubs, local political organizations, and churches. Temperance meetings and religious revivals were efforts to ensure that citizens were upstanding and that good towns would be built.

If associational democracy was present all along, it nevertheless became especially key when the psychological distance between heartlanders and Washington increased. Local organizations were the antidote, Tocqueville said, to authoritarian government. In the 1920s Kansans moved from farms to towns, and improved the quality of town life with electricity and better streets. When the Depression was over and the war won, citizens returned to the project of town improvement. The quiet conservatism of the 1950s focused on town life. Families with young children turned their attention to local schools. Churches became centers of voluntary activities for the complete family, and moderate Republican conservatism that assisted local communities while emphasizing fiscal conservatism was profoundly appealing.

But local communities were never insulated from wider national developments. They were affected by international trade agreements that influenced agricultural markets. The connections of individual citizens to the federal government grew in World War II through the draft, rationing, and higher taxes. Social Security and veterans benefits, home loans, farm programs, and television furthered the connections in the 1950s. Churches were intensely local and yet increasingly shaped by participation in national denominations. When theological conflicts and controversies over civil rights and the Vietnam War emerged, churches and churchgoers were affected. It is difficult to overestimate the significance of these events in the late 1960s. Kansans were predisposed to take a conservative position on most of the emerging issues by virtue of the state's Republican heritage and the small-town roots of its churches. Churchgoers reacted to what they perceived as liberalizing influences in their denominations and on the nation's campuses.

The subsequent strength of the Religious Right cannot be explained apart from the demographic shifts that assisted in elevating to prominence conservative Protestant churches that had been of minimal importance throughout much of the state's history. There were dramatic membership gains in the 1960s and 1970s within Assemblies of God, Pentecostal, independent Christian, nondenominational, and especially Southern Baptist churches. The demographic shifts that reinforced this growth included movement from small towns to larger cities, especially Wichita and Kansas City, and a hefty influx of migrants from Oklahoma, Missouri, Arkansas, and Texas. Newcomers from states that were heavily populated with Southern Baptists contributed to the rise of conservative churches, as did new residents who had been uprooted from established congregations in their hometowns. Southern Baptists did especially well in rapidly growing urban areas where the population was transient and in many cases had grown up in states that were heavily Southern Baptist.

Methodists' middle-of-the-road evangelistic emphasis on personal faith had done well until the 1960s in discouraging the growth of smaller religious organizations. Methodism's administrative system of superintendence and itinerancy served well in small towns, but faltered in rapidly growing urban communities. All of the established Protestant denominations struggled to find the right balance between local autonomy and supervision at the state, regional, or national level. The Catholic Church struggled as well, but experienced greater overall growth than the established Protestant denominations. The greatest departure from the past was that the Catholic Church's pro-life stance shifted its traditional support of Democratic candidates to Republicans and thus aligned it with conservative Protestants. That alignment created a significant constituency from which Religious Right activists could mobilize campaigns against abortion and same-sex marriage.

How much the Religious Right influenced Kansas politics was a question that analysts answered differently depending on what they defined as influence. There was little doubt that social conservatives achieved legislative victories in regulating abortions. The gains were never as much as antiabortion activists wanted, and they did not substantially reduce the total number of abortions. They did make it harder for late-term abortions to be performed, and probably contributed to the view that abortion except under extreme circumstances was wrong. The constitutional ban on gay marriage and benefits for same-sex couples was the Religious Right's most influential accomplishment. Criticisms of evolution were more difficult to assess as a victory for the Religious Right, at least in the short term.

Whether the Religious Right resulted in the larger ill effects that critics claimed was doubtful. Those effects were said to have occurred mostly by distracting voters from issues that would have benefited their communities and pocketbooks more. But a national study showed that voters actually expressed their economic interests at the polls instead of pursuing Religious Right issues at the expense of these interests. Kansas did remarkably well at supporting schools, attracting businesses, and creating jobs.[1]

The Religious Right's tactics generally demonstrated skill in mobilizing activists. The movement cultivated pastors and churchgoers, generated publicity, encouraged citizens to run for office, and persuaded activists to stay involved over long periods and despite setbacks. The movement understood the importance of local networks, but also realized the value of enlisting large congregations and attracting attention from national leaders. It largely worked through legal channels, and recognized pressure points where legislators, the courts, and school boards could be influenced.

The one tactic in which the Religious Right erred was its focus on Tiller. Although a cardinal rule of movement organizing is to target a concrete villain, the mistake lay in the fact that Tiller was an individual citizen, not a powerful person, such as a national political leader or head of an international corporation. To justify bringing in thousands of activists to blockade the Tiller clinic, and mount smaller vigils week after week and year after year, it became necessary to depict Tiller as a far greater enemy than he was. Only by imagining that he was the very personification of evil and a mass murderer on the scale of Adolf Hitler was it possible to believe that shutting down his clinic would be a great triumph. The truth was that Tiller was interchangeable. Had he quietly retired or been killed sooner, other providers of his services would have taken his place in some other community, if not in Wichita itself.

The larger question of what can be learned about the contested place of religion in U.S. politics is best answered by repeating with slight modification House Speaker Tip O'Neil's famous line about all politics being local. The modification is that all politics also take place within a layered system of state and national influences. The checks and balances that keep U.S. democracy running as well as it does involve not only the separate branches of government but also the fact that what cannot happen at the national level can often occur at the local or state level, and vice versa. Antiabortion activists and opponents of gay marriage made greater headway in local and state elections than they did in shaping national policy. At the same time, moderate Republicans and Democrats won victories that checked the Religious Right.

The Kansas experience suggests an important emendation of the argument that religious organizations serve as mediating structures between the individual citizen and the national government. In that view, religious involvement principally gives individuals civic skills and forges social networks through which individuals exercise power in national politics. The federal government, in turn, protects the right of individuals to participate in religious organizations. What is missing from this view is that religion and politics are organized at several crucial levels between the local group in which the individual participates and the national government. These include regional clusters, such as presbyteries, dioceses, and state conferences, and of course political organization happens at several intermediate levels as well, including precincts, towns, counties, and states. In Kansas, religious groups played key roles at these intermediate levels.

Understanding the public role of religion requires paying close attention to state and local politics. A common view holds that national religious organizations, such as denominations and special interest groups like Operation Rescue, mainly seek to influence the federal government by persuading voters to favor particular candidates or bills. From this perspective, the significance of a state being red or blue is principally its contribution to the outcome of a presidential election, how its leaders shape a president's decisions, and whether it can ratify an amendment to the U.S. Constitution. That stance misses the fact that religious groups play a part in electing and influencing state legislators and governors, and shaping the decisions of school boards and courts.

The Religious Right's successes against abortion in Kansas were most effective at the level of state legislation. Operation Rescue's campaign in Wichita drew national attention, but had few results in either Wichita or Washington. Busloads of pro-life demonstrators traveling to Washington each January to protest *Roe v. Wade* were a symbolic gesture that had few consequences either. The real battles were made possible by the *Webster* decision that permitted states to regulate abortion. Although pro-life activists who viewed abortion as murder wanted a complete ban on abortion, their ability to influence state laws proved to be their most important tool. The campaign against gay marriage similarly was fought at the state level. Influencing state legislators to put a constitutional ban on the ballot and persuading voters to approve the amendment were the points at which conservative religious leaders knew they had to make a difference. Shaping the debate about intelligent design and evolution also occurred at the state level.

The remaining lesson Kansas teaches is that predictions about political influence are always tenuous. Despite the fact that Kansas has been a Republican state through most of its history and has been shaped by conservative religion, little about the state's history could have been anticipated by knowing only that. Partisan politics and religion repeatedly came together in novel ways. Republican factions fought each other too often for the state to have been re- garded as a single-party system. Democrats won frequently enough to stay in the game. Methodists and Catholics competed with each other in ways that sometimes led to violence, but that also cre- ated civic institutions and encouraged members to be good citizens. Moderate centrists opposed the most extreme fringe sects and po- litical movements. Suffragists overcame disappointments. Populists and Prohibitionists had their day. Lucy Stone was at least partly correct. On many occasions, Kansas did lead the way.

NOTES

Prologue

1. Lucy Stone, telegram to Susan B. Anthony, May 10, 1867, in Elizabeth Cady Stanton, Susan B. Anthony, and Matilda Joslyn Gage, eds., *History of Woman Suffrage, Vol. II: 1861–1876* (Rochester, NY: Charles Mann, 1887), 221; "Editorial," *New York Tribune*, May 29, 1867; John Stuart Mill, letter to S. N. Wood, June 2, 1867, in Stanton, Anthony, and Gage, *History of Woman Suffrage*, 252.

2. Susan B. Anthony, "Dear Friend," September 12, 1867, in Stanton, Anthony, and Gage, *History of Woman Suffrage*, 242.

3. Stanton, Anthony, and Gage, *History of Woman Suffrage*, 247. The source of this statement is unclear, but it may have been Gage, who did the later editorial work on the volume.

4. William Allen White, "What's the Matter with Kansas?" *Emporia Gazette*, August 16, 1896; Thomas Frank, *What's the Matter with Kansas? How Conservatives Won the Heart of America* (New York: Metropolitan Books, 2004).

Murder at the Glenwood

1. "Killed Wife with Her False Teeth, Is Charge," *Philadelphia Inquirer*, November 13, 1912.

2. See, for example, "Murder by False Teeth?" *Miami Herald*, November 16, 1912; other accounts, picked up by telegraph from Topeka, were carried in newspapers in Illinois, New York, Washington State, and Oregon.

3. "Defense at the Rev. W. L. Beers Trial States Its Case," *Kansas City Star*, March 14, 1913; "Beers Wanted Wife Back," *Kansas City Star*, March 17, 1913; "Pushed False Teeth Down Wife's Throat," *Philadelphia Inquirer*, March 23, 1913.

4. The prison revival is described in "Prayer Reforms a Prison," *Kansas City Star*, March 30, 1913, 4. The Beth-El Bible School's revival and its relation to the 1906 Azusa Street Revival, generally regarded as the founding event of the twentieth-century Pentecostal movement, is described in Amy Sitar, "Praying for Power: Dispositions and Discipline in the Azusa Street Revival's *Apostolic Faith*," *Poetics* 36 (2008): 450–61. For further information, see Douglas Jacobsen, ed., *A Reader in Pentecostal Theology: Voices from the First Generation* (Bloomington: Indiana University Press, 2006); Grant Wacker, *Heaven Below: Early Pentecostals and American Culture* (Cambridge, MA: Harvard University Press, 2001). On Charles

Sheldon, see James Smylie, "Sheldon's *In His Steps*: Conscience and Discipleship," *Theology Today* 32 (1975): 32–45. Sheldon's role in the *Topeka Daily Capital* is included in the time line in "The *Capital Journal*'s Roots Run Deep," *Topeka Capital Journal*, June 1, 2003, available at http://www.findarticles.com. Sheldon held the pastorate at Central Congregational Church until 1919, when illness forced him to resign.

5. "Slain for Her Religion?" *Kansas City Star*, March 16, 1913.

6. "Religious Troubles in Kansas," *Kansas City Times*, November 1, 1889; "Secret Work of the A.P.A.," *St. Louis Republic*, November 4, 1894; "Why He Is Not A.P.A.," *Kansas City Times*, November 30, 1895; "Criticizing the Catholics," *Kansas City Times*, March 4, 1892; T. C. Moffatt, "The Schools," *Topeka Weekly Capital*, December 22, 1892; "Religious Conventions," *Baltimore Sun*, May 22, 1896; "The M. E. Conference," *Topeka Weekly Capital*, March 14, 1899. The statement quoted is from a lecture given by Reverend George W. Miller, pastor of the Independence Avenue Methodist Episcopal Church in Kansas City, Missouri.

7. "Catholics and Methodists Lined Up by the Fairbanks Incident," *Kansas City Times*, February 7, 1910; "Methodist in Rome Replies to Vatican," *New York Times*, February 28, 1910; "Roosevelt Refuses to Visit Pope," *New York Times*, April 4, 1910; "Ireland Scores Methodists," *New York Times*, April 5, 1910; "Merry del Val Explains," *New York Times*, April 7, 1910; "Resent Farley View of Italy's Festival," *New York Times*, March 19, 1911. An editorial published in the September 1910 issue of the *Methodist Review* termed Archbishop John Ireland's criticisms as "most violent, even ravening abuse and calumny of the Methodist Episcopal Church" (847).

8. "Split on Guilt of Beers," *Kansas City Star*, March 23, 1913; "Trying Preacher for Murder," *Kansas City Times*, November 11, 1913; "Witnesses Can't Remember," *Kansas City Times*, November 12, 1913; "Expect a Beers Acquittal," *Kansas City Times*, November 18, 1913; "Accused Minister Weds," *Kansas City Times*, July 4, 1914. In Wyoming, Beers held Methodist pastorates in Egbert, Hillsdale, and North Burns.

CHAPTER 1

1. Fred W. Brinkerhoff, "Address of the President: The Kansas Tour of Lincoln the Candidate," *Kansas Historical Quarterly* 8 (February 1945), 294–307. I follow the time line offered by Brinkerhoff, who argues that earlier accounts of the timing of Lincoln's arrival in Elwood were wrong. I am grateful to Dr. Lonnie H. Lee of Springfield, Illinois, for posing the question of why Lincoln chose to visit Kansas and for mentioning some examples of Lincoln speaking at churches in Springfield. An interesting discussion of Lincoln's Kansas visit in connection with his national campaign appears in Kenneth Winkle, "'The Great Body of the Republic': Abraham Lincoln and the Idea of a Middle West," in *The American Midwest: Essays on Regional History*, ed. Andrew R. L. Cayton and Susan E. Gray (Bloomington: Indiana University Press, 2001), 111–22. E. W. Howe (*Plain People*

[New York: Dodd, Mead and Company, 1929]) offers an interesting but flawed account of Lincoln's visit based on stories that Howe heard when he moved to Atchison almost two decades later and written a half century after that.

2. Don W. Holter, *Fire on the Prairie: Methodism in the History of Kansas* (Topeka: Kansas State Historical Society, 1969); Everett Dick, *The Sod-House Frontier, 1854–1890: A Social History of the Northern Plains from the Creation of Kansas and Nebraska to the Admission of the Dakotas* (Lincoln: University of Nebraska Press, 1989).

3. Reverend W. R. Davis was pastor of the Methodist Episcopal Church in Baldwin City and president of Baker University. He served as chaplain to the territorial legislature.

4. U.S. Census, 1860, electronic data file; "Appointments for Kansas of the M. E. Church for the Year 1859," *Freedom's Champion* (Atchison, KS), May 7, 1859.

5. The dedication and dimensions of the church are included in "Dedication of the New Methodist Church," *Freedom's Champion*, May 14, 1859. For additional information, see William G. Cutler, *History of the State of Kansas* (Chicago: A. T. Andreas, 1883), chapter on Atchison County; Sheffield Ingalls, *History of Atchison County, Kansas* (Lawrence: Standard Publishing Company, 1916). Holter (*Fire on the Prairie*, 86) gives a lower figure of twenty-five hundred dollars as the church's value in 1861.

6. Abraham Lincoln to James W. Somers, March 17, 1860, in Roy P. Basler, ed., *Collected Works of Abraham Lincoln* (Springfield, IL: Abraham Lincoln Association, 1953), 4:351.

7. U.S. Census, 1860. Atchison's population was 2,616; Leavenworth's was 7,429.

8. Data compiled for 1860 showed that 6,097,943 pounds of freight on 1,280 wagons pulled by 13,640 oxen passed through Atchison; that was approximately 20 percent more than in Leavenworth, but less than half the amount through Kansas City. See W. H. Miller, *The History of Kansas City* (Kansas City: Birdsall and Miller, 1881), 105.

9. "Henry Ward Beecher on Old John Brown," *Freedom's Champion*, November 19, 1859; "Kansas Thoroughly Republican," *Freedom's Champion*, December 17, 1859. Atchison's two newspapers carried news and opinion pieces, and reprinted items from eastern newspapers. Between Lincoln's visit in Atchison and his nomination for president the following May, abolitionist James Redpath's *The Public Life of Capt. John Brown, with an Auto-Biography of His Childhood and Youth* (Boston: Thayer and Eldridge, 1860) appeared and sold more than thirty thousand copies. The book featured Brown's view that he was fighting a holy war. Almost immediately after Brown's death, opinion pieces appeared in abolitionist newspapers arguing that Brown had been planted, not buried, and would rise a hundredfold.

10. Charles S. Gleed, "The First Kansas Railway," *Transactions of the Kansas State Historical Society* (1900): 357–58.

11. "Lincoln in Kansas in 1859," *Kansas City Star*, June 2, 1891; "Abraham Lincoln in Kansas," *Kansas City Times*, June 5, 1908); "Lincoln in Kansas," *Transactions of the Kansas State Historical Society* (1902): 536–52; Brinkerhoff, "Address of the President," reprinted in *Kansas History* 31 (Winter 2008–9): 275–88. See also Craig Miner, *Kansas: The History of the Sunflower State, 1854–2000* (Lawrence: University Press of Kansas, 2002), 79–80; Carol Dark Ayers, *Lincoln and Kansas: Partnership for Freedom* (Topeka: Sunflower Press, 2001).

12. An image of the Methodist Church is included in *Kansas History* 31 (Winter 2008–9), 284. When completed a few weeks after Lincoln's visit, the Baptist Church measured 40 feet by 75 feet, or 3,000 square feet, compared to the Methodist Church at 1,856 square feet. Notices published in *Freedom's Champion* (December 10 and 16, 1859) indicate that bids for the Baptist Church were assigned in March 1859, construction was taking place in August and September, and a donation supper was held at the still-unfinished church on December 16, to which residents were invited to bring "lumber, paints, hardward, lamps, or carpeting" for the purpose of "hastening the completion of the church."

13. Ingalls, *History of Atchison County*, 69; Cutler, *History of the State of Kansas*, Atchison County, part 14, biographical sketches, available at http://www.kancoll.org.

14. John R. Murphy, *Memoir of Rev. James M. Challiss* (Philadelphia: Jas. S. Rodgers, 1870), 312–13.

15. A genealogy showing names, dates, locations, and burials in various Baptist cemeteries in Virginia is available as "Stringfellow of Culpeper, VA," February 21, 2008, available at http://www.genforum.genealogy.com.

16. Frank W. Blackmar, *Kansas: A Cyclopedia of State History* (Chicago: Standard Publishing Company, 1912), 361.

17. References to John H. Stringfellow appear in U.S. Congress, *Report of the Special Committee Appointed to Investigate the Troubles in Kansas* (Washington, DC: Wendell Printing Company, 1856), especially 353–56.

18. Benjamin's proslavery activities are described in Daniel Webster Wilder, *The Annals of Kansas* (Topeka: Kansas Publishing House, 1875), 108–9, 355.

19. Franklin G. Adams, "Reminiscences of Franklin G. Adams," *Transactions of the Kansas State Historical Society* (1902): 539.

20. W.V.N. Bay, *Reminiscences of the Bench and Bar of Missouri* (Saint Louis: F. H. Thomas and Company, 1878), 215–16. Abell's views toward abolitionists are described briefly in Cutler, *History of the State of Kansas*, territorial history chapter, part 6; testimony given by George F. Warren in U.S. Congress, *Report of the Special Committee*, 1097–98.

21. Background on Pomeroy is presented in Edgar Langsdorf, "S. C. Pomeroy and the New England Emigrant Aid Company, 1854–1858," *Kansas Historical Quarterly* 7 (1938): 227–45.

22. "The Baptist Church," *Freedom's Champion*, April 14, 1860.

23. These members and their arrangement to switch to other churches are discussed in Cutler, *History of the State of Kansas*, Atchison County churches section.

24. Rebekah W. Pomeroy Bulkley, *Memoir of Mrs. Lucy Gaylord Pomeroy* (New York: John W. Amerman, 1865).

25. John Boggs and J. B. McCleery, *Personal Recollections of Pardee Butler* (Cincinnati: Standard Publishing Company, 1889).

26. The first meeting of the Atchison and Topeka Railroad Company was held at Challis's office on September 15, 1859, and Luther Challiss, Abell, Pomeroy, and John Stringfellow were among the directors chosen (Cutler, *History of the State of Kansas*, era of peace chapter, part 2). Abell and John Stringfellow were the chief promoters of the Atchison and Fort Riley Railroad Company (Blackmar, *Kansas*, 538).

27. These observations are based on letters and documents available from Territorial Kansas Online, including a June 29, 1857, business agreement between Pomeroy and Theodore Hyatt; an August 6, 1857, letter from Pomeroy to Hyatt in which Pomeroy states, "We can sell lots enough to make such sinners as we are rich as sinners ought to be"; a February 14, 1859, letter from Pomeroy to Hyatt about their railroad interests; a March 21, 1860, letter from Hyatt to a friend in which he complains about Pomeroy; a September 4, 1860, letter from Hyatt to his brother Thaddeus discussing their dealings with Pomeroy; an October 10, 1860, letter from Pomeroy to Hyatt describing Kansas settlers' need for food; and a November 4, 1860, letter to Thaddeus from Pomeroy reporting on starving families in Kansas. Additional information about Atchison's role in the relief effort appears in "Kansas Relief," *Freedom's Champion*, March 2, 1861.

28. "Wm. H. Seward in the West!" *Freedom's Champion*, September 29, 1860. Mention of Lincoln's visit appeared a quarter century later in *Freedom's Champion*'s successor, the *Atchison Daily Globe*, September 18, 1885.

29. Richard Joseph Bollig, *History of Catholic Education in Kansas, 1836–1932* (Washington, DC: Catholic University of America, 1933), 38–40; Peter Beckman, *Kansas Monks: A History of St. Benedict's Abbey* (Atchison: Abbey Student Press, 1941), 46. Stringfellow's donated land was barely largely enough and had to be supplemented by a larger donation from Abell. Beckman says that Stringfellow was "simply trying to attract buyers for the lots in his new subdivision."

30. A letter printed in *Freedom's Champion* (October, 22, 1859), for example, from Colonel James Coulter, Atchison's city marshal, suggested that Democrats were bragging about "voting the Irish two or three times" and making "tools of the Irish."

31. Beckman, *Kansas Monks*, 23.

32. William E. Connelley, *A Standard History of Kansas and Kansans* (Chicago: Lewis Publishing Company, 1918), entry for Charles C. Finney, son of M. C. Finney; available at http://www.skyways.lib.ks.us.

33. Jenifer Talbert, comp., "Finney Obituaries," available at http://www.thesalliehouse.com.

34. See, for example, Lucy Gaylord Pomeroy, in Bulkley, *Memoir*, 115.

35. "Rescued from Convent," *Freedom's Champion*, August 6, 1859.

36. "Communications," *Freedom's Champion*, December 15, 1860.

37. No verbatim record of the speech remains, but a synopsis of the Leavenworth lecture the following day gives no indication that he did, and at the Cooper Institute the single mention of the divine comes in a lengthy 110-word sentence in which Lincoln employs irony to suggest that failing to deter the spread of slavery to the territories would be like "reversing the divine rule, and calling, not the sinners, but the righteous to repentance" (Basler, *Collected Works*, 3:498–502, 550). The Cooper Institute lecture is also available at http://www.quod.lib.umich.edu/lincoln. The Leavenworth synopsis is reprinted as "Abraham Lincoln Speaks at Stockton's Hall: Leavenworth, December 3, 1859," *Kansas History* 31 (Winter 2008–9): 289–93.

38. Abraham Lincoln to Joshua F. Speed, August 24, 1855, in Basler, *Collected Works*, 2:322–23.

39. Horace Greeley, "Overland Journey," *New York Daily Tribune*, May 25, 1859. The details of Greeley's trip are included in Martha B. Caldwell, "When Horace Greeley Visited Kansas in 1859," *Kansas Historical Quarterly* 9 (1940): 115–40.

40. "Speech of Horace Greeley to a Mass Meeting of Citizens of Kansas, Attending the Republican Convention at Osawatomie, May 18, 1859," *New York Daily Tribune*, May 31, 1859, 5.

41. Henry Ward Beecher, "Bibles and Rifles in Kansas," letter, March 28, 1856, reprinted in the *New York Daily Tribune*, April 4, 1856, 5.

42. C. B. Lines, "The Kansas Colony to Mr. Beecher," March 31, 1856, reprinted in the *New York Daily Tribune*, April 4, 1856, 5.

43. "The Vote of Atchison County," *Freedom's Champion*, December 17, 1859.

44. Letter from Sam F. Tappan to Rev. T. W. Higginson, June 27, 1859, available at Territorial Kansas Online.

45. John J. Ingalls, letter to his father, September 5, 1863, quoted in Miner, *Kansas*, 52.

46. "Kansas Politics," *New York Times*, September 16, 1859, 2.

47. Cutler, *History of Kansas*, Doniphan County chapter.

48. Horace Greeley, *Overland Journey from New York to San Francisco* (New York: C. M. Saxton, Barker and Company, 1860), 28.

49. One of the few places in which the guided tour and memorabilia displayed offers a more favorable impression of the early Republicans' opponents is the territorial capital museum and historical collection in Lecompton.

50. Horace Greeley, *Recollections of a Busy Life* (New York: J. B. Ford and Company, 1869), 355. In the quarter century after the Civil War, Republicans "held complete control of state politics," usually brought in the

"old soldier" theme during elections, and painted Democrats as the "slave and sedition" party (James W. Drury, *The Government of Kansas* [Lawrence: University of Kansas Press, 1961], 22–23).

51. Cora Dolbee, "The Fourth of July in Early Kansas, 1858–1861," *Kansas Historical Quarterly* 11 (1942): 130–73.

52. David E. Ballard, "The First State Legislature," in *Collections of the Kansas State Historical Society* (Topeka: Kansas State Historical Society, 1908), 233.

53. Inhabitants of Kansas territory in 1860 included 9,367 born in Illinois, 9,945 born in Indiana, 6,331 born in New York, 11,617 born in Ohio, and 6,463 born in Pennsylvania. Sixty-three percent of Kansans in 1860 not born in the territory were from ten northern states. Twelve percent were foreign born. According to the U.S. Census in 1870 (electronic data file), 96 percent of Kansans could read and 93 percent could write; separate figures for males age twenty-one and over indicated that 94 percent could write.

54. Langsdorf, "S. C. Pomeroy and the New England Emigrant Aid Company," 231; Beckman, *Kansas Monks*, 12–17.

55. U.S. Bureau of the Census, *Population of the United States in 1860 Compiled from the Original Returns of the Eighth Census* (Washington, DC: Government Printing Office, 1864), 656–80. To determine the rates in each state, the number employed in each occupation was divided by the total labor force. Respectively, the rate per 10,000 in Kansas, Iowa, Missouri, Arkansas, Minnesota, and the five state average was: lawyers, 114, 62, 40, 55, 93, 73; public officials, 37, 29, 28, 20, 29, 27; merchants, 203, 140, 142, 152, 155, 158; physicians, 119, 77, 85, 144, 47, 94; printers (newspaper), 32, 26, 24, 19, 32, 27; clergy, 65, 67, 43, 58, 58, 58; and teachers, 104, 166, 101, 113, 121, 121.

56. Data on occupations and churches are from the U.S. Census, 1860. On Congregationalism in Missouri, Miller (*History of Kansas City*, 220) states, "Congregationalism was very little understood in Missouri at that time, and the field was, in many respects, a difficult one." The difficulties faced by northern Methodists in Missouri are chronicled in William M. Leftwich, *Martyrdom in Missouri: A History of Religious Proscription, the Seizure of Churches, and the Persecution of Ministers of the Gospel in the State of Missouri during the Late Civil War and under the "Test Oath" of the New Constitution* (Saint Louis: Southwestern Book and Publishing Company, 1870). The broader tensions between 1844 and 1846 are discussed in Edward H. Myers, *The Disruption of the Methodist Episcopal Church, 1844–1846* (Nashville: J. W. Burke and Company, 1875).

57. My calculations are based on descriptions of congregation foundings in Cutler, *History of the State of Kansas*, Atchison, Leavenworth, and Topeka churches sections. The state legislature meeting is mentioned in Noble L. Prentis, *A History of Kansas* (Winfield, KS: E. P. Greer, 1899), 93.

58. During the 1860s, dramatic population growth occurred throughout the Middle West, most of it after 1865. Nebraska's population shot up

326 percent from 29,000 to 123,000; Minnesota's grew 156 percent from 172,000 to nearly 440,000; Iowa's rose 77 percent from 675,000 to 1.2 million; and Missouri's increased 37 percent from 1.2 million to 1.7 million (U.S. Census, 1860, 1870).

59. U.S. Census, 1870.

60. "Remarks on the Statistics of Churches," U.S. Census, 1870, 501.

61. Wyandotte Constitution, adopted on July 29, 1859, and approved by a popular vote on October 4, 1859; Bill of Rights, section 7. An account of the deliberations is given in John A. Martin, *The Wyandotte Convention: An Address* (Atchison: Haskell and Son, 1882).

62. Franklin B. Hough, *American Constitutions: Comprising the Constitution of Each State in the Union and of the United States* (Albany: Weed, Parsons and Company, 1872), 573–79.

63. Wilder, *Annals of Kansas*, 550–51.

64. Quoted in Perl W. Morgan, *History of Wyandotte County, Kansas* (Chicago: Lewis Publishing Company, 1911), 373–74.

65. Letter from Father Emmanuel Hartig to Father Thomas Bartl, quoted in Beckman, *Kansas Monks*, 132–33.

66. Charles Frederick William Dassler, *Compiled Laws of Kansas* (Topeka: Geo. W. Crane, 1885), 357–58. Reverend Green pastored Methodist churches in Ohio from 1860 to 1862, served in the Union army, became pastor of a church in Manhattan, Kansas, in 1864, and was elected lieutenant governor in 1866 and governor in 1868. On at least one occasion as governor he was publicly accused of "conferring some special powers on the Methodists" ("Sectarian," *Leavenworth Bulletin*, January 25, 1868).

67. *Minutes of the Third Session of the Kansas and Nebraska Annual Conference of the Methodist Episcopal Church Held at Topeka, Kansas Territory, April 15–19, 1858* (Saint Joseph: Pfouts and Cundiff, 1958), 10.

68. Mary Ritchie Jarboe, *John Ritchie: Portrait of an Uncommon Man* (Topeka: Shawnee County Historical Society, 1991). Ritchie was a teetotaler who also participated in an effort in 1855 to rid Topeka of its saloon and pass temperance legislation. There is some ambiguity as to who proposed Prohibition at the Wyandotte convention, however. Martin (*The Wyandotte Convention*, 8), for instance, recalled surveyor H. D. Preston of Topeka introducing a temperance resolution, but does not mention Ritchie's role in the discussion.

69. Cutler, *History of the State of Kansas*, Lawrence section.

70. Wilder, *Annals of Kansas*, 562.

71. Frank A. Root, *The Overland Stage to California* (Topeka: Crane and Company, 1901), 270, 434–37.

72. Letter, June 15, 1857, in Bulkley, *Memoir of Mrs. Lucy Gaylord Pomeroy*, 115.

73. Information about Maria Maher is from a letter sent to her by Thomas Ewing Jr., dated September 14, 1859. The letter states that it is better for her to go to Saint Louis than to stay in Leavenworth or return to Lancaster, suggesting that she may have been from Lancaster, Ohio, where

the Ewings lived prior to taking up residence in Kansas in 1856. Such instances inevitably raise the question of whether Ewing himself may have been the father, but there is of course no hint in the letter itself that Ewing's motives were anything but honorable. The letter does note that "we shall if possible prevent any report getting abroad among your acquaintances"—a measure that would have protected Ewing from scandal as well. The one reference to Maher in a biography of Ewing (Ronald D. Smith, *Thomas Ewing Jr.: Frontier Lawyer and Civil War General* [Columbia: University of Missouri Press, 2008], 80) mentions a letter dated September 5, 1859, in which Ewing reports having had to let her go with a recommendation for further employment because of adverse financial circumstances. Smith (ibid., 4) observes that Ewing's father was a Presbyterian who "tolerated Catholicism" because his wife demanded it of him and that Ewing Jr. "took on more of his father's deist ways." What became of Maher is unknown, although one possibility is that she was Mary Maher, age twenty-seven of Irish birth, or Mary Maher, age twenty-nine of Irish birth, both listed in the 1860 census as residents of the county poor farm in Saint Louis.

74. Julia Hardy Lovejoy, diary, December 10, 1854 through January 5, 1860, 23–26, courtesy of Kansas Memory Collection, Kansas State Historical Society, Topeka.

75. Representative contributions to the church expansion literature include Dean Kelley, *Why Conservative Churches Are Growing: A Study in Sociology of Religion* (Macon, GA: Mercer University Press, 1986); Roger Finke and Rodney Stark, *The Churching of America, 1776–2005: Winners and Losers in Our Religious Economy* (New Brunswick, NJ: Rutgers University Press, 2005); Andrew M. Greeley and Michael Hout, *The Truth about Conservative Christians: What They Think and What They Believe* (Chicago: University of Chicago Press, 2006); Michael Hout, Andrew M. Greeley, and Melissa J. Wilde, "The Demographic Imperative in Religious Change in the United States," *American Journal of Sociology* 107 (2001): 468–500; R. Stephen Warner, *A Church of Our Own: Disestablishment and Diversity in American Religion* (New Brunswick, NJ: Rutgers University Press, 2005).

76. J. M. W. Yerrinton and Henry M. Parkhurst, *Debates and Proceedings of the National Council of Congregational Churches* (Boston: National Council of Congregational Churches, 1865), 269–70.

77. Jerald C. Bauer, *Protestantism in America: A Narrative History* (Philadelphia: Westminster Press, 1965), see especially chapter 12.

78. For the forty-five counties in 1870 that had at least one congregation, the zero-order Pearson correlation coefficient with the total population for the number of church organizations was .886, for the number of edifices was .879, for the number of sittings was .846, and for the total property value was .798—all significant at or beyond the .001 level of probability.

79. U.S. Bureau of the Census, *Compendium of the Eleventh Census: 1890* (Washington, DC: Government Printing Office, 1894), 265.

80. Standardized ordinary least squares multiple regression coefficients for the effect of county population and incorporated towns per county on the total number of organized congregations per county in Kansas in 1890 were .678 and .331, respectively—both significant beyond the .001 level of probability. The number of incorporated towns is from the U.S. Census of 1890 and includes all towns for which population was reported in that year; towns were required to have at least 250 residents to incorporate, although a few fell below that number in 1890. The number of incorporated towns by this measure was 330. An alternative measure of the number of towns per county is drawn from my count of towns shown on *Map of Kansas* (Chicago: Rand McNally, 1890). The comparable standardized multiple regression coefficients using this measure are .545 for the population and .430 for the number of towns—both significant beyond the .001 level of probability. The number of towns by this measure was 1,879.

81. The estimate of 6,000 towns having been attempted is from Daniel C. Fitzgerald, *Ghost Towns of Kansas* (Lawrence: University Press of Kansas, 1988). Working with the Kansas State Historical Society, Fitzgerald spent decades collecting information about the many towns that ended up becoming defunct. Conditions for incorporation were established by the Kansas legislature in 1871: "Whenever a petition, signed by a majority of the electors of any unincorporated town or village within the state, shall be presented to the judge of the district court of the county, setting forth the metes and bounds of their village and commons, and stating as near as may be, the number of the inhabitants of such town or village, and praying that such town or village may be incorporated as a city, with satisfactory proof that such petition has been published in full in some newspaper printed in said town or village, at least once in each week for three consecutive weeks, and such judge shall be satisfied that a majority of the taxable inhabitants of such town or village shall be in favor of such incorporation, and that the prayer of the petitioners is reasonable, and that the number of inhabitants of such town or village exceeds two hundred and fifty, and does not exceed two thousand, such judge may, by order (reciting the substance of such petition and the due publication thereof), declare such town or village incorporated as a city of the third class" (Dassler, *Compiled Laws of Kansas*, 187–88).

82. Figures reported in Lee Shai Weissbach, *Jewish Life in Small-Town America: A History* (New Haven, CT: Yale University Press, 2005), 340. Other sources show a Jewish population in Leavenworth of 455 in 1878 and 350 in 1907, both of which are fairly compatible with the figure recorded in the 1890 census. Weissbach's figures also show that the Jewish population in Wichita was 32 in 1878 and rose to 150 in 1907, and that there were no Jews in Topeka in 1878 but 139 by 1907. Smaller Jewish settlements were established in rural communities as well. For example, Marcea Canfield (interview, conducted July 17, 2007) recalled that her Jewish great-grandfather from Russia lived in a Jewish settlement at Hardtner, Kansas, a hundred miles southwest of Wichita near the Oklahoma line,

sometime in the late nineteenth century. An unusual but informative historical account available to readers in the Kansas City area was that of Oscar S. Straus, "250 Years of Hebrews in America," *Kansas City Times*, November 26, 1905. Positive accounts of the weeklong annual Hebrew Fair in Kansas City during the 1880s were reported. See, for instance, "The Hebrew Fair," *Kansas City Star*, November 20, 1884. A report of a "very swell" Jewish wedding in Emporia was published as "A Hebrew Wedding," *Topeka Daily Capital*, November 23, 1892. On Rabbi Samuel Marks in Leavenworth, "Rabbi Marks Re-Elected," *Topeka Daily Capital*, June 26, 1897. One of the most overtly negative articles about Jews, Robert G. Ingersoll's "The Despised Race" (*Topeka Daily Capital*, December 17, 1897), was written by an atheist who was equally dismissive of Christians. The *Leavenworth Bulletin* carried stories about Purim, weddings, and lectures by visiting Jewish leaders; these reports emphasized that Jews were kind, generous, and on the right side politically. The populist newspapers were less complimentary. See, for example, Jason Theodore Haworth, "Anti-Semitism and Kansas Populism" (master's thesis, University of Missouri at Kansas City, 2006), 71–96. Besides Jewish settlements as such, Jewish merchants followed the railroads west, and alternatively were observant in private or discarded Judaism and joined Christian churches. See, for example, Carolyn Sayler, *Doris Fleeson: Incomparably the First Political Journalist of Her Time* (Santa Fe: Sunstone Press, 2010), 23. Sayler mentions Jewish merchant A. L. Mincer, who established a store in Sterling on the Santa Fe railroad, and writes that other Jewish entrepreneurs in the area joined Presbyterian and Congregational churches.

83. Nell Irvin Painter, *Exodusters: Black Migration to Kansas after Reconstruction* (New York: W. W. Norton, 1992); Glen Schwendemann, "Wyandotte and the First 'Exodusters' of 1879," *Kansas Historical Quarterly* 26 (1960): 233–49; "The Southern Fugitives: Mass Meeting of Colored Citizens," *New York Times*, April 11, 1879.

84. U.S. Census, 1890, religious bodies, electronic data file.

85. U.S. Census, 1880, electronic data file. Of the total Kansas population of 996,096, 652,944 were native born in states other than Kansas: 16.4 percent in Illinois, 11.8 percent in Indiana, 8.6 percent in Iowa, 9.2 percent in Missouri, 6.6 percent in New York, 14.3 percent in Ohio, and 9.1 percent in Pennsylvania, totaling 75 percent from these seven states. Of all organized congregations, Methodists accounted for 33 percent in Illinois in 1870, 45 percent in Indiana, 36 percent in Iowa, 33 percent in Missouri, 31 percent in New York, 33 percent in Ohio, and 21 percent in Pennsylvania, or 32 percent overall.

86. *Minutes of the New York East Conference of the Methodist Episcopal Church* (New York: Methodist Episcopal Church, April 2, 1879), 31st sess., 22.

87. Eastern Kansas here refers to the 31 counties that ran as far west as Dickinson and Marion, and as far south as Neosho and Wilson. There were 439 Methodist organizations and 354 Methodist edifices in these

counties in 1890, compared with 808 organizations and 379 buildings in the remaining counties.

88. Quoted in Thomas Coke and Francis Asbury, *The Doctrines and Discipline of the Methodist Episcopal Church in America with Explanatory Notes* (Philadelphia: Henry Tuckniss, 1798), 172.

89. Based on Kansas Methodist Conference reports, there were 279 incorporated towns in 1890 that had a Methodist church and 42 that did not. Population figures are from the U.S. Census. In 1880, incorporated towns that had a Methodist church by 1890 were already larger, averaging 895 residents compared with 215 residents in towns without a Methodist church. In 1890, the mean population of towns with and without Methodist churches, respectively, was 1,172 and 374; in 1900, it was 1,331 and 456; in 1910, 1,676 and 549; in 1920, 1,886 and 558; in 1930, 2,264 and 539; and in 1940, 2,080 and 515. After 1950, as towns became defunct and new towns emerged, the comparisons become less meaningful, but in 2005, for example, towns that had a Methodist church in 1890 averaged 3,213 residents, compared with 1,479 residents in towns that did not have a Methodist church in 1890.

90. U.S. Census, 1870, 1890. In the nation as a whole, there was one clergyperson for every 858 people in 1870, and one for every 714 people in 1890.

91. These observations are drawn from my analysis of appointments in the northern Kansas conference from 1893 through 1900. Limited information on the size of congregations along with where pastors served before and after these dates restricts the amount of confidence that can be placed in these impressions.

92. For numerous firsthand accounts by Methodist pastors serving the Northwest Kansas Conference as population spread west during the 1870s and 1880s, see William Henry Sweet, *A History of Methodism in Northwest Kansas* (Salina: Kansas Wesleyan University, 1920).

93. "Ministerial Appointments Made at the Southwestern Conference," *Kansas City Times*, September 22, 1891. The meeting was for Methodist assignments in Missouri, which closely resembled those in Kansas.

94. These conclusions are from my analysis of information included in *History of the Southwest Kansas Conference of the Methodist Episcopal Church, Vol I., 1883–1931* (Wichita: Methodist Episcopal Church, 1932). The information includes the pastor's name along with the name and dates of each congregation served. I restricted the analysis to pastors serving any time between 1883 and 1903, excluding pastors who did not serve in congregations or whose place of service was unclear, and used data from the 1890 census as the approximate midpoint for the population. The 249 pastors collectively served a total of 1,853 years, during which 897 moves were made, or an average of a move every 2 years. I attained the 5-year attrition rate of 37 percent by counting the number of pastors serving in each of the years from 1883 through 1898 who were still serving in the conference 5 years later. Twenty-six percent of the first appointments were

in towns averaging 100 people, 34 percent were in towns averaging 320 people, 18 percent were in towns averaging 900 people, 15 percent were in towns averaging 2,400 people, and 7 percent were in towns averaging 7,000 people. Among clergy in towns of 500 people or less, 62 percent of their first moves were to a town larger than their first town, and 53 percent of their second moves were to a larger town. Among clergy in towns of more than 500 people, only 33 percent of their first moves were to a larger town, but 53 percent of their second moves were to a larger town. Although larger towns were generally more desirable than smaller ones, some small towns were attractive because of being near a larger town, and some clergy undoubtedly preferred a smaller town near a previous charge to a larger one farther away.

Individual cases illustrated the variations in career patterns. Reverend John M. Archer, for instance, moved from a town of 367 people to one of more than 1,200, but after 2 years went to a town of fewer than 700 people, then relocated to one of more than 1,600, then to one of fewer than 200, and finally to one of more than 1,000. His ups and downs were mitigated by being in the center of the state near several larger towns. Reverend A. B. Bruner was apparently a more senior or more highly regarded pastor, serving for 6 years in the conference, all in towns with more than 3,000 residents. Reverend S. D. McKibbin was an example of a pastor who held pastorates in 10 different locations over a 20-year period, none in towns of more than 200 people and one involving an extensive circuit.

95. Craig Charles Fankhauser, "The Heritage of Faith: An Historical Evaluation of the Holiness Movement in America" (master's thesis, Pittsburg State University, 1983), chapter 4, especially 70. For a quantitative study of revivalism during this period, see George M. Thomas, *Revivalism and Cultural Change: Christianity, Nation Building, and the Market in the Nineteenth-Century United States* (Chicago: University of Chicago Press, 1989).

96. Anonymous, *A Short History of Conservative Friends* (Richmond, IN), available at http://www.snowcamp.org/shocf.

97. Clarence Hiebert, *The Holdeman People: The Church of God in Christ, Mennonite, 1859–1969* (South Pasadena, CA: William Carey Library, 1973).

98. *Winfield Daily Courier*, January 6, 1876.

99. Quoted in "His Heart on Fire," *Kansas City Times*, January 24, 1888; Kathleen Minnix, *Laughter in the Amen Corner: The Life of Evangelist Sam Jones* (Athens: University of Georgia Press, 1993); Chad Gregory, "Sam Jones: Masculine Prophet of God," *Georgia Historical Quarterly* 86 (2002): 231–52.

100. *Arkansas City Traveler*, January 15, 1879.

101. The information here is from news and notices included in the *Winfield Courier* and *Arkansas City Traveler* between 1876 and 1886. Examples of interdenominational cooperation in constructing church buildings, financing them, and hosting meetings in Johnson, Smith, Ottawa, and

Ellis counties are in Joanna L. Stratton, *Pioneer Women: Voices from the Kansas Frontier* (New York: Simon and Schuster, 1981), 171–83.

102. Patricia Douglass Smith, *Centennial Saga of First United Methodist Church, Garden City, Kansas, 1882–1982: A History of the Church and Its First Records* (Garden City: First United Methodist Church, History Committee, 1982), 1–2; *Topeka Commonwealth*, February 29, 1872.

103. Kansas State Census, 1875, in Kansas Board of Agriculture, *Fourth Annual Report of the Kansas Board of Agriculture* (Topeka: Kansas Board of Agriculture, 1875). Church membership figures in 1875 were compiled as part of the state census, but the numbers for Catholics appear to have been estimated and rounded to the nearest hundred for at least a third of the counties, whereas that was evident in only four counties for Methodist membership. However inaccurate they may have been, the 1875 data were collected more carefully than figures reported in subsequent biennial agriculture reports between 1878 and 1888. The 1878 figures for Catholics, for example, are larger than those obtained in the 1890 federal census for at least a third of the counties, despite population growth during that period, and deviate from the 1875 and 1890 figures by a factor of two in most cases, and a factor of ten to twenty in several instances.

104. Data are from the Kansas State Census, 1875. For the 76 reporting counties, the zero-order Pearson correlation coefficient between the value of Catholic and Methodist edifices was .594, between the number of Catholic organizations and Methodist organizations was .370, and between the number of Catholic and Methodist members was .462.

105. Data on members, organizations, and edifices are from the U.S. Census, 1890. Comparisons are with figures from the Kansas State Census, 1875.

106. Beckman, *Kansas Monks*, 63.

107. Thomas Ambrose Butler, *The State of Kansas and Irish Immigration* (Dublin: Dublin University Press, 1871).

108. U.S. Census, 1890; Cutler, *History of the State of Kansas*, Ellis County section; Ellis County Historical Society, *At Home in Ellis County, Kansas, 1867–1992* (Dallas: Taylor Publishing Company, 1991). The zero-order Pearson correlation coefficient between the percentage of the population that was Catholic in each county and the percentage that was foreign born was .506—significant at or beyond the .001 level.

109. The extent of Catholic clustering is evident in statistical comparisons at the county level with Methodists. For the 105 Kansas counties in 1890, statistics for Catholic and Methodist membership, respectively, are: range, 6,056 versus 3,427; standard deviation, 951.2 versus 645.3; skewness, 2.93 versus 1.16; and kurtosis, 11.40 versus 2.14. The kurtosis measure especially indicates the high degree of deviation from a normal statistical distribution.

110. An indication of the geographic separation of Methodists and Catholics was that in 1890, the standardized ordinary least squares regression coefficient for Catholic members per county by Methodist members

per county, controlling for the total population per county, was −.693, which is significant at or beyond the .001 level.

111. *Axtell Anchor*, November 1, 1889.

112. Dassler, *Compiled Laws of Kansas*, 357–58.

113. Coke and Asbury, *Doctrines and Discipline*, 18, 19, 21.

114. *Topeka Commonwealth*, February 1, 1872. Reverend Mitchell may have been more attuned than average to competition with Catholics from having served in a series of previous appointments in Leavenworth.

115. Butler, *State of Kansas*, 35–36.

116. The two churches remain in their original locations, having been constructed from limestone because of a local ordinance passed after most of the wooden stores in Alma burned in three consecutive years. The construction dates are from Cutler, *History of Kansas*, Wabaunsee County chapter. The story about "damned Catholics" is from an interview with Reverend Robert Grimm of St. John Lutheran Church, conducted August 10, 2007.

117. William James Millikin, *Autobiography* (unpublished manuscript, 1917).

CHAPTER 2

1. Thomas Ambrose Butler, *The State of Kansas and Irish Immigration* (Dublin: Dublin University Press, 1871), 34.

2. Sara T. L. Robinson, *Kansas: Its Interior and Exterior Life* (Boston: Crosby, Nichols and Company, 1856), 85.

3. Frank A. Root, *The Overland Stage to California* (Topeka: Crane and Company, 1901), 510–11.

4. *Arkansas City Republican*, December 4, 1886. For several examples of incidents associated with revivals, see Dee Brown, *Wondrous Times on the Frontier* (New York: August House, 1991), 174–83.

5. Craig Charles Fankhauser, "The Heritage of Faith: An Historical Evaluation of the Holiness Movement in America" (master's thesis, Pittsburg State University, 1983), especially chapter 5.

6. "They Do Not Lack Nerve," *Kansas City Times*, May 16, 1889; H. T. Besse, *Church History* (San Jose: Besse Publishing, 1908), 188. Schweinfurth himself only days before had been notified by "white caps" in Rockford, Illinois, to leave the town, or anticipate being tarred and feathered, then roasted alive. "A Minister Warned by White Caps," *New York Times*, May 9, 1889. White caps were vigilante groups that resembled the Ku Klux Klan. See William Holmes, "Whitecapping: Anti-Semitism in the Populist Era," *American Jewish Historical Quarterly* 63 (1974): 244–61.

7. Glenn R. Goss, *The Scofield Bible and C. I. Scofield* (Philadelphia: Philadelphia College of Bible, 1992). Scofield along with his wife, two children, and two domestic servants are listed in the 1870 U.S. census for Atchison. He returned to Saint Louis in 1873, but his wife and children remained in Atchison, where they continued to attend Catholic services.

Dispensationalism, generally regarded as having been influenced by a reaction to Charles Darwin, taught that the church was in a new era preparing for the end-times. The Scofield Bible sold hundreds of thousands of copies. It provided readers with annotations interpreting prophecy and history.

8. Clippings and notes on file at the Smith County Historical Society, Smith Center, KS. The Meyers are mentioned briefly in Jane Fletcher Geniesse, *American Priestess: The Extraordinary Story of Anna Spafford and the American Colony in Jerusalem* (New York: Doubleday, 2008), 162. The group's appeal also became a cautionary tale in Chicago, as reported in "Are a Strange Sect: Spafford Jerusalem Colony," *Sunday InterOcean*, February 17, 1896.

9. The biographical information is from Frank W. Blackmar, *Kansas: A Cyclopedia of State History* (Chicago: Standard Publishing Company, 1912), 753–54. The election results are from the electronic data file made available in Jerome M. Clubb, William H. Flanigan, and Nancy H. Zingale, *Electoral Data for Counties in the United States, 1840 to 1972* (Ann Arbor: Inter-University Consortium for Political and Social Research, University of Michigan, 1986). On railroad development, see George W. Glick, "To the Voters of the 6th Representative District," *Freedom's Champion*, October 29, 1863.

10. The Glick Church is described in A. A. Graham, *History of Fairfield and Perry Counties* (Chicago: W. H. Beers and Company, 1883), 210–11. The heavy margin in Ellis County may have reflected Glick's role in the Union Pacific Railroad, which eventuated in the town of Ellis being selected in 1873 as a roundhouse and machine shop location for the railroad. From 1867 to 1874, Glick served as attorney for the railroad's central branch.

11. Jim L. Lewis, "'Beautiful Bismarck'—Bismarck Grove, Lawrence, 1878–1900," *Kansas Historical Quarterly* 35 (1969): 225–56. William Henry Sweet (*A History of Methodism in Northwest Kansas* [Salina: Kansas Wesleyan University, 1920]) mentions discussions and temperance committees at annual conferences. Reverend Jeremiah Boynton of Topeka was president of the State Temperance Convention in Leavenworth in 1874. See Daniel Webster Wilder, *The Annals of Kansas* (Topeka: Kansas Publishing House, 1875), 657.

12. Using electoral data for counties, I examined standardized ordinary least squares multiple regression coefficients for variables predicting the Democratic vote, controlling for the total votes cast, in Kansas gubernatorial elections from 1870 through 1898. Catholics as a percent of the total county population did not have a statistically significant effect in 1870, 1872, or 1874. The effect was significant in 1876, strongest in the election of 1878, and continued to be significant through 1888. The effect of Methodists as a percent of the total county population on the Democratic vote was negative in every election from 1870 through 1892, but reached statistical significance only in the elections from 1880 through 1890. See also Louise Elaine Rickard, "The Impact of Populism on Electoral Patterns

in Kansas, 1880–1900: A Quantitative Analysis" (PhD diss., University of Kansas, 1974), which includes several models showing the significant and opposing effects of the percentage of Catholics and Protestants on several electoral outcomes.

13. Walter W. Spooner, *The Cyclopedia of Temperance and Prohibition* (New York: Funk and Wagnalls, 1891), 104–5, which also includes the official tallies for each county.

14. For the percentages voting in favor of the amendment in 1880 in each county and the results of a multiple regression analysis showing that "denomination" was significantly associated with the referendum vote taking account of party affiliation, see Robert Smith Bader, *Prohibition in Kansas: A History* (Lawrence: University Press of Kansas, 1986), 269–71. Yet denomination was coded on the basis of examining religious groups' stance toward Prohibition. I replicated the analysis using the more reliable 1890 federal census data for estimating the percent of Methodists and Catholics, and controlled for the total population, the percent of native born, the total number of religious organizations per county, and the number of towns per county. The standardized ordinary least squares regression coefficient for the percent of Methodists was .272, which is significant at the .02 level, and for the percent of Catholics was −.329, which is significant at the .01 level. The coefficient for the total number of religious organizations per county was .539, which is significant at the .02 level, thus underscoring the importance that both the Methodist and Catholic effects remained significant even controlling for the number of religious organizations. The total population, the percent of native born, and the number of towns were not significant, perhaps casting doubt on arguments about Prohibition as a nativist or antiurban issue.

15. James Humphrey, "The Administration of George W. Glick," *Transactions of the Kansas State Historical Society* 9 (1906): 395–413.

16. Quoted in Bader, *Prohibition in Kansas*, 73.

17. It was also rumored that Glick was not the teetotaler he claimed to be, but these reports were discredited. See "No Truth in the Story That Col. Glick Is a Drinking Man," *Chicago Daily Tribune*, October 2, 1882.

18. Quoted in the *Atchison Globe*, November 10, 1882.

19. J. N. Stearns, *Prohibition Does Prohibit; or Prohibition Not a Failure* (New York: National Temperance Society and Publication House, 1882), 66–69.

20. "The Goubleman Case," *Topeka Daily Capital*, January 17, 1884.

21. As previously noted, multiple regression analysis at the county level of the likelihood of voters opting for Democratic candidates in Kansas gubernatorial elections shows that in 1870, 1872, and 1874, the effects of religion did not reach statistical significance. In 1876, the percent of Catholics had a significant positive effect on voting Democratic and the percent of Methodists had a weak negative effect that was not statistically significant. In 1878, 1880, 1882, 1884, 1886, and 1888, the percent of Catholics had a significant positive effect on voting Democratic and the

percent of Methodists had a significant negative effect. In 1890 through 1898, the effects were generally not significant. In further analysis, the total votes cast in each county for Democratic gubernatorial candidates in the 1878 through 1888 elections was combined, divided by the total Republican votes cast in each county to provide a measure of Democratic partisanship, and then ordinary least squares multiple regression models were computed to examine the effects of population size, the percent of Catholics, the percent of Methodists, the percent of native as well as German born, and the percent that voted for the Prohibition amendment in 1880. The effect of the total population demonstrated that more heavily populated counties were more likely to vote Democratic. The percent of native born was negatively associated with voting Democratic, but the effect was not significant or consistent. The percent of German born was positively associated with voting Democratic. The percent of Catholics remained positively associated with voting Democratic when these other factors were included in the models, and the percent of Methodists remained negatively associated. Adding the Prohibition variable reduced the Methodist effect to insignificance, suggesting that Prohibition was an important factor in the Methodist tendency to vote Republican. The adjusted R-square for the model with only population and native born was .076, adding the percent of Catholics and Methodists increased the R-square to .301, including the percent of German born further increased the R-square to .412, and adding the percent voting for Prohibition increased it to .504. It is important to bear in mind that these are county-level results rather than individual-level measurements.

22. One accusation that was reported to Kansas readers occurred in Baltimore, where a Methodist minister declared liquor traffic, wealth, and Catholic "priestcraft" to be the major threats to U.S. freedom. See "The Red Hat," *Atchison Daily Globe*, July 6, 1886.

23. If they mentioned Catholics at all, temperance publications more often emphasized Catholic Total Abstinence Societies, which were said to be popular among farmers in other parts of the Middle West.

24. I. O. Pickering, "The Administrations of John P. St. John," *Transactions of the Kansas State Historical Society* 9 (1906): 378–94.

25. Quoted in P. T. Winskill, *The Temperance Movement and Its Workers* (London: Blackie and Son, 1892), 117–18.

26. "Buchanan and Brown," *Freedom's Champion*, December 3, 1859.

27. These shortcomings are chronicled in Paul Wallace Gates, *Fifty Million Acres: Conflicts over Kansas Land Policy, 1854–1890* (Ithaca, NY: Cornell University Press, 1954).

28. U.S. Bureau of the Census, *Statistical Abstract of the United States, 1890* (Washington, DC: Government Printing Office, 1891), table 241, 303.

29. Ibid., table 167, 140.

30. William Alfred Peffer, *The Farmer's Side: His Troubles and Their Remedy* (New York: D. Appleton and Company, 1891), 30.

31. E. C. Murphy, "Is Rainfall in Kansas Increasing?" *Transactions of the Annual Meetings of the Kansas Academy of Science* 13 (1891): 16–19; C. J. Mock, "Drought and Precipitation Fluctuations during the Late Nineteenth Century," *Great Plains Research* 1 (1991): 26–57.

32. Powell Moore, "A Hoosier in Kansas: The Diary of Hiram H. Young, 1886–1895: Pioneer of Cloud County, Part Two, 1890–1891," *Kansas Historical Quarterly* 14 (1946): 301.

33. *Topeka Daily Capital*, August 31, 1890.

34. Peffer, *The Farmer's Side*, 156–57.

35. For the best overall history of Kansas populism, see O. Gene Clanton, *A Common Humanity: Kansas Populism and the Battle for Justice and Equality, 1854–1903* (Manhattan, KS: Sunflower University Press, 2004). For a valuable comparative study, see Jeffrey Ostler, *Prairie Populism: The Fate of Agrarian Radicalism in Kansas, Nebraska, and Iowa, 1880–1892* (Lawrence: University Press of Kansas, 1993). For useful general histories, see Robert C. McMath, *American Populism: A Social History, 1877–1898* (New York: Hill and Wang, 1990); Charles Postel, *The Populist Vision* (New York: Oxford University Press, 2007). For an extensive list of references, see Worth Robert Miller, "A Centennial Historiography of American Populism," *Kansas History* 16 (1993): 54–69.

36. Jerry Simpson, "The Political Rebellion in Kansas," in *The Farmers' Alliance History and Agricultural Digest*, ed. Nelson A. Dunning (Washington, DC: Alliance Publishing Company, 1891), 283.

37. Moore, "A Hoosier in Kansas." The Populist vote for governor was 49.5 percent of the total votes cast in Cloud County. Information about Reverend Bushong is from the *Miltonvale Record*, June 5, 1924.

38. Isom P. Langley, "Religion in the Alliance," in *The Farmers' Alliance History and Agricultural Digest*, ed. Nelson A. Dunning (Washington, DC: Alliance Publishing Company, 1891), 316. The biographical details are from *Biographical and Historical Memoirs of Eastern Arkansas* (Chicago: Goodspeed Publishers, 1890). See also Peter H. Argersinger, "Pentecostal Politics in Kansas: Religion, the Farmers' Alliance, and the Gospel of Populism," *Kansas Quarterly* 1 (1981): 24–35.

39. William E. Connelley, *A Standard History of Kansas and Kansans* (Chicago: Lewis Publishing Company, 1918), 2440.

40. "Discuss Social Problems," *Milwaukee Journal*, October 16, 1891.

41. "The Labor Question," *Atchison Daily Globe*, May 14, 1892. On the Omaha Platform and events surrounding it, see Lawrence Goodwynn, *The Populist Movement: A Short History of the Agrarian Revolt in America* (New York: Oxford University Press, 1978); John D. Hicks, *The Populist Revolt: A History of the Farmers' Alliance and the People's Party* (Lincoln, NE: Bison, 1970).

42. "Bishop Fink," *Atchison Daily Globe*, February 13, 1890.

43. "Catholics and the Alliance," *Atchison Daily Globe*, March 10, 1890. An analysis of county-level 1890 election results shows that the standardized ordinary least squares regression coefficient of the percent of

Catholics was −.213 (significant at the .05 level) for the Populist candidate in the U.S. Senate race and −.181 (significant at the .05 level) for the gubernatorial race, with both estimates controlling for the total population and the percent of farms encumbered.

44. Quoted in Emory Lindquist, "The Swedish Immigrant and Life in Kansas," *Kansas Historical Quarterly* 29 (1963): 12. See also "People's Party vs. the Church," *Chicago Daily Tribune*, September 3, 1891).

45. "Botkin for Governor; Nominations of the Kansas Prohibitionists," *New York Times,* July 20, 1888; "Botkin Won't Withdraw," *Kansas City Times*, August 19, 1888.

46. "Rev. Bernard Kelly for Pension Agent," *Topeka Daily Capital*, July 11, 1889; "Unseemly Language Used by a Methodist Elder, Politics at the Bottom," *St. Louis Republic*, September 19, 1891; "Mr. Botkin's Gloomy View," *Kansas City Star*, August 17, 1894.

47. "J. D. Botkins' Flop," *Topeka Daily Capital*, August 23, 1894; "Botkin Is Radical," *Topeka Daily Capital*, September 6, 1894.

48. Phyllis M. Swanson, *City of the Plains: A Story of Leonardville* (Leonardville: Leonardville City Library, 1982).

49. William Allen White, "What's the Matter with Kansas?" *Emporia Gazette*, August 15, 1896.

50. "The Richest Church in Topeka Is the Leading Methodist Organization," *Atchison Daily Globe*, November 12, 1889; Sweet, *History of Methodism in Northwest Kansas*, 93, 188; "Ladies Home Missionary Society of the Methodist Church of Atchison," *Atchison Daily Globe*, March 1, 1890.

51. *Industrial Free Press* (Winfield), January 16, 1891, quoted in Michael Lewis Goldberg, "'An Army of Women': Gender Relations and Politics in Kansas Populism, the Woman Movement, and the Republican Party, 1879–1896" (PhD diss., Yale University, 1992), 212.

52. Zero-order Pearson correlation coefficients between the percentage voting for Populist candidates in each county in eleven statewide elections between 1888 and 1896 and the average value of church buildings per county and the percentage of farms encumbered with mortgages were examined. Standardized regression coefficients for ordinary least squares multiple regression models in which the average value of church buildings and the percent of encumbered farms were included simultaneously were also computed. The coefficients for the value of church buildings were uniformly negative, indicating that counties in which churches were more expensive were less likely to vote Populist than those counties in which the churches were less expensive. The coefficients for the effect of encumbered farms were uniformly positive. All the latter coefficients were statistically significant at or beyond the .01 level of probability. After 1888, seven of the nine coefficients for the value of church buildings were significant at or beyond the .05 level of probability. Due to multicollinearity, the effects of additional variables were examined separately. The effects of the value of church buildings remained significant when controlling for the average value of farmland and farm buildings, indicating that the church effect

was not a surrogate measure for overall economic well-being. The effects of encumbered farms were the strongest and most consistent of any other measure of the mortgage situation, including the average rate of interest and the amount of mortgages as a percentage of farm value.

53. For the complete text of Little's speech, see William Jennings Bryan, *The First Battle: A Story of the Campaign of 1896* (Chicago: W. B. Conkey, 1898), 254–58. For Bryan's "cross of gold" statement, see ibid., 206.

54. "Senator Peffer's Acceptance," *Emporia Daily Gazette*, January 29, 1891. The biographical information is from *Biographical Annals of Cumberland County, Pennsylvania* (Chicago: Genealogical Publishing Company, 1905), 235–38. On Peffer's frustrations in the senate, see Peter H. Argersinger, "No Rights on This Floor: Third Parties and the Institutionalization of Congress," *Journal of Interdisciplinary History* 22 (1992): 655–90; Peter H. Argersinger, *Populism and Politics: William Alfred Peffer and the People's Party* (Lexington: University Press of Kentucky, 1974).

55. "Peffer for Senator," *Milwaukee Sentinel*, January 27, 1891.

56. William Alfred Peffer, *Myriorama: A View of Our People and Their History, Together with the Principles Underlying, and the Circumstances Attending, the Rise and Progress of the American Union* (Clarksville, TN: Buck and Neville, 1869). Myriorama in the nineteenth century were popular picture cards, including ones that could be moved in sequence to produce a kind of motion picture.

57. Ibid., 157.

58. Ibid., 174, 216.

59. Ibid., 224.

60. The percentages given here refer to the proportion of the total number of officeholder years held by Republicans. For example, from 1891 through 1899, there were seven seats in the U.S. House of Representatives times ten years, or a total of seventy officeholder years, and Republicans held thirty-three of these, or 47 percent.

61. "Change in Kansas College Faculty," *New York Tribune*, June 13, 1899; "Story of Parties," *Topeka Daily Capital*, March 12, 1897; "Sentiment of the Senate," *Kansas City Times*, July 11, 1894; "A New Deal in Kansas," *Washington Post*, February 24, 1892; "Striving to Divide Kansas," *Washington Post*, November 22, 1892. There was truth in assertions about economic difficulties in western Kansas and the possibility of mortgages being foreclosed in those counties. During the 1890s, the population fell in nearly every county in western Kansas. Grant, Greeley, Haskell, Morton, Stanton, Stevens, and Wallace counties declined by more than 50 percent.

62. According to one contemporary source, the American Protective Association in Kansas aimed "to strike a blow at the Roman Catholic Church and, incidentally, to prevent men of foreign birth from holding office" ("A New Power in Politics," *New York Times*, November 18, 1893). Its strength in the early 1890s included the eastern half of Kansas. See Humphrey J. Desmond, *The A.P.A. Movement* (Washington, DC: New Century Press, 1912), 63. Other sources, however, suggest that the American

Protective Association was less influential in Kansas than in Kansas City, Missouri, where it waged a successful mayoral campaign in 1896. In Kansas, the association was denounced by Populists, and declared itself in favor of McKinley and against "Romanist" candidates. See "A.P.A. Controls Kansas Men," *Chicago Daily Tribune*, April 19, 1896; "O'ermatched," *Los Angeles Times*, June 15, 1896; Clanton, *A Common Humanity*, 219; Seymour Martin Lipset and Earl Raab, *The Politics of Unreason: Right-wing Extremism in America, 1790–1790* (New York: Harper and Row, 1970), 79–92.

63. Data on population, urban population, town size, and farms are from the U.S. Census, 1880 and 1900, electronic data files.

64. The biographical information about Albaugh is from the National Register of Historic Places Registration Form, Morton Albaugh House, U.S. Department of the Interior, National Park Service, October 1990. The Stanley quote is from "Policy Is Outlined: W. E. Stanley Tells What He Intends to Do," *Topeka Daily Capital*, November 15, 1898. The information about Leland appeared in a series of articles titled "My Recollections," *Kansas City Star*, January 26, February 9, February 16, and February 23, 1913.

65. "New Leader in Kansas Party," *Chicago Daily Tribune*, June 19, 1900; "J. R. Burton to Succeed Baker in U.S. Senate," *Topeka Daily Capital*, January 8, 1901; "Marries Rich Widow," *Washington Post*, May 6, 1906; "David Mulvane Estate Is Valued at $1,000,000," *Washington Post*, November 15, 1932; "Joseph R. Burton," *Washington Post*, February 28, 1923; "Hoch Not Hurt by Kissing Tale," *Atlanta Constitution*, May 3, 1906; "Hoch, Editor and Printer," *Kansas City Star*, January 18, 1904; "Picking a Hoch Slate," *Kansas City Star*, January 25, 1904; Edward Wallis Hoch, "Governor's Message to the Legislature of Kansas," January 10, 1905; available at http://www.kslib.info.

66. Hoch, "Governor's Message." See also "Loyal Salina," *Topeka Daily Capital*, June 5, 1890; "Leavenworth," *Topeka Daily Capital*, June 26, 1890. The Law and Order League of the United States changed its name earlier that year to the International Law and Order League following an organizational meeting of Canadian affiliates in Toronto. See "Citizens Aroused," *Topeka Daily Capital* (October 26, 1897.

67. U.S. Bureau of the Census, *Religious Bodies, 1916: Part I: Summary and General Tables* (Washington, DC: Government Printing Office, 1919), table 62, 174–76.

68. "W. E. Stanley," *Kansas City Star*, November 14, 1898.

69. "Troutman at Emporia," *Topeka Daily Capital*, January 7, 1898; "Olpe Women Threaten to Smash Joints," *Topeka Daily Capital*, February 19, 1901; "District Conference Endorses Mrs. Nation and Her Work," *Topeka Daily Capital*, February 19, 1901; "Law and Order Contest in Hutchinson," *Topeka Daily Capital*, March 15, 1901; "Methodist Conference Assignment," *Topeka Daily Capital*, March 19, 1901; "Hoch to Talk Prohibition," *Kansas City Star*, April 30, 1908.

70. Burton had "no philosophy of life" and was elected, White charged, only because of influence from the railroad companies. See "Stern Lesson in Fall of Burton," *Chicago Daily Tribune*, March 29, 1904.

71. "Truly Good Kansas Town," *Washington Post*, June 11, 1911; "Sees Religious Duty in Vote," *Chicago Daily Tribune*, October 17, 1910; Lee L. Bloomenshine, *Prairie around Me: Childhood Memories* (San Diego: Raphael Publications, 1972), 8; Mary Potter Boyd, *Life in Corbin, Kansas* [1907–18], unpublished memoir, available at http://www.wizardofkansas .com/Corbin.

72. U.S. Bureau of the Census, *Statistical Abstract of the United States, 1900* (Washington, DC: Government Printing Office, 1901), table 133, 425; Lida H. Hardy, "Training the Mothers," *Topeka Daily Capital*, December 18, 1900; "A Solid Phalanx," *Topeka Daily Capital*, March 22, 1889.

73. Quoted in "Kansas Methodist Minister Accused of Being Heretic," *Chicago Daily Tribune*, March 21, 1902.

74. "Evolution at Kansas Wesleyan," *New York Tribune*, June 11, 1901.

75. *Constitution of the State of* Kansas, available at http://www.kslib .info/constitution.

76. Gerard V. Bradley, "The Blaine Amendment of 1876: Harbinger of Secularism," *Notre Dame Legal Studies Paper No. 07-02* (January 30, 2007). Blaine's 1884 margin of victory in Kansas was exceeded only in Minnesota and Vermont.

77. "No Sectarian Education," *Omaha World Herald*, February 25, 1896; "Cockrell Amendment Wins," *Omaha World Herald*, April 23, 1896; "Against Money for Sects," *Kansas City Star*, February 4, 1898; "No More Money for Sectarian Schools," *Chicago Daily Tribune*, January 23, 1899.

78. The relevant sections are: Kansas Constitution, article 6, sec. 8; 1876 laws, chapter 122, article 10, sec. 21, and article 11, sec. 23; 1897 laws, chapter 179, sec. 4. All are included in W. D. Ross, *Laws Relating to the Common Schools of Kansas* (Topeka: State Printing Office, 1913), 50, 61, 197.

79. One example was a student named Philip Billard, who was suspended from the Quincy school in North Topeka in 1902 for refusing to participate in religious exercises. See "Theism versus Atheism," *Lucifer the Light Bearer* (Topeka), February 27, 1902.

80. Office of the Attorney General, *Biennial Report to the Governor* (Topeka: Office of the Attorney General, 1886), 118.

81. "To Amend the Constitution," *Kansas City Star*, December 28, 1891; "Are You a Patriotic American?" *Kansas City Times*, June 18, 1894; "The School Board's Reply," *Kansas City Times*, May 20, 1895; "New Political Society," *Kansas City Times*, June 8, 1893; "No Pay for Sectarian School Teachers," *Kansas City Star*, March 14, 1894; "Patriotic Sons of America," *Topeka Daily Capitol*, June 27, 1889.

82. Quoted in "Is Knowledge Dangerous?" *Lucifer the Light Bearer*, February 15, 1889.

83. "Teachers to Ask Legislature for Supplementary Book Law," *Kansas Semi-Weekly Capital* (Topeka), December 28, 1900.

84. "Shots at Rome," *Topeka Daily Capital*, November 20, 1900; "Urges Church to Activity," *Los Angeles Times*, May 26, 1914.

CHAPTER 3

1. John James Ingalls, *Essays, Addresses, and Orations* (Kansas City, MO: Hudson Kimberly, 1902), 483, 486, 488.

2. Herbert Hoover, "The Harvest of National Progress," speech at the Stanford University stadium in Palo Alto, California, on August 11, 1928, quoted in Stewart Beach, "The Story of the Week," *Independent*, August 18, 1928, 166. On the composition of the Kansas state legislature, which included ninety Republicans and thirty-three Democrats in the House of Representatives along with thirty-two Republicans and eight Democrats in the U.S. Senate in 1924, see Marvin Harder and Carolyn Rampey, *The Kansas Legislature: Procedures, Personalities, and Problems* (Lawrence: University Press of Kansas, 1972), 16. The national election results from electronic data files were provided by the Inter-University Consortium for Political and Social Research, University of Michigan, Ann Arbor.

3. Don W. Holter, *Fire on the Prairie: Methodism in the History of Kansas* (Topeka: Methodist Publishing House, 1969), 177–82; "A New Methodist Hospital," *Kansas City Star*, June 21, 1922; "Radio for New Church," *Kansas City Star*, June 13, 1922; "Methodists Gain in 1922," *Kansas City Star*, December 29, 1922; "New Methodist Building in Capital," *Kansas City Star*, November 23, 1922; "Methodists in Russia," *Time*, March 3, 1923; "Trends," *Time*, March 24, 1923; "Methodists and Bolshevists," *Time*, November 26, 1923.

4. These statistics are reported in U.S. Bureau of the Census, *Statistical Abstract of the United States*, for the years indicated.

5. Mark O. Hatfield, ed., *Vice Presidents of the United States, 1789–1993* (Washington, DC: Government Printing Office, 1997), 373–81; Homer Socolofsky, *Arthur Capper: Publisher, Politician, and Philanthropist* (Lawrence: University of Kansas Press, 1962).

6. Walter Roscoe Stubbs, "Message to the Kansas Legislature," January 12, 1909, available at http://www.kslib.info; George Hartshorn Hodges, "Message to the Kansas Legislature," March 10, 1913, available at http://www.kslib.info; "Kansas Primary Law," *New York Tribune*, August 17, 1909; C. A. Dykstra, "The Reorganization of State Government in Kansas," *American Political Science Review* 9 (1915): 264–72; Craig Miner, *Kansas: The History of the Sunflower State, 1854–2000* (Lawrence: University Press of Kansas, 2002), 225–26; Arthur Capper, "Governor's Message," January 12, 1915, available at http://www.kslib.info.

7. Bessie E. Wilder, *Governmental Agencies of the State of Kansas, 1861–1956* (Lawrence: University of Kansas, Governmental Research Center, 1957); "Allen Changed Atchison," *Kansas City Star*, October 21,

1914; Henry J. Allen, "Message to the Kansas Legislature," January 12, 1919, available at http://www.kslib.info.

8. U.S. Bureau of the Census, *Census of Religious Bodies, 1926* (Washington, DC: Government Printing Office, 1930).

9. These conclusions are drawn from examining the standardized residuals for actual Methodist and Catholic memberships for 105 counties in 1926, compared with predicted memberships based on 1906 distributions along with the total population in 1900 and 1920. For example, the largest standardized residual for Methodists was 3.88 for Sedgwick County and the largest standardized residual for Catholics was 4.84 for Wyandotte County. The county-level variations in 1926 Methodist membership are well predicted by 1906 Methodist membership and the total population in 1900 and 1920 (an adjusted R-squared of .916). The Catholic membership in 1926 is predicted by the Catholic membership in 1906, the total population in 1900 and 1920, and the foreign-born population in 1900 and 1920 (with each variable significant at or beyond the .001 level, and an adjusted R-square of .931). As an indication of differences in patterns of concentration, the 5 counties with the largest numbers of Catholics comprised 36 percent of the state's overall Catholic population, whereas the 5 counties with the largest numbers of Methodists made up only 18 percent of the state's Methodists.

10. In U.S. Census data (electronic data files) for incorporated places, 346 towns reported population figures in 1900 and 519 did in 1920; 290 incorporated towns in 1900 had one Methodist church, and the population in these towns increased from an average of 1,272 residents to an average of 1,838. Seven towns had two Methodist churches in 1900, and these towns grew from 12,472 to 20,072 between 1900 and 1920. For contemporary discussions of changes in urban and rural churches, see Arthur E. Holt, "Religion," *American Journal of Sociology* 34 (1928): 172–76; Warren H. Wilson, "What the Automobile Has Done to and for the Country Church," *Annals of the American Academy of Political and Social Science* 116 (1924): 83–86; W. C. Waterman, "Present Tendencies in Rural Sociology," *Social Forces* 7 (1928): 50–58; H. Paul Douglass, *How Shall Country Youth Be Served?* (New York: George H. Doran, 1925).

11. Robert S. Lynd and Helen Merrell Lynd, *Middletown: A Study in Modern American Culture* (New York: Harcourt Brace Jovanovich, 1929), 315.

12. Caroline Henderson, *Letters from the Dust Bowl*, ed. Alvin O. Turner (Norman: University of Oklahoma Press, 2001), 87–90. Henderson lived across the border in Oklahoma, but the church was in Elkhart, the closest market town. She had been a member twelve or thirteen years prior to the incident. "We joined," she wrote, "more because we wished to be associated with Christian people in worship and work for community welfare than because we had given close attention to the theology of the church" (87).

13. "Governor Stubbs a Preacher," *Kansas City Star*, November 15, 1909; "George H. Hodges," in William E. Connelley, ed., *A Standard*

History of Kansas and Kansans (Chicago: Lewis Publishing Company, 1918).

14. "Capper Calls the Church," *Kansas City Star*, September 6, 1915; Arthur Capper, "Methodist Church the Prophet of Prohibition," in *Addresses and Messages* (Topeka: Capper Printing Company, 1921), 415; W. G. Clugston, *Rascals in Democracy* (New York: Richard R. Smith, 1940), 245. One of Capper's gospel team appearances is mentioned in "Capper Packed Sunday Meetings," *Kansas City Star*, December 6, 1915. In *Arthur Capper*, Socolofsky pays little attention to Capper's religious involvement or appearances at churches. An insight into Capper's personal views toward religion can be gleaned from a journal entry written by Capper on Sunday, June 21, 1891, after attending services at a Baptist church in Chicago: "No one can enjoy a good sermon more than I do, even though I may be something of a sinner" (Homer E. Socolofsky, "The Private Journals of Florence Crawford and Arthur Capper, 1891–1892," *Kansas Historical Quarterly* 30 [1964]: 15–64).

15. Henry J. Allen, "Why I Go to Church," *Kansas City Star*, April 22, 1922. For a description of Allen's gospel team, see "Gospel Teams Win 6,000," *Kansas City Star*, January 8, 1914. On his YMCA work, see "Henry Allen's Good Work," *Kansas City Star*, August 1, 1918.

16. "Governor Hodges on the Saloon," *Kansas City Star*, November 13, 1913; "Governor Answers Attack on Prohibition in Kansas," *Christian Science Monitor*, March 27, 1915; "Good Business," *Kansas City Star*, June 29, 1915.

17. William Allen White, "As It Looks," *Emporia Gazette*, August 17, 1914. On Botkin, see Socolofsky, *Arthur Capper*, 91; Clugston, *Rascals in Democracy*, 236.

18. "Oh, Look Who's Here," *Kansas City Star*, August 9, 1914; "G. O. P. Losing in Kansas," *Kansas City Star*, August 16, 1914; "For New System in Kansas," *Kansas City Star*, April 14, 1915.

19. Capper, *Addresses and Messages*, 31–33. The cost-of-living index numbers are reported in U.S. Bureau of the Census, *Statistical Abstract of the United States, 1930* (Washington, DC: Government Printing Office, 1930), table 347, 327; the average national unit values of wheat are noted in ibid., table 352, 331; public debt, ibid., table 195, 198; state, municipal, and local taxes in Kansas, ibid., table 204, 207.

20. "Allen's Campaign Unique," *Kansas City Star*, August 4, 1918.

21. The full resolution is included in "Methodists Favor Votes for Women," *New York Times*, May 24, 1916; "Would Stop Liquor Ads," *Washington Post*, November 27, 1916; "Tobacco Ban in 1924 Aim of W.C.T.U.," *New York Tribune*, August 3, 1919.

22. "Work for Sunday School," *Kansas City Star*, February 21, 1917. Broader developments are detailed in Ben Primer, *Protestants and American Business Methods* (Ann Arbor: UMI Research Press, 1978. On the resistance to automobiles, fears that they would reduce churchgoing, and indications that they facilitated it, see Ronald R. Kline and Trevor Pinch,

"Users as Agents of Technological Change: The Social Construction of the Automobile in the Rural United States," *Technology and Culture* 37 (1996): 763–95.

23. Kansas State Historical Society, "This Day in Kansas History," available at http://www.kshs.org; "Combine to Fight Allen," *Kansas City Star*, October 27, 1920; W.E.B. DuBois, "The Republicans and the Black Voter," *Nation*, June 5, 1920, 757–58; "Church Aid Is Needed," *Kansas City Star*, May 21, 1921; "Labor Harmed by Strike," *Kansas City Star*, September 8, 1922; "See Good in Labor Court," *Kansas City Star*, October 11, 1922; "No 'Good Will' in Horton," *Kansas City Star*, December 24, 1922; Domenico Gagliardo, *The Kansas Industrial Court: An Experiment in Compulsory Arbitration* (Lawrence: University of Kansas Press, 1941; *Debate between Samuel Gompers and Henry J. Allen at Carnegie Hall, New York, May 28, 1920* (New York: E. P. Dutton, 1920).

24. James C. Juhnke, "Mob Violence and Kansas Mennonites in 1918," *Kansas Historical Quarterly* 43 (1977): 334–50; "Indict 7 Pacifists," *Kansas City Star*, October 12, 1917; "Klan at Revival Meeting," *Kansas City Star*, October 23, 1922; "Governor Capper's Slacker Files," Kansas Memory Collection, Kansas State Historical Society, Topeka, available at http://www.kansasmemory.org. One of the larger Klan meetings occurred on July 30, 1924, when two thousand members attended a meeting west of El Dorado. Three days later, five thousand Klan members paraded in Leavenworth.

25. "Attorney General Hopkins Coming Here to Probe Ku Klux Klan," *Arkansas City Traveler*, July 6, 1922; "Ku Klux Klan: Governor Bars Mask Wearing in State," *Arkansas City Traveler*, July 8, 1922; "Governor Allen on the Ku Klux Klan," *Outlook*, December 27, 1922; "Council of Churches Urged to War on Klan," *Washington Post*, December 14, 1923; "In Kansas," *Time*, October 6, 1924; Rory McVeigh, "Power Devaluation, the Ku Klux Klan, and the Democratic National Convention of 1924," *Sociological Forum* 16 (2001): 1–30; David J. Goldberg, "Unmasking the Ku Klux Klan: The Northern Movement against the KKK, 1920–1925," *Journal of American Ethnic History* 15 (1996): 32–48. In January 1925, Klan supporters won a measure in the Kansas Senate that exempted them from the ban on out-of-state organizations, but the measure failed by eight votes in the house, where Clifford R. Hope Jr., who opposed the Klan, was speaker. See Clifford R. Hope Jr., *Quiet Courage: Kansas Congressman Clifford R. Hope* (Manhattan, KS: Sunflower University Press, 1997), 50.

26. "Intolerance," *Time*, December 14, 1925. For one of the more useful collections of essays examining secularization in this period, in which the contingencies and role of human agents are emphasized to a greater extent than in many earlier treatments of secularization, see Christian Smith, ed., *The Secular Revolution: Power, Interests, and Conflict in the Secularization of American Public Life* (Berkeley: University of California Press, 2003).

27. The figures reported here are from my tabulations of annual charters listed in the two-volume edition of Kirke Mechem, ed., *The Annals*

of Kansas, 1886–1925 (Topeka: Kansas Historical Society, 1956). The nonbusiness charters relevant to civil society were given in three categories: churches and affiliated organizations; fairs along with agricultural and civic organizations; and lodges, clubs, unions, and benevolent societies. The dates and locations of regional and statewide meetings were also included.

28. On secondary education, indicating that during the 1923–24 school year 43,807 girls and 37,761 boys were enrolled in public high schools, see U.S. Bureau of the Census, *Statistical Abstract of the United States, 1925* (Washington, DC: Government Printing Office, 1925), table 109, 103. See also Elizabeth Moore, *Maternity and Infant Care in a Rural County in Kansas* (Washington, DC: U.S. Department of Labor Children's Bureau, 1917). The influenza outbreak in Fort Riley in March 1918 has been well documented. For the speculative notion that the epidemic started among hogs in Haskell County, see John M. Barry, *The Great Influenza: The Epic Story of the Deadliest Plague in History* (New York: Penguin, 2005). Subsequent writers who lacked knowledge of Kansas geography have sometimes added confusion by locating Fort Riley in Haskell County. See, for example, Gerald N. Callahan, *Infection: The Uninvited Universe* (New York: Touchstone, 2006); Jeffrey Greene and Karen Moline, *The Bird Flu Pandemic: Can It Happen?* (New York: St. Martin's Press, 2006).

29. U.S. Bureau of the Census, *Statistical Abstract of the United States, 1925*, table 77, 75. The total U.S. deaths in registration areas in 1924 included 79,594 from tuberculosis, and 76,146 from influenza and pneumonia. In 1923, there were 11,666 automobile fatalities in the United States. See "Automobile Deaths Here Exceed General U.S. Rate," *Washington Post*, December 3, 1923; C. E. Shermerhorn, "Fire Prevention in the Home," *New York Times*, October 5, 1924; H. A. Smith, "The Fire Prevention Work of Stock Fire Insurance Companies," *Annals of the American Academy of Political and Social Science* 130 (1927): 103–7.

30. Information on Elmer Monroe, Susan Monroe, and Reverend Simon Monroe is from letters and newspaper articles transcribed by Evelyn A. Swan, October 1994, available at http://www.kansasheritage.org.

31. "Grand Old Party," *Time*, June 11, 1928.

32. Antonia Felix, "Abbey Mode," available at http://www.kuhistory. com. For the Billy Sunday and Frank Strong quotes, see John H. McCool, "Sunday's Sermon, May 4, 1916," available at http://www.kuhistory.com.

33. "Methodists Rebuke a Fundamentalist," *New York Times*, May 3, 1928. The fundamentalist being rebuked was a pastor from Haddonfield, New Jersey.

34. "Methodist Leaders Urge Presbyterian Merger at Meeting," *Washington Post*, May 9, 1928.

35. Democratic National Committee, Anti-Catholic Literature Collection, 1924–28, American Catholic History Research Center, Catholic University of America, Washington, DC. Smith received 67 percent of the vote in Ellis County and 44 percent in Leavenworth. On Hoover's farm policy

as well as religion as a factor in Kansas and Missouri, see Richard V. Oulahan, "Western Missouri Split on 'Religion,'" *New York Times*, October 1, 1928; William F. Ogburn and Nell Snow Talbot, "A Measurement of the Factors in the Presidential Election of 1928," *Social Forces* 8 (1929): 175–83. Patrick H. Callahan is quoted in "Factors in Defeat of Smith Reviewed," *New York Times*, December 2, 1928. See also "Bishop McConnell Challenges Sects," *New York Times*, January 14, 1929; "Chicago Churchmen to Assail 'Whispers,'" *New York Times*, September 14, 1928. The best available measure of opposition to Prohibition in 1928 was the percentage in each county that voted against repeal in 1934. Catholic and Methodist memberships were from the *Census of Religious Bodies, 1926*, and standardized by total population from the 1930 U.S. Census. In ordinary least squares regression models for the percentage voting for Hoover in 1928, the standardized coefficient for Catholics was −.888 (significant at the .001 level) and for Methodists the coefficient was not significant. In a model with Catholics and the percent against repeal, the respective coefficients were −.549 and .698, both significant at the .001 level. In a model with all three variables, the coefficient for Catholics was −.601 and the percent against repeal was .711, both significant at the .001 level, and the coefficient for Methodists was not significant.

36. Herbert Hoover, *The Memoirs of Herbert Hoover, Vol. II: The Cabinet and the Presidency, 1920–1933* (New York: Macmillan, 1952), 207–8, 222; "Allen Sees Mudslinging Ahead," *Atlanta Constitution*, October 29, 1928.

37. Roy Buckingham, "Kansas Wheat Men Cold to Farm Plan," *New York Times*, August 22, 1929. The business failures were reported in U.S. Bureau of the Census, *Statistical Abstract of the United States, 1930* (Washington, DC: Government Printing Office, 1930), table 338, 318. The business failure rate in 1929 in Kansas was .54 percent—higher only than in North and South Dakota, Louisiana, and Arizona.

38. Selected figures reported by the U.S. Department of Agriculture and the U.S. Department of Labor, and included in the U.S. Bureau of the Census, *Statistical Abstract of the United States, 1934* (Washington, DC: Government Printing Office, 1935). W. G. Clugston, "Kansas Perplexed by Much Confusion," *New York Times*, January 4, 1931.

39. "Landon Brands Demo Governor as Hypocrite," *Winfield Daily Courier*, October 13, 1932; "Liquor Campaign Issue," *Winfield Daily Courier*, November 4, 1932; "To Discuss Candidates," *Winfield Daily Courier*, November 4, 1932; Ann L. Galloway, "Prayer Needed," *Winfield Daily Courier*, November 5, 1932.

40. Harry M. Chalfant, "The Anti-Saloon League—Why and What?" *Annals of the American Academy of Political and Social Science* 109 (1923): 279–83; "Now in Kansas," *Chicago Daily Tribune*, December 12, 1925; Philip Kinsley, "Churches Frown on Anti-Saloon League Methods," *Chicago Daily Tribune*, January 29, 1926; Philip Kinsley, "How Dry League Chieftain Bled Kansas Shown," *Chicago Daily Tribune*, January 30, 1926;

W. G. Clugston, "The Anti-Saloon League's Lost Virtue," *Nation*, February 24, 1926, 203–4.

41. "Presbyterians Act against Board Here," *New York Times*, January 9, 1924; "Other May Conventions," *Time*, May 28, 1923. On the Methodist emphasis on personal experience as an inhibiting factor in fundamentalist appeals and the denomination's reluctance to engage in creedal disputes, see George M. Marsden, *Fundamentalism and American Culture: The Shaping of Twentieth-Century Evangelicalism, 1870–1925* (New York: Oxford University Press, 1980), 104.

42. "Speaking the Public Mind," *Kansas City Star*, April 25, 1922.

43. For an extended argument for tolerance and liberality in matters of belief, see "The Clash between Church Liberals and Fundamentalists," *Kansas City Star*, June 16, 1922; Miriam Allen DeFord, "After Dayton: A Fundamentalist Survey," *Nation*, June 2, 1926, 604–5; "Irony," *Time*, May 16, 1927; "Fundamentalist," *Washington Post*, January 15, 1928.

44. Jim Grebe, "Leon Milton Birkhead," Unitarian Universalist Historical Society, available at http://www25.uua.org. All Souls Unitarian Church was in the fashionable Country Club section of suburban Kansas City, Missouri, approximately two miles from the Kansas line.

45. Holter, *Fire on the Prairie*, 188. The total support for pastors (not including parsonage) in the three Kansas conferences was $1,067,980 in 1930, $831,494 in 1932, $646,076 in 1934, and $668,319 in 1939; the total benevolences were $997,495 in 1930, $624,491 in 1932, $421,691 in 1934, and $437,914 in 1939. See "Methodist Reports Reflect Optimism," *Wichita Eagle*, October 11, 1935. Religious construction dropped most dramatically in the early 1930s, from $92.8 million in 1930 to $27.3 million in 1932, and then $18.3 million in 1934, and rose only to $38.4 million by 1939. See U.S. Bureau of the Census, *Statistical Abstract of the United States, 1940* (Washington, DC: Government Printing Office, 1940), table 890, 893.

46. The quotation from the Coldwater Christian Church member is in *Comanche County History, Vol. I*, 168–70, available at http://www.rootsweb.ancestry.com/~kscomanc. The Logan County quotation is from Gloria Gafford, whose father pastored the Keystone Church from 1935 to 1937, included in oral history material, available at http://www.keystonegallery.com. The Liberal story is from Reverend Jesse C. Fisher, quoted in Holter, *Fire on the Prairie*, 191–92. Other families and churches fared better; for example, McPherson County Mennonite Mil Penner (*Section 27: A Century on a Family Farm* [Lawrence: University Press of Kansas, 2002], 150) recalled dust storms and poor crops, but said that the dust bowl "caused barely a ripple in our complacency."

47. U.S. Bureau of the Census, *Census of Religious Bodies, 1936* (Washington, DC: Government Printing Office, 1939), table 3, 66–69. I examined electronic data files on church membership at the county level for Kansas in comparison with 1926 and 1952 data, and computed standardized residuals taking into account the total population in 1930 and 1940. On

the quality of the data, see especially Rodney Stark, "The Reliability of Historical United States Census Data on Religion," *Sociological Analysis* 53 (1992): 91–95.

48. Earl Hayes, quoted in "Farming Fixture," *Hutchinson News*, September 5, 2007. See also Jim Sullinger, "Olathe Honors FDR's 1936 Whistlestop," *Kansas City Star*, April 14, 2009; Franklin Delano Roosevelt, "Rear Platform Remarks at Olathe, Kansas," October 13, 1936, available at http://www.presidency.ucsb.edu.

49. Franklin Delano Roosevelt, "Address at Wichita, Kansas," October 13, 1936, available at http://www.presidency.ucsb.edu.

50. Raymond Gram Swing, "Alf Landon Is Not Cal Coolidge," *Nation*, January 8, 1936, 39–41; D. W. Brogan, "Landon and Kansas," *Washington Post*, September 11, 1936; "Kansas Candidate," *Time*, May 18, 1936; Alfred M. Landon, "Accepting the Republican Nomination for President of the United States," July 23, 1936, available at http://www.kshs.org/research/topics/politics. Donald R. McCoy (*Landon of Kansas* [Lincoln: University of Nebraska Press, 1966], 415) notes that after his defeat in 1936, Landon became more active in religious affairs and served as a delegate to the Methodist's Uniting Conference in Kansas City in 1939.

51. William Allen White, "Landon: I Knew Him When," *Saturday Evening Post*, July 18, 1936, 70.

52. George Gallup, "Roosevelt Is Strongest with Catholics, Jews," *Washington Post*, October 11, 1936. The information was drawn from more than one hundred thousand ballots distributed nationally by mail; other results indicated that 82 percent of Jews were for Roosevelt, Lutherans leaned toward Landon by a 54 percent margin, and Congregationalists favored Landon by 78 to 22 percent. Gallup cautioned readers against attaching too much significance to the religious differences, writing, "Religious preference is only an interesting sidelight in the 1936 campaign and the bitter animosities and undercover feuds of the Hoover-Smith campaign have been forgotten."

53. "Alf Landon, G.O.P. Standard-Bearer, Dies at 100," *New York Times*, October 13, 1987; Anne O'Hare McCormick, "The Big Moment— The Two Men," *New York Times*, November 1, 1936. Gallup poll, February 3–6, 1937, conducted among approximately twenty-three hundred randomly selected adults; electronic data file courtesy of iPoll, available at http://www.ropercenter.com. Using these data, standardized ordinary least squares multiple regression coefficients were computed for all respondents in the United States and respondents in eight Middle West states (Wisconsin, Minnesota, Iowa, Missouri, North Dakota, South Dakota, Nebraska, and Kansas). Nationally, voters who expressed an anti-Catholic sentiment by saying that they would not vote for a Catholic for president who was well qualified for the job were significantly less likely to vote for Roosevelt than other voters, and that was true taking account of other factors, such as age, gender, occupation, region of the country, and whether a person lived in a small town, city, or on a farm. Among voters in the eight

Middle West states including Kansas, the effect of anti-Catholic sentiment in suppressing votes for Roosevelt was stronger than in the nation at large. Among respondents who said that they would vote for a qualified Catholic, 64 percent said they had voted for Roosevelt, while among those who would not have voted for a Catholic, only 44 percent voted for Roosevelt.

54. Peter Fearon, *Kansas in the Great Depression: Work Relief, the Dole, and Rehabilitation* (Columbia: University of Missouri Press, 2007); R. Alton Lee, "[Not] a Thin Dime: Kansas Relief Politics in the Campaign of 1936," *Historian* 67 (2005): 474–88.

55. Robert S. Lynd and Helen Merrell Lynd, *Middletown in Transition: A Study in Cultural Conflicts* (New York: Harcourt and Brace, 1937); John Steinbeck, *The Grapes of Wrath* (New York: Viking, 1939); Sinclair Lewis, *Elmer Gantry* (New York: Harcourt and Brace, 1927); Timothy Egan, *The Worst Hard Time: The Untold Story of Those Who Survived the Great American Dust Bowl* (New York: Houghton Mifflin, 2006); Gallup poll, November 15–20, 1941, electronic data file, courtesy of http://www.ropercenter.uconn.edu. The face-to-face survey included 53 respondents from Kansas; among 443 respondents in the eight Middle West states, 45 percent said religious interest had decreased in the past decade, 18 percent said it had increased, and 31 percent said it had stayed the same.

56. Pamela Riney-Kehrberg, *Rooted in Dust: Surviving Drought and Depression in Southwestern Kansas* (Lawrence: University Press of Kansas, 1994). Her information also included interesting examples of divisions occurring among Mennonites in southwest Kansas.

57. Florence Mason Caywood Stout, "History concerning My Father," November 19, 1968, available at http://skyways.lib.ks.us/genweb/rice; Roger Hormley, *Roger's Remembrances*, n.d., available at http://rogerghormley.wordpress.com; Winton Slagle Sipe, *Memories of a Kansas Farm Boy*, n.d., available at http://www.kancoll.org/articles; Susan Chaffin, "Kansas in the Dust Bowl: 'We Aim to Stay,'" *Voices* (1998), available at http://www.kancoll.org.; Lawrence Svobida, *Farming the Dust Bowl: A First-Hand Account from Kansas* (Lawrence: University Press of Kansas, 1986), 190; Reverend Jesse C. Fisher, quoted in Holter, *Fire on the Prairie*, 191–92.

58. For an examination of popular views of Kansas in the national press, see Robert Smith Bader, *Hayseeds, Moralizers, and Methodists: The Twentieth-Century Image of Kansas* (Lawrence: University Press of Kansas, 1988). Leo E. Oliva ("Kansas: A Hard Land in the Heartland," in *Heartland: Comparative Histories of the Midwestern States*, ed. James H. Madison [Bloomington: Indiana University Press, 1988], 264, 266) argues that Kansas "ceased to be innovative and became concerned with a moral fervor that led to all kinds of petty prohibitions," and observes that "the combination of lagging behind in economic development, reactionary restrictions on individual freedoms, and the image of a dust-blown, God-forsaken land caused many Kansans to be ashamed rather than proud of their state between the world wars."

59. More of Coburn's apocryphal stories are included in "Kansas a Victim of Lies," *Los Angeles Times*, June 25, 1897. Other examples are from "Kansas," *Los Angeles Times*, November 29, 1892; William Allen White, "What's the Matter with Kansas?" *Emporia Gazette*, August 15, 1896. The editor was Ewing Herbert of the *Hiawatha Daily World*, in "Kansas Is Okeh, Scribe Asserts," *Los Angeles Times*, August 28, 1923.

60. Elmer T. Peterson, "Prohibition in Kansas in 1925," *McClure's Magazine*, July 1925, 348–53.

61. H. L. Mencken, "On Law Enforcement," *Chicago Daily Tribune*, December 11, 1927.

62. Clugston, "Kansas Perplexed."

63. Mildred Adams, "Dry Kansas Ponders a Rising Wet Tide," *New York Times*, December 4, 1932.

64. "73% Favor Repeal in Prohibition Poll," *New York Times*, April 29, 1932.

65. Henry J. Allen, "Kansas Bewildered by the Demon Rum," *New York Times*, April 15, 1934; Bader, *Hayseeds, Moralizers, and Methodists*, 81.

66. Among the more interesting studies by social scientists is Earl H. Bell, *Culture of a Contemporary Rural Community: Sublette, Kansas* (Washington, DC: U.S. Department of Agriculture, Bureau of Agricultural Economics, Rural Life Studies, 1942). *The Plow That Broke the Plains* (1936) was written and directed by Pare Lorentz, and the music was composed by Virgil Thomson; the film was produced and distributed by the U.S. Resettlement Administration. "Kansas Is Restless," *Washington Post*, October 10, 1931. *The Washington Masquerade* was an adaptation of Henry Bernstein's play *The Claw*, and was produced by Metro-Goldwyn-Mayer in 1932; it featured a country lawyer from Kansas who is elected to the U.S. Senate and falls in love with a sophisticated blond. *The Worst Woman in Paris* was a Fox production that screened in 1933; one review was titled "Kansas vs. Paris," *New York Times*, November 25, 1933. The LeSueur quote is in Bader, *Hayseeds, Moralizers, and Methodists*, 72–73.

67. The statement about "rubes" was made by Republican western region director Harrison Spangler, quoted in "Slur Develops into Boomerang for Mr. Farley," *Chicago Daily Tribune*, May 28, 1936. The incident was examined in Franklyn Waltman, "Politics and People," *Washington Post*, May 22, 1936.

68. Sidney Olson, "A.F.L. Grades Roosevelt High as Labor Ally," *Washington Post*, October 18, 1936; Franklyn Waltman, "Landon Calm as Campaign for President Gains Impetus," *Washington Post*, April 6, 1936; Franklyn Waltman, "Landon Owes Rise to Firm Dislike of Reckless Experimentation," *Washington Post*, May 17, 1936.

69. Landon, quoted in Isaac Siegel, "Concerning the Campaign," *New York Times*, July 25, 1936.

70. "Landon Fight Wins Praise," *Los Angeles Times*, October 5, 1936; "Landon Supported by Felix Warburg," *New York Times*, September 21, 1936; James A. Hagerty, "Hoover and Landon Discuss Campaign," *New*

York Times, October 2, 1936; "New Deal Is Doomed Says A.M.E. Head," *Chicago Defender*, March 28, 1936; "Ex-Yale Dean Calls Roosevelt Playboy," *New York Times*, October 9, 1935.

71. Mark Sullivan, "Roosevelt Must Be 'Nice' to Business to Win," *Wichita Eagle*, October 13, 1935.

72. The information and quotation about the 1935 Kansas Republican convention are in "Anxious for Hand in Planks," *Wichita Eagle*, October 13, 1935. The seventeen counties in which at least 30 percent of the farmland was in wheat in 1935 were Barton, Edwards, Ellsworth, Ford, Harper, Harvey, Kingman, McPherson, Pawnee, Pratt, Reno, Rice, Rush, Saline, Sedgwick, Stafford, and Sumner. These counties were part of a block of thirty-one counties in which Roosevelt's gains were largest in the state. These counties extended from Butler and Cowley on the east, to Seward, Haskell, Finney, and Scott on the west, and from the Oklahoma line north as far as Russell and Ellis.

73. Standardized multiple regression coefficients were computed from ordinary least squares models for Kansas counties' voting in 1936 (the percentage for FDR). The coefficient for the effect of 1932 voting on 1936 was .588, which demonstrated continuity but also left room for other factors to matter. In a model including 1932 voting and the percentage of farmland in wheat in 1935, the coefficient for the percentage of farmland in wheat (.498) was stronger than the remaining effect for 1932 voting (.473). A model that included these two variables showed an additional weaker but significant negative effect of having voted for Landon for governor in 1934. Another model showed a weak negative effect of having voted against repeal in 1934, but that effect became statistically insignificant when the 1934 Landon vote was included. The effect of the percentage of Catholics in 1936 was not significant. (The caveats noted previously about religious membership figures in 1936 must be considered, although the Catholic figures appear to have been relatively stable compared with predicted values taking account of earlier and later figures and population.) The Southwest Kansas Methodist Conference met in Winfield, on the same day as the 1935 Kansas Republican convention, and voted unanimously to prohibit alcoholic beverages having more than .5 percent alcoholic content. The legislative initiative that became known as three-two beer passed. *Lyons Daily News* editor Jones served as a publicity director for Landon's campaign.

74. "Browder Opposed Draft," *New York Times*, June 29, 1936; "Browder Heads Communist Slate," *New York Times*, June 29, 1936; "Earl Browder in 'Red' Net," *Kansas City Star*, August 27, 1922.

75. "The Outer Darkness," *Time*, October 20, 1952. Browder was described with some amusement as a "home-grown, corn-fed and hand-spanked Anglo-Saxon native of Kansas" in "Earl Browder Visits City," *Los Angeles Times*, May 30, 1939. Browder's release in 1942 was supported by the Bedford-Stuyvesant Citizens' Committee to Free Earl Browder, which was led by a committee of Brooklyn clergy members. See "Start Drive for Browder," *New York Amsterdam Star-News*, March 28, 1942.

76. John H. McCool, "1924: Radio Days," available at http://www .kuhistory.com; Mary Kinnane, "The History of Station KFKU, 1923–1954" (master's thesis, University of Kansas, 1954). Brinkley has been the subject of several biographies, including Gerald Carson, *The Roguish World of Doctor Brinkley* (New York: Holt, Rinehart and Winston, 1960); Gene Fowler and Bill Crawford, *Border Radio* (Austin: Texas Monthly Press, 1987); R. Alton Lee, *The Bizarre Careers of John R. Brinkley* (Louisville: University Press of Kentucky, 2002); Pope Brock, *Charlatan: America's Most Dangerous Huckster, the Man Who Pursued Him, and the Age of Flimflam* (New York: Crown, 2008). On the more general role of radio in rural areas, see Ronald R. Kline, *Consumers in the Country: Technology and Social Change in Rural America* (Baltimore: Johns Hopkins University Press, 2000), 113–27.

77. "Third Party: The Malcontents," *Barron's*, June 29, 1926; Mary Christine Athans, "A New Perspective on Father Charles E. Coughlin," *Church History* 56 (1987): 224–35; Alan Brinkley, *Voices of Protest: Huey Long, Father Coughlin, and the Great Depression* (New York: Knopf, 1982); Tona J. Hangen, *Redeeming the Dial: Radio, Religion, and Popular Culture in America* (Raleigh: University of North Carolina Press, 2002); Geoffrey S. Smith, *To Save a Nation: American Counter-Subversives, the New Deal, and the Coming of World War II* (New York: Basic Books, 1973); Donald Warren, *Radio Priest: Charles Coughlin: The Father of Hate Radio* (New York: Free Press, 1996).

78. U.S. Bureau of the Census, *Census of Religious Bodies, 1926*; U.S. Bureau of the Census, *Census of Religious Bodies, 1936*.

79. See the section devoted to churches of the disinherited in H. Richard Niebuhr, *The Social Sources of Denominationalism* (New York: Meridian Books, 1929), 26–76.

80. "Methodists Meet for Merger Today," *New York Times*, April 26, 1939; "Landon Holds Church Unity Step to Peace," *Washington Post*, April 25, 1939; "Calls Coughlin 'National Menace,'" *New York Times*, February 26, 1939; "Blow at Bigotry," *Washington Post*, May 24, 1939; "Willkie's Chances Bright in Kansas," *New York Times*, October 23, 1940; "Kansas Primary Silent Marvel," *Los Angeles Times*, August 4, 1940; "Kansas Reunion Awaits Nominee," *Los Angeles Times*, September 16, 1940.

81. "Diary, 1942–1943." The diary was transcribed after the woman's death by her daughter. The woman's name was withheld, and some identifying details were altered. Alfred Lord Tennyson, quoted in *In Memoria* (London: Macmillan, 1906), 196.

CHAPTER 4

1. Technically, Eisenhower was not a native son of Kansas, having been born in Denison, Texas, in 1890, but the family had been early settlers in Kansas and returned to Abilene when he was two months old, and Eisenhower considered Abilene his boyhood home.

2. John M. Collins, "Opposition to AAA Spreads in Kansas," *New York Times*, September 25, 1938; *Report of Social Welfare* (Topeka: Kansas State Board of Social Welfare, 1937), 6; "Let Farmers Alone," *Capper's Weekly*, January 29, 1938; Hugo Wall, "Social Welfare in Kansas," *Bulletin of the Governmental Research Center* 3 (1947): 1–2; James Schell, "Changes in Social Welfare Financing in Kansas," *Bulletin of the Governmental Research Center* 8 (1953): 1–2. The new Agricultural Adjustment Act was approved on February 16, 1938, as a replacement for the earlier Agricultural Adjustment Act of 1933 that had been struck down by the Supreme Court in 1935, and was too late to be applied to the winter wheat planed in 1937 and harvested in summer 1938. Thus, the Kansas farmers interviewed in Hutchinson in September had only recently been told how much wheat they could plant, and were concerned not only about the current price of wheat but also about how to interpret the new rules and whether they would change, as they had during each of the past five years. See *History of Agricultural Price Support and Adjustment Programs, 1933–84* (Washington, DC: U.S Department of Agriculture, 1985, available at http://www.ers.usda.gov.

3. Charles Hackett, quoted in Denis Boyles, *Superior, Nebraska: The Common-Sense Values of America's Heartland* (New York: Random House, 2008), 84. Gallup poll, November 16–21, 1938, electronic data file. In this data file, the responses from 433 respondents from eight Middle West states, including 58 Kansans, were identified. The figure reported for Landon supporters is based on Middle West respondents. See Gallup poll, October 10–15, 1938, electronic data file, courtesy of http://www.ropercenter.uconn.edu. Only 5 percent of Kansans compared with 19 percent nationally thought "Roosevelt, or a man like Roosevelt as President is essential for the good of the country." Twenty-eight percent of Kansans believed that "Roosevelt may have done many things that need doing but he has made so many mistakes that his usefulness is now over." And 22 percent said, "It is almost a calamity for this country that we must have two more years of Roosevelt." The national proportions were 27 and 13 percent, respectively. The election results for the state legislature are in Marvin Harder and Carolyn Rampey, *The Kansas Legislature: Procedures, Personalities, and Problems* (Lawrence: University Press of Kansas, 1972), 16.

4. C. Hugh Snyder, *The Youngest Brother: On a Kansas Wheat Farm during the Roaring Twenties and the Great Depression* (Lincoln, NE: iUniverse, 2005), 94. On assistance to families and negative attitudes toward the "dole," see Peter Fearon, *Kansas in the Great Depression: Work Relief, the Dole, and Rehabilitation* (Columbia: University of Missouri Press, 2007). On New Deal projects in western states, see Duane A. Smith, *Rocky Mountain Heartland: Colorado, Montana, and Wyoming in the Twentieth Century* (Tucson: University of Arizona Press, 2008), 120–46.

5. Leo P. Ribuffo, *The Old Christian Right: The Protestant Far Right from the Great Depression to the Cold War* (Philadelphia: Temple

University Press, 1983). Also of interest was Winrod's fellow Wichitan, Elmer J. Garner, whose activities are described in Virgil W. Dean, "Another Wichita Seditionist? Elmer J. Garner and the Radical Right's Opposition to World War II," *Kansas History* 17 (1994): 50–64.

6. For primary election returns by county, see *Report of the Kansas Secretary of State* (Topeka: Kansas State Printing Office, 1938). The results are from ordinary least squares multiple regression analysis of Kansas counties for Winrod votes as a percentage of the total Republican primary votes in 1938. The standardized multiple regression coefficients were –.334 for the percentage who voted for FDR in 1936, .356 for the percentage of German born in 1920, and .209 for the percentage of farms encumbered in 1920. The former two coefficients are significant beyond the .001 level, and the last at the .01 level. Similar results were found using an analysis of the percentage of German born in 1930. Encumbrance data were not obtained in 1930. The average farm size in 1930 was negatively associated with the percentage voting for Winrod. Other potential factors such as the total unemployment and farm unemployment in 1937 were not significant. Winrod's largest victories were in Clay County, where he received 48 percent of the Republican primary votes, Wabaunsee County with 44 percent, Jefferson County with 40 percent, and Marshall County with 39 percent. Reverend Fisher had served as the Methodist district superintendent for the liberal district in southwest Kansas. His largest wins were in Finney County with 57 percent of the Republican primary vote, Kearny County with 49 percent, Greeley County with 48 percent, Gray County with 46 percent, and Stevens County with 45 percent. Fisher's success in western Kansas shows the regional character of the primary and underscores the limits of Winrod's appeal.

7. Gallup poll, November 16–21, 1938, electronic data file, courtesy of http://www.ropercenter.uconn.edu. Among the fifty-eight respondents from Kansas, 3 percent favored Germany, 57 percent favored Russia, and 34 percent were undecided. In the eight Middle West states, the proportions were 9, 57, and 29 percent, respectively. There were no differences between those respondents who had voted for Landon and those who had voted for Roosevelt. The strongest support for Germany was in Illinois, with 19 percent.

8. "Kansas Senator Aspirant Denies Nazi Connection," *Chicago Daily Tribune*, July 30, 1938; "Kansas Faces Muddle over Winrod Race," *Washington Post*, July 27, 1938; W. G. Clugston, "Kansas Feuds Help Winrod," *New York Times*, July 31, 1938; W. G. Clugston, "Kansas Sees Bigotry Beaten," *New York Times*, August 7, 1938. A meeting to find an appropriate opponent to Winrod was held on a Sunday afternoon in November 1937 in Topeka at which Hope and Reed were discussed. See Clifford R. Hope Jr., *Quiet Courage: Kansas Congressman Clifford R. Hope* (Manhattan, KS: Sunflower University Press, 1997), 129.

9. "Respects to Warmakers," *Capper's Weekly*, February 2, 1938; L. H. Robbins, "Militant Pacifist," *New York Times*, December 3, 1939.

10. Arthur Capper, "Now Let's Go," *Capper's Weekly*, November 12, 1932.

11. Capper's views on neutrality and a constitutional amendment were stated in a radio broadcast. See National Council for Prevention of War, "Let the People Decide," *Vital Speeches*, November 30, 1937. On his involvement in antiwar groups, see Homer E. Socolofsky, *Arthur Capper: Publisher, Politician, and Philanthropist* (Lawrence: University of Kansas Press, 1962), 202, 264.

12. Arthur Capper, "Where Do We Go from Here?" WIBW radio address, November 8, 1936; "Arthur Capper," *Washington Post*, December 21, 1951; "Senator Capper," *Christian Science Monitor*, December 22, 1951; Socolofsky, *Arthur Capper*, 229–30.

13. Donald R. McCoy, *Landon of Kansas* (Lincoln: University of Nebraska Press, 1966), 404, 414; *National Jewish Monthly* 53, March 1939, 222; "Landon Sees No Third Term for Roosevelt," *Christian Science Monitor*, January 8, 1940; "Roosevelt Said to Be Weighing Coalition Move," *Washington Post*, May 20, 1940; Arthur Evans, "White House Bid to Landon Is Canceled," *Chicago Daily Tribune*, May 21, 1940. Drew Pearson reported in 1943 on a luncheon at which Landon explained that the feeler about becoming War Department secretary had come from Frank Altschul of New York, who was a relative of former Governor Lehman and an associate of Roosevelt. Landon further disclosed that Roosevelt had promised Knox that he would not run for a third term. See "Washington Merry-Go-Round," *Washington Post*, December 6, 1943. Kenneth S. Davis (*FDR into the Storm, 1937–1940: A History* [New York: Random House, 1993], 534–35) argues that Roosevelt seriously considered not running for a third term.

14. Quoted in Stanley High, "Whose Party Is It?" *Saturday Evening Post*, February 6, 1937, 10.

15. James A. Hagerty, "Martin Says Nation Needs 'Sane' Regime," *New York Times*, January 30, 1940; George Gallup, "Kansas Joins Republicans," *Los Angeles Times*, April 17, 1940; Turner Catledge, "Willkie's Chances Bright in Kansas," *New York Times*, October 23, 1940.

16. For a description of the controversy, see Sue Kendall, *Rethinking Regionalism: John Steuart Curry and the Kansas Mural Controversy* (Washington, DC: Smithsonian Institution Press, 1986). For additional interpretations, see Patricia Junker, ed., *John Steuart Curry: Inventing the Middle West* (New York: Hudson Hills Press, 1998); Merrill D. Peterson, *The Legend Revisited, John Brown* (Charlottesville: University of Virginia Press, 2004).

17. "Republican Faults Defined by White," *New York Times*, April 19, 1938; "War? Poof!" *Washington Post*, October 31, 1939.

18. "White, Head of Aid to Allies Committee," *Los Angeles Times*, December 24, 1940; "Religion Ban Danger Told," *Los Angeles Times*, August 8, 1940; "Churches Plan United Appeal for Funds," *Washington Post*, August 22, 1942; Malcolm W. Bayley, "Interpreter of America's Middle West,"

Christian Science Monitor, October 30, 1945; Everett Rich, *William Allen White: The Man from Emporia* (New York: Farrar and Rinehart, 1941); "The Executive's Bookshelf," *Wall Street Journal*, April 8, 1946.

19. Gallup poll, November 15–20, 1941, electronic data file, courtesy of http://www.ropercenter.uconn.edu. The alternative option read, "Stay out of war, even at the risk of letting Germany win." In the eight Middle West states, 67 percent favored doing "everything we can to defeat Germany, even if this means getting into the war ourselves." In Kansas, 65 percent chose that option.

20. Douglas Hurt, *The Great Plains during World War II* (Lincoln: University of Nebraska Press, 2008); U.S. War Department, *State Summary of War Casualties from World War II for Navy, Marine Corps, and Coast Guard Personnel from Kansas* (Washington, DC: War Department, 1946); U.S. War Department, *World War II Honor List of Dead and Missing Army and Army Air Forces Personnel from Kansas* (Washington, DC: War Department, 1946).

21. "Lindbergh Scored by 700 Churchmen," *New York Times*, September 27, 1941; "$10,000 to Combat Lindbergh," *New York Times*, October 31, 1941; Art Wilson, "The Hows and Whys of the Founding of Wichita Baptist Tabernacle," August 1988, available at http://www.friendshipbaptistofwichita.com.

22. "Anti–New Deal Democrats Unite under Woodring to Regain Party," *New York Times*, February 5, 1944.

23. Katherine Von Blon, "'Bright Star' Poignant Drama of Kansas Family," *Los Angeles Times*, November 25, 1944; "Political Letter," *Signal-Enterprise* (Alma, KS), November 16, 1944.

24. Robert H. Ferrell, *Truman and Pendergast* (Columbia: University of Missouri Press, 1999); Rick Montgomery and Shirl Kasper, *Kansas City: An American Story* (Kansas City, KS: Kansas City Star Books, 2007); Arthur Sears Henning, "How Boss Rule and Roosevelt Named Truman," *Chicago Daily Tribune*, July 25, 1944; Letter from M. D. (name withheld) to President Roosevelt, March 8, 1937, *New Deal Network*, available at http://newdeal.feri.org; Kay Thull, quoted in Boyles, *Superior, Nebraska*, 84. For evidence of the continuing influence of the Pendergast machine under James M. Pendergast, a nephew of Thomas Pendergast, see Richard W. Bolling, "Oral History Interview," October 21, 1988, and April 20, 1989, available at http://www.trumanlibrary.org.

25. "Landon Lauds Foreign Policy Truman Plan," *Washington Post*, June 30, 1945; "Presidential Approval Ratings from 1945–2008," *Wall Street Journal*, available at http://online.wsj.com; "Presidential Approval Ratings: Gallup Historical Statistics and Trends," available at http://www.gallup.com/poll; Robert Howard, "Calls for Quiz on Presidential Pardons Action," *Chicago Daily Tribune*, July 8, 1946; "Truman Friends Sigh in Vain for a Bit Less Noise," *Chicago Daily Tribune*, July 20, 1946.

26. The zero-order Pearson correlation coefficients among Kansas counties with total county population in 1940 was not significant for the

percentage won by FDR in 1936—.379 in 1940, and .441 in 1944, both significant beyond the .001 level. The 1944 poll results are from the 1944 National Election Survey, electronic data file, and refer to responses from the west north-central region in which 127 cases were farm or small-town residents, and 76 were residents of cities of 50,000 or more people. Information about Greater Kansas City refers to the Kansas City, Kansas, and Kansas City, Missouri, metropolitan area. Montgomery and Kasper, *Kansas City*; "American Conservatism: A Wave of Anti-Union Legislation," *Manchester Guardian*, April 2, 1943; "The Country Speaks: Kansas," *Christian Science Monitor*, June 15, 1943.

27. Harry S. Truman, "Rear Platform Remarks in Kansas," June 16, 1948, available at http://www.presidency.ucsb.edu; George Gallup, "Final Poll Gives Dewey 49.5%, Truman 44.5% of Popular Vote," *Washington Post*, November 1, 1948; "Spark Touched Off on 'Ike' in '48 Boom," *Christian Science Monitor*, September 11, 1947.

28. The 1950 U.S. Census showed a total population in Kansas of 1.9 million, up from 1.8 million in 1940. The number of children age fourteen and younger was 499,106 in 1950, up from 281,725 in 1940. U.S. Bureau of the Census, *Statistical Abstract of the United States, 1950* (Washington, DC: Government Printing Office, 1950); U.S. Bureau of the Census, *Statistical Abstract of the United States, 1952* (Washington, DC: Government Printing Office, 1952). School data are from Floyd C. Scritchfield, "Local Public School Organization in Kansas," *Bulletin of the Bureau of Government Research* 6 (1950): 1–3. Sixty-eight percent of Kansas public schools were still one-teacher schools in 1949, but only 11 percent of enrolled pupils attended those schools.

29. Census data for incorporated places, 1950, electronic data files, created from information archived at the Missouri Census Data Center, University of Missouri, Jefferson City, MO.

30. For details of the case along with the role of Topeka and schools in other states, see Richard Kluger, *Simple Justice: The History of* Brown v. Board of Education *and Black America's Struggle for Equality* (New York: Vintage Books, 1977); James T. Patterson, Brown v. Board of Education: *A Civil Rights Milestone and Its Troubled Legacy* (New York: Oxford University Press, 2001).

31. Charity LeDelle Allen Kane, *Autobiography*, 1998, 14, available at http://www.kansasheritage.org. The Supreme Court's 1947 decision in *Everson v. Board of Education* determined that public funds could be used to bus children to parochial schools, but was determined on narrow grounds that left open questions about other First Amendment issues.

32. I. O. Savage, *A History of Republic County, Kansas* (Beloit, KS: Jones and Chubbic, 1901). The history of the Courtland Covenant Church is from *Courtland Journal* (Courtland, KS), October 13, 1988; *Salina Journal*, September 12, 1998. A brief history of the Ada Lutheran Church is in *Salina Journal*, September 5, 1998. For information on church activities, see 1947 issues of the *Courtland Journal*.

33. *Courtland Journal*, April 3, 1947.
34. "Dr. Paul W. Rood," *Courtland Journal*, February 6, 1947. Rood was also president of Biola University in Los Angeles, and active in the leadership of the National Evangelicals Association, Youth for Christ, and the Christian Businessmen's Association. See "Biola Hall of Fame," available at http://100.biola.edu.
35. "First Annual Meet of Churches," *Kiowa News*, October 28, 1948; "John Brown's Battle Field Site of New War," *Chicago Defender*, January 10, 1948.
36. The rally in Elkhart in southwestern Kansas is described in "Dodds and Cunningham Lead Temperance Drive in Kansas," *Christian Science Monitor*, August 28, 1948.
37. F. D. Farrell, "Kansas Rural Institutions: V. Three Effective Rural Churches," *Agricultural Experiment Station Circular* (June 1949): 1–36. An ethnographic study drawing similar conclusions was conducted by anthropologist Carl Withers, who wrote under a pseudonym, in southwestern Missouri not far from the Kansas line. See James West, *Plainville, U.S.A.* (New York: Columbia University Press, 1945), 142–64, especially on religion.
38. *Kiowa News*, March 25 and April 1, 1948. WaKeeney examples are from selected issues of the *Western Kansas World* (WaKeeney), 1948–52; the quotations are from December 18 and 15, 1952.
39. Gordon W. Allport, *The Individual and His Religion* (New York: McMillan, 1950).
40. Roger G. Barker, "Recollections of the Midwest Psychological Field Station," *Environment and Behavior* 22 (1990): 503–13; Allan W. Wicker, "The Midwest Psychological Field Station: Some Reflections of One Participant," *Environment and Behavior* 22 (1990): 492–98.
41. Roger G. Barker and Herbert F. Wright, *Midwest and Its Children: The Psychological Ecology of an American Town* (London: Row, Peterson and Company, 1954). Because the study's focus was children, the social interaction of adults received less attention than may have otherwise been the case, and conclusions are scattered throughout the volume. Oskaloosa was identified only as "Midwest," although sufficient details about its location and population made its true identity, which was revealed in later reports, easily ascertained.
42. Ibid., 22–23.
43. Curiously, the study did not mention the Oskaloosa Church of Christ, founded in 1896; the churchgoers described as attending out of town may have been members of the First Baptist Church on the edge of town, founded in 1907.
44. West, *Plainville, U.S.A.*, 162.
45. *Churches and Church Membership in the United States: An Enumeration and Analysis by Counties, States, and Regions* (New York: National Council of Churches, 1956). The figures reported here are from the 1952 data collected among 114 denominations, electronic data file.

46. Edward Prell, "'Ike' Returns; Joy in Kansas is Unconfined," *Chicago Daily Tribune*, June 22, 1945; Kenneth S. Davis, *Soldier of Democracy: A Biography of Dwight Eisenhower* (Garden City, NY: Doubleday, Doran and Company, 1945), 550.

47. "Eisenhower Tells Midwest Its Duty," *New York Times*, June 22, 1945.

48. Robert Smith Bader, *Hayseeds, Moralizers and Methodists: The Twentieth-Century Image of Kansas* (Lawrence: University Press of Kansas, 1988). The quotation is from James B. Adams, "Over There in Kansas," reprinted in *Denver Daily Post*, November 10, 1952. Davis was born in Salina, educated at Kansas State, served as a war correspondent, and later wrote a definitive multivolume biography of Franklin Delano Roosevelt. Kenneth S. Davis, "That Strange State of Mind Called Kansas," *New York Times*, June 26, 1949.

49. Davis, *Soldier of Democracy*.

50. Will Herberg, *Protestant-Catholic-Jew: An Essay in American Religious Sociology* (New York: Doubleday, 1955), 84; "President-Elect Says Soviet Demoted Zhukov Because of Their Friendship," *New York Times*, December 23, 1952.

51. "Remark Called Casual," *New York Times*, July 11, 1952; "President-Elect Says Soviet," *New York Times*, December 23, 1952.

52. "Avoidance of Bias in Campaign Hailed," *New York Times*, November 10, 1952; President Dwight D. Eisenhower, "Remarks upon Receiving the America's Democratic Legacy Award at a B'nai B'rith Dinner in Honor of the 40th Anniversary of the Anti-Defamation League," Mayflower Hotel, Washington, DC, November 23, 1953, available at http://www .presidency.ucsb.edu.

53. John Gunther, *Eisenhower: The Man and the Symbol* (New York: Harper and Brothers, 1952). The quotation is included in Erwin D. Canham, "A Contemporary Portrait of an 'Uncomplicated Leader of Men,'" *New York Times*, January 27, 1952. Therese Pfannenstiel, "Why I Believe in the United States of America," *Western Kansas World*, November 27, 1952.

54. "Ike Assails Reds in Colleges," *Chicago Daily Tribune*, January 17, 1953; A. L. Schultz, "In Kansas Politics," *Signal-Enterprise*, January 22, 1953; Marquis Childs, "Hubbub in Kansas," *Washington Post*, March 14, 1953; "Storm in Kansas," *Time*, March 30, 1953.

55. The unpopularity of Benson's farm policies was evident in Gallup polls between 1953 and 1958, showing approval of his handling of his job as Secretary of Agriculture in the 28 to 35 percent range. See iPoll, available at http://roperweb.ropercenter.uconn.edu.

56. "Farm Block Leader Confident," *New York Times*, February 12, 1953. The International Council for Christian Leadership was the forerunner of the fellowship, which continued sponsorship of the National Prayer Breakfast. See D. Michael Lindsay, *Faith in the Halls of Power: How Evangelicals Joined the American Elite* (New York: Oxford University Press, 2007), 35.

57. In 1959, sociologist Blanche Geer went from New York to Lawrence, where she conducted field research among first-year students at KU. Her observations focused too little on religion to provide reliable evidence, but one remark fit well with the idea that the activity church and generic beliefs associated with it were taken-for-granted aspects of community life. She wrote in her field notes that the students did not "talk down" religion or "talk it up" but instead merely revealed that it was "very much a part of their lives" as they discussed other topics. Blanche Geer, "First Days in the Field," in *Sociologists at Work: The Craft of Social Research*, ed. Phillip E. Hammond (Garden City, NY: Doubleday, 1964), 376.

58. "Secular Psych Study Banned for Catholics," *Chicago Daily Tribune*, September 3, 1956. The higher-than-expected growth in the numbers of Catholics refers to comparisons of actual membership in each county as reported in the 1952 National Council of Churches electronic data file, and predicted values based on Catholic membership in 1926, the total population in 1930, and the total population in 1950. The counties with standardized residuals greater than .5 were Atchison, Brown, Butler, Cherokee, Cloud, Crawford, Ellis, Finney, Ford, Geary, Johnson, Kingman, Labette, Marshall, Montgomery, Nemaha, Neosho, Saline, Shawnee, and Sumner. On the Christian Rural Overseas Program effort, see William M. Blair, "Two Relief Trains Quit the Midwest," *New York Times*, August 27, 1948. Leonard M. Lowe, who headed the Kansas effort, described it as one of unusual cooperation among religious groups; Mennonites sponsored their own effort, however, and in 1952 the Lutheran and Catholic programs became separate.

59. "Resolution Opposes a Catholic President," *Washington Post*, April 29, 1960; Donald Janson, "Humphrey Joins Kennedy Briefly," *New York Times*, March 5, 1960.

60. Philip Geyelin, "The Religious Issue: Anti-Catholicism Runs Deeper Than Expected, May Backfire on GOP," *Wall Street Journal*, September 12, 1960.

61. The regional results were obtained from the electronic data file for the May 1960 Gallup poll, courtesy of iPoll, available at http://www.ropercenter.uconn.edu. Of 3,044 respondents in the survey, 2,792 gave answers to the question about a Catholic for president, 322 lived in the eight states that the survey classified as West Central (Wisconsin, Minnesota, Iowa, Missouri, North Dakota, South Dakota, Nebraska, and Kansas), and 27 respondents were from Kansas. It was unclear how representative those respondents may have been, but a newspaper poll conducted in western Kansas suggested that support for Kennedy was stronger than expected. See "Kansas Appears to Lean to Nixon," *New York Times*, October 30, 1960.

62. The earlier Gallup poll was conducted in March 1940 and included alternate wordings. When asked, "Would you vote for a Catholic for president who was well qualified for this position?" 33 percent of the respondents said no, and 61 percent said yes; when asked, "If your party nominated a generally well-qualified man for president this year, and he happened to be

a Catholic, would you vote for him?" 31 percent of the respondents said no, and 62 percent said yes. See http://ropercenter.uconn.edu.

63. The factionalism in 1956 was between supporters of Governor Fred Hall and Republican national committeeperson Harry Darby. See "Kansas Governor Suffers Setback," *New York Times*, March 25, 1956. On efforts to reform the state legislature, see Harder and Rampey, *The Kansas Legislature*, 11–37. On the changing role of the farm population, see William M. Blair, "Farm Belt Found Uneasy," *New York Times*, October 22, 1958. Wichita's population grew from 168,279 in 1950 to 254,698 in 1960 as the aviation industry located there expanded. Most of the growth around Kansas City was in suburban Johnson County. For example, Olathe grew from 5,593 in 1950 to 10,987 in 1960, Overland Park was unincorporated in 1950 and grew to 21,110 in 1960, and Shawnee increased from 845 to 9,072. Kansas City, Kansas, declined slightly from 129,553 to 121,901. Docking's reelection in 1958 was attributed to a large turnout in Wichita and Kansas City. See "Kansas Re-elects Gov. Docking: First Democrat to Keep Office," *New York Times*, November 5, 1958. Docking's 63 percent victory in Sedgwick County gave him a margin of 25,122 votes there, and his 70 percent victory in Wyandotte County gave him a margin there of 22,046 votes. Those gains more than made up for losses in the twenty-six less populous counties. He also won a 68 percent victory in traditionally Democratic Ellis County.

64. Of the 54 signatory leaders of the Voluntary Committee of Kansas Clergy and Educators Opposed to Amendment No. 3, 7 were Catholic clergy and 10 were Protestant clergy members. On the other side, Kansans for the Right to Work was led by Louis Weiss, owner of Midland Industries, and Reed Larson of the Coleman Company. Weiss went on to become a board member of the National Right to Work Legal Defense Foundation, and Larson headed the national Right to Work Office ("'Soft Words, Hard Arguments' Will Be Missed," *National Right to Work Newsletter*, August 2005). For a general history of the right-to-work movement, see Gilbert J. Gall, *The Politics of Right to Work: The Labor Federations as Special Interests, 1943–1979* (New York: Greenwood Press, 1988). On the right-to-work initiative in Kansas, see Craig Miner, *Kansas: The History of the Sunflower State, 1854–2000* (Lawrence: University Press of Kansas, 2002), 341–47. The Kansas right-to-work amendment was supported in 93 of the state's 105 counties, and passed by a substantial margin of 90,000s. At the time, only Arizona, Arkansas, Nebraska, Nevada, North Dakota, and South Dakota had constitutional right-to-work amendments. Florida, Mississippi, and Oklahoma subsequently approved right-to-work amendments. See A. H. Raskin, "5 of 6 States Beat 'Work' Proposals," *New York Times*, November 6, 1958.

CHAPTER 5

1. David S. Broder and Leroy F. Aarons, "Kennedy Set to Announce Today," *Washington Post*, March 16, 1968; Warren Weaver Jr., "McCarthy

Gets about 40%," *New York Times*, March 13, 1968; Robert J. Donovan, "Kennedy Declares Antiwar Campaign," *Los Angeles Times*, March 17, 1968; Jimmy Breslin, "RFK," *Los Angeles Times*, April 14, 1968; "14,500 Cheer Kennedy at Kansas State," *Chicago Tribune*, March 19, 1968.

2. Robert F. Kennedy, "Remarks at the University of Kansas," March 18, 1968, available at http://www.jfklibrary.org; "Charisma amidst the Chaos," *Kansas Alumni*, October–November 1994. Kennedy's remark to Breslin is quoted in Thurston Clarke, *The Last Campaign: Robert F. Kennedy and 82 Days That Inspired America* (New York: Macmillan, 2008), 50. Letter from Robert Wuthnow to Kathryn Wuthnow, March 19, 1968.

3. John Hill, "Perspective 68," *Jayhawker Magazine* (Fall 1968): 1.

4. For information about the history and activity of these and other SAC bases, see, for instance, http://www.strategic-air-command.com.

5. For a photograph showing some of the thirty-one thousand Topeka schoolchildren in Topeka practicing duck and cover during a 1960 civil defense drill, see Alice L. George, *Awaiting Armageddon: How Americans Faced the Cuban Missile Crisis* (Chapel Hill: University of North Carolina Press, 2003), 148.

6. Political Behavior Program, *American National Election Studies: 1964 Pre-Post Election Study Codebook* (Ann Arbor: University of Michigan, 1964), electronic data file, courtesy of the Inter-University Consortium for Political and Social Research, University of Michigan. The study was conducted among 1,834 nationally representative respondents. The sample included no respondents from Kansas, but 272 respondents were from the Middle West (Arkansas, Iowa, Minnesota, Missouri, Nebraska, North and South Dakota, and Oklahoma), largely from metropolitan areas such as Saint Louis and Minneapolis. A separate analysis of these respondents revealed no significant differences on these questions from the national results.

7. For descriptions of the 1964 campaign, see Rick Perlstein, *Before the Storm: Barry Goldwater and the Unmaking of the American Consensus* (New York: Hill and Wang, 2001); Robert Alan Goldberg, *Barry Goldwater* (New Haven, CT: Yale University Press, 1997). Binary logistic regression analysis of the responses in the 1964 National Election Survey for 272 respondents in nine Middle West states showed a significant positive relationship between saying that farmers and businesspeople would not be able to do business with Communist countries and planning to vote for Goldwater (an odds ratio of 3.25), controlling for race, gender, religious preference (Catholic), attendance at religious services, and view of the Bible. Other than race, which was highly significant, the only other significant variable in the model was one's view of the Bible, in which those who thought all of the Bible is true were *less* likely to prefer Goldwater than those who thought the Bible "was written by men inspired by God but it contains some human errors." Among respondents nationally, the model showed that Catholics were less likely than Protestants to favor Goldwater, but that relationship was not significant among Middle West respondents. Substituting the anti-Castro item for the trade item yielded similar results (an odds ratio of 3.37).

8. In ordinary least squares analysis of the percentage in each Kansas county voting for Goldwater in 1964, the standardized multiple regression coefficient for the percentage having voted for Winrod in 1938 was .514 (significant beyond the .001 level), controlling for the total population in 1960 (which was negatively associated, –.228, significant beyond the .01 level). With the Republican vote in 1960 added to the model, the coefficients were .305 for percent for Winrod, .657 for a Republican vote in 1960 (both significant beyond the .001 level), and –.017 for the 1960 population (not significant). For a description of the state fair interviews, see Godfrey Sperling Jr., "Mid-U.S. Sounded Out," *Christian Science Monitor*, November 22, 1963.

9. "Goldwater Loses Kansas G.O.P. Bid," *New York Times*, April 19, 1964; Governor John Anderson, "Interview with Bob Beatty," December 15, 2003, courtesy of Kansas Memory Collection, Kansas State Historical Society, Topeka, available at http://www.kansasmemory.org; Joseph D. Mathewson, "Young Republicans," *Wall Street Journal*, November 2, 1964; F. Clifton White and William J. Gill, *Suite 3505: The Story of the Draft Goldwater Movement* (Columbia, MO: John M. Ashbrook Center for Public Policy, 1992), 152; David K. Willis, "GOP Seeks to Ignite Enthusiasm on Campus," *Christian Science Monitor*, May 11, 1965; "Young G.O.P. Elects Backer of Goldwater," *Chicago Tribune*, June 19, 1965; David S. Broder, "Goldwater Man Wins G.O.P. Post," *New York Times*, June 19, 1965; William Chapman, "Reagan Ready for Fast Run at Nomination," *Washington Post*, August 2, 1968; "Conservative Group Labels Nixon Record Disappointing," *Chicago Tribune*, March 3, 1969; David S. Broder, "Two Major Talent Factories Struggle to Dominate the GOP," *Washington Post*, February 17, 1970; "Interview with Paul Beck, Government History Documentation Project, Regional Oral History Office" (Berkeley: University of California, 1982), 31.

10. Mary C. Brennan, *Turning Right in the Sixties: The Conservative Capture of the GOP* (Chapel Hill: University of North Carolina Press, 1995), 64; Ben A. Franklin, "Right-wing Group Backs Goldwater," *New York Times*, July 24, 1964; "Conservative Gives Views," *New York Times*, May 29, 1966; "Wallace on Kansas Ballot," *New York Times*, June 5, 1972.

11. John H. Redekop, *The American Far Right: A Case Study of Billy James Hargis* (Grand Rapids, MI: Eerdmans, 1968); Seymour Martin Lipset and Earl Raab, *The Politics of Unreason: Right-wing Extremism in America, 1790–1970* (New York: Harper and Row, 1970), 273–75; Ronald Lora and William Henry Longton, *The Conservative Press in Twentieth-Century America* (New York: Greenwood, 1999).

12. Robert Howard, "Conservatives Cool to Speech by Ike Backer," *Chicago Daily Tribune*, September 18, 1955; "Rally of We the People Opens Today," *Chicago Daily Tribune*, September 19, 1958; "We the People Elect a Tulsa Evangelist," *Chicago Daily Tribune*, September 21, 1959; "Conservative Voters Told to Hold Together," *Chicago Daily Tribune*, September 20, 1959.

13. "Parley of We the People to Hear Welch," *Chicago Daily Tribune*, September 14, 1961; John Wicklein, "Evangelist Asks Push on U.S. Reds," *New York Times*, August 6, 1961; "We the People Meeting Will Hear Ezra Benson," *Chicago Tribune*, September 20, 1963; Donald Janson, "Hargis Group to Back Goldwater despite Some Members' Attacks," *New York Times*, August 9, 1964.

14. John Wicklein, "Christian Group Aims at Politics," *New York Times*, February 1, 1962; Lora and Longton, *The Conservative Press*.

15. Rusty L. Monhollon, *This Is America? The Sixties in Lawrence, Kansas* (New York: Palgrave Macmillan, 2004); Chalmers M. Roberts, "Ex-Chief Justice of Arizona 'High Priest' of Ultra Group," *Washington Post*, December 20, 1961; Lora and Longton, *The Conservative Press*; Morton Mintz, "Income of Right-wing Groups Reportedly Tripled in 5 Years," *Washington Post*, September 14, 1964; David Talbot, *Brothers: The Hidden History of the Kennedy Years* (New York: Free Press, 2008); Dick Russell, *The Man Who Knew Too Much* (New York: Carroll and Graf, 2003). The poll results are from the 1964 National Election Survey and refer to the 272 respondents from the Middle West states, and among those, the 61 respondents who said they were familiar with the Christian Anti-Communism Crusade.

16. Howard Buffett's son Warren Buffett, who became one of the nation's wealthiest investors, broke with conservative Republicans after his father's death in 1964 and supported McCarthy in 1968. See Daniel Gross, *Bull Run: Wall Street, the Democrats, and the New Politics of Personal Finance* (New York: Public Affairs, 2000), 151.

17. The audio of Reagan's speech, titled "A Time for Choosing," is available at http://www.americanrhetoric.com. For analyses of the speech, see Jonathan M. Schoenwald, *A Time for Choosing: The Rise of Modern American Conservatism* (New York: Oxford University Press, 2001), 195; James Berger, *After the End: Representations of Post-Apocalypse* (Minneapolis: University of Minnesota Press, 1999), 37. For Reagan's campaign activities at the time, see Seymour Korman, "TV's Reagan Speaks Up Tonight for Barry," *Chicago Tribune*, October 27, 1964; Edmund Morris, *Dutch: A Memoir of Ronald Reagan* (New York: Modern Library, 2000). What drew Reagan's attention to Rice County was unclear, although some discussion of the case had taken place in Congress the previous summer, according to one report ("Headlines Ahead," *Chicago Tribune*, June 7, 1964), and in newsmagazines ("U.S. Aid, Wanted or Not: Report on One County," *U.S. News and World Report*, April 1963, 40). For the Area Redevelopment Agency's program criteria, see Frank T. Bachmura, "The Manpower Development and Training Act of 1962: Its Significance for Rural Areas," *Journal of Farm Economics* 45 (1963): 61–72.

18. The proportion in Rice County that voted for Goldwater in 1964 (.39) was only 60 percent as large as the proportion that voted for Nixon in 1960 (.65). Gray County was the only county in which the decline was greater. Rice County residents were forgiving, allocating Reagan 58 percent

of their votes in 1980, but that placed them in the bottom quarter of Kansas counties. Statistical analysis deriving projected voting patterns in 1980 from presidential voting in previous elections suggests that Reagan's tally in Rice County was 3 percent lower than it should have been. The *Lyons Daily News* (November 2, 1964) printed a brief comment about Reagan's speech: "Ronald Reagan, appearing in behalf of Senator Barry Goldwater, Republican candidate for president, re-told the now widely known, but erroneous, story of this county being declared a depressed area, under the Democrats Area Redevelopment Administration. He then mentioned the hundreds of flowing oil wells and the millions of dollars in savings in county banks." The paper carried extensive coverage of the Johnson and Goldwater campaigns during the weeks prior to the election, described Johnson's visit to Wichita and Dole's campaign in Rice County, and during the week prior to the election carried daily full-page advertisements for Goldwater, in which Goldwater declared himself to be a good Christian as well as a strong anti-Communist, and a multipage insert by the Dole campaign. Goldwater won only three of the county's twenty-six precincts, and Dole won only four.

19. Interview, conducted April 8, 2008 (name withheld); "Ground Breaking Ceremony for Mankato Packing Plant," *Jewell County Record*, June 23, 1966; "Virtually All Rice County Eligible Wheatland Under '64 Program," *Lyons Daily News*, May 27, 1964; David W. Keller, "Letter to the Editor," *Lyons Daily News*, October 31, 1964; Governor John Anderson Jr., "Message to the Special Session of the Kansas Legislature," February 17, 1964, available at http://www.skyways.org/KSL/messages.

20. Lisa McGirr, *Suburban Warriors: The Origins of the New American Right* (Princeton, NJ: Princeton University Press, 2001), 76; Sheilah R. Koeppen, "The Republican Radical Right," *Annals of the American Academy of Political and Social Science* 382 (1969): 73 –82.

21. According to Alan F. Westin, sixteen of the John Birch Society's twenty-five National Council members were top executives or former heads of corporations, and were distinguished from other corporate leaders by heading family firms or being a "single 'I did it myself' entrepreneur." See his "The John Birch Society: 'Radical Right' and 'Extreme Left' in the Political Context of Post World War II," in *The Radical Right*, ed. Daniel Bell (Garden City, NY: Doubleday, 1963), 249. For information about the Koch family, see Jane Mayer, "Covert Operations," *New Yorker*, August 30, 2010.

22. Clyde Wilcox, "Sources of Support for the Old Right: A Comparison of the John Birch Society and the Christian Anti-Communism Crusade," *Social Science History* 12 (1988): 429–49, especially the multivariate logit regression results, table 4, 444. A similar conclusion about the relative underinvolvement of fundamentalists in the John Birch Society is also drawn by Lipset and Raab (*The Politics of Unreason*, 29 –302), who also note a study of the California Bay Area showing this to be true even among supporters of Schwarz's movement. The quote about Wichita is from Westin,

"The John Birch Society," 251. See also Fred W. Grupp Jr. and William M. Newman, "Political Ideology and Religious Preference: The John Birch Society and the Americans for Democratic Action," *Journal for the Scientific Study of Religion* 12 (1973): 401 –13. Interesting among other misinformation is the fact that John Birch Society National Committee leader and public spokesperson Tom Anderson, a Tennessean who would be nominated in 1976 as the conservative American Party's presidential candidate, was mistakenly identified in the press as a Kansan. See "Great Kennedy Power Hit by Birch Leader," *Los Angeles Times*, July 4, 1963.

23. Ray Morgan, "Pearson Has Edge in Kansas," *Washington Post*, August 1, 1966; Bob Beatty, "Interview with Governor William Avery," December 5, 2003, at Kansas Memory Collection, Kansas State Historical Society, Topeka; Bob Beatty, "'You Have to Like People': A Conversation with Former Governor William H. Avery," *Kansas History* 31 (2008): 48–67; Joel Paddock, "Democratic Politics in a Republican State: The Gubernatorial Campaigns of Robert Docking, 1966–1972," *Kansas History* 17 (1994): 108–23.

24. Lincoln Montgomery, quoted in Dave Hendrick, "The Quest for Equality: Wichita Blacks Remember Local Battles, Too," *Wichita Eagle*, January 18, 1992.

25. Walter A. Huxman, Arthur J. Mellott, and Delman C. Hill, "The Topeka, Kansas Case Decision," *Journal of Negro Education* 21 (1952): 522–27. For contemporary reactions and the situation in Topeka, see Mary L. Dudziak, "The Limits of Good Faith: Desegregation in Topeka, Kansas, 1950–1956," *Law and History Review* 5 (1987): 351–91; Anita Fleming-Rife and Jennifer M. Proffitt, "The More Public School Reform Changes, the More It Stays the Same: A Framing Analysis of the Newspaper Coverage of *Brown v. Board of Education*," *Journal of Negro Education* 73 (2004): 239–54. Historical treatments of the Supreme Court case include Richard Kluger, *Simple Justice: The History of* Brown v. Board of Education *and Black America's Struggle for Equality* (New York: Vintage, 1977); James T. Patterson, Brown v. Board of Education: *A Civil Rights Milestone and Its Troubled Legacy* (New York: Oxford University Press, 2001). De facto school segregation in Kansas City, Kansas, was still present a decade later. See "Kansas Schools Still Segregated, High Court Is Told in Hearing," *Call and Post*, February 13, 1965; "Review Refused Kansas School Imbalance," *Washington Post*, March 2, 1965. The 1956 poll results are from the 1956 National Election Survey, electronic data file, obtained from the Inter-University Consortium for Political and Social Research, University of Michigan, Ann Arbor, and analyzed to compare the answers from respondents in the nine Middle West states (Arkansas, Iowa, Kansas, Minnesota, Missouri, Nebraska, North and South Dakota, and Oklahoma) with the rest of the country (the reference to rural respondents refers to those not living in Standardized Metropolitan Areas).

26. The two 1957 surveys are Gallup polls conducted between September 19–24 and October 10–15. National results are available from

the Roper Center for Public Opinion Research, University of Connecticut, Storrs. The third survey was the 1958 National Election Survey, analyzed with the same classification of Middle West states as the 1956 survey.

27. The population figures for Kansas counties are from the 1960 U.S. Census, electronic data file. In the census, 91,549 African Americans were included, 61,038 of who lived in Sedgwick, Shawnee, and Wyandotte counties. In percentages, Wyandotte included the largest proportion of African Americans, making up 16.7 percent of the county's population; the proportions in Sedgwick and Shawnee were 6.0 and 6.7 percent, respectively. The population of Geary County, the home of Fort Riley, was 11.7 percent African American. For a description of the 1958 Wichita sit-in, see Gretchen Cassel Eick, *Dissent in Wichita: The Civil Rights Movement in the Midwest, 1954–72* (Urbana: University of Illinois Press, 2001), 55–59. On the Kansas civil rights law, "Another State Outlaws Segregation," *Afro-American* (Baltimore), April 4, 1959; "NAACP Helps Pass Kansas Rights Law," *Chicago Defender*, April 11, 1959. On Kansas City, "Sit-ins Win in Kansas City," *Chicago Defender*, July 30, 1960; "200 Cafes Open to Negro Patrons," *Chicago Defender*, August 24, 1960.

28. The Dockum Drug Company had advertised in Wichita's Negro newspapers since the 1920s and benefited from its African American customers, who were increasingly outspoken about the discrimination they experienced at the store. "Oh, by the way," a writer complained to the *Wichita Post-Observer* (August 28, 1953), "you can now stand up at Dockum and eat your hotdog. They say it's good for digestion. At least they're thinking about our health along with discrimination."

29. "Kansas CME Conference Speaks Out for Rights," *Afro-American*, September 8, 1956; "Kansas Civic Leader Dies," *Los Angeles Sentinel*, February 26, 1959; Eick, *Dissent in Wichita*, 55–59; interview with Rabbi Michael Davis, Congregation Emanu-El, conducted October 15, 2009.

30. For an account that emphasizes leadership and theology, see Charles Marsh, *God's Long Summer: Stories of Faith and Civil Rights* (Princeton, NJ: Princeton University Press, 1997). For an examination of the social bonds that develop in churches and lead to activism, see Charles Marsh, *The Beloved Community: How Faith Shapes Social Justice, from the Civil Rights Movement to Today* (New York: Basic Books, 2004). For especially instructive analyses about emotional expression and the development of leadership skills, see Marla F. Frederick, *Between Sundays: Black Women and Everyday Struggles of Faith* (Berkeley: University of California Press, 2003); Vicki L. Crawford, Jacqueline Anne Rouse, and Barbara Woods, eds., *Women in the Civil Rights Movement: Trailblazers and Torchbearers, 1941–1965* (Indianapolis: Indiana University Press, 1993). For insightful explorations of the relationships between the church as sacred space and neighborhoods, see Omar M. McRoberts, *Streets of Glory: Church and Community in a Black Urban Neighborhood* (Chicago: University of Chicago Press, 2003); Timothy Nelson, *Every Time I Feel the Spirit: Religious Experience and Ritual in an African American Church* (New York: New

York University Press, 2004). Many other relevant studies are referenced in these works.

31. Eick, *Dissent in Wichita*, 55–59; Christina M. Woods, "Saturday Event Will Recognize Dockum Sit-in Civil Rights History," *Wichita Eagle*, October 18, 2006; Beccy Tanner, "Civil Rights Campion, Mentor Dies," *Wichita Eagle*, May 2, 2003; Bud Norman, "Virgil E. Watson, a Giver: He Was a Political, Religious Leader," *Wichita Eagle*, September 21, 1994; "Local Leader in Church, Civic Affairs Recognized," *Chanute Tribune*, November 30, 2002; Sheila Ellis, "Rosa: The Face of Yuma Street," *Manhattan Mercury*, November 25, 2007; Cleon Rickel, "Pastor Left a Lasting Mark," *Ottawa Herald*, February 17, 2003; Ronald Walters, "The Great Plains Sit-in Movement, 1958–60," *Great Plains Quarterly* 16 (1996): 85–94; personal communication with author, Dr. Ronald Walters and Kevin Myles, Wichita NAACP, June 14, 2010. Walters is the primary source for the claim that the Wichita sit-in was an integral part of the chain of events that led to the wider civil rights movement in the South. For an alternative perspective that attaches less significance to the Wichita sit-in, see Aldon D. Morris, *The Origins of the Civil Rights Movement: Black Communities Organizing for Change* (New York: Free Press, 1986).

32. Monhollon, *This Is America*, 54; Joel Mathis, "Celebrated Writer's Church Recognized for Place in History," *Lawrence Journal-World*, August 26, 2001; Louise Hollowell and Martin C. Lehfeldt, *The Sacred Call: A Tribute to Donald L. Hollowell, Civil Rights Champion* (New York: Four-G Publishers, 1997); Mark E. McCormick, "A Legend Overlooked," *Wichita Eagle*, February 22, 1998.

33. "Lesson in Equality: Historic Case Went Deeper Than Integrating Schools," *Lawrence Journal-World*, May 14, 2004; Bill Roy, "Be Proud of Attorneys in Segregation Lawsuit," *Wichita Eagle*, February 10, 2004; Diane Carroll, "Struggle Goes on for True Equality," *Kansas City Star*, May 16, 2004.

34. Margalit Fox, "Zelma Henderson, Who Aided Desegregation, Dies at 88," *New York Times*, May 22, 2008; Sharon Woodson-Bryant, "Tokenism and Triumph in Topeka," *Kansas City Star*, May 18, 1994; Michael F. Blevins, "Remembering Lucinda Todd: The Initiating Plaintiff in *Brown v. Board of Education of Topeka*, May 17, 1954," *Brown Quarterly* 6 (2004), available at http://brownvboard.org.

35. Christina Jackson was also a member at St. John African Methodist Episcopal Church. See "Cristina Jackson Interview," September 20, 1991, available at http://www.kansasmemory.org. Kluger (*Simple Justice*, 395, 408) describes the Brown family as a "religious household" that poured much of their time into the church, and notes that "few of its members had anything to do with the NAACP." Kluger also mentions that McKinley Burnett, the local NAACP branch head associated with the case, belonged to the Church of God, held meetings there, and was "a leader of the congregation" (409). Lena Carper, another plaintiff in the case, was said to have been instrumental in founding the Church of God Seventh Day Adventist.

See "Obituary," *Topeka Capital-Journal*, November 20, 2002. One of the other plaintiffs, Maude Lawton, was a neighbor of Charles Scott and a friend of McKinley Burnett. According to Cheryl Brown Henderson, the plaintiffs were recruited by "talking to fellow church members, NAACP members, personal friends." Quoted in "Black/White and Brown: Brown versus the Board of Education of Topeka," KTWU/Channel 11, Topeka, May 3, 2004.

36. "Methodists Act to End System of Setting Negro Units Apart," *New York Times*, June 9, 1963; "Times for Growth," History of the First Methodist Church in Lawrence; "NAACP State Units Seek Laws on Housing, Jobs," *Chicago Daily Defender*, April 23, 1963; Monhollon, *This Is America*, 57; "Extremists Scored by Church Women," *New York Times*, October 9, 1964; George Dugan, "Presbyterians Urged to Oppose Bans on Interracial Marriages," *New York Times*, May 22, 1965; D.J.R. Bruckner, "Kansas Rights Groups Battle Governor Avery," *Los Angeles Times*, April 27, 1966.

37. Kristine M. McCusker, "'The Forgotten Years' of America's Civil Rights Movement: Wartime Protests at the University of Kansas, 1939–1945," *Kansas History* 17 (1994): 26–37; King's eulogy for Reeb, "A Witness to Truth," available at http://thatsalabama.com; Douglas Harvey, "We Shall Overcome," *KU History* (2007), available at http://www.kuhistory.com; Eick, *Dissent in Wichita*, 100; Laurie Kalmanson, "Wichita-Born Civil Rights Martyr Reeb to Be Honored," *Wichita Eagle*, March 13, 1993; Bill Hirschman, "Chet Lewis, Who Fought Injustice in Wichita Courtrooms, Dies at 61," *Wichita Eagle*, June 22, 1980; Christina M. Woods, "Civil Rights' Next Step," *Wichita Eagle*, September 25, 2006.

38. "Tear Gas Disperses Kansas City Negroes," *Los Angeles Times*, July 10, 1967; "Kansas City's Curfew Calm Broken by Fires and Snipers," *Chicago Tribune*, April 12, 1968; David K. Fly, "Reflections on the Kansas City Riot of 1968" (paper presented at the Missouri State Archives, Jefferson City, November 16, 2006), available at http://www.sos.mo.gov/archives; George W. Cornell, "Christian Church Urged to Relate to Revolution," *Los Angeles Times*, October 5, 1968; Paul Hofmann, "Clergy Meeting Strong Resistance to Involvement in Secular Causes," *New York Times*, April 12, 1968.

39. Nan Robertson, "Peaceful Kansas County Wakes to the Heated Issues of the Day," *New York Times*, October 27, 1968.

40. Harris Survey, August 24, 1968, courtesy of the Roper Center for Public Opinion Research, University of Connecticut, Storrs.

41. National Election Survey, 1968, electronic data file. The results are for whites only, of whom there were 1,374, with 229 living in the nine Middle West states. Middle West responses differed by only a percentage point or two from national responses. Seventy-four percent of white Middle West respondents thought Negroes should have a right to live wherever they wanted, and the same percentage thought at least a majority of Negroes favored desegregation. But 75 percent thought the civil rights

movement was mostly violent, 66 percent felt it was pushing too fast, and 71 percent thought it was hurting more than helping.

42. Tim Kane, "Global U.S. Troop Deployment, 1950–2005," *Heritage Foundation Report*, May 24, 2006, available at www.heritage.org/research; "Statistical Information about Casualties of the Vietnam War," National Archives, available at http://www.archives.gov; "Alerts at Bases in Kansas, Georgia, and Hawaii Rumored in Capital," *New York Times*, June 15, 1965; William Barry Furlong, "Training for the Front-All-Around-You War," *New York Times*, October 24, 1965.

43. Gallup polls, September 1965 and February 1968, asking, "Do you approve or disapprove of the way President Johnson is handling the situation in Vietnam?" results and data set, Roper Center for Public Opinion Research, University of Connecticut, Storrs; Donald Janson, "Support in Farm Belt," *New York Times*, February 3, 1965.

44. Quotes are from Everett Groseclose, "Vietnam's Shadow: Dodge City Illustrates War's Growing Impact at Grassroots Level," *Wall Street Journal*, March 24, 1966.

45. Everett Groseclose, "War-Weary Dodge," *Wall Street Journal*, July 12, 1967.

46. Douglas Johnson, *Amalgam Survey—Churches and Society* (Chicago: University of Chicago, National Opinion Research Center, 1968); CBS News poll, November 1969; Rowland Evans and Robert Novak, "A Near-Clean Sweep," *Washington Post*, May 1, 1966; "Kansas Governor Docking Briefed for Vietnam," *Washington Post*, August 9, 1967. Further information on Ellsworth's views can be found in Monhollon, *This Is America*, 114–16. Election results from U.S. Elections Data, electronic data file, courtesy of Inter-University Consortium for Political and Social Research, University of Michigan, Ann Arbor. In 1970 after the killings at Kent State University, Pearson rethought his position on Vietnam, and opposed the bombing of Laos and Cambodia.

47. "Switches by Press on War Reported," *New York Times*, February 18, 1968; Douglas E. Kneeland, "Kansas Skirmish Won by Kennedy," *New York Times*, March 31, 1968; Douglas E. Kneeland, "Midwest Democrats Cooler to Johnson," *New York Times*, March 15, 1968. Gallup polls in March through May 1969 showed approval of how Nixon was handling the situation in Vietnam ranging from 44 to 47 percent, disapproval from 24 to 27 percent, and no opinion from 25 to 32 percent. For details, see http://roperweb.ropercenter.uconn.edu. Polls in March through May 1970 registered approval of 46 to 53 percent, disapproval of 37 to 43 percent, and no opinion of 10 to 13 percent.

48. Anthony Ripley, "Student Parley Rails at Political and College Life," *New York Times*, August 25, 1968; Anthony Ripley, "Student Congress Stresses Power," *New York Times*, August 26, 1968; Max Frankel, "U.S. Study Scores Chicago Violence as a 'Police Riot,'" *New York Times*, December 2, 1968; Gallup poll, September 1–6, 1968, available at http://roperweb.ropercenter.uconn.edu.

49. David Ohle, Roger Martin, and Susan Brosseau, *Cows Are Freaky When They Look at You: An Oral History of the Kaw Valley Hemp Pickers* (Wichita: Watermark Press, 1991); Beth Bailey, *Sex in the Heartland* (Cambridge, MA: Harvard University Press, 1999).

50. Douglas E. Kneeland, "Center of U.S. Seems Far from Presidential Campaign," *New York Times*, August 1, 1968.

51. Interview, conducted July 3, 2008 (pseudonym used).

52. Interviews, conducted January 21, 2008; June 19, 2007; August 24, 2007; November 5, 2007; January 28, 2008 (names withheld).

53. Monhollon, *This Is America*, 128–33.

54. William C. Towns, "Fire and Smoke," *KU History*, 2007, available at http://www.kuhistory.com; Monhollon, *This Is America*, 146–51.

55. Robert B. Semple Jr., "President Urges End to Violence and Intolerance," *New York Times*, September 17, 1970.

56. "Text of Nixon's Talk in Kansas," *Los Angeles Times*, September 17, 1970. An audio of the lecture, including Landon's introduction, is available at http://ome.ksu.edu/lectures/landon/past.html.

57. "President's Hecklers Face Prosecution," *Chicago Tribune*, September 20, 1970; "Kansas Hecklers Spared," *Washington Post*, September 28, 1970; Stephen E. Ambrose, *To America: Personal Reflections of an Historian* (New York: Simon and Schuster, 2002), 139–40; Sara Smarch, "De-Classified," *Lawrence Journal-World*, January 23, 2006. The FBI files are available in the Kansas Collection, University of Kansas Libraries, Lawrence.

58. James M. Naughton, "Democrats Decry a Nixon Telecast," *New York Times*, September 26, 1970; "Democrats Condemn Nixon Hecklers," *Washington Post*, September 24, 1970; Jules Witcover, "Nixon Campaigns for 'Law and Order' through Midwest," *Los Angeles Times*, October 20, 1970; "College Heads Are Found Too Lenient in G.O.P Poll," *Chicago Tribune*, September 27, 1970; Harris survey, October 1970); Gallup poll, July 31–August 2, 1970.

59. Tom Wicker, "In the Nation: Violence, Corrosion, and Mr. Nixon," *New York Times*, September 20, 1970; Bruce S. Eastwood, "President on Dissent," *New York Times*, September 22, 1970.

60. Billy Graham, "The Divine Answer to the National Dilemma," March 4, 1974, available at http://ome.ksu.edu/lectures/landon/past.html.

61. *Churches and Church Membership, 1980*, electronic data file, from the Inter-University Consortium for Political and Social Research, University of Michigan, Ann Arbor. A study was conducted in 1971, but only 53 denominations participated, whereas 114 participated in 1952 and 111 did so in 1980.

62. As a summary measure, the zero-order correlation of the ratio of change in Methodist membership to the change in population with the total county population in 1950 was −.255; with the population in 1980, it was −.262; and with the growth in population from 1950 to 1980, it was −.264. In the five countries that grew the most (Johnson, Douglas, Riley, Seward,

and Sedgwick), the population increased 131 percent between 1950 and 1980, while Methodist membership grew only 56 percent. The five largest counties in 1980 were Sedgwick, Johnson, Wyandotte, Shawnee, and Douglas. They had grown 109 percent in total population since 1950, but experienced only a 48 percent increase in Methodist membership.

63. For further details, see Robert Wuthnow, "Depopulation and Rural Churches in Kansas, 1950–1980," *Great Plains Research* 15 (2005): 117–34.

64. Interview, conducted February 23, 2007 (name withheld).

65. The exception among established Protestant denominations were Presbyterians, of whom 56 percent lived in the seven most populous counties in 1980. Much of the growth was in Johnson County, where the number of congregations tripled and membership rose sevenfold.

66. Jeffrey K. Hadden, *The Gathering Storm in the Churches: The Widening Gap between Clergy and Laymen* (Garden City, NY: Doubleday, 1969).

67. Phillip E. Hammond, *Campus Clergymen* (New York: Basic Books, 1966); Wade Clark Roof, *Community and Commitment: Religious Plausibility in a Liberal Protestant Church* (New York: Pilgrim Press, 1983); Gertrude J. Selznick and Stephen Steinberg, *The Tenacity of Prejudice* (New York: Harper and Row, 1969).

68. A small but interesting piece of evidence about Methodists' ability to span social class differences in small towns emerged in 1964 when investigators did a follow-up to the 1951 study of Oskaloosa. Although the research focused mostly on other topics, details about a mother-daughter banquet at the Methodist Church showed 112 people in attendance, of whom 81 were categorized by the investigators as middle class, 20 as lower class, and 11 as upper middle class. See Phil Schoggen, *Behavior Settings: A Revision and Extension of Roger G. Barker's Ecological Psychology* (Stanford, CA: Stanford University Press, 1989), 143.

69. Judy Colvin, Connie Redford, Jeannine Bryan, and Art Hays, *History of First Baptist Church, Burden, Kansas, 1885 to 2009* (Burden: First Baptist Church, 2009), available at http://eccchistory.org /BurdenBaptist.htm.

70. For a brief description of the history of connections between Wichita and Oklahoma, see Stan Hoig, *Cowtown Wichita and the Wild, Wicked West* (Albuquerque: University of New Mexico Press, 2007).

71. The number of churches and founding dates are from the Annual Church Profile for Southern Baptist Convention Churches –Sunday School, 1980, electronic data file, courtesy of the Association of Religion Data Archives, University Park, PA, available at http://www.thearda.com. For speculation on the possible effects of conservative southern Protestantism spreading northward, see Mark A. Shibley, *Resurgent Evangelicalism in the United States: Mapping Cultural Change since 1970* (Columbia: University of South Carolina Press, 1996). The move of Southern Baptists into Kansas from Oklahoma, Arkansas, Missouri, and Texas is one of the

most important ways in which the state's religious restructuring differed from the national story that I described in *The Restructuring of American Religion: Society and Faith since World War II* (Princeton, NJ: Princeton University Press, 1988).

72. Illustrative of the connections among these independent churches and Bible institutes, one of the first interim pastors of the Wichita Bible Church was Dr. F. William May, founder of the Midwest Bible and Missionary Institute in Salina, who commuted from Salina and had previously served as president of the Kansas City Bible Institute. In 1938, the Wichita Bible Church purchased a building previously occupied by Winrod's Defenders of the Christian Faith organization. The Kansas City and Salina Bible institutes were loosely associated with the Midwest Bible College in Missouri, the Calvary Bible College in Kansas, and the Ozark Bible Institute in Arkansas. Additional information is available at various online histories of these organizations. Where other information is lacking, some original dates of formation are listed under business entities with the Kansas Secretary of State, available at http://www.accesskansas.org.

73. For a brief summary of the formation of the Christian Churches and Churches of Christ denomination, see J. Gordon Melton, *Encyclopedia of American Religions* (Detroit: Gale, 2009), 479. For a discussion of the split's impact on the geographic distribution of churches in the Disciples tradition, see Roger W. Stump, "Spatial Patterns of Growth and Decline among the Disciples of Christ, 1890–1980," in *A Case Study of Mainstream Protestantism: The Disciples' Relation to American Culture, 1880–1989*, ed. D. Newell Williams (Grand Rapids, MI: Eerdmans, 1991), 445–68. The western Kansas counties in which all the Christian Churches affiliated with the more conservative Christian Churches and Churches of Christ were Ford, Hamilton, Haskell, Meade, Morton, Rooks, Rush, Stevens, and Trego. For national data on the relationship between denominational mergers and schisms, see Robert C. Liebman, John Sutton, and Robert Wuthnow, "Exploring the Social Sources of Denominationalism: Schisms in American Protestant Denominations, 1890–1980," *American Sociological Review* 53 (1988): 343–52.

74. The information about churches and membership is drawn from Churches and Church Membership, 1980, electronic data file. The older established denominations that scholars generally associate with the term "mainline" in these data include American Baptist, Christian Church, Episcopal, Evangelical Lutheran Church in America, Friends, Mennonites, Presbyterian Church (U.S.A.), Unitarian, United Church of Christ, and United Methodist. Conservative churches, also sometimes termed sects or fundamentalist denominations, for the present purposes include Assemblies of God, Baptist Missionary, several Brethren denominations, Christian and Missionary Alliance, Christian Church and Churches of Christ, Churches of Christ, Missouri Synod Lutheran, several Church of God denominations, several Pentecostal and Holiness denominations, Salvation Army, Foursquare Gospel, and Southern Baptist. Missouri Synod Lutherans were

usually classified with the more conservative denominations on the basis of national surveys asking about theological beliefs; for example, Hadden (*The Gathering Storm*, 39) included data showing that 76 percent of Missouri Synod Lutherans believed in a "literal or nearly literal interpretation of the Bible," compared with 43 percent of American Lutheran Church members.

75. Donald O. Cowgill, "The Ecology of Religious Preference in Wichita," *Sociological Quarterly* 1 (1960): 87–96.

76. U.S. Census, 1980, electronic data file, courtesy of the Missouri Census Data Center, University of Missouri, Jefferson City.

77. Charles Y. Glock and Rodney Stark, *Christian Beliefs and Anti-Semitism* (New York: Harper and Row, 1966), 195.

78. "Churches Flay AF Manual Linking Them with Reds," *Washington Post*, February 17, 1960; John Wicklein, "Extremists Try to Curb Clergy," *New York Times*, March 28, 1960; Mary Dee Smith, "History," Metropolitan Baptist Church, available at http://www.metrobaptist.com.

79. Louis Cassels, "Schools Use of Prayers Will Not Change Much," *Washington Post*, July 11, 1962; "Kennedy Defines Role of Religion," *New York Times*, March 2, 1962; "Colony of Atheists Planned in Kansas," *New York Times*, July 3, 1963; Don Irwin, "Battle over Prayer Heating Up in Congress," *Los Angeles Times*, April 19, 1964. Murray's atheist colony did not materialize. In 1972, Republican challenger Charles D. "Chuck" McAtee campaigned in the second congressional district against incumbent Democrat Bill Roy, who he criticized for opposing a constitutional amendment favoring school prayer and the forced busing of schoolchildren. McAtee won in rural Dickinson, Brown, and Doniphan counties, but lost by large margins in Topeka and Leavenworth. For an examination of the court's rulings and their effects, see Kenneth M. Dolbeare and Phillip E. Hammond, *The School Prayer Decisions: From Court Policy to Local Practice* (Chicago: University of Chicago Press, 1971).

80. For the Catholic statistics, see David Baker, James Youniss, and Maryellen Schaub, *System for Catholic Research, Information, and Planning* (Washington, DC: Catholic University of America, Life Cycle Institute, 1990), electronic data files, 1940, 1950, 1960, 1970, 1980, 1990, courtesy of the Association of Religion Data Archives, available at http://www.thearda.com.

81. Andrew M. Greeley, William C. McCready, and Kathleen McCourt, *Catholic Schools in a Declining Church* (Chicago: Sheed and Ward, 1976), 125; Andrew M. Greeley, *The American Catholic: A Social Portrait* (New York: Basic Books, 1977), 132.

82. For an examination of the changing fertility rates, see Charles F. Westoff, "The Blending of Catholic Reproductive Behavior," in *The Religious Dimension: New Directions in Quantitative Research*, ed. Robert Wuthnow (New York: Academic Press, 1979), 231–40.

83. The conservative Americans for Constitutional Action gave the two senators a score of sixty-seven on an approval scale of one hundred, and

the four representatives a rating of seventy-nine. The liberal Americans for Democratic Action and the AFL-CIO's Committee on Political Education gave scores ranging from 16 to 34 percent. See Charles F. Scanlan, "Inside Kansas," *Kiowa News*, January 2, 1975; Warren Weaver Jr., "Dole's Chief Virtue Is That He Fits Right In," *New York Times*, August 22, 1976. Bennett was the first governor to serve under the state's new constitutional provision for a four-year term.

84. Virgil W. Dean, "Seeking 'Realism and a Little Rationality' in Government: The Observations of Former Governor Robert F. Bennett," *Kansas History* 31 (2008): 112.

Chapter 6

1. Three months after Tiller's murder, antiabortion activists from Kansas launched a massive campaign against an abortion clinic in Bellevue, Nebraska.

2. *Trends in Abortion in Kansas, 1973–2005* (New York: Guttmacher Institute, 2008). A national poll conducted by the Opinion Research Corporation from September 11 to 29, 1975, showed that 70 percent of the public were "personally most concerned" about the "high cost of food," 67 percent about "crime and violence," 62 percent about "inflation," 60 percent about the "high cost of medical care," 53 percent about the "high cost of gasoline," and 53 percent about "corruption in government." See Roper Center for Public Opinion Research, University of Connecticut, Storrs, available at http://www.ropercenter.uconn.edu.

3. U.S. Bureau of Economic Analysis, gross domestic product, 1963–2006, electronic data file; Governor Robert F. Bennett, *Message to the Kansas Legislature* (January 23, 1975), available at http://www.skyways.org/KSL/messages.

4. "Attendance at Mass Declines," *Washington Post*, November 16, 1973; Andrew M. Greeley, *The American Catholic: A Social Portrait* (New York: Basic Books, 1977); Dean M. Kelley, *Why Conservative Churches Are Growing: A Study in Sociology of Religion* (1972; rev. and repr., Macon, GA: Mercer University Press, 1986).

5. Russell Chandler, "Thompson Seen New Council Leader," *Los Angeles Times*, October 11, 1975; George Dugan, "Stated Clerk of Presbyterians Is Elected Head of National Council of Churches," *New York Times*, October 12, 1975; "William Phelps Thompson," *Christian Century*, June 8, 1966; "Presbyterians: The Layman Leader," *Time*, June 3, 1966; Christian T. Iosso, "Bill Thompson, Choice, and Balance: An After-Remembrance Reflection," *Perspectives* (Presbyterian Church [U.S.A.], Louisville), March 2007.

6. Nancy Tatom Ammerman, *Baptist Battles: Social Change and Religious Conflict in the Southern Baptist Convention* (New Brunswick, NJ: Rutgers University Press, 1990); Edward B. Fiske, "Backlash against 'Those Liberals,'" *New York Times*, April 16, 1972; John Dart, "Conservative Catholic Laymen to Organize," *Los Angeles Times*, December 9, 1967.

7. Lynn Taylor, "Churches Not United on Question of Abortions," *Chicago Tribune*, February 12, 1973; Dan L. Thrapp, "Churches Split Seriously on Abortion Issue," *Los Angeles Times*, August 13, 1972; Marjorie Hyer, "Abortion, Congress, Churches, Convictions," *Washington Post*, January 22, 1974.

8. Stanley K. Henshaw and Kathryn Kost, *Trends in the Characteristics of Women Obtaining Abortions, 1974 to 2004* (New York: Guttmacher Institute, 2008).

9. Jerome M. Clubb, William H. Flanigan, and Nancy H. Zingale, *Electoral Data for Counties in the United States: Presidential and Congressional Races, 1974–1976* (Ann Arbor: Inter-University Consortium for Political and Social Research, University of Michigan, 1986), electronic data file. The significance of Dole's victory in Sedgwick County is evident in standardized residuals obtained from ordinary least squares regression analysis in which votes by county for Dole are predicted from the total votes cast and the votes cast for Bennett for governor. The standardized residual for Sedgwick County is 4.12, the largest for any county, followed by 2.49 for Johnson County, whereas the standardized residual for Shawnee County is –6.06 and for Douglas County is –3.72. Comparing actual and predicted votes, Dole received approximately thirty-five hundred more votes than would have been expected in Sedgwick, two thousand more in Johnson, five thousand less in Shawnee, and three thousand less in Douglas. For background on the campaign, see Stephen Darst, "How It Is Playing in Emporia," *New York Times*, October 20, 1974; Nicholas M. Horrock, "Anti-Abortion Ad Funds Accepted by Dole in '74," *New York Times*, August 25, 1976; "Dole Ex-Aide Linked to Anti-Abortion Ad," *New York Times*, August 28, 1976. William Roy's account is from a PBS interview, "Stories of Bob," *Frontline*, May 1, 1996, available at http://www.pbs.org.

10. Spencer Rich, "GOP Unit Backs Abortion Plank," *Washington Post*, August 11, 1976; Haynes Johnson, "Unease Goes beyond Abortion Issue," *Washington Post*, July 16, 1976; Jerald terHorst, "Gambling with the Catholic Vote," *Chicago Tribune*, July 21, 1976; Richard Bergholz, "Carter Would Tax Churches —Dole," *Los Angeles Times*, October 2, 1976.

11. B. D. Colen and Judy Mann, "Abortion Passions Rise on Both Sides," *Washington Post*, January 23, 1979; Kenneth A. Briggs, "A Poll of Catholics Points Up Diversity," *New York Times*, March 3, 1978.

12. Bruce McKinney, quoted in "Wichita Vote Plays Important Role in the Movie 'Milk,'" *KSN News* (Wichita), June 25, 2009; "Voting against Gay Rights," *Time*, May 22, 1978; "Anti-Gay Movement, Wichita," *ABC Evening News*, May 8, 1978, courtesy of Vanderbilt Television News Archive.

13. Quoted in Kristi Lowenthal, "Conservative Thought and the Equal Rights Amendment in Kansas" (PhD diss., Kansas State University, 2008), 215–16. On Schlafly and Hobbs, see especially Ruth Murray Brown, *For a "Christian America": A History of the Religious Right* (New York: Prometheus Books, 2002).

14. Ibid., 224. Based on an interview, conducted on September 12, 2007; Lowenthal's analysis of letters is summarized in ibid., 221–36. Narratives similar to Lowenthal's are included in a study among women in Fargo, North Dakota. See Faye D. Ginsburg, *Contested Lives: The Abortion Debate in an American Community* (Berkeley: University of California Press, 1989).

15. Keith Sebelius, "Thank You Kansans," campaign advertisement run in Kansas newspapers, October 26, 1978; Ronald Reagan, "First Inaugural Address," January 20, 1981. Text versions sometimes omit the last part of Reagan's statement (see, for example, http://www.bartleby.com), but the video includes it (http://www.youtube.com).

16. Reagan, "First Inaugural Address."

17. William Endicott, "Carter, Reagan Win Easily in Wisconsin and Kansas," *Los Angeles Times*, April 2, 1980; Ronald Reagan, "Official Announcement of Candidacy for President," November 13, 1979; text of "1980 Ronald Reagan/Jimmy Carter Presidential Debate," October 28, 1980, Miller Center, University of Texas, available at http://www.reagan.utexas.edu.

18. Quotes from a sampling of community newspapers, October 1980.

19. Fred Barbash, "Protesters Deny Woman Judgeship," *Washington Post*, December 23, 1981; Bob Beatty and Mark Peterson, "Interview with Former Kansas Governor John W. Carlin," March 10, 2008, transcript on file in Kansas Memory Collection, Kansas State Historical Society, Topeka, available at http://www.kansasmemory.org, and edited in Bob Beatty, "'Be Willing to Take Some Risks to Make Things Happen': A Conversation with Former Governor John W. Carlin," *Kansas History* 31 (2008): 132.

20. Lawrence H. Tribe, *Abortion: The Clash of Absolutes* (New York: W. W. Norton, 1990), 161–65.

21. Ronald Reagan, "Rebuilding America," Landon Lecture, Kansas State University, September 9, 1982, audio file, available at http://ome.ksu.edu/lectures/landon.

22. Names, locations, and founding dates as listed by the Internal Revenue Service from Form 990 filings as of 2008; Birthright, Birthline, or Pregnancy Crisis centers were located in Chanute (1976), Dodge City (1976), El Dorado (1987), Emporia (1980), Fort Scott (1978), Great Bend (1975), Junction City (1980), Lawrence (1983), Leavenworth (1988), Topeka (1973), and Wichita (1985). "Baby Bill Defeated in Senate," *Wichita Eagle*, March 27, 1985; "Live-Abortion Custody Bill Clears Senate," *Wichita Eagle*, April 10, 1986; Ramona Jones and Jim Cross, "Docking and Hayden Square Off," *Wichita Eagle*, September 24, 1986.

23. "Pontiff Defends Unborn: U.S. Visit Ends with Challenge," *Wichita Eagle*, September 20, 1987; "Evangelicals Praise Pope," *Wichita Eagle*, September 19, 1987; "Rallies in 150 Cities Back Abortion Rights," *Wichita Eagle*, November 13, 1989; Lori Linenberger, "Abortion Rivals Find Survey Encouraging," *Wichita Eagle*, September 25, 1989.

24. Mary C. Segers and Timothy A. Byrnes, eds., *Abortion Politics in American States* (New York: M. E. Sharpe, 1995); Mark A. Graber, *Rethinking Abortion: Equal Choice, the Constitution, and Reproductive Politics* (Princeton, NJ: Princeton University Press, 1999).

25. Alexis de Tocqueville, *Democracy in America* (New York: Harper and Row, 1966). For the original 1977 text in which the authors coined the term mediating structures, and discussed the role of churches, neighborhoods, families, and voluntary associations, see Peter L. Berger and Richard John Neuhaus, *To Empower People: From State to Civil Society* (Washington, DC: AEI Press, 1996).

26. "Abortion Measure Is Tabled," *Wichita Eagle*, March 30, 1989; "KU Center Abortion Ban Fails," *Wichita Eagle*, April 1, 1989; Lori Linenberger, "Killing Fetus Not Crime," *Wichita Eagle*, October 28, 1989; "Hospitals Drop Abortions," *Wichita Eagle*, September 18, 1989; Tom Schaefer, "Catholic Activist Won't Back Down," *Wichita Eagle*, October 21, 1989; Tom Schaefer, "Kansans Say Sanctions Would Be Unlikely Step," *Wichita Eagle*, December 2, 1989.

27. Stan Finger, "St. Francis Asks for Title X Grant: Hospital Would Not Do Abortion Referrals," *Wichita Eagle*, September 16, 1989; John Jenks, "School Board Questions Optional Sex-Ed Lessons," *Wichita Eagle*, October 10, 1989; Stan Finger, "Irked Board of Health Ends Contract," *Wichita Eagle*, November 10, 1989.

28. Judy Lundstrom, "Abortion Clinic Protest leads to 79 Arrests," *Wichita Eagle*, July 16, 1989.

29. Governor John Michael Hayden, "State of the State Message," January 8, 1990, available at http://www.skyways.org/KSL/messages; Judy Lundstrom Thomas, "Relentless Debate on Abortion Rages On," *Wichita Eagle*, January 23, 1990; Martha Sevetson, "68 arrested at Abortion Protest," *Wichita Eagle*, February 11, 1990; David Shribman, "Upside-Down Kansas Gubernatorial Race Offers Voters Choice between 2 Unpopular Candidates," *Wall Street Journal*, October 9, 1990; Jim Cross, "Abortion Foes Want to Be GOP's Kingmakers," *Wichita Eagle*, December 4, 1990.

30. Terry quoted in William Martin, *With God on Our Side: The Rise of the Religious Right in America* (New York: Broadway Books, 1996), 322.

31. Catholic data for the Wichita diocese are from the System for Catholic Research, Information, and Planning, 1990, electronic data file, courtesy of the Association of Religion Data Archives, University Park, PA, available at http://www.thearda.com. Protestant data for Sedgwick County are from Churches and Church Membership in the United States, 1990, electronic data file, also from the Association of Religion Data Archives, or in M. B. Bradley, Norman M. Green Jr., Dale E. Jones, Mac Lynn, and Lou McNeil, *Churches and Church Membership in the United States* (Washington, DC: Glenmary Research Center, 1992). For clergy member information and quotes, see Tom Schaefer, "Resilient Dick Kelsey Has Learned Ways to Link Religion and Politics," *Wichita Eagle*, November 18, 1990;

Tom Schaefer, "A Delicate Balance: Abortion Issue Splits Local Clergy, Congregations," *Wichita Eagle*, August 10, 1991; "Judge Criticizes Bishop over Abortion Protest," *New York Times*, August 14, 1991.

32. Schaefer, "A Delicate Balance."

33. Tom Schaefer, "Ministers Say They Won't Be Initiating Blockades," *Wichita Eagle*, August 15, 1991; "What Wichita Thinks about Operation Rescue," *Wall Street Journal*, August 15, 1991; Van Williams, "Abortion Foes Form Coalition," *Wichita Eagle*, August 17, 1991; "125 Arrested as Wichita Protesters Storm Clinic," *Washington Post*, August 18, 1991; Bud Norman and Judy Lundstrom Thomas, "Abortion Rights Groups Seek Peaceful Force," *Wichita Eagle*, August 20, 1991; "More Are Arrested in Wichita, Including a Leader of Protests," *New York Times*, August 21, 1991; Don Terry, "25,000 Opponents of Abortion Rally in Wichita," *New York Times*, August 26, 1991.

34. Judy Lundstrom Thomas, "Tiller Rejects Compromise on Protests," *Wichita Eagle*, September 6, 1991; "Antiabortion Arrests Resume in Kansas," *Washington Post*, September 8, 1991; Lisa Agrimonti, "Local Anti-Abortion Group Says It Didn't Inspire Invasion of Clinic," *Wichita Eagle*, September 16, 1991; Judy Lundstrom Thomas, "Abortion Foe Arrested upon Return," *Wichita Eagle*, October 5, 1991; Bud Norman, "Abortion Opponents Draw a 9-Mile Line," *Wichita Eagle*, October 7, 1991.

35. Catholic school data, System for Catholic Research, Information, and Planning, electronic data files, 1960, 1970, 1980, 1990. Private Christian school information from school Web sites and IRS 990 filings. For a discussion of school controversies, see Martha Sevetson, "Recall Effort Draws Attention to Thorp's Religious Support," *Wichita Eagle*, March 22, 1992.

36. Schaefer, "Resilient Dick Kelsey."

37. Martha Sevetson, "Thorp: Berger, Religion Not My Issues," *Wichita Eagle*, February 10, 1992; Martha Sevetson, "Voters Thump Thorp," *Wichita Eagle*, April 8, 1992; "District News Roundup," *Education Week*, April 22, 1992.

38. Laurie Kalmanson, "Ways to Keep Kids on High Road Studied," *Wichita Eagle*, February 1, 1992; Susan L. Rife, "Champion Is Out to Battle Evil with His Faith," *Wichita Eagle*, February 8, 1992; Laurie Kalmanson, "Giving Teens a Christian Experience Is Aim of Local Crusade," *Wichita Eagle*, February 15, 1992; Gina Spade, "Teens Hear Message about Faith," *Wichita Eagle*, February 23, 1992.

39. "Bill Limiting Access to Abortion Is Signed by Governor of Kansas," *New York Times*, April 24, 1992.

40. Judy Lundstrom Thomas, "Protests over Abortion Get More Personal," *Wichita Eagle*, November 17, 1991; Judy Lundstrom Thomas, "Tiller Speaks Out after Altercation at Clinic," *Wichita Eagle*, March 21, 1992; Bud Norman and Judy Lundstrom Thomas, "Hand Grenade, Chants Color Opening Day," *Wichita Eagle*, June 7, 1992.

41. "Anti-Abortion Protests Again in Wichita," *Christian Science Monitor*, July 16, 1992; Jim Cross, "Abortion Views and the 4th District," *Wichita Eagle*, July 5, 1992.

42. Anne Fitzgerald, "Experienced Politician Facing Newcomer in 89th," *Wichita Eagle*, October 10, 1992; Jim Cross, "Glickman Rejects Slant on 'Values,'" *Wichita Eagle*, September 21, 1992; Bud Norman, "Churches' Messages Steer Clear of Political Endorsements," *Wichita Eagle*, August 3, 1992; Thomas B. Koelting, "Southern Hospitality, Laced with Fire, Is Falwell's Style," *Wichita Eagle*, August 3, 1992; Tim Boyd, quoted in Jim Cross, "Support for Yost Stops Short of Baptists' Pulpit," *Wichita Eagle*, September 30, 1992.

43. Anne Fitzgerald, "GOP Wins Control of State House," *Wichita Eagle*, November 4, 1992; Mark Gietzen, quoted in Judy Lundstrom Thomas, "Rallying the Faithful," *Wichita Eagle*, September 20, 1992.

44. Rochelle Olson, "Abortion Bill Said to Ban Some Types of Birth Control," *Wichita Eagle*, March 20, 1993; Robert Short, "Abortion Foes Get Raucous Greeting," *Wichita Eagle*, April 24, 1993; Linda Greenhouse, "Supreme Court Says Klan Law Can't Bar Abortion Blockades," *New York Times*, January 14, 1993.

45. Judy Lundstrom Thomas, "Clinics Pushed into a Corner," *Wichita Eagle*, April 18, 1993; Joe Rodriguez, "No Remorse over Shooting," *Wichita Eagle*, October 3, 1993; "Prayer Movement Focus on Abortion," *Wichita Eagle*, October 2, 1993; Robert Short, "Butler County Will Weigh Picketing Law," *Wichita Eagle*, October 19, 1993.

46. Ben Wear, "Conservatives Summon Candidates, School Board Next Battleground," *Wichita Eagle*, January 25, 1993; Judy Lundstrom Thomas, "Conservatives about to Move Legislative Proposals," *Wichita Eagle*, June 7, 1993.

47. Robertson, Landon Lecture, Kansas State University, October 12, 1993, quoted in Judy Lundstrom Thomas, "'Demented Acts of Violence,'" *Wichita Eagle*, October 13, 1993.

48. Linda Greenhouse, "Court Rules Abortion Clinics Can Use Rackets Law to Sue," *New York Times*, January 25, 1994; "State Reports," *Daily Reports Archive*, October 25, 1995, available at http://www.kaisernetwork.org.

49. Kansas Legislature, *Journals of the House and Senate*, March 19–May 4, 1997.

50. "Opinion Line," *Wichita Eagle*, June 28, 1998; Tom McCann, "What's the Role of Morality in the Governor's Race?" *Wichita Eagle*, August 1, 1998.

51. Judy Lundstrom Thomas, "Parents Lobby against Values-Based Teaching," *Wichita Eagle*, December 5, 1992; Julie Wright, "Parents Told to Fight 'Humanism,'" *Wichita Eagle*, May 31, 1992; Judy Lundstrom Thomas, "'700 Club' Report Turns Cameras on State School Reform," *Wichita Eagle*, August 12, 1993; Representative Elizabeth Baker, quoted

in Julie Wright, "A Slam at Religious Right," *Wichita Eagle*, February 24, 1993.

52. Johnson County Election Office, 1996 primary and general election results; Grace Christian Fellowship Church, available at http://www .gcfc.net; "Around Kansas City," *Kansas City Star*, May 24, 1996; Roberta Johnson Schneider, "2 Republicans Vie for Education Spot," *Kansas City Star*, July 19, 1996; Kate Beem, "Private Faith Molds Actions in Public Arena," *Kansas City Star*, May 9, 1999.

53. Laura Scott, "Old-liners Want Their Party Back," *Kansas City Star*, October 25, 1996; John Petterson, "Graves Offers to Help Bid to End State Panel," *Kansas City Star*, December 5, 1996.

54. Paul Ackerman and Bob Williams, *Kansas Tornado: 1999 Science Curriculum Standards Battle* (El Cajon, CA: Institute for Creation Research, 1999); Willis, quoted in Erik Petersen, "Scientists Publicize," *Lawrence Journal-World*, June 10, 1999; "Kansas Catholic Conference Opposes Statement Wording," *Wichita Eagle*, September 26, 1999.

55. Diane Carroll, "Evolution Question Left to Schools," *Kansas City Star*, August 12, 1999; Scott Rothschild, "In the Eye of the Evolution Storm," *Wichita Eagle*, September 5, 1999; James Glanz, "Science vs. the Bible: Debate Moves to the Cosmos," *New York Times*, October 9, 1999; "Science Panel Feels Slighted by School Board," *Salina Journal*, May 13, 1999; Linda Holloway, "Two Reactions to the Kansas Board's Evolution Decision," *Kansas City Star*, December 18, 1999.

56. John D. Morris, foreword to *Kansas Tornado: 1999 Science Curriculum Standards Battle*, by Paul Ackerman and Bob Williams (El Cajon, CA: Institute for Creation Research, 1999), 7. For Johnson's and other creationists' reactions, see Amy Binder, *Contentious Curricula: Afrocentrism and Creationism in American Public Schools* (Princeton, NJ: Princeton University Press, 2004).

57. Allan J. Cigler, Mark Joslyn, and Burdett A. Loomis, "The Kansas Christian Right and the Evolution of Republican Politics," in *The Christian Right in American Politics: Marching to the Millennium*, ed. John C. Green, Mark J. Rozell, and Clyde Wilcox (Washington, DC: Georgetown University Press, 2003), 145–66. The poll found Kansans more divided on human origins (49 percent thought God created humans in their present form, while 42 percent thought humans evolved over millions of years with God guiding the process), but the Kansas results were almost identical to national opinion in a Gallup poll. Diane Carroll, "Evolution Critic Cheers Board Vote," *Kansas City Star*, August 27, 1999; Diane Carroll, "Kansas Evolution Dispute," *Kansas City Star*, October 12, 1999; Reverend Ken Liles, quoted in "Evolution Revolution," *NewsHour*, November 9, 1999; Scott Rothschild, "Evolution Gets Boot," *Wichita Eagle*, August 12, 1999; Carroll, "Evolution Question Left to Schools"; "John L. Petterson, "Elected Board Again a Target," *Kansas City Star*, August 18, 1999; Reverend Ronald Yarnell, "God Calls Us to Understand His Creation,"

Salina Journal, August 17, 1999; Peter Hancock, "Creationists Won't Compromise Beliefs," *Lawrence Journal-World*, November 14, 1999.

58. Steve Kraske, "Want to Toss Your Hat in the Ring?" *Kansas City Star*, August 15, 1999; William K. Piotrowski, "The Kansas Compromise," *Religion in the News* 2 (Fall 1999).

59. Kansas Secretary of State, Kansas primary election results, 2000, available at http://www.kssos.org/elections; Melodee Hall Blobaum, "Holloway Guides Efforts to Establish Private Academy," *Kansas City Star*, May 12, 2001.

60. Lori Arnold, "Churches Challenging IRS Rules by Endorsing from the Pulpit," *Christian Examiner*, November 2008.

CHAPTER 7

1. Dale E. Jones, Sherry Doty, Clifford Grammich, James E. Horsch, Richard Houseal, John P. Marcum, Kenneth M. Sanchagrin, and Richard H. Taylor, *Religious Congregations and Membership in the United States, 2000: An Enumeration by Region, State, and County Based on Data Reported for 149 Religious Bodies* (Nashville, TN: Glenmary Research Center, 2002), electronic data file, available at http://www.thearda.com. The numbers refer to adherents, providing the most comparable data for Protestants and Catholics. Conservative Protestant figures refer to denominations coded by the Glenmary researchers as "evangelical," and include Southern Baptists, independent Christian churches, Lutheran Churches Missouri Synod, Assemblies of God, and smaller denominations such as the Churches of Christ and Church of God.

2. U.S. Census, decennial censuses, incorporated places, 1980, 1990, 2000; electronic data file, courtesy of the Missouri Census Data Center, University of Missouri, Jefferson City. Wichita grew from 13,500 acres in 1940, to 32,600 acres in 1960, to 64,600 acres in 1980, to 86,900 acres in 2000.

3. U.S. Census, public use microsample, 2000, electronic data file. Missouri, Oklahoma, and Texas were the three most common birth states other than Kansas, and comprised approximately 15 percent of the total Kansas population. The locations of United Methodist churches in 2007 were obtained from online information provided by the Kansas Conference of the United Methodist Church, and for Southern Baptist churches in 2007 from information provided by Richie Stanley of the Southern Baptist Convention. The Southern Baptist data include congregations classified as church-type missions.

4. Interviews with staff and members, conducted October 29, 2007; November 7, 2007; November 20, 2008 (names withheld). For an articulation of the pastor's emphasis on the complexity of abortion, homosexuality, evolution, and other controversial issues, see Adam Hamilton, *Seeing Gray in a World of Black and White* (Nashville: Abingdon Press, 2008).

5. Renee M. Hanrahan, *Magdalen Parish Survey: Final Report* (Wichita: Church of the Magdalen, 2007); staff interview, conducted July 29, 2009.

6. The Church of the Magdalen was established in 1950 near the center of Wichita, but did not move to its present location until 2002. See "History," Church of the Magdalen. Garfield University subsequently became Friends University. William G. Cutler, *History of the State of Kansas* (Chicago: A. T. Andreas, 1883); Frank T. Blackmar, *Higher Education in Kansas* (Washington, DC: Government Printing Office, 1900), 156–57; Register of Deeds, Sedgwick County, *National Register of Historic Places Nomination Form*, June 13, 1975; "Mary Ellen Lease Will Preach," *Chicago Daily Tribune*, February 13, 1896; "Notice," *Los Angeles Times*, April 5, 1896. The church did hire a protégé of Lease, Dr. Elmer Wiley, on her recommendation, but fired him before his tenure began after learning that his wife was suing for divorce on the grounds of physical and verbal abuse. See "Protégé of Mrs. Lease," *Chicago Daily Tribune*, March 26, 1896; Abe Levy, "A Church in Limbo," *Wichita Eagle*, October 30, 2004; Dan Close, "Thomas Parish Spread the Gospel Throughout His Life," *Wichita Eagle*, October 23, 1987; Daniel Thomas Johnson, *History and Backgrounds of Manhattan Bible College* (Manhattan, KS: Manhattan Christian College, 2002), available at http://www.mccks.edu.; Mike Hutmacher, "Lift High the Cross," *Wichita Eagle*, October 7, 1999; John Jenks, "'New Age' Teachings Chafe Ministers," *Wichita Eagle*, November 18, 1989; Stephen J. Hedges, David Bowermaster, and Susan Headden, "Abortion Rights Advocates Have Alleged a Conspiracy," *U.S. News and World Report*, November 14, 1994. The prayer, given on January 23, 1996, was reported the next day in the *Kansas City Star* and subsequently reprinted on numerous Web sites. See Abe Levy, "A Pastor Preaches His Mind," *Wichita Eagle*, July 4, 2004.

7. Tom Schaefer, "Baptist Struggle Getting Ugly," *Wichita Eagle*, October 31, 1987; Tom Schaefer, "Churches Fast Becoming Believers in Marketing," *Wichita Eagle*, December 30, 1989; Laura Addison, "From Pulpit to Pew," *Wichita Eagle*, February 22, 1997; Joe Wright, "'Things Are Moving' on South Broadway," *Wichita Eagle*, February 7, 2002.

8. Melodee Hall Blobaum, "Jerry Falwell to Visit Local Church," *Kansas City Star*, September 20, 1997; Joe Gose, "If We Build It, They Will Come," *Kansas City Star*, April 10, 1998; Judy L. Thomas, "Lax Financial Oversight Riles Some Followers," *Kansas City Star*, March 11, 2007.

9. Todd Krehbiel, *Final Report and Recommendations Based on Observations Made at Sedgwick County General Election Polling Sites* (Wichita: Sedgwick County Voter Coalition, 2007). The Central Christian Church, where 5,229 registered voters were assigned, was one of the locations at which religious objects were not covered. At several other locations campaign signs appeared on church lawns.

10. Religion and Politics Survey, 2000, in which a nationally representative sample of 5,603 respondents was included; electronic data file, courtesy of the Association of Religion Data Archives. Sixty-eight percent

of Kansas respondents attended religious services at least once or twice a month, and 84 percent said they believed God was fully revealed in Jesus Christ.

11. The survey was an exit poll conducted in November 2000 among seven hundred registered voters. See National Election Pool General Election Exit Polls, 2000, electronic data file. Sarah Kessinger, "David Miller Profile," *Harris News Service*, July 14, 1998.

12. Laurie Goodstein, "Conservative Church Leaders Find a Pillar in Bush," *New York Times*, January 23, 2000.

13. Phillip Brownlee, "KRA Struggling to Be Relevant," *Wichita Eagle*, October 16, 1999.

14. General election turnout numbers, 1992, 1996, 2000, 2004, Kansas State Secretary of State, available at http://www.kssos.org. Lillian Zier Martell, "Kansas Businesses Keep Eye on Election," *Wichita Eagle*, October 15, 2000; Lori Lessner, "Abortion Showdown," *Wichita Eagle*, July 31, 2000; Lori Lessner, "Delegates Put Focus on Party Unity," *Wichita Eagle*, August 4, 2000; Jim Baker, "Crusaders Return Home," *Lawrence Journal-World*, May 12, 2000; Brian Lewis, "Pulpit, Pews, and Politics," *Wichita Eagle*, September 2, 2000.

15. "Kansans Cheer Bush Abortion Rule," *Salina Journal*, January 23, 2001; Lori Lessner, "Roberts' Votes Lean More to the Right," *Wichita Eagle*, February 18, 2001.

16. Information on file at the Kansas Business Center in Topeka shows that Kansas Legislative Education and Research, Inc., filed as a not-for-profit corporation on August 10, 1999, with Corkins as its resident agent and the Kansas Conservative Caucus as its previous name. For a description of the formation of the Kansas Conservative Caucus, see Peter Hancock, "Conservative Lawmakers Form In-house Think Tank," *Lawrence Journal-World*, September 29, 1999. For a profile of Hawkins, see Steve Painter, "Leaders Calling," *Wichita Eagle*, February 5, 2001.

17. Interview with Tim Cruz, conducted March 12, 2008; Scott Rothschild, "Single Issue Factions Credited for Conservative Blitz," *Lawrence Journal-World*, August 8, 2002; Carol Crupper, "Fliers Stir Church, Politics Debate," *Hays Daily News*, September 1, 2002; Jesse Tuel, "Kansas Board of Education Candidate Takes a Stand," *Chanute Tribune*, November 2, 2002.

18. Stan Finger, "Week of Abortion Protests Begins, Ends Peacefully," *Wichita Eagle*, July 21, 2001.

19. Steve Painter, "Abortion Row Kills So-called Megaffin Bill," *Wichita Eagle*, May 2, 1999; Wes Johnson, "Priest Counters Tiller's Abortion Plan," *Hutchinson News*, January 21, 2000. The background on Carmody's concerns is in an April 22, 1998, letter from Carmody to the *Kansas City Star*, available from Kansans for Life in Topeka.

20. Steve Painter, "Mental Health Exception Is Abortion Debate's Flashpoint," *Wichita Eagle*, March 12, 2000.

21. Martin Hawver, "A Trend on the Doorsteps?" *Hawver's Capitol Report*, July 18, 2002.

22. Attorney General Opinion No. 2003-17, June 18, 2003, Attorney General Phill Kline and Assistant Attorney General Camille Nohe to State Senator Mark S. Gilstrap.

23. Internal Revenue Service, 990 forms for nonprofit organizations in Kansas, by ruling date; Steve Painter, "Group Challenges Law Requiring Sex Reporting," *Wichita Eagle*, October 8, 2003; Claude R. Marx, "Catholic Prelate to Lead Anti-Abortion Campaign," *Wichita Eagle*, January 19, 2002; Annie Calovich, "Stand for Values," *Wichita Eagle*, August 3, 2003; "Senator Leading Abortion Effort," *Salina Journal*, November 3, 2003; "Kline Pick Draws Criticism," *Lawrence Journal-World*, January 28, 2003; "Governor Vetoes Bill on Standards for Abortion Clinics," *Lawrence Journal-World*, April 22, 2003. Abortion statistics from the Guttmacher Institute and Kansas Department of Health.

24. Tom Meagher, "ACLU Leads KU Religion vs. State Debate," *Lawrence Journal-World*, February 16, 2000. The use of biblical language during interrogations became a central issue in *State of Kansas v. Artis Termain Cobb*, Court of Appeals cases 85,309 and 85,445, in 2002.

25. "Kline Says Marriage, Consent Laws in Danger," *Pittsburg Morning Sun*, September 16, 2003; "Court Upholds Harsher Sentence for Illegal Sex," *Newton Kansan*, January 30, 2004; "Kline Critical of Ruling," *Salina Journal*, November 19, 2003.

26. Debbie Schiffelbein, "News," *Garden City Telegram*, August 13, 2003; "Episcopal Church Approves Same-Sex Blessing Ceremonies," *Chanute Tribune*, August 8, 2003; "United Methodist Church Will Again Debate Homosexuality," *Hutchinson News*, April 7, 2003; "Pope Disapproves of Civil Unions," *Salina Journal*, December 29, 2003.

27. Abe Levy, "Defining the Moral Battle Line," *Wichita Eagle*, July 5, 2003; Dylan T. Lovan, "Presbyterians Retain Ban on Ordaining Noncelibate Gays," *Wichita Eagle*, February 23, 2002; "Church Opens Doors to Gays," *Lawrence Journal-World*, April 20, 2004; Sharon Montague, "Formidable Task," *Salina Journal*, March 14, 2005; "Churches Confront Gay Issue," *Hutchinson News*, March 15, 2004; "Position Statement of the Gove Methodist Church," *Hays Daily News*, June 22, 2003; Aaron Hastings Gilbreath, "'A Little Place Getting Smaller': The Depopulation and Social Spatialization of Gove County, Kansas" (master's thesis, University of Kansas, 2007).

28. "Readers Oppose Ban," *Manhattan Mercury*, February 29, 2004; "Time Our Nation Gave Gays Equal Protection," *Hays Daily News*, April 19, 2004.

29. "Bush Wants Marriage Amendment," *Wichita Eagle*, February 25, 2004; National Annenberg Election Survey, 2004, electronic data file, conducted by Princeton Survey Research Associates and Schulman, Ronca and Bucuvalas Inc., for the Annenberg School for Communication, University of Pennsylvania, as a rolling survey among approximately eighty-one thousand respondents nationally, including approximately nine hundred respondents in Kansas. The 39 percent in Kansas who strongly favored

a constitutional ban on gay marriage was only 4 percent higher than the national average, and was lower than the percentage in twenty other states.

30. Abe Levy, "Pastors Push for Marriage Amendment," *Wichita Eagle*, March 22, 2004; Abe Levy, "Gay Union Fight Not Over," *Wichita Eagle*, March 28, 2004; "Negotiators Agree on Ban on Gay Marriage, Civil Unions," *Pittsburg Morning Sun*, April 30, 2004; Dion Lefler, "Bid to Ban Gay Unions Resurfaces," *Wichita Eagle*, April 30, 2004; Abe Levy, "Gay Marriage Issue May Be Resurrected," *Wichita Eagle*, April 26, 2004.

31. Terry Fox and Joe Wright, "Same-Sex Ban Needed," *Wichita Eagle*, April 28, 2004.

32. Abe Levy, "Senate Okays Marriage Amendment," *Wichita Eagle*, May 2, 2004; Steve Painter and Abe Levy, "Effort to Ban Gay Marriage Falls Short," *Wichita Eagle*, May 5, 2004; Lori O'Toole Buselt, "Hot Issues, Heated Elections," *Wichita Eagle*, May 9, 2004.

33. The exit poll results are from 572 Kansas voters, of whom 30 percent were white born-again or evangelical Christians. See National Election Pool General Election Exit Polls, 2004, electronic data file. The results also showed that Senator Brownback won 83 percent of white evangelical votes and that 77 percent of white evangelical voters approved of the way that Bush was handling his job as president. Steve Painter, "New Issue Groups Are Successful in Swaying Outcomes," *Wichita Eagle*, August 5, 2004; John A. Dvorak, Jim Sullinger, and Diane Carroll, "Conservatives Win 24 of 35 Contested House Seats," *Kansas City Star*, August 5, 2004; Bud Norman, "Falwell Speaks on '04 Election," *Wichita Eagle*, September 24, 2004; Brad Cooper, "Falwell Urges Crowd to Get Involved," *Kansas City Star*, September 23, 2004; Roy Wenzl, "Preachers Take 'War' to Topeka," *Wichita Eagle*, November 7, 2004.

34. Abe Levy and Fred Mann, "Senate to Speed Up Gay Marriage Bill," *Wichita Eagle*, January 11, 2005; Tim Carpenter, "Issue Divides Ralliers," *Topeka Capital-Journal*, January 11, 2005; Chris Moon, "Supporters Take Floor," *Topeka Capital-Journal*, January 26, 2005; Chris Moon, "State Prepares for Ads on Gay Unions," *Topeka Capital-Journal*, February 3, 2005.

35. Lori O'Toole Buselt and Steve Painter, "Whirlwind Campaign," *Wichita Eagle*, March 30, 2005; Suzanne Perez Tobias, Joe Rodriguez, and Steve Painter, "Amendment Passes," *Wichita Eagle*, April 6, 2005; Janis Ropp, "Reader Views," *Wichita Eagle*, April 8, 2005.

36. Joe Rodriguez, "Christian Leaders Ponder Next Moves," *Wichita Eagle*, April 6, 2005; "Conservatives Seek to Shift Debate," *Salina Journal*, September 15, 2006.

37. Joe Rodriguez, "Service, Reception to Honor Central Christian's Joe Wright," *Wichita Eagle*, November 18, 2006; Joe Rodriguez, "He's Where He's Supposed to Be," *Wichita Eagle*, April 28, 2007.

38. Joe Rodriguez, "Deacons Offer Insight into Fox Resignation," *Wichita Eagle*, September 2, 2006; Joe Rodriguez, "Pastors Ax Their Radio Program," *Wichita Eagle*, September 28, 2006; Joe Rodriguez, "Fox's New Church Meets for First Time," *Wichita Eagle*, September 4, 2006; Bill

Wilson, "Terry Fox to Keep on Preaching at Park Site," *Wichita Eagle*, July 10, 2007.

39. Judy L. Thomas, "Lax Financial Oversight Riles Some Followers," *Kansas City Star*, March 11, 2007.

40. Morris's faith was amply described in her autobiography, Connie Morris, *From the Darkness: One Woman's Rise to Nobility* (Lafayette, LA: Huntington House, 2002). For other quotes and biographical information about the other board members, see the Kansas State Board of Education Web site (available at http://www.ksde.org) and news reports, including Tim Carpenter, "Republican Has Voice of Parent," *Lawrence Journal-World*, September 20, 1998; Lori Kurtzman, "Rundell Trails Morris," *Hutchinson News*, August 7, 2003; Scott Rochat, "Board Race a Rematch," *Emporia Gazette*, October 15, 2002; Mary Clarkin, "Willard and Anstine Vie for State Board Post," *Hutchinson News*, October 28, 2002; "Conservative Liberally Criticized," *Lawrence Journal-World*, September 15, 2003; "Moderates Worry Social Science Standards Are New Battleground," *Hays Daily News*, July 19, 2004. The moderates on the board in 2005 were Janet Waugh, Sue Gamble, Bill Wagnon, and Carol Rupe.

41. Interview with William Harris and Kathy Harris, conducted December 15, 2008; John Calvert, "Creationism vs. Evolution in Schools," *CNN Transcripts*, February 13, 2001; Josh Funk, "Designs for Change," *Wichita Eagle*, March 22, 2005.

42. Michael Strand, "Intelligent Design Ideas Rejected," *Salina Journal*, January 28, 2005.

43. John Hanna, "After Marriage Victory, Evolution an Issue for Some Clergy," *Hays Daily News*, February 6, 2005; Josh Funk, "Plans Take Shape," *Wichita Eagle*, February 10, 2005.

44. For a firsthand account of the meeting at the Derby Middle School, see Josh Funk, "Evolution Divides Public at Hearing," *Wichita Eagle*, February 11, 2005; John Richard Schrock, "Kansas Schools Getting Bum Rap on Evolution," *Wichita Eagle*, March 2, 2005. Calvert and Fox, quoted in Peter Slevin, "Battle on Teaching Evolution Sharpens," *Washington Post*, March 14, 2005.

45. Audio recordings of the Kansas State Board of Education are available at http://www.ksde.org. For additional descriptions and comments, see Josh Funk, "Board Gets a Taste of Evolution Debate," *Wichita Eagle*, April 14, 2005; Steve Painter, "Evolution's Defenders Will Testify," *Wichita Eagle*, April 20, 2005; George Diepenbrock, "Evolution vs. Creation," *Southwest Daily Times* (Liberal, KS), April 22, 2005; Jodi Wilgoren, "In Kansas, Darwinism Goes on Trial Once More," *New York Times*, May 6, 2005; Ron Bowell, "Local Comment," *Salina Journal*, November 17, 2005.

46. *Summary of Key Changes to Kansas Science Standards Adopted by the Kansas State Board of Education*, November 8, 2005, available at http://kansascience2005.com. For the board members' quotes, see Steve Painter, "The New Standard," *Wichita Eagle*, November 9, 2005.

47. Mirecki circulated an email to a Listserv group on November 19, 2005, in which he wrote about his forthcoming class on intelligent design, "The fundies want it all taught in a science class, but this will be a nice slap in their big fat face by teaching it as a religious studies class under the category 'mythology,'" and when this and other emails became public, conservative activist John Altevogt of the Kansas City area called on KU chancellor Robert Hemenway to fire Mirecki. See Chris Moon, "Religion E-Mails Called 'Vicious,'" *Topeka Capital-Journal*, December 1, 2005; Ron Knox and Eric Weslander, "Mirecki Hospitalized after Beating," *Lawrence Journal-World*, December 5, 2005; Amanda O'Toole, "Students Censure Those Who Beat Professor," *Wichita Eagle*, December 7, 2005; Dion Lefler, "KU Religion Professor Steps Aside," *Wichita Eagle*, December 8, 2005; "Judge Says Intelligent Design Is Unlawful," *Wichita Eagle*, December 21, 2005; Carl Manning, "Moderates Predict Changes in State Board of Education," *Hays Daily News*, August 9, 2006. For a description of the Dover case, see Kenneth R. Miller, *Only a Theory: Evolution and the Battle for America's Soul* (New York: Viking, 2008); Kenneth R. Miller, *Finding Darwin's God: A Scientist's Search for Common Ground between God and Evolution* (New York: Harper, 2007).

48. Interview, conducted July 17, 2007 (name withheld). More than two-dozen superintendants, principals, and teachers were asked to comment briefly about their views.

49. Extensive coverage appeared on national television, in newspapers, and on Web sites. For the most complete single story describing Tiller's death and the activities leading to it, see David Barstow, "An Abortion Battle, Fought to the Death," *New York Times*, July 26, 2009. Roeder was convicted of murder, and on April 1, 2010, was sentenced to life in prison without parole eligibility for fifty years.

50. Eugene H. Lee, personal communication, August 11, 2009; interview with James E. Taylor III, whose father worked for a number of years as Tiller's body guard, conducted June 15, 2009; interview with Rabbi Michael Davis, conducted October 15, 2009. Comments from former patients, supporters, and critics of Tiller were posted on numerous Web sites, including http://voices.kansascity.com, http://www.aheartbreakingchoice.com, http://jezebel.com, and http://inmedias.blogspot.com.

51. Interoffice Memorandum from Phill Kline to Bill Roche and Sylvia Chapman, "Church Efforts," August 8, 2006; "Pastors Pushing Tiller Case in the Kansas Legislature," *Newton Kansan*, March 16, 2007.

52. Kansas State Secretary of State, General Election Official Vote Totals, 2006, available at http://www.kssos.org. Koch Industries was the top donor to Heart PAC with a contribution of $10,000 in 2006; its contributions of $10,000 also made it the top donor in 2004 and 2008, as did contributions of $5,000 in 2000 and 2002. During the 2006 election cycle, Heart PAC spent more than $120,000, including $4,500 for Kansans for Life, $5,000 for Congressperson Ryun, and $5,000 for Congressperson Tiahrt; Tiahrt's campaign in turn donated $5,000 to Kansans for Life.

Koch affiliates contributed $10,000 to Kline's campaign. The financial information is from the Center for Responsive Politics (available at http://www.opensecrets.org) and the Kansas Governmental Ethics Commission (available at http://www.kssos.gov). A national exit poll in 2006 that included only eighty-one respondents in Kansas, of whom twenty-seven were white evangelicals, was too small for reliable results, but suggested that a majority of white evangelicals probably voted for Governor Sebelius and that approval of President Bush among white evangelicals had sunk to a bare majority, but that "values issues such as same sex marriage or abortion" were "extremely important" to white evangelicals in their votes for Congress. See National Election Pool General Election Exit Polls, 2006, electronic data file. In the 2004 National Annenberg Election Survey, the responses in Kansas were divided, just as they were toward same-sex marriage: 40 percent said they strongly favored banning late-term abortions, while 36 percent were strongly opposed; the percentage strongly in favor was only 2 percentage points higher than the national average and was lower than the percentage in twenty-one other states.

53. Martha Burk, "What's Up with Kansas?" *Ms. Magazine*, Spring 2007; Joseph Wright, "Reducing Abortion in Kansas: Expanding Jobs and Health Insurance for Families and Opportunities for Children," Catholics United for the Common Good, May 2007; "IRS Probes Kansas Church's Political Activity," Associated Press, August 18, 2007.

54. Information from the Catholic Diocese of Wichita, Operation Rescue, Kansas Coalition for Life, and Kansans for Life Web sites; Barstow, "An Abortion Battle, Fought to the Death."

55. Kristen Luker, *Abortion and the Politics of Motherhood* (Berkeley: University of California Press, 1985).

56. Art Gentry, "It's Time for Truth," *Wichita Eagle*, November 5, 2006; "Coerced Abortions at Kansas Abortion Clinic," available at http://www.tldm.org.

57. Interviews, conducted January 14, 2009; January 29, 2009; March 10, 2009 (names withheld).

58. Interview, conducted July 25, 2009 (name withheld); comments posted on the day of Tiller's murder, available at http://www.freerepublic.com.

59. Interview, conducted August 4, 2009 (name withheld).

60. Interviews, conducted February 25, 2009; February 7, 2008; February 5, 2009 (names withheld).

61. Jackson was introduced in chapter 5; interview, conducted July 3, 2008 (pseudonym used).

62. Interview, conducted July 27, 2009 (quoted with permission).

63. President William Jefferson Clinton, "Inaugural Dole Lecture," May 21, 2004, transcript, KU University Relations, Lawrence.

64. Sebelius was tapped by President Obama to become the U.S. secretary of health and human services, and assumed that office on April 28, 2009, whereupon she played a central role in the administration's successful

efforts to pass comprehensive health reform legislation. She was succeeded as governor by Lieutenant Governor Mark Parkinson, a Republican member of the Kansas House of Representatives before switching parties to join the Sebelius ticket in 2006. The enduring strength of the Republican Party in Kansas was evident in the 2010 midterm elections, in which conservative Senator Moran was reelected by a 70 to 26 percent margin, all four of the state's Republican candidates for the U.S. House of Representatives won, and conservative Senator Brownback was elected governor by a 63 to 32 percent margin.

65. United Methodist Church of the Resurrection, information packet for visitors and prospective members, and interviews with staff and members.

66. Ibid.

67. Interviews, conducted October 29, 2007; November 2, 2007 (names withheld).

68. Interview, conducted January 6, 2009 (quoted with permission).

Epilogue

1. For an expression of the criticism that the Religious Right was undermining the state's economic well-being, see Thomas Frank, *What's the Matter with Kansas? How Conservatives Won the Heart of America* (New York: Metropolitan Books, 2004). The study that partly refuted this criticism examined the issues nationally that influenced voting in the 2004 election. See Larry M. Bartels, "What's the Matter with *What's the Matter with Kansas*," *Quarterly Journal of Political Science* 1 (2006): 201–26. See also Larry M. Bartels, *Unequal Democracy: The Political Economy of the New Guilded Age* (New York: Russell Sage Foundation, 2008), 83–97.

SELECTED BIBLIOGRAPHY

Ackerman, Paul, and Bob Williams. *Kansas Tornado: 1999 Science Curriculum Standards Battle.* El Cajon, CA: Institute for Creation Research, 1999.

Adams, Franklin G. "Reminiscences of Franklin G. Adams." *Transactions of the Kansas State Historical Society* (1902): 539–43.

Allport, Gordon W. *The Individual and His Religion.* New York: McMillan, 1950.

Ambrose, Stephen E. *To America: Personal Reflections of an Historian.* New York: Simon and Schuster, 2002.

Ammerman, Nancy Tatom. *Baptist Battles: Social Change and Religious Conflict in the Southern Baptist Convention.* New Brunswick, NJ: Rutgers University Press, 1990.

Argersinger, Peter H. "No Rights on This Floor: Third Parties and the Institutionalization of Congress." *Journal of Interdisciplinary History* 22 (1992): 655–90.

———. "Pentecostal Politics in Kansas: Religion, the Farmers' Alliance, and the Gospel of Populism." *Kansas Quarterly* 1 (1981): 24–35.

———. *Populism and Politics: William Alfred Peffer and the People's Party.* Lexington: University Press of Kentucky, 1974.

Athans, Mary Christine. "A New Perspective on Father Charles E. Coughlin." *Church History* 56 (1987): 224–35.

Ayers, Carol Dark. *Lincoln and Kansas: Partnership for Freedom.* Topeka: Sunflower Press, 2001.

Bachmura, Frank T. "The Manpower Development and Training Act of 1962: Its Significance for Rural Areas." *Journal of Farm Economics* 45 (1963): 61–72.

Bader, Robert Smith. *Hayseeds, Moralizers, and Methodists: The Twentieth-Century Image of Kansas.* Lawrence: University Press of Kansas, 1988.

———. *Prohibition in Kansas: A History.* Lawrence: University Press of Kansas, 1986.

Bailey, Beth. *Sex in the Heartland.* Cambridge, MA: Harvard University Press, 1999.

Baker, David, James Youniss, and Maryellen Schaub. *System for Catholic Research, Information, and Planning.* Washington, DC: Catholic University of America, Life Cycle Institute, 1990.

Ballard, David E. "The First State Legislature." In *Collections of the Kansas State Historical Society*, 232–37. Topeka: Kansas State Historical Society, 1908.

Barker, Roger G. "Recollections of the Midwest Psychological Field Station." *Environment and Behavior* 22 (1990): 503–13.

Barker, Roger G., and Herbert F. Wright. *Midwest and Its Children: The Psychological Ecology of an American Town.* London: Row, Peterson and Company, 1954.

Barry, John M. *The Great Influenza: The Epic Story of the Deadliest Plague in History.* New York: Penguin, 2005.

Bartels, Larry M. *Unequal Democracy: The Political Economy of the New Guilded Age.* New York: Russell Sage Foundation, 2008.

———. "What's the Matter with *What's the Matter with Kansas.*" *Quarterly Journal of Political Science* 1 (2006): 201–26.

Basler, Roy P., ed. *Collected Works of Abraham Lincoln.* Springfield, IL: Abraham Lincoln Association, 1953.

Bauer, Jerald C. *Protestantism in America: A Narrative History.* Philadelphia: Westminster Press, 1965.

Bay, W.V.N. *Reminiscences of the Bench and Bar of Missouri.* Saint Louis: F. H. Thomas and Company, 1878.

Beatty, Bob. "'Be Willing to Take Some Risks to Make Things Happen': A Conversation with Former Governor John W. Carlin." *Kansas History* 31 (2008): 114–40.

———. "'You Have to Like People': A Conversation with Former Governor William H. Avery." *Kansas History* 31 (2008): 48–67.

Beckman, Peter. *Kansas Monks: A History of St. Benedict's Abbey.* Atchison: Abbey Student Press, 1941.

Bell, Earl H. *Culture of a Contemporary Rural Community: Sublette, Kansas.* Washington, DC: U.S. Department of Agriculture, Bureau of Agricultural Economics, Rural Life Studies, 1942.

Berger, James. *After the End: Representations of Post-Apocalypse.* Minneapolis: University of Minnesota Press, 1999.

Berger, Peter L., and Richard John Neuhaus. *To Empower People: From State to Civil Society.* Washington, DC: AEI Press, 1996.

Besse, H. T. *Church History.* San Jose: Besse Publishing, 1908.

Binder, Amy. *Contentious Curricula: Afrocentrism and Creationism in American Public Schools.* Princeton, NJ: Princeton University Press, 2004.

Blackmar, Frank W. *Higher Education in Kansas.* Washington, DC: Government Printing Office, 1900.

———. *Kansas: A Cyclopedia of State History.* Chicago: Standard Publishing Company, 1912.

Blevins, Michael F. "Remembering Lucinda Todd: The Initiating Plaintiff in *Brown v. Board of Education of Topeka,* May 17, 1954." *Brown Quarterly* 6 (2004). Available at http://brownvboard.org.

Bloomenshine, Lee L. *Prairie around Me: Childhood Memories.* San Diego: Raphael Publications, 1972.

Boggs, John, and J. B. McCleery. *Personal Recollections of Pardee Butler.* Cincinnati: Standard Publishing Company, 1889.

Bollig, Richard Joseph. *History of Catholic Education in Kansas, 1836–1932*. Washington, DC: Catholic University of America, 1933.

Boyles, Denis. *Superior, Nebraska: The Common-Sense Values of America's Heartland*. New York: Random House, 2008.

Bradley, Gerard V. "The Blaine Amendment of 1876: Harbinger of Secularism." *Notre Dame Legal Studies Paper No. 07–02* (January 30, 2007).

Bradley, M. B., Norman M. Green Jr., Dale E. Jones, Mac Lynn, and Lou McNeil. *Churches and Church Membership in the United States*. Washington, DC: Glenmary Research Center, 1992.

Brennan, Mary C. *Turning Right in the Sixties: The Conservative Capture of the GOP*. Chapel Hill: University of North Carolina Press, 1995.

Brinkerhoff, Fred W. "Address of the President: The Kansas Tour of Lincoln the Candidate." *Kansas Historical Quarterly* 8 (February 1945), 294–307.

Brinkley, Alan. *Voices of Protest: Huey Long, Father Coughlin, and the Great Depression*. New York: Knopf, 1982.

Brock, Pope. *Charlatan: America's Most Dangerous Huckster, the Man Who Pursued Him, and the Age of Flimflam*. New York: Crown, 2008.

Brown, Dee. *Wondrous Times on the Frontier*. New York: August House, 1991.

Brown, Ruth Murray. *For a "Christian America": A History of the Religious Right*. New York: Prometheus Books, 2002.

Bryan, William Jennings. *The First Battle: A Story of the Campaign of 1896*. Chicago: W. B. Conkey, 1898.

Bulkley, Rebekah W. Pomeroy. *Memoir of Mrs. Lucy Gaylord Pomeroy*. New York: John W. Amerman, 1865.

Butler, Thomas Ambrose. *The State of Kansas and Irish Immigration*. Dublin: Dublin University Press, 1871.

Caldwell, Martha B. "When Horace Greeley Visited Kansas in 1859." *Kansas Historical Quarterly* 9 (1940): 115–40.

Callahan, Gerald N. *Infection: The Uninvited Universe*. New York: Touchstone, 2006.

Capper, Arthur. *Addresses and Messages*. Topeka: Capper Printing Company, 1921.

Carson, Gerald. *The Roguish World of Doctor Brinkley*. New York: Holt, Rinehart and Winston, 1960.

Chalfant, Harry M. "The Anti-Saloon League—Why and What?" *Annals of the American Academy of Political and Social Science* 109 (1923): 279–83.

Cigler, Allan J., Mark Joslyn, and Burdett A. Loomis. "The Kansas Christian Right and the Evolution of Republican Politics." In *The Christian Right in American Politics: Marching to the Millennium*, ed. John C. Green, Mark J. Rozell, and Clyde Wilcox, 145–66. Washington, DC: Georgetown University Press, 2003.

Clanton, O. Gene. *A Common Humanity: Kansas Populism and the Battle for Justice and Equality, 1854–1903*. Manhattan, KS: Sunflower University Press, 2004.

Clarke, Thurston. *The Last Campaign: Robert F. Kennedy and 82 Days that Inspired America.* New York: Macmillan, 2008.

Clubb, Jerome M., William H. Flanigan, and Nancy H. Zingale. *Electoral Data for Counties in the United States, 1840 to 1972.* Ann Arbor: Inter-University Consortium for Political and Social Research, University of Michigan, 1986.

———. *Electoral Data for Counties in the United States: Presidential and Congressional Races, 1974–1976.* Ann Arbor: Inter-University Consortium for Political and Social Research, University of Michigan, 1986.

Clugston, W. G. *Rascals in Democracy.* New York: Richard R. Smith, 1940.

Coke, Thomas, and Francis Asbury. *The Doctrines and Discipline of the Methodist Episcopal Church in America with Explanatory Notes.* Philadelphia: Henry Tuckniss, 1798.

Colvin, Judy, Connie Redford, Jeannine Bryan, and Art Hays. *History of First Baptist Church, Burden, Kansas, 1885 to 2009.* Burden: First Baptist Church, 2009.

Connelley, William E. *A Standard History of Kansas and Kansans.* Chicago: Lewis Publishing Company, 1918.

Cowgill, Donald O. "The Ecology of Religious Preference in Wichita." *Sociological Quarterly* 1 (1960): 87–96.

Crawford, Vicki L., Jacqueline Anne Rouse, and Barbara Woods, eds. *Women in the Civil Rights Movement: Trailblazers and Torchbearers, 1941–1965.* Indianapolis: Indiana University Press, 1993.

Cutler, William G. *History of the State of Kansas.* Chicago: A. T. Andreas, 1883.

Dassler, Charles Frederick William. *Compiled Laws of Kansas.* Topeka: Geo. W. Crane, 1885.

Davis, Kenneth S. *FDR into the Storm, 1937–1940: A History.* New York: Random House, 1993.

———. *Kansas: A Bicentennial History.* New York: W. W. Norton, 1976.

———. *Soldier of Democracy: A Biography of Dwight Eisenhower.* Garden City, NY: Doubleday, Doran and Company, 1945.

———. *The Years of the Pilgrimage.* Garden City, NY: Doubleday, 1948.

Dean, Virgil W. "Another Wichita Seditionist? Elmer J. Garner and the Radical Right's Opposition to World War II." *Kansas History* 17 (1994): 50–64.

———. "Seeking 'Realism and a Little Rationality' in Government: The Observations of Former Governor Robert F. Bennett." *Kansas History* 31 (2008), 104–13.

Debate between Samuel Gompers and Henry J. Allen at Carnegie Hall, New York, May 28, 1920. New York: E. P. Dutton, 1920.

Desmond, Humphrey J. *The A.P.A. Movement.* Washington, DC: New Century Press, 1912.

Dick, Everett. *The Sod-House Frontier, 1854–1890: A Social History of the Northern Plains from the Creation of Kansas and Nebraska to the Admission of the Dakotas.* Lincoln: University of Nebraska Press, 1989.

Dolbeare, Kenneth M., and Phillip E. Hammond. *The School Prayer Decisions: From Court Policy to Local Practice*. Chicago: University of Chicago Press, 1971.

Dolbee, Cora. "The Fourth of July in Early Kansas, 1858–1861." *Kansas Historical Quarterly* 11 (1942): 130–73.

Douglass, H. Paul. *How Shall Country Youth Be Served?* New York: George H. Doran, 1925.

Drury, James W. *The Government of Kansas*. Lawrence: University of Kansas Press, 1961.

DuBois, W.E.B. "The Republicans and the Black Voter." *Nation*, June 5, 1920, 757–58.

Dudziak, Mary L. "The Limits of Good Faith: Desegregation in Topeka, Kansas, 1950–1956." *Law and History Review* 5 (1987): 351–91.

Dykstra, C. A. "The Reorganization of State Government in Kansas." *American Political Science Review* 9 (1915): 264–72.

Egan, Timothy. *The Worst Hard Time: The Untold Story of Those Who Survived the Great American Dust Bowl*. New York: Houghton Mifflin, 2006.

Eick, Gretchen Cassel. *Dissent in Wichita: The Civil Rights Movement in the Midwest, 1954–72*. Urbana: University of Illinois Press, 2001.

Ellis County Historical Society. *At Home in Ellis County, Kansas, 1867–1992*. Dallas: Taylor Publishing Company, 1991.

Fankhauser, Craig Charles. "The Heritage of Faith: An Historical Evaluation of the Holiness Movement in America." Master's thesis, Pittsburg State University, 1983.

Farrell, F. D. "Kansas Rural Institutions: V. Three Effective Rural Churches." *Agricultural Experiment Station Circular* (June 1949): 1–36.

Fearon, Peter. *Kansas in the Great Depression: Work Relief, the Dole, and Rehabilitation*. Columbia: University of Missouri Press, 2007.

Ferrell, Robert H. *Truman and Pendergast*. Columbia: University of Missouri Press, 1999.

Finke, Roger, and Rodney Stark. *The Churching of America, 1776–2005: Winners and Losers in Our Religious Economy*. New Brunswick, NJ: Rutgers University Press, 2005.

Fitzgerald, Daniel C. *Ghost Towns of Kansas*. Lawrence: University Press of Kansas, 1988.

Fleming-Rife, Anita, and Jennifer M. Proffitt. "The More Public School Reform Changes, the More It Stays the Same: A Framing Analysis of the Newspaper Coverage of *Brown v. Board of Education*." *Journal of Negro Education* 73 (2004): 239–54.

Fowler, Gene, and Bill Crawford. *Border Radio*. Austin: Texas Monthly Press, 1987.

Frank, Thomas. *What's the Matter with Kansas? How Conservatives Won the Heart of America*. New York: Metropolitan Books, 2004.

Frederick, Marla F. *Between Sundays: Black Women and Everyday Struggles of Faith*. Berkeley: University of California Press, 2003.

Gagliardo, Domenico. *The Kansas Industrial Court: An Experiment in Compulsory Arbitration*. Lawrence: University of Kansas Press, 1941.

Gall, Gilbert J. *The Politics of Right to Work: The Labor Federations as Special Interests, 1943–1979*. New York: Greenwood Press, 1988.

Gates, Paul Wallace. *Fifty Million Acres: Conflicts over Kansas Land Policy, 1854–1890*. Ithaca, NY: Cornell University Press, 1954.

Geer, Blanche. "First Days in the Field." In *Sociologists at Work: The Craft of Social Research*, ed. Phillip E. Hammond, 372–98. Garden City, NY: Doubleday, 1964.

Geniesse, Jane Fletcher. *American Priestess: The Extraordinary Story of Anna Spafford and the American Colony in Jerusalem*. New York: Doubleday, 2008.

George, Alice L. *Awaiting Armageddon: How Americans Faced the Cuban Missile Crisis*. Chapel Hill: University of North Carolina Press, 2003.

Gilbreath, Aaron Hastings. "'A Little Place Getting Smaller': The Depopulation and Social Spatialization of Gove County, Kansas." Master's thesis, University of Kansas, 2007.

Ginsburg, Faye D. *Contested Lives: The Abortion Debate in an American Community*. Berkeley: University of California Press, 1989.

Gleed, Charles S. "The First Kansas Railway." *Transactions of the Kansas State Historical Society* (1900): 357–58.

Glock, Charles Y., and Rodney Stark. *Christian Beliefs and Anti-Semitism*. New York: Harper and Row, 1966.

Goldberg, David J. "Unmasking the Ku Klux Klan: The Northern Movement against the KKK, 1920–1925." *Journal of American Ethnic History* 15 (1996): 32–48.

Goldberg, Michael Lewis. "'An Army of Women': Gender Relations and Politics in Kansas Populism, the Woman Movement, and the Republican Party, 1879–1896." PhD diss., Yale University, 1992.

Goldberg, Robert Alan. *Barry Goldwater*. New Haven, CT: Yale University Press, 1997.

Goodwynn, Lawrence. *The Populist Movement: A Short History of the Agrarian Revolt in America*. New York: Oxford University Press, 1978.

Goss, Glenn R. *The Scofield Bible and C. I. Scofield*. Philadelphia: Philadelphia College of Bible, 1992.

Graber, Mark A. *Rethinking Abortion: Equal Choice, the Constitution, and Reproductive Politics*. Princeton, NJ: Princeton University Press, 1999.

Graham, A. A. *History of Fairfield and Perry Counties*. Chicago: W. H. Beers and Company, 1883.

Greeley, Andrew M. *The American Catholic: A Social Portrait*. New York: Basic Books, 1977.

Greeley, Andrew M., and Michael Hout. *The Truth about Conservative Christians: What They Think and What They Believe*. Chicago: University of Chicago Press, 2006.

Greeley, Andrew M., William C. McCready, and Kathleen McCourt. *Catholic Schools in a Declining Church*. Chicago: Sheed and Ward, 1976.

Greeley, Horace. *Overland Journey from New York to San Francisco*. New York: C. M. Saxton, Barker and Company, 1860.

———. *Recollections of a Busy Life*. New York: J. B. Ford and Company, 1869.

Greene, Jeffrey, and Karen Moline. *The Bird Flu Pandemic: Can It Happen?* New York: St. Martin's Press, 2006.

Gregory, Chad. "Sam Jones: Masculine Prophet of God." *Georgia Historical Quarterly* 86 (2002): 231–52.

Gross, Daniel. *Bull Run: Wall Street, the Democrats, and the New Politics of Personal Finance*. New York: Public Affairs, 2000.

Grupp, Fred W., Jr., and William M. Newman. "Political Ideology and Religious Preference: The John Birch Society and the Americans for Democratic Action." *Journal for the Scientific Study of Religion* 12 (1973): 401–13.

Gunther, John. *Eisenhower: The Man and the Symbol*. New York: Harper and Brothers, 1952.

Hadden, Jeffrey K. *The Gathering Storm in the Churches: The Widening Gap between Clergy and Laymen*. Garden City, NY: Doubleday, 1969.

Hamilton, Adam. *Seeing Gray in a World of Black and White*. Nashville: Abingdon Press, 2008.

Hammond, Phillip E. *Campus Clergymen*. New York: Basic Books, 1966.

Hangen, Tona J. *Redeeming the Dial: Radio, Religion, and Popular Culture in America*. Raleigh: University of North Carolina Press, 2002.

Hanrahan, Renee M. *Magdalen Parish Survey: Final Report*. Wichita: Church of the Magdalen, 2007.

Harder, Marvin, and Carolyn Rampey. *The Kansas Legislature: Procedures, Personalities, and Problems*. Lawrence: University Press of Kansas, 1972.

Hatfield, Mark O., ed. *Vice Presidents of the United States, 1789–1993*. Washington, DC: Government Printing Office, 1997.

Haworth, Jason Theodore. "Anti-Semitism and Kansas Populism." Master's thesis, University of Missouri at Kansas City, 2006.

Henderson, Caroline. *Letters from the Dust Bowl*. Edited by Alvin O. Turner. Norman: University of Oklahoma Press, 2001.

Henshaw, Stanley K., and Kathryn Kost. *Trends in the Characteristics of Women Obtaining Abortions, 1974 to 2004*. New York: Guttmacher Institute, 2008.

Herberg, Will. *Protestant-Catholic-Jew: An Essay in American Religious Sociology*. New York: Doubleday, 1955.

Hicks, John D. *The Populist Revolt: A History of the Farmers' Alliance and the People's Party*. Lincoln, NE: Bison, 1970.

Hiebert, Clarence. *The Holdeman People: The Church of God in Christ, Mennonite, 1859–1969*. South Pasadena, CA: William Carey Library, 1973.

Hoig, Stan. *Cowtown Wichita and the Wild, Wicked West*. Albuquerque: University of New Mexico Press, 2007.

Hollowell, Louise, and Martin C. Lehfeldt. *The Sacred Call: A Tribute to Donald L. Hollowell, Civil Rights Champion*. New York: Four-G Publishers, 1997.

Holmes, William. "Whitecapping: Anti-Semitism in the Populist Era." *American Jewish Historical Quarterly* 63 (1974): 244–61.

Holt, Arthur E. "Religion." *American Journal of Sociology* 34 (1928): 172–76.

Holter, Don W. *Fire on the Prairie: Methodism in the History of Kansas*. Topeka: Kansas State Historical Society, 1969.

Hoover, Herbert. *The Memoirs of Herbert Hoover, Vol. II: The Cabinet and the Presidency, 1920–1933*. New York: Macmillan, 1952.

Hope, Clifford R., Jr. *Quiet Courage: Kansas Congressman Clifford R. Hope*. Manhattan, KS: Sunflower University Press, 1997.

Hough, Franklin B. *American Constitutions: Comprising the Constitution of Each State in the Union and of the United States*. Albany: Weed, Parsons and Company, 1872.

Hout, Michael, Andrew M. Greeley, and Melissa J. Wilde. "The Demographic Imperative in Religious Change in the United States." *American Journal of Sociology* 107 (2001): 468–500.

Howe, E. W. *Plain People*. New York: Dodd, Mead and Company, 1929.

Humphrey, James. "The Administration of George W. Glick." *Transactions of the Kansas State Historical Society* 9 (1906): 395–413.

Hurt, Douglas. *The Great Plains during World War II*. Lincoln: University of Nebraska Press, 2008.

Huxman, Walter A., Arthur J. Mellott, and Delman C. Hill. "The Topeka, Kansas Case Decision." *Journal of Negro Education* 21 (1952): 522–27.

Ingalls, John James. *Essays, Addresses, and Orations*. Kansas City, MO: Hudson Kimberly, 1902.

Ingalls, Sheffield. *History of Atchison County, Kansas*. Lawrence: Standard Publishing Company, 1916.

Jacobsen, Douglas, ed. *A Reader in Pentecostal Theology: Voices from the First Generation*. Bloomington: Indiana University Press, 2006.

Jarboe, Mary Ritchie. *John Ritchie: Portrait of an Uncommon Man*. Topeka: Shawnee County Historical Society, 1991.

Johnson, Daniel Thomas. *History and Backgrounds of Manhattan Bible College*. Manhattan, KS: Manhattan Christian College, 2002.

Johnson, Douglas. *Amalgam Survey—Churches and Society*. Chicago: University of Chicago, National Opinion Research Center, 1968.

Jones, Dale E., Sherry Doty, Clifford Grammich, James E. Horsch, Richard Houseal, John P. Marcum, Kenneth M. Sanchagrin, and Richard H. Taylor. *Religious Congregations and Membership in the United States, 2000: An Enumeration by Region, State, and County Based on Data Reported for 149 Religious Bodies*. Nashville, TN: Glenmary Research Center, 2002.

Juhnke, James C. "Mob Violence and Kansas Mennonites in 1918." *Kansas Historical Quarterly* 43 (1977): 334–50.

Junker, Patricia, ed. *John Steuart Curry: Inventing the Middle West.* New York: Hudson Hills Press, 1998.

Kansas Board of Agriculture. *Fourth Annual Report of the Kansas Board of Agriculture.* Topeka: Kansas Board of Agriculture, 1875.

Kelley, Dean M. *Why Conservative Churches Are Growing: A Study in Sociology of Religion.* Macon, GA: Mercer University Press, 1986.

Kendall, Sue. *Rethinking Regionalism: John Steuart Curry and the Kansas Mural Controversy.* Washington, DC: Smithsonian Institution Press, 1986.

Kinnane, Mary. "The History of Station KFKU, 1923–1954." Master's thesis, University of Kansas, 1954.

Kline, Ronald R. *Consumers in the Country: Technology and Social Change in Rural America.* Baltimore: Johns Hopkins University Press, 2000.

Kline, Ronald R., and Trevor Pinch. "Users as Agents of Technological Change: The Social Construction of the Automobile in the Rural United States." *Technology and Culture* 37 (1996): 763–95.

Kluger, Richard. *Simple Justice: The History of* Brown v. Board of Education *and Black America's Struggle for Equality.* New York: Vintage Books, 1977.

Koeppen, Sheilah R. "The Republican Radical Right." *Annals of the American Academy of Political and Social Science* 382 (1969): 73–82.

Krehbiel, Todd. *Final Report and Recommendations Based on Observations Made at Sedgwick County General Election Polling Sites.* Wichita: Sedgwick County Voter Coalition, 2007.

Langley, Isom P. "Religion in the Alliance." In *The Farmers' Alliance History and Agricultural Digest,* ed. Nelson A. Dunning, 313–17. Washington, DC: Alliance Publishing Company, 1891.

Langsdorf, Edgar. "S. C. Pomeroy and the New England Emigrant Aid Company, 1854–1858." *Kansas Historical Quarterly* 7 (1938): 227–45.

Lee, R. Alton. *The Bizarre Careers of John R. Brinkley.* Louisville: University Press of Kentucky, 2002.

———. "[Not] a Thin Dime: Kansas Relief Politics in the Campaign of 1936." *Historian* 67 (2005): 474–88.

Leftwich, William M. *Martyrdom in Missouri: A History of Religious Proscription, the Seizure of Churches, and the Persecution of Ministers of the Gospel in the State of Missouri during the Late Civil War and under the "Test Oath" of the New Constitution.* Saint Louis: Southwestern Book and Publishing Company, 1870.

Lewis, Jim L. "'Beautiful Bismarck'—Bismarck Grove, Lawrence, 1878–1900." *Kansas Historical Quarterly* 35 (1969): 225–56.

Lewis, Sinclair. *Elmer Gantry.* New York: Harcourt and Brace, 1927.

Liebman, Robert C., John Sutton, and Robert Wuthnow. "Exploring the Social Sources of Denominationalism: Schisms in American Protestant Denominations, 1890–1980." *American Sociological Review* 53 (1988): 343–52.

Lindquist, Emory. "The Swedish Immigrant and Life in Kansas." *Kansas Historical Quarterly* 29 (1963): 1–24.

Lindsay, D. Michael. *Faith in the Halls of Power: How Evangelicals Joined the American Elite*. New York: Oxford University Press, 2007.

Lipset, Seymour Martin, and Earl Raab. *The Politics of Unreason: Right-wing Extremism in America, 1790–1790*. New York: Harper and Row, 1970.

Lora, Ronald, and William Henry Longton. *The Conservative Press in Twentieth-Century America*. New York: Greenwood, 1999.

Lowenthal, Kristi. "Conservative Thought and the Equal Rights Amendment in Kansas." PhD diss., Kansas State University, 2008.

Luker, Kristen. *Abortion and the Politics of Motherhood*. Berkeley: University of California Press, 1985.

Lynd, Robert S., and Helen Merrell Lynd. *Middletown: A Study in Modern American Culture*. New York: Harcourt Brace Jovanovich, 1929.

——. *Middletown in Transition: A Study in Cultural Conflicts*. New York: Harcourt and Brace, 1937.

Marsden, George M. *Fundamentalism and American Culture: The Shaping of Twentieth-Century Evangelicalism, 1870–1925*. New York: Oxford University Press, 1980.

Marsh, Charles. *The Beloved Community: How Faith Shapes Social Justice, from the Civil Rights Movement to Today*. New York: Basic Books, 2004.

——. *God's Long Summer: Stories of Faith and Civil Rights*. Princeton, NJ: Princeton University Press, 1997.

Martin, John A. *The Wyandotte Convention: An Address*. Atchison: Haskell and Son, 1882.

Martin, William. *With God on Our Side: The Rise of the Religious Right in America*. New York: Broadway Books, 1996.

Mayer, Jane. "Covert Operations." *New Yorker* (August 30, 2010), online.

McCoy, Donald R. *Landon of Kansas*. Lincoln: University of Nebraska Press, 1966.

McCusker, Kristine M. "'The Forgotten Years' of America's Civil Rights Movement: Wartime Protests at the University of Kansas, 1939–1945." *Kansas History* 17 (1994): 26–37.

McGirr, Lisa. *Suburban Warriors: The Origins of the New American Right*. Princeton, NJ: Princeton University Press, 2001.

McMath, Robert C. *American Populism: A Social History, 1877–1898*. New York: Hill and Wang, 1990.

McRoberts, Omar M. *Streets of Glory: Church and Community in a Black Urban Neighborhood*. Chicago: University of Chicago Press, 2003.

McVeigh, Rory. "Power Devaluation, the Ku Klux Klan, and the Democratic National Convention of 1924." *Sociological Forum* 16 (2001): 1–30.

Mechem, Kirke, ed. *The Annals of Kansas, 1886–1925*. Topeka: Kansas Historical Society, 1956.

Melton, J. Gordon. *Encyclopedia of American Religions*. Detroit: Gale, 2009.

Miller, Kenneth R. *Finding Darwin's God: A Scientist's Search for Common Ground between God and Evolution.* New York: Harper, 2007.

——. *Only a Theory: Evolution and the Battle for America's Soul.* New York: Viking, 2008.

Miller, W. H. *The History of Kansas City.* Kansas City: Birdsall and Miller, 1881.

Miller, Worth Robert. "A Centennial Historiography of American Populism." *Kansas History* 16 (1993): 54–69.

Miner, Craig. *Kansas: The History of the Sunflower State, 1854–2000.* Lawrence: University Press of Kansas, 2002.

Minnix, Kathleen. *Laughter in the Amen Corner: The Life of Evangelist Sam Jones.* Athens: University of Georgia Press, 1993.

Mock, C. J. "Drought and Precipitation Fluctuations during the Late Nineteenth Century." *Great Plains Research* 1 (1991): 26–57.

Monhollon, Rusty L. *This Is America? The Sixties in Lawrence, Kansas.* New York: Palgrave Macmillan, 2004.

Montgomery, Rick, and Shirl Kasper. *Kansas City: An American Story.* Kansas City, KS: Kansas City Star Books, 2007.

Moore, Elizabeth. *Maternity and Infant Care in a Rural County in Kansas.* Washington, DC: U.S. Department of Labor Children's Bureau, 1917.

Moore, Powell. "A Hoosier in Kansas: The Diary of Hiram H. Young, 1886–1895: Pioneer of Cloud County, Part Two, 1890–1891." *Kansas Historical Quarterly* 14 (1946): 297–352.

Morgan, Perl W. *History of Wyandotte County, Kansas.* Chicago: Lewis Publishing Company, 1911.

Morris, Aldon D. *The Origins of the Civil Rights Movement: Black Communities Organizing for Change.* New York: Free Press, 1986.

Morris, Connie. *From the Darkness: One Woman's Rise to Nobility.* Lafayette, LA: Huntington House, 2002.

Morris, Edmund. *Dutch: A Memoir of Ronald Reagan.* New York: Modern Library, 2000.

Murphy, E. E. "Is Rainfall in Kansas Increasing?" *Transactions of the Annual Meetings of the Kansas Academy of Science* 13 (1891): 16–19.

Murphy, John R. *Memoir of Rev. James M. Challiss.* Philadelphia: Jas. S. Rodgers, 1870.

Myers, Edward H. *The Disruption of the Methodist Episcopal Church, 1844–1846.* Nashville: J. W. Burke and Company, 1875.

National Council of Churches. *Churches and Church Membership in the United States: An Enumeration and Analysis by Counties, States, and Regions.* New York: National Council of Churches, 1956.

Nelson, Timothy. *Every Time I Feel the Spirit: Religious Experience and Ritual in an African American Church.* New York: New York University Press, 2004.

Niebuhr, H. Richard. *The Social Sources of Denominationalism.* New York: Meridian Books, 1929.

Office of the Attorney General. *Biennial Report to the Governor.* Topeka: Office of the Attorney General, 1886.

Ogburn, William F., and Nell Snow Talbot. "A Measurement of the Factors in the Presidential Election of 1928." *Social Forces* 8 (1929): 175–83.

Ohle, David, Roger Martin, and Susan Brosseau. *Cows Are Freaky When They Look at You: An Oral History of the Kaw Valley Hemp Pickers.* Wichita: Watermark Press, 1991.

Oliva, Leo E. "Kansas: A Hard Land in the Heartland." In *Heartland: Comparative Histories of the Midwestern States,* ed. James H. Madison, 248–75. Bloomington: Indiana University Press, 1988.

Ostler, Jeffrey. *Prairie Populism: The Fate of Agrarian Radicalism in Kansas, Nebraska, and Iowa, 1880–1892.* Lawrence: University Press of Kansas, 1993.

Paddock, Joel. "Democratic Politics in a Republican State: The Gubernatorial Campaigns of Robert Docking, 1966–1972." *Kansas History* 17 (1994): 108–23.

Painter, Nell Irvin. *Exodusters: Black Migration to Kansas after Reconstruction.* New York: W. W. Norton, 1992.

Patterson, James T. Brown v. Board of Education: *A Civil Rights Milestone and Its Troubled Legacy.* New York: Oxford University Press, 2001.

Peffer, William Alfred. *The Farmer's Side: His Troubles and Their Remedy.* New York: D. Appleton and Company, 1891.

———. *Myriorama: A View of Our People and Their History, Together with the Principles Underlying, and the Circumstances Attending, the Rise and Progress of the American Union.* Clarksville, TN: Buck and Neville, 1869.

Penner, Mil. *Section 27: A Century on a Family Farm.* Lawrence: University Press of Kansas, 2002.

Perlstein, Rick. *Before the Storm: Barry Goldwater and the Unmaking of the American Consensus.* New York: Hill and Wang, 2001.

Peterson, Merrill D. *The Legend Revisited, John Brown.* Charlottesville: University of Virginia Press, 2004.

Pickering, I. O. "The Administrations of John P. St. John." *Transactions of the Kansas State Historical Society* 9 (1906): 378–94.

Piotrowski, William K. "The Kansas Compromise." *Religion in the News* 2 (Fall 1999).

Political Behavior Program. *American National Election Studies: 1964 Pre-Post Election Study Codebook.* Ann Arbor: University of Michigan, 1964.

Postel, Charles. *The Populist Vision.* New York: Oxford University Press, 2007.

Prentis, Noble L. *A History of Kansas.* Winfield, KS: E. P. Greer, 1899.

Primer, Ben. *Protestants and American Business Methods.* Ann Arbor: UMI Research Press, 1978.

Redekop, John H. *The American Far Right: A Case Study of Billy James Hargis.* Grand Rapids, MI: Eerdmans, 1968.

Redpath, James. *The Public Life of Capt. John Brown, with an Auto-Biography of His Childhood and Youth.* Boston: Thayer and Eldridge, 1860.

Ribuffo, Leo P. *The Old Christian Right: The Protestant Far Right from the Great Depression to the Cold War.* Philadelphia: Temple University Press, 1983.

Rich, Everett. *William Allen White: The Man from Emporia.* New York: Farrar and Rinehart, 1941.

Rickard, Louise Elaine. "The Impact of Populism on Electoral Patterns in Kansas, 1880–1900: A Quantitative Analysis." PhD diss., University of Kansas, 1974.

Riney-Kehrberg, Pamela. *Rooted in Dust: Surviving Drought and Depression in Southwestern Kansas.* Lawrence: University Press of Kansas, 1994.

Robinson, Sara T. L. *Kansas: Its Interior and Exterior Life.* Boston: Crosby, Nichols and Company, 1856.

Roof, Wade Clark. *Community and Commitment: Religious Plausibility in a Liberal Protestant Church.* New York: Pilgrim Press, 1983.

Root, Frank A. *The Overland Stage to California.* Topeka: Crane and Company, 1901.

Ross, W. D. *Laws Relating to the Common Schools of Kansas.* Topeka: State Printing Office, 1913.

Russell, Dick. *The Man Who Knew Too Much.* New York: Carroll and Graf, 2003.

Savage, I. O. *A History of Republic County, Kansas.* Beloit, KS: Jones and Chubbic, 1901.

Sayler, Carolyn. *Doris Fleeson: Incomparably the First Political Journalist of Her Time.* Santa Fe: Sunstone Press, 2010.

Schell, James. "Changes in Social Welfare Financing in Kansas." *Bulletin of the Governmental Research Center* 8 (1953): 1–2.

Schoenwald, Jonathan M. *A Time for Choosing: The Rise of Modern American Conservatism.* New York: Oxford University Press, 2001.

Schoggen, Phil. *Behavior Settings: A Revision and Extension of Roger G. Barker's Ecological Psychology.* Stanford, CA: Stanford University Press, 1989.

Schwendemann, Glen. "Wyandotte and the First 'Exodusters' of 1879." *Kansas Historical Quarterly* 26 (1960): 233–49.

Scritchfield, Floyd C. "Local Public School Organization in Kansas." *Bulletin of the Bureau of Government Research* 6 (1950): 1–3.

Segers, Mary C., and Timothy A. Byrnes, eds. *Abortion Politics in American States.* New York: M. E. Sharpe, 1995.

Selznick, Gertrude J., and Stephen Steinberg. *The Tenacity of Prejudice.* New York: Harper and Row, 1969.

Shibley, Mark A. *Resurgent Evangelicalism in the United States: Mapping Cultural Change since 1970.* Columbia: University of South Carolina Press, 1996.

Simpson, Jerry. "The Political Rebellion in Kansas." In *The Farmers' Alliance History and Agricultural Digest*, ed. Nelson A. Dunning, 280–83. Washington, DC: Alliance Publishing Company, 1891.

Sitar, Amy. "Praying for Power: Dispositions and Discipline in the Azusa Street Revival's *Apostolic Faith*." *Poetics* 36 (2008): 450–61.

Smith, Christian, ed. *The Secular Revolution: Power, Interests, and Conflict in the Secularization of American Public Life*. Berkeley: University of California Press, 2003.

Smith, Duane A. *Rocky Mountain Heartland: Colorado, Montana, and Wyoming in the Twentieth Century*. Tucson: University of Arizona Press, 2008.

Smith, Geoffrey S. *To Save a Nation: American Counter-Subversives, the New Deal, and the Coming of World War II*. New York: Basic Books, 1973.

Smith, H. A. "The Fire Prevention Work of Stock Fire Insurance Companies." *Annals of the American Academy of Political and Social Science* 130 (1927): 103–7.

Smith, Patricia Douglass. *Centennial Saga of First United Methodist Church, Garden City, Kansas, 1882–1982: A History of the Church and Its First Records*. Garden City: First United Methodist Church, History Committee, 1982.

Smith, Ronald D. *Thomas Ewing Jr.: Frontier Lawyer and Civil War General*. Columbia: University of Missouri Press, 2008.

Smylie, James. "Sheldon's *In His Steps*: Conscience and Discipleship." *Theology Today* 32 (1975): 32–45.

Snyder, C. Hugh. *The Youngest Brother: On a Kansas Wheat Farm during the Roaring Twenties and the Great Depression*. Lincoln, NE: iUniverse, 2005.

Socolofsky, Homer E. *Arthur Capper: Publisher, Politician, and Philanthropist*. Lawrence: University of Kansas Press, 1962.

———. "The Private Journals of Florence Crawford and Arthur Capper, 1891–1892." *Kansas Historical Quarterly* 30 (1964): 15–64.

Spooner, Walter W. *The Cyclopedia of Temperance and Prohibition*. New York: Funk and Wagnalls, 1891.

Stanton, Elizabeth Cady, Susan B. Anthony, and Matilda Joslyn Gage, eds. *History of Woman Suffrage, Vol. II: 1861–1876*. Rochester, NY: Charles Mann, 1887.

Stark, Rodney. "The Reliability of Historical United States Census Data on Religion." *Sociological Analysis* 53 (1992): 91–95.

Stearns, J. N. *Prohibition Does Prohibit; or Prohibition Not a Failure*. New York: National Temperance Society and Publication House, 1882.

Steinbeck, John. *The Grapes of Wrath*. New York: Viking, 1939.

Stratton, Joanna L. *Pioneer Women: Voices from the Kansas Frontier*. New York: Simon and Schuster, 1981.

Stump, Roger W. "Spatial Patterns of Growth and Decline among the Disciples of Christ, 1890–1980." In *A Case Study of Mainstream*

Protestantism: The Disciples' Relation to American Culture, 1880–1989, ed. D. Newell Williams, 445–68. Grand Rapids, MI: Eerdmans, 1991.

Svobida, Lawrence. *Farming the Dust Bowl: A First-Hand Account from Kansas.* Lawrence: University Press of Kansas, 1986.

Swanson, Phyllis M. *City of the Plains: A Story of Leonardville.* Leonardville: Leonardville City Library, 1982.

Sweet, William Henry. *A History of Methodism in Northwest Kansas.* Salina: Kansas Wesleyan University, 1920.

Talbot, David. *Brothers: The Hidden History of the Kennedy Years.* New York: Free Press, 2008.

Tennyson, Alfred Lord. *In Memoria.* London: Macmillan, 1906.

Thomas, George M. *Revivalism and Cultural Change: Christianity, Nation Building, and the Market in the Nineteenth-Century United States.* Chicago: University of Chicago Press, 1989.

Tocqueville, Alexis de. *Democracy in America.* New York: Harper and Row, 1966.

Tribe, Lawrence H. *Abortion: The Clash of Absolutes.* New York: W. W. Norton, 1990.

U.S. Bureau of the Census. *Census of Religious Bodies, 1926.* Washington, DC: Government Printing Office, 1930.

———. *Census of Religious Bodies, 1936.* Washington, DC: Government Printing Office, 1939.

———. *Compendium of the Eleventh Census: 1890.* Washington, DC: Government Printing Office, 1894.

———. *Population of the United States in 1860 Compiled from the Original Returns of the Eighth Census.* Washington, DC: Government Printing Office, 1864.

———. *Religious Bodies, 1916: Part I: Summary and General Tables.* Washington, DC: Government Printing Office, 1919.

———. *Statistical Abstract of the United States, 1890.* Washington, DC: Government Printing Office, 1891.

———. *Statistical Abstract of the United States, 1900.* Washington, DC: Government Printing Office, 1901.

———. *Statistical Abstract of the United States, 1925.* Washington, DC: Government Printing Office, 1925.

———. *Statistical Abstract of the United States, 1930.* Washington, DC: Government Printing Office, 1930.

———. *Statistical Abstract of the United States, 1934* (Washington, DC: Government Printing Office, 1935).

———. *Statistical Abstract of the United States, 1940.* Washington, DC: Government Printing Office, 1940.

———. *Statistical Abstract of the United States, 1950.* Washington, DC: Government Printing Office, 1950.

———. *Statistical Abstract of the United States, 1952.* Washington, DC: Government Printing Office, 1952.

U.S. Congress. *Report of the Special Committee Appointed to Investigate the Troubles in Kansas*. Washington, DC: Wendell Printing Company, 1856.

U.S. War Department. *State Summary of War Casualties from World War II for Navy, Marine Corps, and Coast Guard Personnel from Kansas*. Washington, DC: War Department, 1946.

——. *World War II Honor List of Dead and Missing Army and Army Air Forces Personnel from Kansas*. Washington, DC: War Department, 1946.

Wacker, Grant. *Heaven Below: Early Pentecostals and American Culture*. Cambridge, MA: Harvard University Press, 2001.

Wall, Hugo. "Social Welfare in Kansas." *Bulletin of the Governmental Research Center* 3 (1947): 1–2.

Walters, Ronald. "The Great Plains Sit-in Movement, 1958–60." *Great Plains Quarterly* 16 (1996): 85–94.

Warner, R. Stephen. *A Church of Our Own: Disestablishment and Diversity in American Religion*. New Brunswick, NJ: Rutgers University Press, 2005.

Warren, Donald. *Radio Priest: Charles Coughlin: The Father of Hate Radio*. New York: Free Press, 1996.

Waterman, W. C. "Present Tendencies in Rural Sociology." *Social Forces* 7 (1928): 50–58.

Weissbach, Lee Shai. *Jewish Life in Small-Town America: A History*. New Haven, CT: Yale University Press, 2005.

West, James. *Plainville, U.S.A.* New York: Columbia University Press, 1945.

Westin, Alan F. "The John Birch Society: 'Radical Right' and 'Extreme Left' in the Political Context of Post World War II." In *The Radical Right*, ed. Daniel Bell, 239–68. Garden City, NY: Doubleday, 1963.

Westoff, Charles F. "The Blending of Catholic Reproductive Behavior." In *The Religious Dimension: New Directions in Quantitative Research*, ed. Robert Wuthnow, 231–40. New York: Academic Press, 1979.

White, F. Clifton, and William J. Gill. *Suite 3505: The Story of the Draft Goldwater Movement*. Columbia, MO: John M. Ashbrook Center for Public Policy, 1992.

Wicker, Allan W. "The Midwest Psychological Field Station: Some Reflections of One Participant." *Environment and Behavior* 22 (1990): 492–98.

Wilcox, Clyde. "Sources of Support for the Old Right: A Comparison of the John Birch Society and the Christian Anti-Communism Crusade." *Social Science History* 12 (1988): 429–49.

Wilder, Bessie E. *Governmental Agencies of the State of Kansas, 1861–1956*. Lawrence: University of Kansas, Governmental Research Center, 1957.

Wilder, Daniel Webster. *The Annals of Kansas*. Topeka: Kansas Publishing House, 1875.

Wilson, Warren H. "What the Automobile Has Done to and for the Country Church." *Annals of the American Academy of Political and Social Science* 116 (1924): 83–86.

Winkle, Kenneth. "'The Great Body of the Republic': Abraham Lincoln and the Idea of a Middle West." In *The American Midwest: Essays on Regional History*, ed. Andrew R. L. Cayton and Susan E. Gray, 111–22. Bloomington: Indiana University Press, 2001.

Winskill, P. T. *The Temperance Movement and Its Workers*. London: Blackie and Son, 1892.

Wuthnow, Robert. "Depopulation and Rural Churches in Kansas, 1950–1980." *Great Plains Research* 15 (2005): 117–34.

———. *The Restructuring of American Religion: Society and Faith since World War II*. Princeton, NJ: Princeton University Press, 1988.

Yerrinton, J.M.W., and Henry M. Parkhurst. *Debates and Proceedings of the National Council of Congregational Churches*. Boston: National Council of Congregational Churches, 1865.

News Sources

ABC Evening News
Afro-American (Baltimore)
Arkansas City Republican
Arkansas City Traveler
Associated Press
Atchison Daily Globe
Atlanta Constitution
Axtell Anchor
Baltimore Sun
Barron's
Call and Post
Capper's Farmer
Capper's Weekly
Chanute Tribune
Chicago Daily Tribune
Chicago Defender
Chicago Tribune
Christian Beacon
Christian Century
Christian Crusade
Christian Examiner
Christian Science Monitor
CNN Transcripts
Courtland Journal (Courtland, KS)
Daily Reports Archive
Denver Daily Post
Education Week

Emporia Gazette
Freedom's Champion (Atchison, KS)
Frontline
Garden City Telegram
Harris News Service
Hawver's Capitol Report
Hays Daily News
Hutchinson News
Independent
Jayhawker Magazine
Jewell County Record
Kansas Alumni
Kansas City Star
Kansas City Times
Kansas Farmer
Kansas Semi-Weekly Capital (Topeka)
Kiowa News
KSN News (Wichita)
KTWU/Channel 11 (Topeka)
KU History
Lawrence Journal-World
Leavenworth Bulletin
Los Angeles Sentinel
Los Angeles Times
Lucifer the Light Bearer (Topeka)
Lyons Daily News
Manchester Guardian
Manhattan Mercury
McClure's Magazine
Methodist Review
Miami Herald
Miltonvale Record
Milwaukee Journal
Milwaukee Sentinel
Ms. Magazine
Nation
National Catholic Reporter
National Jewish Monthly
National Journal
NewsHour
Newton Kansan
New York Amsterdam Star-News
New York Daily Tribune
New Yorker
New York Times
New York Tribune

Omaha World Herald
Ottawa Herald
Outlook
Perspectives (Presbyterian Church [U.S.A.], Louisville)
Philadelphia Inquirer
Pittsburg Morning Sun
Salina Journal
Saturday Evening Post
Signal-Enterprise (Alma, KS)
Southwest Daily Times (Liberal, KS)
St. Louis Republic
Sunday InterOcean (Chicago)
Time
Topeka Capital-Journal
Topeka Commonwealth
Topeka Daily Capital
Topeka Weekly Capital
Union (Atchison)
U.S. News and World Report
Vital Speeches
Wall Street Journal
Washington Post
Western Kansas World (WaKeeney, KS)
Wichita Beacon
Wichita Eagle
Wichita Post-Observer
Winfield Daily Courier

COLLECTIONS

American Catholic History Research Center, Catholic University of America, Washington, DC
Association of Religion Data Archives, University Park, PA
Ellis County Historical Society
Finney County Historical Society Museum, Garden City, KS
Inter-University Consortium for Political and Social Research, University of Michigan, Ann Arbor
Kansas Collection, University of Kansas Libraries, Lawrence
Kansas Memory Collection, Kansas State Historical Society, Topeka
Missouri Census Data Center, University of Missouri, Jefferson City
Roper Center for Public Opinion Research, University of Connecticut, Storrs.
Shawnee County Historical Society, Topeka
Smith County Historical Society, Smith Center, KS
Stafford County Historical Society Museum, Topeka
Territorial Kansas Online

ELECTRONIC DATA

Annual Church Profile for Southern Baptist Convention Churches, 1980
Churches and Church Membership in the United States, 1952, 1972, 1980, 1990, 2000
Electoral Data for Counties in the United States, 1840–1990
Gallup poll, 1937–1960
Kansas election results, 1998–2008
National Election Pool General Election Exit Polls, 2000, 2004, 2006
National Election Survey, 1944–2006
Religion and Politics Survey, 2000
State Legislative Returns in the United States, 1968–93
System for Catholic Research, Information, and Planning, 1940–90
U.S. Bureau of Economic Analysis, gross domestic product, 1963–2006
U.S. Census, decennial censuses, county data, 1860–2000
U.S. Census, decennial censuses, incorporated places, 1870–2000
U.S. Census, public use microsamples, 1960–2000
U.S. Census, religious bodies, 1870, 1890, 1906, 1916, 1926, 1936, 1952
Voter News Service General Election Exit Polls, 2000

INDEX

Abell, Peter T., 24–25

Abilene, Kansas: Eisenhower in, *203*; as Eisenhower's home, 169, 200–202, 405n1

abolitionism, 3, 21, 30–31

abortion: as campaign issue, 8, 274–76, 288, 298–99; Catholic Church and opposition to, 263, 273, 291, 329; churches as centers of antiabortion activism, 292–93; clergy and activism against, 292–93; clinic blockades and protests, ix, 267, 287–88, 289–94, 298, 301; conception as beginning of life, 273, 282, 284–85, 326, 328; and counseling services, 273–74, 284, 287, 297; freedom of speech and protest rights, 300; legislative restrictions on, 274, 284, 288, 295, 297–300, 302, 367, 369; medical record confidentiality and, 328–29, 348; and moral crisis, 351, 352; Operation Rescue and antiabortion activism, 268, 288–94, 300, 302, 305, 319, 369; parental consent requirements, 275, 281, 285, 286, 288, 297; party affiliation and position on, 288, 295, 299–300, 367; popular opinion in Kansas, 302; proposed constitutional amendment to ban, 275, 281–82; providers in Kansas, 269; and religion in the political sphere, 268; results of efforts to reduce, 328–29; *Roe v. Wade* decision, 2, 265, 269, 273–74, 284, 288; RU-486 (abortion pill), 300; state-level reforms and, 285–86, 369; Summer of Mercy campaign, 267, 289–94; Tiller murder, 2, 267–68, 351–52, 368, 441n49; and tolerance as value, 352–54; violence at clinics,

298, 300 (*see also* Tiller murder *under this heading*); *Webster v. Reproductive Health Services* decision, 285–86, 369

Abrams, Steve, 308, 321, 341–42, 346

activity churches, 7, 189–96, 209, 413n57

Adams, Cecil, 288

Adams, Franklin G., 24–25

Adams, Mildred, 156

African American churches: African Methodist churches, 5, 52, 160, 182, 198, 199, 231–32, 234–35, 238; Baptist churches, 117; Churches of God, 165; civil rights movement and, 234–35

African Americans: *Brown v. Board of Education* and school desegregation, 2, 7, 188, 230, 235–36, 237; demographic information, 185; efforts to exclude, 44; "Exodusters" in Kansas, 52, 236; population data, 51–52; racial segregation of churches, 44, 61–62; suffrage, 3. *See also* civil rights

Agnew, Spiro, 250–51

Agricultural Adjustment Act, 172, 176, 184, 406n2

agriculture: crop prices and farm income, 81–82, 139, 160–61, 171–72, 226, 269; decline in farm population, 216, 264; drought and crop failures, 82, 90–92; as economic sector, 213; Eisenhower's farm policy, 206; farm ownership, 82, 99; farmers as voting constituency, 160–61, 213; federal assistance and subsidies for, 226; Great Depression and, 139–40; inequality within, 99; modernization and, 130, 139; mortgages and foreclosures on farms, 82–83, 89,

ineffective, 364; New Deal and roots of skepticism about, 6, 8, 160, 169, 171–73, 176, 179, 183, 364; Reagan and, 279–83, 286, 365; Religious Right and, 365

bipartisanship, 171, 177–78, 185, 208, 214, 354–55, 364

Birkhead, Leon Milton, 144, 166, 182

birth control, 7–8, 245, 247, 263–64, 295. *See also* abortion

Blaine, James G., 79, 105–6

Blaine amendment, 105–7

"bleeding Kansas," 3–4, 79

Bloomenshine, Lee, 104

Blount, Mrs. O. M., 231–32

Bluemont Central College, 43, 44

"Bone Dry Law" signed by Capper, 122, *123*

Botkin, Jeremiah D., 87–90, 122

Botkin, Tom, 89

Boyd, Mary Potter, 104

Boyd, Tim, 299

Bright Star (play), 183

Brinkerhoff, Fred W., 22

Brinkley, John R., 164

Bristow, Joseph L., 125

broadcasting, religious, 119, 173, 190, 221–24, 228, 273, 310–11, 313, 337–38

Browder, Earl W., 162–63

Brown, Bryan, 299

Brown, Charles R., 160

Brown, John, 21–22, 26, 80–81, 180, 363

Brown, Oliver L., 235–36

Brown v. Board of Education, 2, 7, 188, 230, 235–36, 237

Bryan, Charles, 113

Bryan, William Jennings, 92–93, 96, 143

Bryl, Ellen, 354

Bucklin Methodist Church, 55

Buddhism, 130, 270, 355

Buffett, Howard, 224

Buffett, Warren, 417n16

Burton, J. R., 100, 101, 103

Bush, George W., 300, 321–24, 335; Religious Right and, 321–22, 331

Bushong, Peter and Mrs., 84

Butler, Pardee, 25

Butler, Thomas, 65

Byrd, J. H., 25

Callahan, Patrick H., 137–38

Calvert, John, 342–44

camp meetings, 69–70. *See also* revival meetings

campaigns, political: anti-Semitism in, 159, 173–74; candidate's faith as factor in, 210–12, 321–24, 417n18; "family values" as issue in, 279–81, 295, 301, 329; moral values as issue in, 184–85, 249–51, 299–300, 302–3, 358; profession of personal faith during, 321–24, 417n18; religion as influence on, 4; taxes as issue in, 122, 123–24, 135, 213, 224–25, 269, 281, 302–3; tolerance promoted in, 136–38, 202–5, 210–12; voter demographics and, 216. *See also specific politicians*

capital punishment (death penalty), 11, 269, 357

Capper, Arthur, 103, 112, 115–17, 120–26, 128, 132, 134–35, 139, 140, 149, 187, 396n19; death of, 177; government efficiency and, 115–16, 123–24, 176; and isolationism, 176–77; New Deal and, 153, 176, 183; newspaper and radio ventures, 125, 152, 163–64; Prohibition and, 125, 142; signing the "Bone Dry Law," *123*

Capper's Farmer (newspaper), 115, 125, 152, 163–64

Capper-Volstead Act, 115–16

Carlin, John, 281

Carlson, Frank, 205, 207, 210, 262, 313

Carmody, Tim, 327

Carroll, Mark K., 209–10

Carter, Jimmy, 265, 269, 275–76, 280

Cathedral of the Immaculate Conception (Leavenworth), 39–40, *41*

Cather, Willa, 40

censuses, 20; churches as defined in, 37–38; and decline of churches during Great Depression, 145–46; National Council of Churches as

of gay clergy, 331; same-sex union ceremonies and, 331

Episcopalians, 117, 199; political affiliation and, 149

Equal Rights Amendment (ERA), 277–79, 295

ethnicity, 210; bigotry and, 28; churches and ethnic enclaves, 50–51, 58; "clustering," 61–63; and denomination, 27–28, 66; politics and, 73, 174–75. *See also specific ethnic groups*

euthanasia, 275, 351

Evangelical Free churches, 292; membership in, 292

evangelicalism, 58

Everson v. Board of Education, 410n31

evolution: antiabortion activism and opposition to, 304, 306; "creationism" as alternative to, 2, 305, 308, 309, 344; "intelligent design" and, ix, 2, 339–47; popular opinion regarding, 344; Religious Right and, 268–69, 303–4; in school curriculums, 7, 105, 143, 268–69, 303–11, 345–46, 367; Scopes Trial, 7, 143

Ewing, Thomas Jr., 46, 378n73

"Exodusters," 52, 236

Falwell, Jerry, 272, 284–85, 299, 301, 302, 310, 313, 322, 335, 339

Family Research Council, 313, 323, 327, 337

"family values" as campaign issue, 279–81, 295, 301, 329

Farley, James Aloysius, 158

Farmer's Alliance. *See* Populism

Farmers Liberty League, 172

Farrell, F. D., 193–94

Fascism, 173–75, 182

Faubus, Orval, 230–31

federal government: agricultural subsidies and allotments, 140, 197–98, 206, 226; ambivalence toward, 226; and antipathy toward "big" government, 8, 224, 299, 301–2, 364–65; and education issues, 305–6; National Prayer Breakfasts in Washington, 205, 262,

313; New Deal and dissatisfaction with, 6, 8, 160, 169, 171–73, 176, 179, 183; as politically distant and disinterested in Kansas, xii, 80–81, 170, 177, 187, 193, 197–98, 208, 213–14, 224, 365–66; Reagan and government as "problem," 279–83, 286, 365; state- or local-level influence and, 369–70

Fink, Louis, Bishop, 86–87

Finney, Charles C., 28, 291

Finney, Joan, 288

Finney, Katherine Kathrens, 28

Finney, Michael C., 28

fires and fire prevention, 132–34

First Congregational Church, Topeka, 36

fiscal conservatism, xi, 100, 169, 179, 218, 224–25, 279–83, 365–66; as campaign issue, 213; deficit spending and, 322; efficiency in government and, 6, 113, 115–16, 123–24, 127–28, 150

Fisher, Hugh D., 20

Fisher, Jesse C., 175

Flying Fundamentalists, 143–44, 153

football, 103

Ford, Gerald, 265, 269, 275–76, 322

Ford, James W., 162–63

Foursquare Gospel churches, 260

Fox, Terry, 319, 348

Frank, Thomas, xi, 2

freedom of religion, 39, 65, 337; Wyandotte convention and guarantees of, 38, 44

Freedom's Champion (newspaper), 21, 27, 28–29, 77, 80

Frellick, Gerri von, 223

Friends of Democracy, 166, 182

Friends University, 105

Frist, Bill, 331

fundamentalism, religious, 192; anti-Catholicism and, 210–11; churches and rejection of, 356–59; contexts for emergence of, 6, 7, 142–52; demographic shifts and growth of, 256–61; education of clergy, 258–59; and establishment of independent churches, 258–59; and opposition to abortion, 273; origins

religiosity: and church attendance,
195; Cold War anxieties and, 171;
during Great Depression, 142–44,
150–52, 165; revival meetings and
fanaticism, 68–70; during WW II,
166–68, 182
Religious Right: abortion activism
(*see* Religious Right, abortion
activism); antigay rights activism,
ix, 301, 331–36, 339, 367, 370; big
government opposed by, 301–2;
and constitutional ban on same-sex
marriage, ix, 331–36, 339, 367,
370; demographic shifts and rise
of, 256–61, 366; differentiation of
churches from, 356–59; and direct
political engagement of clergy and
churches, 268, 298–99, 303–4, 367–
68; education issues and, 301 (*see
also* and evolution in the curriculum
under this heading; Kansas Board
of Education controlled by *under
this heading*); and evolution in
the curriculum, 268–69, 303–11,
367; and feminism as threat to
values, 301; financial resources of,
441n53; and gambling as issue,
296; George W. Bush and, 321–24;
as institutionalized organization,
284, 312–14, 324, 333; Kansas
Board of Education controlled by,
304–5, 306–10; legislative efforts
of, ix, 274, 284–86, 288, 295,
297–300, 302, 331–36, 339, 367,
369–70; local vs. federal politics
and, 368, 369–70; and mobilization
of activists, 3, 268, 269, 368; and
morality as campaign issue, 302–3;
and school board or local elections,
296–97, 303–4; school reforms as
focus of, 268–69, 287, 288, 295–97,
301, 303–11, 305, 307, 367;
"stealth tactics" in local elections,
304–5; violence linked to activism,
298, 300–301
Religious Right, abortion activism, 367;
churches as center of, 292–93; clinic
blockades and protest as tactic of,
ix, 267, 287–88, 289–94, 298, 301;
and conception as beginning of

life, 273, 282, 284–85, 326, 328;
freedom of speech and protest
rights, 300; legislation and, 274,
284, 288, 295, 297–300, 302, 367,
369; medical record confidentiality
and, 328–29, 348; Operation
Rescue and, 268, 288–94, 300, 302,
305, 319, 369; parental consent
requirements and, 275, 281, 285,
286, 288, 297; political campaigns
and, 8, 274–76, 288, 298–99; and
political mobilization of, 268,
269; and proposed constitutional
amendment, 275, 281–82; and
reduction in abortions, 328–29;
Roe v. Wade anniversary events,
276, 288, 317, 324, 350; state-level
reforms and, 285–86, 369; Summer
of Mercy campaign, 267, 289–94;
Tiller, and demonization of, 351–52,
368; and Tiller murder, 2, 267–68,
351–52, 368, 441n49; violence at
clinics, 298, 300 (*see also* Tiller
murder *under this heading*);
*Webster v. Reproductive Health
Services* decision, 285–86, 369
reproductive rights. *See* abortion
Republican National Convention
(1928), 135
Republican Party: "antiboss" faction
within, 100–101; anti-Catholicism
and, 97; and campaigning on
credentials, 97; conservatism
and, 2–3; decline of, 212–13; as
dominant political force in Kansas,
5, 27, 72, 95–104, 111–16, 146–47,
212–13, 355, 362, 370; factionalism
within, 26–37, 208–9, 212–13,
220, 363, 370, 414n63; and free
state status of Kansas, 30–33;
funding and resources of, 99–100;
law and order movement within,
101–4; local development and, 6–7;
nativism and, 97; as opposition
party, 6; organization in Kansas, 8,
21; patronage and, 7; Populism as
challenger to, 79–97; Prohibition as
issue, 101–4; Protestant churches
and affiliation with, 5, 15–16, 15–
17, 27–28, 78–79, 141, 149,

parade in, *148*; as state capital, 32, 36
Transcendental Meditation, 270
transportation and travel, 126, 131, 139
trend watching, xi
Troutman, James A., 102–3
Truman, Harry S, 6, 169, 186–87, 208
Tubbs, Frank D., 105
Tucci, Keith, 289

Unification Church (Moonies), 270–71
Union Party, 163
Unitarian churches, 5, 38, 166; civil rights movement and, 232; same-sex marriage supported in, 331–32
United Brethren, 117; membership in, 52, 199; and opposition to abortion, 273; restructuring and denominational mergers, 259–60
universities. *See* colleges and universities
University of Kansas (KU), 116, 136; abortions and KU Medical Center, 286, 288; antiwar activism and, 248–50; birth control controversy at, 245; civil rights activism at, 229, 237–38; creationism and, 309–10, 346; "Days of Rage," 248–49; Purity Palace at, 136; racial discrimination at, 238; radio station at, 163–64; Robert J. Dole Institute of Politics at, 354
University of Wichita, 213
urbanization, 366; and shifting denominational membership, 253–61, 315–16, 366; and shifting voting patterns, 185

"values voters," xi
Van Meter, Iris, 341–42, 346
Van Meteren, Kristian, 325
Van Sickle, Tom, 220–21
Verheide, Abraham, 207
Vietnam War, xii, 7, 215–16, 241–44, 247–48, 265, 273, 366; antiwar protests, 244–45, 248–50; casualties, 241–42; churches and antiwar activism, 243; domestic unrest and, 242–43

violence: civil rights activism and, 237–39; Prohibition and, 101–4; religious intolerance and, 13, 64, 66; and the Religious Right, 298, 300–301, 346; revival meetings and, 69. *See also* murder

WaKeeney, Kansas, 194, 205
Walker, Edwin, 224
Wallace, George C., 221, 224, 240, 244
Walters, Maxine, 234
Walters, Ron, 234
Ward, Henry, 21
Watergate, 269–70, 274
Watson, Virgil E., 234
Webster v. Reproductive Health Services, 285–86, 369
Weddington, Sarah, 288
Weede, Charles R., 142
Welch, Robert, 222, 227, 228
welfare, human: churches and establishment of institutions, 43–45, 358; Johnson administration and welfare programs, 224; as moral issue, 357–59; Prohibition as social welfare issue, 45, 121–22, 155; state spending on, 124–25, 172, 279; voluntary organizations and, 182; women's suffrage and attention to, 76, 115–16, 131–32
Welsh, David, 337
Westin, Alan F., 228
We the People, 222
What's the Matter with Kansas (Frank), xi, 2
"What's the Matter with Kansas" (White), 2, 4, 89–90, 153–54, 303
Wheeler, James, 19
White, William Allen, ix, 2, 4, 89–90, 113, 122, 128–30, *129*, 149, 153, 155, 163, 175, 180–81, 186
Whittaker, Judith, 281
Wichita, Kansas: civil rights ordinance in, 236, 277; defense industry in, 182, 218; demographics, 51, 98, 117, 231, 257, 260–61; Dockum Drug Store sit-ins, 231, *233*, 233–34, 238; as site of abortion activism, 268, 288–94, 300, 302, 305, 319,